The Course of Ideas

The Course of Ideas

COLLEGE WRITING AND READING

JEANNE GUNNER
University of California at Los Angeles

ED FRANKEL
University of California at Los Angeles

1817

HARPER & ROW, PUBLISHERS, NEW YORK

Cambridge, Philadelphia, San Francisco, Washington, London, Mexico City, São Paulo, Singapore, Sydney

Sponsoring Editor: Phillip Leininger
Project Editor: Ellen MacElree
Text Design: Gayle Jaeger
Text Art: NetworkGraphics
Photo Research: Mira Schachne
Production: Delia Tedoff
Compositor: ComCom Division of Haddon Craftsmen, Inc.
Printer and Binder: R. R. Donnelley & Sons Company
Cover Design: Karen Salsgiver
Cover Painting: de Chirico, Giorgio. *The Seer*. 1915. Oil on canvas, 35½ × 27½″ (89.6 ×
   70.1 cm). Collection, The Museum of Modern Art, New York. James Thrall Soby Bequest.
   Photograph © 1985 The Museum of Modern Art, New York.

THE COURSE OF IDEAS: College Writing and Reading

Library of Congress Cataloging-in-Publication Data

Gunner, Jeanne, 1954–
   The course of ideas.

   1. College readers. 2. English language—Rhetoric.
I. Frankel, Ed. II. Title.
PE1417.G86   1986   808′.0427   85-24834
ISBN 0-06-042549-0

   88 9 8 7 6 5

Contents

CHAPTER 2

Religious Beliefs and Attitudes   83

MAP AND TIME LINE

CHAPTER 3

Continuity in Science 141

TIME LINE

CHAPTER 5

Political Theory and Practice *303*

TIME LINE

CHAPTER 6

Philosophical Attitudes 385

Foreword

The Course of Ideas marks an important and much needed change in the way we think about developmental writing at the college level. It offers a curriculum that is accessible yet challenging, and challenging in a way that helps students build the proficiency in academic writing they must have if they are to make the most of higher education. Gunner and Frankel do not give us grammar drills but, rather, exercises that invite students to exlore a broad range of their reading and writing abilities. Gunner and Frankel eschew the typical fare of developmental readers and give us, instead, essays on religion, philosophy, science, politics, and the arts. By carefully integrating reading and writing, they avoid splitting these connected processes into disparate pedagogical universes. They acknowledge their students as members of the academic community and set out to guide them through its conventions. Gunner and Frankel do not, in a word, condescend.

But this is <u>not</u> to say that they are out of touch. They are master teachers, and their sensitivity and their technique are continually evident in the pages of *The Course of Ideas.* The readings are carefully chosen—in some cases edited, in a few cases written especially for this book—so that they progress in difficulty. They are preceded by overviews and headnotes that situate them for the student, as well as by explanations of techniques that can aid comprehension. After the readings come questions that invite the student to reconsider the readings and to write about them in ways that bring previously learned skills and knowledge to bear on present material. Finally, students are continually—and systematically—involved in writing about the readings that more and more closely approximates the writing they must do in the academy.

It sounds funny to label "daring" a book that offers a fairly traditional set of readings on the history of Western thought. But this book is daring. It invites us to reconsider the assumptions that underlie a good many developmental writing programs. And, to my mind, these assumptions are in desperate need of review, for they have restricted rather than enhanced the growth of our student writers. It is unusual and exciting when a textbook can spark such thinking.

MIKE ROSE

To the Student

BEGINNINGS

This book began as an experimental curriculum designed for our students at UCLA. Having taught Freshman English for many years, we increasingly felt that the books we were using weren't doing enough for us or our students. We knew from experience that our students needed background knowledge to enhance their writing and reading skills. We found that students could write more effectively—they could generate, organize, and develop ideas—when they wrote about academic topics that came from readings we studied and talked about in class. By "background knowledge" we mean the historical context, theoretical basis, intellectual/academic vocabulary, and modern context of a concept, issue, theory, person, or text.

READING AND WRITING

The reading skills in the book are designed to help you read <u>academically,</u> which implies reading with a purpose, perhaps looking for specific information and ideas, or defining an author's beliefs and point of view. We emphasize the need for you to read actively and get intellectually involved with all your academic reading.

The writing assignments represent typical academic assignments you'll probably encounter in your other college courses. When you read and write for a course in history, political science, sociology, psychology, or other fields, you'll be asked to summarize material, analyze it, use comparison and contrast, and respond in some way. These are the skills you'll be practicing throughout this book.

When you respond to our assignments, we assume that your instructor is your audience. You'll be writing for someone who knows the reading material, so your job will be demonstrating that you also understand it and can apply original analytical thought to the information.

ORGANIZATION

This book offers conceptual background for a writing and reading course. The readings present an overview of Western intellectual history through a representative sampling of fields and periods. Chapter 1 provides a sense of the Western world's ancient Greek background and covers five fields: religion, science, art, politics, and philosophy. The next five chapters focus on one field and follow it through from the medieval period up to modern times. Reading and writing instruction is attached to the readings, and the exercises and assignments draw on the skills and readings you accumulate as you work through the book. In other words, the book has continuity in both subject and skills.

WHY THE HISTORY OF WESTERN IDEAS?

Any book that selectively presents Western history, omitting the history of other cultures and civilizations, is open to the charge of ethnocentrism, which is the assumption that one's own culture is superior to others. We recognize the importance of other cultures and civilizations. But we also know that many of our students lack the background in Western ideas that they need and are assumed to have when they enter Western colleges and universities. Much college reading assumes student familiarity with the essential ideas, themes, events, and figures of Western culture. We designed this book to help you build up a sense of the Western intellectual context.

ACKNOWLEDGMENTS

We have many people to thank because this book, like most things, has a complex history. Mike Rose deserves the primary credit. He recognized the value of the curriculum and first suggested that we develop it in book form. From start to finish, his ideas and encouragement helped us in our work. Our other UCLA Writing Program colleagues have also given us support as reviewers and advisors: We thank Dick Lanham, Carol Hartzog, and Diane Dugaw. Michael Cohen gave us generous WANDAH computer support. Writing Programs overall provided the best atmosphere that could exist in any academic department for creating and testing a curriculum.

We are grateful for the research help of Brian Lenertz, Cecilia Wittman, Jack Bernhardt, and Christe and Bruce McMenomy. Kathy Bordua and Kris Kirschbaum helped us complete the manuscript, and our editor, Phil Leininger, gave us the freedom to shape the book as we envisioned it. Bob, Ida, and Mili have been both patient and supportive all the way. To them, to our students, and great friend Mike Rose, we dedicate our work.

JEANNE GUNNER

ED FRANKEL

The Course of Ideas

This map of ancient Greece and its surroundings depicts the area known as the "cradle of civilization." Compare it with the modern map. Countries have changed, in name and boundaries. Many countries of antiquity no longer exist. But the actual sites of ancient life still do, though in a transformed way. When you look at an ancient and a modern map, you're looking at the real experience of history. The Western world evolved from the ancient world.

Knowing where a person lived, where an event took place, where a story was set, in short, literally locating the physical origins of Western ideas, can help you understand and remember them. Place is a concept that allows you to build a whole picture. Together with place, time tells you how those people, events, and ideas form a logical sequence. Their meaning depends on their relation to other people, events, and ideas that came before. Together, time and place create the historical context. And understanding context—seeing the whole picture— characterizes the knowledgeable mind.

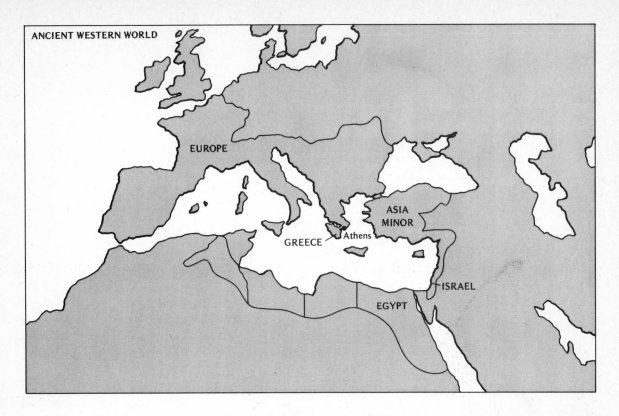

ANCIENT WESTERN WORLD

EUROPE

ASIA MINOR

GREECE — Athens

ISRAEL

EGYPT

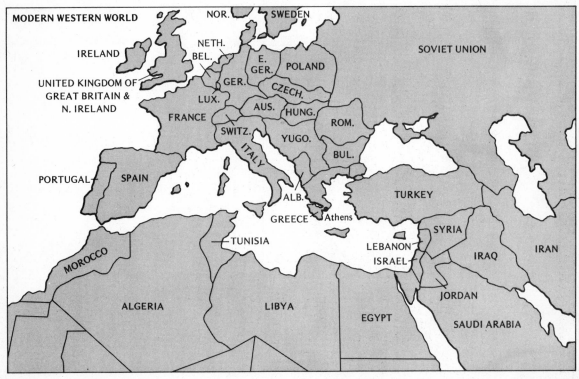

MODERN WESTERN WORLD

NOR.   SWEDEN

IRELAND

NETH.
BEL.

SOVIET UNION

E. GER.   POLAND

UNITED KINGDOM OF
GREAT BRITAIN &
N. IRELAND

GER.

CZECH.

LUX.

AUS.   HUNG.

FRANCE

SWITZ.

ROM.

YUGO.

ITALY

BUL.

PORTUGAL — SPAIN

TURKEY

ALB.

GREECE — Athens

TUNISIA

LEBANON

SYRIA

IRAN

ISRAEL

IRAQ

MOROCCO

JORDAN

ALGERIA

LIBYA

EGYPT

SAUDI ARABIA

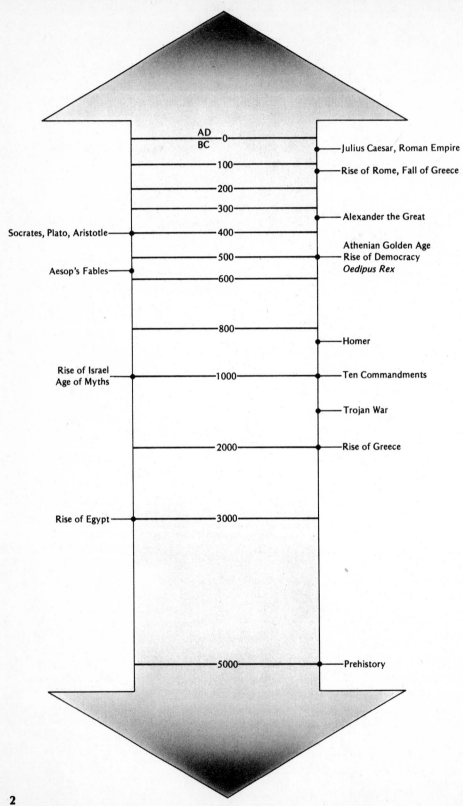

AD
—— 0
BC

Julius Caesar, Roman Empire

100

Rise of Rome, Fall of Greece

200

300

Alexander the Great

Socrates, Plato, Aristotle

400

Athenian Golden Age
Rise of Democracy
Oedipus Rex

500

Aesop's Fables

600

800

Homer

Rise of Israel
Age of Myths

1000

Ten Commandments

Trojan War

2000

Rise of Greece

Rise of Egypt

3000

5000

Prehistory

CHAPTER *1*

The Golden Age of Athens

INTRODUCTION

The reading and writing skills in this chapter combine to form some basic building blocks of academic discourse. We present each skill individually, but when you approach an essay, as a reader and as a writer, you'll probably draw on several at once. Because reading and writing are complex activities, they involve the near-simultaneous play of a number of mental processes. Ancient rhetoricians, or speechmakers, practiced the discrete* skills of building arguments, using figures of speech,* and modulating* the voice, yet when they presented their speeches publicly, they synthesized all these skills into one impressive performance. Reading and writing are related skills; in your academic work, you usually won't employ one skill without the other. When you read and write, you may find yourself moving through the whole range of composition, from discrete skill to a unified product, though you probably won't do so in a linear way, from start to finish.

separate / poetic expressions / controlling the tone

In Chapter 1 you'll read and write about the culture of ancient Athens. Chapter 1 is the only chapter in the book that is not organized chronologically. Instead it introduces the five subject areas covered individually in later chapters: religion, science, art, politics, and philosophy. We hope that by looking at these subjects in ancient Athens, you can develop a sense of how they relate to each other. As you read further in the book, you should also develop a sense of Athens' intellectual life and its relation to later Western thought.

The readings focus on Athens because it greatly influenced the form of Western civilization. Many religious, philosophical, political, scientific, and artistic concepts of today had their origins in the Golden Age of Athens. Mythology, the subject of the first reading, is the Greek equivalent of religion in that it defines a person's relationship to the gods and the world, suggests a moral code, and even explains natural phenomena. Edith Hamilton's essay "Introduction to Classical* Mythology" discusses the nature of the Greek myths and what they reveal about the people who created and perpetuated them. Mythical characters, creatures, places, and events provide us today with ways of naming concepts in psychology, morality, and art. "Echo and Narcissus" and "Oedipus," for example, demonstrate how imagery drawn from mythology pervades* our language and thought.

ancient Greek and Roman

spreads through

"The Founders of Western Philosophy" by Thomas H. Greer describes the development of early Greek philosophical systems. Philosophical ties to science during this period are clear: philosophers and scientists had not yet split their work into what today are the different pursuits of philosophical inquiry and scientific theorizing. Greek philosophers — especially Plato — formulated ways of viewing the world that profoundly changed how we perceive the individual, religion, and the nature of life. Philosophy to this day retains the imprint of Platonic thought. The excerpt from Plato's Symposium illustrates how we can come to know the abstract world of ideas by beginning with the material world, where appreciating physical beauty helps us to recognize abstract beauty, goodness, and truth.

As Greek philosophers developed systematic thought, Greek scientists gave us scientific methodology. In "Greek Science: Origins and Methods," Marshall Clagett places ancient science in the context of modern science to show how indebted we are to ancient scientific endeavors and discoveries, despite their sometimes flawed methods and conceptions. Hippocrates' teachings on epilepsy, "The Sacred Disease," shows how the empirical* method came to overthrow superstition and magic.

based on observation

Moses I. Finley in "Politics" discusses the origin of political thought in Greece. The notions of democracy and utopia began in Athens, as did abstract analysis of government. Again, a modern theoretical system, in this case politics, found its origin in Athens. Finley argues that Athens alone made the critical distinction between "politics" and practical government. Despite its fame as the first democracy, Athens bears the shame of being Socrates' executioner; excerpts from Plato's "The Apology of Socrates" and "Phaedo" recreate Socrates' trial and death.

A. D. DeRidder's "Art in Greece" explains the Greek aesthetic* doctrine of the useful and the beautiful. One of many fundamental aesthetic concepts of Greek culture, the "useful and beautiful" doctrine ruled the creation and evaluation of art and literature through the modern period. Greek art defined the genres* of epic, lyric poetry, tragedy, and comedy. DeRidder helps to explain the Greeks' purpose in such artistic

theory of artistic beauty

literary forms

endeavors. A fable from Aesop and an excerpt from Homer's Odyssey *illustrate art's dual function in ancient aesthetics.*

READING AND WRITING SKILLS OF CHAPTER 1

This chapter presents the following fundamental reading/writing skills:

Surveying the text	*Identifying topic sentences*
Paraphrasing	*Locating the author's thesis*
Developing a paragraph	*Reading for and writing with a thesis*
Revising paragraphs	*Writing a summary*
Critical reading	*Organizing an essay*
Defining terms	*Revising a thesis and essay*

You'll probably employ most of these skills with any academic reading and writing assignments you do. Surveying a text and reading it critically will improve your reading comprehension and make you an "active reader," not just a sponge for information. Locating topic sentences is a useful reading device when you're having difficulty understanding a paragraph or a whole essay, or when you plan to write a summary or outline of an assignment. Finding an author's thesis — the logical skeleton of an essay or book — enables you to read a passage with its logical outline already in mind. You'll find the skill of writing a summary or definition (which is really both a reading and a writing skill that involves paraphrasing an author's ideas) helpful throughout your college studies. And learning to develop paragraphs, organize essays, and revise them effectively are crucial elements in the process of academic writing.

Religion in the Ancient World

READING SKILL: *Surveying the Text*

Before reading anything in depth you should first employ the prereading technique of surveying the material. Surveying the text gives you a background, a framework that will help you organize the information you will get from a particular reading. Surveying resembles the process that musicians go through when they review a score before playing it or that competitive athletes experience when they study pregame tapes. Professional surveyors set up parameters*   boundaries before construction begins. In the same way, good readers set up a framework for assimilating new information presented in their reading by gaining a perspective on the text.

You can survey Edith Hamilton's essay by following these steps:

Focus on the title, "Introduction to Classical Mythology." The title seems straightforward: you're probably going to get just what it says.

Find out who the author is, and question what you already may know about him or her. Check for biographical information, which might reveal an author's scholarly, political, or religious affiliations and in turn suggest his or her views or methods. Some books include a list of the author's complete works, which can give you a sense of his or her major interests and areas of expertise. If you have the time, you can also look up the author's name in a college library's card catalog to see his or her other work. If you checked entries on Edith Hamilton, you'd find that she has written several books on Greek and Roman antiquity, an indication of special scholarship on the topic.

Check the passage's source and date of publication. Knowing an excerpt's origin might tell you its proper context. Knowing when a piece was written is important because cultural and social views change; you'll need to distinguish contemporary perspectives from those of another age. Remember that terms like "modern" and "contemporary" are relative. Edith Hamilton's book was published in 1942, but it can still be considered a modern work, given that it deals with antiquity; it's not the work of a medieval commentator, for instance. But it's also not a work of the 1980s and therefore doesn't reflect recent changes in social and political perspectives.

Look for pictures, graphs, or other illustrations. Such extras often can give you a sense of what to expect in the reading. In this case, no illustrations appear, but in other cases you may benefit from paying attention to the extras.

Read the first sentence of each paragraph. In many cases, this will be the topic sentence, which is the main idea of the paragraph. Look at paragraph 1: the first sentence tells us that the author is probably going to discuss mythology as a way of understanding the ancient mind.

Read the introductory and concluding paragraphs. One or both may summarize the author's main points. The Hamilton excerpt doesn't contain her actual opening and closing paragraphs, so you should focus on her topic sentences instead. Most essays and book chapters do begin and end with general statements, however.

Look for annotation. Read any introductions, chapter overviews, or interim summaries. Take note of headings and subheadings. Are some words underlined or in italics? This may mean there is a glossary* or that words are defined for you in footnotes or page margins. Here, asterisks indicate that a word is defined in the margin. For example, look at the word "nymph*" on page 9: the meaning "beautiful female divinity" appears to the right of the line. Boldface identifies key concepts that have been defined separately from the reading. See below, where **real and unreal,** a philosophical notion of different spheres of existence, is explained in a section called "Key Concepts" before the opening of the passage.

list of words / definitions

Edith Hamilton (1867–1963) in her introduction to Mythology *(1942) discusses the role of mythology in Greek life. She approaches myths as explanations of natural phenomena, a common interpretation though not the only possible one. Myths can be analyzed psychologically as well, or anthropologically, or theologically. They held religious significance for the earliest Greeks, but, by the time of the Golden Age of Athens (fifth century B.C.), myths were usually not believed literally. The Romans adapted Greek mythology, changing the names of most gods and slightly altering their nature. The Romans, too, had little actual faith in the gods. With the start of Christianity, about 400 years after the Golden Age, mythology was suppressed as pagan* literature. In the Renaissance, it was resurrected as artistic material; Botticelli's "Birth of Venus" (1485), reprinted here, shows the continuing presence of Greek myth in Western culture. As astronomers discovered the planets, they named them for ancient Roman gods (Mars, Jupiter, Venus, Mercury, Uranus, Saturn, Neptune, and Pluto). Much modern poetry has also incorporated mythological imagery, evident from the Renaissance through the twentieth century. Retelling the myths continues today, in both prose and recent films* (Clash of the Titans).

non Judeo-Christian

EDITH HAMILTON
"Introduction to Classical Mythology"

KEY CONCEPTS
THE REAL AND THE UNREAL (page 9) and the **INVISIBLE AND VISIBLE WORLD** (page 11) refer to philosophical concepts of different spheres of existence. Related concepts are "body and spirit," "material and ideal," the observable world or world of the senses vs. the abstract world or the world of ideas.

ANTHROPOCENTRISM and **ANTHROPOMORPHISM** are related anthropological concepts. The root "anthropo" means "human." An anthropocentric view of the world, which Hamilton expresses when she writes, "Mankind became the center of the universe," on page 10,

Sandro Botticelli, *The Birth of Venus,* ca. 1480. Canvas. The Granger Collection.

and "The Greeks made their gods in their own image" (page 10), places humans at the center, in interest and importance. Anthropomorphism is the application of human characteristics to things or natural phenomena. This concept appears on pages 12–13.

PRIMEVAL is an adjective that refers to the first state of humankind, or elemental human experiences.

● Greek and Roman mythology is quite generally supposed to show us the way the human race thought and felt untold ages ago. Through it, according to this view, we can retrace the path from civilized man who lives so far from nature, to man who lived in close companionship with nature; and the real interest of the myths is that they lead us back to a time when the world was young and people had a connection with the earth, with trees and seas and flowers and hills, unlike anything we ourselves can feel. When the stories were being shaped, we are given to understand, little distinction had as yet been made between **the real and the unreal**. The imagination was vividly alive and not checked by the reason, so that anyone in the woods might see through the trees a fleeing nymph,* or   beautiful female divinity
bending over a clear pool to drink behold in the depths a naiad's* face.   female water divinity

But a very brief consideration of the ways of uncivilized people everywhere and in all ages is enough to prick that romantic bubble. Nothing is

clearer than the fact that primitive man, whether in New Guinea today
or eons ago in the prehistoric wilderness, is not and never has been a
creature who peoples his world with bright fancies and lovely visions.
Horrors lurked in the **primeval** forest, not nymphs and naiads. Terror lived
there, with its close attendant, Magic, and its most common defense,
Human Sacrifice. Mankind's chief hope of escaping the wrath of whatever
divinities were then abroad lay in some magical rite, senseless but powerful, or in some offering made at the cost of pain and grief.

This dark picture is worlds apart from the stories of classical mythology.
The study of the way early man looked at his surroundings does not get
much help from the Greeks. How briefly the anthropologists treat the
Greek myths is noteworthy.

Of course the Greeks too had their roots in the primeval slime. Of
course they too once lived a savage life, ugly and brutal. But what the
myths show is how high they had risen above the ancient filth and fierce-
ness by the time we have any knowledge of them. Only a few traces of that
time are to be found in the stories.

We do not know when these stories were first told in their present
shape; but whenever it was, primitive life had been left far behind. The
myths as we have them are the creation of great poets. The first written
record of Greece is the *Iliad.** Greek mythology begins with Homer,
generally believed to be not earlier than a thousand years before Christ.
The *Iliad* is, or contains, the oldest Greek literature; and it is written in
a rich and subtle and beautiful language which must have had behind it
centuries when men were striving to express themselves with clarity and
beauty, an indisputable proof of civilization. The tales of Greek mythology
do not throw any clear light upon what early mankind was like. They do
not throw an abundance of light upon what early Greeks were like — a
matter, it would seem, of more importance to us, who are their descendants intellectually, artistically, and politically, too. Nothing we learn about
them is alien to ourselves.

> Homer's epic poem on the Trojan War

People often speak of "the Greek miracle." What the phrase tries to
express is the new birth of the world with the awakening of Greece. "Old
things are passed away; behold, all things are become new." Something
like that happened in Greece. Why it happened, or when, we have no idea
at all. We know only that in the earliest Greek poets a new point of view
dawned, never dreamed of in the world before them, but never to leave
the world after them. With the coming forward of Greece, **mankind became the center of the universe, the most important thing in it.** This was
a revolution in thought. Human beings had counted for little heretofore.
In Greece man first realized what mankind was.

The Greeks made their gods in their own image. That had not entered
the mind of man before. Until then, gods had had no semblance of reality.
They were unlike all living things. In Egypt, a towering colossus,* immo-
bile, beyond the power of the imagination to endow with movement, as
fixed in the stone as the tremendous temple columns, a representation of

> a gigantic statue

the human shape deliberately made unhuman. Or a rigid figure, a woman with a cat's head suggesting inflexible, inhuman cruelty. Or a monstrous mysterious sphinx, aloof from all that lives. In Mesopotamia,* bas-reliefs* of bestial shapes unlike any beast ever known, men with birds' heads and lions with bulls' heads and both with eagles' wings, creations of artists who were intent upon producing something never seen except in their own minds, the very consummation* of unreality.

ancient Middle Eastern region / sculpture with raised figures

fulfillment; endpoint

These and their like were what the pre-Greek world worshiped. One need only place beside them in imagination any Greek statue of a god, so normal and natural with all its beauty, to perceive what a new idea had come into the world. With its coming, the universe became rational.

Saint Paul said **the invisible must be understood by the visible.** That was not a Hebrew idea, it was Greek. In Greece alone in the ancient world people were preoccupied with the visible; they were finding the satisfaction of their desires in what was actually in the world around them. The sculptor watched the athletes contending in the games and he felt that nothing he could imagine would be as beautiful as those strong young bodies. So he made his statue of Apollo. The storyteller found Hermes among the people he passed in the street. He saw the god "like a young man at that age when youth is loveliest," as Homer says. Greek artists and poets realized how splendid a man could be, straight and swift and strong. He was the fulfillment of their search for beauty. They had no wish to create some fantasy shaped in their own minds. All the art and all the thought of Greece centered in human beings.

Human gods naturally made heaven a pleasantly familiar place. The Greeks felt at home in it. They knew just what the divine inhabitants did there, what they ate and drank and where they banqueted and how they amused themselves. Of course they were to be feared; they were very powerful and very dangerous when angry. Still, with proper care a man could be quite fairly at ease with them. Zeus, trying to hide his love affairs from his wife and invariably shown up, was a capital figure of fun. The Greeks enjoyed him and liked him all the better for it. Hera was that stock character of comedy, the typical jealous wife, and her ingenious tricks to discomfit* her husband and punish her rival, far from displeasing the Greeks, entertained them as much as Hera's modern counterpart does us today. Such stories made for a friendly feeling. Laughter in the presence of an Egyptian sphinx or an Assyrian bird-beast was inconceivable; but it was perfectly natural in Olympus, and it made the gods companionable.

thwart; defeat

On earth, too, the deities were exceedingly and humanly attractive. In the form of lovely youths and maidens they peopled the woodlands, the forests, the rivers, the sea, in harmony with the fair earth and the bright waters.

That is the miracle of Greek mythology — a humanized world, men freed from the paralyzing fear of an omnipotent* Unknown. The terrifying incomprehensibilities which were worshiped elsewhere, and the fearsome spirits with which earth, air and sea swarmed, were banned from

all-powerful

Greece. It may seem odd to say that the men who made the myths disliked the irrational and had a love for facts; but it is true no matter how wildly fantastic some of the stories are. Anyone who reads them with attention discovers that even the most nonsensical take place in a world which is essentially rational and matter-of-fact. Hercules, whose life was one long combat against preposterous monsters, is always said to have had his home in the city of Thebes. The exact spot where Aphrodite was born of the foam could be visited by any ancient tourist; it was just offshore from the island of Cythera. The winged steed Pegasus, after skimming the air all day, went every night to a comfortable stable in Corinth. A familiar local habitation gave reality to all the mythical beings. If the mixture seems childish, consider how reassuring and how sensible the solid background is as compared with the Genie who comes from nowhere when Aladdin rubs the lamp and, his task accomplished, returns to nowhere.

The terrifying irrational has no place in classical mythology. Magic, so powerful in the world before and after Greece, is almost nonexistent. There are no men and only two women with dreadful, supernatural powers. The demoniac* wizards and the hideous old witches who haunted Europe and America, too, up to quite recent years, play no part at all in the stories. Circe and Medea are the only witches and they are young and of surpassing beauty — delightful, not horrible. Astrology, which has flourished from the days of ancient Babylon down to today, is completely absent from classical Greece. There are many stories about the stars, but not a trace of the idea that they influence men's lives. Astronomy is what the Greek mind finally made out of the stars. Not a single story has a magical priest who is terribly to be feared because he knows ways of winning over the gods or alienating them. The priest is rarely seen and is never of importance. In the *Odyssey** when a priest and a poet fall on their knees before Odysseus, praying him to spare their lives, the hero kills the priest without a thought, but saves the poet. Homer says that he felt awe to slay a man who had been taught his divine art by the gods. Not the priest, but the poet, had influence with heaven — and no one was ever afraid of a poet. Ghosts, too, which have played so large and so fearsome a part in other lands, never appear on earth in any Greek story. The Greeks were not afraid of the dead — "the piteous dead," the *Odyssey* calls them.

The world of Greek mythology was not a place of terror for the human spirit. It is true that the gods were disconcertingly* incalculable. One could never tell where Zeus's thunderbolt would strike. Nevertheless, the whole divine company, with a very few and for the most part not important exceptions, were entrancingly beautiful with a human beauty, and nothing humanly beautiful is really terrifying. The early Greek mythologists transformed a world full of fear into a world full of beauty.

This bright picture has its dark spots. The change came about slowly and was never quite completed. The gods-become-human were for a long time a very slight improvement upon their worshipers. They were incom-

devil-like

Homer's epic poem on Odysseus' return from Troy

unsettlingly; confusingly

parably lovelier and more powerful, and they were of course immortal;
but they often acted in a way no decent man or woman would. In the *Iliad*
Hector is nobler by far than any of the heavenly beings, and Andromache
infinitely to be preferred to Athena or Aphrodite. Hera from first to last
is a goddess on a very low level of humanity. Almost every one of the
radiant divinities could act cruelly or contemptibly.* A very limited sense   despicably
of right and wrong prevailed in Homer's heaven, and for a long time after.

Other dark spots too stand out. There are traces of a time when there
were beast-gods. The satyrs are goat-men and the centaurs are half man,
half horse. Hera is often called "cow-faced," as if the adjective had somehow stuck to her through all her changes from a divine cow to a very
human queen of heaven. There are also stories which point back clearly
to a time when there was human sacrifice. But what is astonishing is not
that bits of savage belief were left here and there. The strange thing is that
they are so few.

Greek mythology is largely made up of stories about gods and goddesses, but it must not be read as a kind of Greek Bible, an account of the
Greek religion. According to the most modern idea, a real myth has nothing to do with religion. It is an explanation of something in nature; how,
for instance, any and everything in the universe came into existence: men,
animals, this or that tree or flower, the sun, the moon, the stars, storms,
eruptions, earthquakes, and all that is and all that happens. Thunder and
lightning are caused when Zeus hurls his thunderbolt. A volcano erupts
because a terrible creature is imprisoned in the mountain and every now
and then struggles to get free. The Dipper, the constellation called also the
Great Bear, does not set below the horizon because a goddess once was
angry at it and decreed that it should never sink into the sea. Myths are
early science, the result of men's first trying to explain what they saw
around them. But there are many so-called myths which explain nothing
at all. These tales are pure entertainment, the sort of thing people would
tell each other on a long winter's evening. The story of Pygmalion and
Galatea is an example; it has no conceivable connection with any event in
nature. Neither has the Quest of the Golden Fleece, nor Orpheus and
Eurydice, nor many another. This fact is now generally accepted; and we
do not have to try to find in every mythological heroine the moon or the
dawn and in every hero's life a sun myth. The stories are early literature
as well as early science.

But religion is there, too. In the background to be sure, but neverthe-
less plain to see. From Homer through the tragedians* and even later,   writers of tragic plays
there is a deepening realization of what human beings need and what they
must have in their gods.

Zeus the Thunderer was, it seems certain, once a rain-god. He was
supreme even over the sun, because rocky Greece needed rain more than
sunshine and the God of Gods would be the one who could give the
precious water of life to his worshipers. But Homer's Zeus is not a fact of
nature. He is a person living in a world where civilization has made an

entry, and of course he has a standard of right and wrong. It is not very high, certainly, and seems chiefly applicable to others, not to himself; but he does punish men who lie and break their oaths; he is angered by any ill treatment of the dead; and he pities and helps old Priam when he goes as a supplicant* to Achilles. In the *Odyssey,* he has reached a higher level. The swineherd* there says that the needy and the stranger are from Zeus and he who fails to help them sins against Zeus himself. Hesiod,* not much later than the *Odyssey* if at all, says of a man who does evil to the suppli- cant and the stranger, or who wrongs orphan children, "with that man Zeus is angry."

petitioner; favor-seeker

hog shepherd

Greek poet, 8th c. B.C.

Then Justice became Zeus's companion. That was a new idea. The buccaneering* chieftains in the *Iliad* did not want justice. They wanted to be able to take whatever they chose because they were strong and they wanted a god who was on the side of the strong. But Hesiod, who was a peasant living in a poor man's world, knew that the poor must have a just god. He wrote, "Fishes and beasts and fowls of the air devour one another. But to man, Zeus has given justice. Beside Zeus on his throne Justice has her seat." These passages show that the great and bitter needs of the helpless were reaching up to heaven and changing the god of the strong into the protector of the weak.

pirate-like

So, back of the stories of an amorous Zeus and a cowardly Zeus and a ridiculous Zeus, we can catch sight of another Zeus coming into being, as men grew continually more conscious of what life demanded of them and what human beings needed in the god they worshiped. Gradually this Zeus displaced the others, until he occupied the whole scene. At last he became, in the words of Dio Chrysostom, who wrote during the second century A.D.: "our Zeus, the giver of every good gift, the common father and savior and guardian of mankind."

The *Odyssey* speaks of "the divine for which all men long," and hun- dreds of years later Aristotle wrote, "Excellence, much labored for by the race of mortals." The Greeks from the earliest mythologists on had a perception of the divine and the excellent. Their longing for them was great enough to make them never give up laboring to see them clearly, until at last the thunder and lightning were changed into the Universal Father.

READING AND WRITING SKILL: *Paraphrasing*

"Paraphrasing" means putting an author's ideas into your own words. When you read, paraphrasing helps you to understand and retain new informa- tion. It also allows you to state an author's point concisely and to test your ability to understand a concept. Only when you can work with an idea in your own words have you fully grasped it. And when you write, you may need to refer to an author's point or idea as support or illustration in your own work. Para- phrasing an author's words is helpful when you don't want to quote long passages but still need to include the basic ideas from the source of your information.

Look at the last paragraph, sentence 1, on page 11: "That is the miracle of Greek mythology — a humanized world, men freed from the paralyzing fear of an omnipotent Unknown." To paraphrase that sentence, you need to do three things:

1. *Find the focus of the sentence — the main idea.* Some ways of finding the main idea include:

   - Deleting transitional words or phrases so that you'll be left with the main elements of the sentence.
   - Identifying who's doing the action, what the action is, and what the object of the action is.

   In this case, the "miracle of Greek mythology" created/depicted "a humanized world . . . (and) freed (men) from the paralyzing fear of an omnipotent Unknown." This process can make a long, complex sentence easier to understand. Note that some sentences are already in simple and direct form. For example, the topic sentence in paragraph 7 reads: "The Greeks made their gods in their own image."

2. *Think of synonyms for the main words or phrases.* (You shouldn't change key words or terms, like "mythology" or "Greek," however, nor should you change names or proper nouns, such as "Hamilton" or "the Greeks." But you can substitute a number of other words and thus simplify things. Don't use synonyms that are unusual or less precise than the original word (don't say "fairy" instead of "nymph," and don't use a long descriptive phrase instead of "mythology").

3. Finally, *restate the idea in your own words and sentence structure.*

You can paraphrase Hamilton's line in several different ways, depending on your purpose. If you're paraphrasing an idea in order to comprehend it better, you may want a short marginal note which uses some of the author's words but changes the sentence structure into a simple structure telling "who" is "doing what action" to "whom or what": "Greek mythology (who/what) humanized the world and freed man (did what action) from fear of unknown gods (in this case, from whom or what)."

If you're writing a paragraph and need to paraphrase an author's idea, refine your paraphrase so that it's not only in your own sentence structure but also uses your own words. A sentence like "The Greek miracle in mythology was making the world human and freeing men from the fear of an omnipotent Unknown" is not a concise restatement and approaches plagiarism by repeating the majority of the author's actual words directly. A more useful and correct paraphrase might read, "Greek mythology depicted a world where man was unafraid of an all-powerful Unknown."

The following exercise asks you to paraphrase material from Hamilton's essay. Word your paraphrases the way you speak, but be sure they still communicate Hamilton's ideas. Paraphrase her lines first as you would to improve your reading comprehension. Then write each one in your own words as you would if you were including her ideas in a paragraph of your own.

1. Paraphrase the following sentence by isolating the action, the doer of it, and its object:

   > The terrifying incomprehensibilities which were worshiped elsewhere, and the fearsome spirits with which earth, air and sea swarmed, were banned from Greece.

   > First, find the verb: what is the action?
   > . . . were banned . . .
   > Next, ask who is the doer of the action?
   > Greece, or the Greeks
   > Finally, ask what did they do?
   > The Greeks banned _____. (Reword the key ideas "terrifying incomprehensibilities" and "fearsome spirits.")

2. Restate the final sentence of paragraph 5: "Nothing we learn about them is alien to ourselves."

3. Paraphrase the following sentence: "Mankind's chief hope of escaping the wrath of whatever divinities were then abroad lay in some magical rite, senseless but powerful, or in some offering made at the cost of pain and grief."

4. In paragraphs 7 to 9, Hamilton discusses the anthropomorphic nature of the Greek gods. Paraphrase the distinction she makes between the Greek image of a god and the Egyptian or Mesopotamian image.

5. Paraphrase paragraph 5 in one or two sentences.

You can paraphrase an entire paragraph in various ways. You can read over the paragraph carefully, and then state the gist of it in your own words, cutting out information you consider nonessential. When the reading material is complex, however, this method may not be helpful. You might try locating the topic idea first, paraphrase it, and then check the rest of the sentences in the paragraph to see if they're directly relevant to the topic idea. Paraphrase those that are important for the paragraph's meaning. Another way — one that should work well for this assignment — is to go through the paragraph you want to paraphrase, group the sentences logically, and then paraphrase the main idea of each group of sentences. Look at paragraph 5 in Hamilton's essay. The sentences can be grouped logically to make paraphrasing easier. One grouping might be as follows:

> We do not know when these stories were first told in their present shape; but whenever it was, primitive life had been left far behind. The myths as we have them are the creation of great poets.

Locate the central idea in these sentences and paraphrase it:

The next group of sentences all relate to the *Iliad* and can be logically grouped together:

> The first written record of Greece is the *Iliad.* Greek mythology begins with Homer, generally believed to be not earlier than a thousand years before Christ. The *Iliad* is, or contains, the oldest Greek literature; and it is written in a rich and subtle and beautiful language which must have had behind it centuries when men were striving to express themselves with clarity and beauty, an indisputable proof of civilization.

Identify the essential information related to the *Iliad* and paraphrase it:

The final three sentences complete the paragraph's main point and can be expressed in one sentence. Paraphrase these lines to complete your assignment:

> The tales of Greek mythology do not throw any clear light upon what early mankind was like. They do not throw an abundance of light upon what early Greeks were like — a matter, it would seem, of more importance to us, who are their descendants intellectually, artistically, and politically, too. Nothing we learn about them is alien to ourselves.

6. In your own words, characterize the behavior of the Greek gods, as Hamilton describes it in paragraph 12.

7. In paragraphs 17 and 18, Hamilton discusses three different possible purposes of myth. Locate the purposes and state them in your own words.

Survey the following two readings. Read the titles first. Are the names "Echo," "Narcissus," and "Oedipus" already familiar to you? What do you know about these mythological characters? The titles have no author's name included with them; why? Think about other works usually not associated with a particular author: the Bible, folk tales, nursery rhymes. Ancient or traditional stories often can't be attributed to a single author. As you read, you may notice that the following selections are narratives, or stories, unlike Hamilton's article, which is an expository essay (an essay whose purpose is to clarify some point through analysis or argument). Continue surveying the articles on your own. Although you may not want to survey all stories you read, especially if you're reading for pleasure alone, surveying will help you retain and synthesize information when you read for academic purposes.

"Echo and Narcissus"

KEY CONCEPTS

VENGEANCE, or the "avenging goddess" (page 19) represents a moral principle in Greek religious thought. Any offense against the gods, direct or indirect, had to be punished for the moral order to continue. A related notion of vengeance appears in the Old Testament.

Freudian theory uses **NARCISSISM** to denote obsessive concern with the self. Narcissus in this myth "fell in love with himself" (page 19).

● Echo was a beautiful nymph, fond of the woods and hills, where she devoted herself to woodland sports. She was a favorite of Diana, and attended her in the chase. But Echo had one failing; she was fond of talking, and whether in chat or argument, would have the last word. One day Juno* was seeking her husband, who, she had reason to fear, was amusing himself among the nymphs. Echo by her talk contrived to detain the goddess till the nymphs made their escape. When Juno discovered it, she passed sentence upon Echo in these words: "You shall forfeit the use of that tongue with which you have cheated me, except for that one purpose you are so fond of — reply. You shall still have the last word, but no power to speak first." *(margin:* Latin for Hera, queen of the gods)

This nymph saw Narcissus, a beautiful youth, as he pursued the chase upon the mountains. She loved him and followed his footsteps. O how she longed to address him in the softest accents, and win him to conversation! But it was not in her power. She waited with impatience for him to speak first, and had her answer ready. One day the youth, being separated from his companions, shouted aloud, "Who's here?" Echo replied, "Here." Narcissus looked around, but seeing no one called out, "Come." Echo answered, "Come." As no one came, Narcissus called again, "Why do you shun* me?" Echo asked the same question. "Let us join one another," said the youth. The maid answered with all her heart in the same words, and *(margin:* avoid)

SOURCE: *Bulfinch's Mythology* by Thomas Bulfinch (Thomas Y. Crowell, Co.). Copyright © 1970 by Harper & Row, Publishers, Inc. Reprinted by permission of the publisher.

hastened to the spot, ready to throw her arms about his neck. He started back, exclaiming, "Hands off! I would rather die than you should have me!" "Have me," said she; but it was all in vain. He left her, and she went to hide her blushes in the recesses of the woods. From that time forth she lived in caves and among mountain cliffs. Her form faded with grief, till at last all her flesh shrank away. Her bones were changed into rocks and there was nothing left of her but her voice. With that she is still ready to reply to any one who calls her, and keeps up her old habit of having the last word.

Narcissus's cruelty in this case was not the only instance. He shunned all the rest of the nymphs, as he had done poor Echo. One day a maiden who had in vain endeavored to attract him uttered a prayer that he might some time or other feel what it was to love and meet no return of affection. The **avenging goddess** heard and granted the prayer.

There was a clear fountain, with water like silver, to which the shepherds never drove their flocks, nor the mountain goats resorted, nor any of the beasts of the forest; neither was it defaced with fallen leaves or branches; but the grass grew fresh around it, and the rocks sheltered it from the sun. Hither* came one day the youth, fatigued with hunting,   *to this place* heated and thirsty. He stooped down to drink, and saw his own image in the water; he thought it was some beautiful water-spirit living in the fountain. He stood gazing with admiration at those bright eyes, those locks curled like the locks of Bacchus or Apollo, the round cheeks, the ivory neck, the parted lips, and the glow of health and exercise over all. **He fell in love with himself.** He brought his lips near to take a kiss; he plunged his arms in to embrace the beloved object. It fled at the touch, but returned again after a moment and renewed the fascination. He could not tear himself away; he lost all thought of food or rest, while he hovered over the brink of the fountain gazing upon his own image. He talked with the supposed spirit: "Why, beautiful being, do you shun me? Surely my face is not one to repel you. The nymphs love me, and you yourself look not indifferent upon me. When I stretch forth my arms you do the same; and you smile upon me and answer my beckonings* with the like." His tears   *calls* fell into the water and disturbed the image. As he saw it depart, he exclaimed, "Stay, I entreat* you! Let me at least gaze upon you, if I may   *beg* not touch you."

With this, and much more of the same kind, he cherished the flame that consumed him, so that by degrees he lost his color, his vigor, and the beauty which formerly had so charmed the nymph Echo. She kept near him, however, and when he exclaimed "Alas! alas!" she answered him with the same words. He pined away and died; and when his shade* passed the   *ghost* Stygian river, it leaned over the boat to catch a look of itself in the waters. The nymphs mourned for him, especially the water nymphs; and when they smote* their breasts Echo smote hers also. They prepared a funeral   *hit* pile and would have burned the body, but it was nowhere to be found; but in its place a flower, purple within, and surrounded with white leaves, which bears the name and preserves the memory of Narcissus.

WRITING SKILL: *Developing a Paragraph*

You've probably read the traditional definition of a paragraph many times: a group of sentences organized around a single topic, whose first line is indented. Although such a formulation is sufficient as a basic definition, it really only describes a physical phenomenon. It doesn't tell you how to write a paragraph or what qualities distinguish a good paragraph from a bad one.

If you approach paragraphing as a thought process instead of a mechanical grouping of ideas, you may get better results. Many students tend to minimize the importance of paragraph-level thought (as do some instructors when they say "Write just a paragraph . . . ," perhaps unintentionally communicating a sense of its unimportance). But paragraphs in most academic writing are developed ideas, not a series of impressions or a list of observations. Paragraphs can be hard to write because academic thinking — analytical, synthetic, logical, original thinking — demands hard work.

Putting as much mental effort as you can into writing your paragraphs pays off, in several different ways. First, you know more about your topic after you've written a paragraph because you've thought about it in depth: you think by writing. Next, you improve the quality of your work and, in turn, the level of your grade (usually a reliable motivator among college students). And finally, by approaching each paragraph you write as inquiry rather than as the filling out of a predetermined form, you can lessen any writing anxiety you may experience. You can stop defining a paragraph as *X* number of lines you have to fill up, whether or not you have a corresponding number of thoughts. Treat a paragraph instead as an organic process — a thought that grows into other, necessarily related thoughts. Your paragraph's length should be determined not by a formula but by the complexity of the core, or topic, idea, and your increasing skill in drawing it out.

We don't advocate that you throw out all previous paragraphing instruction you've received, but we do suggest that you adapt our notion of paragraphing as thinking to any formulaic approach you now use. In one common formula, for example, you're asked to write a topic sentence and then list two supporting ideas and two illustrating examples. You might use this kind of formula as a prewriting exercise. A paragraph formula can help you begin writing. But you haven't finished your basic composing work until your original thought has reworked such a paragraph's formulaic structure. In other words, a good paragraph has more than an organizational plan. It also has intellectual depth and originality resulting from a process of your own questioning, considering, and reconsidering of your topic.

The following model suggests an approach to paragraphing that mixes formula and original thought. The steps outline one possible process for writing a first-draft paragraph.

In general, when you're writing for academic purposes, paragraphs should contain the following elements:

1. *A topic sentence that answers the assignment* <u>*directly*</u>. "Topic sentence" or "topic idea" traditionally means the main point of a

paragraph. You might think of it as an idea you need to explain to your readers, a term you need to define for them, or an example or statement you wish to examine. You can also consider the topic idea as an answer to a question, one assigned by your instructor or one you pose to yourself. Setting up a question/answer framework for a paragraph can help you clarify for yourself and your readers what the real issue of a paragraph is.

When you first begin writing a paragraph, answer the assigned question, or the one you've framed for yourself, directly. By focusing on the topic in your first sentence, you can insure the paragraph's correct focus throughout. Note that the topic sentence should <u>answer</u> the question, <u>not repeat it</u>. You can use an assignment's wording to help you focus your ideas, but <u>your</u> ideas still need to appear in your topic sentence. In the final version of your paragraph, the topic sentence need not be the first sentence, because you may want to use transitional phrases or sentences, or begin with an example or quotation that you later explain. But you may have an easier time developing your ideas in a first draft if you begin with the topic idea.

2. *An analysis or explanation of the topic idea.* To explain or analyze the topic idea, you may again find it helpful to ask yourself questions about it. Do you need to define any terms or concepts? If you've been asked to analyze the nature of one of the Greek gods — Zeus, for instance — do you need first to explain who he is? What is he known for? Why? How does he behave toward the other gods and humankind? The questions <u>who, what, why,</u> and <u>how</u> are usually helpful places to start in this questioning process. And you can get real depth of thought into your paragraphs by questioning your topic idea and then questioning each answer you come up with. If you ask yourself what Zeus is known for, you might answer that he's the god of thunder. Then you should ask more questions: what's the importance of thunder — what does it mean to control it? Thunder is a kind of stormy, natural power. It marks Zeus as a powerful, sometimes angry god. Keep this questioning process going to expand your analysis of the topic and the amount of careful thought in the paragraph.

3. *An explanation of the topic idea's <u>implications</u>.* You've explained the basic logic of your topic idea; now ask yourself, "So what?" Does your analysis allow you to draw a conclusion? Has your thought process led to some new point? Can you evaluate, warn, sum up? Returning to the "Zeus" topic, consider the implications of Zeus's power. So what if he controls thunder and uses it to express anger? What are the effects on humankind? How powerful must he be? What might the consequences of displeasing him be?

We want to emphasize that the questions listed above should be part of a <u>process</u>. You don't need to ask them in a given order (though logically you need to explain an idea before discussing its implications). The topic itself determines which questions you should ask, and how often. The point is for you to get accustomed to using a questioning process so that you engage your topic as an issue demanding careful, thorough, original thought.

Suppose after reading "Echo and Narcissus" you're asked to write a paragraph discussing how Echo's punishment fits her "crime" especially well. You can begin your development process this way:

1. *Answer the question in your topic sentence.* <u>How</u> does her punishment fit the crime well?

Topic sentence: Echo's punishment fittingly matches her crime in that the very "weapon" she used to hurt others — her voice — is turned against her.

The topic sentence only has to <u>announce</u> the answer you'll develop, not explain it. Your explanation comprises the rest of the paragraph.

2. *Explain how the main elements of your topic sentence relate to each other.* <u>How</u> is Echo's voice a "weapon" used in a "crime"? <u>How</u> is her voice turned against her?

First stage of development. Echo's constant chatter prevents Juno from pursuing her philandering* husband. Juno, as Zeus's wife, is the queen of the goddesses and deserves Echo's respect. But Echo detains Juno with her talk and so protects Zeus and the other nymphs, frustrating Juno's pursuit and causing her anger. Juno's sentence, that Echo may never again speak first but only repeat others' words, takes the cause of Juno's anger and makes it the cause of Echo's pain. *unfaithful*

You're now set for the next stage of development.

3. *Explain why the topic idea makes sense, is logical, has come to be.* <u>Why</u> is turning Echo's voice against her particularly fitting?

Second stage of development. Like Hammurabi's code, which demands an eye for an eye, Juno's decree makes Echo give up the right to assert her wishes, as Echo's persistent talk did to Juno. Echo insisted on having the last word in every conversation, even with a goddess. Her punishment therefore forces her to give the last word, literally, of any conversation she has. With every word she speaks she is forced to recognize both her "crime" and her punishment at the same time.

4. *Now you're ready to make some statement about the preceding material.* What does it <u>mean</u> — for you, for Echo, for the Greeks, for moral beliefs? Does it teach something, explain something — what is its purpose? Its effect? Keep thinking of questions to ask that help you explore the topic idea's implications.

Final stage of development. Juno's divine retribution against Echo serves several purposes. First, it reinforces a moral code, one that says you must pay for any crime with punishment of equal seriousness. Next, because

Echo's sentence is harsh, for it leads to her eventually fading away, it forces the reader to recognize how serious her sin of disrespect really was. Her punishment also explains what was once a mysterious natural phenomenon, the echo, and the full account of Echo's "crime" and punishment helped satisfy the early human need to understand the physical world. Finally, Juno's matching of punishment to transgression enhances the story, making for a balanced plot in this classic myth.

The paragraph's basic structure and content are now ready for revision (see pages 24–26) and proofreading, the final steps in the writing process that, along with the thinking process modeled above, make the difference between work that is at best adequate and work that reflects college-level thought. The process is what is important here. It shows why no two authors writing on the same assignment will produce the same paragraph. No one single answer to the assigned question exists. The individual author using his or her original thought on a topic creates an answer by going through the thinking/writing process.

Whether you discuss the questions that follow all the readings in this book in class or write paragraph responses to them, we suggest that you adapt the thinking process described here to your work.

WRITING SKILL EXERCISES

Respond to the following questions in paragraphs that reflect your process of thought on each topic. We've suggested an approach to some of the questions, but you should adapt our interpretation to your own view on the topics. When you write you'll be explaining the topic to an academic audience. "Audience" refers to your reader or readers. In this case, you're asked to write for your instructor, who knows the Hamilton article and the myths, but who doesn't know how you see the material, what connections you can make, or what other relevant ideas you can bring in. You need to explain your ideas as fully as possible; try to anticipate the reader's questions and incorporate your responses into your paragraph.

[1] How does Narcissus' punishment fit his crime especially well?

You can use the paragraph developed above as a guide to developing your answer to this question, which asks you to focus on Narcissus instead of Echo. His "crime" and "punishment" are different from hers, however, so you'll need to use your own analytical ability to develop the paragraph's content.

[2] Hamilton says that myths often explain natural phenomena. Apply her view to "Echo and Narcissus."

This question asks you to take information from one reading — Hamilton's essay — and use it to explain another passage — here, "Echo and Narcissus." You'll be synthesizing information or joining ideas together to come up with new knowledge about one or both. You might begin by rewording the assignment to name your task exactly: how does "Echo and

Narcissus" explain natural phenomena? The question asks you to discuss the entire myth, so you need to look at both Echo <u>and</u> Narcissus, and how and why they become the echo and the narcissus flower.

[3] In what way does "Echo and Narcissus" illustrate Hamilton's idea that myths reflect a world where man was closely in touch with nature?

You can clarify the question's focus as we did in Question 2 by "translating" it into your own words or simpler terms. Isolate the main element of the sentence, just as you did in the paraphrasing exercises: "Echo and Narcissus" illustrates Hamilton's idea that myth shows man in close touch with nature because it _____ . Now clarify what you're being asked to do:

"In what way" = "how?" How does the myth illustrate Hamilton's idea? Begin developing your paragraph by answering the question directly. Then follow through with further analytical questioning.

[4] Does Hamilton's depiction of the Greek view of the gods apply to their depiction in the Echo myth?

You'll need to paraphrase Hamilton's depiction of the Greek view of the gods at your paragraph's start to clarify your answer for the reader. First, find the section in Hamilton's essay where she discusses the Greek view, mark it, and review it. Paraphrase it first for reading comprehension. Then begin your response to the assignment, changing your paraphrase as necessary.

WRITING SKILL: *Revising Paragraphs for Focus and Development*

Revising your writing is not a one-step process of reading over your work. Revision is an integral* part of the composition process. It consists of several   essential
different activities happening on several different levels. Its purpose is to correct and improve your written work by rethinking it, so that you've produced a piece of intelligent, clear thought expressed in appropriate style.

You should revise your work on the cumulative* levels of sentence, para-   accumulating; collecting
graph, and essay. Sentence-level revision involves checking your grammar: are your thoughts expressed in complete clauses? Do the subjects and verbs agree? Do the pronouns and antecedents? Check your punctuation as well. Remember that if you revise the wording of one sentence, you need to check the other sentences in the paragraph, too, in case you've changed a word from singular to plural, or vice versa, and you refer to it elsewhere with a pronoun.

We'll focus on paragraph revision here (a discussion of essay-level revision appears at the end of the chapter). Because an essay is made up of paragraphs, they are central to the essay's overall success. Paragraphs are the units of real thought in an essay. Without good paragraphs, an essay can't be effective.

The following excerpts from unrevised paragraphs were written by our students in response to Question 2, page **23**. We'll illustrate paragraph revision for you by showing you where some of our students' paragraphs ran into problems and how they could have revised them.

Assignment. Hamilton says that myths often explain natural phenomena. Apply her view to "Echo and Narcissus."

Chulho: In "Echo and Narcissus," the reader learns about the natural phenomena of hearing an echo and seeing oneself in clear water.

This student has run into some problems in his first sentence. His focus is good: he has answered the assignment directly by stating that "Echo and Narcissus" explains two natural phenomena. But he's made a reading comprehension error. The nymph Echo does become the echo we hear in woods and caves, according to the myth, but Narcissus becomes a flower, not a reflection. A first step in revising is checking content correctness. If you haven't understood what you've read, you'll have difficulty writing about it effectively. A reading comprehension error can occur on the level of the assignment itself. When you begin an assignment, you should read it carefully and "translate" it into your own words if necessary. Identify the sections of your reading that it refers to. Review the relevant paragraphs. Then you're ready to think about the assignment and formulate a response. When you revise that response, check its content for accuracy. A well-written paragraph containing a factual error is still a problem paragraph.

Christine: The myth "Echo and Narcissus" explains the natural phenomenon of echoes.

Christine's paragraph went on to explain very well how the myth accounts for the phenomenon of echoes, but look at her topic sentence's focus. It's too narrow — it doesn't deal with Narcissus as well as Echo. Another step in the revision process will help here: check your topic sentence and paragraph for a complete response to the assignment. When you've completed a paragraph, reread the assignment, and then read your paragraph to see if you've answered all parts of the assigned question. If not, expand your topic sentence and develop the new material in the body of the paragraph. The above two topic sentences should also be expanded to include the information that Edith Hamilton is the source of the idea that myths explain natural phenomena.

Rowena: As in most myths, "Echo and Narcissus" explains some natural phenomena. By creating a story about a phenomenon such as an echo, the ancient Greeks were able to explain it. Myths were their way of explaining the everyday occurrences they did not understand. Myths gave way to early science as a way of explaining how things came to be.

This paragraph's focus problem happens not in the topic sentence but in the development of the topic idea. A questioning process could help here. First, what does the myth explain? The writer should explain that it gives the origin of the echo and the narcissus flower. How does it account for them? The writer should then explain how Echo became an echo and Narcissus a flower. Why did Echo become an echo instead of any other natural phenomenon? The writer should analyze the connection between Echo's character and "crime" and the characteristics of an echo, a repetition of sound. Why did Narcissus become a flower? His self-absorption is related to a flower's solitary beauty. Finally, the writer might want to comment on the value of Greek myths as explanations of nature, on the Greek imagination, or might make some other relevant statement. This student's connection of myth and science is very good and shows original, synthetic thought. To revise the rest of the paragraph, she should try to explain, analyze, and discuss the topic idea in greater depth.

> *Dave:* According to Edith Hamilton, the ancient Greeks created stories to help them understand life's mysteries. In "Echo and Narcissus," Greek writers tried to explain why a person's voice is repeated in an echo and why the narcissus came into being. The myth tells us that Echo was a nymph who loved to talk. She angered a powerful goddess by talking too much and she was punished. From that moment on she could not speak except to repeat the last words spoken to her. She fell in love with a boy named Narcissus, who rejected her love. Echo eventually faded away until nothing remained except her voice. It is her voice we hear answering us when we speak in caves, forests, or mountains. Narcissus treated all nymphs cruelly and one asked for vengeance against him. His punishment was to fall deeply in love with his own image in a pond. Narcissus was so infatuated with himself that he refused to eat or drink, and he eventually died. His body was transformed into a flower. The narcissus grows along the edge of water so that it can see its reflection, just as Narcissus did. Through this myth the Greeks explained two natural phenomena in an imaginative and satisfying way.

Dave's paragraph is a very good response to the assignment. First, it reflects good reading comprehension. Second, its topic sentence provides a clear and complete answer to the assignment. And it develops the topic idea in detail, explaining how and why the myth accounts for the natural phenomena of an echo and a narcissus. The student has also checked all sentences for correct grammar.

We'll discuss further steps in the revision process later in this chapter and throughout the following ones. At this point you should be revising your paragraphs for:

- Content correctness through careful reading of the assignment and the reading material it refers to.
- Paragraph focus through a complete topic sentence response.
- Paragraph development through a thorough questioning process to explain, analyze, and discuss the topic fully.

"Oedipus"

KEY CONCEPTS

The **OEDIPUS COMPLEX** is another Freudian term. Freud theorized that young boys go through a stage in which they desire their mothers and resent their fathers, to the point of wishing them dead.

DESTINY is the idea that every individual has a predetermined life; certain things will happen to him or her regardless of choices made or actions taken.

VENGEANCE AND ATONEMENT appear again in this myth. King Laius was murdered; (see page 29, **unatoned blood**) his people, the Thebans, suffer a curse until the murderer is found and punished.

● Among all the descendants of Cadmus, the most famous and the most unhappy was Laius's son, doomed by an oracle* **to be the death of his own father and the husband of his mother.** Forewarned of such a fate, when his queen Jocasta bore a boy, Laius had him cast out on Mount Cithaeron, with his feet tightly bound to make the child more helpless against speedy death. But the goatherd charged with this cruel errand took pity on the wailing infant, and, though he told the king that his bidding was done, in truth he had given it to another herd, who took it to his master Polybus, king of Corinth. By him the boy was kindly received, and brought up under the name of Oedipus ("Swollen foot"); while Laius and Jocasta, making sure he had been torn to pieces by wild beasts, believed themselves to live childless, and thus hoped to cheat the oracle.

a god's message

Polybus and his childless wife Merope adopted the outcast boy as their own son; then, as years went on, few at Corinth remembered how he was not so in truth. Oedipus grew to manhood never doubting but that these foster-parents were his father and mother, till one day, at a feast, some drunken fellow mocked at him for a base-born foundling.* In wrathful concern he sought to know from Merope whose son he truly was. She tried to put him off, yet could not deny that he was a stranger by birth. The dismayed youth turned to Polybus, who also gave him doubtful answers, bidding him ask no more, since it would be a woeful misfortune if ever he came to know his real parents.

abandoned baby

But these hints only made Oedipus more eager to learn the truth, and he bethought himself of Apollo's oracle. Leaving Corinth secretly, he travelled on foot to Delphi, where the priestess vouchsafed* no plain answer to his question, but only this fearful warning —

gave

"Shun thy father, ill-omened* youth! Shouldst thou meet with him, he will fall by thy hand; then, wedding thine own mother, thou wilt leave a race destined to fresh crimes and woe."

having bad luck; cursed

Oedipus turned away with a shudder. Now he believed himself to understand why Polybus and Merope had made a mystery of his birth. Fearing affliction for them, who loved him so well, he vowed never to go back to Corinth, but to seek some distant land, where, if madness came upon his mind to drive him to such wicked deeds, he might be far from the parents he took for threatened by so dire* a curse.

terrible

From Delphi he was making for Boeotia, when in a narrow hollow way where three roads met, he came upon an old man in a chariot, before

SOURCE: Reprinted from *Classic Myth and Legend*, trans. by A. Hope-Moncrieff, the Gresham Publishing Co., Ltd.

which ran an arrogant servant bidding all stand aside to let it pass. Oedipus, used to bid rather than to be bidden, answered the man hotly, and felled him to the ground; then his master flung a javelin at this presumptuous* youth. With his staff Oedipus struck back, overturned the old man from the chariot, and left him dead by the roadside. In the pride of victory Oedipus went his way, ignorant that the proud lord he had slain in a chance quarrel was no other than his own father, Laius. A traveller who found the king's corpse buried it where it lay; and the news was brought to Thebes by the charioteer, who, having fled from that one bold assailant, to excuse his own cowardice gave out that a band of robbers had fallen upon them in the hollow pass.

bold; impertinent

Wandering from city to city, Oedipus reached Thebes, to find it all in mourning not only for the death of its king, but from the dread of a monster that haunted the rocky heights beyond the wall. This was the Sphinx, which men took to be a sister of Cerberus, that three-headed hound of Hades. To anyone coming near it, the creature put a riddle, which if he failed to answer, it devoured him on the spot. Till some man should have guessed its riddle, the Sphinx would not be gone; and so long as it brooded over the city, blight* and famine wasted the fields around. One or another Theban daily met death in setting his wit against this monster's, and its last victim had been a son of Creon, Jocasta's brother, who for a time ruled the kingless land. Seeing himself unable to get rid of the Sphinx, Creon proclaimed that whoever could answer its riddle, were he the poorest stranger, should have as reward the kingdom of Thebes, with all the dead king's treasures, and the hand of his widow, Jocasta, in marriage.

disease

As Oedipus entered the city, a herald* went through the streets to make this proclamation, that set the friendless youth pricking up his ears. Life seemed not dear to him; all he desired was to escape that **destiny** of crime threatened by the oracle. At once he presented himself before Creon, declaring that he was not afraid to answer the Sphinx.

messenger

They led him outside the walls to the stony wilderness it haunted, strewn* with the bones of those who had failed to get its riddle. Here he must seek out the creature alone, for its very voice made men tremble. Soon was he aware of it perched on a rock, a most grisly monster, with the body of a lion, the wings of an eagle, and the head of a woman. But Oedipus, caring little whether he lived or died, shrank not from its appalling looks.

covered; spread about

"Put thy riddle!" he cried; and the Sphinx croaked back —

"What creature alone changes the number of its feet? In the morning it goes on four feet, at midday on two, in the evening on three feet. And with the fewest feet, it has ever the greatest strength and swiftness."

Fixing her cruel eyes on the youth, she frowned to see him not at a loss, nay, he smiled in her stony face, answering forthwith —

"The riddle is easy. It is man that in childhood goes on all-fours, then walks firmly on two feet, and in his old age must lean upon a staff."

Furious to hear her riddle guessed for the first time, the Sphinx gave a shrill scream, flapped her gloomy wings, and vanished among the rocks, never more to be seen at Thebes. With shouts of joy the watching citizens poured out to greet that ready-witted youth that had delivered them from such a scourge.* They hailed him as their king; and he was married to the widowed Jocasta, the more willingly on his part, as he believed himself thus made safe against the unnatural union predicted by the oracle, for he held Merope to be his mother, for all her denial.

    plague

    Years, then, he reigned at Thebes in peace and prosperity, gladly obeyed by the people, who took this young stranger for a favorite of the gods. He loved his wife Jocasta, older than himself as she was; and they had four children, the twin-sons Eteocles and Polynices, and two daughters, Antigone and Ismene. But when these were grown to full age, the fortune of the land seemed to change. For now a sore plague fell upon it, so that the people cried for help to their king, who sent to Delphi his brother-in-law, Creon, to ask of the oracle how the pestilence* might be stayed.

    plague

    The answer was that it came as punishment for the **unatoned blood** of Laius. Now, for the first time, Oedipus set on foot enquiries as to his predecessor's death. Vowing to do justice on the criminal, whoever this might prove to be, he consulted Tiresias the seer,* struck with blindness in his youth because he had spied upon the goddess Athena, who again, taking pity on him for the loss of his eyes, gave him marvellous sharpness of ear, so that he understood the voice of all birds, also she filled his mind with mystic knowledge of things past and of things to come. But the blind seer was loath* to tell what Oedipus sought to know.

    prophet

    reluctant

    "Bitter is knowing when ignorance were best. Let me go home, with a perilous* secret hid in my bosom!"

    dangerous

    In vain the people besought* him, in vain the king bid him speak. At last Oedipus angrily reviled* him as having himself had a hand in the murder he would not disclose. This rash accusation made the old man speak.

    begged

    abused and accused

    "Hear then, oh king, if thou must learn the truth. Thou thyself art the man that slew Laius in the hollow way to Delphi. For thy sake, and no other, this curse is come upon the city."

    Now with a start Oedipus remembered that old lord in the chariot whom he had slain in quarrel as he came from Delphi. Anxiously he pressed Jocasta with questions about her first husband. She described his gray hair, his haughty* bearing, his black steeds; she told that he had been killed by robbers in a hollow pass where three ways met; and every word made Oedipus surer of the truth. But his wife mocked at the seer's wisdom.

    overly proud

    "Even the god's oracle may speak falsely," she said, "for Laius was warned at Delphi that he should fall by the hand of his own son, who, moreover, should marry his mother. Yet we never had but one child, and he was thrown out to die on Mount Cithaeron when not three days old, that thus our house should escape so dark a doom."

    Among the bystanders chanced to be that goatherd charged long ago with the child's death; and him Jocasta called to confirm her words. But the old man fell on his knees, confessing how he had not had the heart to leave a helpless babe to be torn by wolves and eagles, but had given it alive to a servant of the king of Corinth.

Jocasta raised a cry, for she knew her husband passed for a son of that king, and she began to guess the truth, now clear to the awestruck Oedipus, that he and no other had unwittingly* fulfilled the oracle by slaying his own father and wedding his mother. While he stood aghast,* veiling his face for shame and horror, she fled to her chamber, like one out of her senses, barring herself in with her unspeakable woe. When the door was broken open, she had hanged herself with her girdle* rather than look again upon the husband who was no other than her son.

"Thy sorrows are ended; but for me death were too light a punishment!" he wept upon her dead body. And with the buckle of Jocasta's girdle he bored out the sight of both his eyes, so that night came upon him at noonday.

A blind old man, his hair grown suddenly gray, Oedipus groped his way out of the palace, poorly dressed as he had entered it a travel-worn youth; and leaning on the staff with which he had been the death of his father. His people turned away from him shuddering. His own sons held aloof.* Only his daughters, Antigone and Ismene, followed him tearfully, begging him to stay. He would not be entreated; and when they had led him out of the city, Ismene took leave of him and went back to her brothers, already quarreling over the kingdom.

But Antigone vowed that she would never desert her father, and with him she wandered away from her birthplace. Led by her, he went from city to city as a blind beggar, till they came to Athens, where Theseus was king. He gave the exiles refuge in a temple at Colonus. In this sanctuary Oedipus lived on for some years, poor and sorrowful, pitied by his neighbors as a victim of fate, and gently tended by Antigone till death came to end his strange misfortunes.

(margin glosses) unknowingly
horrified

sash; belt

apart

QUESTIONS FOR DISCUSSION AND WRITING

Responding to the following questions in writing should help you clarify and better understand what you've read. Study the questions; be sure you know what you're being asked to do before you begin writing. Find the sections in the text that relate to each question and review them to help you focus your thoughts. Then begin your writing process. Remember that revision is an essential part of that process.

[1] Why did Oedipus leave his home in Corinth? What does his action reveal about his character?

Your response to this question should connect Oedipus' motive for leaving Corinth with his character. You might ask yourself what alternatives he had and what his actual choice shows about the kind of person he is. Think about some possible interpretations: Was he selfish? Proud? How did *he feel about leaving, happy or sad? Think about his character <u>before</u> you begin writing.*

[2] Jocasta kills herself when she learns the truth about her marriage, but Oedipus says that death is "too light a punishment" for him. Why does he think that living with his shame is greater punishment than death?

After you examine Oedipus' reasons for choosing life over suicide, take your discussion further. Consider the implications of Oedipus' decision to live. He makes a <u>moral</u> choice; what is the moral of his action and the myth?

[3] In addition to explaining natural phenomena, myths reflect a moral code, according to Hamilton. What moral issues can you identify in the Oedipus myth?

This assignment asks you to use Hamilton's ideas to analyze the Oedipus myth. As in Question 2, you'll be locating the morals of the myth.

[4] Of the three mythological figures you've read about, which do you consider the most tragic — Echo, Narcissus, or Oedipus?

Sometimes assignments seem to request a one-sentence, or even one-word, answer. In almost every case, however, such assignments imply the question "why?" Your process of questioning your ideas to develop a paragraph should lead you to explain your response fully, even when an assignment doesn't specifically ask "why?" To address the above question fully, you should explain why the character you choose as the most tragic suffers the greatest emotional pain, loses the most, and faces the worst fate.

Philosophy: The Beginnings of Rational Thought

READING SKILL: *Critical Reading*

When you read academic texts, particularly material that is difficult or new, you shouldn't read passively. You shouldn't think of reading merely as getting new information from a printed page and inserting it into an empty file space someplace in your head. Instead, academic reading should be an active process in which you constantly question, check, and review what you already know about the subject while you're reading, and then respond to it in some way.

Behind the words on the pages you read is an author, a person. Think of what it's like when you talk to someone in person who is explaining something to you or telling you a story. If you don't understand something the person has said, you may stop him or her and ask for clarification. If you disagree with something, you may break in and say so, or at least think about your objection. If you agree, you may say a few words of assent, mumble "uh huh," or just nod. You may laugh or make a sarcastic remark, but in any case, you usually do react or respond, either aloud or to yourself.

Good readers, when they read critically, respond in the same way to a text and to the authors behind the text. The authors aren't there to answer back the way they might in a live conversation, but if they are good writers, they try to anticipate questions the reader may ask, giving background information and organizing their material logically to make it accessible.

As a critical reader it's your responsibility to ask questions, to stop, think, agree, disagree, and suspend judgment until you read further and ultimately synthesize what you've read with what you already know. The authors of your reading material may not be physically present, but you should respond as if they were. Stop every couple of lines and think about what you've read. Paraphrase the author's ideas. Respond with a marginal note, even if it's as short as something like "new info" or "tough reading."

Critical reading is slow reading, probably just as slow as a real conversation with a real instructor might be. But you should find it efficient, particularly with material that is difficult or unfamiliar. And critical reading can make uninteresting material more enjoyable because it forces you to get involved with the text.

Survey the following essay. Notice that this article includes an overview which sets the tone for the reading. Notice that it also has subheadings that divide it into three sections: "Pioneers of Rational Thought," "Socrates and Plato," and "Aristotle." Be sure to read such overviews and chapter headings as part of your survey.

Once you begin reading, stop to ask questions about the material. In the following excerpt from the passage, the questions in brackets are ones the active critical reader might ask:

> The earliest Greek philosophers (sixth century B.C.) began by criticizing the prevailing nature-myths. [What is a nature-myth?] They found it hard to believe that earthquakes were caused by the stamping of Poseidon [Who is Poseidon? Do I need to know?] or that lightning was a bolt from Zeus. They made the crucial intellectual leap from a primitive **anthropomorphic view** [What is an anthropomorphic view? The term is in boldface — what does that indicate?] of nature to a rational, analytic view. [How? What _is_ a _rational_ view?]

Read the following article actively, stopping to question its ideas and judgments, pinning down its terminology, and calling to mind any knowledge you already have about Greek philosophy.

Thomas H. Greer wrote "The Founders of Western Philosophy" in 1977. As Greer points out, the Golden Age Greeks originated systematic philosophical thought. They explored theories of the material world — Greek philosophies often bordered on what we consider scientific issues — as well as devel-

oping a theory of idealism. Plato was this original and greatly influential theorist. Later, Platonic theory was incorporated into Christian thought and thus survived throughout the Middle Ages and Renaissance. Nineteenth-century thought also expanded idealist theory. (Following Greer's article you'll find an excerpt from Plato's Symposium *which helps illustrate how idealism works.) Aristotle's works have had similar historical importance, especially in science and literature. As Greer explains, Aristotle defined a systematic method of inquiry.*

THOMAS H. GREER
"The Founders of Western Philosophy"

KEY CONCEPTS

MATERIALISM vs. **IDEALISM** (Plato's "Doctrine of Ideas, page 36), or a belief in "unseen essence" (page 34), is a fundamental concept in Western philosophy. Materialists claim that existence has a real foundation in the objects we perceive; idealists believe that existence is an idea, an essence, perceivable through thought, not sense.

ABSOLUTE vs. **RELATIVE TRUTH** is a logical concept used throughout this passage. It helps us to distinguish context: does a thing or idea depend on another thing or idea for its meaning, or does it have a constant, universal meaning?

EMPIRICAL EVIDENCE, or "the evidence of the senses" (page 34), is information gained through observation.

THEORY OF KNOWLEDGE (page 36) is also called **EPISTEMOLOGY,** the study of the source and characteristics of knowledge.

IDEA OF THE SOUL (page 36) is another way of saying **METAPHYSICS —** what is the nature of the spiritual world?

SOPHISTS, SOCRATIC METHOD, DIALECTICS, THE ACADEMY, PLATONIC DOCTRINE OF IDEAS, UTOPIA, and **THE GOLDEN MEAN** are terms whose definition you will find from their context in the article. These terms will appear in your academic reading quite often because they represent some of the greatest Greek contributions to Western thought.

● The earliest Greek philosophers (sixth century B.C.) began by criticizing the prevailing nature-myths. They found it hard to believe that earthquakes were caused by the stamping of Poseidon or that lightning was a bolt from Zeus. They made the crucial intellectual leap from a primitive, anthropomorphic view of nature to a rational, analytic view.

SOURCE: "The Founders of Western Philosophy" by Thomas H. Greer in *A Brief History of Western Man,* Third Edition. Harcourt Brace Jovanovitch, Inc., 1977.

Pioneers of rational thought

One of the basic questions they sought to answer through rational analysis relates to the composition of the physical universe: What are the elements from which all **material things** are made? Around 600 B.C., Thales of Miletus (in Asia Minor) hypothesized that water is the basic ingredient. This was a logical inference,* since water seems to be present, in various forms, throughout the world of space and matter. It fills the sea, rivers, and springs; it falls from the sky; it is found in the flesh and the organs of animal bodies. And, under varying conditions of temperature and pressure, it changes from a liquid to a solid or a vapor. Thales was no doubt aware that his hypothesis did not explain all the varied appearances of matter; but he and other Greek thinkers were convinced that nature, in its **unseen essence,** is far simpler than it appears to be.

conclusion derived from evidence

Though later philosophers rejected Thales' belief that everything can be reduced to water, they agreed that he was on the right track. Some believed the prime substance to be air or fire; others concluded that there are four basic elements: earth, air, fire, and water. But during the fifth century B.C. Democritus of Abdera (in Thrace) developed the hypothesis that all physical things are formed by combinations of tiny particles, so small that they are both invisible and indivisible. He called them atoms. Democritus' atoms are identical in substance but differ in shape, thus making possible the great variety of perceived objects in the world. They are infinite in number, everlasting, and in constant motion. They account, said Democritus, for everything that has been or ever will be. Democritus offered no **empirical evidence** to prove the existence of atoms, but the fact that he could conceive this remarkable hypothesis demonstrates the far-reaching achievement of Greek rational thought.

By sheer logic another philosopher, Parmenides of Elea (in southern Italy), convinced himself that everything in the universe must be eternal and unchangeable. Change required motion, he reasoned, and motion required empty space. But empty space equals nonexistence, which by definition does not exist. Therefore, he concluded, motion and change are impossible. Parmenides readily admitted that some things appear to move and change; but this must be an illusion of the senses, he said, because it is contradicted by logic. And logic, the Greek philosophers thought, is the most reliable test of truth.

Logic did not always lead to the same answers, however. While Parmenides satisfied himself that matter was unchanging and permanent, another Greek reached the opposite conclusion. Heraclitus of Ephesus (in Asia Minor) insisted that the universe, instead of standing still, is in continuous motion. He declared that a person cannot step into the same river twice — in fact, the river is changing even as one steps into it. This doctrine proved most disturbing, for if everything is constantly changing (including ourselves), how can we gain true knowledge of anything? By the time our mind has been informed, the object of our attention is no longer what it was!

Discomforting suggestions such as these led many Greeks to abandon the effort to find **absolute or final truth.** As philosophic inquiry began to center in Athens during the fifth century B.C., serious thinkers there turned from baffling questions about physical matter, permanence, and change to the more immediate and engaging problems of human existence. A group of professional teachers, called **Sophists** because they claimed to make their pupils wise (sophos), played a leading part in this shift. Most prominent among them was Protagoras, who lived and taught in Athens. He declared, "Man is the measure of all things, of what is and of what is not." Completely skeptical* of general truths, even about the gods, he insisted that truth is different for each individual. What was true (or right) for a Spartan might be false (or wrong) for an Athenian. Furthermore, as Heraclitus had suggested, our bodies and minds are changing every moment, and our perceptions and ideas change with them.

doubting

The Sophists concluded that it is pointless to look for **absolute truth** about nature or morals. Since **truth is relative** to each individual, it is important only to know what one finds agreeable and useful, such as the arts of persuasion or how to succeed in life. As news of this teaching circulated in Athens and elsewhere in Greece, the more conservative citizens became shocked and alarmed. It smacked* of blasphemy* and threatened to subvert* the laws and moral codes of the state. Protagoras protested that his theories did not call for the denial of authority (anarchy) and cautioned his pupils, "When in Athens do as the Athenians." Social order, he agreed, requires reasonable conformity to the laws of the community, whether or not they are absolutely true or right. But the conservative elders were not reassured. It was upsetting to them to think that one person's ideas are as "true" as another's. And the laws of gods and mortals, they argued, cannot be properly respected and upheld unless the citizens believe them to be true and just — in an **absolute sense.**

strongly suggested / impiety; religious disrespect / undercut; weaken

Socrates and Plato

The greatest teacher of the fifth century was Socrates, who met the Sophist view of how to get on in life with the full force of his intellect and will. He was not a defender of the Olympian* religion or of traditional morality; he was convinced, rather, of the existence of a higher truth. Socrates did not claim to know this truth but spoke of himself only as a seeker after knowledge. Because of his skeptical approach and his primary interest in human affairs, Socrates was often mistaken for one of the Sophists. He believed that knowledge must proceed from doubting, and he was forever posing questions and testing the answers people gave him. The Athenians resented having to justify their ways and ideas to Socrates, and he became increasingly unpopular. But he persisted in his arguments and discussions, for, he felt, "The unexamined life is not worth living."

ancient Greek gods of Mt. Olympus

Socrates believed that a technique of careful questioning can lead to the discovery and elimination of false opinions, which often pass for "truth." He cross-examined his associates on their definitions of justice, right, and beauty, moving them constantly toward answers that seemed more and more certain. This **"Socratic method,"** sometimes called the **"dialectical method,"** is simply a procedure for reaching toward truth by means of a dialogue or directed discussion. Socrates did not believe it necessary to observe and collect data in order to find **absolute knowledge;** he had a deep conviction that truth is implanted in the mind but becomes obscured* by erroneous **sense impressions.** The function of the philoso-pher is to <u>recover</u> the truth that lies buried in the mind.

<small>blurred; concealed</small>

Socrates' **theory of knowledge** is closely related to his **idea of the soul** (the seat of the mind). Almost all we know about his idea of the soul, as well as his other views, comes to us through the writings of his brilliant pupil, Plato. In the dialogue of the *Phaedo,* Plato describes the final hours of his great teacher. Condemned to death by an Athenian jury on charges of corrupting the youth and doubting the gods, Socrates faces his fate cheerfully. He does so because he believes the soul is immortal, though during life it is hindered* by the troubles and "foolishness" of the body. Death brings release for the soul and the opportunity to see the truth more clearly than before. And for Socrates the real aim of life is to know the truth, rather than to seek the satisfactions of the body. His devotion to the search for truth persisted unto death.

<small>hampered</small>

It is difficult to say where the ideas of Socrates end and those of Plato begin. Plato wrote masterly literary works in the form of dialogues in which Socrates usually appears as the chief speaker. It seems clear that Plato took up the main thoughts of his teacher and carried them through a full and positive development. It is even possible that Socrates would have challenged some of the conclusions reached by his pupil. Plato, after traveling widely through the Mediterranean lands, founded a philosophi-cal school at Athens (385 B.C.). The **Academy**, as it was called, became the most influential intellectual center of the ancient world. It endured after its founder's death for over nine hundred years, and it served as a model for similar schools in other cities.

Plato continued the Socratic attack on the Sophist theory of relative truth. He refused to admit that the world consists of nothing more than imperfect nature in a constant state of flux.* Turning back to the conjec-tures* of the earlier Greek thinkers, who had been concerned with the "stuff" of the universe and with the question of permanence and change, Plato felt that the imperfect surface of things conceals a perfect, absolute, and eternal order. With daring imagination, he constructed a picture of the universe that satisfied the demands of his intelligence and his conserv-ative temperament.

<small>flow; movement
guesses based on logic</small>

In his famous **"Doctrine of Ideas,"** Plato conceded that the **physical world** is just what Heraclitus and the Sophists suggested: imperfect, changeable, and different in appearance to every individual. But the phys-ical world is superficial, possibly only an illusion of our senses; above and beyond it, Plato asserted, is the "real" **world of spirit**. This consists of perfect Ideas (Forms) authored by "God," which exist unchanged through all the ages. There are, for example, the Ideas of Man, Horse, Tree, Beauty,

Justice, and the State. These exist independent of individuals and can be known to them only through the mind (soul). The physical objects that the senses report are at best imperfect reflections or copies of the master Ideas; hence, though they may offer clues to the Ideas, they have no intrinsic* value. Philosophers should turn away from these sensory impressions and focus upon the discovery and contemplation of the perfect, the eternal, the real. It is in the realm of Ideas (Forms) that they will discover absolute truths and standards.

internal; natural

Plato and thinkers of similar outlook have found this conception sublimely* illuminating and satisfying. It is a possible explanation of the universe, though not a convincing one for persons who place faith primarily in their senses. Many arguments can be marshaled to support it, and centuries later Plato's view was to prove adaptable to the teachings of Christianity. For the Christians, also, subordinated physical things and urged believers to think upon the world of spirit — the "other" world of divine order and perfection.

nobly; grandly

Affairs on earth, according to Plato, are best guided by absolute principles as interpreted by true philosophers. Partly to provide a model society and government (state), he wrote the best known of his dialogues, the *Republic*. The book is rich with suggestions on education, literature, and the arts, but its major influence has been on social and political thought. Plato believed that human institutions should aim, not at complete individual freedom and equality, but at social justice and order. Justice, to Plato, meant harmony of function within each individual and among the individual members of a state. (An aristocrat by birth and inclination, Plato admired Spartan* institutions and had contempt for democratic ways.) Reflecting his view of the state as an organic unity, he argued that the foot should not try to become the head — nor the head the stomach. Every part of the human body and every member of the body politic should do the job it was designed to perform. Only then can friction, envy, and inefficiency — the chief sources of human and social sickness — be eliminated.

of Sparta, ancient Greek military state

To reach this objective, Plato felt, the state must be structured according to natural capacities. The bulk of citizens would make up the class of Workers (producers), who would be sorted into various occupations according to their aptitudes. Above them would be the Guardian class, which would be trained in the arts of war. From this disciplined class would be chosen, with the greatest care, the rulers of the state. While the Workers would be permitted to live "naturally," procreating and raising families, the Guardians would follow a most austere* and regulated life. Matings among them would be arranged by the state, to ensure the production of superior offspring. Any infant showing a physical defect would be left to die of exposure, and normal infants would be taken from their mothers and placed in a community nursery. Parents would not be permitted to know their own children, nor would they be allowed to possess personal property. Such extreme measures are necessary, thought Plato,

without excess; extremely simple

if rulers are to become truly selfless and dedicated to the welfare of the whole community.

The education of the Guardians, the same for males and females, was to be closely controlled. Only the "right" kind of music, art, and poetry would be taught, so that pupils would receive the desired moral indoctrination.* Men and women chosen to be the rulers would have additional training in philosophy and would serve a period of political apprenticeship before taking their place as directors of the state. The Republic of Plato remains to this day an example for believers in aristocracy, planned society, equality for women, and state control over education and the arts. It was the first of a series of **utopias**, or model states, that have offered radical solutions for the problems of human society.

training in a specific belief

Aristotle

Plato's own pupil, Aristotle, combined the brilliant imagination of his master, who had made mind the sole reality, with a sense of the reality of the physical world. Born in Stagira (in Thrace), Aristotle made his way early to Plato's Academy in Athens; years later he founded a school of his own there — the Lyceum (335 B.C.). Far more than his teacher, Aristotle was interested in the **evidence of the senses**. He was, in fact, the greatest collector and classifier in antiquity. His interests ranged from biology to poetry and from politics to ethics.

Aristotle accepted Plato's general notion of the existence of Ideas (Forms), but he held that physical matter also is a part of reality and not to be despised. Matter, he thought, constitutes the "stuff" of reality, though its shapes and purposes come from the Forms that Plato had postulated.* By logical thinking, men can gain knowledge of the purposes of things and of their interrelations, knowledge that will give meaning and guidance to their lives and bring them at the same time closer to God — whom Aristotle conceived as pure spirit and the source of the forms. To Aristotle, logic is the indispensable key to truth and happiness. For this reason, he worked out precise and systematic rules for logical thinking, rules that have been respected for centuries.

assumed; hypothesized

In his study of society and government, Aristotle began by examining existing constitutions and states. In his classic work, the *Politics,* he analyzed and evaluated the major types of political organization. He did not derive from these a model organization suitable for all cities; rather, he recognized that there are differences in local conditions and classes of inhabitants. Aristotle identified three basic types of government: rule by the one, the few, and the many. Each of these types, if dedicated to the general welfare, is legitimate, but any one of them becomes a "perversion" when the rulers pursue their own interest alone. (The worst government of all, he thought, is a perversion of rule by the many.) Under whatever constitution, Aristotle favored a strong role for the "middle class" of citizens. The more numerous poor, he stated, lack experience in directing others; the very rich are not used to obeying. The middle class knows what it is both to command and to obey and may be counted on to avoid political extremes.

The same spirit of moderation — "nothing in excess" — marks Aristotle's comments on what constitutes the "good life." In accordance with his theory that all things have a purpose, he taught that every organ and organism should function according to its design. The function of the eye is to see; the function of the ear is to hear; the function of man is to live like a man. This last calls for a harmonious balance of faculties, of both body and mind. But, since the mind is the crowning and unique part, it is clear that individuals should be governed by reason rather than by their appetites. Further, Aristotle insisted, it is not enough just to be a man; the "good life" must be nobly lived, with every act and faculty aimed at excellence.

But what makes an act excellent (virtuous)? Aristotle admitted that this is a difficult question, which cannot be answered by any exact rule. Excellence is more than a matter of knowledge or science; it is an art that each individual must develop through practice. He advised that, in general, excellence in a particular faculty lies somewhere between extremes. In battle, a warrior should exhibit neither a deficiency of nerve (cowardice) nor an excess (foolhardiness). Rather, he should strike a happy medium (courage). A work of sculpture or architecture should be judged by asking whether it might be improved, either by taking something away or by adding something to it. If it cannot, the work is "just right" — excellent.

Aristotle warned that his advice did not apply to things that are good or bad in themselves. Truth and beauty, for example, should be sought in the highest degree, while murder, theft, and adultery are evil in any degree. But in most affairs each person should find, through trial and self-criticism, the desired mean between extremes. This insistence on moderation has come to be known as the philosophy of **the Golden Mean**. It does not signify a pale average, or mediocre, standard; rather, it calls for the best performance of mind and body working together in harmony.

QUESTIONS FOR DISCUSSION AND WRITING

The following questions might be similar to questions you asked yourself as you read; they derive from a critical reading of the text.

[1] In everyday speech we often use the term "philosophy" to mean "view of life" or individual opinion. But philosophy as an academic subject differs from how we use the term generally. In the above essay, Greer emphasizes the methodical basis of Greek philosophy. As you read, did you find that this systematic approach coincides with your impression of philosophical procedure, or does it differ from it — in other words, do the ideas and concerns of the Greek philosophers strike you as <u>philosophical</u> issues? If not, how do your impressions differ?

To respond to this question, first clarify the assignment. What is it asking you to do? The question guides you by setting up a distinction between the academic meaning of "philosophy" and the word's meaning in its everyday use. You need to examine both meanings. First, what did "philosophy" mean to the ancient Greek thinkers? Then, think about what it means to you. Are the two usages alike or different? Your topic sentence should address this similarity or difference.

[2] Aristotle was Plato's student but later broke with some major Platonic teachings. What sense of their different interests and emphases did you get from reading Greer?

The first sentence tells you that Plato and Aristotle had different philosophical views. Before you begin writing, you need to clarify what each believed by reviewing the appropriate sections in Greer's article. Then examine the two philosophers' beliefs for the major differences. Your response should include a paraphrase of the main beliefs of each.

[3] The Greek philosophers developed rational thought, but rationalism did not overpower the Greek imagination, which shows itself in the Greeks' continuing interest in mythology. How might we account for the coexistence of these two apparently antithetical* interests?   directly opposite

Translate the question into your own words to clarify its focus. The question doesn't refer to any specific ideas in Greer's article; instead, you need to use your own analytical and creative thought to arrive at an answer. Consider why the Greeks might have found satisfaction in both rational and imaginative pursuits.

READING AND WRITING SKILL: *Defining Terms*

As a reader, you will often need to look up words in a dictionary to understand their meaning in a given text. You may also run across terms in your reading that refer to some historical event or that name a scientific phenomenon or a political theory. A dictionary can't always help you in these cases. You may have to consult an encyclopedia or other reference book, or else derive the definition from the term's context in a work (see page 114). When you're the writer using such terms, you can avoid confusing or distracting your readers by defining your terms for them. Because most academic writing is expository — writing whose purpose is to clarify and explain information — you should be careful to define your terms and explain how you're using them in your paragraph or essay. Definition is a skill that you'll find useful in almost any kind of paper you write.

You can approach the task of defining your terms in many different ways, ranging from an informal parenthetical remark "In Sparta (an ancient Greek city), . . ." to a formal definition extending over several paragraphs. How central a term is to your paragraph or essay and whether or not it's familiar to a general academic audience determine how much space you devote to its definition.

When you want simply to clarify a word or provide brief background information for a name, term, or concept, you can paraphrase a dictionary definition or give specific historical details within parentheses or a nonrestrictive clause. In the following examples, the definition part of each sentence is underlined:

> Echo, a nymph of the forest, fell in love with Narcissus.

> Plato's *Republic* (a work of the fourth century B.C.) outlines a utopian society.

> Plato's philosophy is a form of idealism, which stresses that the world of mind or spirit is the true basis of reality.

> Freud theorized that young boys suffer from the Oedipal complex (a term deriving from the myth of Oedipus, who killed his father and married his mother).

If a term is generally unfamiliar or unusual, or if it refers to a central idea in your paragraph or essay, you may want to provide your readers with an extended definition so that they can follow your point more easily. Again, depending on your purpose in using the term, you may need to define it in a few sentences or even several paragraphs. Definition can make up whole essays, if defining a term or concept is your central purpose in writing. When you write an extended definition, some elements to include might be:

- A paraphrase of a general dictionary definition.
- A further explanation in your own words clarifying how you use the term specifically.
- Examples to illustrate the term or concept.
- A contrast to clarify what the term does not mean.

The following paragraph builds a definition of the term "anthropomorphic" by first paraphrasing, then providing further explanation, and finally giving concrete examples:

> The Greeks viewed their gods anthropomorphically. An anthropomorphic view is one that assigns human features or characteristics to nonhuman things. Instead of being described objectively, an anthropomorphized object may be discussed as if it had human emotions, motivations, or rational thought. The Greeks depicted their gods as humans who loved, argued, felt jealous, appreciated beauty. They ate and drank, they made love, and they protected individual mortals as if they were their children. The gods, according to the Greek mythmakers, looked and acted like humans do.

If the writer of this paragraph wanted to analyze the Greek view, he or she might continue the paragraph by explaining why the Greeks anthropomorphized their gods and what significance we might attach to their view. The reader can follow the discussion more easily once the writer's central term — "anthropo-morphized" — is clearly defined.

The following paragraph topics ask you to analyze or discuss concepts from Greek philosophy. Read each question critically to decide what its focus is. Define each concept to the extent you consider necessary for a typical academic reader. In some cases you may want simply to paraphrase; in others you may need several sentences or an entire paragraph to define the concept clearly. We've underlined the terms that most likely will need to be defined for your readers.

1. Some ancient Greeks considered Sophist philosophy immoral. Why did they think it "smacked of blasphemy," as Greer puts it in paragraph 7?
2. Why did Plato consider the Republic to be a utopian society?
3. Explain the basic steps of the Socratic method.
4. What is the central quality of Aristotle's Golden Mean?

Socrates was one of the greatest thinkers in Western history, but he wrote nothing. His student Plato, however, did record Socrates' philosophical thought. Plato's works are mainly dialogues or arguments between several speakers, and usually the major speaker is Socrates. Plato wrote the dialogue Symposium *around the beginning of the fourth century B.C. "Symposium" means "drinking party." Here, Socrates entertains and instructs the other guests by telling a story. He imagines a conversation between himself and Divine Wisdom, represented by the goddess Diotima. As you read, focus on Diotima's explanation of how physical experience in the material world can lead to comprehension of ideal beauty, goodness, and truth.*

PLATO
FROM *Symposium*

● So far, Socrates, I have dealt with love-mysteries* into which even you could probably be initiated, but whether you could grasp the perfect revelation to which they lead the pilgrim* if he does not stray from the right path, I do not know. However, you shall not fail for any lack of willingness on my part: I will tell you of it, and do you try to follow if you can.

The man who would pursue the right way to this goal must begin, when he is young, by applying himself to the contemplation of physical beauty, and, if he is properly directed by his guide, he will first fall in love with one particular beautiful person and beget noble sentiments in partnership with him. Later he will observe that physical beauty in any person is

difficult concepts; secrets

traveler to a sacred place

SOURCE: From Plato: *The Symposium,* trans. by Walter Hamilton (Penguin Classics 1951). Copyright © Walter Hamilton, 1951.

closely akin to physical beauty in any other, and that, if he is to make beauty of outward form the object of his quest,* it is great folly* not to acknowledge that the beauty exhibited in all bodies is one and the same; when he has reached this conclusion he will become a lover of all physical beauty, and will relax the intensity of his passion for one particular person, because he will realize that such a passion is beneath him and of small account.

search; journey / foolishness

The next stage is for him to reckon beauty of soul more valuable than beauty of body; the result will be that, when he encounters a virtuous soul in a body which has little of the bloom of beauty, he will be content to love and cherish it and to bring forth such notions as may serve to make young people better; in this way he will be compelled to contemplate beauty as it exists in activities and institutions, and to recognize that here too all beauty is akin,* so that he will be led to consider physical beauty taken as a whole a poor thing in comparison.

related

From morals he must be directed to the sciences and contemplate their beauty also, so that, having his eyes fixed upon beauty in the widest sense, he may no longer be the slave of a base and mean-spirited devotion to an individual example of beauty, whether the object of his love be a boy or a man or an activity, but, by gazing upon the vast ocean of beauty to which his attention is now turned, may bring forth in the abundance of his love of wisdom many beautiful and magnificent sentiments and ideas, until at last, strengthened and increased in stature by this experience, he catches sight of one unique science whose object is the beauty of which I am about to speak. And here I must ask you to pay the closest possible attention.

The man who has been guided thus far in the mysteries of love, and who has directed his thoughts towards examples of beauty in due and orderly succession, will suddenly have revealed to him as he approaches the end of initiation a beauty whose nature is marvelous indeed, the final goal, Socrates, of all his previous efforts. This beauty is first of all eternal; it neither comes into being nor passes away, neither waxes nor wanes; next, it is not beautiful in part and ugly in part, nor beautiful at one time and ugly at another, nor beautiful in this relation and ugly in that, nor beautiful here and ugly there, as varying according to its beholders*; nor again will this beauty appear to him like the beauty of a face or hands or anything corporeal,* or like the beauty which has its seat in something other than itself, be it a living thing or the earth or the sky or anything else whatever; he will see it as **absolute**, existing alone with itself, unique, eternal, and all other beautiful things as partaking* of it, yet in such a manner that, while they come into being and pass away, it neither undergoes any increase or diminution* nor suffers any change.

viewers

of the flesh

sharing; having part

lessening; reduction

When a man, starting from this sensible world and making his way upward by a right use of his feeling of love for boys, begins to catch sight of that beauty, he is very near his goal. This is the right way of approaching or being initiated into the mysteries of love, to begin with examples of beauty in this world, and using them as steps to ascend continually with that absolute beauty as one's aim, from one instance of physical beauty to two and from two to all, then from physical beauty to moral beauty, and from moral beauty to the beauty of knowledge, until from knowledge of various kinds one arrives at the supreme knowledge whose sole object is that absolute beauty, and knows at last what absolute beauty is.

This above all others, my dear Socrates, is the region where a man's life should be spent, in the contemplation of absolute beauty. Once you have seen that, you will not value it in terms of gold or rich clothing or of the beauty of boys or young men, the sight of whom at present throws you and many people like you into such an ecstasy that, provided that you could always enjoy the sight and company of your darlings, you would be content to go without food and drink, if that were possible, and to pass your whole time with them in the contemplation of their beauty.

What may we suppose to be the felicity* of the man who sees absolute   happiness
beauty in its essence, pure and unalloyed,* who, instead of a beauty   unmixed
tainted* by human flesh and color and a mass of perishable rubbish, is able   corrupted
to apprehend divine beauty where it exists apart and alone? Do you think
that it will be a poor life that a man leads who has his gaze fixed in that
direction, who contemplates absolute beauty with the appropriate faculty
and is in constant union with it? Do you not see that in that region alone
where he sees beauty with the faculty capable of seeing it, will he be able
to bring forth not mere reflected images of goodness but true goodness,
because he will be in contact not with a reflection but with the truth? And
having brought forth and nurtured* true goodness he will have the privi-   supported; nourished
lege of being beloved of God, and becoming, if a man ever can, immortal
himself.

QUESTIONS FOR DISCUSSION AND WRITING

Be sure to define any philosophical terms you use in your responses to the following questions.

[1] Paraphrase the steps that allow one to move from the physical world to knowledge of the ideal, absolute realm, as Diotima explains them. Mark the appropriate sections of paragraphs 2–7 to begin your paraphrasing process.

[2] In paragraph 5, Diotima defines ideal beauty by listing its characteristics, but she uses poetic language. Paraphrase her definition. By explaining it in your own words, you should improve your understanding of the concept and you will also make it easily understandable for an academic audience.

[3] At the end of the dialogue, Diotima says that humans may become immortal by contemplating ideal beauty. Use a questioning process to develop a paragraph explaining how and why knowledge of the ideal world can allow a human to experience the immortal world. Refer to pages 20–23 to review the process of building paragraphs by questioning your topic idea.

[4] Both myths (in Hamilton's view) and philosophy are attempts to explain something about our world or experience. What different purposes do they have?

Ancient Science

READING SKILL: *Identifying Topic Sentences*

The topic sentence of a paragraph contains its key idea, its focus or main point. Identifying a paragraph's topic sentence can clarify its meaning because it states the paragraph's essential point in concise, direct form. Often the first sentence or sentences of a paragraph form the topic idea; sometimes, however, the last sentence of a paragraph sums up the topic. Occasionally, a paragraph has no topic sentence. You then have to infer a topic sentence through context. Identifying topic sentences helps you to clarify an article's thesis. It will also help you when you must write a summary, for summaries consist of your paraphrases of topic ideas.

Remember that academic prose in particular has been written by a person who is probably following the same writing conventions that you are. Just as you have been taught to write with concise topic sentences, so many of the writers you read will use them. Nevertheless, you will encounter academic writers whose prose lacks clarity, conciseness, or logic. Sometimes you'll have to work through an inelegant, wordy, or obtuse* style to get to a main point, and   unclear
sometimes you may find that no clear main point exists. Before you reach that conclusion, however, be sure that the difficulty lies in the text, not in your reading of it.

If you can't locate a topic sentence, ask yourself what the paragraph is actually doing. Is it listing examples, proving something, describing something, comparing or contrasting? If you can clarify the purpose of a paragraph's information, you may be able to work backwards to find the topic sentence or, if none exists, to infer the topic idea.

Survey the following article. Read it actively — stop to question and synthesize. And this time underline the topic sentence of each paragraph as you read.

Clagett wrote Greek Science in Antiquity, *from which this article is taken, in 1957. He points out that in science, as in philosophy, rationalism distinguished the Greek approach from that of earlier civilizations, like the Egyptians. The nations that would later base their scientific discoveries on Greek ideas and methods did not yet exist; Europe was inhabited by tribes that were to become the English, French, Germans, Italians, and so on. The Greeks led the intellectual world in systematic thought applied to scientific investigation.*

The Romans and later the Christians pursued other goals — empire and theol-
ogy — at the expense of continued scientific study and experiment. Late Mid-
dle Ages scholars took up the Greeks' knowledge, kept alive during the so-
called dark ages by the Arab world. In his essay Clagett explains the stages of
Greek scientific development and defines its major methods (which the title
of his work should suggest to you as you preread).

MARSHALL CLAGETT
"Greek Science: Origins and Methods"

KEY CONCEPTS

NATURAL PHILOSOPHY OR SCIENCE (page 46) refers to the life sciences.

EPICUREAN PHILOSOPHY (page 47) states that pleasure, or the
avoidance of pain, is the highest good. **STOIC PHILOSOPHY**, on the other
hand, emphasizes acceptance of life's pleasures and troubles with a
sense of moderation and patience. See Chapter 6, page 392.

NEO-PLATONISM (page 48) joins the Christian idea of spirit to Platonic
idealism.

DEDUCTION and **INDUCTION** (page 48) are logical patterns of inquiry.
Deductive reasoning tests an idea or observation against a general law;
inductive reasoning works from particular observations to formulating
a general law.

ARISTOTELIAN METHOD (page 49) involves making deductions from
general principles or observations.

● Much has been written concerning the seemingly sudden emergence
in the Greek Ionian colonies of the sixth century B.C. of a **natural philoso-**
phy or science rational and surprisingly secular in character. In fact, historians, in recognition of the gulf that separates the approach of this
natural philosophy from that of the cosmology of the Egyptians and the
Babylonians, have called this phenomenon the "Greek Miracle." Study of
the antecedents* in earlier Greek and Near Eastern cultures does some-   predecessors
thing to lessen the miraculous element but leaves us with considerable
admiration for the first two centuries of Greek science and philosophy,
from about 600 B.C. to about 400 B.C.

We cannot hope to detail here the developments leading to the "Greek
Miracle." But we can suggest certain crucial factors. We recognize the
importance of the change from a Bronze Age* civilization to an Iron Age*   between prehistoric Stone
civilization, a change made possible by the improvement of the tech-   and Iron Ages; use of
niques for reducing and working iron. These improved techniques appear   bronze for tools /
toward the end of the second millennium* B.C. The cheap production of   prehistoric time; use of
tools and weapons resulting from that change must have been an impor-   iron for tools / 1000-year
tant factor in the ability of the smaller Greek city-states to compete suc-   period

SOURCE: "Greek Science: Origins and Methods" by Marshall Clagett in *Greek Science in*
Antiquity. Abelard-Schumann Ltd, 1957.

cessfully in trade with the more centralized monarchies of the Near East.

Of at least equal importance, no doubt, was the development of the alphabet, which tradition would have us believe originated in Phoenicia about 1200 B.C. and which spread to areas of Greek culture sometime after the turn of the millennium. Adoption of alphabetic writing did not, of course, initiate anything like popular education. But the comparative ease with which alphabetic writing can be learned certainly made possible a wider distribution of learning than had prevailed in the earlier monarchies, where writing and reading were the property of an exclusively scribal-priestly* class.

clerical and religious

The independence of the commercial-minded inhabitants of Miletus, an Ionian city on the coast of Asia Minor, the possible weakness of the ties between the governing classes of Miletus and older religious orthodoxy* of the cities of the mainland, the immediate contact with the more cultured peoples of Asia Minor, who had drawn their culture from Mesopotamia and Egypt, and the occasional direct contacts with the culture of Mesopotamia and Egypt themselves — all these factors and no doubt others helped to produce the natural philosophy associated with the "school" of Miletus and its traditional founder, Thales (fl.* 575 B.C.).

official doctrine

flourished; the high point

But lest we ignore the intellectual past of Greece in favor of uncertain, although probable, social factors, we should not set aside the undoubted effect of the changing mythology on the evolution of natural philosophy and science among the Greeks. H. Diels, the greatest of the modern editors of the fragments remaining from the writers of the pre-Socratic period, conjectures* as to the very probable development of Greek thought out of earlier mythological speculations. And one of our most distinguished students of Greek culture, W. Jaeger, has led us carefully along the road from the mythological cosmogonies* of early Greece to the "natural" theology that is evident among the so-called "materialists" of Ionia.

guesses based on logic

theories of the universe

It is convenient to divide the period of Greek science into four main chronological divisions. The first and formative period is that usually called by the historians of philosophy the pre-Socratic period, from about 600 B.C. until just before 400 B.C. The second is the fourth century, the century of Plato and Aristotle and, later, of the creation of the **Epicurean** and **Stoic** philosophies. The third period is the so-called Hellenistic period, 300–100 B.C., when Greek culture behind the conquests of Alexander began to spread over the Near East and react more directly with the remains of the older cultures. This was the great period of Greek science, the period of Euclid, Archimedes, Apollonius, and many others. And the last is the Greco-Roman period, from about 100 B.C. to A.D. 600, a period in which Greek science was affected by the spiritual and nonrational currents that were in part responsible for the rise of Christianity. It was in this period that the Greek science which was to pass later to the Arabs and through them to the Latin West was epitomized,* reorganized, and subjected to extensive commentaries.

summarized

Initially we must insist upon the general "rational," critical, often secular and nonmythological tone that the natural philosophers of the pre-Socratic period gave to much of Greek thought and science. We hasten to add that this does not mean that Greek philosophy in general was atheistic. The briefest reading of such Pythagorean fragments as appear genuine, the references in the Ionian fragments themselves, and the subsequent **Neo-Platonic** development make any such judgment ridiculous. But the critical spirit that emerges from this period is of great moment for the subsequent growth of science.

Another distinctive feature of Greek thought that emerged during the first period was the basic concept of a "generalized" science as distinct from a set of empirical rules. It most clearly appears in the creation of a theoretical and abstract geometry. The Egyptians were accustomed in their mathematical papyri to give specific problems, such as the finding of the area of a particular field with particular dimensions. The theoretical geometry behind these empirical operations remained unexpressed and latent.* Now with the Greeks it was the theoretical and abstract geometry that became the object of attention. They arrived at the general solution for the area of any triangle, starting with fundamental definitions, axioms, and postulates.   dormant

Closely connected with the rise of the concept of a generalized, theoretical, and abstract science and closely connected also with the rising critical spirit among the Pre-Socratic philosophers, particularly in the so-called Eleatic school of philosophy, was the evolution among the Greeks of a strict methodology* of reason, or logic. Together with its kindred*   system / related disciplines of mathematics, logic is a fundamental instrument of science. Observed data, whether assembled by the most careful experimental means or not, would mean little if we had no rules for testing the truth and falsity of arguments. It would, of course, be impossible to say when man first used rules of logic — say, for example, the principle of noncontradiction. But it is clear that conscious and critical study of the rules of reasoning is a Greek discovery.

It is, then, among the Eleatic philosophers of the sixth and fifth centuries B.C. that we can find important beginnings in logic, particularly in **deductive logic,** which was used so skillfully by Plato, was formulated as a discipline by Aristotle, and served as the chief instrument for the extraordinary mathematics of Euclid and Archimedes — in fact, for the Hellenistic science generally (from about 300 B.C.). The Greeks, then, became masters of deduction, the drawing of <u>necessary</u> inferences from given premises.

On the other hand, less satisfactory was the Greek understanding of **induction**, the drawing of <u>probable</u> general conclusions from a multiplicity of particulars, the relative probability of the general conclusion depending on the relative completeness of the set of particulars. Also unsatisfactory was the discussion by the Greeks of the relation of argument to experience, although in practice they often exhibited an almost intuitive understanding of the proper relation of a scientific theory to observed data.

A word must be said about the very difficult question of **Aristotle's scientific method**. Although his *Posterior Analytics* is his chief discussion of this question, there is much elsewhere to throw light on it. In the first place the object of a science is to find its principles, its elements, or its causes. This is as true of physics as it is of zoology. "The natural way of doing this is to start from the things which are more knowable and observable to us and proceed toward those things which are clearer and more knowable by nature." That is, we proceed initially from complex effects to simple causes; and once we have found causes or principles we have scientific knowledge. But how do we proceed to causes? Herein lie the difficulties of Aristotelian procedure.

We have already briefly suggested above that the Greeks often had a happy faculty for following what was essentially sound use of empirical observation as a foundation of and check on theory. For example, the whole course of Greek astronomy, as one mathematical system after another attempts to account for the solar, lunar, and planetary movements, was fashioned with the avowed intention of "saving the phenomena" — i.e.,* accounting for appearances — and it seems that one or another of the earlier systems was rejected precisely on the grounds that the theory could not account for the phenomena, or rather that the phenomena directly contradicted some deductive conclusion of the theory. Thus the system of concentric spheres introduced by Eudoxus in the fourth century B.C. and taken up and popularized by Aristotle foundered* on the fact that the apparent size of the moon and planets varies. This indicates that these bodies are not always the same distance from the earth, and they would have to be as a necessary conclusion of the theory of concentric spheres.

Somewhat different was the role of observation and experience in the formation of the early systems of natural philosophy of Thales and his successors. These systems seem to have originated in the grossest analogies and patently insufficient observational data. Thus it is supposed that such gross facts as the plenitude* of water on the earth's surface and its ready change of form to ice or vapor led Thales to assume water as the fundamental stuff of nature and to build a system around this assumption. It may be that the insufficiency of the ties between theory and experience in the early systems is merely representative of the fact that these were the first stages of science and philosophy. It was recognized as important that there be some ties between the theoretical explanation of nature and our experience of nature; but the necessity of a multiplicity of such ties and of their surety* was not apparent. In a sense, the growth of modern science has been brought about on the one hand by the increasing sophistication of theoretical explanation, due largely to the use of mathematics, and on the other hand by the development of experimental ways to establish the surety and firmness of manifold* bonds that unite theory with experience.

It would of course, be incorrect to state that there was no experimentation in antiquity, whether for the purpose of uncovering new facts about

LATIN "id est": that is

broke down

great quantity

certainty; security

multiple

nature or for the purpose of confirming scientific theory. Even at the earliest stages of Greek science, in the sixth and fifth centuries B.C., there was experimentation by Pythagoras and the early Pythagoreans. Thus Pythagoras or his followers clearly established by experiment the relationship between the lengths of vibrating strings and the pitch of the notes emitted by the strings. It is true that the equally famous experiment of Empedocles (490–435 B.C.) with a water vessel to prove the corporality* of air was more a notation of common experience than a deliberately planned and controlled test to confirm theory. But numerous controlled experiments are recorded in the Hippocratic medical treatises, which date from the fifth and fourth centuries B.C., and when we examine the activity of the successor of Theophrastus at the famous Lyceum, Strato the Physicist, we are confronted with activity deliberately experimental for purposes of scientific investigation.

physical existence

If, then, scientific investigation in antiquity involved considerable experimental activity, we may well ask why it was that Greek science falls short of modern science. It falls short in the maturity and the universality of its use of mathematical-experimental techniques. There is no question that a mathematical-experimental science existed in nascent* form, at least, in optics, in statics, and in applied mechanics; that a mathematical-experimental science was present in astronomy; and that an experimental science existed in zoology and physiology. But the techniques of these sciences were not yet commonly considered as the necessary methods in all fields of natural investigation. Before mathematical and experimental techniques had become the common property of Greek science, that science began to level off. The leveling off (note that reference is made to "leveling off" rather than to "dying out") of Greek science in late antiquity took place for a number of important political and social reasons: Rome's rise to political power and domination of the Mediterranean area, the rise of Christianity and the consequent funneling off of many scholars who might have been scientists into dogmatic activities, and the general effect of noncritical spiritual forces that beset* the Mediterranean world from at least late Hellenistic times.

beginning

came upon; plagued

READING AND WRITING SKILL EXERCISES

[1] On page 45 we suggested that you underline the topic sentence of each paragraph as you read. You can check the topic sentences you've underlined against the ones we've listed here.

Paragraph 1 The first sentence is the topic sentence, but its overly formal construction clouds the message. The sentence begins a general introductory paragraph. The key idea here states that secular, rational natural philosophy or science began in sixth-century Greece.

Paragraph 2 Taken together, the first two sentences tell you that the paragraph will outline the "crucial factors" leading to the development of the ''Greek Miracle,'' in this case, Greek science. This kind of topic sentence prepares you for the topic idea instead of naming it directly. You need to read further to get an accurate sense of the paragraph's specific information.

Paragraph 3 The topic sentence here, in contrast to paragraph 2, actually names a factor in the rise of Greek science: development of the alphabet.

Paragraph 4 This paragraph, in fact one long sentence, gives you specific, supporting information before it states the topic idea in the final clause, beginning with ''all these factors . . . helped to produce the natural philosophy associated with the 'school' of Miletus.''

Paragraph 5 The paragraph opens with a transitional phrase followed by the topic idea. Be sure to focus on the main idea, not the transitional idea. Notice that a main point can be stated negatively and still be the focus of the paragraph. Here, ''we should not set aside the undoubted effect of the changing mythology on the evolution of natural philosophy and science among the Greeks,'' really says that mythology is another major factor in the development of Greek science.

Paragraph 6 Like Paragraph 2, this paragraph prepares the reader for the main points instead of naming them directly. It still outlines the paragraph's content for you.

Paragraph 7 The opening is a long, formal topic sentence. Restate it for yourself so that it reads simply, ''Greek thought and science took on a rational tone and left mythology behind.''

Paragraph 8 The first sentence is a direct, simply stated topic sentence.

Paragraph 9 A clear topic idea appears in the first sentence, but you need to extract it from the complex sentence structure: ''. . . the evolution among the Greeks of a strict methodology of reason, or logic'' names the topic issue of the paragraph.

Paragraph 10 The whole paragraph develops the general idea of paragraph 9. It refines the issue of logical methodology to ''deductive logic.'' When you encounter a very long topic sentence like this one, separate the topic idea from the illustrations included in the sentence.

Paragraph 11 This paragraph starts with a clear topic sentence and forms a logical unit with paragraph 10: they talk about two aspects of the issue presented in paragraph 9.

Paragraph 12 The topic sentence that opens this paragraph directly announces what will follow, that is, the difficult question of Aristotle's scientific method.

Paragraph 13 The first sentence tells you that the paragraph repeats the discussion of Greek empirical method.

Paragraph 14 The topic sentence which opens this paragraph can be identified easily because it is part of a logical progression from paragraphs 12 and 13.

Paragraph 15 The first sentence demonstrates again a negatively stated topic idea. Restate it positively to avoid confusing yourself as you read: ''There was experimentation in antiquity.''

Paragraph 16 The first sentence of this concluding paragraph sums up the whole article's topic and places it in an historical context, the relationship of ancient to modern science. Often the topic sentence of a conclusion will summarize main points and place them in some perspective.

[2] Underline the topic sentences in Greer's article on Greek philosophy. Review the suggestions for identifying topic sentences on page **45**.

Hippocrates lived c.* 460–c.377 B.C. You've probably heard that he is the "Father of Medicine" and that doctors take "the Hippocratic oath." His approach to medical science and his method for studying disease mark the beginnings of applied empirical method. The following excerpt from his scientific writings illustrates some of Clagett's major points. Hippocrates here argues against the usual perception of epilepsy as a "sacred disease."

LATIN circa; about, approximately, around

HIPPOCRATES
"The Sacred Disease"

● I am about to discuss the disease called "sacred." It is not, in my opinion, any more divine or more sacred than other diseases, but has a natural cause, and its supposed divine origin is due to men's inexperience, and to their wonder at its peculiar character. Now while men continue to believe in its divine origin because they are at a loss to understand it, they really disprove its divinity by the facile* method of healing which they adopt, consisting as it does of purifications* and incantations.* But if it is to be considered divine just because it is wonderful, there will be not one sacred disease but many, for I will show that other diseases are no less wonderful and portentous,* and yet nobody considers them sacred. For instance, one can see men who are mad and delirious from no obvious cause, and committing many strange acts; while in their sleep, to my knowledge, many groan and shriek, others choke, others dart up and rush out of doors, being delirious until they wake, when they become as healthy and rational as they were before, though pale and weak; and this happens not once but many times.

My own view is that those who first attributed a sacred character to this malady were like the magicians, purifiers, charlatans and quacks of our own day, men who claim great piety and superior knowledge. Being at a loss, and having no treatment which would help, they concealed and sheltered themselves behind superstition, and called this illness sacred, in order that their utter ignorance might not be manifest. They added a plausible story, and established a method of treatment that secured their

overly simple
cleansings / magical chants

significant; meaningful

SOURCE: Reprinted by permission of the publishers and The Loeb Classical Library from Hippocrates, *The Sacred Disease,* translated by W. H. S. Jones, Cambridge, Mass.: Harvard University Press, 1923.

own position. They used purifications and incantations; they forbade the use of baths, and many foods that are unsuitable for sick folk. These observances they impose because of the divine origin of the disease, claiming superior knowledge and alleging other causes, so that, should the patient recover, the reputation for cleverness may be theirs; but should he die, they may have sure fund of excuses, with the defense that they are not at all to blame, but the gods. Having given nothing to eat or drink, and not having steeped their patients in baths, no blame can be laid, they say, upon them. So I suppose that no Libyans dwelling in the interior can enjoy good health, since they lie on goat-skins and eat goats' flesh, possessing neither coverlet nor cloak nor footgear that is not from the goat; in fact they possess no cattle save goats. But if to eat or apply these things engenders and increases the disease, while to refrain works a cure, then neither is godhead to blame nor are the purifications beneficial; it is the foods that cure or hurt, and the power of godhead disappears.

This disease styled sacred comes from the same causes as others, from the things that come to and go from the body, from cold, sun, and from the changing restlessness of winds. These things are divine. So that there is no need to put the disease in a special class and to consider it more divine than the others; they are all divine and all human. Each has a nature and power of its own; none is hopeless or incapable of treatment. Most are cured by the same things as caused them. One thing is food for one thing, and another for another, though occasionally each actually does harm. So the physician must know how, by distinguishing the seasons for individual things, he may assign to one thing nutriment and growth, and to another diminution and harm. For in this disease as in all others it is necessary, not to increase the illness, but to wear it down by applying to each what is most hostile to it, not that to which it is conformable. For what is conformity gives vigor and increase; what is hostile causes weakness and decay. Whoever knows how to cause in men by regimen moist or dry, hot or cold, he can cure this disease also, if he distinguish the seasons for useful treatment, without having recourse to purifications and magic.

QUESTIONS FOR DISCUSSION AND WRITING

[1] How does Hippocrates' method differ from nonrational approaches to medical diagnosis and treatment?

[2] Throughout history, epilepsy has been considered a "sacred" disease or a form of spiritual possession. What characteristics of the disease might have suggested this misconception?

[3] Some of Hippocrates' medical beliefs and practices conform to modern ones; some are clearly wrong or outdated. Isolate the "modern" part of his work.

Political Systems

READING SKILL: *Locating the Author's Thesis*

A thesis is the main point or argument of an essay. It logically formulates the author's main ideas and their implications. All articles, whether argumentative, analytical, descriptive, or narrative, have a thesis, either directly stated or only implied. By articulating an author's thesis, you clarify the main idea for yourself, or, in other words, you <u>understand</u> the article.

Your survey of an article may reveal its thesis, which often appears in the title, the introduction, the first paragraph, or the concluding paragraph. To find the thesis, begin by reading the first several paragraphs, its usual location. A thesis may be one sentence or a full paragraph in length. You will recognize it by its general speculations or claims, unsupported by details or illustrations, and undeveloped by abstract explanation. It may also be recognized as opinion instead of factual or obvious statement. Ask yourself the following questions:

1. What is the <u>focus</u> of the article? What does it discuss, what does it deal with?
2. Is the author trying to prove something about the general topic? How does he view it?
3. What are the major topic ideas? Taken together, they should add up to be the thesis.
4. State the thesis in your own words, highlighting the main idea and including the abstract supporting ideas.

Read the following article and then try to find and state the thesis. A model appears at the end of the passage. To read the article actively, you might begin by asking yourself what you already know about Greek democracy, or democracy in general. As you read, decide which historical personages are relevant. All of the names — Protagoras, Euripides, Theseus — have appeared in earlier readings. Consider why Greek politics influenced later Western governments, unlike political systems developed in other ancient countries.

M. I. Finley is a well-known historian of the ancient world. This essay first appeared in The Legacy of Greece *in 1981. Finley describes how the development of "politics" represents yet another fundamental Greek contribution to the Western world. Keep in mind as you read about Greek "democracy," however, that the Greeks did not share our notion of equality; non-native-born men, women, freedmen,* and slaves were denied the right to participate in Athenian political life. Democracy as we know it derived from eighteenth-century philosophical thought and popular revolutions. Between the Golden Age of Athens and the French and American Revolutions, democracy was only political theory, not applied government.*

persons freed from slavery

MOSES I. FINLEY
"Politics"

KEY CONCEPTS

The **CODE OF HAMMURABI** is the first known written legal system. Hammurabi was a Babylonian king; his code declared that all crimes should be met with punishment of equal seriousness ("an eye for an eye"), regardless of the criminal's social status.

REVELATION is a religious concept naming a direct experience of God or his "divine plan."

A **TYRANT** is a head of state who rules absolutely without the necessary consent of the people.

In a **DEMOCRACY,** people have a direct say in their government or elect their own representatives.

● In Athens, explained the Sophist Protagoras, "when the subject of their deliberation involves political wisdom . . . they listen to every man, for they think that everyone must share in this virtue; otherwise there could be no poleis*." Euripides made the same point in his *Suppliant Women,* [cities] produced in the 420s: quoting the words of the herald at a meeting of the assembly, "What man has good advice to give the city (polis) and wishes to make it known?," Theseus comments, "This is freedom. He who wishes is illustrious; who is unwilling remains silent. For the city, what is more fair than that?"

The judgments of Protagoras and Euripides were possible only because of a fundamental Greek innovation — politics. Government is another matter: every society of any complexity requires a machinery for laying down rules and administering them, for performing community services, military and civil, and for settling disputes. Every society also requires a sanction for both the rules and the machinery, and a notion of justice. But the Greeks took a radical step, a double one: they located the source of authority in the polis, in the community itself, and they decided on policy in open discussion, eventually by voting, by counting heads. That is politics, and fifth-century Greek drama and historiography* reveal how far [body of historical writings] politics had come to dominate Greek culture.

Of course there was discussion about policy in neighboring and earlier societies, in the court circles of the kings of Egypt, Assyria, and Persia, or, on lower levels, in the courts of the Persian satraps* and the circles of the [governors] Homeric "heroes." Such discussions did not constitute politics, however, for they were neither open nor binding. The king or satrap received advice, but he was not obligated to heed it or even to request it. Those with

SOURCE: "Politics" by M. I. Finley. Copyright © Oxford University Press 1981. Reprinted from *The Legacy of Greece: A New Appraisal,* edited by M. I. Finley (1981) by permission of Oxford University Press.

access to him planned, maneuvered,* and sometimes conspired to direct his decisions, in a procedure that has been called government by ante-chamber (rather than government by "chamber"). The same was true of Greek **tyrants,** whose existence was therefore a denial of the polis-idea, and in whose regimes politics ceased to exist.

    managed; manipulated

It must be acknowledged that there were also some early non-Greek political communities, among the Phoenicians and the Etruscans at any rate. Nevertheless, it remains correct to say that, effectively, the Greeks "invented" politics. In the western tradition, the history of politics has always started from the Greeks; that is symbolized by the word "politics" itself, with its root in polis. In no Near Eastern society, furthermore, was the culture politicized as it was among the Greeks.

Nor did any previous society secularize* government in all its aspects, the ideological* as well as the practical, as did the Greeks. Nothing could be further removed from, for example, **Hammurabi's code.** The lengthy preamble* says in its opening paragraph: "Anum and Illil for the prosper-ity of the people called me by name Hammurabi, the reverend God-fearing prince, to make justice to appear in the land, to destroy the evil and the wicked that the strong might not oppress the weak." Solon of Athens, in contrast, was assigned the task of codification* by mutual agree-ment among the contending factions; he claimed neither divine guidance nor revelation nor "royal blood."

    remove from religious control / theoretical

    introduction

    written law

This insistence on the secular quality of public life appears to overlook the ubiquitous* piety* of the Greeks. Altars were everywhere; no public actions (and not many serious private ones) were taken without a prelimi-nary sacrifice; the oath was the standard sanction* in public agreements; the gods were consulted through oracles and other media; successes were shared with the gods; the management of major religious festivals was the state's responsibility, as was the punishment of impiety* and blasphemy.* Yet in neither the classical nor the Hellenistic period did this vast amount of ritual activity normally or seriously impinge* on, or divert, political decisions. A battle might be delayed for a few days, a conviction for impiety might damage an individual's career, but there is no known case when the Delphic oracle, for example, determined a state's course of action (as distinct from providing a retrospective* explanation of a failure). In the Hellenistic east after Alexander, perhaps even more significantly, kings of Egypt and Syria became gods, stressed their divinity in cult, on their coins, occasionally in their epithets* (Epiphanes = God Manifest), but their laws and edicts* were invariably issued in the name of men, not gods, and violation was never treated as a sacrilege.*

    ever-present / respect

    legal approval

    religious disrespect / irreverence; religious treason
    interfere with

    hindsight; backward-looking

    descriptive phrases or names / commands

    religious crime

Likewise in the courts: witnesses continued to testify under oath, but the oath had become a ceremony, not a formal proof as it had once been. It was now necessary to persuade the judges and jurymen; the threat that perjury* would bring down the wrath of the gods was no longer of itself persuasive. How, then, were justice and injustice to be defined and deter-mined? That is, of course, the problem that runs through both archaic*

    lying under oath

    ancient; outdated

and classical Greek literature, more sharply among the philosophers beginning with the Sophists. But it was equally a problem at the level of
practical affairs, not in abstract or general terms but in the day-to-day
decisions of assemblies, magistrates, and courts. Since Greek religion as far
back as we can trace it lacked the component of **revelation** — oracles and
other forms of communication from the supernatural powers referred to
specific actions, not to principles — or even of what may be called the
"quasi-revelation" of a Hammurabi, man had to fall back on himself and
his ancestors (tradition or custom) for the answers. At critical moments,
the Greeks may have turned to a "lawgiver" to codify the right answers,
but that step was no departure from the rule of human self-reliance.

For such a society to function, not to tear itself apart, a broad consensus
was essential, a sense of community and a genuine willingness on the part
of its members to live according to certain traditional rules, to accept the
decisions of legitimate authorities, to make changes only by open debate
and further consensus; in a word, to accept the "rule of law" so frequently
proclaimed by Greek writers. The process thus produced both new rules
and their sanction simultaneously, and, as has already been said, that is
politics. In a world, furthermore, in which inequalities were sharp even
among the members of the community (quite apart from those, such as
slaves, who were wholly excluded), and in which communities were small
in both territory and population, issues were relatively clear and obvious,
and conflict was often acute. The Greek word for political conflict was
stasis,* a very awkward term with a gamut* of connotations* ranging from   unchanged state / wide
day-to-day "party conflict" (to use an anachronistic* modern phrase) to   range / suggestions;
open civil war, which marks the final breakdown of consensus and the   unspoken meanings / out
abandonment of politics. Civil wars, with their attendant bloodshed, ex-   of date or time period
iles, and property dislocations, were frequent in the classical city-states,
with such notable exceptions as Athens and Sparta. They were the subject
of much concern among the great surviving political writers — Thucydides, Plato, and Aristotle — and we therefore tend to misjudge the situation. Only in *Utopia* can there be a society without dissent over important
issues; in a political society, "party conflict" is essential for its continued
existence and well-being, and it is as wrong to regard all instances in the
Greek poleis pejoratively* as it would be to denigrate* contemporary   negatively / downgrade
party politics in the same way.

Today the right to vote is widely believed to be the most essential
privilege (and duty) of a citizen, and that was also the case, within limits,
in the Roman Republic. In the Greek polis, however, though it was an
important right, it was only one of several equally exclusive rights — the
right to own real property, the right to contract a legal marriage with
another citizen, the right to participate in various major cult activities —
and it was available to all citizens only in the **democracies,** whereas the
other rights were universal, normally even under **tyrannies.** Hence membership in the body of "active citizens" and membership in the "commu-   happening at the same
nity of all citizens" were often not coterminous*; hence, too, the fre-   time

quency with which stasis for access to political rights erupted into civil war.

The political rights over which they contended included but transcended* the right to select officials and legislative bodies. At issue was the direct share, by voice and vote, in the decision-making process and in the judicial process (understood broadly enough to include evaluation of the performance, and if necessary punishment, of civil and military officials). The right to vote, in other words, meant above all the right to vote in a legislative or judicial body, not merely at an election. That is why classical Greek governments, whether oligarchic* or democratic, are classified as "direct," in contrast to "representative." When, as in Athens and other democracies, every citizen became a member, barring a few excluded for specified personal offences, "rule by the people" eventually acquired a literal connotation never approached before or since in western history.

No one, however, not even the most "radical" democrat, wished to break the traditional "community" of male citizens, a closed body of families whose members succeeded each other in the orderly progress of the generations. In Greek usage, the Athenians (never "Athens") declared war on the Spartans (not "Sparta"). If one were not an indigenous* Athenian, only a formal act of the sovereign* body could admit one to the community. Not only were women, children, and slaves excluded, which is no surprise, but so were freed slaves (unlike the Roman practice), or free men who migrated from other Greek states or from the "barbarian" world, or even their children, born and raised in the cities that labelled them aliens. In the classical period, grants of citizenship to outsiders were rare and were always the consequence of exceptional actions or circumstances. Aristotle, writing at the end of the classical era, observed that more open-handed policy was a temporary measure in times of severe manpower shortage, abandoned as soon as the crisis was over. Democracies, it is worth adding, appear to have been particularly jealous of citizenship.

In political terms, the power possessed by the community was total. That is to say, within the limits imposed by "rule of law," however that was understood, and by certain taboos in the fields of cult and sexual relations, the sovereign body was unrestrictedly free in its decision-making. There were areas or facets of human behavior in which it normally did not interfere, but that was only because it chose not to, or did not think to do so. There were no natural rights of the individual to inhibit action by the state, no inalienable rights granted or sanctioned by a higher authority. There was no higher authority.

went beyond

led by a group of people

native
ruling

READING AND WRITING SKILL: *Reading for and Writing with a Thesis*

1. In the introduction to Finley's essay, we asked you to find and state his thesis. Compare the thesis you found or formulated with the following description of the whole process:

Paragraph 1 has a lot of illustrations. Notice that the author gives no opinion here; he <u>illustrates</u> an abstract idea instead of expressing the abstract idea itself. Finley uses the words of Protagoras, Euripides, and Theseus to prepare us for his version of the concept "politics," but he doesn't explain the concept. Therefore paragraph 1 does not contain the thesis. Paragraph 2 begins with a sentence that refers back to the essay's title. Greek politics is by this point clearly the essay's focus. Now you need to ask what the author wants to prove about Greek politics. How does he view the topic? As you continue reading with these questions in mind, you'll notice that sentences 2 and 3 can't be the thesis because they are too general and do not refer to the topic of Greek politics. Sentence 4 stands out as Finley's opinion or argument on the topic: "But the Greeks took a radical step, a double one: they located the source of authority in the polis, in the community itself, and they decided on policy in open discussion, eventually by voting, by counting heads." Finley must go on to explain and support this opinion that the Greeks' action was radical and innovative.

2. What supporting arguments does Finley use to back up his thesis? Isolate topic sentences to identify these points.
3. Write your own thesis concerning a contemporary political issue. To develop a thesis, follow these logical steps:
   (a) <u>Read</u> the assignment carefully. Focus on its actual topic(s). Think of your thesis as an answer to questions posed in the assignment. Make sure you understand the question(s) before you formulate your answer. In this case the assignment's focus is a <u>contemporary political</u> issue.
   (b) List some current political issues, particularly those that really interest you. Some examples include the legal drinking age, women and the draft, affirmative action, and free access to birth control. Choose the topic that both interests you <u>and</u> offers good possibilities for essay development.
   (c) Once you have your topic, you need to take a position on it. This position becomes the main point of your thesis.
   (d) State the logical basis of your position. Without a logical basis, you've given an opinion, not a reasoned thesis. A possible thesis for this assignment reads "Including women in the draft promotes the view of them as equals, allows them to become eligible for economic benefits, and increases the draft pool."

As you know from a previous reading in this chapter, Plato re-created in his dialogues Socrates' conversations with various Athenians. Plato probably reformulated Socrates' actual words (again, Socrates himself wrote nothing) to fit with Plato's own philosophical beliefs. The following excerpt, taken from Plato's "The Apology of Socrates" and "Phaedo," covers Socrates' trial and execution. The Athenian leaders charged him with impiety — failing to show proper respect for the gods — and with corrupting the young men of Athens through his ideas. Socrates was at the center of Athenian intellectual life and therefore was often involved in political affairs, though he never belonged to any lawmaking body. As you read, consider how Socrates' speech reflects Athenian political practice as Finley describes it. How does it differ from our contemporary practices?

PLATO
FROM *"The Apology of Socrates"* **and** *"Phaedo"*

● Order, please, gentlemen! Remember my request to give me a hearing without interruption; besides, I believe that it will be to your advantage to listen. I am going to tell you something else, which may provoke a storm of protest; but please restrain yourselves. I assure you that if I am what I claim to be, and you put me to death, you will harm yourselves more than me. Neither Meletus nor Anytus can do me any harm at all; they would not have the power, because I do not believe that the law of God permits a better man to be harmed by a worse. No doubt my accuser might put me to death or have me banished or deprived of civic rights; but even if he thinks, as he probably does (and others too, I dare say), that these are great calamities, I do not think so; I believe that it is far worse to do what he is doing now, trying to put an innocent man to death. For this reason, gentlemen, so far from pleading on my own behalf, as might be supposed, I am really pleading on yours, to save you from misusing the gift of God by condemning me. If you put me to death, you will not easily find anyone to take my place. It is literally true (even if it sounds rather comical) that God has specially appointed me to this city, as though it were a large thoroughbred horse which because of its great size is inclined to be lazy and needs the stimulation of some stinging fly. It seems to me that God has attached me to this city to perform the office of such a fly; and all day long I never cease to settle here, there, and everywhere, rousing, persuading, reproving* every one of you. You will not easily find another like me,   *correcting; reprimanding* gentlemen, and if you take my advice you will spare my life.

[The jury decides for the death penalty and Socrates is imprisoned until he can be executed. The following passage from "Phaedo" recounts Socrates' final hours.]

It was now nearly sunset. Socrates came and sat down, fresh from the bath; and he had only been talking for a few minutes when the prison officer came in, and walked up to him. "Socrates," he said, "at any rate I shall not have to find fault with you, as I do with others, for getting angry with me and cursing when I tell them to drink the poison — carrying out Government orders. I have come to know during this time that you are the noblest and the gentlest and the bravest of all the men that have ever come here, and now especially I am sure that you are not angry with me, but with them; because you know who are responsible. So now — you

SOURCE: Reprinted from Plato: *The Last Days of Socrates*, trans. by Hugh Tredennick (Penguin Classics, revised edition, 1959). By permission of Penguin Books Ltd.

know what I have come to say — goodbye, and try to bear what must be as easily as you can." As he spoke he burst into tears, and turning round, went away.

Socrates looked up at him and said, "Goodbye to you, too; we will do as you say." Then addressing us he went on, "What a charming person! All the time I have been here he has visited me, and shown me the greatest kindness; and how generous of him now to shed tears for me at parting! But come, Crito, let us do as he says. Someone had better bring in the poison, if it is ready prepared; if not, tell the man to prepare it."

"But surely, Socrates," said Crito, "the sun is still upon the mountains; it has not gone down yet. Besides, I know that in other cases people have dinner and enjoy their wine, and sometimes the company of those whom they love, long after they receive the warning; and only drink the poison quite late at night. No need to hurry; there is still plenty of time."

"It is natural that these people whom you speak of should act in that way, Crito," said Socrates, "because they think that they gain by it. And it is also natural that I should not; because I believe that I should gain nothing by drinking the poison a little later — I should only make myself ridiculous in my own eyes if I clung to life and hugged it when it has no more to offer. Come, do as I say and don't make difficulties."

At this Crito made a sign to his servant, who was standing nearby. The servant went out and after a considerable time returned with the man who was to administer the poison; he was carrying it ready prepared in a cup. When Socrates saw him he said, "Well, my good fellow, you understand these things; what ought I to do?"

"Just drink it," he said, "and then walk about until you feel a weight in your legs, and then lie down. Then it will act of its own accord."

As he spoke he handed the cup to Socrates, who received it quite cheerfully, without a tremor,* without any change of color or expression, and said, looking up under his brows with his usual steady gaze, "What do you say about pouring a libation* from this drink? Is it permitted, or not?"

shaking

liquid sacrifice

"We only prepare what we regard as the normal dose, Socrates," he replied.

"I see," said Socrates. "But I suppose I am allowed, or rather bound, to pray the gods that my removal from this world to the other may be prosperous. This is my prayer, then; and I hope that it may be granted." With these words, quite calmly and with no sign of distaste, he drained the cup in one breath.

Up till this time most of us had been fairly successful in keeping back our tears; but when we saw that he was drinking, that he had actually drunk it, we could do so no longer; in spite of myself the tears came pouring out, so that I covered my face and wept broken-heartedly — not for him, but for my own calamity in losing such a friend. Crito had given up even before me, and had gone out when he could not restrain his tears. But Apollodorus, who had never stopped crying even before, now broke out into such a storm of passionate weeping that he made everyone in the room break down, except Socrates himself, who said:

"Really, my friends, what a way to behave! Why, that was my main reason for sending away the women, to prevent this sort of disturbance; because I am told that one should make one's end in a tranquil frame of mind. Calm yourselves and try to be brave."

This made us feel ashamed, and we controlled our tears. Socrates walked about, and presently, saying that his legs were heavy, lay down on his back — that was what the man recommended. The man (he was the same one who had administered the poison) kept his hand upon Socrates, and after a little while examined his feet and legs; then pinched his foot hard and asked if he felt it. Socrates said no. Then he did the same to his legs; and moving gradually upwards in this way let us see that he was getting cold and numb. Presently he felt him again and said that when it reached the heart, Socrates would be gone.

The coldness was spreading about as far as his waist when Socrates uncovered his face — for he had covered it up — and said (they were his last words): "Crito, we ought to offer a cock to Asclepius. See to it, and don't forget."

"No, it shall be done," said Crito. "Are you sure that there is nothing else?"

Socrates made no reply to this question, but after a little while he stirred; and when the man uncovered him, his eyes were fixed. When Crito saw this, he closed the mouth and eyes.

Such was the end of our comrade, who was, we may fairly say, of all those whom we knew in our time, the bravest and also the wisest and most upright man.

QUESTIONS FOR DISCUSSION AND WRITING

[1] Does Socrates' execution reflect badly on the Athenian democracy?

[2] The Athenian leaders were enraged by Socrates' "apology," or self-defense. What in his attitude may have seemed a willful challenge of the state's authority?

[3] In his calm acceptance of death, Socrates asserts his philosophical beliefs. Given what you know of Platonic philosophy, much of which derives from Socrates' thought, why should he find no fear in death?

Ancient Art

READING SKILL: *Writing a Summary*

A summary concisely restates an article's thesis and main ideas. Like paraphrasing, summarizing involves rephrasing an author's point in your own words and sentence structure. Summarizing helps you clarify an article's ideas and retain the information. When you write about an article, you need a sense of its skeletal content so you can avoid having to remember five or possibly five hundred pages of detailed information.

The following steps illustrate one method of writing a summary:

1. After reading the article critically, find the topic idea of each paragraph. Remember, some paragraphs may not have explicitly stated topic sentences, and other paragraphs may contain material that is unessential to an overview of the article's content. Don't feel compelled to include unessential information. Some paragraphs illustrate a point already made in an earlier paragraph. Don't be repetitious in a summary.
2. Paraphrase the topic sentences or ideas.
3. If the article has a clearly stated thesis, begin your summary by paraphrasing it. Some articles may begin with the thesis; some end with it; others have an implied thesis which you will have to articulate.
4. Put the paraphrased thesis and topic ideas in a paragraph. Remember to use transitional words and phrases to show logical connection between ideas.

Survey the following article and then read it critically, remembering to ask questions as you read. What is the article's purpose? If you're unable to locate the thesis, find the topic sentences and supporting details, and then restate them as the thesis.

"The Useful and the Beautiful" appeared in A. D. DeRidder's Art in Greece, *written in 1927. DeRidder explains a fundamental classical aesthetic that many Western artists over the centuries have endorsed: art must be both beautiful and purposeful. Greek vases are one example of art objects that serve a purpose. Poetry has been used to teach moral principles and even record scientific data (a practice common in eighteenth-century Europe).*

A. D. DeRIDDER
"The Useful and the Beautiful"

KEY CONCEPTS

The **ELITE** (page 64) hold special privileges in a society because of their heritage or social standing.

INNATE VS. ACQUIRED CHARACTER (page 64), also referred to as *nature vs. nurture*, reflects a major philosophical issue comprised of two opposing views: biology determines an individual's nature vs. environment shapes an individual's nature.

AESTHETICS is the study of the nature of art: how do we judge its beauty and value?

BEAUTIFUL AND USEFUL ART (or "dulce et utile") is an ancient aesthetic discussed at length in this article. According to this idea, good art not only pleases but also serves some practical end.

ART FOR ART'S SAKE (page 66), another aesthetic doctrine, opposes the view of art as useful and beautiful. This doctrine asserts that good art serves no end but its own.

The **RENAISSANCE** took place in the fourteenth through sixteenth centuries in most Western European countries. The term itself means "rebirth" in French and in more general contexts indicates a new beginning or flourishing.

● It is generally admitted that the Greeks were an artist people; with them good taste and a refined appreciation of the beautiful were not the prerogatives* of the **elite,** but were common to all. "Not a thing that has been dug up in Hellenic* soil but has this flower of elegance, this exquisite and sober feeling for harmony, which gives the impression of a race supremely gifted for art." In the humblest monuments of industrial art one feels that the workman is every whit* as fully alive to the lines of his vase or the proper adaptation of his decoration as a great painter or sculptor. This notion, however, must not be exaggerated, as has sometimes been done, if we are to avoid hasty generalizations and that lack of fine discrimination combined with realization of complexity which mars* so many works on Greek art. Though the average of artistic production in Greece may be much superior to that of other lands, it should be acknowledged frankly that many of the objects dug up in the course of excavations do not justify rapturous admiration. But let us freely admit, since it is the obvious truth, that nowhere else is there so close a relationship between the productions of "high art" and the "minor arts," nor so general a care for the beauty of form and line independently of the value or destination of the object.

rights; privileges

Greek

bit

injures

Is this instinctive — a natural gift — with the Greeks, or is it the result of especially favorable social conditions? Here, as throughout science, we are faced with the eternal problem, the question of an **innate or an acquired character.** Countless anecdotes and innumerable features bear witness to the greater refinement of **aesthetic sensibility** to be found among the Greeks than anywhere else, a refinement which is responsible for their having outdistanced other ancient peoples, less gifted in this respect than themselves, so that they were able to impose their own conceptions on such peoples wherever they have come into contact with them, and this before ever they imposed them on Rome and through Rome on the modern world.

Nevertheless, the expression of aesthetic feeling was facilitated by the

SOURCE: "The Useful and the Beautiful" by A. D. DeRidder in *Art in Greece.* Barnes & Noble Books, 1927. Reprinted by permission.

role which the Greeks recognized as belonging to art. For them it is no mere luxury to be enjoyed only by the privileged few, nor is beauty exclusively reserved for rare and costly articles. Art is a necessity linked up with the very existence of the city and the individual and it is always with them in all they do from the smallest to the most important acts of their lives. Beauty as beauty does not exist unto itself but has ever a practical end in view. This principle, whose effects are to be seen in the earliest productions and which is maintained more or less markedly throughout the existence of Greek art, was elevated into a doctrine by the philosophers, and Socrates admits that the agreeable, the good, the true and the beautiful are one. And for him **the beautiful is that which is useful,** and all practical articles which exactly fulfill their purpose are beautiful. That which the Greeks admired in the human body such as it is repre- sented in statuary* is assuredly the lines and contours and the rhythms of the pose and gestures, but it is also its perfect physical development fitting it for the duties of a citizen who has to compete in the exercises of the palaestra* and in the great national games, to be ready to fight against his country's foes. The beauty of these athletes' bodies lies in the harmonious concordance* of their form, their muscles in action, and the act which they have to accomplish; it varies from one to another, "as a man who is skilled in racing differs from a man who is a skilled wrestler; as the beauty of a shield devised for defense differs completely from the beauty of a javelin designed to be thrown with force and speed. An otherwise un- decorated vase of harmonious shape which is well turned, perfectly fired and faultlessly glazed is a work of art just as is a statue; the potters are as ready to put their signatures upon it as upon an expensively decorated piece, and on the same grounds.

sculpted forms

public gym

agreement

When we admire Greek vases, the delicacy of their design and the elegance of their contours, we sometimes forget that they contained liq- uids — oils and wines — and that this was their true function, which came before delighting the eye. The Greek, however, has never forgotten that the principal role of industrial art is utility. Unlike modern artisans, he would never have conceived a piece of furniture whose overcrowded decoration and involved lines render it unfit for use and which invite the reproach Cochin addressed to his contemporaries when he asked them "not to change the purpose of things but to remember that a candlestick must be straight and upright in order to hold a light, and that the grease- guard of the socket must be concave in order to catch the running wax and not convex so that it overflows in cascades onto the candlestick." In Greece the decoration is not an addition stuck on like a non-essential plating, but is an integral* part of the object and often has a practical purpose in itself. The triumph of Attic* ceramics, which is to be seen towards the close of the 6th century in all the rival ceramic markets, as, for instance, that of Corinth, arises not so much from the beauty of its shapes and decoration but pre-eminently* from commercial considera- tions — it conserves the liquids better and gives them a better flavor.

essential
Athenian

supremely

On the other hand, for a Greek a statue or a painting is not the product

of an entirely disinterested* art. It always had some purpose — to repre-   without selfish motive
sent a divinity and to link that divinity with his or her temple; to honor
such divinity by making a votive offering; to commemorate the dead by
his presentment and by recording his deeds; to tell and teach the great
facts of religion and of national life. "Among the ancients the beautiful is
only the high relief of the useful" (Stendhal). The existence of all these
works of art is justified solely by their role in the social life. The theory of
"art for art's sake," the germ of which is possibly to be found in the
Hellenistic writers, would have been incomprehensible to Phidias, Poly-
clitus and their contemporaries. Yet, in no period, not even when art
becomes more individualistic and more detached from social life, does the
practical aim of art yield place entirely to exclusively aesthetic and emo-
tive* considerations. It has often been said that "the foundation of Greek   emotional
aesthetics is the beautiful harnessed to the service of the useful" (Pottier).

The useful and the beautiful, "high art" and the "minor arts," are not
yet divorced from one another. For the Greek there is no gulf dividing the
plain earthen undecorated vase which holds wine and oil from the sculpture of Phidias; there is simply a quantitative difference in the formula of
beauty and utility of which both are compounded. Knowing that all techniques have their part to play in social life, the artist of the one no more
considers that it is derogatory* to him to decorate an industrial article than   insulting
did the **Renaissance** artists. But there was not that division which nowadays separates a potter from a painter or a stonecutter from a sculptor. The
ancients, in fact, never clearly distinguished between artists and craftsmen; both belong to the class of manual workers. In primitive times they
were despised, but this prejudice disappeared with time except in certain
Dorian cities, such as Sparta, where a citizen is forbidden to gain a living
by a trade. Solon obliged the Athenians to give evidence of their means
of subsistence; Pericles praises work: "It is no shame for any man to
acknowledge poverty; but it is shameful not to work to overcome it."
Socrates recommends wholesome work to Aristarchus: "Which are the
wiser men, those who remain at ease or those who occupy themselves in
doing something useful? Which are more in the right, those who work
or those who, without doing anything, deliberate on the means of subsistence*?"   basic needs for existence

It is essential, if one would understand the fundamental character of
Greek art, to take note of this perpetual interpenetration of two elements
which to modern folk appear to be independent or even antagonistic. In
the study of ancient ceramics it is erroneous to attribute to its authors
thoughts that were above all aesthetic, when they were preoccupied with
practical problems both technical and economic. It is an analogous* error   comparable
to study the works of the great sculptors without considering the purpose
of the work or the religious or civil idea it contains, in short to eliminate
anaesthetic* elements. Beauty is not an end in itself in Greece, but a   unemotional, having no
means to an end.   effect

Beauty, for all that, is not neglected; the artist does not allow himself
to be subjugated* by the needs of social life to such an extent as to leave   overcome

them masters of the field. His work is not solely useful in the cult of the gods and of the dead, or in the glorification of the city: over and above this it is clothed with beauty. It is just this which distinguishes Greek art from so much other art, such as that of Egypt or of Mesopotamia where the aesthetic aim is subordinate to the social aim. And this secondary importance attaching to beauty is one of the causes which has prevented these arts from following in the same steps as the art of Greece and from freeing themselves, as Greek art has done, from the old conventions which regulated them despotically* up to the very end.

tyrannically

Thanks to its profoundly utilitarian essence, art in Greece, however admirable it became, remains what it has always been and everywhere will be in its beginnings, a language, a means of expressing human thoughts and needs, that communion between men which Tolstoy claims that it should be. The thoughts it materialized in visual forms are highly diverse but they are always comprehended within this limit; it is for the archaeologist to understand these forms and read them. What are they? They are the necessities of the Greek city — its religion, political constitution, social ranks, historical events, and manners.

READING AND WRITING SKILL EXERCISES

[1] Suppose that you have been asked to write a summary of DeKidder's essay. The following model shows the actual steps in the process.

(a) The topic sentence of paragraph 1 does not appear until the end. Its very formal language needs to be paraphrased simply:

> But let us freely admit, since it is the obvious truth, that nowhere else is there so close a relationship between the productions of "high art" and the "minor arts," nor so general a care for the beauty of form and line independently of the value or destination of the object.

Paraphrase:

> The Greeks made no distinction in value between decorative art and functional craft.

(b) The topic sentence in paragraph 2 again appears at the end in a long, complicated statement that can be cut down easily:

> Countless anecdotes and innumerable features bear witness to the greater refinement of aesthetic sensibility to be found among the Greeks than anywhere else, a refinement which is responsible for their having outdistanced other ancient peoples, less gifted in this respect than themselves, so that they were able to impose their own conceptions on such peoples wherever they have come into contact with them, and this before ever they imposed them on Rome and through Rome on the modern world.

Paraphrase:

> The Greeks had both a highly developed and widely influential sense of art.

(c) Paragraph 3 begins with the topic sentence:

> Nevertheless, the expression of aesthetic feeling was facilitated by the role which the Greeks recognized as belonging to art.

Note the statement's generality. Your paraphrase should name the role directly:

> Greek art flourished in part because of the Greek view that art should be not only beautiful but also useful.

(d) The second sentence of paragraph 4 is the topic sentence:

> The Greek, however, has never forgotten that the principal role of industrial art is utility.

Paraphrase:

> Utility remained the Greek industrial artist's prime concern.

(e) In paragraph 5, the topic sentence is the first one:

> On the other hand, for a Greek a statue or a painting is not the product of an entirely disinterested art.

Paraphrase:

> The Greeks believed that decorative art always had a purpose.

(f) The topic sentence opens paragraph 6:

> The useful and the beautiful, "high art" and the "minor arts," are not yet divorced from one another.

Paraphrase:

> The Greeks did not distinguish "art" from "craft."

(g) Again the next paragraph begins with the topic sentence:

> It is essential, if one would understand the fundamental character of Greek art, to take note of this perpetual interpenetration of two elements which to modern folk appear to be independent or even antagonistic.

Paraphrase:

> The basic characteristic of Greek art is the union of the beautiful and the useful.

(h) The first sentence of paragraph 8 is the topic sentence:

> Beauty, for all that, is not neglected; the artist does not allow himself to be subjugated by the needs of social life to such an extent as to leave them masters of the field.

Paraphrase:

> Beauty is no less important than usefulness.

(i) The final paragraph begins with the topic sentence:

> Thanks to its profoundly utilitarian essence, art in Greece, however
> admirable it became, remains what it has always been and everywhere
> will be in its beginnings, a language, a means of expressing human
> thoughts and needs, that communion between men which Tolstoy claims
> that it should be.

Paraphrase:

> Greek art served a truly human purpose.

To write the actual summary, you should begin by stating the thesis in
your own words, citing author and essay title in your first sentence:

> In "Art in Greece," DeRidder argues that the Greek conception of art
> combines beauty and usefulness.

Read your paraphrases of all the topic sentences. Are any irrelevant to the
thesis? Omit such sentences from the summary. Sentence 2 does not clearly
relate to the author's main point and serves a secondary purpose in the
essay: that of giving a general historical context for the main idea. Are any
of the paraphrases repetitious? Omit these sentences as well. Sentence 7
repeats the thesis and the main point of paragraph 3, so it can be left out.
 Write the summary paragraph and add transitional words and phrases.

[2] Summarize Hamilton's "Introduction to Classical Mythology."
Remember to omit minor or irrelevant points and to avoid repetition.

Aesop, who lived and wrote in the late sixth century B.C., created fables,
which are stories that teach a lesson. In fables like the "Tortoise and the Hare"
and the "Fox and the Grapes," Aesop used animals to illustrate human foibles*   minor faults
and shortcomings. The following fable exemplifies DeRidder's thesis in that it
both entertains imaginatively and instructs practically.

AESOP
"Diogenes on a Journey"

● Diogenes, the Cynic, was traveling along a road when he came to a
stream in flood and stood there wondering how to get across. A man who
often carried people over saw his difficulty and came and took him across.
Diogenes was grateful for this kindness and was just grumbling at the
poverty which prevented his rewarding this benefactor when the man
saw another traveler who couldn't get across and ran to do the same thing.
Then Diogenes went to him and said, "Well, I won't waste any more

SOURCE: Reprinted from *Aesop Without Morals,* trans. by Lloyd Daly, (A. S. Barnes & Co.,
1961). By permission of the publisher.

gratitude on you since I see that you do this as a hobby and without any discrimination."

Men who do good services for the undeserving as well as for the worthy get no reputation for benefaction but are labeled as stupid.

———————————

Homer's Iliad *and* Odyssey *are two of the oldest and best known Western literary works. "Homer" may have actually been several poets, who sang the poems aloud to entertain an audience. The* Iliad *tells the story of the Trojan War, which in legend started when the Trojan prince Paris abducted the beautiful Helen from her Greek homeland. Her husband Menelaus and his brother Agamemnon gather the greatest Greek armies to fight against the Trojans. Achilles, the greatest of all the Greek heroes, joins in the battle against Troy, as does Odysseus, a hero known for his cunning and bravery. Troy falls and the Greeks return home. The* Odyssey *relates the adventures of Odysseus as he returns from Troy to his Greek homeland, Ithaca. In the following excerpt (presented here in prose form), Odysseus and his crew have been taken prisoner by the cannibalistic, one-eyed giant, Cyclops. Odysseus prepares a red-hot, sharpened stake as a weapon to aid in his own and his crew's escape. Aside from its literary value, the episode illustrates a Greek cultural value, embodied by Odysseus. Read the passage, keeping in mind DeRidder's discussion of useful and beautiful art.*

HOMER
FROM *The Odyssey*

● "Here, Cyclops: drink some wine, now you've eaten human flesh, and see what kind of drink our ship held. I brought it as a gift for you, hoping you would pity me and send me home. But you're an unbearable savage — Monster! What man will ever come to visit you, now that you've done such wrong?"

The Cyclops took the wine and drank it down. He was terribly pleased with the sweet drink, and asked for some more.

"Please be so good as to give me still more, and tell me your name right now, so I can give you a guest-gift, one you will like. For the fruitful fields give even to the Cyclopes great clusters of grapes, and Zeus of the rains makes them grow. But your wine is a bit of nectar and ambrosia."

So he spoke, and again I offered a bowl of bright wine to him. I brought it and served him three times; three times he foolishly drank it. And when the wine had gone to his head, I spoke to him in charming words:

"Cyclops, you ask my well-known name? Well, then, I shall tell you. But you must give me the guest-gift, just as you promised. My name is Nobody. My mother and my father and all my companions call me Nobody."

But once I told him, the Cyclops answered me cruelly: "I will eat Nobody last of his company — the rest of them first. That will be your gift."

Then he leaned back and fell flat. There he lay, his thick neck bent to one side, and sleep, which masters all, overcame him. Heavy with wine, he vomited. Wine and scraps of men poured out of his mouth. I pushed my stake under a heap of embers to heat it, and with a speech encouraged my companions, so none would cower in fear. Just as the olive-wood stake — green as it was — was about to catch, and was glowing brightly, I snatched it from the fire, and my companions stood by me. A great god breathed courage into us. Then we took the sharp-pointed stake and plunged it into the Cyclops' eye; I, perched above, whirled it around, just as a man bores a ship-beam with a drill, and those below, taking hold on either side, keep it spinning with a strap, and it runs steadily. That is how we took hold of the fire-sharpened stake and twisted it into his eye.

Blood bubbled out and boiled around the burning stake. The fiery smoke from the burning eyeball singed off the eyelids and the eyebrows all around. The roots of the eyeball hissed in the fire. As when a smith* dips a great axe into hissing cold water to temper it — for that is what makes it strong — so his eye sizzled around the olive stake. He bellowed* horribly, and the rocks resounded with it. We backed off in terror. He pulled the stake, all spattered with blood, from his eye. Then, in a frenzy, he threw it from him and called loudly to the Cyclopes who lived in the neighboring caves on the windy heights. They heard his cry and ran from every direction. They stood outside the cave and asked what his trouble was.

"What has happened to you, Polyphemus, to make you bellow through the peaceful night and ruin our sleep? Is someone stealing your sheep? Is someone trying to kill you?"

Mighty Polyphemus answered them from the cave: "Friends, Nobody is trying to kill me!"

Answering him quickly, they said, "Well, if you are alone and nobody is attacking you, you must be ill. There is no way to avoid disease, which comes from Zeus. You should pray to your father, Lord Poseidon."

They said this, and then they went away. My heart began to laugh, because my name and cleverness had deceived them. The Cyclops, groaning in agony with the pain, groped around and moved the stone from the door. He sat down in the doorway and spread out his hands, to try to catch anyone sneaking out with the sheep. He probably hoped in his heart I would be so foolish. But I was planning how to work out an escape for myself and my men. I thought of all kinds of plots and tricks to save our lives, for great danger was very near. This seemed the best plan to my heart:

There were some rams there, well-bred, heavy and fleecy, large and handsome, with dark gray wool. Silently, I tied these animals together with the flexible willows on which the monstrous Cyclops slept, brute that he was. I bound together three at a time. The one in the middle carried a man; the other two walked on either side, guarding my comrade. So three sheep carried each man. For me, I chose a ram, the best of all the

metalworker

yelled loudly

flock by far. Taking hold of his back, I curled up beneath his fleecy belly. I held on, my hands entwined firmly in the amazing fleece, waiting patiently. Thus we waited, trembling, for bright Dawn.

As soon as the rosy-fingered dawn appeared, the rams rushed out to pasture, but the ewes bleated about the pen, unmilked, their udders full to the bursting point. Their master, racked* with terrible pain, felt all over the backs of the standing sheep. But the fool never realized how the men were fastened underneath the sheeps' fleecy breasts. Last of the flock, my ram walked to the door, weighed down by his fleece and by me, clever plotter that I am. Great Polyphemus, feeling him all over, said:

tormented

"Dear ram, why do you leave the cave last of all my flock? You never used to be left behind the other sheep, but, with your long strides, you used to be the first to graze on the tender blooms of grass; you were the first to return to the fold in the evening. But now you are the last. Maybe you miss your master's eye, which a wicked man and his wretched companions put out, after my wits were muddled with wine. That was Nobody, and I swear he hasn't escaped destruction yet. If only you could think like me, and become able to speak so you could say where he is hiding from my anger. Then, I tell you, his brains would be smashed around the cave, and splatter on the floor, and my heart would be relieved of some of the sorrows that this good-for-nothing Nobody brought upon me."

Saying this, he let the ram go outside. I came some way from the cave and the yard, then let go of the ram and released my companions. We quickly drove off the fat, long-legged sheep, looking back many times, until we came to the ships. Those of us who had escaped death were a cheerful sight to our dear friends, but they missed the others, and began to mourn loudly for them. I forbade their lamentations with a frown to each one. I told them to load the fleecy sheep quickly into the ships and sail away over the salty water. They boarded in haste and sat down at the oarlocks; sitting in order they beat the gray sea with their oars. But before we were too far away for the Cyclops to hear us, I called out these taunts:

"Cyclops, it was not your fate to eat some timid man's companions in your hollow cave. Your wicked deeds were discovered, you brute — you who dared to eat guests in your own home. That is why Zeus and the other gods have punished you."

So I spoke, and he grew still angrier in his heart. He broke off the top of a great hill, and hurled it at us. It splashed just in front of our dark-prowed ship, failing to reach the rudder's tip. The water gushed under the falling stone, and the backwash, like a wave from the deep sea, pushed us immediately back toward the land, and brought us close to shore. I took a very long pole in my hands, and pushed us off again. I encouraged my companions, and ordered them, with nods of my head, to fall to their oars again so we could get away from this danger. They leaned forward and rowed. Now when we had gone twice as far out to sea, again I was going to call to the Cyclops. But my companions all tried to restrain me, muttering in soft tones:

"Reckless fellow! Why do you want to enrage this wild savage? He just now forced the ship back to land by throwing a rock into the sea, and we thought we were lost all over again. If he had heard us speak or cry out, he would have pounded our heads and our ships' beams together, by hurling a jagged boulder at us, for he can throw very far."

So they said, but they did not dissuade my bold spirit. I taunted him again, with rage in my heart:

"Cyclops, if any mortal man asks you about the hideous blinding of your eye, say it was Odysseus who deprived you of sight — the spoiler* of cities, the son of Laertes, whose home is in Ithaka!"

plunderer; ruiner

QUESTIONS FOR DISCUSSION AND WRITING

[1] The character of Odysseus exemplifies an ideal of heroic behavior. Name the characteristics that make Odysseus a hero.

[2] At one point in the narrative, Odysseus says to Polyphemus that "Zeus and the other gods have punished you." But Polyphemus is the son of the god Poseidon. Why is Odysseus not guilty of impiety for assaulting the semi-divine Cyclops? What purpose does his behavior serve in the Greek moral code?

[3] Despite pleas from his comrades, Odysseus continues to taunt the Cyclops and reveals his name to him. Why does Odysseus insist on bragging about his actions and revealing his identity?

WRITING SKILL: *Organizing an Essay*

We discussed paragraph development as a thought process that focused on topic idea and paragraph structure. In the same way, essay development depends on clarifying your thesis, or main idea, and deriving from it some logical points for systematic analysis. Your thesis should both begin your essay and provide its main points or thoughts.

To write a good thesis in response to an essay assignment, clarify your subject, topic, and main idea, along with its supporting points. An assignment's subject, or category, should be obvious, for it most likely reflects your current class topic. Essay assignments in this chapter, for example, will deal with the ancient Greek world in relation to religion, philosophy, science, politics, or art. A topic differs from the larger subject in that it names an actual issue, not a general heading. Under the subject heading "ancient Greek art" you might be asked to write on the topic "useful and beautiful art," which names a particular aesthetic. Your actual thesis should address that topic in some definitive way, directly answering the assigned question, taking a stand, comparing/contrasting it to something else. Your assignment usually will direct your response.

Many students assume that once they've answered an assignment's main question, they've completed their thesis. But a response unsupported by logic

remains a subjective response, an opinion. A <u>thesis</u>, on the other hand, is a
logical contention* that a given response is true <u>because</u> of specific contributing   argument
factors or reasons. A complete thesis, therefore, clarifies both your response to
an assigned question and your logic behind that response. Include the <u>logical
bases</u> that support your main point in your thesis sentence (or sentences, or
paragraph — it's up to <u>you</u> to determine the thesis statement's appropriate
form).

Again as in paragraph development, thesis development can begin with a
model or formula, but you need to adapt such a predetermined structure to your
assignment's and your essay's particular nature. Writing is thinking, and no
formula can reflect your individual thought. A thesis formula can, however, help
you think about essay organization. To use your thesis as a guide to organizing
your essay, you need to write a clearly focused and well-developed thesis.
Remember that a thesis should <u>answer</u> an assignment, <u>not repeat</u> it. And it
should include the major reasons behind that answer. The more you develop
your thesis, the easier it will be to develop your essay.

Suppose you're asked to write an essay on the subject "Greek art," the
topic being the contemporary value of the "useful and beautiful" aesthetic. Your
thesis should respond with your assessment of the aesthetic's value today and
with reasons for your view. One possible formulation might be as follows:

> *Thesis:* The ancient Greek aesthetic of the "useful and beautiful" holds
> no relevant value for art and artists today. The aesthetic ties artistic
> creation to an outdated moral code that would alienate contemporary
> artists and audiences. It also artificially limits artistic subjects and forms
> that could reflect modern values and ideas particularly well because it
> emphasizes not only morality but "beauty," an emphasis that excludes
> many contemporary experiences.

The above thesis is <u>abstract:</u> it presents ideas, not concrete examples. Use
examples in the essay's body to support and illustrate your ideas, but use the
thesis to outline the ideas themselves, clarifying the essay's main point for you
and the reader.

Treating your thesis as your essay's logical outline helps you organize your
thoughts. Paragraph topics derive from the thesis, which, if well written, tells you
what you <u>must</u> discuss as well as what you should <u>not</u> — what is off the point.
Isolate the key thesis elements, decide on their logical order, and develop each
one in as many paragraphs as you need to explain the idea.

A good thesis tells you what the main paragraph topics should be. In the
model thesis above, the key elements are:

1. No relevant value exists in the "useful and beautiful" aesthetic.
2. The aesthetic is outdated.
3. It alienates modern artists and audiences.
4. It limits artistic subjects and forms.
5. It excludes many contemporary experiences from artistic treatment.

The topics outlined in the thesis should be the topic ideas developed in the
essay's paragraphs.

Your next task is to put these topic ideas in some logical order. Your topic ideas should build on each other logically. If you're using a special term in your essay, for example — in this case, "useful and beautiful art" — you should define it in a paragraph before you move on to analyzing or applying it. In the above essay, you can't really claim Topic 1 is true unless you've first explained your reasons, the main idea's logical bases. Topic 1 really forms the essay's premise and logical conclusion, and so should come after discussion of all the other topics. Topic 2, however, suggests a basic view of the aesthetic and also demands that you define it; your discussion of it should precede your discussion of Topics 1, 3, 4, and 5. Note that Topic 2 has split into at least two paragraphs already, one defining the term "useful and beautiful" and one explaining how and why the aesthetic is outdated. Each of these paragraphs may split into two or more other paragraphs, depending on how thoroughly you analyze each topic idea.

Let's stop here to emphasize a point about essay length. You, the writer, control the number of paragraphs and pages in anything you write. An assignment that asks for three pages can have the same kind of thesis as one that requires thirty; your subdivision of paragraph topic ideas determines the depth of your analysis, degree of support, amount of description, number of definitions, and so on. You can take an idea like Topic 2 and treat it in two paragraphs for a basic discussion, or you can develop its elements and implications in ten pages. Clarify for yourself what your instructor expects and what your topic demands before you decide on a paragraphing approach and essay length.

Once you've decided to discuss Topic 2 in your essay's first section, you can then examine the point's logical result, which should be named by one of the other key thesis elements. Here, an outdated aesthetic alienates modern artists and audiences, according to the thesis. This effect should be analyzed in the next stage of your discussion. Subdivide the idea of alienation, discuss it in however many paragraphs you need, and move on to the next logical element.

By joining together your skill in developing paragraphs and your ability to develop a thesis and use it as a logical outline, you should be able to produce thoughtful, well-organized essays. Revising for focus, logic, and support, and proofreading for correct diction, grammar, and punctuation, will insure that your work reflects your real ability. Some student examples follow the chapter essay assignments. They illustrate the difference between an incomplete, unfocused thesis and an effective one that should lead to a well-organized essay. We then discuss techniques for essay-level revision, which you should now practice in addition to your paragraph-level revision skills.

CHAPTER 1 ESSAY ASSIGNMENTS

When you write essays in your college courses, you're writing for several purposes. First, by writing on a topic, you improve your comprehension of the material. Your written response to an assignment demonstrates your understanding of the subject to the instructor. Essay assignments give you an opportunity to practice and improve your academic reading and writing skills. And perhaps most importantly, writing, because it is a thinking process, allows you to increase your knowledge on a topic and build the academic skills of critical, interpretative, and synthetic thought. The following assignments ask you to go beyond repetition of information. They ask you to apply your original, creative thought to the material you've read.

[1] The Greeks studied and practiced philosophy, science, politics, and even art according to a rational method. Explain the concept of "rational method" and analyze how the Greeks used a logical system of thought in each of the above fields.

This assignment has five basic parts. First identify them to clarify your focus. You need to define "rational method" before you can apply the idea to Greek philosophy, science, politics, and art. Greer's article would be a good place to start because it focuses on rational methods. Then review the other relevant articles and ask the question, "What method did the Greeks employ here?" Look at Clagett's article on science, Finley's on politics, and DeRidder's on art. You might also be able to use examples from Plato's dialogues, Hippocrates' essay, and Homer's Odyssey.

[2] What do you see as the major contributions of Greek culture to Western civilization? Which are most apparent or most important in contemporary life?

Identify the main parts of this assignment. The second question basically asks you why the contributions you identify are major ones. See the discussion below for further examination of this question.

[3] Odysseus, in Homer's *Odyssey,* and Socrates, as Plato depicts him in the "Apology" and "Phaedo," are both heroes, though one is fictional and the other historical. What qualities make them both heroic, and why?

You might want to begin your essay with some background information on each figure to explain who each one is and what he's like. Your essay should focus on the heroic qualities of both, however. Think about their situations; what kind of dangers and threats did they both face? How did they both react? What qualities do they both display?

[4] Echo, Narcissus, and Oedipus all suffered, though for different reasons. Choose one character and analyze the causes of his or her suffering. Examine the moral issue(s) of the situation. You might consider Echo's harsh lesson in respect or the costs of narcissism. If you choose to write on Oedipus, focus on one moral issue in the myth: the sins of patricide or pride, or his fate of self-sacrifice to save the city.

This assignment reads straightforwardly: What suffering did the character undergo? Why? What moral, if any, is intended? Your thesis should outline the answers you'll develop in the essay's paragraphs.

[5] We've all encountered narcissistic behavior in others and, perhaps, ourselves. Why might a person be narcissistic? What needs might narcissism fill? Discuss its possible effects on individuals and society.

This assignment focuses on the concept of narcissism. Because the concept will be central to your essay, you might want to clarify its definition in a paragraph before you begin analyzing its causes, purposes, and effects.

[6] Reread the definition of anthropomorphism. In many ways, we "anthropomorphize" things around us, like animals or technology. In what ways do we discuss pets or computers as if they had human characteristics?

Like Question 5, this question asks you to focus your essay on a concept that might first need clarification through careful definition. The question directly asks "in what ways" we anthropomorphize certain things; remember to address the implied "why?" in your thesis and the paragraphs that develop it.

WRITING SKILL: *Revising a Thesis and Essay*

The following thesis samples were written by our students in response to Question 2. The first thesis created some problems for the writer; the second one was a more successful beginning.

> *Dave:* The Greeks led the Western world in scientific investigation, and their culture influenced later Western civilization. The major contributions of their culture to Western civilization are mainly focused on art, architecture, and science. The most important figures of the fifth and fourth centuries B.C. were Sophocles, Democritus, Euripides, Socrates, Plato, Aristotle, and Hippocrates.

To check the effectiveness of this thesis statement, first read the assignment and then look for a direct and complete answer in the thesis. We'll repeat the assignment: "What do you see as the major contributions of Greek culture to Western civilization? Which are most apparent or most important in contemporary life?"

Here, Dave names what he considers the major Greek contributions to be: art, architecture, and science. So far, so good. But why are these of major importance? Where do we see their influence today? None of the sentences in his thesis addresses these issues. He may find it difficult to develop a complete essay because he hasn't given himself a complete thesis to think and write about. The final sentence in his thesis is a factual list of names, which doesn't give him any topic to discuss in the essay's body. It's not helpful as part of the thesis and should be eliminated. When he discusses Greek scientific contributions in a later paragraph, he might then want to bring in Aristotle and Hippocrates, but just mentioning their names in the thesis is of little value, for the essay's writer or reader.

Rich: The main contributions of Greek culture to Western civilization are scientific knowledge and the development of politics. The Greeks based their scientific work on a rational method, so that today we no longer rely on magic or other irrational systems to explain the world. Democracy is a Greek political idea that has become a successful modern-day form of government.

Rich's thesis answers all parts of the assignment. He knows — and therefore is able to tell his readers from the essay's start — what his main topics and his reasons for his answers are: our scientific and political practices today derive from Greek innovations; they have freed us from nonrational beliefs and have helped us organize our society.

Rich's thesis also provides him with a logical framework for his essay. Look at it again to see how it outlines these main topics:

- Greek scientific knowledge.
- Development of politics.
- Rational method.
- No reliance on magic/irrational systems.
- Democracy.
- Successful modern government.

Once placed in logical order, these topics should lead to a well-organized, well-developed essay. A possible logical organization of the topic ideas follows:

- Greek scientific knowledge leading to the development of:
- a rational method, causing a:
- release from irrational systems;
- the Greeks also developed politics, leading to:
- Greek democracy, a model for:
- successful modern government

You could organize the essay in other ways, too. It could be organized historically, for example, moving from Greek innovations in science and politics, to scientific and political practices today, to an analysis of how important the Greek roots of both are. Having some logical plan in mind before you begin writing is the important issue here. Once you've answered your assignment clearly and completely, clarified your main topics, and worked out a logical order of discussion, you're set to start work on developing the individual paragraphs. Remember the importance of paragraph development as we discussed it earlier. Paragraphs are the units of thought in an essay. Good paragraphs — paragraphs that consist of thorough analysis and original interpretation — insure effective and interesting essays.

When you are revising a complete essay, you should be looking at your work on the sentence level, to check for grammar and coherence, the paragraph level, to check for development and logic, and the essay level, to check your thesis, organization, and overall development.

The Thesis

As we discussed above, one useful way to check for a good thesis is to read the assignment first and then the essay's thesis, to see if it provides a direct and complete answer. Doing this can help you check your essay for proper focus and a complete response to all parts of the assignment.

Organization

To check an essay for a good logical framework, try reading only its thesis and topic sentences. Together they should form the essay's logical skeleton. Do all the topic ideas connect to the ideas in the thesis? Are there any main ideas in the thesis that don't appear in a topic sentence? Is the sequence of topic ideas logical?

Development

Look at the length of each paragraph. Although it's possible to have short paragraphs, be sure to check any very short one for full content development. Have you discussed the topic idea in detail? Can you analyze it further by telling how it works or why it's true? Can you provide an example to illustrate the topic idea and then explain it for the reader? Did you develop the implications of the topic idea: why is it important, what effects has it caused, how should the reader view it? Check any very long paragraph for a possible focus error. If you discuss two different topics, split the discussion into two paragraphs so the reader can follow your ideas easily.

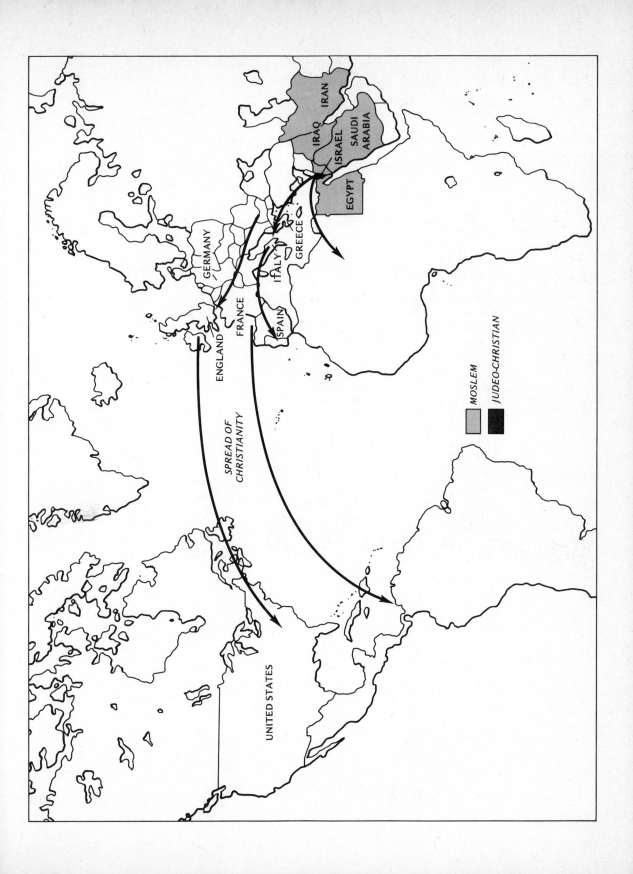

IRAN

IRAQ

SAUDI
ARABIA

ISRAEL

EGYPT

GERMANY

ITALY

GREECE

FRANCE

ENGLAND

SPAIN

SPREAD OF
CHRISTIANITY

UNITED STATES

MOSLEM

JUDEO-CHRISTIAN

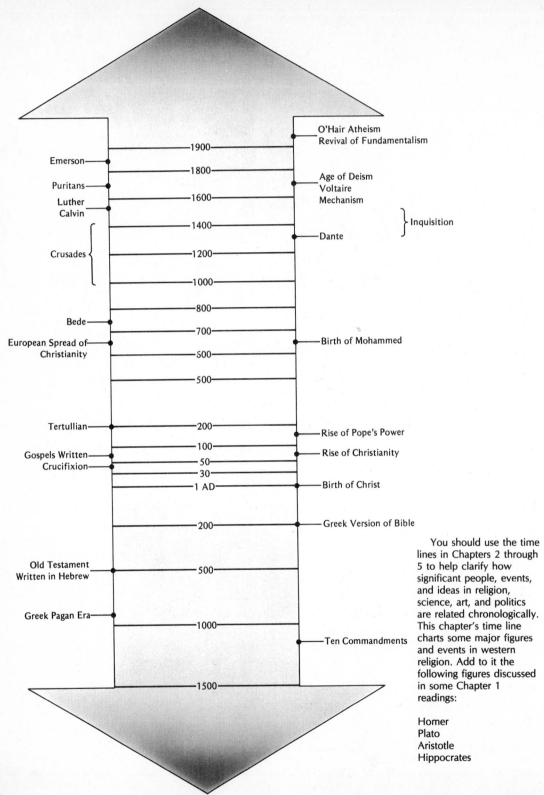

O'Hair Atheism
Revival of Fundamentalism

1900

Emerson
1800

Puritans
1600
Age of Deism
Voltaire
Mechanism

Luther
Calvin
1400
} Inquisition

Dante
1200

Crusades
1000

800

Bede
700

European Spread of
Christianity
500
Birth of Mohammed

500

Tertullian
200
Rise of Pope's Power

Gospels Written
100
Rise of Christianity

Crucifixion
50
30

1 AD
Birth of Christ

200
Greek Version of Bible

Old Testament
Written in Hebrew
500

Greek Pagan Era
1000

Ten Commandments

1500

You should use the time lines in Chapters 2 through 5 to help clarify how significant people, events, and ideas in religion, science, art, and politics are related chronologically. This chapter's time line charts some major figures and events in western religion. Add to it the following figures discussed in some Chapter 1 readings:

Homer
Plato
Aristotle
Hippocrates

CHAPTER *2*

Religious Beliefs and Attitudes

INTRODUCTION

The readings in this chapter discuss some of the major issues and concepts in Western religious thought. Religion is not simply a matter of personal faith in God; throughout history, religion has been intimately tied up with the development of cultural and political institutions, and even, at times, with philosophy, science, and art. The first two readings juxtapose* the ancient Hebrew and Christian religions. These two Bible stories—the first from the Old Testament, the second from the New Testament—show how perceptions of God and divine law changed: the all-powerful Hebrew Jehovah who embodied vengeance and mercy becomes in the Christian tradition the seldom-seen God the Father, whose benevolent son, Jesus Christ, promises God's love and compassion for all.

The selection from Tertullian illustrates the dogmatic attitudes of the early Church Fathers as Christianity became institutionalized during the first five centuries A.D. Patristic* writers reshaped Christ's precepts into a stringent* and rigorously demanding doctrine and moral code.

An excerpt from the Venerable Bede's Life of Cuthbert shows how Christian beliefs were taught by the use of stories called "lives of the saints." Bede's narrative, an early Middle Ages chronicle, rejects the ancient rational tradition in favor of belief in the saving and miraculous qualities of the Christian faith.

In the selection from A Distant Mirror: The Calamitous Fourteenth Century, Barbara W. Tuchman, a leading contemporary historian, analyzes the role the Church played in medieval life. The passage shows how

place side by side

early Christian

severe

closely interwoven religious and political life was at the time. Tuchman discusses some of the Church's internal problems that led to various religious reform movements in the sixteenth century.

Harvey Cox, another contemporary scholar, examines some Western misconceptions and prejudices about Islam, the Moslem religion. Islam began in the seventh century A.D.; as it grew, it clashed with the Western Christian tradition. Out of this clash came cultural animosity* and religious prejudice. Cox's essay underlines the fundamental similarities between Islam and Christianity, which he argues fuel mistrust and rivalry between the two religions.

hostility

The selection from Dante's Divine Comedy *gives a prose version of Canto XXVIII of the* Inferno. *Its graphic imagery of fire and infernal suffering reflects medieval conceptions of Hell. The selection illustrates Cox's thesis that Westerners viewed Mohammed as a particularly sinful and bestial pagan. It also illustrates Tuchman's thesis that Hell and its tortures were very real to the people of medieval times.*

Harold J. Grimm in "The Growth of Lutheranism" analyzes Luther's beliefs that led to the Reformation, a split in the organized Catholic Church. With Luther begins the Protestant era, carried further by Calvin, whose doctrine was less tolerant and hopeful than Luther's. Calvin taught that only people specifically marked by God—the "elect"—could ever hope for salvation.

Thomas J. Wertenbaker's "The Rule of Conduct" describes the rigid code of behavior in American Puritan life. The Puritans' suspicion of leisure and entertainment derived from their Calvinistic heritage, which taught that the devil lay in wait to tempt weak and idle people to sin and damnation.

In "God as Divine Clockmaker," Ian G. Barbour sums up some of the growing rationalist perceptions of God. As scientists increased our understanding of the physical universe, they speculated on God's role in a mechanistic world. To them, God was a designer and the universe his well-running machine.

Voltaire was one of the greatest voices of the Age of Reason. He presents a deist's view of a benevolent, rational God, whose existence is independent of any organized church. "Of Universal Tolerance" shows Voltaire's belief in God's universal accessibility.

Reacting to the Age of Reason, the Romantics sought to free the individual from a mechanistic view of life and nature. Ralph Waldo Emerson, a famous American Romantic poet and essayist, was among the leaders of the transcendentalists, people who believed in spirituality rather than organized religious doctrine. In "Emerson," Brooks Atkinson explains the transcendentalists' notion of the universe as a great and holy spirit of which all people are part.

Atheism shows the continued historical progression of religion away from a unified force in government and society to a less public, more individual practice. Madalyn Murray O'Hair, a contemporary American atheist who is an active advocate for the separation of church and state, presents in "Refutation" a modern atheist's response to religion. She refutes earlier arguments for the existence of God.

READING AND WRITING SKILLS OF CHAPTER 2

The skills in this chapter include:

Locating an implied thesis	*Marking the text*
Paragraphs of comparison and contrast	*Deriving definitions*
	Understanding analogies
Detecting an author's bias or assumptions	*Formulating a response to an argument*

The above list mixes reading and writing skills because reading, writing, and thinking are interconnected. When you begin a reading assignment, you need first to establish what *it is that you're reading. Marking a text, locating an implied thesis, and deriving definitions give you access to what an author is trying to say and to the information you need. Understanding analogies and looking for bias and assumptions help you evaluate an author's ideas. The final stage in gathering and interpreting information is being able to synthesize and react to it critically, to compare, contrast, or respond.*

The Ancient World

READING SKILL: *Locating an Implied Thesis*

Usually, your academic readings will have a thesis, whether the work is descriptive, narrative, or expository.* Often, however, authors do not state a thesis directly. Finding a thesis that is implied instead of directly stated challenges your skill as a careful reader.

writing whose purpose is to examine and clarify

The first two passages in this chapter are narratives: they tell a story. The purpose of narratives, or stories, isn't always to entertain. Usually they suggest some moral, opinion, or argument—they imply a thesis—which you must identify. Remember that a thesis can be considered the answer to a question. To find an implied thesis, you can begin by formulating questions suggested by the narrative, or by your active critical reading of the narrative:

- What is the topic of the passage?
- What is its focus?
- What is the conflict? Most narratives consist of conflicting/opposing ideas, issues, points of view, characters, or actions. In a way, the thesis is the resolution of the conflict, or tension, of the narrative. For example, you've read Socrates' speech in Plato's "Apology." The topic of the piece is Socrates' trial; its focus is on his self-defense. The conflicts involved include Socrates versus his Athenian judges or, more specifically, Socrates' sense of his worth to the community versus the judges' belief in his corruption and their fear and dislike of him. The judges sentence him to death; his death means that fear and hatred have won out over individual honesty in criticizing the state. Plato implies that Socrates' trial and conviction reflect the Athenian leaders' failure or even political corruption.
- What is its purpose? If you read a parable, like "The Prodigal Son," or a fable, like Aesop's "Diogenes on a Journey," you know its purpose is to teach some moral or lesson. The implied thesis should be the same moral or lesson that the author wishes to teach or illustrate. By clarifying an author's purpose, you should be able to extract the thesis.

Read the following narrative for its implied thesis. At the end you'll find a model of one way to locate and state it.

The Old Testament is a collection of the writings of ancient Hebrew scholars and the teachings of the Hebrew prophets. We can trace the origins of some Bible stories, such as the great flood, back through the Egyptians, Babylonians, and Assyrians. The Judeo-Christian tradition considers the Bible the "word of God," but others view it as moral philosophy written by several different hands, probably from the eighth through second centuries B.C.

In either case, Old Testament teachings and imagery continue to have a strong influence on Western thought. The New Testament, deriving from the teachings of Jesus Christ and passed on orally until the second century A.D., has also greatly influenced all aspects of Western culture. Both parts of the Bible survive today as the definitive beliefs of the Jewish and Christian religions.

"The Golden Calf"

KEY CONCEPTS

IDOLATRY consists of object-worship; instead of a spiritual notion of God, idolators worship a representation of God, usually some sort of statue. Here, the people say, ". . . make us a god."

The Old Testament notion of **ATONEMENT** means you must pay for your sins with an equivalent sacrifice.

● When the people became aware of Moses' delay in coming down from the mountain, they gathered around Aaron and said to him, "Come, **make us a god** who will be our leader; as for the man Moses who brought us out of the land of Egypt, we do not know what has happened to him." Aaron replied, "Have your wives and sons and daughters take off the golden earrings they are wearing, and bring them to me." So all the people took off their earrings and brought them to Aaron, who accepted their offering, and fashioning this gold with a graving tool, made a molten* calf. Then they cried out, "This is your God, O Israel, who brought you out of the land of Egypt." On seeing this, Aaron built an altar before the calf and proclaimed, "Tomorrow is a feast of the Lord." Early the next day the people offered holocausts* and brought peace offerings. Then they sat down to eat and drink, and rose up to revel.* [made from melted metal] [burnt sacrifices] [celebrate]

With that, the Lord said to Moses, "Go down at once to your people, whom you brought out of the land of Egypt, for they have become depraved. They have soon turned aside from the way I pointed out to them, making for themselves a molten calf and worshiping it, sacrificing to it and crying out, 'This is your God, O Israel, who brought you out of the land of Egypt!' I see how stiff-necked* this people is," continued the Lord to Moses. "Let me alone, then, that my wrath may blaze up against them to consume them. Then I will make of you a great nation." [stubborn]

But Moses implored the Lord, his God, saying, "Why, O Lord, should your wrath blaze up against your own people, whom you brought out of the land of Egypt with such great power and with so strong a hand? Why should the Egyptians say, 'With evil intent he brought them out, that he might kill them in the mountains and exterminate them from the face of the earth'? Let your blazing wrath die down; relent* in punishing your [be less stubborn or stern] people. Remember your servants Abraham, Isaac and Israel, and how you swore to them by your own self, saying, 'I will make your descendants as numerous as the stars in the sky; and all this land that I promised, I will give your descendants as their perpetual heritage." So the Lord relented in the punishment he had threatened to inflict on his people.

Moses then turned and came down the mountain with the two tablets of the Commandments in his hands, tablets that were written on both sides, front and back; tablets that were made by God, having inscriptions on them that were engraved by God himself. Now, when Joshua heard the noise of the people shouting, he said to Moses, "That sounds like a battle in the camp." But Moses answered, "It does not sound like cries of victory, nor does it sound like cries of defeat; the sounds that I hear are sounds of revelry." As he drew near the camp, he saw the calf and the dancing. With that, Moses' wrath flared up, so that he threw the tablets down and broke them on the base of the mountain. Taking the calf they had made, he fused it in the fire and then ground it down to powder, which he scattered on the water and made the Israelites drink.

Moses asked Aaron, "What did this people ever do to you that you should lead them into so grave a sin?" Aaron replied, "Let not my lord be angry. You know well enough how prone the people are to evil. They said to me, 'Make us a god to be our leader; as for the man Moses who brought us out of the land of Egypt, we do not know what has happened to him.' So I told them, 'Let anyone who has gold jewelry take it off.' They gave it to me, and I threw it into the fire, and this calf came out."

When Moses realized that, to the scornful joys of their foes, Aaron had let the people run wild, he stood at the gate of the camp and cried, "Whoever is for the Lord, let him come to me!" All the Levites then rallied to him, and he told them, "Thus says the Lord, the God of Israel: Put your sword on your hip, every one of you! Now go up and down this camp, from gate to gate, and slay your own kinsmen, your friends and neighbors!" The Levites carried out the command of Moses and that day there fell about three thousand of the people. Then Moses said, "Today you have been dedicated to the Lord, for you were against your own sons and kinsmen, to bring a blessing upon yourselves this day."

On the next day Moses said to the people, "You have committed a grave sin. I will go up to the Lord, then; perhaps I may be able to make **atonement** for your sin." So Moses went back to the Lord and said, "Ah, this people has indeed committed a grave sin in making a god of gold for themselves! If you would only forgive their sin! If you will not, then strike me out of the book that you have written." The Lord answered, "Him only who has sinned against me will I strike out of my book. Now, go and lead the people whither I have told you. My angel will go before you. When it is time for me to punish, I will punish them for their sin."

Thus the Lord smote* the people for having had Aaron make the calf   struck; afflicted
for them.

READING AND WRITING SKILL EXERCISES

The following steps illustrate one method for stating an implied thesis in your own words. You may find the Chapter 1 discussions of paraphrasing and locating topic sentences helpful when you're working with implied thesis statements.

[1] First, read the passage. Then, name its focus: God's anger at the Israelites' construction of a false idol, a molten calf.

[2] Identify the conflict: who or what are the opposing forces? Often you must think chronologically: what happened first and what happened later to create tension or conflict? In "Echo and Narcissus," for example, the overly talkative Echo prevented Hera from catching up with the philandering Zeus, which led to Hera's anger and her punishment of Echo. The action in "The Golden Calf" is the construction of a molten calf, which contradicted one of God's previous commands.

[3] How is the conflict resolved—what is the solution? Here, the sinners are punished and the commandment is reaffirmed. You should state that commandment directly as the thesis of the narrative. In this case the thesis might read, "The Israelites must honor God alone." Remember that multiple thesis statements are possible in an essay or narrative, so try to formulate several possibilities to get at all of the author's main points.

If you have difficulty figuring out an implied thesis using this model, you can try another approach, that of directly questioning the author's purpose. What point does he or she want to make? If you know something of the author's philosophy or work, you can surmise* his or her position on the   figure out
passage's topic. In the following parable, your knowledge of Christianity may allow you to make assumptions about Jesus' attitude toward the sinful son. Use one of the above techniques to help you clarify the parable's implied thesis and state it in your own words.

"The Prodigal* Son"   extremely wasteful

● A certain man had two sons. And the younger of them said to his father, "Father, give me the share of the property that falls to me." And he divided his means between them.

And not many days later, the younger son gathered up all his wealth, and took his journey into a far country; and there he squandered his fortune in loose living. And after he had spent all, there came a grievous famine over that country, and he began himself to suffer want. And he went and joined one of the citizens of that country, who sent him to his farm to feed swine.* And he longed to fill himself with the pods that the   pigs
swine were eating, but no one offered to give them to him.

But when he came to himself, he said, "How many hired men in my father's house have bread in abundance, while I am perishing here with hunger! I will get up and go to my father, and will say to him, Father, I have sinned against heaven and before thee. I am no longer worthy to be called thy son; make me as one of thy hired men." And he arose and went to his father.

But while he was yet a long way off, his father saw him and was moved with compassion, and ran and fell upon his neck and kissed him. And the son said to him, "Father, I have sinned against heaven and before thee. I am no longer worthy to be called thy son." But the father said to his servants, "Fetch quickly the best robe and put it on him, and give him a ring for his finger and sandals for his feet; and bring out the fattened calf and kill it, and let us eat and make merry; because this my son was dead, and has come to life again; he was lost, and is found." And they began to make merry.

Now his elder son was in the field; and as he came and drew near to the house, he heard music and dancing. And calling one of the servants he inquired what this meant. And he said to him "Thy brother has come, and thy father has killed the fattened calf, because he has got him back safe." But he was angered and would not go in.

His father, therefore, came out and began to entreat* him. But he answered and said to his father, "Behold, these many years I have been serving thee, and have never transgressed* one of thy commands; and yet thou hast never given me a kid that I might make merry with my friends. But when this thy son comes, who has devoured his means with harlots, thou hast killed for him the fattened calf."

beg

sinned against

But he said to him, "Son, thou art always with me, and all that is mine is thine; but we were bound to make merry and rejoice, for this thy brother was dead, and has come to life; he was lost, and is found."

QUESTIONS FOR DISCUSSION AND WRITING

[1] Paraphrase the events of the parable. What conflict arises? How is it resolved?

[2] The parable's purpose is to teach a major Christian precept.* What are the implications of the father's forgiveness of his prodigal son? In other words, what precept does the parable seek to teach?

moral rule

WRITING SKILL: *Paragraphs of Comparison and Contrast*

When you compare two things, you identify their similarities. When you write a paragraph of comparison, a good way to begin is to write a topic sentence that names a point of comparison. You can develop such a paragraph, as we have done below, by explaining and elaborating on the similarity of the two points you're comparing. You might want to include specific examples or supporting quotations to illustrate how they are alike. Adapt the paragraph development techniques discussed in Chapter 1 to paragraphs whose purpose is the comparison of things or ideas. Try asking <u>how</u> and <u>why</u> the two things are the same in terms of the topic idea, and then ask <u>so what</u>: what are the similar results or implications?

Example: Compare the actual sins committed in the two Bible stories.

The following topic sentence provides one possible response to the assignment:

> Both the Israelites and the prodigal son rejected their responsibility to a figure of authority.

To develop the comparison named in the topic sentence, you could first analyze <u>how</u> the two sins are alike:

> In the Israelites' case, they had a pact with God to be his chosen people. God expected them to adore him alone. By building the idol, the calf, they failed to meet God's expectations and they transferred their devotion from him to a "false god." The prodigal son also rejected his duty, in this case to his father. A good son would have observed his father's wishes and would have devoted himself to work, not to revelry.

You can develop the paragraph further by analyzing <u>why</u> their behavior was sinful:

> Both the Israelites and the prodigal son chose self-indulgence over discipline and respect. They should have remained faithful to their agreement, the Israelites to God and the prodigal son to his filial* duty.

pertaining to being a son or daughter

Keep the paragraph coherent by emphasizing the comparison: explain the similar results of their sins:

> Their sins caused them both humiliation, pain, and, for the Israelites, even death. By disrespecting figures whom they should have honored, both the Israelites and the prodigal son committed grave sins and were forced to seek forgiveness and redemption.

The above paragraph demonstrates one possible way of developing a comparison. It's a <u>balanced</u> comparison because it analyzes both Bible stories equally. It also includes words that emphasize the comparison: "both" and "also."

Using the steps outlined above, write a paragraph of comparison on the following topics.

1. An "intermediary" is a go-between, someone who relays information from one party to another. Jesus, the Son of God, tells his followers the story of the prodigal son to teach them of God's will. In a paragraph, compare Jesus and Moses as intermediaries.
2. Both Echo and Narcissus disrespected the gods or disregarded their power. Compare the "sin" of Echo or Narcissus to the sin of the Israelites or the prodigal son.

3. You've read four narratives: "Echo and Narcissus," "Oedipus," "The Golden Calf," and "The Prodigal Son." Explain how all of the narratives have a purpose apart from entertainment: what is their major similarity?
4. One can consider the God/believer relationship to be similar to that of parent/child. Develop the comparison in a paragraph.

When you contrast two things, you point out their differences. The topic sentence in a paragraph of contrast should focus on a single point of difference so that you can develop the contrast fully, in a balanced discussion. Develop the paragraph by explaining <u>how</u> and <u>why</u> the two things you're contrasting differ and what their different results or implications might be.

Example: Contrast how the sinners in the two Bible stories came to recognize their sins.

Topic Sentence:

The Israelites and the prodigal son recognized their sins through different sources.

Explain <u>How</u>:

Moses, the intermediary between God and the Israelites, tells his people that they have violated God's law. Their source of recognizing their sins is external. The prodigal son, on the other hand, has no one to tell him of his sin; only through suffering does he come to recognize his wrongdoing. His conscience, an internal force, leads him to both recognize his sin and repent for it. The Old Testament story emphasizes law and public recognition of sin, while the New Testament story, the parable, emphasizes conscience and personal awareness.

In the above paragraph, terms such as "different," "on the other hand," and "while" emphasize that you're <u>contrasting</u> two things. Such terms help focus the reader's attention on the specific contrast you're developing.

Write a paragraph of contrast on each of the following topics.

1. Every religion defines "God" differently and ascribes different characteristics to him. The God of the Old Testament differs from the God of the New Testament. In a paragraph, contrast God's treatment of human beings as represented in the Old Testament story, "The Golden Calf," with his attitude toward human beings as represented in Jesus' parable, "The Prodigal Son." Consider the issues of vengeance, atonement, and forgiveness.
2. Hamilton discusses the Greeks' very human portrayal of their gods; the depiction of gods in "Echo and Narcissus" illustrates her point. Contrast the Greek conception of god with the view of God seen in the Old or New Testament story.
3. Contrast the sin of Oedipus with the Israelites' or the prodigal son's. Consider intention or motive, their view of themselves upon confronting their sins, and how they atoned for them.

4. Consider your reactions to the image of God represented in the four narratives. Contrast your own perception of God to the one that appeared most different from it.
5. You've read about three kinds of moral systems: the Greek, the Old Testament, and the New Testament. You've also read about the basis of scientific method in Clagett's "Greek Science." Contrast the characteristics of religious faith with scientific thought.

The Middle Ages

READING SKILL: *Detecting an Author's Bias or Assumptions*

We've already stressed the importance of recognizing an author as a real person, someone who holds a set of beliefs about the world. Knowing an author's association with a particular religious, political, or philosophical school can help prepare you for reading his or her work. If you're dealing with a persuasive essay, biographical information becomes even more important. Few writers are completely objective; most of us write with assumptions and biases. "Bias" in this sense means a frame of reference, not necessarily a prejudice. For instance, our bias in this book is a common one of English instructors: we value good reading, writing, and thinking skills regardless of the task, be it an English essay or a lab report. Because of their biases, authors make assumptions in their writing. They take for granted that certain things are true and they need not explain or defend their point of view for the reader. As a reader, you're responsible for detecting authors' biases and their underlying assumptions. If you don't examine biases and assumptions as you read, you may accept ideas, explanations, or arguments which you should question instead.

As a reading skill, knowing a writer's bias gives you a framework for approaching the reading. If you know, for example, that the Pope has written or even endorsed a certain article on contraception, you can assume that the article will have a bias against artificial means of birth control. You can't always assume that writers inject their personal biases in their writings, for many writers aim at objectivity, but looking for biases and assumptions should always be part of the questioning process in your critical reading.

Look at the biographical sketch that precedes the following reading. Consider the title as well. Before you read the essay, think about the author's possible bias. Does the title lead you to believe that he has made certain assumptions about marriage? His title suggests two alternatives; can you infer his opinion of marriage from them?

_____

Tertullian (160–230 A.D.), one of the Fathers of the Church, helped define and consolidate Catholic theology. His major works emphasize the values of asceticism* and the monastic life. Tertullian's writings and attitudes typify   strict self-discipline for religious purposes early Christian thought, which finds its greatest expression in the philosophical writings of St. Augustine (354–430 A.D.). The ascetic tradition continued up to the medieval period, when a more humanistic, scholarly approach emerged with the rise of the great universities. St. Thomas Aquinas (1225–1274) is the most famous Christian theorist of that age.

TERTULLIAN
"Better to Marry Than to Burn"

● I have written this essay so that I can explain the doctrine of the Apostle* Paul. In the first place, I think I will not be considered ungodly if I call attention to a remark which he himself makes, that when he grants permission for marriage he is acting according to his own judgment, that is, according to a human way of looking at things, and is not repeating a precept* which God has given him. For even after he explains that widows and single people should marry if they cannot practice continence,* since it is better to marry than to burn, he turns to another class of people and says: But to those who are married, it is not I but the Lord who gives commandments on how they should behave.

a disciple of Jesus

rule

abstaining from sex

Now this statement, though it refers exclusively to those who are single or widowed at the time when they are converted to the faith, is cited by all those people who want to justify marriage for any reason whatever. But I want to make clear what sort of "good" it is which is suggested as better than the pain of a punishment, a "good" which cannot be viewed as good except when it is compared with the greatest of all evils, so that only in this relative sense is it good to marry—only because it is worse to burn!

A thing deserves to be called "good" only if it is good in an absolute sense, without any reference to something that is evil or even to something else that is good. Something that is truly good, if it is compared with another good and found inferior, remains, nevertheless, good in itself. But if we are obliged to call it "good" by comparison with something that is evil, then it is not so much a good as it is a kind of lesser evil. If you take away the term of comparison, "than to burn," let me ask whether you would presume to say simply, "It is better to marry," without naming precisely what marriage is better than? By removing the term of comparison that says marriage is better than some evil, you remove the element which allows us to speak of it as good.

We should understand, then, that it is better to marry than to burn in the same sense that it is better to have one eye than none. Once you get away from the term of comparison, you see immediately that it is not really better to have just one eye, since this itself is not a good. Therefore, no one should cite Paul's argument in seeking to defend a position he has adopted. Strictly speaking, it has reference only to those who are single or widowed, and who are thus not actually bound by marriage ties. Yet

SOURCE: "Better to Marry Than to Burn" by Tertullian from *Treatises on Marriage and Remarriage*. Trans. by William P. LeSaint. Newman Press, 1956.

even these people, as I hope I have shown, ought to understand the nature of the permission which is granted to them.

READING SKILL EXERCISES

[1] Tertullian says that he should "not be considered ungodly" if he points out that St. Paul, not God, said marrying is better than burning with the sin of lust. Tertullian assumes that his readers will judge how good or faithful a Christian he is. What kind of audience does he assume he is writing for?

[2] Is Tertullian biased against marriage? Which lines in his essay reveal his attitude?

[3] Authors may write with more than one kind of bias. In "The Apology of Socrates" and "Phaedo," Plato presents Socrates' trial and death in a tragic light. He shows his moral and political biases. What is this implied judgment of the Athenian leaders, Socrates' persecutors?

[4] Does DeRidder in "Art in Greece" write with any particular bias? If so, what is it? Does his bias extend to the point of endorsing the doctrine of beautiful and useful art?

[5] In "Politics," M. I. Finley writes about Greek politics in an admiring tone. What does he assume about his readers' political beliefs?

WRITING SKILL EXERCISES: PARAGRAPHS OF COMPARISON AND CONTRAST

[1] Both Tertullian in his sermon and Jesus in his parable have a moral purpose. Compare their actual purposes and their sense of a typical person's weaknesses.

[2] In one paragraph, discuss the similarities between Tertullian's threats regarding sexual indulgence and God's revenge on the faithless Israelites. In a second paragraph, contrast the actions and temptations that Tertullian and "The Golden Calf" warn against.

[3] Contrast the human-God relationship as Hamilton presents it in Greek mythology, "The Golden Calf" represents it in the Old Testament, and "The Prodigal Son" in the New Testament. Consider divine expectations of the human being, the human expectations of God, and the role of sin, vengeance, atonement, and forgiveness.

[4] Think about the purpose of religion in human life. Compare how Greek mythology, Judaism, and Christianity all meet specific human needs.

The Venerable Bede (c.672–735) wrote histories of England in the early Middle Ages. His most famous work is Ecclesiastical History of the English People. *The title of the work reveals his interest; he was a chronicler of the Church, a Christian historian of the Anglo-Saxon peoples' conversion from* paganism to Christianity. It was Bede who began dating events according to their relation to Christ's birth: he was the first to use "A.D." as a measure of time.

The following passage comes from Bede's chronicle of St. Cuthbert, a seventh-century religious figure. Bede writes his chronicle not as true, objective history, but as an uncritical recounting of the miracles attributed to the saint. As you read, consider Bede's possible (or probable) bias toward his material. What might his <u>purpose</u> be in writing about St. Cuthbert's life? What assumptions does Bede make about his audience's beliefs and attitudes toward Christian doctrine?

BEDE
FROM *Life of Cuthbert*

● From having shown what power the venerable Cuthbert had against the deceits and frauds of the devil, we can now go on to reveal his strength in combating the fiend's undisguised fury. There was a sheriff of King Ecgfrith, called Hildmer, a man dedicated to good works along with all his household and therefore specially loved by Cuthbert. He visited Hildmer whenever he happened to be in the neighborhood. His wife, though zealous in almsgiving* and all the other fruits of virtue, was suddenly possessed of a devil. She was so sorely vexed* that she would gnash* her teeth, let out frightful howls, and fling her arms and legs about. It was terrifying to see or hear her. The convulsions gradually exhausted her, and she was already at death's door, or so it seemed, when her husband galloped off to fetch Cuthbert.

giving money or food to the poor / troubled or disturbed / grind

"My wife is ill," he pleaded. "She is very near her end. Send a priest before she goes, to give her the Body and Blood of the Lord and to bury her in holy ground."

He was ashamed to admit that she whom Cuthbert was used to seeing well was now out of her mind. Cuthbert went off to see whom he could send when it suddenly came to him that she was in the grip of no ordinary illness; she was possessed. He returned.

"I will not send anyone else. I ought to go back with you and see her myself."

As they were going along the sheriff began to weep. The bitterness of his anguish was apparent from the floods of his tears. He was afraid that when Cuthbert found that she was mad he might think she had served God up to now only in feigned* faith. But the man of God gently soothed his fears.

pretended, false

"Do not weep. Your wife's condition will not astonish me. I know, even though you are ashamed to admit it, that she is afflicted by a demon. I know too that before I arrive the demon will have left her and that she herself will come running out to meet us as sound as ever. She will take

SOURCE: From *Life of Cuthbert* by Bede. Trans. by J. F. Webb (Penguin Books, 1965). Copyright © 1965 by J. F. Webb.

the reins, bid us come in quickly, and treat us with all her usual attention. It is not only the wicked who are stricken down in this way. God, in his inscrutable designs, sometimes lets the innocent in this world be blighted*   destroyed by the devil, in mind as well as body.

Cuthbert continued to console and instruct his friend in this vein,* and   manner as they approached the house the evil spirit, unable to bear the coming of the Holy Spirit with whom Cuthbert was filled, suddenly departed. The woman, loosed from the chains of the devil, jumped up as though woken from a deep sleep, rushed out in gratitude to the saint, and caught hold of his bridle. Her bodily and mental strength soon completely returned. She asked him to dismount and come in to bless the house and waited on him with her most devoted attention. She admitted quite openly that at the first touch of his bridle all trace of her affliction had vanished.

QUESTIONS FOR DISCUSSION AND WRITING

[1] How does St. Cuthbert explain the sheriff's wife's illness?

[2] What is Bede's implied thesis in the narrative?

[3] Bede uses Cuthbert to illustrate the qualities of a saint. What are Cuthbert's saintly characteristics?

[4] In "The Sacred Disease," Hippocrates argued against the idea of "possession." He stated that all diseases have physical causes and cures. Contrast Hippocrates' views on possession with the Christian views suggested by Bede's narrative.

READING SKILL: *Marking the Text*

Books used for learning and teaching are meant to be written in. You will find that many of the books that your teachers use for lectures are covered with notes, remarks, reminders, question marks, exclamation points, and underlinings. We encourage you to mark your textbooks as well for two reasons: first, by writing your comments in a book while you read, you force yourself to read critically. Second, marking the text can aid you in organizing and retaining information as you read and study. It can help you establish the importance of ideas and the relationship between facts and ideas.

Everyone has a different way of marking texts. Develop a comfortable method for yourself and then stick with it. Here are a few suggestions:

Consider underlining the main idea in one color ink and the supporting ideas in another, or put one line under the main idea and two under the supporting ideas.

Sometimes students underline too much. Try to underline only the key words in a sentence.

Try underlining or marking after you read a paragraph or section. This technique will force you to think about what you have read and is more effective for studying than underlining and marking as you read.

Write the purpose or function of each paragraph in the margin.

Develop a set of abbreviations or symbols for yourself, for example:

      ex.—example

      def.—definition

      sum.—summary

      test q.—possible test question

      ?—confusing idea; ask the instructor

      ! or *—important idea

Circle words you don't know but that seem important for context; write their definitions in the margin.

Look for logical connectors or words in the text which signal listings of important ideas, causes, or reasons, such as "first," "next," "finally." Number the lists in the margin.

We've marked the following passage in four different ways:

1. Single underlining indicates the main idea of a paragraph.
2. Double underlining marks support or expansion of a main idea.
3. Right-hand marginal notes number concrete examples.
4. Left-hand marginal notes summarize a paragraph's function.

Begin your own marking process in paragraph 11. You'll find that some paragraphs don't conform to the topic sentence–supporting development–concrete examples model. Paragraph 6, for instance, has two topic ideas because it names first a problem and then a solution; therefore, it has two single-underlined sentences. Sometimes an author restates a paragraph's topic idea to emphasize its importance; you should mark a main idea only once to avoid repetitious marking. Your marking should reflect the different functions a paragraph may serve.

Barbara Tuchman wrote A Distant Mirror *in 1978. She's an historian, not a theologian like Tertullian, and her account of medieval religion focuses on its role in the everyday lives of people. This was the era of the great heresies, expounded by sects that split from the main Church over doctrinal differences. They met with aggressive repression at the hands of the Inquisition. None of the contemporary Protestant religions—which successfully challenged Catholic, or papist, hegemony*—yet existed.*   dominance

BARBARA W. TUCHMAN

FROM *A Distant Mirror*

KEY CONCEPTS

PENITENCE/ABSOLUTION and **REPENTANCE/SALVATION** both refer to the process of atoning for sin and being rewarded with forgiveness for doing so.

The **CHOSEN,** like the Israelites in the Old Testament, are those selected by God for protection or salvation.

The term **INHERENT CONDITIONS** makes the same distinction as the term **INNATE VS. ACQUIRED** (see page 63).

ASCETICISM involves leading a life of renunciation, in which a person gives up wealth, physical comforts, and sexual relations to devote himself or herself to spiritual contemplation.

MYSTICAL experience involves direct, intuitive knowledge of God.

In the sin of **HERESY,** considered by the Church to be one of the most serious sins, a person challenges God's law or the Church's interpretation of it.

The **INQUISITION** was the Church's organized campaign against heresy, which threatened its authority. Inquisitors often used torture to extract confessions and in some cases put heretics to death.

A believer in the **SUPREMACY OF THE STATE** recognizes national law over ecclesiastical, or Church, law.

NOMINALISM, unlike idealism, recognizes no essential ideas or objects; all things are distinct in their existence.

● In daily life the Church was comforter, protector, physician. The Virgin and patron saints gave succor in trouble and protection against the evils and enemies that lurked along every man's path. Craft guilds,* towns, and functions had patron saints, as did individuals. Archers and crossbowmen had St. Sebastian, martyr of the arrows; bakers had St. Honore, whose banner bore an oven shovel argent and three loaves gules; sailors had St. Nicholas with the three children he saved from the sea; travelers had St. Christopher carrying the infant Jesus on his shoulder; charitable brotherhoods usually chose St. Martin, who gave half his cloak to the poor man; unmarried girls had St. Catherine, supposed to have been very beautiful. The patron saint was an extra companion through life who healed hurts, soothed distress, and in extremity could make miracles. His image was carried on banners in processions, sculpted over the entrance to town halls and chapels, and worn as a medallion on an individual's hat.

Above all, the Virgin was the ever-merciful, ever-dependable source of comfort, full of compassion for human frailty, caring nothing for laws and judges,

[margin notes: analysis of Church's role; associations; ex. 1 patron saints' role; ex. 2 patron saints' role]

ready to respond to anyone in trouble; amid all the inequities,* injuries, and senseless harms, the one never-failing figure. She frees the prisoner from his dungeon, revives the starving with milk from her own breasts. When a peasant mother takes her son, blinded by a thorn in his eye, to the Church of St. Denis, kneels before Our Lady, recites an Ave Maria, and makes the sign of the cross over the child with a sacred relic, the nail of the Saviour, "at once," reports the chronicler, "the thorn falls out, the inflammation disappears, and the mother in joy returns home with her son no longer blind."

A hardened murderer has no less access. No matter what crime a person has committed, though every man's hand be against him, he is still not cut off from the Virgin. In the *Miracles of Notre Dame*, a cycle of popular plays performed in the towns, the Virgin redeems every kind of malefactor* who reaches out to her through the act of **repentance**. A woman accused of incest with her son-in-law has procured his assassination by two hired men and is about to be burned at the stake. She prays to Notre Dame, who promptly appears and orders the fire not to burn. Convinced of a miracle, the magistrates free the condemned woman, who, after distributing her goods and money to the poor, enters a convent. The act of faith through prayer was what counted. It was not justice one received from the Church but forgiveness.

More than comfort, the Church gave answers. For nearly a thousand years it had been the central institution that gave meaning and purpose to life in a capricious world. It affirmed that man's life on earth was but a passage in exile on the way to God and the New Jerusalem, "our other home." Life was nothing, wrote Petrarch to his brother, but "a hard and weary journey toward the eternal home for which we look; or, if we neglect our salvation, an equally pleasureless way to eternal death." What the Church offered was salvation, which could be reached only through the rituals of the established Church and by the permission and aid of its ordained priests. *"Extra ecclesium nulla salus"* (No **salvation** outside the Church) was the rule.

Salvation's alternative was Hell and eternal torture, very realistically pictured in the art of the time.

threat of Hell

In Hell the damned hung by their tongues from trees of fire, the impenitent burned in furnaces, unbelievers smothered in foul smelling smoke. The wicked fell into the black waters of an abyss* and sank to a depth proportionate to their sins: fornicators* up to the nostrils, persecutors of their fellow man up to the eyebrows. Some were swallowed by monstrous fish, some gnawed by demons, tormented by serpents, by fire or ice or fruits hanging forever out of the reach of the starving. In Hell men were naked, nameless, and forgotten. No wonder salvation was important and the Day of Judgment present in every mind. Over the doorway in every cathedral it was carved in vivid reminder, showing the numerous sinners roped and led off by devils toward a flaming cauldron* while angels led the fewer elect to bliss in the opposite direction.

ex. 1

bottomless pit

people engaging in illicit sexual intercourse

ex. 2
ex. 3
ex. 4

a large pot

ex. 5

damnation + salvation

No one doubted in the Middle Ages that the vast majority would be eternally damned. *Salvandorum paucitas, damnandorum multitudo* (Few saved, many damned) was the stern principle maintained from Augustine to Aquinas. Noah and his family were taken to indicate the proportion of the saved, usually estimated at one in a thousand or even one in ten thousand. No matter how few were to be chosen, the Church offered hope to all. Salvation was permanently closed to non-believers in Christ, but not to sinners, for sin was an inherent condition of life which could be canceled as often as necessary by penitence and absolution. "Turn thee again, turn thee again, thou sinful soul," spoke a Lollard preacher, "for God knoweth thy misgovernance* and will not forsake thee. Turn thou to me saith the Lord and I shall receive thee and take thee to grace."

ex. 1
ex. 2

ex. 1

poor management

Church gives sense of dignity + beauty

The Church gave ceremony and dignity to lives that had little of either. It was the source of beauty and art to which all had some access and which many helped to create. To carve the stone folds of an apostle's gown, to paste with infinite patience the bright mosaic* chips into a picture of winged angels in a heavenly chorus, to stand in the towering space of a cathedral nave* amid pillars rising and rising to an almost invisible vault and know this to be man's work in honor of God, gave pride to the lowest and could make the least man an artist.

The Church, not the government, sponsored the

pieces of colored stones

main part of a church from altar to entrance

ex. 1

church + poor

care of society's helpless—the indigent* and sick, or-   impoverished
phan and cripple, the leper, the blind, the idiot—<u>by
indoctrinating the laity in the belief that alms
bought them merit and a foothold in Heaven.</u> Based   *example*
on this principle, the impulse of Christian charity was
self-serving but effective. Nobles gave alms daily at   *ex. 1*
the castle gate to all comers, in coin and in leftover
food from the hall. Donations from all sources poured
into the hospitals, favorite recipients of Christian   *ex. 2*
charity. Merchants bought themselves peace of mind
for the non-Christian business of making profit by   *ex. 3*
allocating a regular percentage to charity. This was
entered in the ledger under the name of God as the
poor's representative. A Christian duty of particular
merit was the donation of dowries to enable poor
girls to marry, as in the case of a Gascon seigneur* of   nobleman
the 14th century who left 100 livres to "Those whom   *ex. 4*
I deflowered, if they can be found."

Corporate bodies accepted the obligation to help
the poor as a religious duty. The statutes of craft
guilds set aside a penny for charity, called "God's
penny," from each contract of sale or purchase. Parish councils of laymen superintended maintenance
of the "table of the Poor" and of a bank for alms.
On feast days it was a common practice to invite   *extended*
twelve poor to the banquet table, and on Holy   *example*
Thursday, in memory of Christ, the mayor of a
town or other notable would wash the feet of a beggar. When St. Louis conducted the ceremony, his
companion and biographer, the Sire de Joinville,
refused to participate, saying it would make him
sick to touch the feet of such villeins. It was not always easy to love the poor.

transition to criticism of Church

<u>The clergy on the whole were probably no more
lecherous or greedy or untrustworthy than other
men, but because they were supposed to be better or
nearer to God than other men, their failings attracted more attention.</u> If Clement VI was luxury-   *ex. 1*
loving, he was also generous and warm-hearted. The   *ex. 2*
Parson among the Canterbury pilgrims is as benign
and admirable as the Pardoner is repulsive, always
ready to visit on foot the farthest and poorest house
of his parish, undeterred* by thunder or rain.   unstopped

<u>Nevertheless, a wind of discontent was rising.</u>
Papal tax-collectors were attacked and beaten, and
even bishops were not safe. In 1326, in a burst of

anti-clericalism, a London mob beheaded the Bishop
and left his body naked in the street. In 1338 two
"rectors of churches" joined two knights and a "great
crowd of country folk" in attacking the Bishop of
Constance, severely wounding several of his retinue,*
and holding him in prison. Among the religious
themselves, the discontent took serious form. In Italy
arose the Fraticelli, a sect of the Franciscan order, in
another of the poverty-embracing movements that
periodically tormented the Church by wanting to
disendow it. The Fraticelli or spiritual Franciscans
insisted that Christ had lived without possessions,
and they preached a return to that condition as the
only true "imitation of Christ."

people serving someone important

The poverty movements grew out of the essence
of Christian doctrine: renunciation of the material
world—the idea that made the great break with the
classical age. It maintained that God was positive and
life on earth negative, that the world was incurably
bad and holiness achieved only through renunciation
of earthly pleasures, goods, and honors. To gain victory over the flesh was the purpose of fasting and
celibacy, which denied the pleasures of this world for
the sake of reward in the next. Money was evil,
beauty vain, and both were transitory.* Ambition
was pride, desire for gain was avarice,* desire of the
flesh was lust, desire for honor, even for knowledge
and beauty, was vainglory. Insofar as these diverted
man from seeking the life of the spirit, they were
sinful. The Christian ideal was **ascetic**: the denial of
sensual man. The result was that, under the sway of
the Church, life became a continual struggle against
the senses and a continual engagement in sin, accounting for the persistent need for **absolution**.

temporary
greed

Repeatedly, **mystical** sects arose in an effort to
sweep away the whole detritus* of the material
world, to become nearer to God by cutting the earth-
binding chains of property. Embedded in its lands
and buildings, the Church could only react by renouncing the sects as **heretical**. The Fraticelli's stubborn insistence on the absolute poverty of Christ and
his twelve Apostles was acutely inconvenient for the
Avignon papacy,* which condemned their doctrine
as "false and pernicious"* heresy in 1315 and, when
they refused to desist,* excommunicated them and
other associated sects at various times during the

trash

rule by a Pope
harmful
stop

next decade. Twenty-seven members of a particularly stubborn group of Spiritual Franciscans of Provence were tortured by the **Inquisition** and four of
them burned at the stake at Marseille in 1318.

The wind of temporal* challenge to papal su-   worldly
premacy was rising too, focusing on the Pope's right
to crown the Emperor, and setting the claims of the
state against those of the Church. The Pope tried to
excommunicate this temporal spirit in the person of
its boldest exponent,* Marsilius of Padua, whose *De-*   supporter
fensor Pacis in 1324 was a forthright assertion of the
supremacy of the state. Two years later the logic of
the struggle led John XXII to excommunicate William of Ockham, the English Franciscan, known for
his forceful reasoning as "the invincible doctor." In
expounding a philosophy called **"nominalism,"** Ockham opened a dangerous door to direct intuitive
knowledge of the physical world. He was in a sense
a spokesman for intellectual freedom, and the
Pope recognized the implications by his ban. In
reply to the excommunication, Ockham promptly
charged John XXII with seventy errors and seven
heresies.

QUESTIONS FOR DISCUSSION AND WRITING

[1] Jesus teaches Christian forgiveness in "The Prodigal Son." Discuss how
his notion of forgiveness is reflected in the organized medieval Church, as
Tuchman analyzes it. Consider the issues of confession, absolution, and
retribution. Then contrast how a person went about gaining forgiveness in
Jesus' parable and in the medieval Church as Tuchman's article explains the
process.

*This assignment consists of several parts. Break it into separate questions to
clarify what you need to do and how you might go about doing it. Here's
one possible approach:*

*(a) To discuss the notion of Christian forgiveness, you could first define the
term, either in several sentences or, because it's the assignment's
central concept, a whole paragraph. Or you could summarize the
concept as Tuchman discusses it and as Jesus implies its meaning in his
parable.*

*(b) To discuss how the notion is similar in Jesus' parable and Tuchman's
analysis, compare it in terms of "confession, absolution, and
retribution." You'll probably need several paragraphs to compare the
concepts in detail.*

*(c) Then contrast how one gains forgiveness according to Jesus and
according to the medieval Church.*

[2] Compare the medieval Church's doctrine of "no salvation outside the Church" with the Old Testament notion of the chosen people as portrayed in "The Golden Calf." Consider why such a doctrine might be beneficial to both believer and organized religion alike. How did the requirements for attaining salvation differ for Christian and Israelite?

You could approach this assignment as part summary, part definition, part comparison, and part contrast. Summarize the doctrine of "no forgiveness outside the Church" and define the notion of the "chosen people" in separate paragraphs. Then discuss how the concepts are similar in their benefits to the believer and to the organized religion. You should reread "The Golden Calf" and Tuchman's article, looking for the actual requirements for salvation which each outlines or suggests, and mark the appropriate sections.

[3] In some ways, Oedipus served a similar function in his society as the Church served in medieval society. Compare their roles: what did they give to their people? How did their roles differ?

[4] Compare and contrast some of your religion's major doctrines with those described by Tuchman or suggested by the Bible stories.

[5] How has the role of religion in daily life changed from ancient and medieval times to the present day? Consider purpose, practice, and participants.

   The following article discusses the common Western biases and assumptions about Islam, the Moslem religion. The author refers particularly to Canto XXVIII of Dante's *Inferno,* which directly follows this reading. According to the author, what are the common assumptions about Islam, and what biases do they reveal? When you've finished reading, paraphrase the essay's main points.

   Apply your critical reading skills to analyze the essay. After reading each paragraph or section, go back and mark the specific biases and assumptions that the author identifies. Marking the text will help you to locate the ideas you must paraphrase.

   Harvey Cox is a well-known contemporary scholar of theology who currently teaches at Harvard. "Understanding Islam" first appeared in The Atlantic *in 1981. During the "dark ages," from the fall of Rome in 476 A.D. to approximately 900, and into the Middle Ages, the Islamic culture preserved, assimilated, and added to the advances made by Greek scientists and mathematicians. The Islamic holy wars pushed the Moslem empire west, through Spain. The Christian Crusades, which dated from the eleventh through thirteenth centuries, were Christian Europe's attempts to regain control of the holy land, Jerusalem, from the Moslems. This religious and political strife had racial undertones as well and kept cultural exchange to a minimum, though the exchange that did go on was of great value to Western science and philosophy.*

HARVEY COX
"Understanding Islam: No More Holy Wars"

KEY CONCEPTS

According to the psychological theory of Carl Jung, a pioneer of modern psychology early in this century and one of Freud's original pupils, we all have **PRIMAL** experiences, that is, experiences that remind us of some basic human event: birth, for example. The word "primal" derives from the Latin word for "first."

Jung also theorized that our minds recognize certain **ARCHETYPES,** prime, essential models of objects or experiences, such as an archetypal mother.

Freud developed the theory of **PSYCHOANALYSIS,** a method of exploring dreams, memories, and feelings to explain how the individual mind is formed.

Freudian psychology also discusses **SIBLING RIVALRY,** the competition between brothers and sisters for their parents' affection.

The terms **PARTICULAR** and **UNIVERSAL** refer to the relativity or specificity of a thing vs. its general truth.

Church vs. **CIVIL POLITY,** names the conflict of church vs. state in terms of where legal and political power rests.

● Odious* Western images of Muhammad and of Islam have a long and embarrassingly honorable lineage. Dante places the prophet in that circle of hell reserved for those stained by the sin he calls *seminator di scandalo e di scisma* [sewing of scandal and schism]. As a schismatic,* Muhammad's fitting punishment is to be eternally chopped in half from his chin to his anus, spilling entrails and excrement at the door of Satan's stronghold. His loyal disciple Ali, whose sins of division were presumably on a lesser scale, is sliced only "from forelock to chin." There is scandal, too. A few lines later, Dante has Muhammad send a warning to a contemporary priest whose sect was said to advocate the community of goods and who was also suspected of having a mistress. The admonition* cautions the errant* padre that the same fate awaits him if he does not quickly mend his ways. Already in Dante's classic portrait, we find the image of the Moslem linked with revolting violence, distorted doctrine, a dangerous economic idea, and the tantalizing hint of illicit sensuality.

Nothing much has changed in the 600 years since. Even the current

disgusting, offensive

a person who causes a split or division in a religion

warning / someone going off the proper course

SOURCE: From *Understanding Islam* by Harvey Cox. Copyright © 1981. By permission of Atlantic Monthly Co., Boston, Mass.

wave of interest in Eastern spirituality among many American Christians has not done much to improve the popular estimate of Islam. It is fashionable now in the West to find something of value in Buddhism or Hinduism, to peruse the *Sutras** or the *Bhagavad Gita,** to attend a lecture by Swami Muktamanda or the Dalai Lama, even to try a little yoga or meditation. But Americans in general and Christians in particular seem unable to find much to admire in Islam. As G. H. Hansen observes, with only a modicum* of hyperbole,* in his book *Militant Islam,* the mental picture most Westerners hold of this faith of 750 million people is one of ". . . strange bearded men with burning eyes, hieratic* figures in robes and turbans, blood dripping from the amputated hands and from the striped backs of malefactors,* and piles of stones barely concealing the battered bodies of adulterous couples." Lecherous, truculent,* irrational, cruel, conniving,* excitable, dreaming about lascivious* heavens while hypocritically enforcing oppressive legal codes: the stereotype of the Moslem is only partially softened by a Kahlil Gibran who puts it into sentimental doggerel* or a Rudolph Valentino who does it with zest and good humor.

Hindu and Buddhist religious writings / a Hindu religious text

a small amount

exaggeration

priest-like

evil doers

argumentative / scheming

lustful

poorly written poetry

There is, of course, one important exception to the West's rejection of the religious value of Islam. This exception's most visible representatives have been Muhammad Ali and the late Malcolm X. Most Americans who seem genuinely drawn to the call of the minaret* are blacks. But given the racial myopia* that continues to affect almost all American cultural perceptions, this exception has probably deepened the distrust most white Americans feel toward Islam. The dominant image was summed up brilliantly in a Boston newspaper's cartoon showing a Moslem seated in prayer. Over his head the balloon contained one word: "Hate!"

tower of Moslem mosque

nearsightedness

This captious* caricaturing of Moslems and Arabs is not confined to the popular mentality. In his *Orientalism,* Edward Said describes a study published in 1975 of Arabs in American textbooks that demonstrates how prejudices continue to be spread through respectable sources. One textbook, for example, sums up Islam in the following manner:

finding fault easily

> The Moslem religion, called Islam, began in the seventh century. It was started by a wealthy businessman of Arabia, called Muhammad. He claimed that he was a prophet. He found followers among the other Arabs. He told them they were picked to rule the world.

This passage is, unfortunately, not atypical. Although phrased with some degree of restraint, it coheres all too well with the popular medieval picture of Muhammad as a sly trickster or the current comic-book depictions of the sated,* power-mad Arab. Moreover, Dante's unflattering portrait of the prophet was rooted in traditions that existed long before his time. These **primal** shadowgraphs* have notoriously long half-lives, and they continue to darken our capacity to understand Islam to this day.

completely satisfied or full

images made by projecting a shadow on a screen

Allah works in mysterious ways. Through the stubborn geopolitics of oil, Westerners are being forced, like it or not, to learn more about Islam than they ever thought they would. Inevitably this reappraisal has begun to include a rethinking of the relationship between Islam and Christianity. In the fall of 1979, the World Council of Churches sponsored a conference on the subject of Kenya, and Christian scholars with direct experience of Islam were invited from all over the world. The results were mixed since, ironically, theologians from countries where Islam is a small minority seemed much more eager to enter into dialogue with their Moslem counterparts than did those from countries where Christians form a small minority in an Islamic world. Still, the recent upsurge of Islamic visibility will surely increase enrollment in courses on Islam wherever they are offered, and sales of books on the subject are up.

All such activities are welcome. But what about the shadowgraphs? Conferences and courses will help only if their participants become aware of the deep-lying, nearly **archetypal** images that subvert* the whole enterprise from the outset. Along with study and analysis, a kind of cultural archaeology or even a collective **psychoanalysis** may be necessary if we are to leave Dante's *Inferno* behind and live in peace with our Moslem neighbors on the planet Earth. The question is, How can Westerners, and Christians in particular, begin to cut through the maze of distorting mirrors and prepare the ground for some genuine encounter with Moslems?

overthrow or destroy

The first thing we probably need to recognize is that the principal source of the acrimony* underlying the Christian-Moslem relationship is a historical equivalent of **sibling rivalry**. Christians somehow hate to admit that in many ways their faith stands closer to Islam than to any other world religion. Indeed, that may be the reason Muhammad was viewed for centuries in the West as a charlatan and an impostor. The truth is, theologically speaking at least, both faiths are the offspring of an earlier revelation through the Law and the Prophets to the people of Israel. Both honor the Virgin Mary and Jesus of Nazareth. Both received an enormous early impetus* from an apostle—Paul for Christianity and Muhammad for Islam —who translated a **particularistic** vision into a **universal** faith. The word "Allah" (used in the core formula of Islam: "There is no God but Allah and Muhammad is his prophet") is not an exclusively Moslem term at all. It is merely the Arabic word for God, and is used by Arabic Christians when they refer to the God of Christian faith.

bitter hatred

supportive push

There is nothing terribly surprising about these similarities since Muhammad, whose preaching mission did not begin until he reached forty, was subjected to considerable influence from Christianity during his formative years and may have come close—according to some scholars— to becoming an Abyssinian Christian. As Artend van Leeuwen points out in his thoughtful treatment of Islam in *Christianity in World History,* "The truth is that when Islam was still in the initial stages of its development, there was nothing likely to prevent the new movement from being accepted as a peculiar version of Arabian Christianity." Maybe the traditional Christian uneasiness with Islam is that it seems just a little too similar. We sense the same aversion we might feel toward a twin brother who looks more like us than we want him to and whose habits remind us of some of the things we like least in ourselves.

The actual elements of the Koran's message—faith, fasting, alms,* prayer, and pilgrimage—all have Christian analogues.* Despite its firm refusal to recognize any divine being except God (which is the basis for its rejection of Christ's divinity), Islam appears sometimes to be a pastiche* of elements from disparate* forms of Christianity molded into a potent unity. Take the Calvinist emphasis on faith in an omnipotent deity, the pietistic* cultivation of daily personal prayer, the medieval teaching on charity, the folk-Catholic fascination with pilgrimage, and the monastic* practice of fasting, and you have all the essential ingredients of Islam. All, that is, except the confluence* of forces which, through the personality of Muhammad and the movement he set off, joined these elements in the white heat of history and fused them into a coherent faith of compelling attractiveness.

No one should minimize the fact that in any genuine conversation between Christians and Moslems certain real differences in theology and practice will have to be faced, what scholars so often call "rival truth claims." But such conflicting assertions can be properly understood only against the flesh-and-blood history that has somehow made them rivals. Religious teachings do not inhabit a realm apart. They mean what they do to people because of the coloration* given to them by long historical experience. Therefore a previous question has to be asked. It is this: If Christianity and Islam share such common roots and, despite real differences, some striking similarities, why have they grown so bitter toward each other over the centuries? Why did the average white American feel less sympathetic to Islam than to any other world religion even <u>before</u> our current flap* with the ayatollahs*?

Curiously, after being warned for years that our greatest enemies in the world were godless and atheistic, Americans are now faced with a challenge that emanates* from profoundly religious sources. Although Islam has never accepted the dichotomy* between religion and the **civil polity** that has arisen in the West, there can be little doubt that the present Islamic renaissance is not a deviation but an authentic expression of the elements that were there at its origin. So we are now told that, instead of atheists, we are dealing with "fanatics," or "Moslem fundamentalists." This language is not very helpful either.

Sometime soon a real conversation must begin. Perhaps the moment has come to set aside Dante, Urban II, and the rest; to remember instead the two children of Father Abraham, from both of whom God promised to make great nations; to recall that Jesus also cast his lot with the wounded and wronged of his time; to stop caricaturing the faith of Arabia's apostle; and to try to help both Christians and Moslems to recover what is common to them in a world that is just too small for any more wars, especially holy ones.

Margin glosses:

donations to the poor

similarities, counterparts

mixture

different

religiously devoted

pertaining to monks or nuns

flowing together

meaning, implications, characteristics

dispute / Islamic religious leader

originates

split

QUESTIONS FOR DISCUSSION AND WRITING

[1] Compare the beliefs and practices of Christianity and Islam.

[2] Ask someone outside of class about his or her impression of Islam or Moslems. Compare or contrast the response with Cox's argument that most Westerners have a negative view.

[3] Which Islamic beliefs and practices might Tertullian condone? Explain how their views are similar and why they might agree. Use examples and quotations from both Tertullian and Cox.

[4] Think of some historical figure who in your eyes personifies evil. Compare the evil actions and qualities of that individual with those attributed by Westerners to Mohammed. Contrast truly evil characteristics with false impressions produced by bias and assumptions.

DANTE
Inferno, Canto XXVIII

One of the greatest names in Western literature is Dante Alighieri, an Italian poet. Dante wrote his epic poem, The Divine Comedy, *in 1320. The work has three parts:* Inferno, Purgatorio, *and* Paradiso. *In each part, Dante depicts his imaginary voyage through the regions of the afterlife, with the Roman poet Virgil as his guide. He intended his poem to be a theological tract as well as a criticism of his contemporaries, especially those holding political power. His work illustrates Tuchman's thesis that religious concerns were central to medieval life and that people then had a literal notion of hell and damnation. It also illustrates Cox's thesis that the Islamic prophet Mohammed was feared and hated by Christian society of the time.*

In the Inferno, *the source of the following passage, Dante divides Hell into nine circles, each of which has several subdivisions. The more serious your sin, the graver your punishment and the lower your placement in the descending circles. The following passage depicts part of the ninth circle, reserved for "schismatics." A schismatic is one who intentionally causes division or strife, between the individual and the Church, the king, or the family. Heresy was the major and most serious form of schismatic sin in the eyes of the Church.*

Read the passage, here translated from its original Italian verse into English prose form. Dante's characters represent the prevailing views of his era; the poem contains a great deal of blatant religious and racial bias common at the time. As you read, pay particular attention to Dante's depiction of Moslems. When you finish reading, write a paraphrase of Dante's implied thesis.

● Even if someone tried, over and over again, who could ever really tell of all the blood and gore that I now saw before me?

Translated by Jeanne Gunner.

Surely no human language has the words, the meanings, that could convey such awful tales.

Imagine an assembly of all the people who already mourned their dead through the long Trojan war, which the infallible Livy wrote about, and all those who suffered such painful wounds when they fought against Robert Guiscard, and the others whose heaps of bones still lie at Ceperano, where Apulians turned traitors, and at Tagliacozzo, where old Alardo, without weapons, was victorious; imagine one man showing his pierced limb, another holding up his stump for all to see. Even so, none of this would equal the hideous ninth chasm.* pit

I saw a man who looked like a barrel that had lost its staves*: he was split open from his chin to his anus, and his intestines hung down between his legs. All his guts showed, even the pathetic sack that makes filth out of what we swallow. He looked at me, displaying all his innards to my startled stare, and with his hands he ripped apart his chest, saying: pieces of wood that make up a barrel's walls

"Now see how torn up I am! See how mutilated Mohammed is! Before me goes my apostle Ali, crying, with his face split open from chin to scalp. And all the others that you see here, sewers of scandal and schism while they lived, are laid open like this as punishment. Behind us a devil cruelly cuts us in two. As we pass by him on our painful path, he makes new sword-slashes in each of us, because our wounds close up before we pass by again.

But who are you, looking at us, loitering on that bank, perhaps to avoid recognizing the torment that your own conscience sentences you to?"

My guide answered him: "Death hasn't brought him here, nor have sins led him to this place of punishment. I, who am dead, must lead him through every level of hell, to give him full experience here below: and that's as true as my speaking to you."

More than a hundred, when they heard his words, stopped in their tracks, forgetting their torture. They looked at me in wonder.

Another, who had his throat pierced through and his nose cut away from right below his eyebrows, and who had only one ear, stopped with the pack to stare in awe. In front of all the others, he tore open his windpipe, which was soaked with blood through and through, and said:

"You, not damned by sin, I have seen you in your Italian land, if appearances don't deceive me. Think of Pier da Medicina if ever again you see the pretty slope between Vercelli and Marcabo. And let the two best men of Fano, Guido and Angiolello, know that, if our foreknowledge here isn't worthless, they will be thrown from their boat and drowned, near la Cattolica, through the treason of a wicked tyrant. Neptune never saw such an evil deed done by pirates or Argives between the Isle of Capri and Majorca. That traitor who has only one eye, and holds the land that one here with me wishes he had never seen, will call them to a conference with him. Then he'll arrange it so they'll need to make no oath or prayer on the agreement."

I said to him: "If you want me to carry your news, show me, tell me who he is that has such bitter sight." Then he put his hand on the jaw of one of his companions and opened his mouth, crying, "Here's the man himself, but no speech comes from him. This man, an exile, calmed Caesar's doubts, telling him that trouble awaits those who delay."

Oh how shocking Curio appeared, with his tongue carved from his throat—he used to speak so boldly!

And one who had only stumps at the end of each arm, lifting up his mutilated limbs so that blood dripped down and stained his face, cried: "Remember Mosca, too, who said—alas!—what's done is done, which was the start of trouble for the Tuscan people." I added: "And the death of your own." He went on his way, like a mournful madman, grief piled on grief.

But I remained to watch the group, and I saw something that I would be afraid to describe without having a witness other than myself, if my conscience, that good companion that gives a man courage, didn't reassure me; its purity is like armor. I'm sure I saw, and still see in my mind, a trunk without a head go by, just like all the others of this sad crowd passed; and this body held its head by the hair, swinging it like a lantern in its hand. And the head looked at us and said, "Oh me!" For itself, it made of itself a light—it was two in one, and one in two: how that was possible, God only knows. When it was right at the foot of the bridge, it raised its arm up high, with its head in hand—to bring its words near us —and it said:

"Now see this awful punishment, you who, still breathing, walk among the dead: see if any pain is as great as mine. And so that you can bring news of me, know that I am Bertran de Born, who gave the young King such wicked guidance. I made father and son turn against each other; Achitophel created no greater malice between Absalom and David. Because I divided once-united people, I carry my brain, alas! divided from my body, its former home. Divine revenge shows itself in me."

QUESTIONS FOR DISCUSSION AND WRITING

[1] Tuchman claims that the medieval vision of Hell was very literal (see pages 101–102). How does this passage from Dante confirm her interpretation?

[2] Which of the Western biases against Moslems analyzed by Cox does Dante's passage illustrate?

[3] Given what you know of Tertullian's thought, do you believe that he would approve of Dante's depiction of Hell?

[4] Consider Dante's depiction of Hell in the context of contemporary images. Would most modern people find it outdated and alien or real and familiar?

[5] Describe some probable purposes which Dante may have had in mind as he wrote the *Inferno.* Consider edification,* entertainment, artistic expression, political polemic.*

education

strong argument

Reform Movements

READING SKILL: *Deriving definitions*

Texts often include clear, simple definitions of the main concepts they deal with. But sometimes definitions are not given directly. They may be mixed in with narration and analysis. As a critical reader, you may need to derive (to draw out, extract) a usable definition of any main concept you're studying. In the following passage, the author assumes that his readers already know what Lutheranism is, and he therefore doesn't include a formal definition of it in his essay. He moves immediately to analyzing the elements of Lutheranism against their historical background.

To derive a definition from such an analytical essay, you should mark sections of the text that specify the given topic's characteristics. Only with a clear definition of a given topic can you understand an author's discussion of it. As you read, mark the text for information that explicitly or implicitly defines Lutheranism, with the idea of writing an extended definition in mind.

Harold J. Grimm wrote "The Growth of Lutheranism" in 1963. His article traces the rise of Lutheranism during the Reformation. This period—the early sixteenth century—marks a major change in Western Christianity. The Church of Rome lost much of its authority and power to Protestant factions. Political repercussions included animosity between Catholic and Protestant countries or opposing factions within nations; England, France, and Spain saw continuing religious/political conflict over the next few centuries. Even today, the Protestant/Catholic split causes political turmoil; Northern Ireland is a violent example.

HAROLD J. GRIMM
"The Growth of Lutheranism"

KEY CONCEPTS

The **REFORMATION**, which challenged the authority of the Catholic Church, took place in the sixteenth century under the leadership of Martin Luther.

CONSERVATISM refers to a political attitude, specifically one that involves resistance to change.

A **DUALISTIC** doctrine proposes that two forces exist in the universe, a positive/good one and a negative/evil one.

● The fear of popular unrest, expressed by religious and secular* authorities during the first years of the **Reformation**, had been well founded. It seemed as though every German with grievances looked to Luther for redress,* especially after the publication of his revolutionary pamphlets of 1520. Luther's own religious program, which he expressed in a forcible idiomatic* German as well as in Latin, became the program of the masses, and such words as gospel and liberty became the watchwords* of a movement that tended to become much broader than the purely religious reforms envisioned by Luther.

non-religious, worldly

correction, satisfaction

common regional speech

slogans

Luther at the Wartburg and the radicals at Wittenberg

At the Wartburg Luther had an opportunity to consider those events that had driven him inexorably* from the position of a monk, professor, and preacher demanding reforms in conformity with his new theology to the position of a leader of a widespread national movement against Rome. Frequently he was troubled by doubts whether he, one person among many thousands, was able to oppose the entire medieval Church supported by the Empire. But he eventually dispelled such doubts by doing hard work of a constructive nature. By gradually building an evangelical* church separated from Rome, he carried into practice, as far as circumstances would permit, his new theology and demonstrated his innate **conservatism**.

relentlessly

Protestant, pertaining to the New Testament

Luther's inner conflict during his stay of almost ten months at the Wartburg was accentuated by his physical inactivity, by lack of contact with his friends, and by disturbing news from the outside. This conflict found characteristic expression in his many references to the devil. He was quick to see in every opponent and obstacle the work of Satan. This tendency is an indication of the religious **dualism** that became so pronounced in his theology. Although God's grace was for him a dynamic* force for good, struggling for the soul of man and his regeneration, he picturesquely conceived of evil, engineered by the devil, as a dynamic force working for the destruction of the soul. By faith in God the individual permitted the forces of good to operate successfully against the forces of evil; but because evil was not vanquished in this life, the struggle continued until the soul was released from the body. One's own ability and the use of force were of no avail, for only the preaching of the gospel would provide victory.

energetic

SOURCE: From *The Reformation Era*, Second Edition, by Harold J. Grimm. Copyright © 1973 by Harold J. Grimm. Edited with permission from Macmillan Publishing Company.

This certainty that God would combat the forces of evil without man's efforts was reflected in all Luther's letters and sermons sent to his friends from the Wartburg. The many rumors and the popular excitement that followed his disappearance after the Diet of Worms were soon allayed* when he established contact with his friends, without divulging* the exact location of his "island of Patmos," or "region of the birds." By his voluminous* correspondence he attempted to keep the Reformation in line with his own doctrines and to prevent the uncertainty and violence that, he felt, would destroy all that had thus far been achieved. He urged Melanchthon and others to preach the evangelical message in the vernacular,* made suggestions for reorganizing the University of Wittenberg, gave encouragement to those who feared the future, and answered the polemical* tracts of his enemies.

calmed

revealing

large, filling volumes

common native language of a country or area

argumentative

Meanwhile Luther applied still further his new doctrines to Christian life and practice. In a pamphlet, *Concerning Confession, Whether the Pope Has Power to Order It,* he adduced* Bible passages to show that the Christian had the right to confess his sins to God alone; that priestly confession and absolution, though not denied by the Bible, were inventions designed to enslave Christians; and that the power of forgiving sins was given by Christ to the entire Church, not only to the clergy. Even more significant was his opposition to what he considered the distorted views concerning the role of the clergy in the Church. Arguing that the Bible and the early Church sanctioned* the marriage of priests and that the Western Church had imposed celibacy as a further means for suppressing freedom, Luther came to the defense of one of his students, a priest, who had taken a wife and whom his ecclesiastical* superior had accused of an infraction* of the canon* law.

gave as evidence

approved of

of the church
breaking of a law / church laws

Luther's attack upon the unique position of the clergy was extended to the monks in his work *On Monastic Vows,* also written at the Wartburg. He maintained that because virtually all monks took the monastic vows in the hope of earning merits on a higher plane than ordinary Christians— contrary to the "New Testament reign of liberty and faith"—these vows were not binding, despite ecclesiastical authority to the contrary. Moreover, the chastity that they vowed was contrary to human nature and reason. The vow of poverty, he insisted, was in most instances a sham,* for the monks did not seek out those monasteries that rigidly practiced that virtue but used monasticism* to obtain false religious security and live lives of ease. Obedience was generally looked upon as mere obedience to a prior,* whereas the true Christian was obedient to God above all; and God demanded an active life of service to others, not withdrawal from the community. Although he stated his case against monastic vows with dogmatic* certainty, he cautioned his friends at Wittenberg to permit monks and nuns to exercise complete freedom in determining whether or not they should revoke their vows. Yet when he returned to Wittenberg, only the prior had remained in the Augustinian monastery.

falsehood, deception

life as a monk or nun

head of a monastery

strictly held

Luther was also compelled to give his attention to the practical question of the celebration of the Mass and Communion in both kinds when Carlstadt, his colleague at the university, and Gabriel Zwilling, a forceful preacher of the Augustinian order, attempted to enforce changes in Wittenberg. In order to clarify still further the doctrines that he had expressed in *The Babylonian Captivity,* he wrote his pamphlet *On the Abrogation of Private Mass.* Like the priestly hierarchy of the Middle Ages, he maintained, the Mass as a sacrifice had no sanction in the New Testament, which refers only to a memorial of Christ's sacrifice.

The news that Luther received concerning the overzealous* activities of some of his followers in carrying out his reforms filled him with forebodings* of serious social as well as religious disturbances. Although he wrote Spalatine and Elector Frederick, criticizing them for withholding from publication some of his polemical writings, and demanded of the archbishop of Mainz that he cease encouraging superstitious practices by permitting the sale of indulgences, he consistently refrained from inciting revolt and urged his followers to carry on reforms through duly constituted political authorities.

In defiance of the Edict of Worms and contrary to the wishes of his elector, Luther traveled incognito* to Wittenberg to learn firsthand how serious the disturbances had become. Upon his return to the Wartburg he once more made clear his views with respect to the importance of obeying the political authorities in his *Faithful Exhortation to All Christians to Guard Against Revolt and Tumult.* Although he can be justly criticized for not realizing that a revolt against ecclesiastical authority might lead to a revolt against the political and social order, he cannot be accused of inconsistency. His entire concern centered in a religious problem and excluded political, economic and social considerations, except insofar as these could be improved by praying, hearing the Gospel, and requesting reforms of the established authorities.

In further preparation for the preaching of the gospel of Christ, which he considered his chief mission, Luther continued his study of Hebrew and Greek. As an aid to those preachers who could not write their own sermons, he prepared his first collection of short sermons, called *Postils* or *Homilies,* in which he expounded his evangelical doctrines in simple, homely language, free of all scholastic subtleties.* As the father of the modern evangelical sermon, he demonstrated how the Bible could be made a lively, dynamic force. For him the entire Bible was primarily a testimony of Christ that he, like Paul, felt compelled to bring to all people.

Undoubtedly, the greatest product of the Wartburg days was Luther's translation into German of the New Testament, achieved in the unbelievably short period of eleven weeks. Numerous translations of the New Testament and the Bible as a whole had previously been made; but this was the first one not based on the Vulgate translation of Jerome. Luther used the second edition of Erasmus' New Testament, published in 1519. By using the official German of the Saxon Chancery, not his own colloquial Saxon dialect, he helped create a standard German for all Germany.

overenthusiastic

fears; premonitions

disguised

very fine points

Organization and spread of Lutheranism

As soon as order had been established at Wittenberg, Luther and his friends took up the task of constructing an evangelical church along conservative lines. Although urging leaders to follow moderation and tolerance toward those who had not yet comprehended the significance of the Gospel, Luther insisted that those who had should be firm in their opposition to the forces of evil.

Contrary to Luther's expectations, the simple preaching of the Gospel did not solve all difficulties and differences of opinion. Consequently he resorted* upon occasion to vigorous practical measures for the maintenance of order. He went on numerous missions to those centers where serious controversies had developed and wrote many letters and pamphlets urging vigorous action in abolishing the Mass, relic worship, and other nonevangelical usages. He also persisted in his demands that his elector put an end to the old practices in All Saints Church in Wittenberg until the latter finally agreed to do so in 1524. Like Carlstadt during the Wittenberg disturbances, Luther now argued that in matters of the conscience a Christian should obey God rather than man.

turned to

Meanwhile, Luther also reformed the order of service in the parish church at Wittenberg, substituting for the defunct* daily Masses a short daily worship, in which the chief emphasis was placed upon reading and expounding the Bible. In the Sunday service, in which the Lord's Supper was celebrated, the preaching of the Gospel in the vernacular likewise received chief emphasis, although Luther retained most of the medieval liturgy,* including the Gloria, the Hallelujah, the Nicene Creed, the Sanctus, and the Agnus Dei. With the assistance of two able musicians he adapted the Gregorian music to the German translation with happy artistic results. Communion in both kinds followed the sermon. But Luther did not insist that congregations elsewhere follow the service at Wittenberg in every detail, for he maintained that freedom should be practiced in all externals, such as the use of vestments,* candles, and music. Although the private Mass was abolished, individual confession before Communion was permitted. The great concern in making changes in the service was to make it intelligible to the participants; therefore the vernacular was used both in the liturgy and in the singing of the hymns.

no longer existing

religious services

clergyman's robes

The Baptismal service was also translated into German, for Luther wished to make the parents of those baptized aware of the importance of this sacrament, by means of which the infant became regenerated, was "delivered from the devil, sin and death," and was made a member of the Christian communion of saints. Although he wished to simplify the rite, he retained it in its traditional form, for he did not want to offend weak Christians.

Luther's emphasis upon the preaching of the Gospel and the participation of the members of the congregation in the religious services was reflected also in his plans for the administration of the Church. In his significant work *On Secular Government,* he distinguished between the spiritual realm, which consisted of preaching the Gospel and in which no force should be used, and the secular realm, which was divinely ordained to maintain order and which the Christians must obey in secular matters. The ideal society, according to Luther, would be the one in which the Christian government would protect all divinely created classes in their respective callings and maintain order in the preaching of the Gospel. Thus preaching and governing were, according to him, complementary* callings, the former operating in the sphere of religion and ethics, the latter in matters pertaining to order.

> completing or perfecting something

In his attempts to approximate the conditions of the primitive Christian Church, Luther replaced the ecclesiastical hierarchy of the medieval Church with the spiritual democracy of the New Testament. He insisted that the congregation had the right not only to decide doctrinal matters and call pastors and teachers but to appropriate and administer ecclesiastical revenues* for the good of the whole community. Accordingly, a common treasury received money from the entire community, and from it the congregations paid their teachers and preachers, maintained schools, and cared for the poor. The wishes of the congregation were usually executed by both the city council as the chief administrative body and the chief pastor as a superintendent, or bishop.

> income from taxes

READING AND WRITING SKILL EXERCISES

When an essay doesn't explicitly provide the definition of its main idea or concept, you can try several different techniques to derive it for yourself. Some useful methods include: (1) prereading; (2) marking key words and signal words; and (3) noting repeated ideas.

Prereading: Ask yourself what you already know about the term you need to define. In this case, you may already recognize Lutheranism as a Protestant religion. A Protestant church is one that protested against Rome, against the Pope's total authority. You may also be familiar with the term "Reformation." Protestants re-formed Christianity in certain ways. With this general background knowledge you're prepared to read for specific information on the changes that define Lutheranism, a particular Protestant movement.

Marking key words: Sometimes key words describe the term's characteristics; they may be synonyms or vocabulary words common to the topic or its class. Since you know that the topic here relates to the reform of a religion, words related to change and doctrine may be key words.

Marking signal words: Watch for words or phrases that "signal" discussion of the term's defining characteristics. Common expressions include "means," "is characterized by," "believed," "consists of." In this case, the term we're defining refers to Luther's

reforms and doctrines, so common signal words might be
"believed," "preached," "conceived of," "applied," "thought."
Repetition: Look through sentences you've marked to identify repeated
<u>general</u> terms. These terms probably name major characteristics of
the term you need to define.

We've marked the following sentences from Grimm's first four paragraphs
for key words and signal words, as you should do when you're reading to
formulate a definition. Continue marking the text for words that point out
Lutheranism's characteristics.

1. ". . . gospel and liberty became the <u>watchwords</u> . . ."
2. ". . . <u>building</u> an evangelical church <u>separated from Rome</u>" and "<u>he
carried into practice</u> . . . his new theology and <u>demonstrated</u> his innate
conservatism."
3. ". . . conflict <u>found characteristic expression</u> in his many references to
the devil."
4. "This <u>tendency</u> is an indication of the <u>religious dualism</u> that became so
pronounced in his <u>theology</u>."
5. "This certainty that God would combat the forces of evil without
man's efforts <u>was reflected</u> in all Luther's letters and sermons . . ."
6. "He <u>urged</u> . . . to preach the evangelical message in the vernacular . . ."
7. ". . . he <u>adduced</u> Bible passages to show . . . the Christian had the
right to confess his sins to God alone . . . priestly confessions and
absolution . . . enslave Christians . . ."
8. ". . . <u>significant</u> was his <u>opposition to</u> . . . distorted views concerning
the role of the clergy . . ."

In this reading, the following words show up repeatedly:

<u>new theology</u> (religious program, doctrines)
<u>evangelical doctrine</u> (evangelical church, hearing the Gospel)

We can define Lutheranism as a <u>new theology</u> (or a new religious program,
a new doctrine, reform). Now we have the first part of the definition. The
other repeated word is Gospel or evangelical doctrine, the main
characteristic of Luther's new theology. By analyzing its parts, you'll name
Luther's identifying characteristics or elements.

If you're familiar with the thing or idea you're defining, you may not
need to work through all the above steps. In this case, if you know that
Lutheranism is a doctrine of theological reform, you can focus on the signal
words which lead to specific information about Luther's beliefs and reforms.
We've already marked the signal words in the above sentences. Some signal
words may lead to dead ends, but others help you focus on Luther's beliefs
directly. For example, in sentence 3, the phrase "conflict found
characteristic expression" leads you to evidence of Luther's literal belief in
the devil, the first identifying characteristic to appear in the article. If you
can mark your text for main points of definition indicated by the signal
words and sift through the information for the overall major points in your

head, do so. Otherwise, make a list of the information, as we have done, and then go through it, striking out repetitious, irrelevant, or clearly minor details.

Separate the list into general issues and supporting details, eliminating repetitions. Then paraphrase the major points. The final definition may be stated this way:

> Lutheranism began as a conservative, evangelical church separate from Rome. Luther believed in dualism, God's ability to fight evil without man's efforts, and the need to preach God's message in everyday language. He argued <u>against</u> the clergy, Mass, confession, and <u>for</u> individual prayer, hearing the Gospel in everyday language, Church reform, and individual participation in and control of the Church.

Thomas Wertenbaker's discussion of the Puritan code of behavior appeared in his book, The First Americans *(1927). You probably have heard the term "Puritan," and may have a mental picture of men and women in simple, modest dress, working and praying, and celebrating Thanksgiving with the Indians. You can draw a more detailed and accurate definition of the term from the following passage. Puritans practiced a form of Calvinism, a Protestant religion like Lutheranism, but one that emphasized human sinfulness and the uncertainty of redemption. The American Puritan ethic defined the earliest non-Indian American culture. Its restrictive nature eventually led to a kind of social and religious revolution—transcendentalism—in the nineteenth century, which you'll read about later in this chapter.*

THOMAS J. WERTENBAKER
"The Rule of Conduct"

KEY CONCEPTS

THE ELECT, a Calvinist term, refers to those people whom God has chosen for salvation.

A **THEOCRACY** is a form of government in which religious leaders administer the state and determine its laws.

● To the Puritan, this world seemed a place of temptation and danger. On trial before an exacting* God, he was constantly subjected to the wiles of Satan and his minions.* In what form the spirits of evil would assail him he knew not, so that safety lay only in unceasing vigilance. "Was ever man more tempted . . . ," wrote Cotton Mather in his *Diary*. "Should I tell, in how many Forms the Divel* has assaulted me, and with what Subtilty and Energy, his assaults have been carried on, it would strike my Friends with

severely demanding
followers

devil

Horrour." Again and again this eminent divine implored "the Help of Heaven" against "the Buffetings* of Satan." With eternal happiness or eternal punishment hanging in the balance, the Puritan had for earthly pleasures a mingled feeling of contempt and fear. They were but baubles* placed before him in seductive forms by the Evil One to divert him from the great goal of salvation.

blows

cheap jewelry

This state of mind brought about constant self-searchings and a rigid code of personal conduct. The Puritan had few diversions, and these few he took with some qualms* of conscience. To go out into the country in quest of chestnuts, to smoke a pipe, to read a beautiful poem, to play shuffleboard, amusements innocent in themselves, might afford some opening to Satan to lure the godly man from the path of duty. Safety could be assured only by constant meditation on religious matters, regular attendance at divine service, copious* reading of the Bible, much prayer, and sobriety* in the tasks of everyday life.

twinges

plentiful

seriousness

Nor was the Puritan content with maintaining this rigid standard for himself—he insisted that his neighbor should conform to it also. Sin and worldliness, dread diseases of the soul, are no less contagious than diseases of the body, and like them must be stamped out in order to insure the safety of the community, save **the elect** from annoyance, and protect God from mockery. The New England leaders set up for their Zion* the most severe moral code; that their system interfered seriously with individual liberty did not in the least give them pause.

holyland

Laws for the observance of the Sabbath* were everywhere rigidly enforced. In Massachusetts a law was passed in 1653 which made it a misdemeanor to waste time by taking walks on the streets or by visiting ships in the port on Sunday. It was forbidden to travel, cook, sweep or make up beds on that day. In New London, John Lewis and Sarah Chapman were brought before the court in 1670, "for sitting together on the Lord's day, under an apple tree, in Goodman Chapman's orchard." From time to time laws were passed in various New England colonies against observing Christmas, indulging in mixed dances, playing cards, or performing on certain musical instruments. God's time must not be frittered* away, as anyone who read the book of Proverbs well understood.

Sunday; religious day of rest

wasted

This asceticism* entailed no great hardship upon the moving spirits of the **theocracy** themselves. For them there were many compensations—the interest that comes from creative leadership, the inspiration derived from reading and study, the anticipated joy of a heaven easily within the grasp of their imaginations. Beyond doubt the virile, rosy-cheeked John Cotton delighted in his religion quite as today the great surgeon and the captain of industry feel the thrill of accomplishment. But for those in the humbler walks of life—the farmer, the fisherman, the ship carpenter or the blacksmith—the system of repression must have been irksome.* The reverence which they entertained for their leaders, their fear of damnation, their respect for the law might keep them within the narrow limits of Puritan life, but the effort was hard. Even in the days of the exodus,*

religious self-denial

annoying

Puritans' flight to America

when men's minds were fired with zeal* for the new state which they   enthusiasm
were building in the forests of America, there must have been in many a
humble breast the fierce beating of suppressed desire.

QUESTIONS FOR DISCUSSION AND WRITING

[1] Derive a definition for the term "Puritan." Review the possible
techniques for deriving definitions on pages 119–120.

[2] In what ways can dancing, card-playing, or taking walks be construed as
sinful activities?

[3] How does the Puritan differ from the Lutheran? What major theological
beliefs separate the two religious schools?

[4] Wertenbaker refers to the Puritans' "asceticism." Tertullian was also an
ascetic. What were the shared goals of such believers?

READING SKILL: *Understanding Analogies*

Definition is more than an academic exercise. In intellectual history, scientists and philosophers have faced the major task of defining both material and
physical phenomena in order to make sense of what was, without definition, a
chaotic world. The growth of Western scientific thought that began with the
Renaissance saw great thinkers struggling to define some of the most basic
human concerns: the nature of God, humans and the universe.

But how do you define such abstractions? The difficulty lies in expressing
the specific characteristics of the unobservable, the unseen. Analogies can allow
you to discuss abstractions in concrete terms. They equate an unknown idea or
thing with something familiar as a means of defining the unknown. Mystics who
claim to have communed with God often cannot say what they experienced,
but many have said what their experience was like: "God is like a brilliant light
or fire, one that does not burn, but instead illuminates the mind and warms the
heart." In his "Allegory of the Cave," Plato makes an analogy between his
theory of perception and knowledge and a man facing the wall of a cave, seeing
only reflections of the "real world." Learning to perceive reality is like finding
your way out of the cave: from the distorted reflections you move to the source
of light, or understanding. Plato explains his abstract theory of ideas through his
extended analogy made up of concrete illustrations.

The following passage discusses some very common analogies used by
sixteenth- and seventeenth-century scientists to define "God." As you read,
underline the analogies which appear in Barbour's essay. Consider the abstract
theory they attempt to express.

---

*Ian Barbour wrote the following article in 1966. It covers the age of ration-
alism (the late sixteenth and seventeenth centuries), which saw the rise of
modern scientific method and major scientific discoveries, like Newton's the-*

*ory of gravity and his development of calculus. The search for knowledge
through rational thought altered theological views, as Barbour here explains.
It also led to the Age of Reason, or the Enlightenment, in the eighteenth
century.*

IAN G. BARBOUR
"God as Divine Clockmaker"

KEY CONCEPTS

In a **MECHANISTIC** view of the universe, all forces and objects run
according to a prearranged plan, like parts in a machine, one thing
infallibly causing another thing to happen.

REVELATION involves direct experience of God's existence or his
divine plan; see page 125.

PROVIDENCE refers to God's ordained plan for the universe, or a kind
of Christian fate.

The **FIRST CAUSE** is God, who built the universe and set the
mechanism in motion.

DIVINE IMMANENCE is the belief that we can know God by observing
the order of the universe, that is, God's existence in the actual parts of
the universal machine.

STATUS QUO is the middle-of-the-road or generally accepted position;
it usually implies a desire to maintain conditions unchanged.

DEISM is a form of Christian faith outside the organized Church,
emphasizing God's benevolence and rationality.

The **PRIMACY OF SPIRIT OVER MATTER** is another way of naming
Platonic idealism (see page 126).

PANTHEISTIC ABSOLUTE is similar to **DIVINE IMMANENCE** but emphasizes
God's existence in all natural things.

● Nowhere was the impact of scientific on religious thought greater than
in the modification of views of the function of God in relation to nature.
God became primarily the divine Architect, though various attempts were
made to find a place for God's continuing activity within **a mechanical
natural order**. Boyle's favorite analogy for the world was the famous clock
at Strasbourg. The analogy served him well in arguing for the divine
Clockmaker, for a clock is obviously not the work of chance but of skillful
artifice* by its original creator. But the analogy also makes clear the diffi-   craftsmanship
culties in finding any room for present divine activity, for a clock once
started runs its own independent mechanical course.

Most of the virtuosi,* at least until the end of the century, were willing   accomplished scholars or
practitioners

SOURCE: Ian G. Barbour, *Issues in Science and Religion*, Copyright © 1966, pp. 40–43.
Reprinted by permission of Prentice-Hall, Inc., Englewood Cliffs, NJ.

to make an exception to the rule of law in the case of biblical miracles, which they felt to be part of their Christian heritage. God may intervene on rare occasions for special reasons since he is not bound by his creation. Some authors felt that miracles and the fulfillment of prophecies were evidence for the validity of **revelation**; they claimed that miracles were public events observable by the senses and attested* by reliable witnesses. Other interpreters showed more ambivalent attitudes; having used the regularity of the world as their main argument for God, they did not want to make too much of the irregularities. Thus Boyle started by affirming God's freedom to rule his creatures, but ended by asserting that God's wisdom was displayed primarily in planning things so he would not have to intervene. God demonstrated his care for the welfare of his creatures in the perfection of the original creative act, which was itself the greatest miracle. Laws are the instruments through which he governs, and he violates them "very rarely." The unfailing rule of law, not miraculous intervention, is the chief evidence of God's wisdom.

certified as true

There were various attempts to preserve the doctrine of **providence**. Some writers simply affirmed a mechanical universe and a God who cares about each detail, without attempting to reconcile the two assertions. Others equated providence with God's prevision; foreseeing the chain of causes, he could adjust his agents in advance to secure his providential ends without violating the ensuing* order. More commonly, providence received a very general interpretation. Not the particular events but the total design represented God's benevolence. He set things in motion in a harmonious way, planning the overall structure and order of the world for the welfare of his creatures. Once started, the operation of nature would follow fixed laws, with material causes acting from their own necessity.

coming after

God's function in the present was thus reduced to the preservation of the cosmic order. God's concurrence* had traditionally been conceived as an active participation, and some of the virtuosi so interpreted it. Boyle, like Descartes, stated that if the Almighty were to discontinue his support of the universe it would collapse. Continuing divine involvement is necessary, he said, since a law is not a real power but only a pattern of regularity. But it was the clock analogy that provided the basic interpretive image of the world as a perfect machine, autonomous* and self-sufficient, with natural causes acting in independence of God. "Divine preservation" started as an active sustenance,* became passive acquiescence,* and was then forgotten.

power; jurisdictional role

operating independently

that which supports life / peaceful agreement

Perhaps partly because he did not want to see God's role limited to that of **First Cause**, and partly because his scientific data were inaccurate, Newton asserted that God has a continuing function in adjusting the solar system. He believed that there is no scientific explanation for the pattern of the planets, holding that coplanar orbits with velocities in the same direction cannot be accounted for by natural causes. There are also continuing irregularities in motion, he said, which would build up if God did not occasionally step in to correct them. In addition, God somehow prevents the stars from collapsing together under gravitational attraction.

Newton also identified absolute space and time with God's omnipresence*   *being everywhere*
and eternity, but this was a purely passive role. God was represented
primarily as the Maker external to what he has made; like the clockmaker,
he could act only by intervening from outside. The traditional idea of
divine immanence in nature was virtually lost until its recovery by eighteenth-century Romanticism* and, in a different form, by Protestant liber-   *literary movement*
alism in the light of evolution in the nineteenth century.   *sanctifying nature*

The scientific inadequacy of Newton's references to divine interven-
tion became obvious in the next century; Laplace's nebular* hypothesis   *cloudlike clusters of gases*
was able to account for the coplanar character of the solar system, and the   *or far-distant stars*
"irregularities" were shown to be due either to inaccurate observations or
to perturbations* that would eventually cancel each other out. Laplace   *disturbances*
was correct in saying of God's role in planetary motion, "I had no need of
that hypothesis." The theological inadequacy of Newton's assertions was
pointed out by Leibniz: a perfect God would not have created an imperfect mechanism requiring periodic correction. We might object further
that God the Cosmic Plumber, mending the leaks in his system, would be
the Ultimate Conservative, concerned only to maintain the **status quo**.
This was "the God of the gaps," introduced to explain areas of scientific
ignorance, and destined to retreat in the light of new knowledge to become the Retired Architect, the inactive God of **Deism**.

Most of the virtuosi thus ended by reducing God's role to that of First
Cause; the divine benevolence was expressed in his original act of creation and not in continuing fatherly care. But they defended this limited
fatherly role with vigor, for they wanted to assert the **primacy of spirit over
matter** without compromising the orderliness of the universe. Against
Hobbes, they maintained that the universe is the product of intelligent
purpose, not of blind chance. Against Leibniz, they maintained that creation was an act of God's will and freedom, not of rational necessity. Against
Spinoza, they maintained that God is separate from the world and external
to it, not identical with the nexus* of inexorable* law. Though the func-   *central point / unstoppable*
tion of God was drastically reduced, the conception of God was still the
traditional one of personal intelligence and will, not the **pantheistic Absolute**.

READING SKILL EXERCISES

*The article's title makes an analogy between God and a clockmaker. First
consider what a clockmaker does and what a clock is. Then analyze how
the universe is like a clock and God like a clockmaker: God designed the
planets and their motion just as a clockmaker designed the cogs, gears,
and wheels within a clock. The designers of each built the machine and
set it in motion. A clock requires periodic adjustment; this analogy
suggests that God observes the workings of the universe and steps in only
when his intervention is needed for the universe to continue on its path.
The analogy also implies that the universe runs according to rules and that
all things have a purpose designed by God.*

[1] Explain how the analogy of God as "divine Architect" works and what its implications about the nature of God and the universe are.

[2] Explain God as the "Cosmic Plumber." What particular attitude toward God does such an analogy suggest?

[3] How does the term "Retired Architect" change the original analogy of God as an architect?

[4] Explain how the punishment of the sinners in Dante's ninth circle of Hell is analogous to their specific crime, sowing "scandal and schism," that is, causing religious, political, or family dissent.

One view of the history of religion in the West states that its decline in importance parallels a general decay in Western culture and values. Another view states that religion loses its importance and relevance in proportion to the rise of science and rational explanations of the world. Read the following passage for Voltaire's implied thesis. Which view of religion might he support? The title gives you some indication of his beliefs. Consider how Voltaire's views differ from previous religious parables, arguments, and analyses you have read so far.

The French philosopher and writer Voltaire (1694–1778) embodied the beliefs of the typical Enlightenment thinker: reason as the prime value, tolerance for religious and intellectual differences, and freedom to pursue and express one's beliefs. Voltaire was one of the "encyclopédistes," the group of French thinkers who put together the first encyclopedia. He is also known as the author of Candide, *a philosophical tale advocating that we each "cultivate our garden," or accept the conditions of our life and do what we can to make life worthwhile. You'll read about another Enlightenment figure, Alexander Pope, in Chapter 4. The theorists behind the American Revolution were Enlightenment thinkers: Locke, Montesquieu, Paine, Jefferson. Deism, the belief that God created the world but that man was responsible for his own actions and was not under divine guidance, flourished in the eighteenth century. Here, Voltaire, a deist, writes satirically on Christian intolerance.*

VOLTAIRE
"Of Universal Tolerance"

KEY CONCEPT
INFALLIBILITY, a major Roman Catholic doctrine, states that the Pope's doctrinal decisions come directly from God and therefore cannot be wrong.

● It doesn't take great art or refined eloquence to prove that Christians ought to have tolerance for each other. I will go even further: I say that we should consider all men as brothers. What! A Turk my brother? A Chinese my brother? A Jew? A Siamese? Yes, certainly; aren't we all children of the same father, and creatures of the same God?

But these people scorn us; but they treat us as idolaters! Oh well—I will tell them that they're wrong. It seems to me that I would be able at least to astonish the conceited obstinacy of an imam* or Buddhist priest, if I said something like this to them: Persian priest

"This little globe, which is just a speck, revolves in space, just like so many other globes; we're lost in the universe. Mankind, in the neighborhood of about five feet tall, surely isn't much in all of creation. One of these imperceptible beings says to some of his neighbors, in Arabia or Africa: Listen to me, because the God of all these worlds enlightened me: there are 900,000,000 ants like us on earth, but only my ant-hill is dear to God; all the others, for all eternity, are loathsome to him; mine alone will prosper, and all the others will be eternally unlucky."

They would stop me then, and they would ask me who the madman was who said this nonsense. I would be obliged to tell them: "You yourselves." Then I would try to soothe them, but that would be very difficult.

I would speak now to the Christians, and I would dare to say to, for example, a fervent Dominican Inquisitor: "My brother, you know that each province in Italy has its slang, and that people don't speak alike from Venice to Bergamo to Florence. The Crusca Academy has set the language; one must not deviate from the rule of its dictionary, and Buonmattei's *Grammar* is an **infallible** guide that one has to follow; but do you believe that the Academy's consul, and Buonmattei, in his absence, would have been able to cut out the tongue of all the Venetians and all the Bergamese who persisted in their dialect?"

The Inquisitor answers me: "Differences always exist; what matters here is the salvation of your soul: it's for your own good that the Grand Inquisitor orders your arrest on the testimony of a single individual, even if he be a hardened criminal; that you have no lawyer to defend you; that you never know the name of your accuser; that the Inquisitor first promise you grace, and then condemn you; that he put you through five different tortures, and then that you be either whipped, or sentenced to hard labor, or burned at the stake. This pious practice doesn't suffer contradiction." I would take the liberty of answering him: "My brother, you may perhaps be right; I'm sure you want to do me good; but can't I be saved without all that?"

It's true that these absurd horrors don't daily stain the face of the earth; but they have been frequent, and one would easily be able to compose from them a volume much heavier than the Gospels that damn them. Not only is it terribly cruel in this short life to persecute those who don't think as we do, I don't know that it isn't risky to pronounce their eternal damna-

Translated by Jeanne Gunner

tion. It seems to me that it's not for little specks of time like us to anticipate the Creator's decrees. I'm far from opposing this sentence: "No salvation outside the Church"; I respect it, and all that it teaches, but, really, do we know all the ways of God and the full extent of his mercy? Isn't it allowed to hope in him as much as to fear him? Isn't it enough to support the Church? Must each individual person usurp* the rights of Divinity and decide before him the eternal fate of all men? take over

When we wear mourning for the king of Sweden, or Denmark, or England, or Prussia, do we say that we're mourning for one of the damned who burns eternally in hell? In Europe there are 40,000,000 inhabitants who don't belong to the Church of Rome; will we say to each of these: "Sir, considering that you are infallibly damned, I don't want to eat, do business, or converse with you"?

What French ambassador, having been presented to some great lord, would say from deep down inside his heart, Your Majesty will infallibly burn for all eternity, because you submitted to circumcision? If he really believed that the great lord is God's mortal enemy and the object of his vengeance, would he be able to talk to him? Should he have been sent to him? With what man would one be able to do business, what duty of civil life would one be able to fulfill, if in effect one was convinced of this idea that he was dealing with the damned?

O sectarians* of a merciful God! if you have had a cruel heart; if, while adoring him whose whole law consists of these words: "Love God and your neighbor," you have overworked this pure and holy law with sophisms* and incomprehensible arguments; if you have kindled* discord, now for a single word, now for a single letter of the alphabet; if you have assigned eternal punishment to the omission of a few words, a few rites that people elsewhere cannot possibly know, I would say to you, shedding tears on all humankind, "Come with me to the day of final judgment, where God will treat each one according to his deeds. narrow-minded people
clever but incorrect arguments / started, as a fire

I see all the dead from centuries past and present brought before his presence. Are you very sure that our Creator and our Father will say to the wise and virtuous Confucius, to the lawmaker Solon, to Pythagoras, to Zaleucus, to Socrates, to Plato, to the divine Antoninus, to good Trajan, to Titus, the delights of the human race, to Epictetus, and so many others, models of humanity: Go, monsters, go suffer punishment infinite in intensity and duration; so that your torment will be as eternal as I am! And you, my beloved, Jean Chatel, Ravaillac, Damiens, Cartouche, etc., who died with the prescribed ceremonies, sit forever at my right hand and share my empire and my bliss."

You recoil in horror from these words; and, after they have escaped me, I have nothing more to say to you.

WRITING SKILL: FORMULATING A RESPONSE TO AN ARGUMENT

One of the most traditional ways of formulating an argument is first to summarize an opposing view and then refute it. You clarify the beliefs of* to prove false *each side by implicitly defining and contrasting them. When you formulate the response of one author to another author or to a given issue, you need to draw on your skills of reading for an implied thesis, detecting bias and assumptions, and summarizing. To write the summary and response, you need to paraphrase the authors' ideas carefully.*

[1] Summarize Voltaire's views on tolerance. How would Tertullian react to them?

[2] Formulate the attitude of the medieval Church towards religious tolerance, using Tuchman's discussion and Dante's poem. According to the parable of the prodigal son, should universal tolerance be encouraged?

[3] Review your definitions of Lutheranism and Puritanism. Summarize Luther's teachings on salvation. What would the Puritan's response be?

[4] Summarize the "clockmaker" view of God's role in the universe and respond with your own notion of a divine presence in life.

[5] Which of the attitudes toward tolerance or salvation represented in the readings on religion do you find the least "tolerable"? Summarize the view and then respond with your own argument.

Ralph Waldo Emerson was a major American writer and philosopher of the nineteenth century. He's known for his poems and essays, which are considered Romantic works. Romanticism (a topic you'll read about in Chapter 4) was a philosophy that influenced art and religion especially. Romanticism is not one systematic philosophy but is more an attitude, a trend of thought. Most Romantic thinkers emphasized the freedom of the individual and the oppressive nature of organized society and religion. Emerson was a major spokesperson for the American brand of Romanticism. In his life, he moved slowly away from the Unitarian Church to what was then considered a radical doctrine of spirituality. He believed that spiritual nature came from an all-encompassing higher force, the Oversoul. To get in touch with the spiritual world, one had to <u>transcend</u> the material world, to move beyond physical reality into the realm of the spirit. Romantics in general believed that the world of nature helped people to connect with the spiritual realm. Emerson helped define the American version of Romanticism by emphasizing civic life in addition to the natural world. Like Walt Whitman, the American poet who shared some of Emerson's beliefs, he taught that the real American spirit involved action as well as thought. Romantic thought can be seen as a reaction to the Age of Reason (which Voltaire was part of and Barbour wrote about); Emerson and the American Romantics can be seen as the antithesis or reaction to the previous centuries' Puritan culture. In the following essay, Brooks Atkinson, a contemporary scholar of American literature, explains Emerson's transcendentalism.

BROOKS ATKINSON
"Emerson"

KEY CONCEPTS
A **TRANSCENDENTALIST** seeks truth in the realm of ideas or spirits, rejecting the material world and believing instead in his or her own mind, experience, and energy.

IDEALISM is the philosophical basis of transcendentalism. As Plato first formulated it, idealism stated that reality resides in ideas, not things. The **MATERIALIST**, on the other hand, believes that sense perceptions tell us about the real nature of the world. See Chapter 1, page 33.

INTUITION is usually considered an irrational mental process, the opposite of reason, related to emotion, not logic.

PANTHEISM is a form of religious belief. A pantheist adores nature, taking it to be the physical presence of God.

● Emerson was a **transcendentalist**. He believed in the "over-soul"—the universal soul of which everything living was a part. Even in Emerson's own day the word "transcendentalism" was considered confusing, and the popular meaning of the word is still "vague, obscure, visionary." Scholars accustomed to exact knowledge could not make head or tail of Emerson's school of thought. That was not surprising. Transcendentalism had no system; it was more poetry than thought. "What is popularly called transcendentalism among us is **idealism**," Emerson once said. In contrast with the **materialist**, who reasoned from facts, history, and the animal wants* of man, the idealist believed in "the power of thought and of will, in inspiration, in miracle, in individual culture."

desires

To a young country just beginning to enjoy its independence and lustily expanding in all directions, this style of thinking was natural and satisfying. It believed that anything could be accomplished. Systems of thought and methods of reasoning seemed stifling to people of exultant* temperament who were looking on all the fruits of the earth and finding them good. It was easy for them to give their **intuitions** authority over experience. Not what had been done but what might be done seemed to them the greater truth. Life flowed into the transcendentalist from the flowers, the clouds, the birds, the sun, the chill and warmth of the weather, the beauty of the evening, and from the farms, the shops and the railroads where life was stirring and good things seemed to be happening.

joyful

Although Emerson's philosophy was not a system, it had something of

SOURCE: From *The Selected Writings of Ralph Waldo Emerson,* edited by Brooks Atkinson. Copyright © 1940 by Random House, Inc. Reprinted by permission of Random House.

a plan in the way he developed it. His attitude toward life was based on his love of nature and is stated in his first book, *Nature*. A short book, published anonymously, it was generally dismissed by the reviewers as **pantheistic** rapture, charmingly written but without much significance. Yet it represented several years of deliberate thought when Emerson was trying to put his ideas in order. He began in the introduction with a definition of terms: "Nature, in the common sense, refers to essences unchanged by man: space, the air, the river, the leaf. Art is applied to the mixture of his will with the same things, as in a house, a canal, a statue, a picture." He rejoiced that man is of nature and that nature is his home. The most significant statement he made is that man becomes a part of God when he surrenders himself to association with nature: "I become a transparent eyeball; I am nothing; I see all; the currents of the Universal Being circulate through me; I am part or parcel of God."

Five years later Emerson published his first book of *Essays*, made from lectures he had been reading chiefly in Boston. The new book contained the essay on "The Over-Soul" which may be regarded as the cornerstone of his faith. In the notes to the complete works, Emerson's son has pointed out that the first series of essays derive from a plan set down in the journals:

> *There is one soul.*
> *It is related to the world.*
> *Art is its action thereon.*
> *Science finds its methods.*
> *Literature is its record.*
> *Religion is the emotion of reverence that it inspires.*
> *Ethics is the soul illustrated in human life.*
> *Society is the finding of this soul by individuals in each other.*
> *Trades are the learning of the soul in nature by labor.*
> *Politics is the activity of the soul illustrated in power.*
> *Manners are silent and mediate expressions of soul.*

Not everybody was willing to follow Emerson so far from the material world into the world of intuition. Identifying man with God seemed like heresy to some of the clergy.* Others thought it was mere rhapsody* or wishful thinking. And, of course, many hardheaded men did not know what he was talking about. But the effect of this belief on Emerson was transcendent. To believe himself part of universal wisdom gave him a wonderful sense of freedom. It was the ultimate liberation. It was creative. Life seemed good fundamentally; nature and man could be trusted. Life was something not to be learned but to be lived. Now was the appointed hour for making a fresh start. The doctrine was a receptive one. Better an imperfect theory, with glimpses of the truth, than digested systems that were dead.

Emerson's faith was dynamic. And that was why he seemed to the

church ministers / ecstatic expression

young people of his time to be the great cultural liberator. He was always on the side of imaginative exploration. In "The American Scholar," he said the sole use of books is to inspire: "One must be a creator to read well." The scholar's preoccupation with bookish learning seemed moribund* to   death-like
him. He urged the scholar to become a man of action and learn directly from life: "Life is our dictionary. Years are well spent in country labors; in town; in the insight into trades and manufactures; in frank intercourse with many men and women; in science; in art; to the end of mastering in all facts a language by which to illustrate and embody our perceptions." He enkindled* the hearts of the young divinity students with the same   inspired; fired up
criticisms of institutions and the same invitation to life. Religion should have a common accent away from the cloister*: "The time is coming when   monastery
all men will see that the gift of God to the soul is not a vaunting,* overpow-   boastful
ering, excluding sanctity,* but a sweet, natural goodness, a goodness like   holiness
thine* and mine, and that so invites thine and mine to be and to grow."   yours
He complained that religion was treated in the pulpit "as if God were dead."

QUESTIONS FOR DISCUSSION AND WRITING

[1] Summarize the definition of transcendentalism.

[2] Contrast the transcendentalist values to the Puritan ethic.

[3] Think about religious attitudes and practices in America today. How are both sides of our tradition—the Puritan and the Romantic, or transcendentalist—still evident?

WRITING SKILL: *Summary/Response Essay*

As you read the following passage, note the form of O'Hair's address. Her thesis appears in the third paragraph; she organizes her work in the form of summary/response. First she presents the historical arguments for the existence of God, and then she refutes* them.   proves false

---

Madalyn Murray O'Hair is a contemporary advocate of atheism and atheists' rights. Atheism, or disbelief in God and religion, is largely a twentieth-century phenomenon, perhaps because in the twentieth century people with nontraditional views on religion have met with more tolerance than they would have in earlier times. Atheism has emerged as a contemporary issue particularly in the current school prayer controversy, which involves the constitutional issue of separation of church and state. O'Hair's essay (transcribed from a radio broadcast) attempts to refute major arguments for the existence of God.

MADALYN MURRAY O'HAIR
"Arguments for God, Historical and Contemporary, with Refutation"

KEY CONCEPTS

ARISTOTELIAN SYLLOGISTICS refers to Aristotle's method of deductive reasoning; see page 135.

An **EMPIRICAL ARGUMENT** depends on observable evidence to prove its point.

An **A PRIORI** statement is an assumption, a given.

A **COSMOLOGICAL** view addresses the whole universe as a single entity.

A **TELEOLOGICAL** view claims that life has some detectable design, some purpose; see page 137.

An **ONTOLOGICAL** view is a metaphysical view: God must exist because we can imagine something called "God."

● Good evening. This is Madalyn Murray O'Hair, American Atheist, back to talk to you again.

The Society of Separationists, my sponsors, sell booklets, and some of these are authored by me. One of them is titled, "Why I Am an Atheist." This booklet is a capsule description of what a theist is, what an atheist believes and what an atheist thinks about religion.

A part of it deals with the so called "Arguments for god" and "his existence." I would like to read some of this to you tonight, for it is imperative that you know that religious people of all the time of recorded history have admitted that there is no god.

You are not hearing things at all. They have admitted this.

When? When? Who?

Just listen.

We all agree, you and I and all of the religious people, everybody, on one rule of logic when we discuss things logically. The rule is that when anyone postulates* a theory, that person has the burden of proof. He must show the proof of his theory. The classic example is Newton. When he postulated a theory of gravity, which later became a law, it was necessary for him to prove that his theory was correct before it was accepted by the world community of scholars, and by people in general.

takes as true

It is not a surprise then, to you, to discover here with me tonight that the religious community, its scholars, teachers and theologians, churchmen of every kind, have admitted that god is only a theory. They have admitted this by their constant attempts to offer proof of their proposition and theory. They put forth more and different proofs in a constant stream in order to do this. Now, If a god really <u>was</u>, it would not be necessary for

SOURCE: From "What on Earth Is An Atheist" by Madalyn Murray O'Hair. Copyright © 1972. Reprinted by permission of American Atheist Press.

them to do this. From the way they define him, it is obvious that he would be able to offer this proof and not leave it to their puny efforts. He could just appear, just once, or give incontrovertible* proof in some set of laboratory conditions and that would end the argument for all time. He does not, of course, because there is no god. He can't be called forth because he doesn't exist.

unable to be disproved

The theories, however, are interesting. The religionists have been putting them forth for thousands of years. Knowing that the burden of proof is on them, the religionists have assumed that burden.

We Atheists merely evaluate and categorize their arguments, and decide if we wanted to accept them or reject them. For us, it is as simple as that. So, any good Atheist simply acquaints himself with every argument that has been set forth in support of the god theory since human history began.

This is impossible, you say? Not at all. The arguments are not too good and there are not too many of the basic arguments. There are elaborations on certain theme arguments, but the basics are simple. It will surprise you to hear that in thousands of years of arguments, there have only been a half a dozen basic arguments. That's right—six of them.

But, think of this a moment. Why would even six arguments be needed? If there were a god, his existence would be argument enough. There would be no need to prove it a half a dozen times, would there? It is only when you lose an argument that you need so much proof. Isn't it curious that with all of this, every religious person says, "I believe in god"? He does not say, "There is a god." It only indicates that the proposition is indeed very tenuous,* even with the help of **Aristotelian syllogistics**.

shaky; flimsy

I am sure you are impatient. What are the possible arguments for a belief in god? First, I must give you those arguments which have been abandoned.

The first group of arguments cluster around the idea of direct sensory experience. This is the **empirical argument**. Someone says he has actually talked to god, or heard him, or seen him, or smelled him, or touched him. Today when people say this, the psychiatrists say they are having hallucinations, and classify the hallucinations as auditory,* visual, tactile,* or olfactory,* but an hallucination, no less. Have you seen god? Have you personally talked to him? Well, you can trust your own senses if you are a normal human being. If you have not seen him, felt him, talked with him, smelled him, you know no one else has. Included in this category of arguments are the ideas of "mystical insights," which "tell" you there is a god, and "intuition," which does the same. The group of ideas concerned with direct sensory experience (real or imagined) and insight or intuition (real or imagined) has been abandoned now for many years and is not any longer considered as valid argument.

pertaining to hearing / pertaining to sense of touch / pertaining to smell

The second group of arguments has to do with "Faith." This is your accepting someone else having experienced the first group of ideas, your blind acceptance of someone else's talking with god, or seeing him, or having "insight," or "intuition" which tells him there is a god. When two people share a delusion like this, the psychiatrist calls it "folie à deux"* and when a large group shares this delusion, it is popularly called "religion." For the most part the modern theologians have abandoned this argument too.

shared delusion

The third group of older arguments has to do with authority, and depends on your acceptance of that authority. There are different kinds of authority here involved. The authority of an institution, a book, an individual person. If you accept the authority of an institution, this is the authority of a particular church: the Moslem church, the Hindu church, the pagan church, the Roman Catholic Church, your particular protestant church.

You choose what you want to choose, unless you live in an era when choice is not approved, and then you have a certain religion rammed down your throat, whether you like it or not, by a powerful institution. If you accept the authority of a book, again you have a lot of choices: the Koran, the Veda, the Old Testament, the New Testament, the Apocrypha, the Upanishads, the Torah.

Again, what would have happened to you in old Mexico had you said that you did not accept their holy book? The old Aztecs would have torn your heart out of your body on one of their altars. If you accept the authority of a person, again you have a lot of choices: Mohammed, Confucius, Buddha, Moses, Fatima, Christ, Quoxichochtle. Authority, whoever is in power, rules. That is why this argument has been abandoned.

The fourth group of arguments has to do with rational and/or logical proofs. The Roman Catholic Church was the longest holdout before turning to this group. But even now that church expects arguments to be logical. The kicker in the woodpile is that these so-called rational or logical proofs are based simply on **a priori** grounds. This is a so-called high fallutin' way of saying that the religionists start out with so-called "self-evident truths." One of these is "In the beginning was the word." One then gets into nonsense for that sentence has absolutely no meaning at all. Understanding this we can proceed tongue in cheek. Rational arguments can be reduced to three main categories also: the **cosmological**, the **teleological**, and the **ontological**. Let's just look at these jawbreakers for a moment.

The cosmological argument is the most popular. This is the oldest argument and was advanced by Thomas Aquinas. It is based on the principle of cause and is called the principle of "causality." It holds that everything requires a cause to account for its existence. John Stuart Mill is the person who is credited with having put the K.O. to this argument. He tells the story that it was his little child who revealed the truth to him.

He was holding forth on this argument one day about everything needing to be caused, and his pre-school age child was listening. He said that since everything had to be caused, god caused everything. His child interrupted and said, "Daddy, if everything is caused, who caused god?"

At first sight, of course, this argument does sound convincing, but a very brief consideration reveals that it offers no real proof at all. That is, the theorist cannot solve his dilemma by postulating an uncaused first cause, when by his first premise everything must have a cause. That is to say, who gave god the wherewithal to begin everything? Who caused god? Who is god's mother? The cosmological argument is worthless.

The old Indian myths were that the world rested on an elephant, and the elephant rested on a tortoise (a huge turtle) and then a little Indian boy who tended elephants said, "Well, what does the turtle rest on?" and the great religious philosophers there said, "Let's change the subject."

The Atheist is very practical about this. We say simply, we do not know how the universe came into being, or what caused life at all. Let us all admit our ignorance and attempt to find out the answer through science and research.

Be man enough to say with us, "We don't know, either."

The second argument, the teleological argument, is also known as the natural law argument. This was the favorite of the eighteenth century, especially under the influence of Sir Isaac Newton and the cosmographists. Generally it goes this way: as we look at the world around us, we observe an order and design which makes the assumption of a planning intelligence unavoidable. Look at the stars, the moon, the plants, the seasons, day and night, with rhythm. Actually, though, the teleological argument lies open to such easy attack that the modern theologians avoid it. What very little evidence there is of a purpose in this world, is overwhelmed by the conspicuous lack of benevolent purpose. The most unprejudiced mind can only allow that the universe appears indifferent to the life that swarms over it. Surely only a very evil deity, a very evil god, would create and smile upon the diseases of man, on war, earthquakes, defective children, floods, drought, hurricanes, polio. The teleological argument is worthless.

The ontological argument is the chief hope of the theologians. This holds that god's existence is implied by his nature, which the theologians define. This is an argument by definition. If we can define perfection, then it must exist. Oh, come now! It is impossible to prove existence merely by the process of definition. If I try to describe an elf to you, or a leprecaun, no matter how much detail can be given, this does not make that elf exist. Dickens could describe his characters like no other author. Yet this did not make David Copperfield become a real-live person. The ontological argument is worthless.

Immanuel Kant tried to introduce the "moral" argument for god. This was that goodness, justice, truth, love and wisdom flow from god and therefore he exists. However, it left unsolved the problem of badness, injustice, untruth, hate and folly, and this argument fails also. After all, if god is omnipotent, omnipresent, omniscient,* omnibenevolent, i.e. all powerful, always present, all knowing and always good, how could he permit evil? This argument fails.

The latest argument, coming from America, is the pragmatic* argument and this asks us, "Does it work?" Is mankind advanced or retarded

knowing all things

practical

by faith in a god? Well, you have history to answer that. Religion has caused more misery to all men in every single stage of history than any other single idea. I need only recount human sacrifices, the use of humans to build pyramids, the religious wars, the crusades, the crime of the Inquisition, the burning of witches, even here in America, the internecine* warfare between religious groups. If that does not answer the question, then we propose that the question be asked, "has not the idea of Santa Claus alone brought more happiness?" Of course it has. The pragmatic argument fails.

internally divisive and destructive

We Atheists might be pleased to accept the idea of god if a god was invented who loved people—a kind and good and honorable god. Until he is invented someday by man, we merely look at your arguments and your beliefs and your conduct and say, "This is not for us. We want something better for people."

WRITING SKILL EXERCISE

[1] Summarize O'Hair's argument against religious faith. Respond with your own beliefs, criticizing or defending her ideas.

[2] Review Tertullian's argument against marriage. Summarize it and then respond to it, agreeing or disagreeing.

[3] Explain how the "clockmaker" view of God is mechanistic. Can you accept the view of the universe as a well-running machine, or does such a view seem limiting or unrealistic to you? Consider both sides: science has detected physical laws, universal patterns, but human beings suffer inexplicable tragedies nonetheless.

CHAPTER 2 ESSAY ASSIGNMENTS

[1] Analyze the influence various religions have had on other social institutions or pursuits. Think of religious influences in art, music, literature, government, or science. You may find the essays of Tuchman, Cox, Grimm, and Atkinson useful in preparing your response.

[2] Consider the following religious systems represented in the readings: Greek mythology, Judaism, Christianity, Islam, transcendentalism, and atheism. Under which system would a woman, a Jew, a Black, or a homosexual enjoy the most freedom? Under which would he or she face the greatest persecution? Support your answers with textual evidence.

[3] Both religion and philosophy deal with similar topics and fulfill similar human needs. Analyze the purposes they each serve. What fundamental difference makes them separate pursuits?

[4] Religion plays an essential role in the historical development of society. Every religion changes, and with each change comes some social reaction,

which may be considered constructive or destructive. Discuss both the constructive and the destructive influences religion has had on Western society, and argue whether the dominant historical force has been the constructive or destructive side. Use specific examples from the readings to support your argument.

[5] Western thinkers have offered two fundamental ways to understand the world: through religious beliefs and rational methods, or science. Historically, the two approaches have often come into conflict. Analyze the possible reasons for scientific contradiction and resentment of religious teachings and authority. Then consider the possible causes of the Christian Church's mistrust of and resistance to scientific thought.

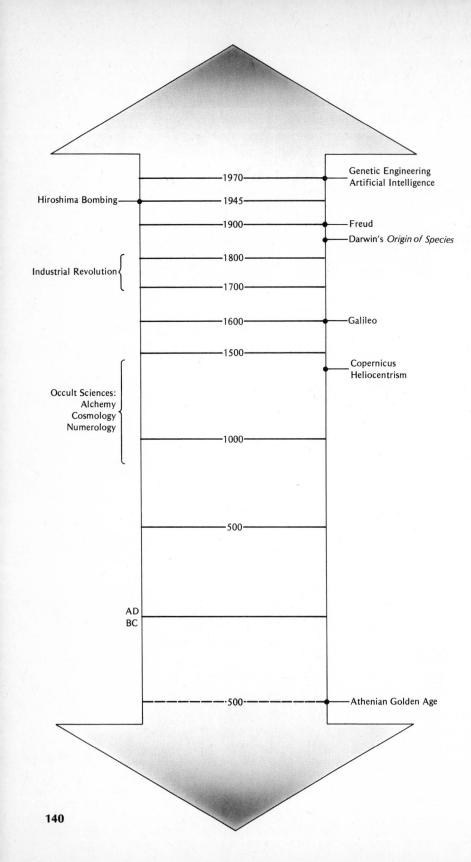

1970 — Genetic Engineering
Artificial Intelligence

Hiroshima Bombing — 1945

1900 — Freud
— Darwin's *Origin of Species*

Industrial Revolution {
1800
1700

1600 — Galileo

1500

Copernicus
Heliocentrism

Occult Sciences:
Alchemy
Cosmology
Numerology

1000

500

AD
BC

500 — Athenian Golden Age

Science has been intimately connected with the ancient Greek civilization and religious belief and practices over the centuries. In this chapter you'll be reading about scientific developments, but keep the religious background in mind as you read. To help yourself do this, chart the following names and events from Chapter 2 readings onto the science time line:

the death of Christ
the Patristic era
the rise of Islam
the Inquisition
the Puritans
the deists
transcendentalism

CHAPTER *3*

Continuity in Science

INTRODUCTION

In Chapter 1, you read about the Greeks' development of scientific method. A major difference between ancient science and science after the Christian period is that ancient science, then called natural philosophy, was not necessarily in opposition to religion and philosophy, nor was it used as a basis for technological development. But in the medieval and Renaissance periods, science came into conflict with religious belief and study. And since the eighteenth century—the beginning of the industrial revolution—up to our time, science has worked hand in hand with technology and so has had a very direct effect on people's daily lives. This chapter focuses on some of the issues raised by scientific inquiry and development as they challenge many of the traditional religious and philosophical beliefs that you've been reading about and have gone on to create new social and psychological effects.

The chapter begins with issues in twentieth-century science and then goes back to a chronological organization, from the time of medieval science through Freud in the early part of our century. The first four essays deal with major contemporary topics: artificial intelligence (abbreviated as AI), genetic engineering, and atomic warfare. Together, the topics represent some human issues that science has raised—usually unintentionally—since the Middle Ages, issues that seem to be continually relevant and problematic. Over the centuries, science has created different hopes, fears, and social problems. The specific hopes, fears, and problems seen in each period help define the historical age by illustrating its

*particular concerns and priorities. You are most likely familiar with these
issues as they have arisen in the twentieth century; we present them first
so that you can locate and evaluate them in earlier periods and then go
on to build a sense of science's historical continuity.*

In Machines Who Think, *Pamela McCorduck summarizes the pros and
cons of continued advancement in artificial intelligence research, or
scientific attempts to build computers that "imitate our essential human
property of intelligence." Will AI improve our quality of life and help us
better understand the human mind, or will it dehumanize our society and
change us as a species?*

*Caryl Rivers, in "Grave New World," touches on similar issues raised by
genetic engineering research. If we learn to manipulate genetics, will we
be creating a beneficial medical tool or do we risk altering our biological
nature? And there are moral repercussions: do we have the right to alter
nature?*

*Atomic energy, what many call the "ultimate human challenge,"
became a global concern when the first atomic bomb was dropped on
Hiroshima in August 1945. The readings in this chapter give you two
different perspectives on the event: an American newspaper account one
day after the bombing, and then eyewitnesses' accounts of the actual
human suffering inflicted by the bomb.*

*The chapter's chronological readings begin with a selection from
Friedrich Heer's* The Medieval World, *a book that examines a period when
science was subordinate to theology and was seeking "a legitimate niche
in society." Scientists then studied not only chemistry, astronomy, and
mathematics, but also emphasized alchemy, astrology, and numerology as
pursuits of equal scientific value and importance.*

*Bertrand Russell's essay on religion and science, "The Copernican
Revolution," explores the impact of the heliocentric theory proposed by
Copernicus and Galileo in a Christian world which believed that God
created human beings to be the center of his universe. The Church's
struggle with the new scientific theories was carried on through the
Inquisition, whose leaders burned or imprisoned many early scientists,
Galileo among them.*

*The industrial revolution is the eighteenth-century forerunner of our
technological age. In "The Scientific Background to the Industrial
Revolution," Christe McMenomy outlines the major scientific innovations
of the age and analyzes their diverse social effects. With increasing
industrialization came urbanization—the rise of densely populated cities.
Overcrowding, poverty, and child labor abuse were some of the problems
caused by the demographic* shift from an agricultural to an*   relating to population
industrial-based society.

*Charles Darwin is a name you'll encounter throughout readings in
science and the humanities. As Bertrand Russell explains in "Evolution,"
Darwin's theory directly challenged theological and scientific beliefs about
human origin. His nineteenth-century writings on natural science continue*

to have religious and political implications into the twentieth century. You'll read about the scientific theory of natural selection as well as George E. Simpson's "Early Social Darwinism." In Hitler's "Man Must Kill," you'll see the ultimate application of Social Darwinism, which reworked Darwin's principle of "survival of the fittest."

Freud's theories were the psychological equivalent of Darwin's biological work as they redefined the nature of the human mind. Freudian theory, here explained in Kagan and Havemann's "Psychoanalytic Theory," has implications not just for science but for art and philosophy as well. According to Freud, one can read a person's behavior and dreams as symbols of his or her unconscious conflicts. In "The Freudian Revolution Analyzed," Alfred Kazin discusses how Freudian psychology has shaped our perception of the individual in modern times.

READING AND WRITING SKILLS OF CHAPTER 3

Reading selectively
Drawing inferences
Using comparison and contrast

Some Contemporary Scientific Issues

READING SKILL: *Reading Selectively*

Many humanities courses are organized thematically: "Women in Politics"; "History of American Trade Unions"; "Mythological Sources of Modern Literature." In such courses you'll often be required to read secondary materials which contain specific information related to the course theme. Given a mass of material, you'll have to read selectively so that you can extract the information that relates directly to your course theme or specific assignment. To select the specific information you need from pages of general information, you can follow these steps:

1. Write down the course theme, breaking it into as many specific subtopics as you consider relevant.
2. Make a chart using the course theme and subtopics as headings. As you read, write down the specific ideas you find under the appropriate heading.
3. Read for explicit references to the course theme and subtopics. Look for related key words and synonyms. Mark the text or paraphrase the information on your chart.
4. Question the text for implicit connections to the theme or subtopics. Take your chart headings and, after reading a paragraph or section, stop to ask whether <u>you</u> can relate the information to the theme/subtopics.

The readings in this chapter suggest several prominent concerns historically raised by science which we'll take as our chapter themes:

The <u>goals</u> and <u>motives</u> involved in scientific advances.
The <u>fears</u> and <u>threats</u> resulting from scientific theories and technological developments.
The <u>social</u> and <u>psychological effects</u> arising from some major changes in our scientific knowledge and practice.

Read the following essay selectively for the themes we've listed. The following chart contains some of the relevant information. Most of the goals, fears, and possible effects are stated explicitly, but be sure to question the text for implicit connections as well. The chapter writing assignments will be based on these themes, so your charts for each reading will help prepare you to write.

McCorduck's book was published in 1979. Artificial intelligence is a recent development in computer science technology, but the idea of a brain divorced from a human body has long fascinated writers and readers of science fiction and fantasy literature, and has provided the premise for several films, such as 2001: A Space Odyssey. Robotics, the engineering field devoted to developing mechanical simulations of human physical abilities, has also suggested some common images and plots in popular literature and film; the robots in Star Wars *are examples of AI. In such stories the computer, robot, or other AI creation often turns on its creators, threatening human control and possibly existence. McCorduck's article deals with more contemporary, though, from her point of view, not necessarily more realistic, popular fears about AI.*

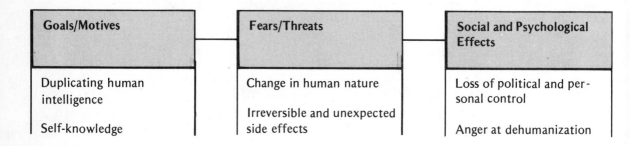

Goals/Motives	Fears/Threats	Social and Psychological Effects
Duplicating human intelligence	Change in human nature	Loss of political and personal control
Self-knowledge	Irreversible and unexpected side effects	Anger at dehumanization

PAMELA McCORDUCK
FROM *Machines Who Think*

KEY CONCEPTS

ARTIFICIAL INTELLIGENCE is a field of computer science research whose goal is to create programs that duplicate human thinking.

A **MECHANISTIC MODEL OF HUMANS** suggests that human thought and behavior follow discernible physical or biological laws; see **MECHANISTIC VIEW OF THE UNIVERSE**, Chapter 2, page 124.

In mythology and theology, **RETRIBUTION** means inflicting punishment of a severity equal to the sin committed.

The **FREUDIAN MODEL** of human behavior states that our behavior expresses unconscious libidinal* urges and neuroses resulting from repression.   sexual

HUMANISTS emphasize the primacy* of human intellect and study of the liberal arts.   first importance

The **COPERNICAN REVOLUTION**, discussed later in this chapter in Bertrand Russell's article of that name, refers to Copernicus's discovery that the sun, not the earth, is at the center of the universe.

● **Artificial intelligence** is the latest manifestation of an enduring human impulse to create artifacts that will imitate our essential human property of intelligence. In the midst of such an act, we participate in two related and equally enduring impulses: the one to know ourselves as deeply and in as much detail as possible; the other to render that knowledge in a way that is accessible to our fellow creatures—always the hope of the biological and behavioral sciences, philosophy, and in some ways, art. Thus artificial intelligence strikes me as a happy phrase for what this field seems to be about.

Artificial intelligence as a science has been less apparently successful than its founding fathers hoped, but its progress in the twenty or so years of its existence has been enough to confound its critics—it performs better and better, slowly breaking down each barrier the critics declared could never be surmounted. Whether it will surmount them all remains to be seen. Each step toward a fully realized intelligent artifact suggests that it can be done, but it hasn't been yet. Each of these steps, however, forces us to refocus our view of ourselves, and at such points people who ponder the human condition have the right, the responsibility, to consider our proper place in the universe, our possibilities and limitations, our individual and collective purposes.

Are there domains where computers, even if they somehow can, ought not to intrude? Joseph Weizenbaum suggests three such places: where computers could represent an attack on life itself; where the effects can easily be seen to be irreversible and the side effects are not entirely foreseeable; and where it is proposed to substitute a computer system for a human function that involves interpersonal respect, understanding, and love.

But life itself is an attack on life, when it comes to that. Women still die in childbirth, and we eat living plants and animals to sustain ourselves. We consider it good to go on having children (and making childbirth as safe as we possibly can), and we try to be good stewards* of other forms of life, ⟶ caretakers though the meaning of "good" has been highly variable throughout our history. We can expect our notion of good to continue to change, so we must be wary of blanket proscriptions.* ⟶ condemnations

Computers ought not be introduced where the effects can easily be seen to be irreversible and the side effects are not entirely foreseeable. I've met no one in computing who disagrees with this, though Buchanan makes the reasonable point that almost anything interesting will have these properties. This may then be an argument for preserving the status quo, but few people are altogether in love with things as they are. John McCarthy argues that intelligent machines will be helpful in these kinds of predictions, able to foresee by simulation effects and events we ourselves might not.

No computer system should be substituted for a human function that involves interpersonal respect, understanding, and love. Weizenbaum's examples here are two, a psychoanalyst and a judge. On judges, John McCarthy says in his review, "The second quotation from me is the rhetorical question, 'What do judges know that we cannot tell a computer?' I'll stand on that if we make it 'eventually tell' and especially if we require that it be something that one human can reliably teach another." Lederberg agrees that no computer system should be substituted for such human functions, but goes on to make the point that we'd better be equally sure about those humans in whom we invest respect, understanding, and love.

This brings us to the notion of artificial intelligence as alien, as not having shared our human experience, and being therefore deficient. When Weizenbaum and I were discussing this idea—and indeed he makes the point in his book—he again said how difficult it is, perhaps impossible, for somebody from one culture to act as judge in another. I laughed, and said that I probably spoke for most women, minorities, and others excluded from power in my own culture when I said I'd rather take my chances with an impartial computer. Our human experience is a fact of our existence, but how much we share with one another is limited not only by gender and class and color of skin, but also by temperament: one person's irresponsibility is another's high spirits. McCarthy also reminds us that we know next to nothing about what constitutes the nature of human experience or understanding; when we know more about them we will be able to reason about whether a machine can have a simulated or vicarious experience normally confined to humans, and we will be able to define whether a machine understands something or not.

Have we embraced the machine metaphor too readily? I suppose what is meant here is that many more people feel unable to control their lives than in the past, that a political and personal impotence has seized a significant portion of the population, that things are in the saddle and ride mankind (a nineteenth-century sentiment, it might be good to remember).

Have large numbers of people adopted the machine metaphor to describe themselves? Weizenbaum offers us workers Studs Terkel interviewed in *Working* who complain that others seem to regard them as machines but that they themselves certainly don't; hence their grievance.* This attitude is exactly the opposite of Weizenbaum's point. No, I fail to see that we have assumed the machine metaphor wholesale for ourselves as individuals, although we do feel legitimate anger at systems in society that operate as if humans can be regarded that way. This anger often expresses itself in yeasty* forms of protest.

complaint; objection

active

On the other hand, a **mechanistic model of humans**, which views us as part of the natural world and therefore just as comprehensible as any other part of it, has some attractions. It relieves human suffering when we discover that a virus behaves biochemically in certain human tissues, instead of assuming that a diseased person is suffering as **retribution** for sinful thoughts. I doubt that Weizenbaum would deny this statement, but there's bias in his next step, the choice of mechanistic models to explain human mental functioning. His choice seems based less on science than personal preference. One could argue that the information-processing model of human mental functioning, which Weizenbaum attacks, is in fact more general and accounts for much more cultural and gender variation—and is a lot less bizarre—than the **Freudian model**, which Weizenbaum proffers* without question, judging from his analysis of the compulsive programmer. In places in his book, and certainly in conversation, he concedes that the information-processing model has its uses. His objection, then, is that AI workers are single-minded about the model as the sole means of encompassing the human experience. That isn't my impression. Their writings are enthusiastic but tentative: they think they're onto a good thing, maybe one of the best so far, as an approach to explaining human cognition.* But they read novels and poetry, compose and play music, see movies and write stories, and make the same noises about the value of doing those things as the rest of us.

presents; offers

acquisition of knowledge

Perhaps Weizenbaum means that by regarding humans mechanistically, we think we can escape our moral responsibility to one another and to the society in which we all live. That's an amazing leap, and when it gets made, suggests at the very least an impoverished moral education. Then again, human cussedness* will always find an excuse for itself, call it original sin, bad company, disadvantaged background, or what we will.

stubbornness

Finally, Weizenbaum worries that to regard humans as another instance of information-processing machines seems to imply that "there's nothing unique about the human species." Strictly speaking, our definition as a species makes us unique. He doesn't say why regarding ourselves as another instance of information-processing machines automatically precludes* regarding ourselves in other ways too. But the real question is whether humans as a species deserve more special treatment and consideration than other species. The **humanist** has traditionally answered a resounding yes to that question, but that yes is fraught with problems. Faith in our specialness has often been used as license to plunder and exploit. It's a good corrective,* and in the long run self-preserving, to meditate on our connection with other things instead of our disjunctions.* We are part, not monarchs, of the universe.

prevents, excludes

treatment, cure
separations, gaps

And if we introduce into our universe machines who think, will we owe them our trust and love and respect? AI researchers say of course not, and people outside the field are even horrified by the question. But I suspect we need all the practice in humility, in loving and respecting others that we can get. We'll find out soon enough if it's misplaced.

So the question of whether an artificial intelligence can be made may be put aside with a tentative, qualified yes. Whether it should be done is still open for examination, and to ask how such machines will make us appear in our own eyes gets closer to the nub of what troubles us about AI. This question refers not to the technical feasibility of artificial intelligence, but to what we will have to face about ourselves, the possibility that we may have to undergo still another redefinition of ourselves as a species, another **Copernican revolution** that will move us further yet from the center of the universe.

QUESTIONS FOR DISCUSSION AND WRITING

[1] What is the author's position on AI? Quote lines from the essay to support your interpretation. You may want to refer to the discussion of authorial bias and assumptions in Chapter 2.

[2] McCorduck, in defending AI, suggests that we might need to be more suspicious of humans than computers. What are her concerns or fears about human judgment?

[3] What are the advantages of a "mechanistic model" of human beings—how can computers help us better understand ourselves?

[4] The ancient Greek foundations of Western scientific and philosophical thought emphasized that logic was a human faculty and defined the uniqueness of the human mind. Is artificial intelligence an extension of human logic, or is it a dehumanizing force that threatens the continuity of the Western logical tradition?

The following essay explores how genetic engineering might change the nature of human life. Read for the three chapter themes, or subtopics, and set up a chart to list the specific issues as they appear in the article.

Caryl Rivers' essay appeared in the Saturday Review *in April 1972. Her topic, genetic engineering, reflects the culmination of years of scientific specu- lation and experiment, and centuries of human longing and effort to find the "key" to life or to eternal youth. The medieval alchemists in their chemical experiments searched for the secret of wisdom and immortality; Spanish ex- plorers in the New World sought the legendary "fountain of youth." With various techniques of manipulating genetics, such as cloning and in vitro fertilization, now in practice, twentieth-century science is closer than ever to making human intervention in the life process routine. Rivers explores the moral issues and fears raised by advances in this scientific field.*

CARYL RIVERS
"Grave New World"

KEY CONCEPTS
A **HUXLEIAN NIGHTMARE** refers to Aldous Huxley's vision of the future in his novel, *Brave New World,* where humans are bred in bottles and have predetermined intelligence levels.

LAISSEZ-FAIRE is a French term commonly used in English to mean a policy of noninterference.

● A society matron proudly introduces her two sons and her daughter. They are her children by every biological rule but one: She has never been pregnant. Sex cells from her body and her husband's body were implanted three times in the womb of a "proxy* mother," who was paid a union wage to carry each fetus and give birth.

stand-in, substitute

An astronaut is carried aboard a space vehicle destined to probe the outer limits of this galaxy. He has no legs. Legs would be only an inconvenience during the years in which the astronaut will be confined to his spaceship. For this reason he was programmed to be born legless.

A Latin American dictator has some skin tissue scraped from his left arm. Nine months later, five hundred babies emerge from a factory that contains five hundred artificial wombs. The babies are genetic carbon copies of the dictator.

Although fiction today, these events could become realities with relatively slight advances in man's most adventurous and morally complex science, genetic engineering.

This new science is experimenting with a technique that would make possible the manipulation of an embryo during gestation* so as to change its physical characteristics. It may offer an alternative to natural human reproduction—a process that would allow the implantation of a fertilized ovum in the womb of a "host" mother or in an artificial womb inside a laboratory. Not too far off, according to specialists in the field, is the possibility of creating children with only one parent who will be biological duplicates of that single parent. Genetic engineering, in short, is on the brink of revolutionizing the traditional concepts of man, God, and creation.

period of pregnancy

The moral questions posed by recent advances in this and related life sciences are no longer speculative. They have to be faced as practical realities, and, in parts of the scientific community, this is now being done. Indeed, a heated debate is in progress. Some scientists encourage genetic experimentation, putting their faith in man's rational power. They say, in effect, that the only thing too sacred to tamper with is scientific investigation itself. Others, however, point to numerous instances in which technology has outrun man's wisdom (nuclear stockpiles, for example), and they warn that if guidelines in genetic technology are not immediately set forth, geneticists may bring into being a terrifying, uncontrollable **Huxleian nightmare**.

Those who urge restraint say it is past time to start thinking about controls for genetic technology. Scientific advances have already made it possible to change fundamentally the human reproductive process. The Caesarean section is now a common operation and constitutes a basic tampering with the way in which babies are born. There have already been successful blood transfusions to unborn children in cases of Rh blood

SOURCE: "Grave New World" by Caryl Rivers. Copyright © 1972 by *Saturday Review Magazine*, April 8, 1972. Reprinted by permission.

incompatibility. An estimated 25,000 women whose husbands are sterile resort to artificial insemination in this country each year, and more than a third of them give birth as a result.

Perhaps the most advanced work in the field is being done at Cambridge University in England by Drs. Robert G. Edwards and P. S. Steptoe. They have produced the best evidence to date of true in vitro fertilization* and are presently attempting to implant the fertilized egg in the uterus of the donor. They obtain the ova for their experiments from volunteer women who are seeking to overcome infertility. One woman, for example, had blocked Fallopian tubes that made normal conception impossible.

conception outside the uterus, "in a bottle"

Once an ovum can be successfully implanted in the womb, the way is open for "proxy mothers." A fertilized ovum could be removed from the womb of a woman after she had conceived and then be implanted in the uterus of another woman who would ultimately give birth. The child, of course, would carry the genetic identity of its true parents. The proxy mother would be only a temporary host, with no genetic relationship to the child. Technology could go one step further and simply eliminate the process of pregnancy and childbirth altogether. A human embryo could be removed from the uterus and placed in an artificial womb.

French biologist Jean Rostand speculated that, once the size of the human brain is not limited by the size of the female pelvis, it might be possible to double the number of fetal brain cells. Would this produce superintelligent people or monstrous misfits? Where will the line be drawn between legitimate medical practices and a Frankenstein-like toying with the human condition? And who will draw the line?

Another possibility of genetic engineering that raises serious moral questions is the creation of what are called clones—carbon copies of a human being already in existence, resulting from a process much more revolutionary than the merging of sperm and egg in a test tube.

Normally, the sexual process by which life begins guarantees the diversity of the species. The child inherits characteristics from both the mother and the father so that, while he may resemble either or both of them, he is unique. There are two kinds of cells in the human body—sex cells (ova and sperms) and body cells. Each body cell has a nucleus containing forty-six characteristic-determining chromosomes. Sex cells have only half that number. A merger of two sex cells is required for the resulting zygote to have a complete set of chromosomes and to begin dividing.

But human reproduction could take another route. Body cells contain the requisite* number of chromosomes to start a new individual, but they cannot divide the way the fertilized egg does. The body cells have very specialized jobs to do. Some go into making hair, others teeth, others skin, and so forth. Only the part of the body-cell mechanism that is useful in its specific job gets "switched on." If a body cell could receive a signal to switch on all of its mechanisms, it would divide and subdivide and multiply, finally developing into a new human being.

necessary, required

Accordingly, if such a "switching on" technique were developed, a body cell could be taken from a donor—scraped from his arm, perhaps—and be chemically induced to start dividing. The cell could be implanted in an artificial womb or in the uterus of a woman where, presumably, it would develop like a normal fetus. The baby would be genetically identical to the donor of the cell—his twin, a generation removed. It would have only one true parent. Its "mother" would be, like the proxy mother, only a temporary host.

The possibilities of human cloning are enough to startle even a science fiction writer. Societies would be tempted to clone their best scientists, soldiers, and statesmen. An Einstein might become immortal through his carbon copies. Or a Hitler. What better way for a dictator to extend his power beyond the grave? A carbon copy might be the ultimate expression of human egoism.

Some scientists estimate that human cloning will be possible by the end of the 1970s. If human cloning were ever practiced on a wide scale, it would drastically affect the course of human evolution. Nobel Prize-winning geneticist Dr. Joshua Lederberg has said he can imagine a time in the future when "clonishness" might replace the present dominant patterns of nationalism and racism.

Cloning is not the only avenue man might take to redesign himself. Advances in molecular biology could lead to genetic surgery: the addition of genes to or removal of them from human cells. In experiments with mouse cells, scientists added healthy new genes to a defective cell. The new genes not only corrected an enzyme deficiency in the cell but were duplicated when healthy new cells began to divide. It is now possible, in principle, to remove defective cells from a human patient, to introduce new genes, and to place the "cured" cells back into the patient.

Genetic surgery might also be put to more ambitious uses. J. B. Haldane, the late, renowned British geneticist, was one of the first to speculate and predict that men would tailor-make new kinds of people for space travel. He suggested the legless man referred to earlier, who would be ideally suited to living in the cramped quarters of a space capsule for long journeys; men with prehensile* feet and tails for life on asteroids where low gravity makes balance difficult; and muscular dwarfs to function in the strong gravitational pull of Jupiter.

adapted for grabbing and holding

Genetic engineering might also bring to life one of the mixtures of man and animal known in all the myths of man: the Minotaur, the Centaur, and the Gorgons. So far, however, human and animal chromosomes have been successfully mingled only in tissue-culture experiments.

Modern medicine may be able to produce not only man-animal combinations but a man-machine combination for which a name has already been coined: cyborg. We are familiar with the use of artificial material in the human body: plastic arteries, synthetics to replace damaged bone, or even an artificial heart. Who will draw the dividing line between man and robot?

There are few existing guidelines for the manipulation of "living" material and human beings. Reports from Britain describe experiments in which pregnant women awaiting abortion have been exposed to certain kinds of sound waves to determine if there will be extensive chromosome damage in the fetus. Is it immoral to damage a fetus for experimental purposes, even though it will be aborted? Does an embryo "grown" in a laboratory have any legal rights?

Even the practice of genetic counseling—guidance based upon an individual's chromosomal make-up—which is becoming increasingly common, raises ethical questions. Would an individual who is marked as a carrier of deleterious* genes carry a social stigma* as well? Dr. Marc Lappe of the Institute of Society, Ethics, and the Life Sciences, a group set up to examine the moral questions posed by science, thinks he would.

harmful, destructive / mark of shame

"It could lead to a subtle shift in the way we identify people as human," he says. "We could say, 'Oh, he has an extra chromosome.' We could then identify him as being qualitatively different. He is somewhat imperfect, perhaps not as human as the rest of us."

Suppose, for example, a genetic counselor knows that a newborn baby has an extra Y chromosome. There is evidence that the extra Y chromosome predisposes an individual to aggressive behavior. Should that become part of his medical record? What impact might that knowledge have on a school principal if a child with an extra Y becomes involved in typical childish pranks? Should the parents know, or would the knowledge have an adverse effect on the way they bring up the child?

The agonizing moral question posed by almost all aspects of genetic engineering has divided the scientific community. Hearing the arguments among scientists, one is reminded of the story about two men in a jail cell. One looked out and saw the mud; the other saw the stars.

Dr. Robert Sinsheimer of the California Institute of Technology sees the promise: "For the first time in all time a living creature understands its origin and can undertake to design its future. Even in the ancient myths man was constrained* by his essence. He could not rise above his nature to chart his destiny."

limited

Dr. Salvador Luria of MIT, a Nobel laureate,* takes the opposite viewpoint, "We must not ignore the possibility that genetic means of controlling human heredity will become a massive means of human degradation. Huxley's nightmarish society might be achieved by genetic surgery rather than by conditioning and in a more terrifying way, since the process would be hereditary and irreversible."

one who has received the Nobel prize

Dr. George Wald, a Nobel laureate at Harvard who has spoken out on a wide range of social issues, emphasizes the fact that every organism alive today represents an unbroken chain of life that stretches back some three billion years. That knowledge, he says, calls for some restraint. The danger he senses in genetic technology is a movement toward reducing man's unpredictability. "With animals we have abandoned natural selection for the technological process of artificial selection. We breed animals for what we want them to be: the pigs to be fat, the cows to give lots of milk, work horses to be heavy and strong, and all of them to be stupid. This is the process by which we have made all of our domestic animals. Applied to men, it could yield domesticated men."

Wald sees the trends of modern life working to erode one of the glories of being human: free will. "Free will is often inefficient, often inconvenient, and always undependable. That is the character of freedom. We value it in men. We disparage* it in machines and domestic animals. Our technology has given us dependable machines and livestock. We shall now have to choose whether to turn it to giving us more reliable, efficient, and convenient men, at the cost of our freedom. We had better decide now, for we are already not as free as we once were, and we can lose piecemeal* from within what we would be quick to defend in a frank attack from without."

belittle

bit by bit

Scientists themselves have shown growing awareness of the moral implications of their work. "Scientists have always had a supreme obligation to be concerned about the uses of their work," Isaac Asimov says. "In the past an ivory-tower scientist was just stupid. Today he's stupid and criminal."

But is it enough that scientists develop sensitivity to the moral complexities of the new technology? Can they alone grapple* with choices so fundamental they could affect the future of human heredity? James Watson has called the idea that science must always move bravely forward "a form of **laissez-faire** nonsense dismally reminiscent of the creed that American business, if left to itself, would solve everybody's problems."

confront, deal with

Seeing a child lying crippled by a genetic disease, one can't help thinking that, if such a scourge* could be lifted from the children of the future, it would be worth the risk of any Brave New Worlds. It is probably unwise and perhaps impossible to barricade any street of scientific inquiry and say: No Admittance. But neither can we blind ourselves to the consequence of travelling that street until it is too late. Dr. Kass has summarized the question posed by genetic engineering: "Human heredity is intricate and mysterious. We must face the prospect of intervention with awe, humility, and caution. We may not know what the devil we are doing."

curse

QUESTIONS FOR DISCUSSION AND WRITING

[1] After reading this article. decide how the author views the issue of genetic engineering. According to Rivers, do the potential benefits outweigh the fears?

[2] What similar fears do both genetic engineering and AI generate? How and why does such research frighten us?

[3] What is the argument against "domesticated men?" (See above.) You may need to define the concept first, before you can explain the argument against it.

Both of the next two essays relate to a single issue: the use of the atomic bomb. Because the articles cover one subject, you can use one chart to organize the thematic content you need to extract from the material. You should identify each entry you make, however, so that you will know where the information came from—number the essays 1 and 2, or abbreviate their sources ("NYT," for *New York Times,* and "UF," for *Unforgettable Fire,* for example).

At the time of this article, World War II was nearing its end. The Allies (the United States, Great Britain, and Russia, along with other countries fighting against Germany, Italy, and Japan) had already defeated the Nazis, and Japan was on the verge of defeat. With the stated goal of ending the war quickly, U.S. military and scientific leaders tested their new "super weapon," the atomic bomb, by exploding it over two Japanese cities, Hiroshima and Nagasaki. The people and their cities were devastated, physically wrecked by the blast and its deadly radiation, and psychologically suffering shock and horror at the new weapon's power. Throughout history, advances in weaponry have changed the nature of warfare, but crossbows and rifles were minor innovations compared to the radical implications of "the bomb."

SIDNEY SHALETT
"First Atomic Bomb Dropped on Japan; Missile Is Equal to 20,000 Tons of TNT; Truman Warns Foe of a 'Rain of Ruin'"

● Washington, Aug. 6—The White House and War Department announced today that an atomic bomb, possessing more power than 20,000 tons of TNT, a destructive force equal to the load of 2,000 B-29s and more than 2,000 times the blast power of what previously was the world's most devastating bomb, had been dropped on Japan.

The announcement, first given to the world in utmost solemnity by President Truman, made it plain that one of the scientific landmarks of the century had been passed, and that the "age of atomic energy," which can be a tremendous force for the advancement of civilization as well as for destruction, was at hand.

At 10:45 o'clock this morning, a statement by the President was issued at the White House that sixteen hours earlier—about the time that citizens on the Eastern seaboard were sitting down to their Sunday suppers—an American plane had dropped the single atomic bomb on the Japanese city of Hiroshima, an important army center.

What happened at Hiroshima is not yet known. The War Department said it "as yet was unable to make an accurate report" because "an impenetrable cloud of dust and smoke" masked the target area from reconnaissance* planes. The Secretary of War will release the story "as soon as accurate details of the results of the bombing become available." spying; information-gathering

But in a statement vividly describing the results of the first test of the atomic bomb in New Mexico, the War Department told how an immense steel tower had been "vaporized" by the tremendous explosion, how a 40,000-foot cloud rushed into the sky, and two observers were knocked down at a point 10,000 yards away. And President Truman solemnly warned:

> It was to spare the Japanese people from utter destruction that the ultimatum of July 26 was issued at Potsdam. Their leaders promptly rejected that ultimatum. If they do not now accept our terms, they may expect a rain of ruin from the air the like of which has never been seen on this earth.

The President referred to the joint statement issued by the heads of the American, British and Chinese governments, in which terms of surrender were outlined to the Japanese and warning given that rejection would mean complete destruction of Japan's power to make war.

[The atomic bomb weighs about 400 pounds and is capable of utterly destroying a town, a representative of the British Ministry of Aircraft Production said in London, the United Press reported.]

What is this terrible new weapon, which the War Department also calls the "Cosmic Bomb"? It is the harnessing of the energy of the atom, which is the basic power of the universe. As President Truman said, "the force from which the sun draws its power has been loosed against those who brought war to the Far East."

The imagination-sweeping experiment in harnessing the power of the atom has been the most closely guarded secret of the war. America to date has spent nearly $2,000,000,000 in advancing its research. Since 1939, American, British and Canadian scientists have worked on it. The experiments have been conducted in the United States, both for reasons of achieving concentrated efficiency and for security; the consequences of having the material fall into the hands of the enemy, in case Great Britain should have been successfully invaded, were too awful for the Allies to risk.

All along, it has been a race with the enemy. Ironically enough, Germany started the experiments, but we finished them. Germany made the mistake of expelling, because she was a "non-Aryan," a woman scientist who held one of the keys to the mystery, and she made her knowledge available to those who brought it to the United States. Germany never quite mastered the riddle, and the United States, Secretary Stimson declared, is "convinced that Japan will not be in a position to use an atomic bomb in this war."

Not the slightest spirit of braggadocio* is discernible* either in the wording of the official announcements or in the mien* of the officials who gave out the news. There was an element of elation in the realization that ITALIAN: bragging / evident; observable / appearance we had perfected this devastating weapon for employment against an enemy who started the war and has told us she would rather be destroyed than surrender, but it was grim elation. There was sobering awareness of the tremendous responsibility involved.

Secretary Stimson said that this new weapon "should prove a tremendous aid in the shortening of the war against Japan," and there were other responsible officials who privately thought that this was an extreme understatement and that Japan might find herself unable to stay in the war under the coming rain of atom bombs.

It was obvious that officials at the highest levels made the important decision to release news of the atomic bomb because of the psychological effect it may have in forcing Japan to surrender. However, there are some officials who feel privately it might have been well to keep this completely secret. Their opinion can be summed up in the comment by one spokesman: "Why bother with psychological warfare against an enemy that already is beaten and hasn't sense enough to quit and save herself from utter doom?"

No details were given on the plane that carried the bomb. Nor was it stated whether the bomb was large or small. The President, however, said the explosive charge was "exceedingly small." It is known that tremendous force is packed into tiny quantities of the element that constitutes these bombs. Scientists, looking to the peacetime uses of atomic power, envisage submarines, ocean liners and planes traveling around the world on a few pounds of the element. Yet, for various reasons, the bomb used against Japan could have been extremely large.

Hiroshima, first city on earth to be the target of the "Cosmic Bomb," is a city of 318,000 which is—or was—a major quartermaster depot and port of embarkation for the Japanese. In addition to large military supply depots, it manufactured ordnance,* mainly large guns and tanks, and machine tools and aircraft-ordnance parts.

weapons and ammunition

President Truman grimly told the Japanese that "the end is not yet. In their present form these bombs are now in production," he said, "and even more powerful forms are in development."

He sketched the story of how the late President Roosevelt and Prime Minister Churchill agreed that it was wise to concentrate research in America, and how great secret cities sprang up in this country, where, at one time, 125,000 men and women labored to harness the atom. Even today more than 65,000 workers are employed.

"What has been done," he said, "is the greatest achievement of organized science in history. We are now prepared to obliterate more rapidly and completely every productive enterprise the Japanese have above ground in any city. We shall destroy their docks, their factories and their communications. Let there be no mistake; we shall completely destroy Japan's power to make war."

The President emphasized that the atomic discoveries were so important, both for the war and for the peace, that he would recommend to

Congress that it consider promptly establishing "an appropriate commission to control the production and use of atomic power within the United States."

"I shall give further consideration and make further recommendations to the Congress as to how atomic power can become a powerful and forceful influence toward the maintenance of world peace," he said.

Secretary Stimson called the atomic bomb "the culmination of years of herculean* effort on the part of science and industry, working in cooperation with the military authorities." He promised that "improvements will be forthcoming shortly which will increase by several fold the present effectiveness."

heroic, great

"But more important for the long-range implications of this new weapon," he said, "is the possibility that another scale of magnitude will be developed after considerable research and development." The scientists are confident that over a period of many years atomic bombs may well be developed which will be very much more powerful than the atomic bombs now at hand.

[The plants which manufactured the atom bombs] were amazing phenonema in themselves. They grew into large, self-sustaining cities, employing thousands upon thousands of workers. Yet, so close was the secrecy that not only were the citizens of the area kept in darkness about the nature of the project, but the workers themselves had only the sketchiest ideas—if any—as to what they were doing. This was accomplished, Mr. Stimson said, by "compartmentalizing" the work so "that no one had been given more information than was absolutely necessary to his particular job."

A special laboratory also has been set up near Santa Fe, N.M., under direction of Dr. J. Robert Oppenheimer of the University of California. Dr. Oppenheimer also supervised the first test of the atomic bomb on July 16, 1945. This took place in a remote section of the New Mexico desert lands, with a group of eminent scientists gathered, frankly fearful to witness the results of the invention which might turn out to be either the salvation or the Frankenstein's monster of the world.

"Atomic fission holds great promise for sweeping developments by which our civilization may be enriched when peace comes, but the overriding necessities of war have precluded the full exploration of peacetime applications of this new knowledge," Mr. Stimson said. "However, it appears inevitable that many useful contributions to the well-being of mankind will ultimately flow from these discoveries when the world situation makes it possible for science and industry to concentrate on these aspects."

Although warning that many economic factors will have to be considered "before we can say to what extent atomic energy will supplement coal, oil and water as fundamental sources of power," Mr. Stimson acknowledged that "we are at the threshold of a new industrial art which will take many years and much expenditure of money to develop."

The War Department gave this supplementary background on the development of the atomic bomb:

> The series of discoveries which led to the development of the atomic bomb started at the turn of the century when radioactivity became known to science. Prior to 1939, the scientific work in this field was world-wide, but more particularly so in the United States, the United Kingdom, Germany, France, Italy, and Denmark. One of Denmark's great scientists, Dr. Neils Bohr, a Nobel prize winner, was whisked from the grasp of the Nazis in his occupied homeland and later assisted in developing the atomic bomb.
>
> It is known that Germany worked desperately to solve the problem of controlling atomic energy.

QUESTIONS FOR DISCUSSION AND WRITING

[1] What justifications did the President and military officials offer for dropping the bomb?

[2] The article does not refer explicitly to the human suffering caused by the bomb. What sense of the declared "enemy," the Japanese people, comes across in the American statements, which might explain how we were able to inflict such widespread destruction on a civilian population?

_____

Unforgettable Fire *is a collection of drawings by survivors of the atomic bomb attacks on Hiroshima and Nagasaki. The book's introduction, reprinted below, describes the heavily populated Hiroshima as it existed before the blast, and then takes us through a detailed account of the first moments, hours, and days following the explosion. Part of the horror lies in the fact that this single attack continues to claim victims even today: many people who lived through the actual event suffer the effects of radiation exposure, with cancer still taking many lives. The article also describes the psychological scars of this "unforgettable fire" which marks all of us in the atomic age.*

THE JAPANESE BROADCASTING CORPORATION
FROM *Unforgettable Fire*

● *That morning . . .*

On August 6, 1945, the morning started with a cloudless blue sky characteristic of the Inland Sea's summer. In March the big Tokyo air raid had killed 120,000 citizens. Many other cities in Japan were also violently bombed and burned by the American air attacks so that many non-combatants continued to be cruelly killed. In April American armed forces landed on Okinawa and the whole island became a battlefield. 90,000

SOURCE: From *Unforgettable Fire* by The Japanese Broadcasting Corporation. Copyright © 1977 by the Japanese Broadcasting Corporation. Reprinted by permission of Random House.

Japanese soldiers were killed and 100,000 civilians died. Japanese people cried loudly that they would fight a decisive battle on the mainland.

Hiroshima remained unharmed. A wild rumor spread that the Americans were not bombing in Hiroshima because it was a religious city with many Buddhist believers. Though not known at the time, in fact, the American military had ordered that Hiroshima be spared from bombing raids in order to later calculate accurately the full effects of the A-Bomb.

Hiroshima developed on the delta* at the mouth of the Ota River that ran from the Chugoku mountains into the Seto Inland Sea. In line with the Meiji government's policy to make the country rich and the army strong, Hiroshima became a strategic center for the Japanese military. From Hiroshima's Ujina Port soldiers recruited from all over Japan were sent to battle on the Asian continent. As World War II continued, Hiroshima developed into a major military city.

area of a river's opening

Before daybreak of August 6 an air raid alarm was given in Hiroshima. At 7:00 A.M. another air raid alarm was sounded. But at 7:31 A.M. the all clear was given. Soldiers at the anti-aircraft machine guns on the roofs of the military installations and munitions* factories were released by an air defense order.

war supplies

Just before the fateful moment the seven rivers which ran through the city looked stagnant because of the high tide and reflected the deep-blue of the summer sky. Wearing work clothes and gaiters,* with air defense hoods thrown back, people were running on the big and small bridges throughout the city. One of these was the Aioi Bridge, an unusual T-type bridge. It was the target of the A-Bomb. The mobilized students, even school girls, were hurrying to the munitions factories by streetcar. A horse-drawn farmer's cart, taking nightsoil* from the city to outlying farms, passed by at a leisurely pace with a clop-clop noise. Small clouds of dust rose here and there among the crowded, tile-roofed houses. These showed that work had begun on pulling down evacuated buildings to make compulsory firelanes. Members of the Women's Society of Labor Service, National Volunteers from the suburban districts, and junior high school students put their lunches in the shade of nearby trees before beginning a long day of sweaty, dusty work.

overshoes

human waste used as fertilizer

In public offices and businesses workers had begun their jobs after their section chiefs had given their morning instructions. In public schools morning assemblies had begun because even during summer vacation, students who had not been evacuated had lessons there. Little children were busy playing in the streets. There were even foreigners in Hiroshima. Several thousand Koreans who had been taken from their country were working as forced laborers in an armament* factory. There were some foreign students from Southeast Asian countries. And there were even Americans, POW Army pilots who had been shot down. Suddenly a bell rang in the broadcasting department of NHK. It was a warning given from the Army Headquarters of Chugoku District Army Information. The radio announcer began to read the bulletin, "Chugoku District Army Information. Three enemy airplanes have been spotted over the Saijo

weapons

area. . . ." Just then there was a dreadful shaking and loud crash of iron and concrete. The announcer was thrown into the air.

The flash: 8:15

The A-Bomb, which was nicknamed "Little Boy," was dropped from the B-29, Enola Gay. It exploded 570 meters above the ground with a light blue flash. The diameter of the fireball was 100 meters and the temperature at its center was 300,000 C.* Soon after the explosion black and white smoke covered the whole city and rose thousands of meters high. The pressure of the blast directly under the center of the explosion was from 4.5 to 6.7 tons per square meter. Wooden houses within a radius of two kilometers of the hypocenter* collapsed and completely burned from the wind and heat. The fires continued for two days. Some people who were near the center of the explosion literally evaporated and only their shadows remained; others were turned to charred corpses. Those who survived were badly burned. Usually their clothes were scorched and burned so they were practically naked. Their skin peeled off and hung down. They rushed to nearby fire prevention water boxes and river banks seeking water. Friends and relatives trapped under collapsed houses were crying for help. But flames surrounded them so closely that they were about to burn.

centigrade; a heat measurement

area directly beneath the bomb blast

Later large black drops of rain poured down. It was a deadly rain which contained mud, ash, and other radioactive fallout. Through burning flames and pouring black rain there was an endless line of injured people heading for the outskirts of the city. The burns on their hands made the skin hang down. Their hands looked like those of ghosts.

"Give me water."

The security functions of the army, police, prefecture,* and city agencies practically ceased. Under such circumstances medical treatment was started by doctors and nurses who were injured themselves. Damage to nearby army posts was rather slight and so soldiers from them first began the relief job. Hospitals soon became full, so public schools around the city were used as first-aid stations. They were also crowded by the rush of wounded persons. Countless dead bodies and seriously wounded people, who barely breathed, were left on the road or the river-banks of the city. Medical supplies were used up immediately because of the unimaginable number of wounded persons. The untreated people took their last breath moaning, "Give me water." What is now called radiation sickness soon appeared. People began suffering from diarrhea as if they had dysentery, losing clumps of their hair, and developing purple colored spots on their skin which made them look like a map. Such people soon died, their bodies full of big maggots they were too weak to remove.

local government

Those who were looking for their relatives walked around in the still smoldering city with the rescue parties. What they saw were dead bodies piled up on the ground and filling up the rivers. Figures of mothers who died protecting their own children were especially heartbreaking. People were deeply scarred by the indiscriminate cruelty of the new styled bomb and the dreadfulness of war itself.

Among those who entered the city later, there were a large number of people who were affected by lingering radioactivity, and died. Cremation of dead bodies continued for many days throughout the city. On top of some wood dead bodies were piled up, oil poured on them, and a fire was lit. The smell of dead bodies and the wail of sutra-chanting* spread over   praying
the vast scorched desolation.

And on August 9, the second A-Bomb was dropped on Nagasaki.

QUESTIONS FOR DISCUSSION AND WRITING

[1] Why does the author give so much detail about life in Hiroshima before the bombing?

[2] What was the victims' prevailing state of mind immediately after the atomic blast?

SECTION ESSAY ASSIGNMENTS

[1] Using the charts you've made for the preceding essays, summarize in a minimum of two paragraphs the major goals/motives, fears/threats, and social/psychological effects generated by the three twentieth-century scientific innovations: AI, genetic engineering, and the atom bomb.

[2] Choose one of the chart subheadings and, using the summary you wrote for Question 1, respond to the issues raised by the various authors. Your response should clarify which issue you think is the most important. Cite reasons for your assessment, explaining them abstractly and illustrating them concretely.

The Historical Context: Medieval and Renaissance Science

READING SKILL: *Drawing Inferences*

In the preceding section of this chapter, you read about contemporary scientific advances in artificial intelligence, genetic engineering, and atomic warfare and analyzed them according to the chapter themes of goals/motives, fears/threats, and social/psychological effects. The following article contains general information about the questionable status of science in the Middle Ages.

Science has made many advances since that time, but one can argue that the same social and philosophical concerns remain.

In this section, you'll still be reading selectively for the chapter themes. But sometimes you'll find that the information is not explicitly, or openly, stated. To isolate information relevant to the themes we're following you may need to question the text to draw inferences. Making or drawing inferences means coming to a conclusion about something that hasn't been explicitly or openly stated. You do this all the time with people when you "read" their "body language": a down-turned mouth, a clenched fist, "smiling" eyes all communicate unstated messages. Making inferences when you read, looking for unstated but implied meaning, requires "reading between the lines," i.e. concluding something from the facts, descriptions, or other statements an author makes.

Many authors want you to come to your own conclusions about ideas they present when they are trying to argue a point or convince you of something. You'll probably agree more strongly with some issue if you've made the logical connections and drawn some conclusions about it yourself, with the author only suggesting or implying those connections and conclusions.

Sometimes authors present facts clearly and you will draw inferences easily, perhaps automatically. Other times you'll have to look for clues, hints, subtle connotations* of words, diction, tone, irony, sarcasm, metaphor, and so on. In "Grave New World," the author cites one scientist who sees genetic engineering as "working to erode one of the glories of being human: free will." Here genetic engineering's threat to free will is clearly stated: genetic engineering threatens free will. If the author had simply said, "Genetic engineering will have an impact on free will," it would be up to you as a critical reader to infer from the author's tone and the statement's context whether the author believed that the impact would be beneficial or threatening.

suggestions; unstated meanings

The first reading question following this article asks you to infer what the motives were for the medieval alchemists' efforts to change common metals into gold. To draw inferences you have to make connections, look for possible results and ramifications, and, above all, ask questions, perhaps like these: What would the personal results be if someone could turn metal into gold? What would the alchemists get? What would they need to accomplish their task? How would they be viewed by their contemporaries? What was the context, the political, social, and cultural world surrounding the alchemists and their work?

———————

Friedrich Heer wrote The Medieval World *in 1961. The rise of science from about the fourteenth century helped bring Europe out of the "dark ages," but at a cost: the new scientific inquiry came into increasing conflict with the established Christian order, which held that theology provided the answers to all human needs. With little knowledge of rational or empirical method—for ancient scientific knowledge had been suppressed—the medieval scientists bear little similarity to scientists in the modern era. What survives of the medieval scientists' work can be seen today in occult* sciences such as astrology and numerology.*

supernatural

FRIEDRICH HEER
FROM *The Medieval World*

KEY CONCEPTS

The eighteenth century is commonly referred to as the Age of
Reason or the **ENLIGHTENMENT**. The period's characteristics include the
rise of deism, a belief in a benign but noninterfering God.

An **EMPIRICAL** view states that we can gain knowledge only through
observation, or the use of our senses.

The **MACROCOSM AND THE MICROCOSM** name two views of the
universe, "macrocosm" referring to the universe as a whole, a single
entity, and "microcosm" referring to a single part of the universe as an
analogy for the whole—in the part you have a model of the whole
system.

● About the middle of the fourteenth century John of Rupescissa, a Franciscan, complained that there were so few genuine and pious natural
philosophers*; most of those who pretended to pursue the sciences were
magicians, sorcerers, swindlers and false coiners. "It is of no avail* to strive
for perfection in this art if a man has not first purified his mind by a devout
life and profound contemplation, so that he not only recognizes nature for
what it is but also understands how to change what can be changed; but
this is given to all too few."

John's own scientific knowledge came to him "through divine enlightenment," during a stay of seven years in prison. His subjects were medicine, chemistry and alchemy,* and he attracted much attention in his own
day by his prophecies of changes in Church and State. He foretold that the
Papacy, then captive at Avignon, would lose its power and worldly possessions and return to apostolic poverty. His years of imprisonment were
passed first at Toulouse, as the prisoner of the Franciscan Provincial of
Aquitaine, and afterwards in a papal jail at Avignon. Primarily "a seeker
out of the secrets of nature," he falls, with other Franciscans, alchemists,
soothsayers* and astrologers, into that line of European natural philosophers which leads through Dr. Faustus, Boyle and Erasmus Darwin down
into the nineteenth century and indeed into the present.

This "seeking out of the secrets of nature" should not be regarded as
something set apart from the religious and political preoccupations of the
moment; it was intimately bound up with the prevailing outlook on the
world. Those most active and most activating in this field were attempting
nothing less than the transformation of the "elements of nature" and of
society, the metamorphosis which should alter the age itself and all human
relations. A high value has often been set on natural science as the coadju-

early organic scientists help

study of turning metals into gold

fortune tellers, prophets

SOURCE: From *The Medieval World* by Friedrich Heer (The New American Library, 1961).
By permission of the publisher.

tor* of religious and political advancement. Erasmus Darwin, for example, assistant the grandfather of Charles Darwin, was at once a doctor of medicine, a religious reformer, a man of the **enlightenment** and a revolutionary. It can be shown that the reforming ideal of using science to "make the world a better place," which in the twentieth century is bound up with the two great questions of the relationship of science and religion and the social and political uses of atomic energy, has a long ancestry. In Europe the pedigree reaches back at least into the twelfth century, though it was mainly in the thirteenth and early fourteenth centuries that the natural sciences began to emerge in their own right, and even then in a peculiarly ambiguous role. Anyone who concerned himself with the "secrets of nature" and was bold enough to seek them out by experiment was committed to a perilous association with magicians, sorcerers and alchemists, that is to say with underground conspirators dedicated to uncovering the secrets God had veiled in mystery, impelled by motives of ambition and vanity or in consequence of a sworn compact with the devil. Gerbert of Aurillac, the tenth century scholar with mathematical and scientific interests who on his election to the Papacy took the name Sylvester II, was famous in the Middle Ages not for his pontificate* but as a magician and term as Pope a sorcerer. As late as the seventeenth century the same German word still served both for "spirit" and for "gas" and the distinction between the two was arrived at only very slowly. Boyle, friend of Newton and the "father of modern chemistry," was a practicing alchemist, and Newton himself derived some of the basic elements of his color theory from the natural philosophers of the thirteenth and fourteenth centuries.

During the Middle Ages those who pursued the natural sciences had no legitimate niche in society, nor were they recognized by the Church. The universities eschewed* technical activities (the necessary basis of experi- avoided ment and of empirical research) as "illiberal arts," banishing them to the backrooms and workshops of small craftsmen and persons of dubious reputation. Theology frowned on any attempt at reaching into the secrets of nature, an unlawful invasion of the sacred womb of the Great Mother. Even in the nineteenth century the Spanish Academy of Sciences could reject on these grounds a proposal for controlling the river Manzanares. Anyone who persisted in flying in the face of public opinion by meddling with science was forced to consort with outcasts of all kinds: with Provencal Jews, because they could translate Arabic texts dealing with alchemy, chemistry, medicine and astrology, and with eccentrics who lived out their lives in dark secluded basements, dedicated to their quest for the "philosopher's stone," the transmutation* of quicksilver into gold. Anyone change in form who like Roger Bacon was bold enough to convert his monastic cell into a cell of early scientific endeavor had to be prepared to exchange it for a prison.

The pattern of development in medieval ideas about the natural sciences provides as conspicuous an example of that broad co-existence of opposites as any we have yet met with: it can never be sufficiently stressed that medieval society, medieval piety and medieval learning were all compounded of numerous contradictory and diverse elements. Scholars who engaged in scientific pursuits did so from a mixture of motives, rational and irrational, scholarly and superstitious; their methods were a combination of **empiricism** and bold speculation. The stresses of contemporary political and religious pressures were such that although these activities may have made a satisfying life's work for an individual, what emerged from them was certainly not science. The different subjects went together in pairs, some of them so closely linked as to become hybrids. Chemistry went with alchemy, astronomy with astrology, mathematics with cosmology* (numbers were regarded as sacred cyphers in which were hidden all the secrets of **the macrocosm and the microcosm**), technology with magic, medicine with philosophy, and optics with mystical ideas about light.

study of the universe's structure

QUESTIONS FOR DISCUSSION AND WRITING

[1] The medieval alchemists sought to transform the "elements of nature" and to change quicksilver into gold. What can you infer about their motives? Review the questions we've suggested you ask yourself as you read (see page 164) to help you draw some logical conclusions about the alchemists' motives.

[2] Medieval universities did not support "technical activities" in relation to science. Infer the social effects of this academic stand. First ask yourself questions about the logical relationship between society and technology: what social changes might technology bring about? What would society be like without technology? Develop more questions on your own to help you draw inferences about the social effects.

[3] Explain the Church's fears about science and the kinds of threats medieval scientists faced. Include both explicit references in the text and any inferences you can draw from the material.

WRITING SKILL: *Using Comparison and Contrast*

How would you explain the term "alchemist" to someone unfamiliar with the history of Western science?

How can we discuss the effects of wide-scale nuclear war, given that it's a theoretical, or abstract, situation?

How might we assess the values and dangers of genetic engineering as a medical tool?

What logic can a person in our computer-saturated society use to illustrate the potential dangers of artificial intelligence?

Sometimes in class discussions or written assignments you'll need to define or analyze an unusual term or a theoretical issue. Or you may want to evaluate a proposal or an experimental practice. You can deal with the above questions and issues by using the logic of comparison and contrast.

Through comparison, you can make the unfamiliar or unknown more comprehendible. You can explain the term "alchemist," for example, by drawing parallels between an alchemist and a scientist: both share a specific goal—understanding physical principles—and use some similar methods—experimentation and testing. Comparison can also help when your topic is theoretical; you can clarify it by placing it in the context of something that is concrete or already known. We know the consequences of atomic war through the attacks on Hiroshima and Nagasaki; we can infer that a wide-scale nuclear war would produce comparable effects, with proportionally larger destruction.

Using contrast, you can make distinctions between things or ideas that are apparently alike but that have essential differences which possibly change their practical consequences or value. Contrast can also help you define a concept: you can explain what it is by explaining what it is not or how it differs from something similar to it. We might evaluate the worth of genetic engineering by looking at the specific cases of fertility drugs and in vitro fertilization. Whereas both may help couples who have been unable to have children, the former method enhances a natural process but the latter raises moral issues of tampering with nature and allowing scientists to manipulate genetics. In the case of continuing advances in computer science, one might argue that simple programs merely aid human mental processes, increasing their speed and reliability, whereas programs that allow for artificial intelligence may move beyond a mechanical stage into the human realm of sensitive and creative thought.

Comparison and contrast are logical processes. As a process of inquiry, both activities help you discover more about your topic. As techniques of paragraph and essay development, they help you communicate your ideas effectively. They are ways of expanding and clarifying your thoughts.

In some college writing assignments, you'll be asked directly to compare and contrast ideas, perhaps to demonstrate that you understand each idea individually and in connection to each other or some broader issue. By responding to an assignment that asks you to compare and contrast Greek science to medieval science, for instance, you demonstrate first that you understand each practice fully. You also show that you can identify abstract principles defining science; whether in antiquity or the Middle Ages, science has the purpose of explaining physical laws. And you show your ability to distinguish fundamentally different characteristics of apparently similar things; Greek knowledge of logic and experimental method made ancient science more advanced than medieval science, which proceeded on assumption and magic as often as it did on experimentation.

But you can use the tools of comparison and contrast in almost any kind of assignment, even if you haven't been asked to compare and contrast specifically. Comparison and contrast are valuable ways to approach an assignment that asks you to define, analyze, evaluate, or to do any combination of expository tasks. Comparison and contrast are useful thinking strategies, not just rigid rhetorical modes.

In Chapter 2 we discussed ways of developing paragraphs that compare and contrast things or ideas. You can incorporate such paragraphs in essays to help develop your topic, or you can write essays composed entirely of comparisons and/or contrasts. Remember that in our discussion of definition we said that it was up to you to determine how significant a part definition would play in a specific essay. In the same way, you need to decide when to use comparison and contrast, and to what extent you should build your essay on these particular modes.

Below are some sample assignments that require differing amounts of comparison and contrast. We discuss how you might approach each assignment, offering our logic for the use of comparison and contrast in each. You may want to use the same process when you begin your writing assignments in this chapter.

1. Compare and contrast the uses of science and philosophy.

Clearly, this assignment asks you to develop your essay entirely as a comparison/contrast. You will need to identify some uses of science and some uses of philosophy. Then <u>synthesize</u> the two lists or, in other words, name abstract <u>bases</u> of comparison and contrast. For example, some uses of science include explaining natural phenomena, harnessing nature for technological purposes, and gaining knowledge. Philosophy can be used to guide human behavior, explain the nature of life, and develop logic and other rational methods of inquiry. You can synthesize the first elements on the lists: explaining natural phenomena and explaining the nature of life are both ways of explaining life in general. Thus, one abstract basis of comparison is that both science and philosophy are useful in explaining life. Another category that can be synthesized, this time from the final elements of the lists, is gaining knowledge. Finally, science, by harnessing nature, and philosophy, by guiding our behavior, help make daily life easier, a third abstract basis of comparison.

Your lists will probably include elements that don't match. These can form the abstract bases of contrast. Science is used to improve or manipulate the physical world. Philosophy, on the other hand, attempts to explain the physical world, not to alter it. Science and philosophy therefore differ in the purposes they're used for. Science has been used for economic gain more often than has philosophy. They also differ in their practical use, a second abstract basis of contrast. You can develop this essay by using each abstract basis of comparison and contrast as paragraph topics. Your conclusion may include an evaluation of the relative worth of the two fields.

2. Medieval scientists were often victims of the Inquisition. In what ways might their work be considered heretical?

This assignment implies a comparison between medieval scientists and heretics. You might begin by defining heresy, either in your introduction or in a paragraph following the thesis. Once you've outlined the characteristics of heresy for the reader, you can draw comparisons between them and the practices and beliefs of medieval scientists. Would you also want to develop contrasts to show how they differed? The assignment seems to emphasize comparison; you should probably minimize or omit contrasts.

3. Opponents of genetic engineering refer to the Frankenstein myth as a warning against its use. Develop an argument countering their claims.

This assignment asks for an argument. Argument essays may draw on many different rhetorical modes; comparison and contrast are especially useful. Here, you might develop the contrasts between the Frankenstein myth and the practice of genetic engineering as a way of defusing its opponents' criticism. You're not limited to contrast, however; you can compare the genetic engineer with Dr. Frankenstein, and then analyze how such comparisons are weak or even false. You can describe the procedure of each, showing how Frankenstein's was unscientific and uncontrolled, and then contrast it to the controlled conditions of the genetic engineer's laboratory. Use comparison to set up similarities which you will then show to be shallow by developing in-depth contrasts.

Read the following essay selectively for the chapter themes, paying particular attention to the ways the Copernican revolution affected people psychologically and socially.

Bertrand Russell, a major twentieth-century mathematician and philosopher, wrote Religion and Science *in 1935. The selection below chronicles the Church's increasingly negative and finally repressive reaction to Copernican theory. Galileo pursued Copernicus's formulation of a heliocentric* universe,*   sun-centered *which contradicted scriptural* authority. The theory not only caused religious*   Biblical *strife but also had psychological ramifications affecting art as well as religion and science.*

BERTRAND RUSSELL
"The Copernican Revolution"

KEY CONCEPTS
IMPIETY is the sin of disrespectfulness toward God or Church teachings.

STOIC philosophy advocates avoiding extremes as a way of assuring a good and happy life; see Chapter 6, page 395.

In theological terms, **INFIDELITY** means unfaithfulness to one's God or to Church doctrine, and is one of the most serious charges possible.

The **INQUISITION** was the Catholic Church's organized campaign against **HERESY;** see Chapter 2, page 100.

● The first pitched battle between theology and science, and in some ways the most notable, was the astronomical dispute as to whether the

SOURCE: Reprinted from *Religion and Science* by Bertrand Russell (1935) by permission of Oxford University Press.

earth or the sun was the center of what we now call the solar system. The orthodox theory was the Ptolemaic, according to which the earth is at rest in the center of the universe, while the sun, moon, planets, and system of fixed stars revolve round it, each in its own sphere. According to the new theory, the Copernican, the earth, so far from being at rest, has a twofold motion: it rotates on its axis once a day, and it revolves round the sun once a year.

The theory which we call Copernican, although it appeared with all the force of novelty in the sixteenth century, had in fact been invented by the Greeks, whose competence in astronomy was very great. It was advocated by the Pythagorean school, who attribute it, probably without historical truth, to their founder Pythagoras. The first astronomer who is known definitely to have taught that the earth moves was Aristarchus of Samos, who lived in the third century B.C. He was in many ways a remarkable man. He invented a theoretically valid method of discovering the relative distances of the sun and moon, though through errors of observation his result was far from correct. Like Galileo, he incurred the imputation* of   accusation, charge
impiety, and he was denounced by the **Stoic** Cleanthes. But he lived in an age when bigots had little influence on governments, and the denunciation apparently did him no harm.

The Greeks had great skill in geometry, which enabled them to arrive at scientific demonstration in certain matters. They knew the cause of eclipses, and from the shape of the earth's shadow on the moon they inferred that the earth is a sphere. Eratosthenes, who was slightly later than Aristarchus, discovered how to estimate the size of the earth. But the Greeks did not possess even the rudiments of dynamics, and therefore those who adhered to the Pythagorean doctrine of the earth's motion were unable to advance any very strong arguments in favor of their view. Ptolemy, about the year A.D. 130, rejected the view of Aristarchus, and restored the earth to its privileged position at the center of the universe. Throughout later antiquity and the Middle Ages, his view remained unquestioned.

The theory of Copernicus, though important as a fruitful effort of imagination which made further progress possible, was itself still very imperfect. The planets, as we now know, revolve about the sun, not in circles, but in ellipses,* of which the sun occupies, not the center, but one of the   ovals
foci.* Copernicus adhered to the view that their orbits must be circular,   points on a line
and accounted for irregularities by supposing that the sun was not quite in the center of any one of the orbits. This partially deprived his system of the simplicity which was its greatest advantage over that of Ptolemy, and would have made Newton's generalization impossible if it had not been corrected by Kepler. Copernicus was aware that his central doctrine had already been taught by Aristarchus—a piece of knowledge which he owed to the revival of classical learning in Italy, and without which, in those days of unbounded admiration for antiquity, he might not have had the courage to publish his theory. As it was, he long delayed publication

because he feared ecclesiastical censure.* Himself an ecclesiastic, he dedicated his book to the Pope, and his publisher, Osiander, added a preface
(which may perhaps have not been sanctioned* by Copernicus) saying that
the theory of the earth's motion was put forward solely as a hypothesis, and
was not asserted as positive truth. For a time, these tactics sufficed, and
it was only Galileo's bolder defiance that brought retrospective* official
condemnation upon Copernicus.

criticism

approved

backward look after the fact

At first, the Protestants were almost more bitter against him than the
Catholics. Luther said that "People give ear to an upstart astrologer who
strove to show that the earth revolves, not the heavens or the firmament,*
the sun and the moon. Whoever wishes to appear clever must devise some
new system, which of all systems is of course the very best. This fool wishes
to reverse the entire science of astronomy; but sacred Scripture tells us
that Joshua commanded the sun to stand still, and not the earth." Melanchthon was equally emphatic; so was Calvin, who after quoting the text:
"The world also is stablished, that it cannot be moved," triumphantly
concluded: "Who will venture to place the authority of Copernicus above
that of the Holy Spirit?" Even Wesley, so late as the eighteenth century,
while not daring to be quite so emphatic, nevertheless stated that the new
doctrines in astronomy "tend toward **infidelity.**"

sky

In this, I think, Wesley was, in a certain sense, in the right. The importance of Man is an essential part of the teaching of both the Old and New
Testaments; indeed God's purposes in creating the universe appear to be
mainly concerned with human beings. The doctrines of the Incarnation
and the Atonement could not appear probable if Man were not the most
important of created beings. Now there is nothing in the Copernican
astronomy to prove that we are less important than we naturally suppose
ourselves to be, but the dethronement of our planet from its central
position suggests to the imagination a similar dethronement of its inhabitants. While it was thought that the sun and moon, the planets and the
fixed stars, revolved once a day about the earth, it was easy to suppose that
they existed for our benefit, and that we were of special interest to the
Creator. But when Copernicus and his successors persuaded the world
that it is we who rotate while the stars take no notice of our earth; when
it appeared further that our earth is small compared to several of the
planets, and that they are small compared to the sun; when calculation and
the telescope revealed the vastness of the solar system, of our galaxy and
finally of the universe of innumerable galaxies—it became increasingly
difficult to believe that such a remote and parochial* retreat could have
the importance to be expected of the home of Man, if Man had the cosmic
significance assigned to him in traditional theology. Mere considerations
of scale suggested that perhaps we were not the purpose of the universe:
lingering self-esteem whispered that, if we were not the purpose of the
universe, it probably had no purpose at all. I do not mean to say that such
reflections have any logical cogency,* still less that they were widely
aroused at once by the Copernican system. I mean only that they were

narrow

reason, validity

such as the system was likely to stimulate in those to whose minds it was vividly present. It is therefore not surprising that the Christian Churches, Protestant and Catholic alike, felt hostility to the new astronomy, and sought out grounds for branding it as heretical.

Galileo Galilei (1564–1642) was the most notable scientific figure of his time, both on account of his discoveries and through his conflict with **the Inquisition**. It was the telescope that led Galileo on to more dangerous ground. Hearing that a Dutchman had invented such an instrument, Galileo reinvented it, and almost immediately discovered many new astronomical facts, the most important of which, for him, was the existence of Jupiter's satellites.

Besides Jupiter's moons, the telescope revealed other things horrifying to theologians. It showed that Venus has phases like the moon; Copernicus had recognized that his theory demanded this, and Galileo's instrument transformed an argument against him into an argument in his favor. The moon was found to have mountains, which for some reason was thought shocking. More dreadful still, the sun had spots! This was considered as tending to show that the Creator's work had blemishes; teachers in Catholic universities were therefore forbidden to mention sun-spots, and in some of them this prohibition endured for centuries. A Dominican was promoted for a sermon on the punning text: "Ye men of Galilee, why stand ye gazing up into the heaven?" in the course of which he maintained that geometry is of the devil, and that mathematicians should be banished as the authors of all **heresies**. Theologians were not slow to point out that the new doctrine would make the Incarnation difficult to believe. Moreover, since God does nothing in vain, we must suppose the other planets inhabited; but can their inhabitants be descended from Noah or have been redeemed by the Savior? Such were only a few of the dreadful doubts which, according to Cardinals and Archbishops, were liable to be raised by the impious* inquisitiveness of Galileo.   disrespectful

The result of all this was that the Inquisition took up astronomy, and arrived, by deduction from certain texts of Scripture, at two important truths:

> The first proposition, that the sun is the center and does not revolve about the earth, is foolish, absurd, false in theology, and heretical, because expressly contrary to Holy Scripture . . . The second proposition, that the earth is not the center, but revolves about the sun, is absurd, false in philosophy, and, from a theological point of view at least, opposed to the true faith.

Galileo, hereupon, was ordered by the Pope to appear before the Inquisition, which commanded him to abjure* his errors, which he did on   renounce
February 26, 1616. He solemnly promised that he would no longer hold the Copernican opinion, or teach it whether in writing or by word of mouth. It must be remembered that it was only sixteen years since the burning of Bruno.*   16th c. Italian philosopher

At the instance of the Pope, all books teaching that the earth moves were thereupon placed upon the Index*; and now for the first time the work of Copernicus himself was condemned. Galileo retired to Florence, where, for a while, he lived quietly and avoided giving offense to his victorious enemies. — list of forbidden works

During the time of Galileo's enforced silence, his enemies had taken the opportunity to increase prejudice by arguments to which it would have been imprudent* to reply. It was urged that his teaching was inconsistent with the doctrine of the Real Presence. The Jesuit Father Melchior Inchofer maintained that "the opinion of the earth's motion is of all heresies the most abominable, the most pernicious, the most scandalous; the immovability of the earth is thrice* sacred; argument against the immortality of the soul, the existence of God, and the incarnation, should be tolerated sooner than an argument to prove that the earth moves." By such cries of "tally-ho" the theologians had stirred each other's blood, and they were now all ready for the hunt after one old man, enfeebled by illness and in process of going blind. — unwise — three times

Galileo was once more summoned to Rome to appear before the Inquisition, which, feeling itself flouted,* was in a sterner mood than in 1616. — treated with contempt

When he reached Rome he was thrown into the prisons of the Inquisition, and threatened with torture if he did not recant.* The Inquisition, "invoking the most holy name of our Lord Jesus Christ and of His most glorious Virgin Mother Mary," decreed that Galileo should not incur the penalties provided for heresy, "provided that with a sincere heart and unfeigned* faith, in Our presence, you abjure, curse, and detest the said errors and heresies." Nevertheless, in spite of recantation and penitence, "We condemn you to the formal prison of this Holy Office for a period determinable at Our pleasure; and by way of salutary penance, we order you during the next three years to recite, once a week, the seven penitential psalms." — take back; deny — sincere

The comparative mildness of this sentence was conditional upon recantation. Galileo, accordingly, publicly and on his knees, recited a long formula drawn up by the Inquisition, in the course of which he stated: "I abjure, curse, and detest the said errors and heresies . . . and I swear that I will never more in future say or assert anything, verbally or in writing, which may give rise to a similar suspicion of me." He went on to promise that he would denounce to the Inquisition any heretics whom he might hereafter find still maintaining that the earth moved, and to swear, with his hands on the Gospels, that he himself had abjured this doctrine. Satisfied that the interests of religion and morals had been served by causing the greatest man of the age to commit perjury, the Inquisition allowed him to spend the rest of his days in retirement and silence, not in prison, it is true, but controlled in all his movements, and forbidden to see his family or his friends. He became blind in 1637, and died in 1642—the year in which Newton was born.

QUESTIONS FOR DISCUSSION AND WRITING

[1] Galileo risked his life by pursuing his scientific research. What can you infer about his motives for continuing his work?

[2] What were the Church's motives for persecuting Galileo?

[3] How can you account for the difference in the ancient Greek world view, which was heliocentric, and the Middle Ages view, which was geocentric? How can you account for the Greeks' knowledge being lost? You'll need to draw inferences from all the information you've read on life and religion in the Middle Ages and Renaissance.

WRITING ASSIGNMENT: *Definition/Contrast Essay*
The Copernican revolution rocked the Western world's notion of a geocentric universe and hence their view of humanity itself. What was the medieval view of the individual's place in the universe? What were the major differences in the post-Copernican revolution view?

The Modern Era

Christe McMenomy is an historian of science. Her article, written in 1984, outlines the causes and effects of the industrial revolution, a major turning point in the nature of Western culture. Our present technological age grew out of this eighteenth-century development. The century saw the invention of steam engines, the rise of factories, and the construction of canals—innovations that we perhaps consider old-fashioned but that changed the eighteenth-century world as drastically as the telephone, radio, television, and computer have changed the twentieth. Again we witness drastic scientific change leading to drastic changes in all spheres of human life.

CHRISTE McMENOMY
"The Scientific Background to the Industrial Revolution"

● The period between Galileo and Darwin was one of great change in the definition of science, its methodology and subject matter, and in the status and education of the scientist. At the end of the middle ages, natural philosophers were trained in the universities of Europe in logic and dialectic, and their texts were primarily commentaries on Aristotle. Scientific method was defined by logical demonstration of known conclusions, as exemplified by Aristotle's discussions of physics and cosmology. The relationship between physics, astronomy, and mathematics was defined in hierarchical terms, and conclusions in one discipline could not be used in demonstrations of conclusions in another discipline.

By the time of Galileo's death in 1642, both the method of training scientists and the methods scientists used were changing. Renaissance *humanism* fostered the development of an educational system emphasizing useful knowledge, not merely theoretical demonstration. Francis Bacon described a national program of scientific investigation, a fact-gathering method of science, with the ultimate goal being the control of nature for the benefit of mankind. While his programs were never adopted as he envisioned them, Bacon's view of nature as knowable and controllable, and science as an enterprise devoted to discovering new facts, rather than proving old observations, reveals a conception of science drastically different from that of the medieval natural philosophers.

Galileo used mathematics to describe the behavior of bodies in motion, and developed a method of experimental mechanics based on measurement of isolatable phenomena. Kepler defined five parts for astronomy, including observations, hypotheses to explain planetary motion, cosmology or metaphysics, prediction, and instruments. For Kepler, development of the cosmology was least important: if hypotheses explaining the observations could be fitted to a cosmological or metaphysical system, that was an advantage, but if not, it was the cosmological system which had to be discarded, not the hypotheses which accounted for the observations. Gilbert, who pioneered work on magnetism, also favored an observational approach which was not bound to outdated theories, and dedicated his work to those men who sought answers not in old books, but in things themselves.

The emphasis on measurement and experimentation, and the new goal of finding useful knowledge, brought theoretical science closer ties with technology. Scientific measurement requires precise instruments. Experimenters were forced to become craftsmen to make instruments to carry out their tests, or at least to explain their needs to craftsmen who could make the instruments for them. The need for certain kinds of knowledge also defined those areas where science could most usefully benefit society. In the two centuries before Galileo, the requirements of navigators sailing out of sight of land for long periods on voyages to the New World had stimulated the spread of knowledge of astronomical calculation and geometric mapping techniques by the end of the sixteenth century. In the seventeenth and eighteenth centuries, the need for better agricultural techniques to support growing populations, the need for more fuel for production and heating, and the need for better timing devices, as well as the needs of warfare, all promoted theoretical investigation in biology, mechanics, mining technology, ballistics* and engineering which resulted   study of firearms
in new technology, and ultimately, in the industrial revolution of the late eighteenth century.

The new view of man as an active intellectual with wide interests and abilities broke down some of the old barriers between the theoretical and practical sciences. The printing press made publication of books by many different authors possible. Craftsmen who produced works on mining, ballistics and architecture were largely self-taught, not scholars of the great universities, and their knowledge came from experience with the coal mines of Germany, and the cannon and fortifications used in Italy. Practical sciences became part of the university curriculum. In London, Gresham College was founded in 1600 to provide free education in mechanical and navigational arts in addition to traditional studies.

The seventeenth century is also the period in which the great scientific societies were founded. The Lincei of Rome, which counted Galileo among its members, was shortlived, but the Royal Society of London and the Académie des Sciences of Paris were permanent foundations, whose goals were the advancement of knowledge for human use. Newton, Boyle, and Hooke were Fellows of the Royal Society; in France, Huygens, and later Lavoisier and Coulomb, belonged either to the Académie or to the Ecole Polytechnique. The societies stimulated the dissemination of theories, experimental methods and results; the development of instruments, and at times, unhealthy rivalry. The status of the scientist had become one of both personal and national prestige, and there was competition between the scientists of England and France, who debated for decades over whether Newton or Leibniz had invented calculus first.

In contrast to the seventeenth century, the early eighteenth century was a period of relatively few important major scientific advances. Instead, there were major technological implementations of the seventeenth century theories, leading to the industrial revolution, which were made possible by the changes in both science and society which had taken place since the middle ages. Besides the new experimental methods of science, and the cooperation of the scientific societies, the dissemination* of scientific ideas was increased by popularizations of new theories. Newton's *Principles of Mathematical Physics* appeared in a new version in the 1730s, written especially for the edification of ladies. Such popularizations interested the general public in the advances and possibilities of scientific theories.

There were other major developments in society which aided the industrial revolution. Economic institutions such as banks, insurance companies and trading companies were willing and able to advance the capital necessary to build new factories and means of transportation, in return for a share of the profits. Religious reformation provided new ways of evaluating success and challenging the authority of old institutions and ideas, and encouraged reception of new ideas. There was a general shift towards practical application of new knowledge in all areas of public and private life, which fed on the closer relationship between theoretical science and technology.

The industrial revolution was really a group of several revolutions. These were changes in transportation, architecture, energy use, and

spread

manufacturing. The transportation and architecture revolutions have their origins in the Renaissance, when the new astronomy made possible navigation beyond sight of land, and the ideas from perspective aided the Italian painters to design new buildings. As long distance voyages became safer, the demand for better shipping increased, to allow manufacturers in Europe to take advantage of cheap raw materials available in the New World. Ships increased in size and sail power, and changed shape to allow for greater maneuverability.

The new relationship between science and technology fostered the science of engineering. Systematic studies of how weight could be supported by beams led to stronger and safer building, road and bridge design, and the development of stronger materials allowed construction of larger factories.

The availability of steam power, iron and steel, and the machines to produce precision tools provided the materials and energy sources necessary for the invention of the railway engine. The earliest engines were used in England for mining, but by the mid-nineteenth century, the railroad had become the major source of goods transportation in England and in America, and was opening the American West to immigration and settlement.

The industrial revolution of the eighteenth and nineteenth centuries emphasized the interdependence of science and technology. Not only in the fields mentioned here, but also in the study of ballistics and chemistry, theoretical science provided the information necessary for improvements in cannon and dyes. Society came to expect that new scientific theories would result in new products, new sources of energy, and a better standard of living. By the nineteenth century, the scientist was a professional, supported by industrial or government institutions as well as academic ones, and his discoveries and inventions brought him prestige among his colleagues, and often financial reward from ownership of patents. The technical craftsman was educated in theoretical science and capable of applying new theories to improve production, make new tools, or invent new machines.

The social impact of the industrial revolution and the scientific discoveries of the seventeenth and eighteenth centuries was tremendous. In medicine, agriculture and factory production, new knowledge and techniques both improved the lives of many people and created new problems for others.

The study of medicine was freed from the authority of Galen and Hippocrates, and Harvey and others determined finally the circulation of the blood. The use of the microscope in medical research led to the discovery of germs and the invention of preventative innoculations for such diseases as small pox. Doctors were able to cure or prevent more diseases, with the result that more people lived longer and more had productive lives.

In agriculture, the enclosure laws permitted the landed gentry* to consolidate their lands, and take over untenanted areas for cultivation. The new attitude toward experimentation and technology led to the introduction of more effective draining techniques, better crop rotation, and the use of new food crops from plants discovered in the New World. Agricultural output increased significantly in England and the United States, with the result that fewer people were needed as farm laborers to produce the food necessary to support the population.

upper middle class

The displacement of poor farmers from the land caused an urban growth crisis. People flooded into the new industrial centers seeking jobs in the factories. Because the machines performed the work, they needed only to be overseen and refitted with supplies of thread or raw cotton. Factory owners set wages for women and children lower than those for men, as was true with farm labor. But factory work required less strength than outdoor labor; women and children were often hired to supervise the machines or work in the mines, leaving many men out of work. The work involved little mental effort but long hours. Children working throughout the day had no time for education, and adults were frustrated by a type of work which emphasized the worth of machines over people.

For those who could afford the new goods of the factories, living standards improved significantly. Cheap cloth from the textile revolution made it possible for all but the very poor to afford a change of clothes. Dishes, pot and pans, and soap improved home food preparation and sanitation, resulting in better general health. Cheaper transportation made a wide variety of other goods available for the first time to many people who would otherwise never have been able to afford them.

The changes brought by the industrial revolution raised new fears and expectations among the people it affected. Traditional jobs and social positions were threatened as women took more wage-earning posts, and populations shifted from the farms to the cities. The landed gentry and aristocracy lost some prestige as enterprising inventors produced new goods and became wealthy enough to influence political decisions. On the other hand, the availability of new products and cheaper goods made possible better standards of living for people who were not wealthy. And the new interdependence between science and technology had already solved energy and health problems and promised to answer more.

QUESTIONS FOR DISCUSSION AND WRITING

[1] The author refers to one social effect of the industrial revolution as an "urban growth crisis." Considering the economic status of the new urban population, make inferences about actual living conditions in the growing cities.

[2] Summarize the causes of the industrial revolution: how can we account for the technological advances that characterize this period?

[3] The theories of Copernicus and Galileo and the industrial age both represent scientific "revolutions." Contrast the social and psychological effects of the two ages.

WRITING ASSIGNMENT: *Definition/Comparison Essay*

Like the eighteenth-century industrial revolution, the twentieth century as a result of scientific innovations has seen a "technological revolution." Using the essays you've read on AI, genetic engineering, and the atom bomb, derive a definition of "technological revolution" and then compare it to the industrial revolution. Focus on the social effects of each.

The following three readings treat Darwin's scientific theory of evolution and its effects on fields outside science, especially on politics. Read for the psychological and social effects of Darwin's theory as well as for the motives behind and threats posed by those people who made Social Darwinism a political tool or weapon.

_____

The following article, like the article on Copernicus and Galileo, comes from Russell's Religion and Science. *Russell explains Darwin's basic scientific theories and their religious, social, and psychological impact. Before Darwin's theory of evolution, most people took the Bible story of creation as a literal account of the world's origin. As recently as 1925, a teacher was convicted of a crime for teaching evolutionary theory in a Tennessee school; the incident is famous as the "Scopes monkey trial." Many people today still read the Bible literally. These "creationists" reject Darwin's theory absolutely. Darwin himself lived during the Victorian era (named for the rule of Queen Victoria) in England, an era characterized by conservative social views usually associated with the middle class. Russell's article describes the hostile reception that Darwin's ideas encountered.*

BERTRAND RUSSELL
"Evolution"

KEY CONCEPTS

When little government regulation of commerce exists, the system is called **LAISSEZ-FAIRE ECONOMICS**.

PROVIDENCE refers to the idea of Christian fate; see Chapter 2, page 124.

● The doctrine of the gradual evolution of plants and animals by descent and variation, which came into biology largely through geology, may be divided into three parts. There is first the fact, as certain as a fact about

SOURCE: "Evolution" in *Religion and Science* by Bertrand Russell (1935) by permission of Oxford University Press.

remote ages can hope to be, that the simpler forms of life are the older, and that those with a more complicated structure make their first appearance at a later state of the record. Second, there is the theory that the later and more highly organized forms did not arise spontaneously, but grew out of the earlier forms through a series of modifications; this is what is specially meant by "evolution" in biology. Third, there is the study, as yet far from complete, of the mechanism of evolution, i.e., of the causes of variation and of the survival of certain types at the expense of others. The general doctrine of evolution is now universally accepted among biologists, though there are still doubts as to its mechanism. The chief historical importance of Darwin lies in his having suggested a mechanism—natural selection—which made evolution seem more probable; but his suggestion, while still accepted as valid, is less completely satisfying to modern men of science than it was to his immediate successors.

Darwin's theory was essentially an extension to the animal and vegetable world of **laissez-faire economics**, and was suggested by Malthus's theory of population. All living things reproduce themselves so fast that the greater part of each generation must die without having reached the age to leave descendants. A female cod-fish lays about 9,000,000 eggs a year. If all came to maturity and produced other cod-fish, the sea would, in a few years, give place to solid cod, while the land would be covered by a new deluge.* Even human populations, though their rate of natural increase is slower than that of any other animals except elephants, have been known to double in twenty-five years. If this rate continued throughout the world for the next two centuries, the resulting population would amount to five hundred thousand millions. But we find, in fact, that animal and plant populations are, as a rule, roughly stationary; and the same has been true of human populations at most periods. There is therefore, both within each species and as between different species, a constant competition, in which the penalty of defeat is death. It follows that, if some members of a species differ from others in any way which gives them an advantage, they are more likely to survive. If the difference has been acquired, it will not be transmitted to their descendants, but if it is congenital* it is likely to reappear in at least a fair proportion of their posterity.* Lamarck thought that the giraffe's neck grew long as a result of stretching up to reach high branches, and that the results of this stretching were hereditary; the Darwinian view, at least as modified by Weismann, is that giraffes which, from birth, had a tendency to long necks, were less likely to starve than others, and therefore left more descendants, which, in turn, were likely to have long necks—some of them, probably, even longer necks than their already long-necked parents. In this way the giraffe would gradually develop its peculiarities until there was nothing to be gained by developing them further.

Darwin's theory depended upon the occurrence of chance variations, the causes of which, as he confessed, were unknown. It is an observed fact that the posterity of a given pair are not all alike. Domestic animals have

flood

from birth / descendants

been greatly changed by artificial selection: through the agency of man cows have come to yield more milk, race-horses to run faster, and sheep to yield more wool. Such facts afforded the most direct evidence available to Darwin of what selection could accomplish. It is true that breeders cannot turn a fish into a marsupial,* or a marsupial into a monkey; but changes as great as these might be expected to occur during the countless ages required by the geologists. There was, moreover, in many cases, evidence of common ancestry. Fossils showed that animals intermediate between widely separated species of the present had existed in the past; the pterodactyl, for example, was half bird, half reptile. Embryologists discovered that, in the course of development, immature animals repeat earlier forms; a mammalian fetus, at a certain stage, has the rudiments* of a fish's gills, which are totally useless, and hardly to be explained except as a recapitulation* of ancestral history. Many different lines of argument combined to persuade biologists both of the fact of evolution, and of natural selection as the chief agent by which it was brought about.

mammals having pouches

basic elements

summary

Darwinism was as severe a blow to theology as Copernicanism. Not only was it necessary to abandon the fixity of species and the many separate acts of creation which Genesis seemed to assert; not only was it necessary to assume a lapse of time, since the origin of life, which was shocking to the orthodox; not only was it necessary to abandon a host of arguments for the beneficence of **Providence**, derived from the exquisite adaptation of animals to their environment, which was now explained as the operation of natural selection—but, worse than any or all of these, the evolutionists ventured to affirm that man was descended from the lower animals. Theologians and uneducated people, indeed, fastened upon this one aspect of the theory. "Darwin says that men are descended from monkeys!" the world exclaimed in horror. It was popularly said that he believed this because he himself looked like a monkey (which he did not). When I was a boy, I had a tutor who said to me, with the utmost solemnity: "If you are a Darwinist, I pity you, for it is impossible to be a Darwinist and a Christian at the same time." To this day in Tennessee [1935], it is illegal to teach the doctrine of evolution, because it is considered to be contrary to the Word of God.

As often happens, the theologians were quicker to perceive the consequences of the new doctrine than were its advocates, most of whom, though convinced by the evidence, were religious men, and wished to retain as much as possible of their former beliefs. Progress, especially during the nineteenth century, was much facilitated by lack of logic in its advocates, which enabled them to get used to one change before having to accept another. When all the logical consequences of an innovation are presented simultaneously, the shock to habits is so great that men tend to reject the whole, whereas, if they had been invited to take one step every ten or twenty years, they could have been coaxed along the path of progress without much resistance. The great men of the nineteenth century were not revolutionaries, either intellectually or politically, though they were willing to champion a reform when the need for it became overwhelmingly evident. This cautious temper in innovators helped to make the nineteenth century notable for the extreme rapidity of its progress.

The theologians, however, saw what was involved more clearly than did the general public. They pointed out that men have immortal souls, which monkeys have not; that Christ died to save men, not monkeys; that men have a divinely implanted sense of right and wrong, whereas monkeys are guided solely by instinct. If men developed by imperceptible steps out of monkeys, at what moment did they suddenly acquire these theologically important characteristics? At the British Association in 1860 (the year after *The Origin of Species* appeared), Bishop Wilberforce thundered against Darwinism, exclaiming: "The principle of natural selection is absolutely incompatible with the word of God."

QUESTIONS FOR DISCUSSION AND WRITING

[1] Caryl Rivers in "Grave New World" states that "if human cloning were ever practiced on a wide scale it would drastically affect the course of human evolution." After reading about Darwin's theory, explain how cloning as the major human reproductive method would change the evolutionary process.

[2] Russell points out that "Darwinism was as severe a blow to theology as Copernicanism." Compare the threats each posed to Christianity.

[3] "Darwin says that men are descended from monkeys!" This reductive* restatement of Darwin's theory is still common today, especially among creationists. Explore possible reasons for such comments: make inferences about motives and about why some people find the monkey-man tie so offensive.

*grossly oversimplified

The writing assignment at the end of this section asks for a definition of Social Darwinism. Mark the text as you read for the doctrine's defining characteristics. Look particularly for the issues which make it a <u>social</u> theory, not a scientific one. If you keep the definition of "Darwinism" in mind as you read, you should be able to detect the ideas the Social Darwinists drew from Darwin's theory.

George E. Simpson's "Early Social Darwinism" (1959) explains the social and political repercussions of Darwin's theories, particularly his notion of "survival of the fittest." Social Darwinists believed that, by nature, the "best" humans rise to positions of power, in terms of wealth, status, and political control; Darwin himself intended no such interpretation. Social Darwinist theory was used to justify aggressive capitalism, colonialism, and imperialism. Rudyard Kipling, a British poet of the period, expressed a Social Darwinist sentiment when he wrote "That they should take who have the power / And they should keep who can." Following Simpson's article you'll find an excerpt

*from a speech by Adolf Hitler, the German National Socialist (Nazi) Party
leader during World War II. His views radically extended the implications of
Social Darwinism to actual racial extermination: the Nazis planned and carried
out the execution of six million European Jews, an atrocity known as the
"Holocaust."*

GEORGE E. SIMPSON
"Early Social Darwinism"

KEY CONCEPTS

COLONIAL EXPANSION means that one nation increases its political or
economic dominance over a subject nation. **IMPERIALISM** is a related
concept; in this case, the stronger nation acquires dominance over the
actual land of the subject nation.

A **NATURALISTIC** world view involves belief in observable physical
laws that determine biology and behavior.

EUGENICS is the study of human breeding, emphasizing continued
physical and mental improvement through genetic manipulation.

● The application of Darwin's principle of natural selection to human
society, with special emphasis on competition and struggle, became
known as "Social Darwinism." This doctrine, congenial to the intellectual
climate of the end of the nineteenth century, was endorsed by the advocates of unrestricted competition in private enterprise, the **colonial ex-
pansionists**, and the opponents of voluntary social change. Among others,
Ernest Haeckel provided scientific sanction for this point of view:

> The theory of selection teaches that in human life, as in animal and
> plant life, everywhere and at all times, only a small and chosen minority
> can exist and flourish, while the enormous majority starve and perish
> miserably and more or less prematurely. . . . The cruel and merciless
> struggle for existence which rages through living nature, and in the
> course of nature must rage, this unceasing and inexorable* competition   unstoppable
> of all living creatures is an incontestable fact; only the picked minority of
> the qualified fittest is in a position to resist it successfully, while the great
> majority of the competitors must necessarily perish miserably. We may
> profoundly lament this tragical state of things, but we can neither
> controvert* nor alter it. "Many are called, but few are chosen." This   disprove
> principle of selection is as far as possible from democratic, on the
> contrary it is aristocratic in the strictest sense of the word.

Herbert Spencer and William Graham Sumner were prominent in
advancing the doctrine of the social Darwinists. Despite differences in

SOURCE: "Early Social Darwinism" by George E. Simpson. First appeared in *The Antioch
Review*, Vol. XIX, No. 1 (Spring 1959). Copyright © 1959 by the Antioch Review, Inc.
Reprinted by permission of the editors.

their philosophies, both saw the poor as the "unfit." Because they are the result of the operations of the laws of evolution, they cannot be assisted and efforts to help them through legislation, public charity, and social reconstruction are evil. According to Spencer, "The whole effort of nature is to get rid of them, and make room for better . . . If they are sufficiently complete to live, they do live, and it is well they should live. If they are not sufficiently complete to live, they die, and it is best they should die."

Although Darwin pointed out that militarism and war occasion reverse selection by exposing the biologically soundest young men to early death or preventing them from marrying during the prime of life and, at the same time, by providing those with poorer constitutions with greater opportunity to marry and propagate* their kind, many of the social Darwinists praised war as a means of furthering social progress. An English scientist, Karl Pearson, wrote: "History shows me one way and one way only, in which a high state of civilization has been produced, namely the struggle of race with race, and the survival of the physically and mentally fitter race. If men want to know whether the lower races of man can evolve a higher type, I fear the only course is to leave them to fight it out among themselves."

breed

Nineteenth century **imperialists**, calling upon Darwinism in defense of the subjugation* of "backward" races, could point to *The Origin of Species* which had referred in its sub-title to *The Preservation of Favored Races in the Struggle for Life.* Darwin had been talking about pigeons but they saw no reason why his theories should not apply to men, and the whole spirit of the **naturalistic** world view seemed to call for a vigorous and unrelenting thoroughness in the application of biological concepts. Darwinian theory was utilized to justify the conflicts of rival empires, the ententes* and the alliances of the "balance of power." Bismarck in Germany, Chamberlain in England, and Theodore Roosevelt in the United States found in social Darwinism a sanction for their theories of force and expansion.

enslavement

agreements

Another aspect of social Darwinism at the turn of the century was the **eugenics** movement. Like other early social Darwinists, the eugenicists equated the "fit" with the upper classes and the "unfit" with the poor. Believing that disease, poverty, and crime are due largely to heredity, they warned against the high reproductive rates of the lower classes.

Social Darwinism in recent years

Adolf Hitler's racism and Nazism have been called perversions of Darwinism. Hitler's virulent* doctrines were the culmination of a half-century of social Darwinistic thinking in Germany. One of his most influential immediate predecessors was General Freidrich von Bernhardi, who said of the Germans that "no nation on the face of the globe is so able to grasp and appropriate all the elements of culture, to add to them from the stores of its own spiritual endowment, and to give back to mankind richer gifts than it received." Bernhardi glorified war as a biological necessity, as the

bitter, poisonous

greatest factor in the furtherance of culture and power, and claimed that the Germans could fulfill their great and urgent duty toward civilization only by the sword.

Hitler's doctrines are so well-known that extended reference to them here is unnecessary. According to *Mein Kampf,* the "Aryan" alone "furnishes the great building-stones and plans for all human progress." The Aryan had subjugated "lower races" and made them do his will, the Jew's "intellect is never constructive," "the mingling of blood . . . is the sole reason for the dying-out of old cultures," and hyperindividualism had cheated Germany of world domination and a peace "founded on the victorious sword of a lordly people. . . ." Hitlerism represents the most extreme variety of social Darwinism and the one which has had the most powerful effects on the destinies of modern peoples.

Conclusion

One hundred years after the publication of *The Origin of Species,* and eighty-eight years after the appearance of *The Descent of Man,* natural selection remains an important concept in biology, anthropology, sociology, even in international relations. Modern man is subject to selection, natural and artificial. If this were not so, all human genotypes would produce surviving children in the same ratio as the occurrence of these genotypes in existing populations. Today the adaptive value of co-operation is more widely acknowledged and the role of ruthless aggression as a factor in the evolution of man, society, and culture is given smaller significance. Social Darwinistic thinking has not disappeared, but increasingly the "nature, red in tooth and claw" version of natural selection is regarded as an outdated brand of Darwinism.

ADOLF HITLER
"Man Must Kill"

KEY CONCEPTS

Darwin theorized that **self-preservation** is the primary natural law; all species seek to maintain their individual existence at any cost. The **struggle for survival** is the process by which an animal (the human included) preserves itself, a process that often involves violence against other animals.

● If men wish to live, then they are forced to kill others. The entire struggle for survival is a conquest of the means of existence which in turn results in the elimination of others from these same sources of sub-

SOURCE: From *Hitler's Words* by Adolph Hitler. Edited by Gordon Prange. Washington, D.C.: American Council on Public Affairs.

sistence.* As long as there are peoples on this earth, there will be nations against nations and they will be forced to protect their vital rights in the same way as the individual is forced to protect his rights.   *basic survival*

There is in reality no distinction between peace and war. Life, no matter in what form, is a process which always leads to the same result. **Self-preservation** will always be the goal of every individual. Struggle is ever present and will remain. This signifies a constant willingness on the part of man to sacrifice to the utmost. Weapons, methods, instruments, formations, these may change, but in the end the **struggle for survival** remains.

One is either the hammer or the anvil.* We confess that it is our purpose to prepare the German people again for the role of the hammer. For ten years we have preached, and our deepest concern is: How can we again achieve power? We admit freely and openly that, if our Movement is victorious, we will be concerned day and night with the question of how to produce the armed forces which are forbidden us by the peace treaty. We solemnly confess that we consider everyone a scoundrel who does not try day and night to figure out a way to violate this treaty, for we have never recognized this treaty.   *metal stand used as a support for hammering*

We admit, therefore, that as far as we are concerned the German army in its present form is not permanent. For us it will serve only as a great cadre* army, that is, as a source of sergeants and officers. And in the meantime we will be continuously at work filling in the ranks. We will take every step which strengthens our arms, which augments* the number of our forces, and which increases the strength of our people.   *special corps*   *increases*

We confess further that we will dash* anyone to pieces who should dare to hinder us in this undertaking. . . . Our rights will never be represented by others. Our rights will be protected only when the German Reich* is again supported by the point of the German dagger.   *smash*   *state*

QUESTIONS FOR DISCUSSION AND WRITING

[1] Define Social Darwinism.

[2] Explain how Social Darwinism was useful to political groups like Nazis or imperialists. Make inferences about their motives for adapting the theory to their nationalistic causes.

[3] How might a poor person respond to the Social Darwinist notion that the poor are "unfit" and that "disease, poverty, and crime are due largely to heredity?" What threats does the doctrine pose for that person, and what social and psychological effects could it have on him or her?

[4] Compare and contrast the practice of Social Darwinism with that of AI and genetic engineering. Consider the possible goals, motives, and threats involved in all three, and come to some conclusion about the social acceptability of each.

[5] What major Darwinist theories does Hitler draw on to justify his political beliefs? How is his use of the theories contrary to Darwin's intentions?

WRITING ASSIGNMENT
Explain "Social Darwinism" as a political doctrine. What are its major teachings? Then examine Hitler's use of Darwin's ideas, comparing and/or contrasting his interpretations to those of the Social Darwinists. Can we consider Hitler an embodiment of or a deviation from Social Darwinism?

The next two articles you'll read give you an overview of Freud's psychological theories as well as some of their specific effects on twentieth-century thought. Read selectively for the impact of Freud's theories: why did they meet such resistance? How did they threaten the accepted image of human nature?

_____

The following textbook excerpt summarizes some of Sigmund Freud's psychological theories. Freud himself "made the comparison of psychoanalysis with Copernican and Darwinian theory in terms of the three historical blows which human narcissism has had to undergo: the cosmological blow administered by Copernicus, the biological blow administered by Darwin and his group, and the psychological blow administered by psychoanalysis."

JEROME KAGAN AND ERNEST HAVEMANN
"Psychoanalytic Theory"

● The most influential personality theory during the past half century has been "psychoanalytic theory," originally formulated by Sigmund Freud. Freud began his career in Vienna in the 1880s as a physician and neurologist. He became interested in psychological processes as the result of his experiences with patients who were suffering from hysteria—that is, from paralysis of the legs or arms that seemed to have no physical cause. His final theories represent a lifetime of treating and observing many kinds of neurotic patients and also of attempting to analyze the unconscious aspects of his own personality.

When Freud introduced his ideas around the turn of the century, they were bitterly attacked. Many people were repelled by his notion that man, far from being a rational animal, is largely at the mercy of his irrational unconscious thoughts. Many were shocked by Freud's emphasis on the role of sexual impulses and particularly by his insistence that young children have intense sexual motives. Over the years, however, the furor has died down. There is considerable controversy over the value of psychoanalytic methods in treating neurotic* patients, but even those who criticize psychoanalysis as a form of therapy accept some of Freud's basic notions about personality and its formation.

showing slight maladjustment

Freud's most influential ideas concerned concepts central to the study of psychology. One of them was the role of anxiety. Freud was a pioneer in emphasizing the importance of anxiety, which he believed to be the central problem in mental disturbance. Another was repression and the other defense mechanisms. Freud believed that these mechanisms, and especially the process of repression,* are frequently used to eliminate from conscious awareness any motive or thought that threatens to cause anxiety. Another influential idea was his concept of the unconscious mind, composed in part of repressed motives and thoughts. Freud was the first to suggest the now widely held theory that the human mind and personality are like an iceberg, with only a small part visible and the great bulk submerged and concealed. All of us, he maintained, have many unconscious motives of which we are never aware but which nonetheless influence our behavior. An example is the case of a man who sincerely believes that he has no hostile motives, yet who in subtle ways performs many acts of aggression against his wife, his children, and his business associates.

blocking out upsetting thoughts

The core of the unconscious mind, according to Freud, is the "id," composed of raw, primitive, inborn forces that constantly struggle for gratification. Even the baby in his crib, Freud said, is swayed by two powerful drives. One is what he called the "libido," embracing sexual urges and such related desires as to be kept warm, well-fed, and comfortable. The other is aggression—the urge to fight, dominate, and where necessary destroy.

The id operates on what Freud called the "pleasure principle," insisting on immediate and total gratification of all its demands. Freud felt, for example, that the baby—though unable to think as yet like a human being and thus more like a little animal—wants to satisfy his libido by possessing completely everything he desires and loves and to satisfy his aggressive urges by destroying everything that gets in his way. As the child grows up, he learns to control the demands of the id, at least in part. But the id remains active and powerful throughout life; it is indeed the sole source of all the psychic energy put to use in behaving and thinking. It is unconscious and we are not aware of its workings, but it continues to struggle for the relief of all its tensions.

The conscious, logical part of the mind that develops as the child grows up was called by Freud the ego—the "real" us, as we like to think of ourselves. In contrast to the id, the ego operates on the "reality principle"; it tries to mediate between the demands of the id and the realities of the environment. Deriving its energies from the id, the ego perceives what is going on in the environment and develops the operational responses (such as finding food) necessary to satisfy the demands of the id. The ego does our logical thinking; it does the best it can to help us lead sane and satisfactory lives. To the extent that the primitive drives of the id can be satisfied without getting us into danger or harm, the ego permits them satisfaction. But when the drives threaten to get us jailed as a thief or rejected by society as a brawler and a rake,* the ego represses them or attempts to satisfy them with substitutes that are socially acceptable.

wild liver

In the ego's constant struggle to satisfy the demands of the id without permitting the demands to destroy us, it has a strong but troublesome ally in the third part of the mind as conceived by Freud—the "superego." In a sense the superego is our conscience, our sense of right and wrong. It is partly acquired by adopting the notions of right and wrong that we are taught by society from the earliest years. However, Freud's concept of the superego represents a much stronger and more dynamic notion than the word "conscience" implies. Much like the id, the superego is mostly unconscious, maintaining a far greater influence over our behavior than we realize. It is largely acquired as a result of that famous process that Freud called the "Oedipus complex," which can be summarized as follows.

According to Freud, every child between the ages of about two and a half through six is embroiled* in a conflict of mingled affection and resentment for his parents. The child has learned that the outer world exists and that there are other people in it, and the id's demands for love and affection reach out insatiably toward the person he has been closest to—the mother. Although the child has only the haziest notion of sexual feelings, he wants to possess his mother totally and to take the place of his father with her. But his anger against his father, the rival with whom he must share her, makes him fearful that his father will somehow retaliate against his mother—so that he becomes overwhelmed with strong feelings of mingled love, anger, and fear toward both parents at once.

caught up

The Oedipus conflict must somehow be resolved; the way this is done, according to Freud, is through identification with the parents. The child ends his mingled love and hate for his parents by becoming like them, by convincing himself that he shares their strength and authority and the affection they have for each other. The parents' moral judgments, or what the child conceives to be their moral judgments, become his superego. This helps him hold down the drives of the id, which have caused him such intense discomfort during the Oedipal period. But, forever after, the superego tends to oppose the ego. As his parents once did, the superego punishes him or threatens to punish him for his transgressions.* And, since its standards were rigidly set in childhood, its notions of crime and guilt are likely to be completely illogical and unduly harsh.

misbehavior

In their own way the demands of the superego are just as insatiable as the id's blind drives. Its standards of right and wrong and its rules for punishment are far more rigid, relentless, and vengeful than anything in our conscious minds. Formed at a time when the child was unable to distinguish between a "bad" wish and a "bad" deed, the superego may sternly disapprove of the merest thought of some transgression—the explanation, according to Freud, of the fact that some people who have never actually committed a "bad" deed nonetheless feel guilty all their lives.

The three parts of the human personality are in frequent conflict. One of the important results of the conflict is anxiety, which is produced in the ego whenever the demands of the id threaten danger or when the superego threatens disapproval or punishment. Anxiety, though unpleasant, is a tool that the ego uses to fight the impulses or thoughts that have aroused it. In one way or another—by using repression and the other defense mechanisms, by turning the mind's attention elsewhere, by gratifying some other impulse of the id—the ego defends itself against the threat from the id or superego and gets rid of the anxiety.

In a sense the conscious ego is engaged in a constant struggle to satisfy the insatiable demands of the unconscious id without incurring the wrath and vengeance of the largely unconscious superego. To the extent that a person's behavior is controlled by the ego, it is sensible and generally satisfying. To the extent that it is governed by the childish passions of the id and the unrelenting demands of the superego, it tends to be foolish, unrewarding, painful, and neurotic.

If the ego is not strong enough to check the id's drives, a person is likely to be a selfish and hot-headed menace to society. But if the id is checked too severely, other problems may arise. Too much repression of the libido can make a person unable to enjoy a normal sex life or to give and take competition. Too strong a superego may result in vague and unwarranted feelings of guilt and unworthiness, and sometimes in an unconscious need for self-punishment.

There can be little question that Freud was an important innovator who had a number of most useful insights into the human personality. He was the first to recognize the role of the unconscious and the importance of anxiety and defenses as a factor in personality. He also dispelled the myth, widely accepted before his time, that children do not have the sexual urges and hostile impulses that characterize adults.

One criticism of Freud is that he may have overemphasized the role of sexual motivation in personality. In Freud's nineteenth and early twentieth century Vienna, with its strict sexual standards, it is perhaps only natural that many of his neurotic patients should have had conflicts and guilt feelings centering around their sexual desires. In today's Western world, with its more permissive attitudes toward sexual behavior, this kind of conflict and guilt seems to be less frequent. Yet people continue to have personality problems and the incidence of serious mental disturbance seems to remain about the same as ever. This would indicate that conflicts over sexuality cannot be the sole or perhaps even the most important cause of personality disturbances. Another frequent criticism of Freud is that many of his ideas about the dynamics of human behavior can be explained more economically without using his concepts of the id, ego, and superego.

The fact that Alfred Kazin, who is a professor of English, has written an article on Freud and psychoanalysis suggests the extent of Freud's influence in fields outside of science. Almost any human endeavor is open to Freudian interpretation because Freud's theories of mind and behavior can be seen as intrinsically part of all human thought and action. Before Freud, psychologists sought to explain mental functions physically or philosophically; the pre-Freudian Western world had no notion of the unconscious mind.

ALFRED KAZIN
"The Freudian Revolution Analyzed"

KEY CONCEPTS

A **determinist** believes that biology or psychology, not free will, directs behavior.

Positivism is a philosophy of science which states that we can observe and understand physical laws and apply them to human nature and behavior, both to explain and predict them.

● It is hard to believe that Sigmund Freud was born over a century ago. Although Freud has long been a household name (and, in fact, dominates many a household one could mention), his theories still seem too "advanced," they touch too bluntly on the most intimate side of human relations, for us to picture Freud himself coming out of a world that in all other respects now seems so quaint.

Freud's influence, which started from the growing skepticism about civilization and morality after the First World War, is now beyond description. Freudianism gave sanction to the increasing exasperation with public standards as opposed to private feelings; it upheld the truths of human nature as against the hypocrisies and cruelties of conventional morality; it stressed the enormous role that sex plays in man's imaginative life, in his relations to his parents, in the symbolism of language.

It is impossible to think of the greatest names in modern literature and art—Thomas Mann, James Joyce, Franz Kafka, T. S. Eliot, Ernest Hemingway, William Faulkner, Pablo Picasso, Paul Klee—without realizing our debt to Freud's exploration of dreams, myths, symbols and the imaginative profundity of man's inner life. Even those who believe that original sin is a safer guide to the nature of man than any other can find support in Freud's gloomy doubts about man's capacity for progress. For quite other

SOURCE: "The Freudian Revolution Analyzed" by Alfred Kazin from *Freud and the Twentieth Century.* Edited by Benjamin Nelson, The World Publishing Company.

reasons, Freud has found followers, even among Catholic psychiatrists, who believe that Freud offers a believable explanation of neurosis and a possible cure, and so leaves the sufferer cured to practice his faith in a rational way.

Many psychologists who disagree with Freud's own materialism have gratefully adopted many of Freud's diagnoses, and although he himself was chary* about the psychoanalytical technique in serious mental illness,   cautious more and more psychiatrists now follow his technique, or some adaptation of it. For no other system of thought in modern times, except the great religions, has been adopted by so many people as a systematic interpretation of individual behavior. Consequently, to those who have no other belief, Freudianism sometimes serves as a philosophy of life.

Freud's extraordinary achievement was to show us, in scientific terms, the primacy* of natural desire, the secret wishes we proclaim in our   central role dreams, the mixture of love and shame and jealousy in our relations to our parents, the child as father to the man, the deeply buried instincts that make us natural beings and that go back to the forgotten struggles of the human race. Until Freud, novelists and dramatists had never dared to think that science would back up their belief that personal passion is a stronger force in people's lives than socially accepted morality. Thanks to Freud, these insights now form a widely shared body of knowledge.

In short, Freud had the ability, such as is given to very few individuals, to introduce a wholly new factor into human knowledge; to impress it upon people's minds as something for which there was evidence. He revealed a part of reality that many people before him had guessed at, but which no one before him was able to describe as systematically and convincingly as he did. In the same way that one associates the discovery of certain fundamentals with Copernicus, Newton, Darwin, Einstein, so one identifies many of one's deepest motivations with Freud. His name is no longer the name of a man; like "Darwin," it is now synonymous with a part of nature.

No one can count the number of people who now think of any crisis as a personal failure, and who turn to a psychoanalyst or to psychoanalytical literature for an explanation of their suffering where once they would have turned to a minister or to the Bible for consolation. Freudian terms are now part of our thought.

For much of this "Freudian" revolution, Freud himself is not responsible. And in evaluating the general effect of Freud's doctrines on the modern scene, especially in America, it is important to distinguish between the hard, biological, fundamentally classical thought of Freud, who was a **determinist**, a pessimist, and a genius, from the thousands of little cultural symptoms and "psychological" theories, the pretensions and self-indulgences, which are often found these days in the prosperous middle-class culture that has responded most enthusiastically to Freud.

There is, for example, the increasing tendency to think that all problems are "psychological," to ignore the real conflicts in society that underlie politics and to interpret politicians and candidates—especially those you don't like—in terms of "sexual" motives. There is the cunning use of "Freudian" terms in advertising, which has gone so far that nowadays there's a pretty clear suggestion that the girl comes with the car. There are all the psychologists who study "motivations," and sometimes invent them, so as to get you to buy two boxes of cereal where one would have done before.

On the other hand, the greatest and most beautiful effect of Freudianism is the increasing awareness of childhood as the most important single influence on personal development. This profound cherishing of childhood has opened up wholly new relationships between husbands and wives, as well as between parents and children, and it represents—though often absurdly overanxious—a peculiar new tenderness in modern life. Similarly, though Freud's psychology is weakest on women, there can be no doubt that, again in America, the increasing acknowledgement of the importance of sexual satisfaction has given to women an increasing sense of their individual dignity and their specific needs.

But the greatest revolution of all, and one that really explains the overwhelming success of Freudianism in America, lies in the general insistence on individual fulfillment, satisfaction and happiness. Odd as it may seem to us, who take our striving toward these things for granted, the insistence on personal happiness represents the most revolutionary force in modern times. And it is precisely because our own tradition works toward individual self-realization, because private happiness does seem to us to be both an important ideal and a practical goal, that Freudianism has found so many recruits in this country.

Freud himself made his initial effect in the most traditional, the most rational, the most human kind of way; he wrote books; he presented evidence; he made claims and gave proofs. People read and believed. Many more did not read, and most of those who read Freud's first great work, *The Interpretation of Dreams,* did not believe any of it. But, after all, very few books ever have a decisive effect on the world. In Freud's case, what counts is that some of the people who read were so stirred that they went on to change other minds.

Freud's work appealed to the increasing regard for individual experience that is one of the great themes of modern literature and art. The sensitiveness to each individual as a significant register of the consciousness in general, the artistic interest in carrying human consciousness to its farthest limits—it was this essential side of modern art that Freud's researches encouraged and deepened. He brought, as it were, the authority of science to the inner prompting of art, and thus helped writers and artists to feel that their interest in myths, in symbols, in dreams was on the side of "reality," of science, itself, when it shows the fabulousness of the natural world.

Now, if we look back for a moment, the impact of these theories seems all the more remarkable in view of the natural human tendency to suspect, to limit and to derogate sexual experience. What Freud proclaimed above all else was that "nature," which is nearest to us in the erotic side of man, and which culture and society are always pushing away as unworthy of man's "higher" nature, has constantly to be brought into man's awareness. Freud saw in man's sexual instinct a force of profound natural urgency, a whole system of energies, which could be repressed and forgotten and pushed back into the unconsciousness only at the cost of unnecessary strain and even of self-destructiveness.

Yet far from preaching "sexuality" itself at any cost, Freud admitted that "civilization" requires the repression or at least the adaptation of sexuality. Civilization as we know it, Freud said, had been built up on man's heroic sacrifice of instinct. Only, Freud issued the warning that more and more men would resent this sacrifice, would wonder if civilization was worth the price. And how profoundly right he was in this can be seen not only in the Nazi madness that drove him as an old man out of Vienna, that almost cost him his life, but in the increasing disdain for culture, in the secret lawlessness that has become, under the conformist surface, a sign of increasing personal irritation and rebelliousness in our society. More and more, the sexual freedom of our time seems to be a way of mentally getting even, of confused protest, and not the pagan enjoyment of instinct that writers like D. H. Lawrence upheld against Freud's gloomy forebodings.

For Freud the continuous sacrifice of "nature" that is demanded by "civilization" meant that it was only through rationality and conscious awareness that maturity could be achieved. Far from counseling license, his most famous formula became—"Where id was, ego shall be"—the id representing the unconscious, the ego our dominant and purposive sense of ourselves. However, consciousness meant for Freud an unyielding insistence on the importance of sexuality. And it was just on this issue that, even before the first World War, his movement broke apart.

Jung went astray, as Freud thought, because he was lulled by the "mystical" side of religion; Adler, through his insistence that not sex but power feelings were primary. Later, Harry Stack Sullivan and Erich Fromm tended to emphasize, as against sex, the importance of personal relatedness to others, and nowadays many psychoanalysts tend to value religion much more highly than Freud ever could. But the root of the dissidence* was always Freud's forthright insistence on the importance of sexuality and his old-fashioned, mid-nineteenth-century **positivism**. For Freud always emphasized the organic and the physical rather than the social and the "cultural."

disagreement, rebellion

Perhaps it is because Freud was born a century ago that he had the old-fashioned belief that nothing—not even a lot of patients—is so important as carrying your ideas beyond the point at which everybody already agrees with you. Nowadays everybody is something of a Freudian, and to many Freudians, the truth is in their keeping, the system is complete. But

what mattered most to Freud was relentlessly* carrying on the revolution   unendingly, steadily
of human thought.

QUESTIONS FOR DISCUSSION AND WRITING

[1] Why is the impact of Freud's theories considered to be of equal
importance to that of Copernicus and Darwin?

[2] Kazin calls Freud a pessimist. Which of his theories suggest a pessimistic
or negative attitude toward human nature? How do those theories threaten
the ideal image of human nature?

[3] Freudianism insists on "individual fulfillment, satisfaction, and
happiness," according to Kazin. How did Freud's theories promote our
contemporary view of the individual as a unique entity, and why might this
view be criticized as a selfish and immoral one?

[4] Kazin states that Freudian theory has powerfully influenced art and
literature. Explain why and how his ideas might affect the creation of art.

WRITING ASSIGNMENT
Religious thinkers like Tertullian seem to define human nature negatively,
suspecting human motives and drives. Other religious views, like those of
the New Testament and Martin Luther, are more tolerant and positive.
Compare and contrast the Christian view of human nature with Freud's
theories of the human mind and behavior. Which is ultimately the harsher
view?

CHAPTER 3 ESSAY ASSIGNMENTS
[1] Summarize the predominant motives you've isolated in the scientific
discoveries and innovations covered in the chapter readings. Overall, do
these motives show science to be mainly a humanistic* endeavor? Consider   concerned with liberal
the role of ego, quest for knowledge, desire for power, and so on.   learning

[2] Compare and contrast twentieth-century fears about science and its
products with fears experienced in earlier centuries. Is the twentieth century
more enlightened and tolerant an age than ages past?

[3] According to one common philosophical view of contemporary society,
many individuals feel alienated from their social and physical surroundings.
In what ways may science over the centuries have caused or contributed to
the sense of loneliness, anxiety, and estrangement* that characterizes   separation
alienation?

Edward Hopper, *Nighthawks,* 1942. Oil on canvas, 33⅛ × 60 in. Courtesy of The Art Institute of Chicago, Friends of American Art Collection.

Edward Hopper, *Room in Brooklyn.* Oil on canvas, 29 × 34 in. (73.6 × 86.3 cm.) Copyright © 1985. All rights reserved. Museum of Fine Arts, Boston, Charles Henry Hayden Fund.

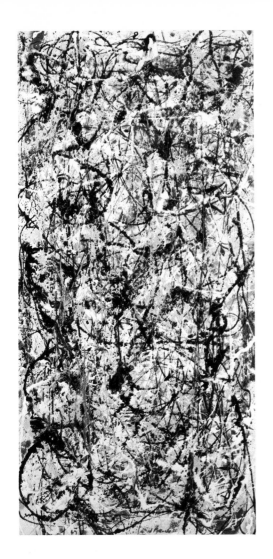

Jackson Pollack (Amer. 1912–1956), *Cathedral,* 1947.
Enamel and aluminum paint on canvas, 71½ × 35¹/₁₆ in.
(l m. 81 cm. × 89 cm. 1 mm.) Dallas Museum of Art, gift of
Mr. and Mrs. Bernard J. Reis.

Jackson Pollock, *Blue Poles.* Courtesy of the Australian
Consulate.

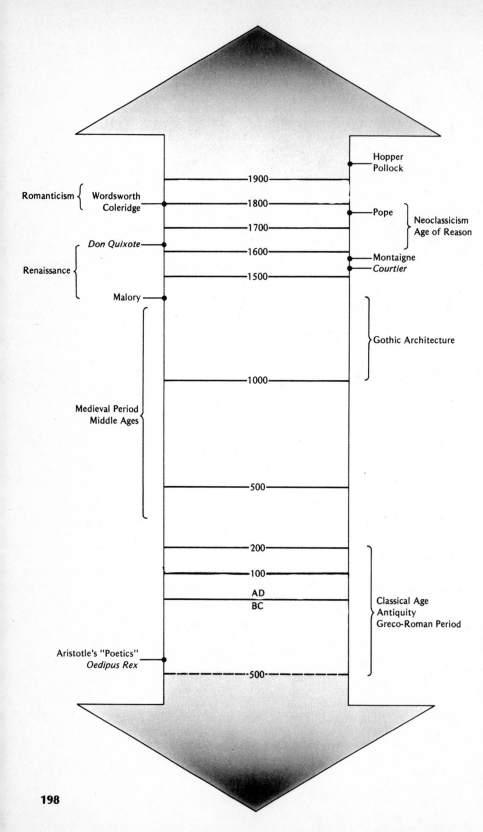

Hopper
Pollock

Romanticism { Wordsworth
Coleridge

1900

1800

Pope

Neoclassicism
Age of Reason

1700

Don Quixote

1600

Montaigne
Courtier

Renaissance {

1500

Malory

Gothic Architecture

1000

Medieval Period
Middle Ages

500

200

100

AD
BC

Classical Age
Antiquity
Greco-Roman Period

Aristotle's "Poetics"
Oedipus Rex

500

Like science, Western art has felt the strong influence of religion. Until the Renaissance, art often served religious purposes, but then it was increasingly used to promote scientific thought as well, which sometimes contradicted religious doctrine.

Include the following historical figures and events in religion and science on this time line to get a sense of how religion, science, and art developed in relationship and reaction to each other.

rise of Christianity
birth of Mohammed
Voltaire
Industrial Revolution
Darwinism
Freud

CHAPTER 4

Forms and Ideas in Art

INTRODUCTION

Art has served many functions in our culture; it's been used for religious purposes, political ends, and simple entertainment. In this chapter we present selected works of art as historical documents, as aesthetic wholes in themselves, and also as social indicators or cultural symbols that both reflect and influence culture. Viewing art as historical document suggests that all works of art may be studied as texts, whether verbal or visual. But to be able to read and understand these documents, you have to be able to decode their signs and symbols.

This chapter covers several different art forms: drama, architecture, prose, poetry, and painting. Performing arts, like music and dance, although not represented here, also can be "read" as texts that tell a story, create a scene or mood, or simply express an artist's ideas or emotions. Such expression usually contains a thesis, an organizational plan, and illustration, equivalent to an essay's elements.

Sophocles' Oedipus Rex stands as one of the most enduring literary and psychological documents of Western culture. Its themes appear in psychological, anthropological, and philosophical studies. As literature, it has been taken as a model tragedy, and as such it has influenced dramatic construction through the modern age. Aristotle refers to Oedipus Rex in his Poetics to illustrate his dramatic principles, which were taken as the "rules" of literary creation at least into the eighteenth century. In the twentieth century, Freud used the story of Oedipus to name what he argued was a universal psychological experience, the Oedipal stage of sexual development. His essay explaining this theory is included here.

Two essays on medieval art (Bernard S. Myers, "The Rise of Gothic Art" and Emile Male, an excerpt from The Gothic Image*) show Gothic architecture and painting to be complex religious, social, and aesthetic texts. The art of the time conformed to a unified symbolic code and manner of expression; a cathedral's mass, ornament, structure, and spatial design were intended specifically to express the individual's relationship to God.*

Texts from different historical periods reflect a culture's changing tastes and beliefs. "Sir Lancelot du Lake," an excerpt from Sir Thomas Malory's Le Morte D'Arthur, *typifies the late medieval idealization of chivalry as Malory reworks the Arthurian legends. A later work, Cervantes'* Don Quixote, *also uses chivalry as its material, but it treats the topic satirically.*

Artistic expression isn't confined to concrete works of art, like paintings, sculptures, literary works, or architecture. Castiglione in The Book of the Courtier *and Montaigne in "Of Not Communicating One's Glory" write about personal style, and in their essays they show how ideals of behavior also reflect an age's aesthetic values. Castiglione's glorification of the highly stylized Renaissance courtier contrasts with Montaigne's seventeenth-century skeptical approach to manners and mores.**   essential customs and laws

Eighteenth- and nineteenth-century English poetry shows a dramatic shift in aesthetic values and world view. The three poems included here document a change from a neoclassical, mechanistic world view to one emphasizing subjective truth and organic change. Alexander Pope in An Essay on Man *epitomizes the neoclassic mechanist in a world where "whatever is, is right." The Romantics William Wordsworth and Samuel Taylor Coleridge in "The Solitary Reaper" and "Kubla Khan," respectively, look to nature and imagination to create individual visions of the world. Essays by George Sherburn and C. M. Bowra ("Alexander Pope" and "The Romantic Imagination," respectively) outline the aesthetics of these two very different literary times.*

Our own contemporary art, often abstract and subjective, sometimes confounds and perplexes the untrained audience. Ladd Terry in "Modern Art in Transition" traces the historical roots of the modernist movement, describing its major innovations in design and material. He argues that modern artists share common aesthetic values despite the split of abstract and representational painting and sculpture, illustrated here by the paintings of Jackson Pollock and Edward Hopper (see Color Plate).

READING AND WRITING SKILLS OF CHAPTER 4

This chapter presents the following reading/writing skills:

Developing a reading strategy
The graphic organizer
Marking the text II

Some Greek Roots: Drama

READING SKILL: *Developing A Reading Strategy*

You've practiced the following reading skills:

Surveying the text
Paraphrasing
Critical reading
Defining terms
Identifying topic sentences
Locating the author's thesis
Writing a summary
Locating an implied thesis
Detecting bias or assumptions
Marking the text
Deriving definitions
Understanding analogies
Reading selectively
Drawing inferences

Developing an effective strategy in any given situation depends on your knowing two things: what your purpose or goal is, and what materials are available for your use. In reading, the purpose or goal is completing your assignment, and the material is your text. Usually, your assignment will, or should, dictate the strategies you need to use. For example, if you're asked to summarize a text, your strategies might include finding a thesis, identifying topic sentences, paraphrasing main ideas, and marking the text. In the last chapter you were asked to read for three specific chapter themes. A good strategy for that assignment might be to use the previously mentioned skills plus the skills of reading selectively and drawing inferences. Developing a strategy means matching skills to task instead of reading haphazardly, without a purpose. You should begin actually reading an assignment only after you've developed a strategy for both approaching and completing it.

Once you've clarified your assignment, you should always draw on your surveying skills. Surveying is one skill that's essential to every assignment. Once you've surveyed a text, you're ready to choose those reading techniques that will help you the most. The second essential skill which you should use every time you read is engaging the text, or reading critically: questioning both the text and your understanding of it.

READING SKILL: *The Graphic Organizer*

The title of the following text should be familiar, for you've already read the Oedipus myth in Chapter 1. You may want to review the events and themes of the myth as part of your survey. You may also want to look at the questions at the end of the play to see if they help you focus your reading. You'll notice that this reading differs in at least two essential ways from the others you've encountered. First, it's a play, a dramatic work, and second, it's considerably longer than anything you've read so far in this book. Your reading strategy will have to take these differences into consideration.

You could begin developing your reading strategy by first thinking about the reading techniques that seem most useful for a long, nonexpository work. Works that are not expository — plays, poems, short stories, and novels, for example — usually have no explicit thesis, nor do they have paragraph topic ideas, if indeed they are even organized into paragraphs. But such works still have an implied thesis, which you must be able to identify. Thus, you'll need to apply your skill in stating an implied thesis (see pages 00).

In a literary text, locating an implied thesis involves reading critically for plot, character, and theme. The "plot" is what actually happens in the work. Simply put, it's the action of the story. The plot consists of a series of related events that create a kind of tension, or conflict of opposites. The plot usually moves toward a climax, the point of highest interest in the work, and perhaps the part that evokes the reader's most intense emotional feeling or reaction. A "dénouement" usually follows the climax. "Dénouement" is the French word for untying or unknotting. In literature it is the outcome of the story.

According to Aristotle, character is less central to a drama than plot. He doesn't mean that characters are unimportant. Instead, he means that plot, or action, reveals and changes character. The plot reveals the characters' motives, concerns, and true nature.

The theme is the main idea of the work. It is an abstract concept that is depicted through plot and character. Examples of specific themes might be vengeance, the conflict of materialism versus idealism, devotion to God, friendship, and so on. In *Oedipus Rex,* the themes include vengeance and self-knowledge. Remember that most works have multiple themes.

How will you keep all of this information organized? You can summarize the play's events, but because a play has no paragraphs or topic ideas, you'll have to adapt your usual summary technique. In your survey you should have noticed that the play is divided into a prologue and four scenes. Try using these formal divisions as a guide to organizing your summary.

Because plot summaries outline concrete information, you can easily depict them by sketching them out, representing them visually in a "graphic organizer." When you read, using a graphic organizer can help you to plot out, clarify, and retain information from any of the arts and sciences. When you read literature, a graphic organizer helps you to keep track of a work's sequential events and character relationships. In this way you can clarify how the plot develops, what happens as a result of some earlier cause, and how characters react to changing events.

To pick out significant plot events and character development, you may want first to read a section of the work and take notes on what happens and then go back over your notes checking for causal relationships (what event brought about some new event, and how the main characters responded). Graph these significant events and changes to show their logical connection. If you're pressed for time, you could just graph the story as you read, rather than going over your notes and then doing the graphic organizer. Adapt these suggestions into a system that is simple and works for you.

In the Prologue and Scene I of *Oedipus Rex,* the events could be represented as we have done below. Keep this diagram with you as you read the first section of the play so that you can check your sense of what's happening against our graph. Complete the organizer as you read the rest of the play, adapting the chart's form to your own style as you wish.

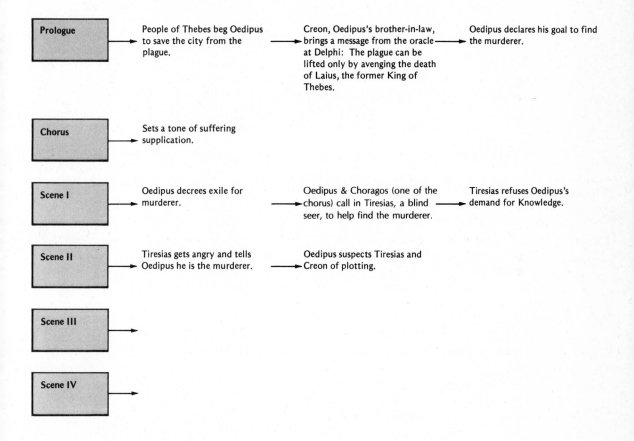

Prologue → People of Thebes beg Oedipus to save the city from the plague. → Creon, Oedipus's brother-in-law, brings a message from the oracle at Delphi: The plague can be lifted only by avenging the death of Laius, the former King of Thebes. → Oedipus declares his goal to find the murderer.

Chorus → Sets a tone of suffering supplication.

Scene I → Oedipus decrees exile for murderer. → Oedipus & Choragos (one of the chorus) call in Tiresias, a blind seer, to help find the murderer. → Tiresias refuses Oedipus's demand for Knowledge.

Scene II → Tiresias gets angry and tells Oedipus he is the murderer. → Oedipus suspects Tiresias and Creon of plotting.

Scene III →

Scene IV →

Sophocles wrote Oedipus Rex *in 429 B.C., and like most ancient tragedians, he drew his literary material from mythology and presented his drama as popular entertainment at religious festivals. Aristotle cited* Oedipus Rex *as the ideal dramatic construction because it had a clear main plot and its hero* *underwent a reversal of his fortunes from good to bad. The play set the literary standards for Renaissance and neoclassical Europe. Voltaire wrote a tragedy based on the Oedipus myth in the eighteenth century, and many other authors have treated the material as well, in various genres.* Sophocles' play continues to be popular with contemporary audiences.*

forms of literary art

SOPHOCLES
Oedipus Rex

KEY CONCEPTS

REVELATION means direct communication from a god.

An **ORACLE** names either the place devoted to divine revelation, or a god's mouthpiece, usually a priest or priestess, or an actual revelation.

An **EXILE** is a criminal or "persona non grata" — an unwanted person — who has been punished by ejection from his or her community or country.

VENGEANCE, or "to take revenge," means claiming retribution for some wrong suffered.

DIVINATION is the art of telling the future from signs in natural phenomena or dreams.

According to the ancient Greek moral code, when one has committed an offense against a god, nature, or the moral code, one is in a state of **POLLUTION.**

STATESMANSHIP refers to the handling of political affairs; a statesman is a leader or diplomat.

REGICIDE means murdering a king.

The word **POLICY** is sometimes used to name behavior that is shrewd, manipulative, or has some ulterior purpose, usually a political one.

ANARCHY is a state of political chaos.

A **TYRANT** maintains absolute power.

Someone who shows irreverence for the gods is guilty of the sin of **BLASPHEMY.**

The Greek notion of **FATE** means that the gods have predestined the course of a person's life.

The word **PRIMAL** refers to an origin or archetypal experience.

Sexual relations between close relatives is called **INCEST.**

A **PARRICIDE** is a person who has killed his father, mother, or other close relative.

To **PURGE** oneself is to cleanse oneself of sin or disease.

PERSONS REPRESENTED:

OEDIPUS	MESSENGER
A PRIEST	SHEPHERD OF LAIOS
CREON	SECOND MESSENGER
TEIRESIAS	CHORUS OF THEBAN ELDERS
IOCASTE	

THE SCENE: *Before the palace of Oedipus, King of Thebes. A central door and two lateral doors open onto a platform which runs the length of the façade. On the platform, right and left, are altars; and three steps lead down into the "orchestra," or chorus-ground. At the beginning of the action these steps are crowded by suppliants** who have brought   people seeking favors *branches and chaplets* of olive leaves and who lie in various attitudes*   garlands; wreaths *of despair.* OEDIPUS *enters.*

Prologue

OEDIPUS: My children, generations of the living
  In the line of Kadmos, nursed at his ancient hearth:*   fireplace
  Why have you strewn yourselves before these altars
  In supplication,* with your boughs and garlands?*   favor-seeking / wreaths
  The breath of incense rises from the city
  With a sound of prayer and lamentation.
                             Children,
  I would not have you speak through messengers,
  And therefore I have come myself to hear you —
  I, Oedipus, who bear the famous name.

                                      [*To a* PRIEST:

  You, there, since you are eldest in the company,
  Speak for them all, tell me what preys upon you,
  Whether you come in dread, or crave some blessing:
  Tell me, and never doubt that I will help you
  In every way I can; I should be heartless
  Were I not moved to find you suppliant here.
PRIEST: Great Oedipus, O powerful King of Thebes!
  You see how all the ages of our people
  Cling to your altar steps: here are boys
  Who can barely stand alone, and here are priests
  By weight of age, as I am a priest of God,
  And young men chosen from those yet unmarried;
  As for the others, all that multitude,

SOURCE: *The Oedipus Rex of Sophocles.* An English version by Dudley Fitts and Robert Fitzgerald. Copyright © 1949 by Harcourt Brace Jovanovich, Inc.; renewed 1977 by Cornelia Fitts and Robert Fitzgerald. Reprinted by permission of the publisher.

They wait with olive chaplets in the squares,
At the two shrines of Pallas, and where Apollo
Speaks in the glowing embers.
　　　　　　　　　　　　Your own eyes
Must tell you: Thebes is tossed on a murdering sea
And can not lift her head from the death surge.
A rust consumes the buds and fruits of the earth;
The herds are sick; children die unborn,
And labor is vain. The god of plague and pyre*　　　　　　cremation site
Raids like detestable lightning through the city,
And all the house of Kadmos is laid waste,
All emptied, and all darkened: Death alone
Battens* upon the misery of Thebes.　　　　　　　　　　clings to

You are not one of the immortal gods, we know;
Yet we have come to you to make our prayer
As to the man surest in mortal ways
And wisest in the ways of God. You saved us
From the Sphinx, that flinty singer, and the tribute
We paid to her so long; yet you were never
Better informed than we, nor could we teach you:
It was some god breathed in you to set us free.

Therefore, O mighty King, we turn to you:
Find us our safety, find us a remedy,
Whether by counsel of the gods or men.
A king of wisdom tested in the past
Can act in a time of troubles, and act well.
Noblest of men, restore
Life to your city! Think how all men call you
Liberator for your triumph long ago;
Ah, when your years of kingship are remembered,
Let them not say *We rose, but later fell* —
Keep the State from going down in the storm!
Once, years ago, with happy augury,*　　　　　　　　predicting the future
You brought us fortune; be the same again!
No man questions your power to rule the land:
But rule over men, not over a dead city!
Ships are only hulls,* citadels* are nothing,　　　　　frames / fortresses
When no life moves in the empty passageways.
OEDIPUS: Poor children! You may be sure I know
All that you longed for in your coming here.
I know that you are deathly sick; and yet,
Sick as you are, not one is as sick as I.

Each of you suffers in himself alone
His anguish, not another's; but my spirit
Groans for the city, for myself, for you.

I was not sleeping, you are not waking me.
No, I have been in tears for a long while
And in my restless thought walked many ways.
In all my search, I found one helpful course,
And that I have taken: I have sent Creon,
Son of Menoikeus, brother of the Queen,
To Delphi, Apollo's place of **revelation**,
To learn there, if he can,
What act or pledge of mine may save the city.
I have counted the days, and now, this very day,
I am troubled, for he has overstayed his time.
What is he doing? He has been gone too long.
Yet whenever he comes back, I should do ill
To scant* whatever duty God reveals.   minimize

PRIEST: It is a timely promise. At this instant
   They tell me Creon is here.
OEDIPUS: O Lord Apollo!
   May his news be fair as his face is radiant!
PRIEST: It could not be otherwise: he is crowned with bay,
   The chaplet is thick with berries.
OEDIPUS: We shall soon know;
   He is near enough to hear us now.

                               [*Enter* CREON

                 O Prince:
Brother: son of Menoikeus:
What answer do you bring us from the god?
CREON: A strong one. I can tell you, great afflictions
   Will turn out well, if they are taken well.
OEDIPUS: What was the **oracle**? These vague words
   Leave me still hanging between hope and fear.
CREON: Is it your pleasure to hear me with all these
   Gathered around us? I am prepared to speak,
   But should we not go in?
OEDIPUS: Let them all hear it.
   It is for them I suffer, more than for myself.
CREON: Then I will tell you what I heard at Delphi.

In plain words
The god commands us to expel from the land of Thebes
An old defilement* we are sheltering.   shameful corruption

It is a deathly thing, beyond cure;
We must not let it feed upon us longer.
OEDIPUS: What defilement? How shall we rid ourselves of it?
CREON: By **exile** or death, blood for blood. It was
Murder that brought the plague-wind on the city.
OEDIPUS: Murder of whom? Surely the god has named him?
CREON: My lord: long ago Laïos was our king,
Before you came to govern us.
OEDIPUS: I know;
I learned of him from others; I never saw him.
CREON: He was murdered; and Apollo commands us now
To take revenge upon whoever killed him.
OEDIPUS: Upon whom? Where are they? Where shall we find a clue
To solve that crime, after so many years?
CREON: Here in this land, he said.
                                        If we make enquiry,
We may touch things that otherwise escape us.
OEDIPUS: Tell me: Was Laïos murdered in his house,
Or in the fields, or in some foreign country?
CREON: He said he planned to make a pilgrimage.
He did not come home again.
OEDIPUS: And was there no one,
No witness, no companion, to tell what happened?
CREON: They were all killed but one, and he got away
So frightened that he could remember one thing only.
OEDIPUS: What was that one thing? One may be the key
To everything, if we resolve to use it.
CREON: He said that a band of highwaymen attacked them,
Outnumbered them, and overwhelmed the King.
OEDIPUS: Strange, that a highwayman should be so daring —
Unless some faction here bribed him to do it.
CREON: We thought of that. But after Laïos' death
New troubles arose and we had no avenger.
OEDIPUS: What troubles could prevent your hunting down the killers?
CREON: The riddling Sphinx's song
Made us deaf to all mysteries but her own.
OEDIPUS: Then once more I must bring what is dark to light.
It is most fitting that Apollo shows,
As you do, this compunction* for the dead.   concern
You shall see how I stand by you, as I should,
To avenge the city and the city's god,
And not as though it were for some distant friend,
But for my own sake, to be rid of evil.
Whoever killed King Laïos might — who knows? —
Decide at any moment to kill me as well.
By avenging the murdered king I protect myself.

Come, then, my children: leave the altar steps,
Lift up your olive boughs!
　　　　　　　　　　One of you go
And summon the people of Kadmos to gather here.
I will do all that I can; you may tell them that.

　　　　　　　　　　　　　　　　　[*Exit a* PAGE

So, with the help of God,
We shall be saved — or else indeed we are lost.
PRIEST: Let us rise, children. It was for this we came,
And now the King has promised it himself.
Phoibos has sent us an oracle; may he descend
Himself to save us and drive out the plague.

　　　　　　　[Exeunt* OEDIPUS *and* CREON *into the palace by the central*　　exit
　　　　　　　door. The PRIEST *and the* SUPPLIANTS *disperse R and L.**　　stage right and stage left
　　　　　　　After a short pause the CHORUS* *enters the* orchestra.　　representative group of
CHORUS: What is God singing in his profound　　　　　　　　　　　　citizens
Delphi of gold and shadow?
What oracle for Thebes, the sunwhipped city?

Fear unjoints* me, the roots of my heart tremble.　　　　　　　　　disturbs

Now I remember, O Healer, your power, and wonder:
Will you send doom like a sudden cloud, or weave it
Like nightfall of the past?

Speak, speak to us, issue of holy sound:
Dearest to our expectancy: be tender!

Let me pray to Athenê, the immortal daughter of Zeus,
And to Artemis her sister
Who keeps her famous throne in the market ring,
And to Apollo, bowman at the far butts of heaven —

O gods, descend! Like three streams leap against
The fires of our grief, the fires of darkness;
Be swift to bring us rest!

As in the old time from the brilliant house
Of air you stepped to save us, come again!

Now our afflictions have no end,
Now all our stricken host* lies down　　　　　　　　　　　　　large gathering of people
And no man fights off death with his mind;

The noble plowland bears no grain,
And groaning mothers can not bear —

See, how our lives like birds take wing,
Like sparks that fly when a fire soars,
To the shore of the god of evening.

The plague burns on, it is pitiless,
Though pallid* children laden* with death   pale; ashen / afflicted;
Lie unwept in the stony ways,   weighed down

And old gray women by every path
Flock to the strand about the altars

There to strike their breasts and cry
Worship of Phoibos in wailing prayers:
Be kind, God's golden child!

There are no swords in this attack by fire,
No shields, but we are ringed with cries.
Send the besieger plunging from our homes
Into the vast sea-room of the Atlantic
Or into the waves that foam eastward of Thrace —

For the day ravages what the night spares —

Destroy our enemy, lord of the thunder!
Let him be riven* by lightning from heaven!   split in two

Phoibos Apollo, stretch the sun's bowstring,
That golden cord, until it sing for us,
Flashing arrows in heaven!
                              Artemis, Huntress,
Race with flaring lights upon our mountains!

O scarlet god, O golden-banded brow,
O Theban Bacchos in a storm of Maenads,

                                   [*Enter* OEDIPUS, C.

Whirl upon Death, that all the Undying hate!
Come with blinding torches, come in joy!

Scene I

OEDIPUS: Is this your prayer? It may be answered. Come,
  Listen to me, act as the crisis demands,
  And you shall have relief from all these evils.

Until now I was a stranger to this tale,
As I had been a stranger to the crime.
Could I track down the murderer without a clue?

But now, friends,
As one who became a citizen after the murder,
I make this proclamation to all Thebans:
If any man knows by whose hand Laïos, son of Labdakos,
Met his death, I direct that man to tell me everything,
No matter what he fears for having so long withheld it.
Let it stand as promised that no further trouble
Will come to him, but he may leave the land in safety.

Moreover: If anyone knows the murderer to be foreign,
Let him not keep silent: he shall have his reward from me.
However, if he does conceal it; if any man
Fearing for his friend or for himself disobeys this edict,*   command
Hear what I propose to do:

I solemnly forbid the people of this country,
Where power and throne are mine, ever to receive that man
Or speak to him, no matter who he is, or let him
Join in sacrifice, lustration,* or in prayer.   ceremonial offering
I decree that he be driven from every house,
Being, as he is, corruption itself to us: the Delphic
Voice of Zeus has pronounced this revelation.
Thus I associate myself with the oracle
And take the side of the murdered king.

As for the criminal, I pray to God —
Whether it be a lurking thief, or one of a number —
I pray that that man's life be consumed in evil and wretchedness.
And as for me, this curse applies no less
If it should turn out that the culprit is my guest here,
Sharing my hearth.
                    You have heard the penalty.
I lay it on you now to attend to this
For my sake, for Apollo's, for the sick
Sterile city that heaven has abandoned.
Suppose the oracle had given you no command:
Should this defilement go uncleansed for ever?
You should have found the murderer: your king,
A noble king, had been destroyed!
                    Now I,
Having the power that he held before me,
Having his bed, begetting* children there   fathering
Upon his wife, as he would have, had he lived —
Their son would have been my children's brother,
If Laïos had had luck in fatherhood!
(But surely ill luck rushed upon his reign) —

I say I take the son's part, just as though
I were his son, to press the fight for him
And see it won! I'll find the hand that brought
Death to Labdakos' and Polydoros' child,
Heir of Kadmos' and Agenor's line.
And as for those who fail me,
May the gods deny them the fruit of the earth,
Fruit of the womb, and may they rot utterly!
Let them be wretched as we are wretched, and worse!

For you, for loyal Thebans, and for all
Who find my actions right, I pray the favor
Of justice, and of all the immortal gods.
CHORAGOS:* Since I am under oath, my lord, I swear   chorus member
  I did not do the murder, I can not name
  The murderer. Might not the oracle
  That has ordained the search tell where to find him?
OEDIPUS: An honest question. But no man in the world
  Can make the gods do more than the gods will.
CHORAGOS: There is one last expedient* —   way, method
OEDIPUS: Tell me what it is.
  Though it seem slight, you must not hold it back.
CHORAGOS: A lord clairvoyant* to the lord Apollo,   able to see the future
  As we all know, is the skilled Teiresias.
  One might learn much about this from him, Oedipus.
OEDIPUS: I am not wasting time:
  Creon spoke of this, and I have sent for him —
  Twice, in fact; it is strange that he is not here.
CHORAGOS: The other matter — that old report — seems useless.
OEDIPUS: Tell me. I am interested in all reports.
CHORAGOS: The King was said to have been killed by highwaymen.
OEDIPUS: I know. But we have no witnesses to that.
CHORAGOS: If the killer can feel a particle of dread,
  Your curse will bring him out of hiding!
OEDIPUS: No.
  The man who dared that act will fear no curse.
                    [*Enter the blind seer* TEIRESIAS, *led by a* PAGE
CHORAGOS: But there is one man who may detect the criminal.
  This is Teiresias, this is the holy prophet
  In whom, alone of all men, truth was born.
OEDIPUS: Teiresias: seer: student of mysteries,
  Of all that's taught and all that no man tells,
  Secrets of Heaven and secrets of the earth:
  Blind though you are, you know the city lies
  Sick with plague; and from this plague, my lord,
  We find that you alone can guard or save us.

Possibly you did not hear the messengers?
Apollo, when we sent to him,
Sent us back word that this great pestilence*   plague
Would lift, but only if we established clearly
The identity of those who murdered Laïos.
They must be killed or exiled.
Can you use
Birdflight or any art of **divination**
To purify yourself, and Thebes, and me
From this contagion? We are in your hands.
There is no fairer duty
Than that of helping others in distress.
TEIRESIAS: How dreadful knowledge of the truth can be
   When there's no help in truth! I knew this well,
   But made myself forget. I should not have come.
OEDIPUS: What is troubling you? Why are your eyes so cold?
TEIRESIAS: Let me go home. Bear your own fate, and I'll
   Bear mine. It is better so: trust what I say.
OEDIPUS: What you say is ungracious and unhelpful
   To your native country. Do not refuse to speak.
TEIRESIAS: When it comes to speech, your own is neither temperate
   Nor opportune. I wish to be more prudent.*   wise and careful
OEDIPUS: In God's name, we all beg you —
TEIRESIAS: You are all ignorant.
   No; I will never tell you what I know.
   Now it is my misery; then, it would be yours.
OEDIPUS: What! You do know something, and will not tell us?
   You would betray us all and wreck the State?
TEIRESIAS: I do not intend to torture myself, or you.
   Why persist in asking? You will not persuade me.
OEDIPUS: What a wicked old man you are! You'd try a stone's
   Patience! Out with it! Have you no feeling at all?
TEIRESIAS: You call me unfeeling. If you could only see
   The nature of your own feelings . . .
OEDIPUS: Why,
   Who would not feel as I do? Who could endure
   Your arrogance toward the city?
TEIRESIAS: What does it matter!
   Whether I speak or not, it is bound to come.
OEDIPUS: Then, if "it" is bound to come, you are bound to tell me.
TEIRESIAS: No, I will not go on. Rage as you please.
OEDIPUS: Rage? Why not!
And I'll tell you what I think:
You planned it, you had it done, you all but
Killed him with your own hands: if you had eyes,
I'd say the crime was yours, and yours alone.

TEIRESIAS: So? I charge you, then,
   Abide* by the proclamation you have made: stay; live
   From this day forth
   Never speak again to these men or to me;
   You yourself are the **pollution** of this country.
OEDIPUS: You dare say that! Can you possibly think you have
   Some way of going free, after such insolence?*   disrespect
TEIRESIAS: I have gone free. It is the truth sustains me.
OEDIPUS: Who taught you shamelessness? It was not your craft.
TEIRESIAS: You did. You made me speak. I did not want to.
OEDIPUS: Speak what? Let me hear it again more clearly.
TEIRESIAS: Was it not clear before? Are you tempting me?
OEDIPUS: I did not understand it. Say it again.
TEIRESIAS: I say that you are the murderer whom you seek.
OEDIPUS: Now twice you have spat out infamy.* You'll pay for it!   evil action
TEIRESIAS: Would you care for more? Do you wish to be really angry?
OEDIPUS: Say what you will. Whatever you say is worthless,
TEIRESIAS: I say you live in hideous shame with those
   Most dear to you. You can not see the evil.
OEDIPUS: It seems you can go on mouthing like this for ever.
TEIRESIAS: I can, if there is power in truth.
OEDIPUS: There is:
   But not for you, not for you,
   You sightless, witless,* senseless, mad old man!   stupid
TEIRESIAS: You are the madman. There is no one here
   Who will not curse you soon, as you curse me.
OEDIPUS: You child of endless night! You can not hurt me
   Or any other man who sees the sun.
TEIRESIAS: True: it is not from me your fate will come.
   That lies within Apollo's competence,
   As it is his concern.
OEDIPUS: Tell me:
   Are you speaking for Creon, or for yourself?
TEIRESIAS: Creon is no threat. You weave your own doom.
OEDIPUS: Wealth, power, craft of **statesmanship**!
   Kingly position, everywhere admired!
   What savage envy is stored up against these,
   If Creon, whom I trusted, Creon my friend,
   For this great office which the city once
   Put in my hands unsought — if for this power
   Creon desires in secret to destroy me!

   He has bought this decrepit* fortune-teller, this   broken down
   Collector of dirty pennies, this prophet fraud —
   Why, he is no more clairvoyant than I am!
                    Tell us:

Has your mystic mummery* ever approached the truth?   hypocritical acting
When that hellcat the Sphinx was performing here,
What help were you to these people?
Her magic was not for the first man who came along:
It demanded a real exorcist. Your birds —
What good were they? or the gods, for the matter of that?
But I came by,
Oedipus, the simple man, who knows nothing —
I thought it out for myself, no birds helped me!
And this is the man you think you can destroy,
That you may be close to Creon when he's king!
Well, you and your friend Creon, it seems to me,
Will suffer most. If you were not an old man,
You would have paid already for your plot.
CHORAGOS: We can not see that his words or yours
    Have been spoken except in anger, Oedipus,
    And of anger we have no need. How can God's will
    Be accomplished best? That is what most concerns us.
TEIRESIAS: You are a king. But where argument's concerned
    I am your man, as much a king as you.
    I am not your servant, but Apollo's.
    I have no need of Creon to speak for me.

    Listen to me. You mock my blindness, do you?
    But I say that you, with both your eyes, are blind:
    You can not see the wretchedness of your life,
    Nor in whose house you live, no, nor with whom.
    Who are your father and mother? Can you tell me?
    You do not even know the blind wrongs
    That you have done them, on earth and in the world below.
    But the double lash of your parents' curse will whip you
    Out of this land some day, with only night
    Upon your precious eyes.
    Your cries then — where will they not be heard?
    What fastness* of Kithairon will not echo them?   remote area
    And that bridal-descant* of yours — you'll know it then,   marriage song
    The song they sang when you came here to Thebes
    And found your misguided berthing.*   home
    All this, and more, that you can not guess at now,
    Will bring you to yourself among your children.

    Be angry, then. Curse Creon. Curse my words.
    I tell you, no man that walks upon the earth
    Shall be rooted out* more horribly than you.   searched out; destroyed
OEDIPUS: Am I to bear this from him? — Damnation
    Take you! Out of this place! Out of my sight!

TEIRESIAS: I would not have come at all if you had not asked me.
OEDIPUS: Could I have told that you'd talk nonsense, that
   You'd come here to make a fool of yourself, and of me?
TEIRESIAS: A fool? Your parents thought me sane enough.
OEDIPUS: My parents again! — Wait: who were my parents?
TEIRESIAS: This day will give you a father, and break your heart.
OEDIPUS: Your infantile riddles! Your damned abracadabra!
TEIRESIAS: You were a great man once at solving riddles.
OEDIPUS: Mock me with that if you like; you will find it true.
TEIRESIAS: It was true enough. It brought about your ruin.
OEDIPUS: But if it saved this town?
TEIRESIAS:

                                              [*To the* PAGE:
                    Boy, give me your hand.
OEDIPUS: Yes, boy; lead him away.
                    — While you are here
   We can do nothing. Go; leave us in peace.
TEIRESIAS: I will go when I have said what I have to say.
   How can you hurt me? And I tell you again:
   The man you have been looking for all this time,
   The damned man, the murderer of Laïos,
   That man is in Thebes. To your mind he is foreign-born,
   But it will soon be shown that he is a Theban,
   A revelation that will fail to please.
                              A blind man,
   Who has his eyes now; a penniless man, who is rich now;
   And he will go tapping the strange earth with his staff
   To the children with whom he lives now he will be
   Brother and father — the very same; to her
   Who bore him, son and husband — the very same
   Who came to his father's bed, wet with his father's blood.

   Enough. Go think that over.
   If later you find error in what I have said,
   You may say that I have no skill in prophecy.
               [*Exit* TEIRESIAS, *led by his* PAGE. OEDIPUS *goes into the*
               palace.
CHORUS: The Delphic stone of prophecies
   Remembers ancient **regicide**
   And a still bloody hand.
   That killer's hour of flight has come.
   He must be stronger than riderless
   Coursers* of untiring wind,   fast horses
   For the son of Zeus armed with his father's thunder
   Leaps in lightning after him;
   And the Furies* follow him, the sad Furies.   avenging goddesses

Holy Parnassos' peak of snow
Flashes and blinds that secret man,
That all shall hunt him down:
Though he may roam the forest shade
Like a bull gone wild from pasture
To rage through glooms of stone.
Doom comes down on him; flight will not avail him;
For the world's heart calls him desolate,
And the immortal Furies follow, for ever follow.

But now a wilder thing is heard
From the old man skilled at hearing Fate in the wingbeat of a bird.
Bewildered as a blown bird, my soul hovers* and can not find   hangs motionless
Foothold in this debate, or any reason or rest of mind,
But no man ever brought — none can bring
Proof of strife between Thebes' royal house,
Labdakos' line, and the son of Polybos;
And never until now has any man brought word
Of Laïos' dark death staining Oedipus the King.

Divine Zeus and Apollo hold
Perfect intelligence alone of all tales ever told;
And well though this diviner works, he works in his own night;
No man can judge that rough unknown or trust in second sight,*   ESP
For wisdom changes hands among the wise.
Shall I believe my great lord criminal
At a raging word that a blind old man let fall?
I saw him, when the carrion* woman faced him of old,   decaying flesh
Prove his heroic mind! These evil words are lies.

Scene II

CREON: Men of Thebes:
  I am told that heavy accusations
  Have been brought against me by King Oedipus.

  I am not the kind of man to bear this tamely.

  If in these present difficulties
  He holds me accountable for any harm to him
  Through anything I have said or done — why, then,
  I do not value life in this dishonor.
  It is not as though this rumor touched upon
  Some private indiscretion.* The matter is grave.   offense
  The fact is that I am being called disloyal
  To the State, to my fellow citizens, to my friends.
CHORAGOS: He may have spoken in anger, not from his mind.

CREON: But did you not hear him say I was the one
   Who seduced the old prophet into lying?
CHORAGOS: The thing was said; I do not know how seriously.
CREON: But you were watching him! Were his eyes steady?
   Did he look like a man in his right mind?
CHORAGOS: I do not know.
   I can not judge the behavior of great men.
   But here is the King himself.

                                          [*Enter* OEDIPUS

OEDIPUS: So you dared come back.
   Why? How brazen* of you to come to my house,   insolent, bold
   You murderer!
                 Do you think I do not know
   That you plotted to kill me, plotted to steal my throne?
   Tell me, in God's name: am I coward, a fool,
   That you should dream you could accomplish this?
   A fool who could not see your slippery game?
   A coward, not to fight back when I saw it?
   You are the fool, Creon, are you not? hoping
   Without support or friends to get a throne?
   Thrones may be won or bought: you could do neither.
CREON: Now listen to me. You have talked; let me talk, too.
   You can not judge unless you know the facts.
OEDIPUS: You speak well: there is one fact; but I find it hard
   To learn from the deadliest enemy I have.
CREON: That above all I must dispute with you.
OEDIPUS: That above all I will not hear you deny.
CREON: If you think there is anything good in being stubborn
   Against all reason, then I say you are wrong.
OEDIPUS: If you think a man can sin against his own kind
   And not be punished for it, I say you are mad.
CREON: I agree. But tell me: what have I done to you?
OEDIPUS: You advised me to send for that wizard, did you not?
CREON: I did. I should do it again.
OEDIPUS: Very well. Now tell me:
   How long has it been since Laïos —
CREON: What of Laïos?
OEDIPUS: Since he vanished in that onset by the road?
CREON: It was long ago, a long time.
OEDIPUS: And this prophet,
   Was he practicing here then?
CREON: He was; and with honor, as now.
OEDIPUS: Did he speak of me at that time?
CREON: He never did;
   At least, not when I was present.
OEDIPUS: But . . . the enquiry?
   I suppose you held one?
CREON: We did, but we learned nothing.

OEDIPUS: Why did the prophet not speak against me then?
CREON: I do not know; and I am the kind of man
  Who holds his tongue when he has no facts to go on.
OEDIPUS: There's one fact that you know, and you could tell it.
CREON: What fact is that? If I know it, you shall have it.
OEDIPUS: If he were not involved with you, he could not say
  That it was I who murdered Laïos.
CREON: If he says that, you are the one that knows it! —
  But now it is my turn to question you.
OEDIPUS: Put your questions. I am no murderer.
CREON: First, then: You married my sister?
OEDIPUS: I married your sister.
CREON: And you rule the kingdom equally with her?
OEDIPUS: Everything that she wants she has from me.
CREON: And I am the third, equal to both of you?
OEDIPUS: That is why I call you a bad friend.
CREON: No. Reason it out, as I have done.
  Think of this first: Would any sane man prefer
  Power, with all a king's anxieties,
  To that same power and the grace of sleep?
  Certainly not I.
  I have never longed for the king's power — only his rights.
  Would any wise man differ from me in this?
  As matters stand, I have my way in everything
  With your consent, and no responsibilities.
  If I were king, I should be a slave to **policy**.

  How could I desire a scepter* more   symbol of authority
  Than what is now mine — untroubled influence?
  No, I have not gone mad; I need no honors,
  Except those with the perquisites* I have now.   benefits
  I am welcome everywhere; every man salutes me,
  And those who want your favor seek my ear,
  Since I know how to manage what they ask.
  Should I exchange this ease for that anxiety?
  Besides, no sober mind is treasonable.
  I hate **anarchy**
  And never would deal with any man who likes it.

  Test what I have said. Go to the priestess
  At Delphi, ask if I quoted her correctly.
  And as for this other thing: if I am found
  Guilty of treason with Teiresias,
  Then sentence me to death! You have my word
  It is a sentence I should cast my vote for —
  But not without evidence!
                      You do wrong
  When you take good men for bad, bad men for good.

A true friend thrown aside — why, life itself
Is not more precious!
                In time you will know this well:
For time, and time alone, will show the just man,
Though scoundrels are discovered in a day.
CHORAGOS: This is well said, and a prudent man would ponder it.
  Judgments too quickly formed are dangerous.
OEDIPUS: But is he not quick in his duplicity?*   deceit
  And shall I not be quick to parry* him?   fight off
  Would you have me stand still, hold my peace, and let
  This man win everything, through my inaction?
CREON: And you want — what is it, then? To banish me?
OEDIPUS: No, not exile. It is your death I want,
  So that all the world may see what treason means.
CREON: You will persist, then? You will not believe me?
OEDIPUS: How can I believe you?
CREON: Then you are a fool.
OEDIPUS: To save myself?
CREON: In justice, think of me.
OEDIPUS: You are evil incarnate.*   in the flesh
CREON: But suppose that you are wrong?
OEDIPUS: Still I must rule.
CREON: But not if you rule badly.
OEDIPUS: O city, city!
CREON: It is my city, too!
CHORAGOS: Now, my lords, be still. I see the Queen,
  Iocastê, coming from her palace chambers;
  And it is time she came, for the sake of you both.
  This dreadful quarrel can be resolved through her.

                                 [*Enter* IOCASTE

IOCASTE: Poor foolish men, what wicked din* is this?   noise
  With Thebes sick to death, is it not shameful
  That you should rake some private quarrel up?

                                [*To* OEDIPUS:

Come into the house.

                — And you, Creon, go now:
  Let us have no more of this tumult* over nothing.   confusion
CREON: Nothing? No, sister: what your husband plans for me
  Is one of two great evils: exile or death.
OEDIPUS: He is right.
                Why, woman I have caught him squarely
  Plotting against my life.
CREON: No! Let me die
  Accurst* if ever I have wished you harm!   cursed
IOCASTE: Ah, believe it, Oedipus!

In the name of the gods, respect this oath of his
For my sake, for the sake of these people here!
CHORAGOS: Open your mind to her, my lord. Be ruled by her, I beg you!
OEDIPUS: What would you have me do?
CHORAGOS: Respect Creon's word. He has never spoken like a fool,
And now he has sworn an oath.
OEDIPUS: You know what you ask?
CHORAGOS: I do.
OEDIPUS: Speak on, then.
CHORAGOS: A friend so sworn should not be baited* so,   teased; tormented
In blind malice,* and without final proof.   hatred
OEDIPUS: You are aware, I hope, that what you say
Means death for me, or exile at the least.
CHORAGOS: No, I swear by Helios, first in Heaven!
    May I die friendless and accurst,
The worst of deaths, if ever I meant that!
        It is the withering fields
            That hurt my sick heart:
        Must we bear all these ills,
            And now your bad blood as well?
OEDIPUS: Then let him go. And let me die, if I must,
Or be driven by him in shame from the land of Thebes.
It is your unhappiness, and not his talk,
That touches me.
                        As for him —
Wherever he goes, hatred will follow him.
CREON: Ugly in yielding, as you were ugly in rage!
    Natures like yours chiefly torment themselves.
OEDIPUS: Can you not go? Can you not leave me?
CREON: I can.
    You do not know me; but the city knows me,
    And in its eyes I am just, if not in yours.

                                                    [*Exit* CREON
CHORAGOS: Lady Iocastê, did you not ask the King to go to his chambers?
IOCASTE: First tell me what has happened.
CHORAGOS: There was suspicion without evidence; yet it rankled*   irritated
    As even false charges will.
IOCASTE: On both sides?
CHORAGOS: On both.
IOCASTE: But what was said?
CHORAGOS: Oh let it rest, let it be done with!
    Have we not suffered enough?
OEDIPUS: You see to what your decency has brought you:
    You have made difficulties where my heart saw none.
CHORAGOS: Oedipus, it is not once only I have told you —
    You must know I should count myself unwise

To the point of madness, should I now forsake you —
　　　You, under whose hand,
　　　　In the storm of another time,
　　　Our dear land sailed out free.
　　　But now stand fast at the helm!

IOCASTE: In God's name, Oedipus, inform your wife as well:
　　Why are you so set in this hard anger?

OEDIPUS: I will tell you, for none of these men deserves
　　My confidence as you do. It is Creon's work,
　　His treachery, his plotting against me.

IOCASTE: Go on, if you can make this clear to me.

OEDIPUS: He charges me with the murder of Laïos.

IOCASTE: Has he some knowledge? Or does he speak from hearsay?*　　gossip; rumor

OEDIPUS: He would not commit himself to such a charge,
　　But he has brought in that damnable soothsayer*　　fortuneteller
　　To tell his story.

IOCASTE: 　　　　　Set your mind at rest.
　　If it is a question of soothsayers, I tell you
　　That you will find no man whose craft gives knowledge
　　Of the unknowable.

　　　　　Here is my proof:

An oracle was reported to Laïos once
(I will not say from Phoibos himself, but from
His appointed ministers, at any rate)
That his doom would be death at the hands of his own son —
His son, born of his flesh and of mine!

Now, you remember the story: Laïos was killed
By marauding* strangers where three highways meet;　　raiding
But his child had not been three days in this world
Before the King had pierced the baby's ankles
And left him to die on a lonely mountainside.

Thus, Apollo never caused that child
To kill his father, and it was not Laïos' fate
To die at the hands of his son, as he had feared.
This is what prophets and prophecies are worth!
Have no dread of them.
　　　　　It is God himself
Who can show us what he wills, in his own way.

OEDIPUS: How strange a shadowy memory crossed my mind,
　　Just now while you were speaking; it chilled my heart.

IOCASTE: What do you mean? What memory do you speak of?

OEDIPUS: If I understand you, Laïos was killed
    At a place where three roads meet.
IOCASTE: So it was said;
    We have no later story.
OEDIPUS: Where did it happen?
IOCASTE: Phokis, it is called: at a place where the Theban Way
    Divides into the roads toward Delphi and Daulia.
OEDIPUS: When?
IOCASTE: We had the news not long before you came
    And proved the right to your succession here.
OEDIPUS: Ah, what net has God been weaving for me?
IOCASTE: Oedipus! Why does this trouble you?
OEDIPUS: Do not ask me yet.
    First, tell me how Laïos looked, and tell me
    How old he was.
IOCASTE: He was tall, his hair just touched
    With white; his form was not unlike your own.
OEDIPUS: I think that I myself may be accurst
    By my own ignorant edict.
IOCASTE: You speak strangely.
    It makes me tremble to look at you, my King.
OEDIPUS: I am not sure that the blind man can not see.
    But I should know better if you were to tell me —
IOCASTE: Anything — though I dread to hear you ask it.
OEDIPUS: Was the King lightly escorted, or did he ride
    With a large company, as a ruler should?
IOCASTE: There were five men with him in all: one was a herald,*   spokesperson
    And a single chariot, which he was driving.
OEDIPUS: Alas, that makes it plain enough!
                        But who —
    Who told you how it happened?
IOCASTE: A household servant,
    The only one to escape.
OEDIPUS: And is he still
    A servant of ours?
IOCASTE: No; for when he came back at last
    And found you enthroned in the place of the dead king,
    He came to me, touched my hand with his, and begged
    That I would send him away to the frontier district
    Where only the shepherds go —
    As far away from the city as I could send him.
    I granted his prayer; for although the man was a slave,
    He had earned more than this favor at my hands.
OEDIPUS: Can he be called back quickly?
IOCASTE: Easily.
    But why?

OEDIPUS: I have taken too much upon myself
    Without enquiry; therefore I wish to consult him.
IOCASTE: Then he shall come.
                        But am I not one also
    To whom you might confide these fears of yours?
OEDIPUS: That is your right; it will not be denied you,
    Now least of all; for I have reached a pitch
    Of wild foreboding.* Is there anyone   sense of coming evil
    To whom I should sooner speak?

    Polybos of Corinth is my father.
    My mother is a Dorian: Meropê.
    I grew up chief among the men of Corinth
    Until a strange thing happened —
    Not worth my passion, it may be, but strange.

    At a feast, a drunken man maundering in his cups*   self-pitying
    Cries out that I am not my father's son!

    I contained myself that night, though I felt anger
    And a sinking heart. The next day I visited
    My father and mother, and questioned them. They stormed,
    Calling it all the slanderous rant* of a fool;   raving
    And this relieved me. Yet the suspicion
    Remained always aching in my mind;
    I knew there was talk; I could not rest;
    And finally, saying nothing to my parents,
    I went to the shrine at Delphi.
    The god dismissed my question without reply;
    He spoke of other things.
                        Some were clear,
    Full of wretchedness, dreadful, unbearable:
    As, that I should lie with my own mother, breed
    Children from whom all men would turn their eyes;
    And that I should be my father's murderer.

    I heard all this, and fled. And from that day
    Corinth to me was only in the stars
    Descending in that quarter of the sky,
    As I wandered farther and farther on my way
    To a land where I should never see the evil
    Sung by the oracle. And I came to this country
    Where, so you say, King Laïos was killed.

    I will tell you all that happened there, my lady.

There were three highways
Coming together at a place I passed;
And there a herald came towards me, and a chariot
Drawn by horses, with a man such as you describe
Seated in it. The groom* leading the horses   stableman
Forced me off the road at his lord's command;
But as this charioteer lurched over towards me
I struck him in my rage. The old man saw me
And brought his double goad* down upon my head   whip
As I came abreast.
                          He was paid back, and more!
Swinging my club in this right hand I knocked him
Out of his car, and he rolled on the ground.
                                              I killed him.

I killed them all.
Now if that stranger and Laïos were — kin,
Where is a man more miserable than I?
More hated by the gods? Citizen and alien alike
Must never shelter me or speak to me —
I must be shunned by all.
                          And I myself
Pronounced this malediction* upon myself!   curse

Think of it: I have touched you with these hands,
These hands that killed your husband. What defilement!

Am I all evil, then? It must be so,
Since I must flee from Thebes, yet never again
See my own countrymen, my own country,
For fear of joining my mother in marriage
And killing Polybos, my father.
                          Ah,
If I was created so, born to this fate,
Who could deny the savagery of God?

O holy majesty of heavenly powers!
May I never see that day! Never!
Rather let me vanish from the race of men
Than know the abomination* destined me!   loathsome act
CHORAGOS: We too, my lord, have felt dismay at this.
   But there is hope: you have yet to hear the shepherd.
OEDIPUS: Indeed, I fear no other hope is left me.
IOCASTE: What do you hope from him when he comes?
OEDIPUS: This much:

If his account of the murder tallies with yours,
Then I am cleared.
IOCASTE: What was it that I said
Of such importance?
OEDIPUS: Why, "marauders," you said,
Killed the King, according to this man's story.
If he maintains that still, if there were several,
Clearly the guilt is not mine: I was alone.
But if he says one man, singlehanded, did it,
Then the evidence all points to me.
IOCASTE: You may be sure that he said there were several;
And can he call back that story now? He can not.
The whole city heard it as plainly as I.
But suppose he alters some detail of it:
He can not ever show that Laïos' death
Fulfilled the oracle: for Apollo said
My child was doomed to kill him; and my child —
Poor baby! — it was my child that died first.

No. From now on, where oracles are concerned,
I would not waste a second thought on any.
OEDIPUS: You may be right.
                        But come: let someone go
For the shepherd at once. This matter must be settled.
IOCASTE: I will send for him.
I would not wish to cross you in anything,
And surely not in this. — Let us go in.

                              [*Exeunt into the palace*

CHORUS: Let me be reverent* in the ways of right,   respectful
Lowly the paths I journey on;
Let all my words and actions keep
The laws of the pure universe
From highest Heaven handed down.
For Heaven is their bright nurse,
Those generations of the realms of light;
Ah, never of mortal kind were they begot,
Nor are they slaves of memory, lost in sleep:
Their Father is greater than Time, and ages not.

The **tyrant** is a child of Pride
Who drinks from his great sickening cup
Recklessness and vanity,
Until from his high crest* headlong   high point
He plummets* to the dust of hope.   falls rapidly
That strong man is not strong.
But let no fair ambition be denied;

May God protect the wrestler for the State
In government, in comely policy,
Who will fear God, and on His ordinance* wait.   command, law

Haughtiness* and the high hand of disdain*   pride / contempt
Tempt and outrage God's holy law;
And any mortal who dares hold
No immortal Power in awe
Will be caught up in a net of pain:
The price for which his levity* is sold.   disrespect; joking
Let each man take due earnings, then,
And keep his hands from holy things,
And from **blasphemy** stand apart —
Else the crackling blast of heaven
Blows on his head, and on his desperate heart;
Though fools will honor impious* men,   blasphemous
In their cities no tragic poet sings.

Shall we lose faith in Delphi's obscurities,*   mysteries
We who have heard the world's core
Discredited,* and the sacred wood   disproved
Of Zeus at Elis praised no more?
The deeds and the strange prophecies
Must make a pattern yet to be understood.
Zeus, if indeed you are lord of all,
Throned in light over night and day,
Mirror this in your endless mind:
Our masters call the oracle
Words on the wind, and the Delphic vision blind!
Their hearts no longer know Apollo,
And reverence for the gods has died away.

Scene III

[*Enter* IOCASTE

IOCASTE: Princes of Thebes, it has occurred to me
To visit the altars of the gods, bearing
These branches as a suppliant, and this incense.
Our King is not himself: his noble soul
Is overwrought* with fantasies of dread,   agitated
Else he would consider
The new prophecies in the light of the old.
He will listen to any voice that speaks disaster,
And my advice goes for nothing.
[*She approaches the altar, R.*
To you, then, Apollo,
Lycean lord, since you are nearest, I turn in prayer.

Receive these offerings, and grant us deliverance
From defilement. Our hearts are heavy with fear
When we see our leader distracted, as helpless sailors
Are terrified by the confusion of their helmsman.

[*Enter* MESSENGER

MESSENGER: Friends, no doubt you can direct me:
    Where shall I find the house of Oedipus,
    Or, better still, where is the King himself?
CHORAGOS: It is this very place, stranger; he is inside.
    This is his wife and mother of his children.
MESSENGER: I wish her happiness in a happy house,
    Blest in all the fulfillment of her marriage.
IOCASTE: I wish as much for you: your courtesy
    Deserves a like good fortune. But now, tell me:
    Why have you come? What have you to say to us?
MESSENGER: Good news, my lady, for your house and your husband.
IOCASTE: What news? Who sent you here?
MESSENGER: I am from Corinth.
    The news I bring ought to mean joy for you,
    Though it may be you will find some grief in it.
IOCASTE: What is it? How can it touch us in both ways?
MESSENGER: The word is that the people of the Isthmus
    Intend to call Oedipus to be their king.
IOCASTE: But old King Polybos — is he not reigning still?
MESSENGER: No. Death holds him in his sepulchre.*   tomb
IOCASTE: What are you saying? Polybos is dead?
MESSENGER: If I am not telling the truth, may I die myself.
IOCASTE: [*To a* MAIDSERVANT:
    Go in, go quickly; tell this to your master.

    O riddlers of God's will, where are you now!
    This was the man whom Oedipus, long ago,
    Feared so, fled so, in dread of destroying him —
    But it was another fate by which he died.

[*Enter* OEDIPUS, C.

OEDIPUS: Dearest Iocastê, why have you sent for me?
IOCASTE: Listen to what this man says, and then tell me
    What has become of the solemn prophecies.
OEDIPUS: Who is this man? What is his news for me?
IOCASTE: He has come from Corinth to announce your father's death!
OEDIPUS: Is it true, stranger? Tell me in your own words.
MESSENGER: I can not say it more clearly: the King is dead.
OEDIPUS: Was it by treason? Or by an attack of illness?
MESSENGER: A little thing brings old men to their rest.
OEDIPUS: It was sickness, then?

MESSENGER: Yes, and his many years.
OEDIPUS: Ah!
   Why should a man respect the Pythian hearth, or
   Give heed to the birds that jangle above his head?
   They prophesied that I should kill Polybos,
   Kill my own father; but he is dead and buried,
   And I am here — I never touched him, never,
   Unless he died of grief for my departure,
   And thus, in a sense, through me. No. Polybos
   Has packed the oracles off with him underground.
   They are empty words.
IOCASTE: Had I not told you so?
OEDIPUS: You had; it was my faint heart that betrayed me.
IOCASTE: From now on never think of those things again.
OEDIPUS: And yet — must I not fear my mother's bed?
IOCASTE: Why should anyone in this world be afraid,
   Since **Fate** rules us and nothing can be foreseen?
   A man should live only for the present day.
   Have no more fear of sleeping with your mother:
   How many men, in dreams, have lain with their mothers!
   No reasonable man is troubled by such things.
OEDIPUS: That is true; only —
   If only my mother were not still alive!
   But she is alive. I can not help my dread.
IOCASTE: Yet this news of your father's death is wonderful.
OEDIPUS: Wonderful. But I fear the living woman.
MESSENGER: Tell me, who is this woman that you fear?
OEDIPUS: It is Meropê, man; the wife of King Polybos.
MESSENGER: Meropê? Why should you be afraid of her?
OEDIPUS: An oracle of the gods, a dreadful saying.
MESSENGER: Can you tell me about it or are you sworn to silence?
OEDIPUS: I can tell you, and I will.
   Apollo said through his prophet that I was the man
   Who should marry his own mother, shed his father's blood
   With his own hands. And so, for all these years
   I have kept clear of Corinth, and no harm has come —
   Though it would have been sweet to see my parents again.
MESSENGER: And is this the fear that drove you out of Corinth?
OEDIPUS: Would you have me kill my father?
MESSENGER: As for that
   You must be reassured by the news I gave you.
OEDIPUS: If you could reassure me, I would reward you.
MESSENGER: I had that in mind, I will confess: I thought
   I could count on you when you returned to Corinth.
OEDIPUS: No: I will never go near my parents again.

MESSENGER: Ah, son, you still do not know what you are doing —
OEDIPUS: What do you mean? In the name of God tell me!
MESSENGER: — If these are your reasons for not going home.
OEDIPUS: I tell you, I fear the oracle may come true.
MESSENGER: And guilt may come upon you through your parents?
OEDIPUS: That is the dread that is always in my heart.
MESSENGER: Can you not see that all your fears are groundless?
OEDIPUS: How can you say that? They are my parents, surely?
MESSENGER: Polybos was not your father.
OEDIPUS: Not my father?
MESSENGER: No more your father than the man speaking to you.
OEDIPUS: But you are nothing to me!
MESSENGER: Neither was he.
OEDIPUS: Then why did he call me son?
MESSENGER: I will tell you:
   Long ago he had you from my hands, as a gift.
OEDIPUS: Then how could he love me so, if I was not his?
MESSENGER: He had no children, and his heart turned to you.
OEDIPUS: What of you? Did you buy me? Did you find me by chance?
MESSENGER: I came upon you in the crooked pass* of Kithairon.   mountain passageway
OEDIPUS: And what were you doing there?
MESSENGER: Tending my flocks.*   sheep herds
OEDIPUS: A wandering shepherd?
MESSENGER: But your savior, son, that day.
OEDIPUS: From what did you save me?
MESSENGER: Your ankles should tell you that.
OEDIPUS: Ah, stranger, why do you speak of that childhood pain?
MESSENGER: I cut the bonds that tied your ankles together.
OEDIPUS: I have had the mark as long as I can remember.
MESSENGER: That was why you were given the name you bear.
OEDIPUS: God! Was it my father or my mother who did it?
   Tell me!
MESSENGER: I do not know. The man who gave you to me
   Can tell you better than I.
OEDIPUS: It was not you that found me, but another?
MESSENGER: It was another shepherd gave you to me.
OEDIPUS: Who was he? Can you tell me who he was?
MESSENGER: I think he was said to be one of Laïos' people.
OEDIPUS: You mean the Laïos who was king here years ago?
MESSENGER: Yes; King Laïos; and the man was one of his herdsmen.
OEDIPUS: Is he still alive? Can I see him?
MESSENGER: These men here
   Know best about such things.
OEDIPUS: Does anyone here
   Know this shepherd that he is talking about?

Have you seen him in the fields, or in the town?
If you have, tell me. It is time things were made plain.
CHORAGOS: I think the man he means is that same shepherd
　　You have already asked to see. Iocastê perhaps
　　Could tell you something.
OEDIPUS:　　　　　　　　Do you know anything
　　About him, Lady? Is he the man we have summoned?
　　Is that the man this shepherd means?
IOCASTE:　　　　　　　　　　Why think of him?
　　Forget this herdsman. Forget it all.
　　This talk is a waste of time.
OEDIPUS:　　　　　　　　How can you say that,
　　When the clues to my true birth are in my hands?
IOCASTE: For God's love, let us have no more questioning!
　　Is your life nothing to you?
　　My own is pain enough for me to bear.
OEDIPUS: You need not worry. Suppose my mother a slave,
　　And born of slaves: no baseness* can touch you.　　　　　　　　degradation
IOCASTE: Listen to me, I beg you: do not do this thing!
OEDIPUS: I will not listen; the truth must be made known.
IOCASTE: Everything that I say is for your own good!
OEDIPUS:　　　　　　　　　　My own good
　　Snaps my patience, then; I want none of it.
IOCASTE: You are fatally wrong! May you never learn who you are!
OEDIPUS: Go, one of you, and bring the shepherd here.
　　Let us leave this woman to brag of her royal name.
IOCASTE: Ah, miserable!
　　That is the only word I have for you now.
　　That is the only word I can ever have.
　　　　　　　　　　　　　　　[Exit into the palace
CHORAGOS: Why has she left us, Oedipus? Why has she gone
　　In such a passion of sorrow? I fear this silence:
　　Something dreadful may come of it.
OEDIPUS:　　　　　　　　　　Let it come!
　　However base my birth, I must know about it.
　　The Queen, like a woman, is perhaps ashamed
　　To think of my low origin. But I
　　Am a child of Luck; I can not be dishonored.
　　Luck is my mother; the passing months, my brothers,
　　Have seen me rich and poor.
　　　　　　　　　　If this is so,
　　How could I wish that I were someone else?
　　How could I not be glad to know my birth?
CHORUS: If ever the coming time were known
　　To my heart's pondering,*　　　　　　　　　　contemplation

Kithairon, now by Heaven I see the torches
At the festival of the next full moon,
And see the dance, and hear the choir sing
A grace to your gentle shade:
Mountain where Oedipus was found,
O mountain guard of a noble race!
May the god who heals us lend his aid,
And let that glory come to pass
For our king's cradling-ground.*   birthplace

Of the nymphs that flower beyond the years,
Who bore you, royal child,
To Pan of the hills or the timberline Apollo,
Cold in delight where the upland clears,
Or Hermês for whom Kyllenê's heights are piled?
Or flushed as evening cloud,
Great Dionysos, roamer of mountains,
He — was it he who found you there,
And caught you up in his own proud
Arms from the sweet god-ravisher
Who laughed by the Muses' fountains?

Scene IV

OEDIPUS: Sirs: though I do not know the man,
  I think I see him coming, this shepherd we want:
  He is old, like our friend here, and the men
  Bringing him seem to be servants of my house.
  But you can tell, if you have ever seen him.
                          [*Enter* SHEPHERD *escorted by servants*
CHORAGOS: I know him, he was Laïos' man. You can trust him.
OEDIPUS: Tell me first, you from Corinth: is this the shepherd
  We were discussing?
MESSENGER: This is the very man.
OEDIPUS: [*To* SHEPHERD
  Come here. No, look at me. You must answer
  Everything I ask. — You belonged to Laïos?
SHEPHERD: Yes: born his slave, brought up in his house.
OEDIPUS: Tell me: what kind of work did you do for him?
SHEPHERD: I was a shepherd of his, most of my life.
OEDIPUS: Where mainly did you go for pasturage?*   grazing land
SHEPHERD: Sometimes Kithairon, sometimes the hills near-by.
OEDIPUS: Do you remember ever seeing this man out there?
SHEPHERD: What would he be doing there? This man?
OEDIPUS: This man standing here. Have you ever seen him before?
SHEPHERD: No. At least, not to my recollection.
MESSENGER: And that is not strange, my lord. But I'll refresh

His memory: he must remember when we two
Spent three whole seasons together, March to September,
On Kithairon or thereabouts. He had two flocks;
I had one. Each autumn I'd drive mine home
And he would go back with his to Laïos sheepfold. —
Is this not true, just as I have described it?

SHEPHERD: True, yes; but it was all so long ago.

MESSENGER: Well, then: do you remember, back in those days,
That you gave me a baby boy to bring up as my own?

SHEPHERD: What if I did? What are you trying to say?

MESSENGER: King Oedipus was once that little child.

SHEPHERD: Damn you, hold your tongue!

OEDIPUS: No more of that!
It is your tongue needs watching, not this man's.

SHEPHERD: My King, my Master, what is it I have done wrong?

OEDIPUS: You have not answered his question about the boy.

SHEPHERD: He does not know . . . He is only making trouble . . .

OEDIPUS: Come, speak plainly, or it will go hard with you.

SHEPHERD: In God's name, do not torture an old man!

OEDIPUS: Come here, one of you; bind his arms behind him.

SHEPHERD: Unhappy king! What more do you wish to learn?

OEDIPUS: Did you give this man the child he speaks of?

SHEPHERD: I did.
And I would to God I had died that very day.

OEDIPUS: You will die now unless you speak the truth.

SHEPHERD: Yet if I speak the truth, I am worse than dead.

OEDIPUS: Very well; since you insist upon delaying —

SHEPHERD: No! I have told you already that I gave him the boy.

OEDIPUS: Where did you get him? From your house? From somewhere
else?

SHEPHERD: Not from mine, no. A man gave him to me.

OEDIPUS: Is that man here? Do you know whose slave he was?

SHEPHERD: For God's love, my King, do not ask me any more!

OEDIPUS: You are a dead man if I have to ask you again.

SHEPHERD: Then . . . Then the child was from the palace of Laïos.

OEDIPUS: A slave child? or a child of his own line?

SHEPHERD: Ah, I am on the brink of dreadful speech!

OEDIPUS: And I of dreadful hearing. Yet I must hear.

SHEPHERD: If you must be told, then . . .
                                    They said it was Laïos' child;
But it is your wife who can tell you about that.

OEDIPUS: My wife! — Did she give it to you?

SHEPHERD: My lord, she did.

OEDIPUS: Do you know why?

SHEPHERD: I was told to get rid of it.

OEDIPUS: An unspeakable* mother!   shameful; horrifying

SHEPHERD: There had been prophecies . . .
OEDIPUS: Tell me.
SHEPHERD: It was said that the boy would kill his own father.
OEDIPUS: Then why did you give him over to this old man?
SHEPHERD: I pitied the baby, my King,
  And I thought that this man would take him far away
  To his own country.
                    He saved him — but for what a fate!
  For if you are what this man says you are,
  No man living is more wretched than Oedipus.
OEDIPUS: Ah God!
  It was true!
          All the prophecies!
                    — Now,
  O Light, may I look on you for the last time!
  I, Oedipus,
  Oedipus, damned in his birth, in his marriage damned,
  Damned in the blood he shed with his own hand!
                    [*He rushes into the palace*
CHORUS: Alas for the seed of men.

What measure shall I give these generations
That breathe on the void* and are void   empty, meaningless world
And exist and do not exist?

Who bears more weight of joy
Than mass of sunlight shifting in images,
Or who shall make his thought stay on
That down time drifts away?

Your splendor is all fallen.

O naked brow of wrath and tears,
O change of Oedipus!
I who saw your days call no man blest —
Your great days like ghósts góne.

That mind was a strong bow.

Deep, how deep you drew it then, hard archer,
At a dim fearful range,
And brought dear glory down!

You overcame the stranger —
The virgin with her hooking lion claws —

And though death sang, stood like a tower
To make pale Thebes take heart.

Fortress against our sorrow!

True king, giver of laws,
Majestic Oedipus!
No prince in Thebes had ever such renown,*   fame
No prince won such grace of power.

And now of all men ever known
Most pitiful is this man's story:
His fortunes are most changed, his state
Fallen to a low slave's
Ground under bitter fate.

O Oedipus, most royal one!
The great door that expelled you to the light
Gave at night — ah, gave night to your glory:
As to the father, to the fathering son.

All understood too late.

How could that queen whom Laïos won,
The garden that he harrowed* at his height,   ploughed
Be silent when that act was done?

But all eyes fail before time's eye,
All actions come to justice there.
Though never willed, though far down the deep past,
Your bed, your dread sirings,*   offspring
Are brought to book at last.
Child by Laïos doomed to die,
Then doomed to lose that fortunate little death,
Would God you never took breath in this air
That with my wailing lips I take to cry:

For I weep the world's outcast.

I was blind, and now I can tell why:
Asleep, for you had given ease of breath
To Thebes, while the false years went by.
                    [*Enter, from the palace,* SECOND MESSENGER
SECOND MESSENGER: Elders of Thebes, most honored in this land,
    What horrors are yours to see and hear, what weight

Of sorrow to be endured, if, true to your birth,
You venerate* the line of Labdakos!   honor
I think neither Istros nor Phasis, those great rivers,
Could purify this place of the corruption
It shelters now, or soon must bring to light —
Evil not done unconsciously, but willed.
The greatest griefs are those we cause ourselves.
CHORAGOS: Surely, friend, we have grief enough already;
    What new sorrow do you mean?
SECOND MESSENGER: The Queen is dead.
CHORAGOS: Iocastê? Dead? But at whose hand?
SECOND MESSENGER: Her own.
    The full horror of what happened you can not know,
    For you did not see it; but I, who did, will tell you
    As clearly as I can how she met her death.

    When she had left us,
    In passionate silence, passing through the court,
    She ran to her apartment in the house,
    Her hair clutched by the fingers of both hands.
    She closed the doors behind her; then, by that bed
    Where long ago the fatal son was conceived —
    That son who should bring about his father's death —
    We heard her call upon Laïos, dead so many years,
    And heard her wail for the double fruit of her marriage,
    A husband by her husband, children by her child.

    Exactly how she died I do not know:
    For Oedipus burst in moaning and would not let us
    Keep vigil* to the end: it was by him   watch
    As he stormed about the room that our eyes were caught.
    From one to another of us he went, begging a sword,
    Cursing the wife who was not his wife, the mother
    Whose womb had carried his own children and himself.
    I do not know: it was none of us aided him,
    But surely one of the gods was in control!
    For with a dreadful cry
    He hurled his weight, as though wrenched out of himself,
    At the twin doors: the bolts gave, and he rushed in.
    And there we saw her hanging, her body swaying
    From the cruel cord she had noosed about her neck.
    A great sob broke from him, heartbreaking to hear,
    As he loosed the rope and lowered her to the ground.

    I would blot out from my mind what happened next!
    For the King ripped from her gown the golden brooches*   jewelry pins

That were her ornament, and raised them, and plunged them down
Straight into his own eyeballs, crying, "No more,
No more shall you look on the misery about me,
The horrors of my own doing! Too long you have known
The faces of those whom I should never have seen,
Too long been blind to those for whom I was searching!
From this hour, go in darkness!" And as he spoke,
He struck at his eyes — not once, but many times;
And the blood spattered his beard,
Bursting from his ruined sockets like red hail.

So from the unhappiness of two this evil has sprung,
A curse on the man and woman alike. The old
Happiness of the house of Labdakos
Was happiness enough: where is it today?
It is all wailing and ruin, disgrace, death — all
The misery of mankind that has a name —
And it is wholly* and for ever theirs.   completely
CHORAGOS: Is he in agony still? Is there no rest for him?
SECOND MESSENGER: He is calling for someone to lead him to the gates
So that all the children of Kadmos may look upon
His father's murderer, his mother's — no,
I can not say it!
                        And then he will leave Thebes,
Self-exiled, in order that the curse
Which he himself pronounced may depart from the house.
He is weak, and there is none to lead him,
So terrible is his suffering.
                        But you will see:
Look, the doors are opening; in a moment
You will see a thing that would crush a heart of stone.
        [*The central door is opened;* OEDIPUS, *blinded, is led in*
CHORAGOS: Dreadful indeed for men to see.
Never have my own eyes
Looked on a sight so full of fear.
Oedipus!
What madness came upon you, what daemon*   demon; evil spirit
Leaped on your life with heavier
Punishment than a mortal man can bear?
No: I can not even
Look at you, poor ruined one.
And I would speak, question, ponder,
If I were able. No.
You make me shudder.
OEDIPUS: God.   God.
Is there a sorrow greater?

Where shall I find harbor in this world?
My voice is hurled far on a dark wind.
What has God done to me?
CHORAGOS: Too terrible to think of, or to see.
OEDIPUS: O cloud of night,
   Never to be turned away: night coming on,
   I can not tell how: night like a shroud!*   burial gown
   My fair winds brought me here.
                      O God. Again
   The pain of the spikes where I had sight,
   The flooding pain
   Of memory, never to be gouged* out.   dug or scratched out
CHORAGOS: This is not strange.
   You suffer it all twice over, remorse* in pain,   great regret
   Pain in remorse.
OEDIPUS: Ah dear friend
   Are you faithful even yet, you alone?
   Are you still standing near me, will you stay here,
   Patient, to care for the blind?
                  The blind man!
   Yet even blind I know who it is attends me,
   By the voice's tone —
   Though my new darkness hide the comforter.
CHORAGOS: Oh fearful act!
   What god was it drove you to rake black
   Night across your eyes?
OEDIPUS: Apollo. Apollo. Dear
   Children, the god was Apollo.
   He brought my sick, sick fate upon me.
   But the blinding hand was my own!
   How could I bear to see
   When all my sight was horror everywhere?
CHORAGOS: Everywhere; that is true.
OEDIPUS: And now what is left?
   Images? Love? A greeting even,
   Sweet to the senses? Is there anything?
   Ah, no, friends: lead me away.
   Lead me away from Thebes.
               Lead the great wreck
   And hell of Oedipus, whom the gods hate.
CHORAGOS: Your fate is clear, you are not blind to that.
   Would God you had never found it out!
OEDIPUS: Death take the man who unbound
   My feet on that hillside
   And delivered me from death to life! What life?
   If only I had died,

This weight of monstrous doom
Could not have dragged me and my darlings down.
CHORAGOS: I would have wished the same.
OEDIPUS: Oh never to have come here
With my father's blood upon me! Never
To have been the man they call his mother's husband!
Oh accurst! Oh child of evil,
To have entered that wretched bed —
                              the selfsame one!
More **primal** than sin itself, this fell to me.
CHORAGOS: I do not know how I can answer you.
You were better dead than alive and blind.
OEDIPUS: Do not counsel me any more. This punishment
That I have laid upon myself is just.
If I had eyes,
I do not know how I could bear the sight
Of my father, when I came to the house of Death,
Or my mother: for I have sinned against them both
So vilely* that I could not make my peace   horribly
By strangling my own life.
                       Or do you think my children,
Born as they were born, would be sweet to my eyes?
Ah never, never! Nor this town with its high walls,
Nor the holy images of the gods.
               For I,
Thrice* miserable! — Oedipus, noblest of all the line   three times
Of Kadmos, have condemned myself to enjoy
These things no more, by my own malediction
Expelling that man whom the gods declared
To be a defilement in the house of Laïos.
After exposing the rankness* of my own guilt,   corruption; rottenness
How could I look men frankly in the eyes?
No, I swear it,
If I could have stifled my hearing at its source,
I would have done it and made all this body
A tight cell of misery, blank to light and sound:
So I should have been safe in a dark agony
Beyond all recollection.
              Ah Kithairon!
Why did you shelter me? When I was cast upon you,
Why did I not die? Then I should never
Have shown the world my execrable* birth.   detestable; hateful

Ah Polybos! Corinth, city that I believed
The ancient seat of my ancestors: how fair
I seemed, your child! And all the while this evil

Was cancerous within me!
                    For I am sick
In my daily life, sick in my origin.

O three roads, dark ravine, woodland and way
Where three roads met: you, drinking my father's blood,
My own blood, spilled by my own hand: can you remember
The unspeakable things I did there, and the things
I went on from there to do?
                         O marriage, marriage!
The act that engendered me, and again the act
Performed by the son in the same bed —
                              Ah, the net
Of **incest**, mingling fathers, brothers, sons,
With brides, wives, mothers: the last evil
That can be known by men: no tongue can say
How evil!
            No. For the love of God, conceal me
Somewhere far from Thebes; or kill me; or hurl me
Into the sea, away from men's eyes for ever.

Come, lead me. You need not fear to touch me.
Of all men, I alone can bear this guilt.

                                    [*Enter* CREON

CHORAGOS: We are not the ones to decide; but Creon here
    May fitly judge of what you ask. He only
    Is left to protect the city in your place.
OEDIPUS: Alas, how can I speak to him? What right have I
    To beg his courtesy whom I have deeply wronged?
CREON: I have not come to mock you, Oedipus,
    Or to reproach* you, either.   criticize; condemn

                              [*To* ATTENDANTS:
                    — You, standing there:
    If you have lost all respect for man's dignity,
    At least respect the flame of Lord Helios:
    Do not allow this pollution to show itself
    Openly here, an affront* to the earth   insult
    And Heaven's rain and the light of day. No, take him
    Into the house as quickly as you can.
    For it is proper
    That only the close kindred* see his grief.   relatives
OEDIPUS: I pray you in God's name, since your courtesy
    Ignores my dark expectation, visiting
    With mercy this man of all men most execrable:
    Give me what I ask — for your good, not for mine.
CREON: And what is it that you would have me do?

OEDIPUS: Drive me out of this country as quickly as may be
   To a place where no human voice can ever greet me.
CREON: I should have done that before now — only,
   God's will had not been wholly revealed to me.
OEDIPUS: But his command is plain: the **parricide**
   Must be destroyed. I am that evil man.
CREON: That is the sense of it, yes; but as things are,
   We had best discover clearly what is to be done.
OEDIPUS: You would learn more about a man like me?
CREON: You are ready now to listen to the god.
OEDIPUS: I will listen. But it is to you
   That I must turn for help. I beg you, hear me.

The woman in there —
Give her whatever funeral you think proper:
She is your sister.
                    — But let me go, Creon!
Let me **purge** my father's Thebes of the pollution
Of my living here, and go out to the wild hills,
To Kithairon, that has won such fame with me,
The tomb my mother and father appointed for me,
And let me die there, as they willed I should.
And yet I know
Death will not ever come to me through sickness
Or in any natural way: I have been preserved
For some unthinkable fate. But let that be.

As for my sons, you need not care for them.
They are men, they will find some way to live.
But my poor daughters, who have shared my table,
Who never before have been parted from their father —
Take care of them, Creon; do this for me.
And will you let me touch them with my hands
A last time, and let us weep together?
Be kind, my lord,
Great prince, be kind!
                    Could I but touch them,
They would be mine again, as when I had my eyes.
                    [*Enter* ANTIGONE *and* ISMENE, *attended*
Ah, God!
Is it my dearest children I hear weeping?
Has Creon pitied me and sent my daughters?
CREON: Yes, Oedipus: I knew that they were dear to you
   In the old days, and know you must love them still.
OEDIPUS: May God bless you for this — and be a friendlier
   Guardian to you than he has been to me!

Children, where are you?
Come quickly to my hands: they are your brother's —
Hands that have brought your father's once clear eyes
To this way of seeing —
                        Ah dearest ones,
I had neither sight nor knowledge then, your father
By the woman who was the source of his own life!
And I weep for you — having no strength to see you —,
I weep for you when I think of the bitterness
That men will visit upon you all your lives.
What homes, what festivals can you attend
Without being forced to depart again in tears?
And when you come to marriageable age,
Where is the man, my daughters, who would dare
Risk the bane* that lies on all my children?   disease
Is there any evil wanting? Your father killed
His father; sowed the womb of her who bore him;
Engendered* you at the fount* of his own existence!   fathered / origin
That is what they will say of you.
                        Then, whom
Can you ever marry? There are no bridegrooms for you,
And your lives must wither away in sterile dreaming.

O Creon, son of Menoikeus!
You are the only father my daughters have,
Since we, their parents, are both of us gone for ever.
They are your own blood: you will not let them
Fall into beggary and loneliness;
You will keep them from the miseries that are mine!
Take pity on them; see, they are only children,
Friendless except for you. Promise me this,
Great Prince, and give me your hand in token of it.
                        [CREON *clasps his right hand*
Children, I could say much, if you could understand me,
But as it is, I have only this prayer for you:
Live where you can, be as happy as you can —
Happier, please God, than God has made your father!
CREON: Enough. You have wept enough. Now go within.
OEDIPUS: I must; but it is hard.
CREON: Time eases all things.
OEDIPUS: But you must promise —
CREON: Say what you desire.
OEDIPUS: Send me from Thebes!
CREON: God grant that I may!
OEDIPUS: But since God hates me . . .
CREON: No, he will grant your wish
OEDIPUS: You promise?

CREON: I can not speak beyond my knowledge.
OEDIPUS: Then lead me in.
CREON: Come now, and leave your children.
OEDIPUS: No! Do not take them from me!
CREON: Think no longer
   That you are in command here, but rather think
   How, when you were, you served your own destruction.
                  [*Exeunt into the house all but the* CHORUS; *the* CHORAGOS
                  chants directly to the audience:
CHORAGOS: Men of Thebes: look upon Oedipus.

   This is the king who solved the famous riddle
   And towered up, most powerful of men.
   No mortal eyes but looked on him with envy,
   Yet in the end ruin swept over him.

   Let every man in mankind's frailty
   Consider his last day; and let none
   Presume on his good fortune until he find
   Life, at his death, a memory without pain.

QUESTIONS FOR DISCUSSION AND WRITING

[1] Describe the character of Oedipus before he hears Tiresias' words. Cite lines from the play that reveal his nature.

[2] A tragic hero is one whose elevating quality ultimately causes a terrible downfall. Name Oedipus' main heroic quality and then apply this formulation to his situation.

[3] Why are the play's events tragic, not merely pathetic and sad?

[4] Jocasta kills herself when she confronts the truth of the situation; Oedipus chooses to live. Examine his final statements in the play to explain his decision.

[5] How does the character of Creon change from the play's beginning to its end?

[6] Study the bitter dialogue between Oedipus and Tiresias on pages 212–216. What kind of character does Tiresias reveal? How does he react to the anger of the King?

[7] Sophocles uses irony throughout *Oedipus Rex.* For example, at the play's start, Oedipus refers to himself saying "I, Oedipus, who bear the famous name." He knows he is famous for solving the Sphinx's riddle; the audience knows he is really infamous for committing parricide and incest. Cite other examples of irony as they appear in the text. How do they increase the play's emotional impact?

READING SKILL: *Marking the Text II*

    In your academic work you'll often be asked to apply one author's ideas, theories, or approach to some other work. At the end of this section you will be asked to apply Aristotle's abstract categories, his "taxonomy" or framework for analyzing tragedy, to *Oedipus Rex.* You'll also be asked to evaluate how well his paradigms* reflect the play's structure and effect. You should develop a reading strategy that conforms to this assignment's demands. In addition to the usual surveying and engaging the text, marking the text is a skill you can adapt to the assignment's particular requirements.   *examples*

    Review our suggestions for marking a text (described in Chapter 2). In addition to identifying main ideas, supporting examples, and paragraph function, you should now mark those ideas or sections that you can apply directly to *Oedipus Rex,* noting the connection in the margin. Look for particular phrases or sentences in Aristotle that you can quote as evidence when you apply Aristotle's ideas about tragedy to Sophocles' play and evaluate how closely they apply. We've marked the first four paragraphs; as you read, continue to mark possible connections between the two works.

    Aristotle's Poetics *was not written by Aristotle: what we call the* Poetics *today is actually a collection of his students' class notes. He taught at the Lyceum in Athens; he and his students were known as the "peripatetics," a term denoting someone who walks about, which apparently was Aristotle's teaching style. The term has come to mean any follower of Aristotelian philosophy. The* Poetics *began the Western tradition of literary criticism, the study of a literary work's elements and a method for evaluating them. Aristotle's literary criticism was actually descriptive — that is, it objectively named the parts of a literary composition — but literary history took it as prescriptive — meaning a set of rules governing composition. In its descriptive approach, Aristotle's criticism reflects his scientific method in that both systems — the critical and the scientific — set up categories and both are applied deductively.*

        ARISTOTLE
FROM *Poetics*

    KEY CONCEPTS

    The theory of **IMITATION** is fundamental to Western art; Aristotle defines it in the following passage. Basically, the theory states that art duplicates life, that it re-creates experience and observation.

    Aristotle's theory of **PURGATION** states that viewing art, tragedy especially, rids the audience of harmful or dangerous emotions.

    RHETORIC is the study of linguistic style, or how we can manipulate language to enhance meaning.

An Aristotelian **whole** is another artistic concept fundamental to Western literature. All works should have a distinct beginning, a developed middle section, and a definite end.

● Poetry in general seems to have sprung from two causes, each of them lying deep in our nature. First, the instinct of **imitation** is implanted in man from childhood, one difference between him and other animals being that he is the most imitative of living creatures, and through imitation learns his earliest lessons; and no less universal is the pleasure felt in things imitated. We have evidence of this in the facts of experience. Objects which in themselves we view with pain, we delight to contemplate when reproduced with minute fidelity,* such as the forms of the most ignoble* animals and of dead bodies.

faithfulness / lowly, base

* enjoyment of Oedipus Rex despite its tragic content.

Tragedy — as also Comedy — was at first mere improvisation. The one originated with the authors of the Dithyramb,* the other with those of the phallic songs,* which are still in use in many of our cities. Tragedy advanced by slow degrees; each new element that showed itself was in turn developed. Having passed through many changes, it found its natural form, and there it stopped.

irregular short poem
cult songs

Epic poetry* agrees with Tragedy in so far as it is an imitation in verse of characters of a higher type. They differ in that Epic poetry admits but one kind of meter,* and is narrative in form. They differ, again, in their length: for Tragedy endeavors, as far as is possible, to confine itself to a single revolution of the sun, or but slightly to exceed this limit; whereas the Epic action has no limits of time. This, then, is a second point of difference, though at first the same freedom was admitted in Tragedy as in Epic poetry.

long narrative verse story of a great event

beat of a poem by syllables

* events of Oedipus Rex cover one day only

Tragedy is an imitation of an action that is serious, complete, and of a certain magnitude; in language embellished* with each kind of artistic ornament, the several kinds being found in separate parts of the play; in the form of action, not of narrative; through pity and fear effecting the proper **purgation** of these emotions.

decorated

true of Oedipus Rex?

Every tragedy, therefore, must have six parts, which determine its quality — namely, plot, character, diction, thought, spectacle, and song. But most important is the structure of the incidents. For Tragedy is an imitation, not of men, but of an action and of life, and life consists in action, and its end is a mode of action, not a quality. Now character determines men's qualities, but it is by their actions that they are happy or the reverse. Dramatic action, therefore, is not with a view to the representation of character: character comes in as subsidiary* to the actions. Hence the incidents and the plot are the end of a tragedy; and the end is the chief thing of all. Again, without action there cannot be a tragedy; there may

subordinate

SOURCE: *Poetics* by Aristotle. Translated by S. H. Butcher, Macmillan Publishing Company, 1932.

be without character. The Plot, then, is the first principle, and, as it were, the soul of a tragedy.

Third in order is Thought — that is, the faculty of saying what is possible and pertinent in given circumstances. In the case of oratory,* this is the function of the political art and of the art of **rhetoric**: and so indeed the older poets make their characters speak the language of civic life; the poets of our time, the language of the rhetoricians. Character is that which reveals moral purpose, showing what kind of things a man chooses or avoids. Speeches, therefore, which do not make this manifest, or in which the speaker does not choose or avoid anything whatever, are not expressive of character. Thought, on the other hand, is found where something is proved to be or not to be, or a general maxim* is enunciated.

speechmaking

truth or saying

Fourth among the elements enumerated comes diction, by which I mean the expression of the meaning in words, and its essence is the same both in verse and prose. Of the remaining elements Song holds the chief place among the embellishments.

The spectacle has, indeed, an emotional attraction of its own, but, of all the arts, it is the least artistic, and connected least with the art of poetry. For the power of Tragedy, we may be sure, is felt even apart from representation and actors. Besides, the production of spectacular effects depends more on the art of the stage machinist than on that of the poet.

These principles being established, let us now discuss the proper structure of the Plot, since this is the first and most important thing in Tragedy.

Now, according to our definition, tragedy is an imitation of an action that is complete, and whole, and of a certain magnitude; for there may be a **whole** that is wanting in magnitude. A whole is that which has a beginning, a middle, and an end. A beginning is that which does not follow anything by causal necessity, but after which something naturally is or comes to be. An end, on the contrary, is that which itself naturally follows some other thing, either by necessity, or as a rule, but has nothing following it. A middle is that which follows something as some other thing follows it. A well-constructed plot, therefore, must neither begin nor end at haphazard,* but conform to these principles.

by chance

It is evident from what has been said that it is not the function of the poet to relate what has happened, but what may happen — what is possible according to the law of probability or necessity. The poet and the historian differ not by writing in verse or in prose. The work of Herodotus might be put into verse, and it would still be a species of history, with meter no less than without it. The true difference is that one relates what has happened, the other what may happen. Poetry, therefore, is a more philosophical and a higher thing than history, for poetry tends to express the universal, history the particular.

Plots are either simple or complex, for the actions in real life, of which the plots are an imitation, obviously show a similar distinction. An action which is one and continuous in the sense above defined, I call simple, when the change of fortune takes place without reversal of the situation and without recognition.

A complex action is one in which the change is accompanied by such reversal, or by recognition, or by both. These last should arise from the internal structure of the plot, so that what follows should be the necessary or probable result of the preceding action. It makes all the difference whether any given event is a case of propter hoc or post hoc.* Reversal *result of some cause* of the situation is a change by which the action veers round to its opposite, subject always to our rule of probability or necessity.

Recognition, as the name indicates, is a change from ignorance to knowledge, producing love or hate between the persons destined by the poet for good or bad fortune. The best form of recognition is coincident with a reversal of the situation, as in the *Oedipus*. This recognition, combined with reversal, will produce either pity or fear; and actions producing these effects are those which, by our definition, Tragedy represents.

A perfect tragedy should, as we have seen, be arranged not on the simple but on the complex plan. It should, moreover, imitate actions which excite pity and fear, this being the distinctive mark of tragic imitation. It follows plainly, in the first place, that the change of fortune presented must not be the spectacle of a virtuous man brought from prosperity to adversity, for this moves neither pity nor fear; it merely shocks us. Nor, again, that of a bad man passing from adversity to prosperity, for nothing can be more alien to the spirit of Tragedy: it possesses no single tragic quality; it neither satisfies the moral sense nor calls forth pity or fear. Nor, again, should the downfall of the utter villain be exhibited. A plot of this kind would, doubtless, satisfy the moral sense, but it would inspire neither pity nor fear; for pity is aroused by unmerited misfortune, fear by the misfortune of a man like ourselves. Such an event, therefore, will be neither pitiful nor terrible. There remains, then, the character between these two extremes — that of a man who is not eminently good and just, yet whose misfortune is brought about not by vice or depravity,* but by *corruption, evil* some error or frailty.* He must be one who is highly renowned and *weakness* prosperous — a personage like Oedipus, Thyestes, or other illustrious men of such families.

Fear and pity may be aroused by spectacular means; but they may also result from the inner structure of the piece, which is the better way, and indicates a superior poet. For the plot ought to be so constructed that, even without the aid of the eye, he who hears the tale told will thrill with horror and melt to pity at what takes place. This is the impression we should receive from hearing the story of the *Oedipus*. But to produce this effect by the mere spectacle is a less artistic method, and dependent on extraneous* aids. Those who employ spectacular means to create a sense *external, uninvolved* not of the terrible but only the monstrous, are strangers to the purpose of Tragedy; for we must not demand of Tragedy any and every kind of pleasure, but only that which is proper to it. And since the pleasure which the poet should afford is that which comes from pity and fear through imitation, it is evident that this quality must be impressed upon the incidents. Let us then determine what are the circumstances which strike us as terrible or pitiful.

Actions capable of this effect must happen between persons who are either friends or enemies or indifferent to one another. If an enemy kills an enemy, there is nothing to excite pity either in the act or the intention — except so far as the suffering in itself is pitiful. So again with indifferent persons. But when the tragic incident occurs between those who are near or dear to one another — if, for example, a brother kills, or intends to kill, a brother, a son his father, a mother her son, a son his mother, or any other deed of the kind is done — these are the situations to be looked for by the poet.

QUESTIONS FOR DISCUSSION AND WRITING

[1] Summarize Aristotle's dramatic elements and categories. In a paragraph, argue how well *Oedipus Rex* fits Aristotle's framework, citing examples from the play and quotations from the *Poetics* to support your view.

[2] Aristotle states that imitation is inherent human behavior. List examples that might support his claim. Think particularly about children's games and play, common types of entertainment, and educational methods.

[3] Spectacle, Aristotle claims, is "the least artistic" of literary elements. Think of contemporary dramatic works on TV or in films. Do they reflect this Aristotelian judgment?

[4] Review the myth of Echo and Narcissus. Is Narcissus' story a tragedy according to the Aristotelian definition? Explain your logic, referring to both the myth and the *Poetics*.

Just as you have applied Aristotle's theory of tragedy to Oedipus Rex, *Freud applies part of his theory of sexual development to the play. He uses Sophocles' literary work as evidence and illustration of his own ideas. Read his essay — after first surveying it — and state its thesis. Then mark the connections he makes between his theory and the play. By isolating the connection of thesis and evidence, you will be able to distinguish the author's ideas from the play's themes and assess the logical validity of his connections. We've marked the first two instances of Freud's use of the play as evidence; continue marking the text from that point. Look for two basic kinds of evidence: example and quotation.*

SIGMUND FREUD
"Oedipus Rex"

KEY CONCEPT

The word **primeval** refers to the "first age," or the earliest and most basic impulses and desires of the human mind.

● In my experience, which is already extensive, the chief part in the mental lives of all children who later become psycho-neurotics* is played by their parents. Being in love with one parent and hating the other are among the essential constituents* of the stock of psychical impulses which is formed at that time and which is of such importance in determining the symptoms of the later neurosis. It is not my belief, however, that psycho-neurotics differ sharply in this respect from other human beings who remain normal — that they are able, that is, to create something absolutely new and peculiar to themselves. It is far more probable — and this is confirmed by occasional observations on normal children — that they are only distinguished by exhibiting on a magnified scale feelings of love and hatred to their parents which occur less obviously and less intensely in the minds of most children.

anxious, disturbed people

parts

This discovery is confirmed by a legend that has come down to us from classical antiquity: a legend whose profound and universal power to move can only be understood if the hypothesis I have put forward in regard to the psychology of children has an equally universal validity. What I have in mind is the legend of King Oedipus and Sophocles' drama which bears his name.

ties play to theory of sexual development

The action of the play consists in nothing other than the process of revealing, with cunning delays and ever-mounting excitement — a process that can be likened to the work of a psychoanalysis — that Oedipus himself is the murderer of Laius, but further that he is the son of the murdered man and of Jocasta. Appalled at the abomination* which he has unwittingly perpetrated,* Oedipus blinds himself and forsakes his home. The oracle has been fulfilled.

unnatural crime
committed

Oedipus Rex is what is known as a tragedy of destiny. Its tragic effect is said to lie in the contrast between the supreme will of the gods and the vain attempts of mankind to escape the evil that threatens them. The lesson which, it is said, the deeply moved spectator should learn from the tragedy is submission to the divine will and realization of his own impotence. Modern dramatists have accordingly tried to achieve a similar tragic effect by weaving the same contrast into a plot invented by themselves. But the spectators have looked on unmoved while a curse or an oracle was fulfilled in spite of all the efforts of some innocent man: later tragedies of destiny have failed in their effect.

If *Oedipus Rex* moves a modern audience no less than it did the contemporary Greek one, the explanation can only be that its effect does not lie in the contrast between destiny and human will, but is to be looked for in the particular nature of the material on which that contrast is exemplified. There must be something which makes a voice within us ready to recognize the compelling force of destiny in the *Oedipus,* while we can dismiss as merely arbitrary* such dispositions* as are laid down in modern

not following any law /
explanations, opinions

SOURCE: "Oedipus Rex" from *The Interpretation of Dreams.* Copyright © 1954 by Basic Books Incorporated.

tragedies of destiny. And a factor of this kind is in fact involved in the story of King Oedipus. His destiny moves us only because it might have been ours — because the oracle laid the same curse upon us before our birth as upon him. It is the fate of all of us, perhaps, to direct our first sexual impulse towards our mother and our first hatred and our first murderous wish against our father. Our dreams convince us that that is so. King Oedipus, who slew his father Laius and married his mother Jocasta, merely shows us the fulfillment of our own childhood wishes. But, more fortunate than he, we have meanwhile succeeded, insofar as we have not become psycho-neurotics, in detaching our sexual impulses from our mothers and in forgetting our jealousy of our fathers. Here is one in whom these **primeval** wishes of our childhood have been fulfilled, and we shrink back from him with the whole force of the repression by which those wishes have since that time been held down within us. While the poet, as he unravels* the past, brings to light the guilt of Oedipus, he is at the same time compelling us to recognize our own inner minds, in which those same impulses, though suppressed, are still to be found. The contrast with which the closing Chorus leaves us confronted —

solves

> . . . Fix on Oedipus your eyes,
> Who resolved the dark enigma, noblest champion and most wise.
> Like a star his envied fortune mounted beaming far and wide:
> Now he sinks in seas of anguish, whelmed* beneath a raging
> tide . . .

overtaken

— strikes as a warning at ourselves and our pride, at us who since our childhood have grown so wise and so mighty in our own eyes. Like Oedipus, we live in ignorance of these wishes, repugnant* to morality, which have been forced upon us by Nature, and after their revelation we may all of us well seek to close our eyes to the scenes of our childhood.

disgusting

There is an unmistakable indication in the text of Sophocles' tragedy itself that the legend of Oedipus sprang from some primeval dream-material which had as its content the distressing disturbance of a child's relation to his parents owing to the first stirrings of sexuality. At a point when Oedipus, though he is not yet enlightened, has begun to feel troubled by his recollection of the oracle, Jocasta consoles him by referring to a dream which many people dream, though, as she thinks, it has no meaning:

> Many a man ere now in dreams hath lain
> With her who bare him. He hath least annoy
> Who with such omens troubleth not his mind.

Today, just as then, many men dream of having sexual relations with their mothers, and speak of the fact with indignation and astonishment. It is clearly the key to the tragedy and the complement to the dream of the dreamer's father being dead. The story of Oedipus is the reaction of the imagination to these two typical dreams. And just as these dreams, when dreamt by adults, are accompanied by feelings of repulsion, so too the legend must include horror and self-punishment. Its further modification originates once again in a misconceived secondary revision of the material, which has sought to exploit it for theological purposes. The attempt to harmonize divine omnipotence with human responsibility must naturally fail in connection with this subject-matter just as with any other.

QUESTIONS FOR DISCUSSION AND WRITING

[1] *Oedipus Rex* is a play based on legend, not fact. How can Freud use legendary material fairly to support a scientific theory? What justification does he offer? Cite evidence from Freud's essay.

[2] For the most part Freud uses *Oedipus Rex* for a nonliterary purpose, but he does discuss the play's dramatic effect. Review Aristotle's literary principles and identify the one that Freud refers to in his essay.

[3] Freud quotes Jocasta's lines in which she tells Oedipus not to worry about his dreams, for they mean nothing. What is Freud's reaction to her advice, and why?

SECTION ESSAY ASSIGNMENTS

The evidence you use to support your ideas in an essay depends on what you want to prove, or what your thesis is. You need to select examples and quotations that fit a particular issue. Therefore, in each of the following assignments, you will have to go through Oedipus Rex *with specific ideas in mind so that you find the most appropriate supporting evidence.*

[1] Hegel, a nineteenth-century German philosopher, defined tragedy as the collision of two "rights," or two good forces, such as having to choose between romantic love and family loyalty, as in the plot of Shakespeare's *Romeo and Juliet.* Using your graphic organizer, name the good forces or impulses that come into opposition in the play. Think about Oedipus' character: what makes him a hero? Then consider what "right" demands his downfall. How does Oedipus help to cause his own tragedy? Develop your ideas in an essay. Your thesis should address the issue of which two forces are in opposition and how Oedipus himself brings on the play's tragic situation. Cite evidence from the text in the form of examples <u>and</u> quotations.

[2] Aristotle's theory of catharsis states that by watching a tragedy, the audience goes through a symbolic process of purgation, experiencing pity, fear, and the release of those emotions. Analyze which elements of *Oedipus Rex* might make it a cathartic experience, according to Aristotle's theory. Which events might cause fear in the spectator? Which events seem designed to arouse pity? How does the play's ending allow for a sense of restored stability? Use examples and quotations from the play and from Aristotle to support your views.

[3] After reviewing Aristotle's and Hegel's theory of tragedy, compare and contrast Oedipus' situation with that of the children of Israel in "The

Golden Calf,'' the son in the New Testament's ''Prodigal Son,'' or Narcissus in the myth ''Echo and Narcissus.'' One point of comparison might be the recognition and reversal faced by all of these figures; for a point of contrast examine all of the stories for a collision of two opposing forces.

[4] In paragraph four, Freud rejects the interpretation of *Oedipus Rex* as a ''tragedy of destiny.'' Develop an argument that defends this interpretation. Cite passages and examples from the play to show that Oedipus faced an inevitable fall.

The Text of Medieval Architecture

READING SKILL EXERCISE: *Using a Graphic Organizer*

In the following article, Bernard S. Myers describes a medieval cathedral's architectural elements. Survey the article, read it, and then arrange the elements into a graphic organizer. You will need to name the categories he describes; looking for topic ideas will help you identify them. The first paragraph is a general introduction to cathedral architecture. The graphic organizer might begin with the main idea of paragraph two, that the cathedral's major element is its mass, its whole effect:

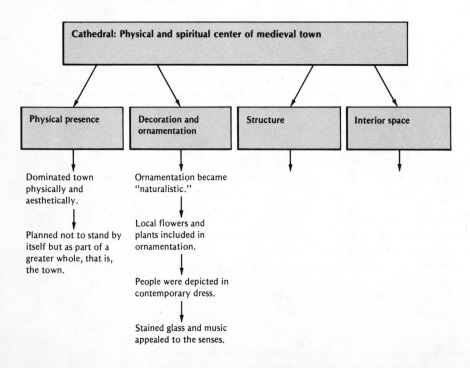

Cathedral: Physical and spiritual center of medieval town

- Physical presence
- Decoration and ornamentation
- Structure
- Interior space

Physical presence:
- Dominated town physically and aesthetically.
- Planned not to stand by itself but as part of a greater whole, that is, the town.

Decoration and ornamentation:
- Ornamentation became ''naturalistic.''
- Local flowers and plants included in ornamentation.
- People were depicted in contemporary dress.
- Stained glass and music appealed to the senses.

Complete the diagram. Use paragraph three's topic idea as the category name and fill in the two subcategories that Myers describes. Take paragraphs five and six together because they both deal with a single category.

The following article appeared in Bernard S. Myers' Art and Civilization in 1967. Although Myers writes on medieval art, not religion, many of his points were raised by Barbara Tuchman in A Distant Mirror (excerpted in Chapter 2). That their discussions of medieval art and religion bear resemblances indicates the pervasive influence of the Christian religion at the time. Generally, the architectural masterpieces of the modern world are government buildings, office buildings, or private homes, not cathedrals as in the medieval era; this difference reflects how changing social and religious values can dictate architectural values. Most of the medieval cathedrals still stand, however, and are preserved as great works of art, relics of the medieval aesthetic.

BERNARD S. MYERS
"The Rise of Gothic Art"

KEY CONCEPTS

An **AESTHETIC** is a standard for judging what is beautiful.

GEOMETRIC art and **NATURALISTIC** art can be considered opposite aesthetics. The first term refers to art that is symmetrical and has basic patterns; the second names art that imitates nature without idealizing it to the point of symmetry.

DOGMATISM is an insistence on strict observation of a given doctrine.

● Standing on one side of the market place, the Gothic cathedral was the physical and spiritual focus of town life. People met there daily for worship and for other purposes. Mystery plays* were performed before it; wandering preachers gave their sermons within its shadow — these were the entertainments of the middle ages. In its sculptures and stained glass the knowledge of the age was summarized for an illiterate public. In the church also, people were baptized, confirmed, married; from this point there still came the power for salvation. — religious dramas

It is little wonder therefore that the cathedral, symbol of the universal church, dominated not only the town itself (even now it is the first thing one sees on approaching many cities) but the **aesthetic** of the times as well. Every art in this period was subject to the architectural idea; even the pages in manuscripts are essays in architecture. Consequently, detail is subordinate to general effect in the ideal Gothic building. The figures on the column shafts are lengthened, as evident on the facade of Chartres, and so long as Gothic art keeps this unified relationship it remains strong. A piece of Gothic cathedral sculpture is seldom able to stand by itself, since it is planned as part of a greater whole, differing from classical sculpture, which is often made to be self-enclosed.

Emerging from the dark shadow of the monastic Middle Ages, ornament* turned from **geometric** to **naturalistic**. For example, instead of the ever-present formalized acanthus* leaf of previous periods, the actual flora* of a given area was now reproduced in art. Although for the most part the Romanesque iconography* and subjects of the monastery churches were retained, they were given a new naturalistic treatment. As early as the thirteenth century, nature and the physical world became part of theology — a significant change for all aspects of medieval life. Even

decoration
plant having large intricate leaves
flowers and plants
images, statuary

Chartres Cathedral. Courtesy of Gates, Frederic Lewis.

historical subjects (e.g., Biblical and Roman themes) were given a certain contemporaneity* of costume. The cathedral in this period epitomized* the new secular spirit by its representation of scenes from everyday life and its generally humanistic approach. It appealed to the senses through the use of color in sculpture, lambent* stained glass, and rich complex sounds in the new polyphonic* music.

> modernness / best represented; embodied
>
> radiant
>
> having many sounds

Structurally the Gothic cathedral, while different from Romanesque, was an extension and outgrowth of the latter. The same basic physical problem remained: to build a large stone-vaulted* fireproof structure. But the monastic Romanesque architects had been limited spiritually and technically to a static and massive conception, whereas their successors aspired to a more open, better-lighted, dynamic,* and higher structure embodying the new striving and idealism, the mystic exaltation of the period. The physical and logical expression of this ideal constitutes the special character of Gothic building.

> having stone ceiling supports
>
> in motion; moving

Dynamic in its total architectural effect, where the Romanesque church was static, the Gothic cathedral is thoroughly preoccupied with problems of space, both as means and as end. While the Romanesque in many cases seemed dark and low, this architecture achieves greater height and illumination, a quality of endlessness symbolic of newer feelings. The sense of infinity is lent in part by the repetition of small details and by avoidance of a terminus.* More important, however, the vaults are raised to hitherto undreamed-of heights, a great number of windows are cut into the walls, and the interior and exterior of the building are connected by the translucent* windows and the general openwork character of the style.

> end point
>
> admitting light

From the outside of the church, its interior spaces can immediately be sensed, just as from the inside the exterior is implied. Instead of the earlier fixed **dogmatism** of heavy inert Romanesque vaults on massive unpierced walls, there is a delicately balanced organic system. The vaults are supported separately by ribs connected to the complex piers rising from the floor and partly by the solid stone outer buttresses rising from the ground. These buttresses are connected to the vaults and to the deliberately thin, window-pierced walls by stone braces called flying buttresses. The walls of the Gothic building are little more than stone curtains hanging from above, with large areas cut away for window openings and gallery spaces. The architect can raise his structure to grandiose heights because of the dynamic balance engendered between the downward and outward thrust of the vaults and the upward thrust of the floor piers combined with the diagonal inward thrust of the flying buttresses. Through this triumph of logic, the Gothic builder produced a thrilling and inspiring religious structure in which the immense, sometimes invisible height of the vaults, the vibrating color of stained glass, and the rich music united to achieve a more effective act of faith. The Gothic architect brought logic and reason to buttress faith.

QUESTIONS FOR DISCUSSION AND WRITING

[1] In the final sentence, Myers states that "the Gothic architect brought logic and reason to buttress faith." Cite some examples from the reading to show how a cathedral's form illustrated specific Christian religious beliefs.

[2] Ornamentation is a common structural element of car design, landscaping, furniture style, food display/presentation, uniforms, personal attire, haircuts, and so on. Select two or three of these subjects and cite examples of both geometric and naturalistic ornamentation.

Look carefully at the drawing of a window at Chartres. Understanding and appreciating the art of a painting or a building require a special kind of "reading" skill. In the same way as a written text, paintings and buildings represent a particular theme, or thesis, presented in some organized way. To understand visual art you have to be familiar with the artist's symbolic language. When you look at a painting, you need to translate its elements into descriptive language in order to discuss it. In the following essay, Emile Male states that "medieval art may be called a sacred script." As you read, pay attention to Male's translations of common medieval artistic symbols.

Emile Male wrote The Gothic Image *in 1958. He explains how medieval artists all used a traditional religious, symbolic language in their works, making their art easily accessible to a person of their time but making it seem distant from the present day. Again, as the essays of Tuchman and Myers pointed out, we see a uniformity in medieval artistic subjects, themes, and symbols: the artists clearly represent an age dominated by the Church. Modern Western art, with its freedom of subject matter and medium,* retains little of the medieval aesthetic, for it stresses the individual over the institution.*

type of expression

EMILE MALE
FROM *The Gothic Image*

KEY CONCEPTS
HERESY is the theological crime of contradicting Church dogma; see Chapter 2, page 100.
  DIVINE INTERVENTION refers to any direct action by God that changes the course of events.

● The Middle Ages had a passion for order. They organised art as they had organised dogma, secular learning and society. The artistic representation of sacred subjects was a science governed by fixed laws which could not be broken at the dictates* of individual imagination. It cannot be questioned that this theology of art, if one may so put it, was soon reduced to a body of doctrine, for from very early times the craftsmen are seen submitting to it from one end of Europe to the other. This science was transmitted by the Church to the lay* sculptors and painters of the thirteenth century who religiously guarded the sacred traditions, so that, even in the centuries in which it was most vigorous, medieval art retained the hieratic* grandeur of primitive art.

orders

non-church affiliated

very stylized

The art of the Middle Ages is first and foremost a sacred writing of which every artist must learn the characters. He must know that the circular nimbus* placed vertically behind the head serves to express sanctity,* while the nimbus impressed with a cross is the sign of divinity which he will always use in portraying any of the three Persons of the Trinity. He will learn that the aureole (i.e., light which emanates from the whole figure and surrounds the body as a nimbus) expresses eternal bliss, and belongs to the three Persons of the Trinity, to the Virgin, and to the souls of the Blessed. He must know that representations of God the Father, God

halo
state of sainthood, holiness

the Son, the angels and the apostles should have the feet bare, while there would be real impropriety in representing the Virgin and the saints with bare feet. In such matters a mistake would have ranked almost as **heresy**. Other accepted symbols enabled the medieval artist to express the invisible, to represent that which would otherwise be beyond the domain of art. A hand emerging from the clouds, making the gesture of benediction* with thumb and two fingers raised, and surrounded by a cruciform nimbus, was recognized as the sign of **divine intervention**, the emblem of providence. Little figures of nude and sexless children, ranged side by side in the folds of Abraham's mantle,* signified the eternal rest of the life to come.

blessing

cloak

There are also accepted signs for objects of the visible world which the artist must learn. Lines which are concentric* and sinuous* represent the sky, those which are horizontal and undulating* represent water. A tree, that is to say a stalk surmounted with two or three leaves, indicates that the scene takes place on the earth; a tower pierced by a doorway is a town, while if an angel watch on the battlements it is the heavenly Jerusalem. Thus we have a veritable* hieroglyphic* in which art and writing blend, showing the same spirit of order and abstraction that there is in heraldic art* with its alphabet, rules and symbolism. These examples, which it would be useless to multiply, will suffice to show in what sense medieval art may be called a sacred script.

encircling / curvy
wavy

true / Egyptian picture writing

family symbols, coats of arms

Medieval art is like medieval literature; its value lies less in conscious talent than in diffused* genius. The personality of the artist does not always appear, but countless generations of men speak through his mouth and the individual, even when mediocre, is lifted by the genius of the Christian centuries.

scattered

QUESTIONS FOR DISCUSSION AND WRITING

[1] What does Male mean when he calls medieval art a "sacred script"?

[2] Male explains that the medieval artist was not free to represent sacred subjects according to his own imagination; he had to follow fixed laws. Why should the artist be restricted in this way? Consider the fact that medieval art is primarily <u>religious</u>.

SECTION ESSAY ASSIGNMENTS

The following assignments ask you to deal with some common structures and designs that surround us everyday as texts that can be read. You can develop and improve your ability to articulate nonverbal thesis statements by examining the "language" of visual art and common objects.

[1] Apply the categories you've listed in your graphic organizer to the following kinds of buildings: a mall; a gas station; a fast-food restaurant. Write an essay on each topic, describing how each element is represented in the particular building, both its interior and exterior, assessing which element(s) is/are most important to the building's function.

[2] We're surrounded every day by different forms of visual symbolism: advertisements, traffic signs, and the like. Choose one form and translate the individual symbols, interpreting their meaning and message.

[3] Compare and contrast the purpose, structure, and ornament of a medieval cathedral with those of a modern office building.

Renaissance Prose

In retelling the Arthurian legends — the story of King Arthur and his Knights of the Round Table — Sir Thomas Malory depicts the late Middle Ages' idealized vision of chivalry. Review our suggestions for deriving a definition outlined in Chapter 2. As you read, mark incidents and actions that symbolize the elements of chivalry. When you finish the reading, your writing assignment will ask for a paragraph defining the term.

Malory wrote Le Morte D'Arthur *in the fifteenth century, well after the age of chivalry had passed. The Arthurian legends have persisted in Western literature and art; in the nineteenth century, Richard Wagner composed the operas* Parsifal *and* Tristan and Isolde, *which are based on Arthurian legends and characters. Readers of the present day still enjoy the legends. They recount Arthur's youth, the influence of his teacher, the magician Merlin, Arthur's claiming of Excalibur, the "sword in the stone," and the rise of his court at Camelot, home to the Knights of the Round Table. Arthur may have been an historical figure, perhaps of Roman lineage (the Romans had once conquered Great Britain). In the legend, Lancelot is Arthur's most devoted knight. Lancelot's love for Queen Guenivere, Arthur's wife, is one of the tragic ironies of the Arthurian stories.*

SIR THOMAS MALORY
FROM *Le Morte D'Arthur*

● Sir Lancelot departed, and when he came to the Chapel Perilous he alighted* and tied his horse to a little gate. As soon as he was within the churchyard he saw on the front of the Chapel many fair rich shields turned upside-down, and many of these shields Sir Lancelot had seen knights bear beforehand. With that, he saw standing by him there thirty huge knights, taller by a yard than any man he had ever seen; they all grimaced and

got down

SOURCE: From *Le Morte D'Arthur* by Sir Thomas Malory. R. M. Lumiansky, ed. Copyright © 1982 by R. M. Lumiansky. Reprinted with permission of Charles Scribner's Sons.

gnashed* at Lancelot. When he saw their countenances,* he was sorely* afraid; so he put his shield before him and took his sword in his hand, ready for battle. The knights were all armed in black armor, ready with their shields and their drawn swords. As Sir Lancelot would have gone through them, they scattered on every side of him and gave him the way. He waxed* all bold and entered into the Chapel, and there he saw no light except a dim lamp burning. Then he was aware of a corpse covered with a cloth of silk, and he stooped down and cut away a piece of that cloth. At that, he felt as if beneath him the earth had quaked a little, and he was frightened. Then he saw a fair sword lying by the dead knight, and he got it in his hand and hurried out of the Chapel.

As soon as he was in the Chapel-yard, all the knights spoke to him with a grim voice and said, "Knight, Sir Lancelot, put that sword from thee or else thou shalt die!"

"Whether I live or die," said Sir Lancelot, "with no such words shall ye* get it again. Therefore fight for it, if ye list.*"

But then he past through them, and beyond the Chapel yard a fair damosel* met him and said, "Sir Lancelot, leave that sword behind thee or thou will die for it."

"I will not leave it," said Sir Lancelot, "for any threats."

"No," she said, "if thou did leave that sword, thou would never see Queen Guenivere."

"Then I would be a fool if I should leave this sword," said Lancelot.

"Now gentle knight," said the damosel, "I require thee to kiss me but once."

"Nay," said Sir Lancelot, "That God forbid."

"Well, sir," said she, "if thou had kissed me thy life-days had been done. But now, alas, I have lost all my labor, for I ordained this chapel for thy sake and for Sir Gawain. I once had Sir Gawain with me, and at that time he fought with that knight who lieth* there dead in yonder chapel, Sir Gylbert the Bastard; and at that time he smote* off the left hand of Sir Gylbert. Sir Lancelot, now I tell thee that I have loved thee for seven years, but no woman may have thy love except queen Guenivere. Since I may not rejoice thee and have thy body alive, I had thought of no greater joy in this world than to have thy body dead. Then I would have embalmed it and wrapped it and so kept it for all my life-days, and daily I would have embraced thee and kissed thee as spite to Queen Guenivere."

"Ye say well!" said Sir Lancelot. "Jesus preserve me from your subtle crafts.*"

He took his horse and departed from her, and as the book sayeth, when Sir Lancelot had departed she made such sorrow that she died within a fortnight.* Her name was Hellawes the Sorceress, Lady of the Castle Nygramous.

Soon Sir Lancelot met the damosel, Sir Melyot's sister, and when she saw him she clapped her hands and wept for joy. Then they rode unto a castle nearby, where Sir Melyot lay, and as soon as Sir Lancelot saw him

---

Margin glosses:

grinded their teeth / face, looks / exceedingly

grew

you
want

lady

is stretched out
cut, hit

spells, plots

2 weeks

he knew him; but he was pale as the earth from bleeding. When Sir Melyot saw Sir Lancelot he kneeled upon his knees and cried on high, "Oh lord, Sir Lancelot, help me!"

At once Sir Lancelot leapt unto him and touched his wounds with Sir Gylbert's sword; then he wiped his wounds with a part of the bloody cloth that Sir Gylbert was wrapped in. At once he was as well as he ever was. Then there was great joy among them, and they made Sir Lancelot all the cheer that they might. So on the morn Sir Lancelot took his leave and bade*   told Sir Melyot to hurry "to the court of my lord Arthur, for it draweth nigh*   near to the feast of the Pentecost; and there by the grace of God ye shall find me." And they parted.

Then Sir Lancelot rode through many strange countries, over moors*   fields and valleys, till by fortune he came to a fair castle. As he passed beyond the castle he thought he heard two bells ring, and then he was aware of a falcon which came flying over his head toward a high elm, with long leashes about her feet. As she flew unto the elm to take her perch, the leashes wrapped about a bough; when she would have taken flight she hung there, held fast by the legs. Sir Lancelot saw how she hung and beheld the fair falcon dangling, and he was sorry for her.

Meanwhile a lady came out of the castle and cried on high, "Oh Lancelot, Lancelot, as thou art the flower of all knights, help me to get my hawk. For if my hawk is lost, my lord will destroy me; I guarded the hawk but she slipped away from me. And if my lord husband knows it, he is so hasty that he will slay me."

"What is your lord's name?" said Sir Lancelot.

"Sir," she said, "his name is Sir Phelot, a knight who belongs to the king of North Wales."

"Well fair lady, since you know my name and require me of knighthood to help you, I will do what I may to get your hawk; yet God knoweth I am a poor climber and the tree is passing high, with few boughs to help me."

Sir Lancelot alighted, tied his horse to the same tree, and prayed the lady to unarm him. When he was unarmed he put off all his clothes except his shirt and breeches.* Then with might and force he climbed up to the   pants falcon and tied the leashes to a large rotten bough and threw the hawk down with the bough. At once the lady got the hawk in her hand.

Sir Phelot came out of the thicket suddenly, he who was her husband, all armed and with his naked sword in his hand. He said "Oh knight Lancelot, now I have found thee as I wished!" — and stood at the bole*   trunk of the tree to slay him.

"Ah, lady," said Sir Lancelot, "why have ye betrayed me?"

"She hath done," said Sir Phelot, "only as I commanded her. Therefore there is no other help, for the hour has come when thou must die."

"That would be shame to thee," said Sir Lancelot: "thou, an armed knight, to slay a naked man by treason."

"Thou gettest no other grace," said Sir Phelot, "and therefore help thyself if thy canst."

"Truly," said Sir Lancelot, "that shall be thy shame. But since thou wilt not do otherwise, take my armor with thee and hang my sword upon a bough where I may get it, then do thy best to slay me if thou canst."

"Nay, nay," said Sir Phelot, "for I know thee better than thou thinkest. Therefore thou gettest no weapon if I may keep you therefrom."

"Alas," said Sir Lancelot, "that ever a knight should die weapon-less!"

Then he looked above him and below him, and over his head he saw a rough limb, a big leafless bough. He broke it off from the trunk; then he came lower and saw where his own horse stood, and suddenly he leapt on the farther side of his horse, away from the knight. Then Sir Phelot lashed at him eagerly, thinking to have slain him, but Sir Lancelot put the stroke away with the rough bough; with it he smote Sir Phelot on one side of the head, so that he fell down in a swoon* on the ground. Then Sir Lancelot   faint
took Sir Phelot's sword out of his hand and struck his neck from the body.

The lady cried, "Alas, why have you slain my husband?"

"I am not the cause," said Sir Lancelot. "With falsehood you would have me slain by treason, and now it has fallen on you both."

Then she swooned as though she would die. Sir Lancelot got all his armor as quickly as he might and put it upon him for fear of further attack, since the knight's castle was so near him. Then as soon as he could he took his horse and departed, thanking God that he had escaped from that hard adventure.

So Sir Lancelot rode in many wild ways throughout moors and marshes, and as he rode in a valley he saw a knight chasing a lady with a naked sword in order to slay her. But just as the knight would have slain this lady, she cried to Sir Lancelot and prayed him to rescue her. When he saw that mischief, he took his horse and rode between them saying, "Knight, fie,*   oh!
for shame! Why wilt thou slay this lady? Thou dost shame unto thee and all knights."

"What hast thou to do between me and my wife?" said the knight. "I will slay her despite thy head."

"That shall ye not," said Sir Lancelot, "for instead we two will have ado*   fight
together."

"Sir Lancelot," said the knight, "thou dost not thy part, for this lady hath betrayed me."

"It is not so," said the lady. "Truly he sayeth wrong about me. Because I love and cherish my cousin-germane,* he is jealous; but as I shall answer   blood relative
to God, there was never sin between us. But sir, as thou art called the most worshipful* knight of the world I require thee of true knighthood to help   honorable
me and save me. For what so ever he says, he will slay me; he is without mercy."

"Have ye no fear," said Lancelot. "It shall not lie in his power."

"Sir," said the knight, "In your sight I will be ruled as ye will have me."

So Sir Lancelot rode with the knight on one side and the lady on the other. They had ridden only a short while when the knight bade Sir

Lancelot turn and look behind him, and said, "Sir, yonder come men of arms riding after us."

So Sir Lancelot turned and suspected no treason. But the knight went to his lady's side and suddenly cut off her head. When Sir Lancelot had spied what he had done, he said, "Traitor, thou hast shamed me forever!" And suddenly he alighted from his horse and pulled out his sword to slay the knight. But he fell flat to the earth and gripped Sir Lancelot by the thighs and cried mercy.

"Fie on thee!" said Sir Lancelot. "Thou shameful knight, thou maist* have no mercy; therefore arise and fight with me."   *may*

"Nay," said the knight, "I will never arise till ye grant me mercy."

"Now I will offer thee fairly," said Lancelot. "I will unarm myself to my shirt, and I will have nothing upon me but my shirt and my sword in my hand. Then if thou canst slay me, thou art quit* forever."   *pardoned, released*

"Nay, Sir, that I will never do."

"Well," said Sir Lancelot, "take this lady and her head and bear them with thee. And here thou shalt swear upon my sword to bear them always upon thy back and never to rest till thou come to Queen Guenivere."

"Sir," said he, "that I will do, by the faith of my body."

"Now," said Lancelot, "tell me, what is your name?"

"Sir, my name is Pedyvere."

"In a shameful hour thou were born," said Lancelot.

So Pedyvere departed with the dead lady and the head and found the queen with King Arthur at Winchester. There he told all the truth.

"Sir Knight," said the queen, "This is a horrible and shameful deed, and a great rebuke for Sir Lancelot; but, not withstanding, his worship is known in many diverse countries. I shall give you this as a penance.* Make   *punishment* ye as good shift* as ye can: ye shall bear this lady with you on horseback   *arrangements* unto the Pope of Rome, and from him receive your penance for your foul deeds. And ye shall never rest one night where ye rest another; if ye go to any bed, the dead body shall lie with you."

He made his oath and so departed. And it telleth the French book, when he came to Rome the Pope bade him go back to Queen Guenivere; and in Rome his lady was buried by the Pope's commandment. Later this knight, Sir Pedyvere, fell into great goodness and was a holy man and a hermit.

QUESTIONS FOR DISCUSSION AND WRITING

[1] Lancelot takes part in four separate adventures in this reading. In each he demonstrates particular virtues that identify him as a great hero of chivalry. Summarize the events of each adventure and then name the heroic qualities that Lancelot demonstrates in each one.

[2] Define the concept of "chivalry." Lancelot is the ideal knight; examine his characteristics and behavior to begin building your definition. Note his

treatment of women and his code of behavior, revealed by what he chooses and what he refuses to do.

[3] Malory wrote *Le Morte D'Arthur* in the early Renaissance, looking back on and idealizing a past age. Which of the story's elements mark it as an idealized treatment as opposed to a realistic treatment of an historical era? Consider the plausibility of the events and the characters' behavior.

The Spanish writer Miguel de Cervantes wrote what is considered to be the first novel in European literature. The following selection presents two episodes from Cervantes' work, completed in 1614. Cervantes treats some of the same themes as Malory did in "Sir Lancelot," but Cervantes' work satirizes* *makes fun of* chivalry. Still, the work has serious elements in addition to its humor; it philosophizes as well as entertains. Read the selection, looking for the same chivalric codes as Malory idealized, and note how Cervantes' treatment becomes a satire and a critique of those codes while allowing Don Quixote himself to be a sympathetic as well as ridiculous hero.

Before Cervantes' work, most long narratives had no unifying plot; they usually consisted of a series of adventures. Don Quixote *also is organized by adventures, but it has progressive character development (meaning that we can understand a character's psychological motivation and can see him or her change throughout the story) and an overall theme.*

CERVANTES
FROM *Don Quixote*

Chapter VIII. Of the valorous* Don Quixote's success in the dreadful and *brave*
never before imagined Adventure of the Windmills.

● At that moment they caught sight of some thirty or forty windmills, which stand on that plain, and as soon as Don Quixote saw them he said to his squire: "Fortune is guiding our affairs better than we could have wished. Look over there, friend Sancho Panza, where more than thirty monstrous giants appear. I intend to do battle with them and take all their lives. With their spoils* we will begin to get rich, for this is a fair war, and *riches* it is a great service to God to wipe such a wicked brood* from the face of *family* the earth."

"What giants?" asked Sancho Panza.

"Those you see there," replied his master, "with their long arms. Some giants have them about six miles long."

"Take care, your worship," said Sancho; "those things over there are not giants but windmills, and what seem to be their arms are the sails, which are whirled round in the wind and make the millstone* turn." *stone used for grinding*

SOURCE: *Don Quixote* by Cervantes. Translated by J. M. Cohen. Copyright © 1950 by J. M. Cohen. Reprinted by permission of the publisher, Penguin Classics.

"It is quite clear," replied Don Quixote, "that you are not experienced in this matter of adventures. They are giants, and if you are afraid, go away and say your prayers, whilst I advance and engage them in fierce and unequal battle."

As he spoke, he dug his spurs into his steed* Rocinante, paying no attention to his squire's shouted warning that beyond all doubt they were windmills and no giants he was advancing to attack. But he went on, so positive that they were giants that he neither listened to Sancho's cries nor noticed what they were, even when he got near them. Instead he went on shouting in a loud voice: "Do not fly, cowards. vile* creatures, for it is one knight alone who assails* you."

    horse

    disgusting
    attacks

At that moment a slight wind arose, and the great sails began to move. At the sight of which Don Quixote shouted: "Though you wield more arms than the giant Briareus, you shall pay for it!" Saying this, he commended himself with all his soul to his Lady Dulcinea, beseeching her aid in his great peril. Then, covering himself with his shield and putting his lance in the rest, he urged Rocinante forward at a full gallop and attacked the nearest windmill, thrusting his lance into the sail. But the wind turned it with such violence that it shivered his weapon in pieces, dragging the horse and his rider with it, and sent the knight rolling badly injured across the plain. Sancho Panza rushed to his assistance as fast as his ass could trot, but when he came up he found that the knight could not stir.* Such a shock had Rocinante given him in their fall.

    move

"O my goodness!" cried Sancho. "Didn't I tell your worship to look what you were doing, for they were only windmills? Nobody could mistake them, unless he had windmills on the brain."

"Silence, friend Sancho," replied Don Quixote. "Matters of war are more subject than most to continual change. What is more, I think — and that is the truth — that the same sage Friston who robbed me of my room and my books has turned those giants into windmills, to cheat me of the glory of conquering them. Such is the enmity* he bears me; but in the very end his black arts shall avail* him little against the goodness of my sword."

    hatred
    help

"God send it as He will," replied Sancho Panza, helping the knight to get up and remount Rocinante, whose shoulders were half dislocated.

As they discussed this last adventure they followed the road to the pass of Lapice where, Don Quixote said, they could not fail to find many and various adventures, as many travellers passed that way. He was much concerned, however, at the loss of his lance, and, speaking of it to his squire, remarked: "I remember reading that a certain Spanish knight called Diego Perez de Vargas, having broken his sword in battle, tore a great bough or limb from an oak, and performed such deeds with it that day, and pounded so many Moors, that he earned the surname of the Pounder, and thus he and his descendants from that day onwards have been called Vargas y Machuca. I mention this because I propose to tear down just such a limb from the first oak we meet, as big and as good as his; and I intend to do such deeds with it that you may consider yourself

most fortunate to have won the right to see them. For you will witness
things which will scarcely be credited.*"   believed

"With God's help," replied Sancho, "and I believe it all as your worship
says. But sit a bit more upright, sir, for you seem to be riding lop-sided.
It must be from the bruises you got when you fell."

"That is the truth," replied Don Quixote. "And if I do not complain of
the pain, it is because a knight errant* is not allowed to complain of any   wandering knight
wounds, even though his entrails* may be dropping out through them."   guts, intestines

"If that's so, I have nothing more to say," said Sancho, "but God knows
I should be glad if your worship would complain if anything hurt you. I
must say, for my part, that I have to cry out at the slightest twinge, unless
this business of not complaining extends to knight errants' squires as well."

Don Quixote could not help smiling at his squire's simplicity, and told
him that he could certainly complain how and when he pleased, whether
he had any cause or no, for up to that time he had never read anything
to the contrary in the law of chivalry.

*Chapter X. In which is related the device Sancho adopted to enchant the
Lady Dulcinea, and other incidents as comical as they are true.*

As soon as Don Quixote had hidden himself in the thicket, or oak wood,
or forest, beside great El Toboso, he ordered Sancho to go back to the city,
and not return to his presence without first speaking to his lady on his
behalf, and begging her to be so good as to allow herself to be seen by her   condescend
captive knight, and to deign* to bestow her blessing on him, so that he
might hope thereby to meet with the highest success in all his encounters   exhausting
and arduous* enterprises. Sancho understood to do as he was commanded,
and to bring his master as favorable reply as he had brought him the last
time.   conversation

This colloquy* Sancho held with himself: "I have seen from countless
signs that this master of mine is a raving lunatic who ought to be tied up
— and me, I can't be much better, for since I follow him and serve him,
I'm more of a fool than he — if the proverb is true that says: tell me what
company you keep and I will tell you what you are; and that other one too:
not with whom you are born but with whom you feed. Well, he's mad —
that he is — and it's the kind of madness that generally mistakes one thing
for another, and thinks white black and black white, as was clear when he   monks / camels
said that the windmills were giants and the friars'* mules dromedaries,*
and the flocks of sheep hostile armies, and many other things to this tune.
So it won't be very difficult to make him believe that the first peasant girl
I run across about here is the lady Dulcinea. If he doesn't believe it I'll
swear, and if he swears I'll outswear him, and if he sticks to it I shall stick
to it harder, so that, come what may, my word shall always stand up to his.
Perhaps if I hold out I shall put an end to his sending me on any more of
these errands, seeing what poor answers I bring back. Or perhaps he'll
think, as I fancy he will, that one of those wicked enchanters who, he says,

have a grudge against him, had changed her shape to vex and spite him."

With these thoughts Sancho quieted his conscience, reckoning the business as good as settled. And there he waited till afternoon, to convince Don Quixote that he had time to go to El Toboso and back. And so well did every thing turn out that when he got up to mount Dapple he saw three peasant girls coming in his direction, riding on three young asses or fillies* — our author does not tell us which — though it is more credible that they were she-asses, as these are the ordinary mounts of village women; but as nothing much hangs on it, there is no reason to stop and clear up the point. To continue — as soon as Sancho saw the girls, he went back at a canter* to look for his master and found him, sighing and uttering countless amorous lamentations. But as soon as Don Quixote saw him, he cried: "What luck Sancho? Shall I mark this day with a white stone or a black?"

female ponies

slow run

"It'll be better," replied Sancho, "for your worship to mark it in red chalk, like college lists, to be plainly seen by all who look."

"At that rate," said Don Quixote, "you bring good news."

"So good," answered Sancho, "that your worship has nothing more to do than to spur Rocinante and go out into the open to see the lady Dulcinea del Toboso, who is coming to meet your worship with two of her damsels."

"Holy Father! What is that you say, Sancho my friend," cried Don Quixote. "See that you do not deceive me, or seek to cheer my real sadness with false joys."

"What could I gain by deceiving your worship?" replied Sancho. "Especially as you are so near to discovering the truth of my report. Spur on, sir, come, and you'll see the princess, our mistress, coming dressed and adorned — to be brief, as befits her. Her maidens and she are one blaze of gold, all ropes of pearls, all diamonds, all rubies, all brocade* of more than ten gold strands; their hair loose on their shoulders, like so many sunrays sporting in the wind and, what's more, they are riding on three piebald* nackneys, the finest to be seen."

woven fabric

spotted horses

"Hackneys* you mean, Sancho."

"There is very little difference," replied Sancho, "between nackneys and hackneys. But let them come on whatever they may, they are the bravest ladies you could wish for, especially the Princess Dulcinea, my lady, who dazzles the senses."

"Let us go, Sancho my son," replied Don Quixote, "and as a reward for this news, as unexpected as it is welcome, I grant you the best spoil I shall gain in the first adventure that befalls me; and, if that does not content you, I grant you the fillies that my three mares will bear this year, for you know that I left them foal on our village common."

"The fillies for me," cried Sancho, "for it is not too certain that the spoils of the first adventure will be good ones."

At this point they came out of the wood and discovered the three village girls close at hand. Don Quixote cast his eye all along the El Toboso

road, and seeing nothing but the three peasant girls, asked Sancho in great
perplexity* whether he had left the ladies outside the city.   confusion

"How outside the city?" he answered. "Can it be that your worship's
eyes are in the back of your head that you don't see that these are they,
coming along shining like the very sun at noon?"

"I can see nothing, Sancho," said Don Quixote, "but three village girls
on three donkeys."

"Now God deliver me from the Devil," replied Sancho. "Is it possible
that three hackneys, or whatever they're called, as white as driven snow,
look to your worship like asses? Good Lord, if that's the truth, may my
beard be plucked out."

"But I tell you, Sancho my friend," said Don Quixote, "that it is as true
that they are asses, or she-asses, as that I am Don Quixote and you Sancho
Panza. At least they look so to me."

"Hush sir!" said Sancho. "Don't say such a thing, but wipe those eyes
of yours, and come and do homage* to the mistress of your thoughts who   honor
is drawing near."

As he spoke he rode forward to receive the three village girls, and
dismounting from Dapple, took one of the girl's asses by the bridle and
sank on both knees to the ground, saying: "Queen and Princess and Duchess of beauty, may your Highness and Mightiness deign to receive into
your grace and good liking your captive knight, who stands here, turned
to marble stone, all troubled and unnerved* at finding himself in your   nervous
magnificent presence. I am Sancho Panza, his squire, and he is the travel-
weary knight, Don Quixote de la Mancha, called also by the name of the
Knight of the Sad Countenance."

By this time Don Quixote had fallen on his knees beside Sancho, and
was staring, with his eyes starting out of his head, and a puzzled look on
his face, at the person whom Sancho called Queen and lady. And as he
could see nothing in her but a country girl, and not a very handsome one
at that, she being round-faced and flat-nosed, he was bewildered and
amazed, and did not dare to open his lips. The village girls were equally
astonished at seeing these two men, so different in appearance, down on
their knees and preventing their companion from going forward. But the
girl they had stopped broke the silence by crying roughly and angrily:
"Get out of the way, confound* you, and let us pass. We're in a hurry."   damn

To which Sancho replied: "O Princess and world famous Lady of El
Toboso! How is it that your magnanimous* heart is not softened when you   generous
see the column and prop* of knight errantry kneeling before your sub-   foundation
limated* presence?"   (here misused; intended:
      beyond description)
On hearing this, one of the two others exclaimed: "Wait till I get my
hands on you, you great ass! See how these petty gentry come and make
fun of us village girls, as if we couldn't give them as good as they bring!
Get on your way, and let us go on ours. You had better!"

"Rise Sancho," said Don Quixote at this, "For I see that Fortune unsatisfied with the ill already done me, has closed all roads by which any comfort may come to this wretched soul I bear in my body. And you, O perfection of all desire! Pinnacle* of human gentleness! Sole remedy of this afflicted heart, that adores you! Now that the malignant* enchanter persecutes me, and has put clouds and cataracts* into my eyes, and for them alone, and for no others, has changed and transformed the peerless* beauty of your countenance into the semblance* of a poor peasant girl, if he has not at the same time turned mine into the appearance of some spectre* to make it abominable to your sight, do not refuse to look at me softly and amorously, perceiving in this submission and prostration,* which I make before your deformed beauty, the humility with which my soul adores you."

    high point
    evil
    disease causing blindness
    without equal
    shape, order

    ghost
    groveling

"Tell that to my grandmother!" replied the girl. "Do you think I want to listen to that nonsense? Get out of the way and let us go on, and we'll thank you."

Sancho moved off and let her pass, delighted at having got well out of his fix. And no sooner did the girl who had played the part of Dulcinea find herself free than she prodded her nackney with the point of a stick that she carried, and set off at a trot across the field. But when the she-ass felt the point of the stick, which pained her more than usual, she began to plunge so wildly that my lady Dulcinea came off upon the ground. When Don Quixote saw this accident, he rushed to pick her up, and Sancho to adjust the strap on the saddle which had slipped under the ass's belly. But when the saddle was adjusted and Don Quixote was about to lift his enchanted mistress in his arms and place her on her ass, the lady picked herself up from the ground and spared him the trouble. For, stepping back a little, she took a short run, and resting both her hands on the ass's rump, swung her body into the saddle, lighter than a hawk, and sat astride like a man.

At which Sancho exclaimed: "By St. Roque, the lady, our mistress, is lighter than a falcon, and she could train the nimblest Cordovan or Mexican to mount like a jockey. She was over the cropper* of the saddle in one jump, and now without spurs she's making that hackney gallop like a zebra. And her maidens are not much behind her. They're all going like the wind."

    back

And so they were, for once Dulcinea was mounted, they all spurred after her and dashed away at full speed, without once looking behind them till they had gone almost two miles. Don Quixote followed them with his eyes, and, when he saw that they had disappeared, turned to Sancho and said:

"Do you see now what a spite the enchanters have against me, Sancho? See to what extremes the malice* and hatred they bear me extend, for they have sought to deprive me of the happiness I should have enjoyed in seeing my mistress in her true person. In truth, I was born a very pattern for the unfortunate, and to be a target and mark for the arrows

    ill will

of adversity.* You must observe also, Sancho, that these traitors were not   trouble, bad luck
satisfied with changing and transforming Dulcinea, but transformed her
and changed her into a figure as low and ugly as that peasant girl's. And
they have deprived her too of something most proper to great ladies,
which is the sweet smell they have from always moving among ambergris*   perfume base
and flowers. For I must tell you, Sancho, that when I went to help my
Dulcinea on to her hackney, as you say it was, though it seemed a she-ass
to me, I got such a whiff of raw garlic as stank me out and poisoned me
to the heart."

"Oh the curs!*" cried Sancho at this. "Oh wretched and spiteful en-   dogs
chanters! I should like to see you strung up by the gills* like pilchards* on   air openings / sardines
a reed. Wise you are and powerful — and much evil you do! It should be
enough for you, ruffians,* to have changed the pearl of my lady's eyes into   bums, criminals
corktree galls, and her hair of purest gold into red ox tail bristles, and all
her features, in fact, from good to bad, without meddling with her smell.
For from that at least we have gathered what lay concealed beneath that
ugly crust. Though, to tell you the truth, I never saw her ugliness, but only
her beauty, which was enhanced and perfected by a mole she had on her
right lip, like a moustache, with seven or eight red hairs like threads of
gold more than nine inches long."

"To judge from that mole," said Don Quixote, "by the correspondence
there is between those on the face and those on the body, Dulcinea must
have another on the fleshy part of her thigh, on the same side as the one
on her face. But hairs of the length you indicate are very long for moles."

"But I can assure your worship," replied Sancho, "that there they were,
as if they had been born with her."

"I believe it friend," said Don Quixote, "for nature has put nothing on
Dulcinea which is not perfect and well-finished. And so, if she had a
hundred moles like the one you speak of on her, they would not be moles,
but moons and shining stars. But tell me, Sancho, that which appears to
me to be a pack-saddle and which you set straight — was it a plain saddle
or a side-saddle?"

"It was just a lady's saddle," replied Sancho, "with an outdoor covering
so rich that it was worth half a kingdom."

"And to think that I did not see all this Sancho!" cried Don Quixote.
"Now I say once more — and I will repeat it a thousand times — I am the
most unfortunate of men."

And that rascal Sancho had all he could do to hide his amusement on
hearing this crazy talk from his master, whom he had so beautifully deceived.

QUESTIONS FOR DISCUSSION AND WRITING

[1] The passage consists of two episodes: the windmill adventure and
Dulcinea's "transformation." Which elements of chivalry does Cervantes
satirize in each instance?

[2] Examine the character of Sancho Panza. To which social class does he belong? Does Cervantes treat him positively or negatively? Could a character like Sancho have appeared in Arthurian legends or Greek myths?

[3] Consider how realistic the adventures in *Don Quixote* are compared to those of "Sir Lancelot." Look at the details in the setting, the psychological depiction of each character, and the plausibility of the actions.

SECTION ESSAY ASSIGNMENTS

[1] Both Malory's story and Cervantes' novel were intended to entertain an audience. Analyze the effects of each work: what emotional reactions do the authors try to elicit through character development and plot events?

[2] Compare and contrast the chivalric codes, the nature of the heroes and heroines, and the authors' attitudes toward both in "Sir Lancelot" and *Don Quixote.* Consider how each author treats the hero, and note how the idealized woman is presented in each. What is the attitude toward devotion, adventure, and daring action?

[3] Is Cervantes completely critical of chivalry in *Don Quixote?* Argue that Quixote is either a purely ridiculous, humorous hero or that he is also sympathetic, perhaps pathetic, or even verging on tragic. Cite specific examples and quotations from the text to support your view. If you choose to argue the second issue, consider Quixote's idealism.

The conversation that makes up the following reading passage takes place in the Renaissance court of an Italian duke. These members of court society are entertaining themselves by playing "parlor games" of a sort. On the evening that this particular conversation takes place, the game involves describing the ideal courtier. By taking part in the game, the participants show off their ability to speak eloquently and wittily at a moment's notice. They admire a certain style of behavior called "sprezzatura," a kind of cool, sophisticated manner that understates one's accomplishments. Read the passage to clarify how spontaneity relates to *sprezzatura.*

The Book of the Courtier (1528) typifies Renaissance literature in its emphasis on stylistic accomplishment in art, conversation, and behavior. The Renaissance was a humanistic period, a rebirth of classical interests and learning. At this time, Western society's power base was shifting from the Church to the great monarchs of Europe. This was the age of Shakespeare, Leonardo da Vinci, Michelangelo, Galileo, Newton; of colonial expansion in the New World; of the Spanish conquistadors' sometimes brutal exploits in South America; of Magellan's circumnavigation of the globe; of Christopher Columbus. The Renaissance was an age of expansion, in both its rediscovery of the ancient world and its exploration of the new.

CASTIGLIONE
FROM *The Book of the Courtier*

● At a sign from the Duchess, Cesare Gonzaga began:

"If I well remember, Count, it seems to me you have repeated several times this evening that the Courtier* must accompany his actions, his [member of a royal court] gestures, his habits, in short, his every movement, with grace. And it strikes me that you require this in everything as that seasoning without which all the other properties and good qualities would be of little worth. And truly I believe that everyone would easily let himself be persuaded of this, because, by the very meaning of the word, it can be said that he who has grace finds grace. But since you have said that this is often a gift of nature and the heavens, and that, even if it is not quite perfect, it can be much increased by care and industry, those men who are born as fortunate and as rich in such treasure as some we know have little need, it seems to me, of any teacher in this, because such benign* favor from [kindly] heaven lifts them, almost in spite of themselves, higher than they themselves had desired, and makes them not only pleasing but admirable to everyone. Therefore I do not discuss this, it not being in our power to acquire it of ourselves. But as for those who are less endowed* by nature [blessed] and are capable of acquiring grace only if they put forth labor, industry, and care, I would wish to know by what art, by what discipline, by what method, they can gain this grace, both in bodily exercises, in which you deem it to be so necessary, and in every other thing they do or say. Therefore, since by praising this quality so highly you have, as I believe, aroused in all of us an ardent desire, according to the task given you by signora Emilia, you are still bound to satisfy it."

"I am not bound," said the Count, "to teach you how to acquire grace or anything else, but only to show you what a perfect Courtier ought to be. Nor would I undertake to teach you such a perfection; especially when I have just now said that the Courtier must know how to wrestle, vault,* [jump] and so many other things which, since I never learned them myself, you all know well enough how I should be able to teach them. Let it suffice that just as a good soldier knows how to tell the smith* what shape, style, [metalworker] and quality his armor must have, and yet is not able to teach him to make it, nor how to hammer or temper* it; just so I, perhaps, shall be able to [make strong] tell you what a perfect Courtier should be, but not to teach you what you must do to become one. Still, in order to answer your question in so far as I can (although it is almost proverbial* that grace is not learned), I say [in traditional wisdom] that if anyone is to acquire grace in bodily exercises (granting first of all that he is not by nature incapable), he must begin early and learn the principles from the best of teachers. And how important this seemed to King Philip of Macedon can be seen by the fact that he wished Aristotle, the famous philosopher and perhaps the greatest the world has ever known, to be the one who should teach his son Alexander the first elements of letters. And among men whom we know today, consider how well and gracefully signor Galeazzo Sanseverino, Grand Equerry of France, performs all bodily exercises; and this because, besides the natural aptitude of person that he possesses, he has taken the greatest care to study with good masters and to have about him men who excel, taking from each the best of what they know. For just as in wrestling, vaulting, and in the handling of many kinds of weapons, he took our messer Pietro Monte as his guide, who is (as you know) the only true master of every kind of acquired strength and agility — so in riding, jousting,* and the rest he has ever had before his eyes those men who are known to be most perfect in these matters.

fighting with lances

"Therefore, whoever would be a good pupil must not only do things well, but must always make every effort to resemble and, if that be possible, to transform himself into his master. And when he feels that he has made some progress, it is very profitable to observe different men of that profession; and, conducting himself with that good judgment which must always be his guide, go about choosing now this thing from one and that from another. And even as in green meadows the bee flits* about among the grasses robbing the flowers, so our Courtier must steal this grace from those who seem to him to have it, taking from each the part that seems most worthy of praise; not doing as a friend of ours whom you all know, who thought he greatly resembled King Ferdinand the Younger of Aragon, but had not tried to imitate him in anything save in the way he had of raising his head and twisting one side of his mouth, which manner the King had contracted* through some malady.* And there are many such, who think they are doing a great thing if only they can resemble some great man in something; and often they seize upon that which is his only bad point.

flies about

caught / illness

"But, having thought many times already about how this grace is acquired (leaving aside those who have it from the stars), I have found quite a universal rule which in this matter seems to me valid above all others, and in all human affairs whether in word or deed: and that is to avoid affectation* in every way possible as though it were some very rough and dangerous reef; and (to pronounce a new word perhaps) to practice in all things a certain *sprezzatura* [nonchalance], so as to conceal all art and make whatever is done or said appear to be without effort and almost without any thought about it. And I believe much grace comes of this: because everyone knows the difficulty of things that are rare and well done; wherefore facility* in such things causes the greatest wonder; whereas, on the other hand, to labor and, as we say, drag forth by the hair of the head, shows an extreme want of grace, and causes everything, no matter how great it may be, to be held in little account.

false airs

ease, ability

"Therefore we may call that art true art which does not seem to be art; nor must one be more careful of anything than of concealing it, because

if it is discovered, this robs a man of all credit and causes him to be held
in slight esteem. And I remember having read of certain most excellent
orators* in ancient times who, among the other things they did, tried to   speakers
make everyone believe that they had no knowledge whatever of letters;
and, dissembling* their knowledge, they made their orations appear to be   hiding
composed in the simplest manner and according to the dictates* of nature   laws
and truth rather than of effort and art; which fact, had it been known,
would have inspired in the minds of the people the fear that they could
be duped by it.

"So you see how art, or any intent effort, if it is disclosed, deprives
everything of grace. Who among you fails to laugh when our messer
Pierpaolo dances after his own fashion, with those capers* of his, his legs   fancy steps
stiff on tiptoe, never moving his head, as if he were a stick of wood, and
all this so studied that he really seems to be counting his steps? What eye
is so blind as not to see in this the ungainliness* of affectation; and not to awkwardness
see the grace of that cool *disinvoltura* [ease] (for when it is a matter of
bodily movements many call it that) in many of the men and women here
present, who seem in words, in laughter, in posture not to care; or seem
to be thinking more of everything than of that, so as to cause all who are
watching them to believe that they are almost incapable of making a
mistake?"

QUESTIONS FOR DISCUSSION AND WRITING

[1] Define the "perfect courtier."

[2] Name the qualities/behavior a perfect courtier does not display, and
explain why.

[3] What is the importance of *sprezzatura*?

Both Castiglione and Montaigne write about the individual's public image
and behavior, but they view the concepts differently. Read the following passage
for Montaigne's assessment of a "glorious" reputation's value. You'll compare
and contrast the two authors' ideas in a writing assignment, so you should read
Montaigne with Castiglione in mind, marking the text for points of connection.
Review the reading questions before you begin the passage as a further means
of focusing your reading.

---

*Michel de Montaigne (1533–1592) was a mixture of the Renaissance man
— someone with skill and knowledge in many areas — and a forerunner of the
age of rationalism, with his famous skepticism and discursive* mind. His*   passing from one topic to
motto, "What do I know?" symbolizes his ironic view of human ideals and   another
*shortcomings. He lived in a time of political turmoil caused by religious fac-
tions in France and other European countries — the era of the Reformation
and its repercussions.*

MICHEL DE MONTAIGNE
"Of Not Communicating One's Glory"

● Of all the illusions in the world, the most universally received is the concern for reputation and glory, which we espouse* even to the point of giving up riches, rest, life, and health, which are effectual* and substantial goods, to follow that vain phantom and mere sound that has neither body nor substance:

> *The fame that charms proud mortals with sweet sound,*
> *And seems so fair, is but an echo, a dream,*
> *The shadow of a dream, beyond repair*
> *Dispersed and scattered by a puff of air.*

And of the irrational humors* of men, it seems that even the philosophers get rid of this one later and more reluctantly than any other.

It is the most contrary and stubborn of all, "because it does not cease to tempt even souls that are making good progress" [Saint Augustine]. There is hardly any other illusion whose vanity reason condemns so clearly; but it has such live roots in us that I do not know whether anyone yet has ever been able to get clean rid of it. After you have said everything and believed everything to disown it, it produces such an ingrained* inclination against your arguments that you have little power to withstand it. For as Cicero says, even those who combat it still want the books that they write about it to bear their name on the title page, and want to become glorious for having despised glory.

All other things can be traded; we lend our goods and our lives to the need of our friends; but to communicate one's honor and endow another with one's glory, that is hardly ever seen.

Catalus Luctatius, in the war against the Cimbrians, after making every effort to stop his soldiers from fleeing before the enemy, himself joined the fugitives and played the coward, so that they should seem rather to be following their captain than fleeing from the enemy. That was abandoning his reputation to cover the shame of others.

When the Emperor Charles V came into Provence in the year 1537, they say that Antonio de Leyva, seeing his master resolved on this expedition and believing that it would add wonderfully to his glory, nevertheless expressed a contrary opinion and advised him against it; to this end, that all the glory and honor of this plan should be attributed to his master, and that it might be said that his good judgment and foresight had been such that, against the opinion of everyone, he had carried out such a splendid enterprise: which for de Leyva, was to honor his master at his own expense.

(margin glosses: espouse — adopt, defend; effectual* — useful; humors* — moods; ingrained* — habitual)*

SOURCE: *The Complete Works of Montaigne.* Trans. by Donald M. Frame. Reprinted with permission of the publishers, Stanford University Press. Copyright © 1943, 1948, 1957, 1958 by Donald M. Frame.

When the Thracian ambassadors, in consoling Argileonis, the mother of Brasidas, for the death of her son, praised him so highly as to say that he had not left his like behind him, she refused this private and particular praise and gave it back to the public: "Don't tell me that," she said; "I know that the city of Sparta has many citizens greater and more valiant than he was."

In the battle of Crecy the prince of Wales, still a very young man, was in charge of the vanguard.* The principal stress of the encounter was at that point. The lords who were with him, finding themselves in a tough fight, sent word to King Edward to come up and help them. He inquired about the condition of his son, and being answered that he was alive and on his horse, he said: "I should be doing him wrong to go now and rob him of the honor of victory in this combat that he has sustained so long; whatever risk there may be, this shall be all his own." And he would not go or send to him, knowing that if he went, it would be said that all would have been lost without his help, and that the credit for this exploit would be attributed to him: "for it is always what is thrown in last that seems to have accomplished the whole thing" [Livy].

front lines

Many in Rome thought, and it was commonly said, that the principal great deeds of Scipio were due in part to Laelius, who was always promoting and seconding Scipio's greatness and glory without any care for his own. And Theopompus, king of Sparta, to the man who told him that the republic remained on its feet because he knew how to command well, said: "It is rather because the people know how to obey well."

As women who succeeded to peerages,* in spite of their sex, had the right to attend and deliberate in cases pertaining to the jurisdiction* of peers, so the ecclesiastical peers, in spite of their profession, were obliged to assist our kings in their wars, not only with their friends and retainers,* but also in person. The bishop of Beauvais, finding himself with Philip Augustus at the battle of Bouvines, participated very courageously in the action; but it seemed to him he should not touch the fruit and glory of this bloody and violent activity. With his own hand he got the better of several of the enemy that day; and he would give them to the first gentleman he found, to cut their throats or take them as prisoners, letting him handle them as he chose; and he so delivered William, earl of Salisbury, to Jean de Nesle. With a like subtlety of conscience he was willing to club a man to death but not to wound him, and therefore fought only with a mace.*

ranks of nobility
authority

attendants, servants

spiked club

Someone in my day, being reproached by the king for having laid hands on a priest, strongly and stoutly denied it: the fact was that he had cudgeled* and kicked him.

clubbed

QUESTIONS FOR DISCUSSION AND WRITING

[1] Judging from Montaigne's views on glory, how do you think he would look on Castiglione's ideal courtier?

[2] Montaigne and Castiglione advocate that people be modest about their accomplishments. How do the two authors' <u>motives</u> for praising modesty differ?

[3] Explain how each of Montaigne's examples supports his view of real glory.

SECTION ESSAY ASSIGNMENTS

[1] Which character most closely fits Montaigne's image of the true hero, Sir Lancelot or Don Quixote? Apply Montaigne's ideal of behavior to both.

[2] The chivalrous knight and the courtier both represent an idealized notion of behavior. Review your definitions of chivalry and the courtier, then compare and contrast the values of each. Consider their actions, appearance, skills, and personal beliefs.

[3] Castiglione and Montaigne present an aesthetic of behavior, a suggested code for daily life. Consider your own beliefs about what comprises your aesthetic of behavior. Ideally, what is the best way for a person to act? Support your definition with concrete examples from your own life or experience with others.

Neoclassical Poetry and the Romantic Revolt

The following excerpt from Pope's poem, *An Essay on Man* (1733–1734), reflects a world view similar to that described in the article, "God as Divine Clockmaker." As part of your prereading, review the article before you read the poem.

Poems differ from prose on many levels and therefore we read them differently. However, in each case you need to read initially for literal understanding: What is the poet saying? Your first task in reading poetry, then, is comprehending the content. Read the poem through once (after carefully surveying it) to get a sense of its literal content without trying to figure out its images and allusions in detail. You may need to translate symbols and images into common language before you can ultimately appreciate the poem as poetry; understanding the poet's actual words is probably the best way to work toward that goal.

Here we're concerned with Pope's poem quite literally as an essay, as a thesis and argument defending his philosophical views. Treat it as a document in intellectual history, one representing an eighteenth-century view of life. Since it's an eighteenth-century poetic work, the language differs from our daily speech, and you may find the diction difficult. What constitutes an effective reading strategy for a long, difficult passage? Paraphrasing and summarizing should probably form the real center of your strategy. Review the techniques covered in Chapter 2. Note that the poem has numbered sections that form convenient units for you to paraphrase and summarize.

We have paraphrased the first five sections for you. Read our paraphrases and then do your own for the remaining sections. Refer to the discussion on paraphrasing in Chapter 1 if necessary.

Alexander Pope stands as one of the greatest English poets, and probably the greatest of the eighteenth-century neoclassical age. He wrote during the Enlightenment, and his poem reflects that age's sense of control, optimism, and reason. Pope and Voltaire were contemporaries. Both authors shared the sense of human progress that foreshadowed and accompanied the industrial revolution. But even the century's greatest minds couldn't predict the human suffering that would ensue.*

follow

ALEXANDER POPE
FROM *An Essay on Man*

KEY CONCEPTS

PROVIDENCE refers to God's control over human life and the world; see Chapter 2, page 124.

In a mechanistic view of the world, God is the **FIRST CAUSE** in the mechanism, or the one who started the machine going.

As the sun, the planets, and the stars revolved, they produced divine, celestial music, according to seventeenth-century astronomers. This harmony was called the **MUSIC OF THE SPHERES**.

The **CHAIN OF BEING** is a theory of natural order. It states that a spiritual hierarchy moves from God down through humans to the lower orders of life.

To Henry St. John Lord Bolingbroke

Epistle I. Of the Nature and State of Man, with Respect to the Universe

Awake my St. John, leave all meaner things
To low ambition, and the pride of kings.
Let us (since life can little more supply
Than just to look about us and to die)
Expatiate* free o'er this scene of man;   discuss at length
A mighty maze! but not without a plan;
A wild, where weeds and flowers promiscuous* shoot,   uncontrolled

Or garden, tempting with forbidden fruit.
Together let us beat this ample field;
Try what the open, what the covert* yield;   hidden
The latent* tracts,* the giddy* heights, explore   unused, inactive / fields /
Of all who blindly creep, or sightless soar;   dizzy
Eye Nature's Walks, shoot folly* as it flies,   foolishness
And catch the manners living as they rise;
Laugh where we must, be candid where we can;
But vindicate* the ways of God to man.   justify

[John, let's forget worldly, material ambition. Let's look at the human condition; it's complex, but orderly and planned. Let's examine the obvious and the hidden, the highs and the lows. Let's be honest but keep our sense of humor, as we try to explain God's plan.]

Say first of God above, or man below,
What can we reason, but from what we know?
Of man, what see we but his station here,
From which to reason, or to which refer?
Through worlds unnumbered though the God be known,
'Tis ours to trace him only in our own.
He, who through vast immensity can pierce,
See worlds on worlds compose one universe,
Observe how system into system runs,
What other planets circle other suns,
What varied Being peoples every star,
May tell why Heaven has made us as we are.
But of this frame the bearings, and the ties,
The strong connections, nice* dependencies,   subtle
Gradations just, has thy pervading soul
Looked through? Or can a part contain the whole?
Is the great chain, that draws all to agree,
And drawn supports, upheld by God, or thee?

[First, regarding God or man, we can only judge from our experience. We can only talk about man in terms of his place in the world. God exists in an infinite universe, and he understands life in this world, on other planets, and throughout the universe. But we only know him in our own world. God understands how all things in the universe are connected. Man doesn't have the ability to see God's whole plan, for man is only one part of it. God, not man, created and controls the chain of being.]

· · ·

Of systems possible, if 'tis confessed
That Wisdom Infinite must form the best,
Where all must full or not coherent be,

And all that rises, rise in due degree;
Then, in the scale of reasoning life, 'tis plain,
There must be, somewhere, such a rank as man:
And all the question (wrangle* e'er so long)   argue
Is only this, if God has placed him wrong?

[This system, made by God's wisdom, must be good; there is a place
for everything, even man. Some people dare to question God, accusing
him of misplacing man.]

Respecting man, whatever wrong we call,
May, must be right, as relative to all.
In human works, though labored on with pain,
A thousand movements scarce one purpose gain;
In God's, one single can its end produce;
Yet serves to second too some other use.
So man, who here seems principal alone,
Perhaps acts second to some sphere unknown,
Touches some wheel, or verges to some goal;
'Tis but a part we see, and not a whole.

[Because we see only a part of "the big picture" and not the entire
picture, man must be in his correct place in the universe, despite the
pain and apparent injustice of human existence.]

When the proud steed shall know why man restrains
His fiery course, or drives him o'er the plains;
When the dull ox, why now he breaks the clod,
Is now a victim, and now Egypt's God:
Then shall man's pride and dullness comprehend
His actions, passions, being's use and end;
Why doing, suffering, checked, impelled; and why
This hour a slave, the next a deity.
   Then say not man's imperfect, Heaven in fault;
Say rather, man's as perfect as he ought:
His knowledge measured to his state and place,
His time a moment, and a point in space.
If to be perfect in a certain sphere,
What matter, soon or late, or here or there?
The blest today is as completely so,
As who began a thousand years ago.

[Just as the horse doesn't understand why his rider controls him; just as
an ox doesn't understand why he is a beast of burden yet also a divine
symbol, it is impossible for man to understand the suffering and joy of
being human. Man is not an imperfect creation of God. Man is just as
he is supposed to be.]

Heaven from all creatures hides the book of Fate,
All but the page prescribed, their present state:
From brutes what men, from men what spirits know:
Or who could suffer being here below?
The lamb thy riot dooms to bleed today,
Had he thy reason, would he skip and play?
Pleased to the last, he crops* the flowery food,   chews
And licks the hand just raised to shed his blood.
O blindness to the future! Kindly given,
That each may fill the circle marked by Heaven:
Who sees with equal eye, as God of all,
A hero perish, or a sparrow fall,
Atoms or systems into ruin hurled,
And now a bubble burst, and now a world.

  Hope humbly then; with trembling pinions* soar;   wings
Wait the great teacher, Death, and God adore!
What future bliss, he gives not thee to know,
But gives that hope to be thy blessing now.
Hope springs eternal in the human breast:
Man never is, but always to be blest:
The soul, uneasy and confined from home,
Rests and expatiates in a life to come.

  Lo! the poor Indian, whose untutored mind
Sees God in clouds, or hears him in the wind;
His soul proud Science never taught to stray
Far as the solar walk, or milky way;
Yet simple Nature to his hope has given,
Behind the cloud-topped hill, an humbler heaven;
Some safer world in depth of woods embraced,
Some happier island in the watery waste,
Where slaves once more their native land behold,
No fiends torment, no Christians thirst for gold!
To be, contents his natural desire,
He asks no angel's wing, no seraph's* fire;   exalted angel
But thinks, admitted to that equal sky,
His faithful dog shall bear him company.

  Go, wiser thou! and, in thy scale of sense,
Weigh thy opinion against **Providence***;*
Call imperfection what thou fancy'st such,
Say, here he gives too little, there too much;
Destroy all creatures for thy sport or gust,*   eating pleasure
Yet cry, if man's unhappy, God's unjust;
If man alone engross* not Heaven's high care,   take up, interest
Alone made perfect here, immortal there:
Snatch from his hand the balance and the rod,

Rejudge his justice, be the God of God!
In pride, in reasoning pride, our error lies;
All quit their sphere, and rush into the skies.
Pride still is aiming at the blest abodes,   dwellings
Men would be angels, angels would be gods,
Aspiring to be gods, if angels fell,
Aspiring to be angels, men rebel:
And who but wishes to invert the laws
Of order, sins against the Eternal Cause.
　　Ask for what end the heavenly bodies shine,
Earth for whose use? Pride answers, "Tis for mine:
For me kind Nature wakes her genial* power,   warm, life-giving
Suckles* each herb, and spreads out every flower;   feeds
Annual for me, the grape, the rose renew
The juice nectareous,* and the balmy* dew;   fruity liquid / warm
For me, the mine a thousand treasures brings;
For me, health gushes from a thousand springs;
Seas roll to waft* me, suns to light me rise;   carry by air
My footstool earth, my canopy* the skies."   ceiling cover
　　But errs not Nature from this gracious end,
From burning suns when livid* deaths descend,   pale
When earthquakes swallow, or when tempests* sweep   storms
Towns to one grave, whole nations to the deep?
"No," 'tis replied, "the **first Almighty Cause**
Acts not by partial, but by general laws;
The exceptions few; some change since all began,
And what created perfect?" — *Why then man?*
If the great end be human happiness,
Then Nature deviates; and can man do less?
As much that end a constant course requires
Of showers and sunshine, as of man's desires;
As much eternal springs and cloudless skies,
As men forever temperate* calm, and wise.   avoiding extremes
If plagues or earthquakes break not Heaven's design,
Why then a Borgia* or a Catiline*?   Italian Renaissance prince /
                                                            ancient Roman orator
Who knows but he whose hand the lightning forms,
Who heaves old ocean, and who wings the storms,
Pours fierce ambition in a Caesar's mind,
Or turns young Ammon* loose to scourge* mankind?   Old Testament figure /
                                                            curse
From pride, from pride, our very reasoning springs;
Account for moral, as for natural things:
Why charge we Heaven in those, in these acquit?
In both, to reason right is to submit.
　　Better for us, perhaps, it might appear,
Were there all harmony, all virtue here;
That never air or ocean felt the wind;
That never passion discomposed the mind:

But ALL subsists by elemental strife;
And passions are the elements of life.
The general ORDER, since the whole began,
Is kept in Nature, and is kept in man.
   What would this man? Now upward will he soar,
And little less than angel, would be more;
Now looking downwards, just as grieved appears
To want the strength of bulls, the fur of bears.
Made for his use all creatures if he call,
Say what their use, had he the powers of all?
Nature to these, without profusion, kind,
The proper organs, proper powers assigned;
Each seeming want compensated of course,
Here with degrees of swiftness, there of force;
All in exact proportion to the state;
*Nothing to add, and nothing to abate.**   lessen, reduce
Each beast, each insect, happy in its own;
Is Heaven unkind to man, and man alone?
Shall he alone, whom rational we call,
Be pleased with nothing, if not blest with all?
   The bliss of man (could pride that blessing find)
Is not to think or act beyond mankind;
No powers of body or of soul to share,
But what his nature and his state can bear.
Why has not man a microscopic eye?
For this plain reason, man is not a fly.
*Say what the use, were finer optics** given,   science of vision
To inspect a mite, not comprehend the heaven?
Or touch, if trembling alive all o'er,
To smart and agonize at every pore?
*Or quick effluvia** darting through the brain,   stream of thought
*Die of a rose in aromatic** pain?   strong smelling
If nature thundered in his opening ears,
And stunned him with the **music of the spheres**,
How would he wish that Heaven had left him still
*The whispering zephyr,** and the purling* rill*?   breeze / flowing / brook
Who finds not Providence all good and wise,
Alike in what it gives, and what denies?

               . . .

   See, through this air, this ocean and this earth,
All matter quick, and bursting into birth.
Above, how high progressive life may go!
Around, how wide! How deep extend below!
Vast Chain of Being! *Which from God began,*
*Natures ethereal,** human, angel, man,   heavenly
Beast, bird, fish, insect, what no eye can see,

No glass can reach! From Infinite to thee,
From thee to nothing — On superior powers
Were we to press, inferior might on ours:
Or in the full creation leave a void,
Where, one step broken, the great scale's destroyed:
From Nature's chain whatever link you strike,
Tenth or ten thousandth, breaks the chain alike.
   And, if each system in gradation roll
Alike essential to the amazing Whole,
The least confusion but in one, not all
That system only, but the Whole must fall.
Let earth unbalanced from her orbit fly,
Planets and suns run lawless through the sky,
Let ruling angels from their spheres be hurled,
Being on being wrecked, and world on world,
Heaven's whole foundations to their center nod,
And Nature tremble to the throne of God:
All this dread ORDER break — for whom? for thee?
Vile worm! — oh madness, pride, impiety!*   disrespect
   What if the foot, ordained the dust to tread,
Or hand, to toil, aspired to be the head?
What if the head, the eye, or ear repined*   complained
To serve mere engines to the ruling Mind?
Just as absurd for any part to claim,
To be another in this general frame:
Just as absurd, to mourn the tasks or pains,
The great directing MIND of ALL ordains.*   orders
   All are but parts of one stupendous whole,
Whose body Nature is, and God the soul;
That, changed through all, and yet in all the same,
Great in the earth, as in the ethereal frame,
Warms in the sun, refreshes in the breeze,
Glows in the stars, and blossoms in the trees,
Lives through all life, extends through all extent,
Spreads undivided, operates unspent,
Breathes in our soul, informs our mortal part,
As full, as perfect, in a hair as heart;
As full, as perfect, in vile man that mourns,
As the rapt* seraph that adores and burns;   enraptured
To him no high, no low, no great, no small;
He fills, he bounds, connects and equals all.
   Cease then, nor ORDER imperfection name:
Our proper bliss depends on what we blame.
Know thy own point: this kind, this due degree
Of blindness, weakness, Heaven bestows on thee.
Submit — In this, or any other sphere,
Secure to be as blest as thou canst bear:

Safe in the hand of one disposing Power,
Or in the natal,* or in the mortal hour.   birth
All Nature is but art, unknown to thee;
All chance, direction, which thou canst not see;
All discord,* harmony not understood;   confusion
All partial evil, universal good:
And, spite of pride, in erring reason's spite,
One truth is clear: WHATEVER IS, IS RIGHT.

QUESTIONS FOR DISCUSSION AND WRITING

[1] To understand this poem on its literal level, you'll need to paraphrase each section. Go through each "paragraph" and restate the main idea in your own words. Some of the "paragraphs" repeat ideas stated earlier in the poem, in order to emphasize them. You don't need to paraphrase such paragraphs. When you've finished paraphrasing Pope's poem, the result should be a useful summary of his argument.

[2] Would you describe Pope as an optimist or a pessimist? Cite examples and quotations to support your view.

[3] What image of God does Pope present in the poem?

[4] Pope poses the question, "Is the great chain that draws all to agree, and drawn supports, upheld by God, or thee?" What attitude does Pope criticize here? How does his image of the universe as a chain supporting all life defend his view of God?

George Sherburn discusses Pope's poetry as representative of eighteenth-century aesthetics. Read the passage, bearing in mind that you will write a comparison and contrast of eighteenth- and nineteenth-century aesthetics. Mark the passage in order to derive a definition of neoclassical aesthetics.

Sherburn's introduction to his book, The Best of Pope, *outlines the major elements of neoclassical aesthetics. The ancient precept of "useful and beautiful art" prevailed among eighteenth-century artists, who took ancient works as models for their compositions. Aristotle's "rules" determined literary form and taste. The age valued stylistic refinement, and thus many neoclassical works may seem remote or inaccessible to untrained modern readers, as Sherburn points out.*

GEORGE SHERBURN
"Alexander Pope"

KEY CONCEPTS

The theory that art ought to **DELIGHT AND INSTRUCT** is related to the idea of the **USEFUL AND THE BEAUTIFUL,** which you studied in Chapter 1.

In this case, art should be useful by teaching some moral principle, in addition to providing entertainment.

DECORUM is a theory of artistic appropriateness and taste. According to this theory, certain words and actions can never be part of a truly artistic work because they are by their nature ugly or unfit in some way.

NEOCLASSIC ART, or "new classical" art, is a seventeenth- and eighteenth-century style that derived from ancient Greek and Latin models.

● Pope's conception of the art of poetry differs fundamentally from that of the nineteenth century and the present day. Poetry for him was the best vehicle of moral instruction. It was the best vehicle because it utilized "the passions" as well as the reason, and the cooperation of passion and reason was regarded essential to moral welfare. He and his contemporaries recognized the validity of Horace's dictum as to poets *aut prodesse aut aut delectare volunt* [wanting to delight and also instruct] but they relegated* [deferred, lowered] delight to a secondary place: poets delighted in order to instruct. It follows that Pope's art was concerned with meanings, not with surfaces; with ideas rather than images. He was early charged with being "an eternal writer of amorous, pastoral* madrigals,*" but his own boast was: [idealized / song for several voices]

> *That not in Fancy's maze he wander'd long,*
> *But stooped to truth, and moralized his song.*

He was, then, no "imagist"; he even spoke slightingly of such triviality, though he recognized the importance of "images" as an ornament to poetry. But human motives and duties — and errors! — were the burden of his song; and when he wrote of outdoor nature, he used the landscape as the natural setting for the genteel* activities of the sportsman. Land- [refined] scape for its own sake apart from humanity is not for him poetic material. He neglects the pictorial and strives rather to present the essential quality of objects.

Another important divergence* of the aesthetic of his day from that of [departure] ours is its impersonality. Ideal conduct for a Chesterfield consisted not in self-expression or "self-realization," but in perfect conformity with a fine pattern of behavior — in "**decorum**." The poet similarly expressed not his personal feelings; for self-expression was by no means his object. He rather gave precepts* for and illustrations of conduct for men in general. Pope [rules, laws] has been accused more than once of insincerity in his praise of retirement and content:

> *Blest, who can unconcern'dly find*
> *Hours, days, and years slide soft away,*

SOURCE: "Alexander Pope" by George Sherburn from *The Best of Pope*, the Ronald Press Company, 1929.

In health of body, peace of mind,
Quiet by day,

Sound sleep by night; study and ease,
together mixt; sweet recreation;
And Innocence, which most does please
With meditation.

Thus let me live, unseen, unknown,
Thus unlamented, let me die,
Steal from the world, not a stone
Tell where I lie.

Even the last lines, in the first person, had best be interpreted in the light of the classical theories of universality and ideality, and not in the light of later theories of self-revelation in poetry. The lines are simply Pope's expression of an ideal theme; they may or may not be what he always thought, but they certainly are "What oft was thought, but ne'er so well express'd."

Pope's art so far is true **Neo-Classic**. The poet follows or imitates nature, and nature is what is normal and universal in human experience: it is common sense, not the particular sense of the individual. In practice, however, and in theory at times Pope differs from Aristotle in a tendency to be realistic rather than idealistic in his attitude toward human nature. The perfect hero of the modern romance seemed to Pope morally imprac-ticable:* "we but read (so the 'Essay on Homer' tells us) with a tender weakness what we can neither apply or emulate.*" Homer's heroes with their boastfulness and "unmanaged roughness" he finds preferable. In a note to the *Odyssey,* he takes the obvious position that "perfection is not to be found in human life, and consequently ought not to be ascribed* to it in poetry." The life and tastes of Pope's readers invite him to the use of materials such as make him seem at times a journalistic rather than a "classical" poet.

Pope's art is essentially cultural as well as intellectual. At its best it belongs with the works of the great musicians of Pope's day, Handel and Bach, or with the exquisite realism of Hogarth.* Unlike more democratic art which has succeeded it, it cannot be appreciated without study; there never was a time when it could be grasped without intellectual effort. It is a sad limitation to one's taste in literature to insist on art that primarily thrills the senses without affecting the mind, and it is a sad error to see in Pope only the journalistic passages that make footnotes essential — or only the malicious* passages that indicate personal spite.

impossible
imitate as a good model

considered part of

18th-century artist

cruel, spiteful

QUESTIONS FOR DISCUSSION AND WRITING

[1] Sherburn writes, "Poetry for [Pope] was the best vehicle of moral instruction." Choose a line from *An Essay on Man* to illustrate Sherburn's statement.

[2] Eighteenth-century poets had a didactic* purpose in writing poetry; they   instructional
sought not only to please but also to instruct. What main idea did Pope
attempt to teach in his poem?

[3] Sherburn acknowledges that Pope's poem is not "democratic art,"
which means it cannot be easily understood by the common person. What
then constitutes "democratic" characteristics in art?

---

*William Wordsworth is an English poet of the same stature as Alexander
Pope, but his artistic beliefs and his poetic style differ greatly from the earlier
poet's neoclassical aesthetics. Reading Wordsworth's "Solitary Reaper" (1805)
in the context of Pope's* Essay *should give you a good sense of what happened
to neoclassical aesthetics and taste in the nineteenth century: you can see how
artistic and cultural values seem to engender their opposites from age to age.
After the mechanism, decorum, and prescriptive precepts of the seventeenth
and eighteenth centuries, literary artists were ready to break out of such
restrictions and embrace a new aesthetic, one that emphasized innovation,
naturalness, and freedom. Romanticism was an artistic response to neoclassicism and contradicted many of the earlier age's practices and beliefs. Romanticism was not a literary phenomenon alone but affected political, social, religious, and philosophical thought as well. The age of democracy is often taken
as a Romantic product; pantheism* and transcendentalism* are Romantic*   nature worship / spiritual
creeds; subjectivism and idealism characterize Romantic philosophy. Words-   belief in the mind's ability
worth's poetry helped define Romantic aesthetics, as did the poetry of Samuel   to rise above matter
*Taylor Coleridge, a Wordsworth contemporary and friend. Together the two
men formulated English Romantic poetic theory. Coleridge's "Kubla Khan"
(1797) follows Wordsworth's poem here. Coleridge claimed that he
"dreamed" "Kubla Khan" while under the influence of opium and wrote
down fragments of it later, which perhaps partially accounts for the poem's
strange and vivid imagery. Following these poems comes an essay defining
Romantic aesthetics. C. M. Bowra's "The Romantic Imagination" explains
how Romanticism represents a radical shift in nineteenth-century aesthetics.*

WILLIAM WORDSWORTH
*"The Solitary Reaper**"*   grain cutter

Pope's poem is a form of philosophical essay; Wordsworth's is more of
a description, both of a scene and his reaction to it. Read the poem carefully
and then paraphrase each stanza, describing the scene and the poet's emotions.

*Behold her, single in the field,
Yon* solitary Highland* Lass*!*   that / Scottish / girl
*Reaping and singing by herself;
Stop here, or gently pass!
Alone she cuts and binds the grain,*

And sings a melancholy strain;*	song
O listen! for the vale* profound	valley
Is overflowing with the sound.	

No nightingale did ever chaunt*	sing
More welcome notes to weary bands	
Of travelers to some shady haunt,*	deserted area
Among Arabian sands:	
A voice so thrilling ne'er was heard	
In spring-time from the cuckoo bird,	
Breaking the silence of the seas,	
Among the farthest Hebrides.*	Scottish islands

Will no one tell me what she sings?	
Perhaps the plaintive* numbers flow	sorrowful
For old, unhappy, far-off things,	
And battles long ago:	
Or is it some more humble lay,*	ballad, song
Familiar matter of today?	
Some natural sorrow, loss or pain,	
That has been, and may be again?	

Whate'er the theme, the maiden sang	
As if her song could have no ending;	
I saw her singing at her work,	
And o'er* the sickle* bending; —	over / cutting tool
I listened, motionless and still;	
And as I mounted up the hill,	
The music in my heart I bore,	
Long after it was heard no more.	

QUESTIONS FOR DISCUSSION AND WRITING

[1] Eighteenth-century neoclassical poets like Pope valued order in the natural world. What does Wordsworth, a nineteenth-century Romantic poet, particularly value about the natural world depicted in the poem?

[2] Wordsworth tells us that he cannot understand the reaper's language, yet he is moved by her song. How does the song captivate him?

[3] Pope's poem consists of grandiose images and large philosophical issues presented in formal diction. How does Wordsworth's poem differ? Consider his poem's setting, the reaper's class status, and the speaker's attitudes and diction.

In addition to natural themes and imagery, the realm of the imagination is another facet of Romanticism. Read through Coleridge's poem for its literal description of Xanadu. Look also for the "tension" of the poem, its opposing forces (similar to the idea of "plot" which you analyzed in *Oedipus Rex*).

SAMUEL TAYLOR COLERIDGE
"Kubla Khan"

A Vision in a Dream, A Fragment

In Xanadu did Kubla Khan*   Chinese ruler
A stately pleasure dome decree:
Where Alph, the sacred river, ran
Through caverns measureless to man
Down to a sunless sea.
So twice five miles of fertile ground
With walls and towers were girdled* round: encircled
And there were gardens bright with sinuous* rills,* curving / brooks
Where blossomed many an incense-bearing tree;
And here were forests ancient as the hills,
Enfolding sunny spots of greenery.

But oh! that deep romantic chasm* which slanted   gorge, crack, crevice
Down the green hill athwart* a cedarn* cover!   across / full of cedar trees
A savage place! as holy and enchanted
As e'er beneath a waning* moon was haunted   setting, shrinking
By woman wailing for her demon lover!
And from this chasm, with ceaseless turmoil seething* boiling
As if this earth in fast thick pants were breathing,
A mighty fountain momently was forced:
Amid whose swift half-intermitted* burst   irregular
Huge fragments vaulted like rebounding hail,
Or chaffy* grain beneath the thresher's* flail:*   unhusked, unpulled /
And 'mid these dancing rocks at once and ever   grain-removing machine /
It flung up momently* the sacred river.   threshing tool
Five miles meandering* with a mazy motion   from moment to moment
Through wood and dale* the sacred river ran,   winding, wandering
Then reached the caverns measureless to man,   valley
And sank in tumult* to a lifeless ocean;   noise
And 'mid this tumult Kubla heard from far
Ancestral voices prophesying war!

The shadow of the dome of pleasure
Floated midway on the waves;
Where was heard the mingled measure
From the fountain and the caves.
It was a miracle of rare device,
A sunny pleasure dome with caves of ice!

A damsel with a dulcimer*   stringed musical instrument
In a vision once I saw:
It was an Abyssinian* maid,   near Eastern land

And on her dulcimer she played,
Singing of Mount Abora.
Could I revive within me
Her symphony and song,
To such a deep delight 'twould win me,
That with music loud and long,
I would build that dome in air,
That sunny dome! those caves of ice!
And all who heard should see them there,
And all should cry, Beware! Beware!
His flashing eyes, his floating hair!
*Weave a circle round him thrice,**   three times
And close your eyes with holy dread,
For he on honey-dew hath fed,*   food of the gods
*And drunk the milk of Paradise.**   drink of the gods

QUESTIONS FOR DISCUSSION AND WRITING

[1] Describe Xanadu and Kubla Khan's pleasure dome in a paragraph, paraphrasing the poem's lines.

[2] What is the tension in the poem? Who threatens whom with war, and who is fearful of the poet's power at the poem's end?

[3] What mental quality does each poet you have read — Pope, Wordsworth, and Coleridge — seem to value most highly?

C. M. BOWRA
FROM *The Romantic Imagination*

Bowra offers a general analysis of Romantic values. Read the passage to develop a specific definition of Romantic aesthetics, which in effect will be an elaboration of Bowra's thesis. Clarify your reading strategy before you begin.

KEY CONCEPTS

The Romantics attempted to create art that was more than an **IMITATION OF LIFE**; in this sense, they differed from the neoclassical age, which accepted Aristotle's theory. See page 33.

METAPHYSICAL thought studies the nature of being; see Chapter 1, page 33.

The Romantics also rejected a **MECHANISTIC** view of life in favor of organicism; instead of viewing life and the world as a smoothly running machine, they saw it more like a tree, which was of a type but was still unique and constantly growing and changing.

An **IDEALIST** believes that reality exists in the unseen world of ideas as opposed to material things.

A **SENSATIONALIST** view of the world states that we know via our sense perceptions only.

INTUITION is a mental quality that derives from imagination as opposed to pure reason.

TRANSCENDENTALISM is a spiritual belief that states that one can move beyond the purely sensual world into an ideal realm through nonrational channels.

● If we wish to distinguish a single characteristic which differentiates the English Romantics from the poets of the eighteenth century, it is to be found in the importance which they attached to the imagination and in the special view which they held of it. On this, despite significant differences on points of detail, Blake, Coleridge, Wordsworth, Shelley, and Keats agree, and for each it sustains a deeply considered theory of poetry. In the eighteenth century imagination was not a cardinal* point in poetical theory. For Pope and Johnson, as for Dryden before them, it has little importance, and when they mention it, it has a limited significance. They approve of fancy, provided that it is controlled by what they call "judgement," and they admire the apt* use of images, by which they mean little more than visual impressions and metaphors.* But for them what matters most in poetry is its truth to the emotions, or, as they prefer to say, sentiment. They wish to speak in general terms for the common experience of men, not to indulge personal whims* in creating new worlds. For them the poet is more an interpreter than a creator, more concerned with showing the attractions of what we already know than with expeditions into the unfamiliar and the unseen. They are less interested in the mysteries of life than in its familiar appearance, and they think that their task is to display this with as much charm and truth as they can command. But for the Romantics imagination is fundamental, because they think that without it poetry is impossible.

This belief in the imagination was part of the contemporary belief in the individual self. The poets were conscious of a wonderful capacity to create imaginary worlds, and they could not believe that this was idle or false. On the contrary, they thought that to curb it was to deny something vitally necessary to their whole being. They thought that it was just this which made them poets. They saw that the power of poetry is strongest when the creative impulse works untrammeled,* and that in their own case this happened when they shaped fleeting* visions into concrete forms and pursued wild thoughts until they captured and mastered them. As the Renaissance poets suddenly found the huge possibilities of the human self

major

fitting
poetic comparisons

fancies, impulses

unrestricted
quickly disappearing

SOURCE: Excerpted by permission of the publishers from *The Romantic Imagination* by Sir Maurice Bowra, Cambridge, Mass.: Harvard University Press, 1949.

and expressed them in a bold and far-flung art, which is certainly much more than an **imitation of life**, so the Romantics, brought to a fuller consciousness of their own powers, felt a similar need to exert these powers in fashioning new worlds of the mind.

The Romantic emphasis on the imagination was strengthened by considerations which are both religious and **metaphysical**. For a century English philosophy had been dominated by the theories of Locke. He assumed that in perception the mind is wholly passive, a mere recorder of impressions from without, "a lazy looker-on on an external world." His system was well suited to an age of scientific speculation which found its representative voice in Newton. The **mechanistic** explanation which both philosophers and scientists gave of the world meant that scanty* respect *meager, little* was paid to the human self and especially to its more instinctive, though not less powerful, convictions. Thus both Locke and Newton found a place for God in their universes, the former on the ground that "the works of nature in every part of them sufficiently evidence a deity," and the latter on the principle that the great machine of the world implies a mechanic. But this was not at all what the Romantics demanded from religion. For them it was a question less of reason than of feeling, less of argument than of experience, and they complained that these mechanistic explanations were a denial of their innermost convictions. So too with poetry. Locke had views on poetry, as he had on most human activities, but no very high regard for it. For him it is a matter of "wit," and the task of wit is to combine ideas and "thereby to make up pleasant pictures and agreeable visions in the fancy."

Locke is the target both of Blake and of Coleridge, to whom he represents a deadly heresy on the nature of existence. They are hostile to his whole system which robs the human self of importance. They reject his conception of the universe and replace it by their own systems, which deserve the name of **"idealist"** because mind is their central point and governing factor. But because they are poets, they insist that the most vital activity of the mind is the imagination. Since for them it is the very source of spiritual energy, they cannot but believe that it is divine, and that, when they exercise it, they in some way partake* of the activity of God. *share*

This is a tremendous claim, and it is not confined to Blake and Coleridge. It was to some degree held by Wordsworth and Shelley and Keats. Each was confident not only that the imagination was his most precious possession but that it was somehow concerned with a supernatural order. Never before had quite such a claim been made, and from it Romantic poetry derives much that is most magical in it.

The perception which works so closely with the imagination is not of the kind in which Locke believed, and the Romantics took pains to dispel any misunderstanding on the point. Since what mattered to them was an insight into the nature of things, they rejected Locke's limitation of perception to physical objects, because it robbed the mind of its most essential function, which is at the same time to perceive and to create.

When they rejected the **sensationalist** view of an external world, Blake and Coleridge prepared the way to restoring the supremacy of the spirit which had been denied by Locke but was at this time being propounded by German metaphysicians. Blake knew nothing of them, and his conclusions arose from his own visionary outlook, which could not believe that matter is in any sense as real as spirit. Coleridge had read Kant and Schelling and found in them much to support his views, but those views were derived less from them than from his own instinctive convictions that the world of spirit is the only reality. Because he was first a poet and only secondly a metaphysician, his conception of a universe of spirit came from his intense sense of an inner life and from his belief that the imagination, working with **intuition**, is more likely than the analytical reason to make discoveries on matters which really concern us.

In rejecting Locke's and Newton's explanations of the visible world, the Romantics obeyed an inner call to explore more fully the world of spirit. In different ways each of them believed in an order of things which is not that which we see and know, and this was the goal of their passionate search. They wished to penetrate to an abiding* reality, to explore its   lasting
mysteries, and by this to understand more clearly what life means and what it is worth. Locke and Newton explain what the sensible world is, but not what it is worth.

The great Romantics, then, agreed that their task was to find through the imagination some **transcendental** order which explains the world of appearances and accounts not merely for the existence of visible things but for the effect which they have on us, for the sudden, unpredictable beating of the heart in the presence of beauty, for the conviction that what then moves us cannot be a cheat or an illusion, but must derive its authority from the power which moves the universe. For them this reality could not but be spiritual, and they provide an independent illustration of Hegel's doctrine that nothing is real but spirit. In so far as they made sweeping statements about the oneness of things, they were metaphysicians, but, unlike professional metaphysicians, they trusted not in logic but in insight, not in the analytical reason but in the delighted, inspired soul which in its full nature transcends both the mind and the emotions.

The Romantics knew that their business was to create, and through creation to enlighten the whole sentient* and conscious self of man, to   feeling, aware
wake his imagination to the reality which lies behind or in familiar things, to rouse him from the deadening routine of custom to a consciousness of immeasurable distances and unfathomable* depths, to make him see that   uncomprehensible, beyond
mere reason is not enough and that what he needs is inspired intuition.   measure
They take a wider view both of man and of poetry than was taken by their staid* and rational predecessors of the eighteenth century, because they   conservative, restrictive
believed that it is the whole spiritual nature of man that counts, and to this they made their challenge and their appeal.

QUESTIONS FOR DISCUSSION AND WRITING

[1] Bowra writes that Romantic poets created poetry in order "to wake [man's] imagination to the reality which lies behind or in familiar things, to rouse him from the deadening routine of custom to a consciousness of immeasurable distances and unfathomable depths." Cite quotations or examples from both Wordsworth and Coleridge to illustrate these intentions.

[2] According to Bowra, in what sense is the Romantic imagination divine?

[3] What main idea in Locke's philosophy did the Romantics reject, and why? Which ideas in Pope complement Locke's philosophical views?

SECTION ESSAY ASSIGNMENTS

[1] Review Bowra's discussion of Locke's philosophy, outlining and paraphrasing the major points. In an essay, show how Locke's philosophical views apply to Pope's Essay on Man.

[2] Drawing on Sherburn, Bowra, and the poems of Pope, Wordsworth, and Coleridge, compare eighteenth- and nineteenth-century aesthetics. The points you might consider include the purpose of poetry, the nature of the poet, and how each views rational and intuitive thought.

[3] Consider the educational value of neoclassical versus Romantic poetry. Which do you believe offers more to the student? If you argue Pope's case, you might defend a view of poetry as instructional material — its purpose is more to teach than to delight. If you argue for Wordsworth and Coleridge, you may take a humanistic position, in which poetry is considered a balance to purely academic purposes.

Twentieth-Century Painting

The paintings reproduced at the beginning of this chapter (see Color Plate) seem very different on the surface: Hopper's are representational — they depict real figures — and Pollock's are abstract — they present design over form or, in other words, in Pollock shapes, patterns, and colors are more important than figures or structures. But the different paintings represent a similar aesthetic of the twentieth century. Read the following passage, which will help you define the modern aesthetic.

Ladd Terry wrote this essay in 1984. Terry is himself an artist and brings a painter's point of view to his subject. He explains how modern art grew out of the nineteenth-century practice and developed its own forms and materials. The untrained viewer may have difficulty detecting any common aesthetic in works as different as Pollock's and Hopper's. In their attempts to suppress point of view, to focus on surface and design, the works of modern artists sometimes seem ahistorical and closed to interpretation. But some critics might argue that modern art, too, is a text that can be read, a text reflecting the artist's culture and personality.

LADD TERRY
"Modern Art in Transition"

KEY CONCEPT
Art for art's sake is an aesthetic that places art itself above any other purpose in artistic creation; it is an antithetical doctrine to "useful and beautiful" art or to art that "delights and instructs."

● Understanding modern art requires a familiarity with social history, art history, and contemporary aesthetic values. It is a broad subject involving over a hundred years of information and a widely varied group of contributors. The influences which created what we refer to as modern art may go back to antiquity; its foundations developed in nineteenth-century Europe, and European aesthetics influenced modern art well into the twentieth century. But there is no single creed* or manifesto* that com- belief system / declaration
pletely defines modern art.

Modern art may be thought of as any aesthetic expression that is new or innovative to the times in which it is expressed. Historically, it has come to mean the period from the late nineteenth century to the early 1960s. What most typifies modern art in the twentieth century is the artist's involvement in the concepts and processes of art. Prior to this period, there was, in general, an emphasis on allegory, storytelling of both histori-cal and religious themes, or illumination of scene and character. Subject or content dominated the style and manner of the work. Religious, politi-cal, and social pressure held sway over style, manner, and even content. The king or Pope or patron* often dictated a painting's subject and style. financial supporter

With exception given to stylistic device, a dominant theme was nature recorded as the artist perceived it. The artist used the forms of nature to describe his view of the world. Whereas the artist modified nature consid-erably to express his or her aesthetic ideas, the essence of the work was the relationship of expression to natural form. In Northern Europe, the northern Renaissance artists included Gothic imagery and angst*-filled anxiety, doubt
brooding atmospheres of dragons, lizards, and skulls. The Venetian Ren-aissance artists of southern Italy, on the other hand, displayed a world of sunshine and blue skies, using pastoral settings to depict the same religious theme as that of the northern Renaissance artist. The natural form may have been idealized or modified to suit the artist's individual or cultural

expression, but generally they tended to see the painting as a window to the outside world.

During the period of modern art, artists began seriously to question what art is and what function it serves. Art became an investigation of the self, as in the Expressionist* and Surrealist* movements, or an investigation of concepts and process, as in the Impressionist,* Cubist,* and Pop Art* movements.

artist-centered / breaking with reality / sense-oriented / geometric / mainstream culture

American artists, at the turn of the century, were still paying homage* to Europe, studying and adopting European styles and techniques. Although America owed a great deal to those European artists and schools that pioneered modernist concepts, by the late 1930s America was the leading exponent of modern art. Aesthetically, the twentieth century is an American century.

honor

There are many opinions as to which influences led to the development of modern art. Certainly, developments in science and technology had a great, if indirect, influence by changing society and the artist's perception of the world. In the early 1900s Freud's theory of the subconscious did much to free the artists in their search for meaning. Also influencing modernism were specific developments like modular* steel construction in architecture, the development and popular dissemination of film, the industrialization and increased urbanization of America, the rise of the middle class, with its growing access to art, the loosening of class distinctions, which allowed the common person to participate in the arts, and the expanding role of America in developing art.

in separate sections

Modern art in America became a search for personal expression which led many artists to abandon realistic imagery in favor of a strong statement of design and individual vision. As the modern artist probed the question of function in art, art came to serve the individual artist's purpose. (**Art for art's sake** is a phrase that captures the sense of what modern art is about.) The canvas became the stage for the artist to act out intellectual or emotional constructs, unrestricted by formal elements of style as dictated by school or manner.

In their search for new ideas and methods in art, many artists developed new ways of making art, but the egoism of personal expression formed the primary consideration. Whether representational or abstract,* modern art reveals the dual concept of saying something while at the same time designing the surface. Space, shape, and form, which prior to modern art merely supported natural imagery, became abstract elements, central to the themes of modern art. The illusion of deep space began to flatten, and color became contrived or arbitrary.*

nonpictorial

not following rules

The Impressionists investigated light and color. With exaggerated brush strokes and heightened color, they created a warm, inviting world of visual and sensual pleasures. Images of sunshine and shadow sparkled with color and form.

The Expressionists used the media to convey emotional statements about the subjects of their work. With thick paint, heavy brush strokes, and strongly stated color, they recaptured on canvas the emotions of the passionate artist.

The Cubists took the images of nature, analyzing the forms and the space around them, then flattened the natural deep space in which these forms usually existed. The natural forms were devices used to develop analytical concepts. Color was used minimally, value used to express variety and developed form.

The Surrealists were hedonists* of the subconscious. Their work was directly related to the theories of Sigmund Freud. His theories helped free the Surrealists from the need to express the contradiction, confusion, and conflict of their world. The Surrealist artists attempted to escape the confines of an objective, rational, experienced world.

pleasure-seekers

The Abstract Expressionists took their inspiration from the abstraction of earlier modernist schools such as the Cubists and Constructionists, and the expression from the Post-Impressionists, Expressionists, and Fauvists. The canvas became large abstractions of real forms, painted with strong movement and action, the paint dripped and moved in a way that was honest to the material.

The Pop Artists were the last of the so-called modernists and they provided a transition for modern art to a new aesthetic format. Their quirky, erotic, humorous, iconoclastic,* deadpan look at the common objects and trendy images of society was a strong social comment that tried to deny comment.

antitraditional

Edward Hopper and Jackson Pollock exemplify the modernist paradox, for their work is seemingly contradictory in form, yet upon investigation has interesting similarities in concept.

Edward Hopper (1882–1967) was a quietly transitional figure in the modernist movement. His work, primarily American East Coast rural landscapes and cityscapes, was greatly influenced by his studies in Europe. These studies produced an infatuation with French art, particularly with Millet and French Realism. He was also influenced by Rembrandt and the Impressionists. Still clinging to the realist idea of the past while designing his canvas in modernist concepts of planes and spaces, his work is both modernist and traditionalist. Hopper's cool, detached landscapes and interiorscapes in a realist mode have as their basic design a flat, geometric patterning that supersedes the subject.

Although often referred to as the most significant American realist in the twentieth century, Hopper more significantly used the realist format as a device to express modernist concepts. Many of his paintings are complicated homages to nineteenth-century European realist paintings. His work also reflects the influence of film, theater, and literature in his framing of the subject and creating a mood or thematic metaphor. The paintings have a geometric frontality in which the images, much like a documented photograph, appear as flat, geometric forms. This frontality places the isolated viewer in the position of a voyeur. The detachment of both viewer and inhabitant of the canvas creates a mirrored state of loneliness, perhaps reflecting the loneliness of Hopper himself. Hopper's intention was to deal with the planes and light of the design. His painting, "Room in Brooklyn" (1932), which shows a couple on a lighted porch at night, is an example of his intention. Hopper has commented that he wasn't interested in the couple on the porch, but rather in the darkness around and beyond the porch and in the light streaming from the porch light. When he does include figures, they are solitary, introspective, and inactive. "Night Hawks" (1942), probably the most recognizable of his paintings, is a dramatic example of the viewer and the people being viewed. The strongly stated geometric planes produce a modernist painting of design and structure rather than social comment. Any comment is left to the viewer of the painting.

Jackson Pollock (1912–1956), an American abstract painter, was the central figure of American painting in the late 1940s and early 1950s. His lifestyle and expressions on canvas became the stuff of myth and legend. He typified the strutting confidence of America, victorious after World War II. But this confidence was fraught with contradiction. Artists had begun to question the dominance of European aesthetic influence and traditions, and a new attitude developed about the meaning of art. Individual expression achieved dominance as American realist traditions of a generation before gave way to the democracy of individual expression.

Pollock, a swaggering, brooding, emotional alcoholic, lived the part of the modern artist. After his regular Tuesday session with his analyst, he could be found at the Cedar Bar, a New York hangout for artists and intellectuals. Passions would turn into brawls. In general, the Abstract Expressionists were emotional and action-oriented. Pollock's work is a good example of this action as painting.

More than any other artist in the late 1940s, it was Pollock who broke the ties to the European influence in art. The confusion in understanding his work has to do with its uniqueness in confrontation with the established European aesthetic ideas, for Pollock's work was not just a new variation; it was completely different, requiring a new way of understanding art. Pollock's art had its foundations in European painting, but it was uniquely American.

Pollock's method has been described as "automatic writing" related to the movement of the hand as in writing script or drawing. His paintings often contain unconventional objects and textures such as sand, broken glass, metal, and wood. Pollock used sticks, trowels, and his hands as he flung or dripped paint onto his canvases.

The large canvases, often painted on the floor, were a mist of pigment, a webbing of dripped and poured paint, covering the surface, leaving no "holes" or figure-ground contrast as in a figure depicted in a scene.

"Blue Poles" (1952), a painting of "heroic" size, is an atmosphere of blue space, an "all-over" painting with rich, lyrical webbing, "drawn" lines, and varying intensity of color. The paint is laid down in flourishes, loops, and spatters. Color is more important than value contrast (dark and light value), much like the Impressionists. The painting is a celebration of color, perhaps "decorative" in its celebration of the "spiritual essence" of experience. In Pollock's words, "My aim has always been the most exact transcriptions possible of my most intimate impressions of nature."

If modern art is considered a transitional period in the history of art, it is perhaps one of the most significant. Hopper and Pollock are but two of many of the artists who found a way of expressing something of themselves in the modernist movement. The movement continues to exert its influence on the concepts and attitudes of artists today.

QUESTIONS FOR DISCUSSION AND WRITING

[1] Terry states that the works of Hopper and Pollock are "seemingly contradictory in form, yet . . . [have] interesting similarities in concept." Explain how the paintings embody comparable modernist ideas.

[2] Terry points out that modernism reflects an "art for art's sake" aesthetic. To what extent do the medieval cathedrals and Pope's poetry share that aesthetic?

[3] Terry argues that neither Hopper's nor Pollock's work contains social comment. As you view their paintings, can you derive any social statement from either?

SECTION ESSAY ASSIGNMENTS

[1] Consider your impressions as you view Hopper's and Pollock's paintings. Choose one painting and analyze its impact on the viewer. Topics you might consider include intellectual content (does the painting suggest an idea or make you think?); aesthetic value (is it attractive in some way?); associations (what does it remind you of?); identification (can you sympathize with the scene or design? Does it draw you in in some way, positively or negatively?).

[2] Compare and contrast the impact of each painting, perhaps using the categories suggested in the above question. Draw on Terry's essay to support your points.

[3] You have studied examples of the following art forms: drama, architecture, prose, poetry, and painting. Develop an argument that painting is as expressive an art form as any of these. Discuss its ability to express aesthetic, intellectual, and emotional ideas.

CHAPTER 4 ESSAY ASSIGNMENTS

[1] You've read both Pope and Sherburn, the former illustrating and the latter analyzing neoclassical aesthetics. Given what you know of modernist

aesthetics from Terry's article and your own impressions of Hopper and Pollock, describe in an essay how a neoclassicist might view modern art.

[2] The medieval world had few actual texts from antiquity, and so its art developed with only indirect influence, drawing instead on Christian philosophy. Compare and contrast ancient and medieval aesthetics to show how each defined art's purpose, its subject matter, and the relationship of common people to the creation and enjoyment of art.

[3] In antiquity, the Middle Ages, and the neoclassical period, the artist's personal ego is not closely identified with his work of art. During the Renaissance, the Romantic era, and the modern period, however, ego becomes a dominant concern and theme. Discuss the presence of a sense of self, or ego, in each period, citing specific examples to show how the works reflect the absence or presence of the individual ego.

[4] In *The Republic,* Plato argues that art is a lie, that it distorts the truth because artistic imitation is several times removed from reality. Choose two examples from the chapter readings to explain and illustrate how art idealizes or alters reality.

[5] You've read pieces on classical art, philosophy, politics, science, and religion; you've also read a selection from Pope's *Essay on Man,* which touches on most of those subjects. Pope's era is the neoclassical age — the "new classical" period. What parallels can you draw between the concerns, interests, beliefs, and values of the two periods?

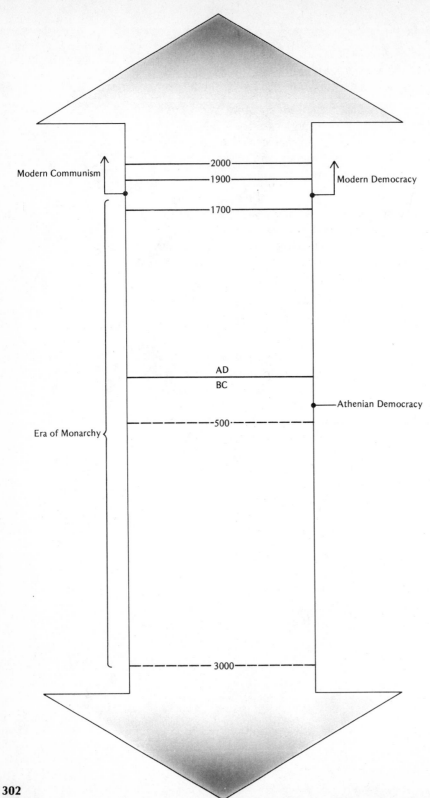

Modern Communism

2000
1900
1700

Modern Democracy

AD
BC

Athenian Democracy

500

Era of Monarchy

3000

Chart the following religious, scientific, and aesthetic figures, works, and movements on this chapter's time-line. Try to infer the relationship between the prevailing types of government at a given time and the changes in the other fields you've read about in the preceding chapters.

The Odyssey
Oedipus Rex
Plato
Scientific method
The New Testament
Medieval era
Dante
Luther
Atom bomb
Alchemy
Social Darwinism
Alexander Pope
Romanticism
The Renaissance

CHAPTER 5

Political Theory and Practice

INTRODUCTION

This chapter's readings present political theory and reflect actual
practice. At the beginning of each section you will read a theoretical
definition of a particular political system or ideology including democracy,
monarchy, communism, imperialism, and terrorism. Each definition is
followed by several passages depicting historical problems that surfaced
when theory was put into practice. The passages focus on the costs and
shortcomings inherent in any political system. We want to emphasize that
the readings highlight discrepancies, contradictions, and dissatisfactions
which inevitably arise in any society's system of government, for no
political system has shown itself to be perfect. Be careful of making
political judgments based on this material alone. Any conclusions you
draw should be based on further study that will enable you to weigh the
theoretical soundness and the practical problems involved.

There are many other political systems and ideologies not covered by
this chapter, and those covered here are treated generally and over large
historical periods. In the first section, on democracy, the readings illustrate
how inequality and oppression in different nations have coexisted with
their avowed beliefs in equality and representation, and how democratic
revolutions can lead to anarchy and terror on the way to freedom. The
section covers the place of women in the ancient Athenian democracy
(Amaury de Riencourt, "Woman in Athens"); the French Revolution's
Reign of Terror (Albert Parry, "Robespierre's Bloody Virtue"); and the
struggle of women and minorities for full rights in American democratic
society (Hiram Wesley Evans, "The Klan's Fight for Americanism,"
Malcolm X, "The Ballot or the Bullet," James Farmer, "A Night of Terror
in Plaquemine, Louisiana, 1963," and Marlene Dixon, "Why Women's

Liberation"). The chapter offers multiple readings on these topics because the issue of equal rights for women and minorities continues to be a pressing contemporary concern.

Although they are fading from the contemporary Western political picture, monarchies were the predominant form of government in Western Europe beginning with the ancient world and continuing to modern times. Monarchy's theoretical basis is surveyed in William Edenstein's "Monarchy." Of the Roman Caesars, Caligula demonstrates the political truism that absolute power corrupts absolutely, in Suetonius, "Gaius [Caligula]." Commenting on his relationship to the Roman people, he said, "Let them hate me, so long as they fear me," a political philosophy related to Machiavelli's dictum* in The Prince, "To be feared is   pronouncement much safer than to be loved." An account of Louis XIV's court at Versailles by W. H. Lewis in "The Court" shows the literal price of aristocracy: royal excess and grandeur paid for by the suffering poor.

Communism is used as an umbrella term for both Marxist thought and socialism. The two essays included in the communism section show communism's past and future costs. In the first, Alexander Weissberg, from The Accused, you'll read a victim's account of Stalin's Great Purge during the 1930's. In the second reading, Dianne Feeley, "Women and Marxism," a radical feminist criticizes the American Communist's party's revisionist position on women's rights. According to Marxist theory, women's full emancipation can only be attained at the cost of abolishing the family as a social unit.

All forms of government — democracies, monarchies, and communist states — have practiced imperialism, the subject of the next section, which is defined in Robin Winks' essay, "Imperialism." George Orwell's story, "Marrakech," and W.E.B. Dubois' essay, "White Masters of the World," each point out the human costs of imperialism to both the oppressed and the oppressor.

The belief that terrorism can be used to bring about political change concerns all of us in the contemporary world. Theoretically, terrorism appears to be an effective instrument for political change, as Baljit Singh explains it in "An Overview of Terrorism." But do the ends justify the means? A newspaper account of a terrorist bombing (Richard Eder, "23 Killed in Dublin Blast") vividly illustrates how the terrorist ideology becomes a bloody reality for its innocent victims.

READING AND WRITING SKILLS OF CHAPTER 5

This chapter presents the following reading/writing skills:

Recognizing rhetorical modes
Using logical connectors to improve comprehension
Writing with logical connectors

Democracy, Oppression, and Violence

Survey the following article, which is an extended definition of democracy. Use an appropriate reading strategy that will enable you to paraphrase the definition and write a summary of it.

SIDNEY HOOK
"Democracy"

KEY CONCEPTS

The Declaration of Independence formulated an ethical principle of **INALIENABLE RIGHTS**, which states that every individual has the right to "life, liberty, and the pursuit of happiness." These rights are "inalienable": they cannot be taken away.

DELEGATION OF AUTHORITY in a democracy means that the people have elected representatives to speak for them.

A **DICTATOR** or **ABSOLUTE MONARCH** has total control of a nation's government and armed forces; the people hold no power over their leader and cannot elect any representatives.

The principle of **MAJORITY RULE** means that whatever most of the people want will become law despite the possibly opposing wishes of the minority.

The modern meaning of a **TYRANNY** is a dictatorship, a form of government by a single leader without the necessity of popular consent.

ANARCHY is the lack of any organized governing system.

The notion of **THE HERD** derives from the notion of the **ELITE;** the first term, an animal image, refers to the masses and carries with it the connotation "stupid"; the second term refers to some group that expects special privileges or recognition based on some quality, like education, that separates them from "the herd."

Big Brother's government in Orwell's *Nineteen Eighty-Four* is an example of a **TOTALITARIAN** regime. It is characterized by authoritarian control of the people.

A **BENEVOLENT DESPOT** holds absolute power over a nation in an attempt to improve or maintain the nation's economic or political condition.

The word "democracy" has many meanings, but in the modern world its use signifies that the ultimate authority in political affairs rightfully belongs to the people. The term characteristically evokes positive emotional responses among those who utter it as well as those who hear it. There was

SOURCE: "Democracy" by Sidney Hook from *Encyclopedia Americana*. Published by Grolier Inc. Copyright © 1984. Reprinted by permission of the publisher.

a time when "democrat" was a term of abuse. Today its connotations are honorable.

Democracy is a form of government in which the major decisions of government — or the direction of policy behind these decisions — rest directly or indirectly on the freely given consent of a majority of the adults governed. This makes democracy essentially a political concept even when it is used — and sometimes misused — to characterize non-political institutions.

Democracy as a political process is obviously a matter of degree — depending on the area of life within the bounds of political experience and the number and qualifications of those considered adults. Because no ideal democracies exist and because there are always some areas in which the voice or wishes of the multitude* can be heard or can make itself felt, the difference between non-democratic and democratic states are sometimes characterized as being "merely" one of degree. This is incontestable, but usually the argument of difference "merely in degree" is employed to minimize, and often confuse, the difference between democratic and non-democratic states.

the masses, common people

Freely given consent

It becomes necessary, therefore, to supplement the above definition with a working conception that will enable us to distinguish democratic regimes from others. One such working conception is the view that a democratic government is one in which the minority or its representatives may peacefully become the majority or the representatives of the majority. The presupposition* is, of course, that this transition is made possible by, and expresses, the freely given consent of the majority of the adults governed. The implications of the presence of freely given consent call attention to the difference between ancient democracies, which stressed only majority rule as a validating principle, and modern democracies, which since the birth of the American republic have stressed the operating presence of **inalienable rights**.

that which is supposed or assumed beforehand

Direct and indirect democracy

Before developing the implications of this distinction, it is necessary to dissolve certain misconceptions that have often plagued discussions of democracy. The first is the view that the only genuine democracy is "direct" democracy in which all citizens of the community are present and collectively pass on all legislation, as was practiced in ancient Athens or as is the case in a New England town meeting. From this point of view an indirect or representative democracy is not a democracy but a constitutional republic or commonwealth. This distinction breaks down because, literally construed,* there can be no direct democracy if laws are defined not only in terms of their adoption but also in terms of their execution. For **delegation of authority** is inescapable in any political assemblage* unless all citizens are in continuous service at all times, not only legislating but

translated, interpreted

group

executing the laws together. The basic question is whether the delegation of authority is reversible — controlled by those who delegated it.

Democracy vs. republic

The second misconception is the identification of, or confusion between, the terms "democracy" and "republic." Strictly speaking, a republican form of government is one in which the chief titular* head of government is not hereditary. A republic can have an undemocratic form of government (for example, Nazi Germany or the Soviet Union) whereas a monarchy can be a democracy (for example, Britain and the Scandinavian countries). There is no organic or logical connection between the two terms.

only in name

Majority rule and minority rights

From one point of view, any community in which a majority of the adult population were slaves cannot be considered democratic. Nonetheless, there is a valid distinction between the kinds of government that existed in antiquity in which the freemen — however limited in numbers — were the source of ultimate political authority and governments in which the authority of government was vested in a **dictator** or **absolute monarch**. The former were ancient democracies even though the free citizenry or its representatives recognized no limitation on the nature and exercise of their rule and others enjoyed no political rights. The result of elections in the ancient democracies often was the civil equivalent of a military victory, and "vae victis" ("woe to the vanquished") often described the fate of the defeated. Under such circumstances "democratic" rule was bloody, disorderly, and often a preface to the emergence of a strong man or dictator. Even where power was in the hands of the majority, there was no democracy in the modern sense for minority rights were not considered.

With the emergence of a theory of human rights beginning in the 17th century and its explicit development in the writings of Thomas Hobbes and, above all, John Locke, the way was prepared for a conception of democracy in which the principle of **majority rule** was a necessary but not a sufficient condition. The will of the majority was to enjoy democratic legitimacy only if it was an expression of freely given consent. The specific provisions of the American Bill of Rights, and the unwritten, but not unspoken, assumptions of the British Constitution after the Cromwellian Revolution expressed, in the idiom* of the time, the limits set by human rights on the power of ruling majorities, minorities, or kings.

common language

Majorities could do everything except deprive minorities of the freedoms — of speech, press, assembly, rights to a fair trial, and so on — the exercise of which might enable the minority peacefully to win over the electorate and come to power. Minorities might do everything within the context of these human rights to present their case. But so long as they accepted the principles of democratic organization, they were bound by

the outcome of the give and take of free discussion and debate until
another opportunity for persuasion might present itself. Since unanimity*   complete agreement
among human beings about matters of great and topical concern is impos-
sible, the majority principle, insofar as it truly respects the existence of
human rights, is the only one that makes democracy a viable alternative
to tyranny. The other alternative to **tyranny** is **anarchy**, which is the rule
of a thousand tyrants.

Conditions for democratic rule

What are the signs of "freely given consent" or under what conditions
is it present? Briefly, when there is no physical coercion or threat of
coercion employed against expression of opinion; when there is no arbitrary restriction placed on freedom of speech, press, and assembly; where
there is no monopoly of propaganda by the ruling party; and where there
is no institutional control over the instruments or facilities of communication. These are minimal conditions for the existence of freely given con-
sent. In their absence a plebiscite,* even if unanimous, is not democrati-   direct vote on an issue
cally valid.

From one point of view these may be considered negative conditions
for the presence of democratic rule. But it may be necessary for a government to take positive measures to ensure that different groups in the
population have access to the means by which public opinion is swayed.
If, for example, an individual or a group had an economic monopoly of
newsprint or television channels and barred those with contrary views
from using them, both the spirit and letter of democracy would be violated.

Informed citizenry

Philosophers of democracy, especially Thomas Jefferson, John Stuart
Mill, and John Dewey, have called attention to certain positive conditions
whose presence quickens and strengthens the democratic process. Foremost of these is the spread of education, allowing for an informed and
critical awareness of the issues and problems of the times. If the avenues
of communication are open, an educated electorate* can become aware   people who vote
of the consequences and costs of past policies and the present alternatives
of action.

If, as Spinoza declared, men may become enslaved by their ignorance,
uninformed freedom of choice may take the road of disaster. It is this fear
of mass ignorance or the stupidity of **the herd** that is one root of opposition
to democracy. H. L. Mencken referred to democracy as "the dictatorship
of the booboisie." The more informed and better educated the electorate,
the healthier is the democracy.

Citizen participation

A second positive condition for the existence of an effective democracy
is the active participation of the citizens in the processes of government.

Participation is all the more essential as government grows in size and complexity and a mood develops that the individual citizen is ineffective and ineffectual in the face of anonymous forces controlling his destiny. The result of such a mood may be widescale apathy and the decay in democratic vitality even when democratic forms are preserved. "The food of feeling," observed Mill, "is action. Let a person have nothing to do for his country, and he will not care for it."

Inviolable rights for minorities

The acceptance of the inviolable rights of minorities reduces the danger of dictatorship by the majority in a democracy. The rights of minorities, however, cannot be construed literally as absolute, independent of the consequences of the actions of such rights on the rights of majorities or on the welfare of society as a whole. In addition, rights may conflict. Freedom of speech may interfere with a man's right to a fair trial and sometimes, as when an orator is inciting* a lynching mob, with the victim's right to life. In such circumstances the rights of a minority may have to be abridged. What, then, is the difference between democratic and **totalitarian** governments? Do not the latter also abridge the rights of citizens in the alleged interests of the common good?

urging on

Democracy vs. totalitarianism

The differences are profound. The first distinction is that democratic government recognizes the intrinsic as well as the instrumental value of civil rights, and when it moves to restrict or abridge them, it does so slowly and reluctantly, prepared to put up with considerable disorder as a price for their preservation. Second, if and when the exercise of a civil right creates a clear and present danger of a social evil that threatens other human rights, it is abridged for a limited period and restored as soon as normalcy returns. Third, the restrictions of government agencies on every level in a democracy are subject to appeal, review, and check by an independent judiciary.*

court system

Arguments against democracy

The most powerful arguments against democratic government have been formulated by its honest opponents from Plato to George Santayana, not by modern totalitarians professing to be democrats. The nub* of these arguments is that most human beings are either too stupid or too vicious, or both, to be entrusted with self-government, that the upshot of majority rule therefore is **tyranny** and terror, and that the nature of the public good — which is the end of government — is so complex, so largely a matter of administrative wisdom and skill, that only an **elite** of the intellectually gifted and spiritually elect can discover and implement* it. "Knowledge, and knowledge alone," writes Santayana, "gives divine right to rule."

main point

enact

The weakness in these arguments was exposed by Plato himself. If most human beings are vicious, who is to control the guardians? Who can guarantee the benevolence of the **benevolent despot**? In his account of the inevitable decline from the ideal aristocracy of his Republic to the depths of the irresponsible tyrant, Plato admits that rule of the philosophers is also flawed. And although he uses the analogy of the ship to argue that just as it makes no sense to elect the pilot of a ship, who must be specifically trained for the task, so it makes no sense to elect the pilot of the ship of state, he overlooks the fact that the destination of the ship is not within the competence of the pilot. Indeed, his other analogies reinforce the argument for democracy. For example, he eloquently points out that it is not the cobbler* who knows best what a good pair of shoes is, but the wearer. The whole philosophy of democracy may be expressed in the implications of the homely maxim that he who wears the shoes knows best where they pinch. Despite all the drawbacks and limitations of democracy, there is considerable point to Winston Churchill's declaration: "Democracy is the worst possible form of government — except all the others that have been tried."

shoemaker

Faith in democracy

The faith in democracy ultimately rests not in the belief in the natural goodness of man but in the belief that most human beings can learn by experience. In a world in which science can command unlimited natural power, it can be said that its basic values, shared knowledge, mutual discussion, and the institutionalization of consent can solve more problems with less friction than is possible by entrusting decisive power to minorities who claim to be better judges of the true interests of citizens than the citizens themselves. It is true that democracies have made foolish decisions. But where such errors have not been rectified* by better and more informed democratic action, salvation has been sought in a dictator or charismatic* leader, and the result has more often than not ended in disaster.

corrected

inspiring; attractive

Democracy, as we have seen, is not indivisible — all or nothing — in the sense that its political form necessitates the extension of the democratic principle to other areas of experience. It only makes an extension possible to those who have the vision, courage, and intelligence to struggle for it. Nor is democracy indivisible on the international scene in the sense that the world must soon become one democratic community. Even under a world government, plural political systems may be feasible if each is prepared to sacrifice some national sovereignty* for the sake of peace.

political authority

What can be expected is that the ideals of freedom in flourishing democratic cultures, which are on their way to solving the problems of poverty and unemployment, will always function as an inspiration to the subjects of totalitarian societies. In time, if peace is preserved, and democratic cultures do not yield to the military threats of totalitarian Communist regimes, the masses in those countries may bring about democratic changes by their own efforts. Freedom is infectious. The appetite for freedom grows on what it feeds. And once the process of liberalization begins, there is no telling where it will end.

QUESTIONS FOR DISCUSSION AND WRITING

[1] Summarize the definition of "democracy."

[2] Ancient democracy shares the notion of "majority rule" with modern democracy, but the author points out that the two systems had different notions of human rights (see page 307). Explain the difference between ancient and modern systems of "majority rule."

[3] One argument against democracy claims that only a select few are capable of leading a nation, that our leaders should come from the "intellectually gifted and spiritually elect." What are the fallacies in this argument?

READING SKILL: *Recognizing Rhetorical Modes*

When you speak — or when you write — you communicate your ideas not only through <u>what</u> you say but <u>how</u> you say it. In the same way, an author manipulates sentences and paragraphs on the level of content <u>and</u> organizational patterns, or rhetorical modes, to achieve his or her purpose.

Both essays, and paragraphs within essays, can be classified into different types. By being able to recognize these organizational patterns while you read, you can improve your comprehension and retention. Essays and paragraphs can be divided into the following categories:

1. Narration: telling a story.
2. Description: using concrete details, physical observations.
3. Process: describing how to do something.
4. Listing: cataloguing items or ideas.
5. Cause/effect: connecting causes and results; actions and reactions.
6. Comparison and contrast: showing similarities and differences between two or more things.
7. Chronological order: establishing a sequential order between ideas or events.
8. Problem/solution: establishing two factors, one stating a problem and the other providing a possible remedy.
9. Statement/support: presenting a thesis or argument followed by evidence.
10. Definition/example: explaining and then illustrating a term or concept.

Recognizing each paragraph's rhetorical mode helps you identify an author's purpose, and by clarifying the purpose of each paragraph, you can improve your comprehension and retention. This skill should be a primary part of your reading strategy.

The rhetorical mode of the following essay is argument. Within the essay, the author uses different rhetorical modes for each paragraph. We've marked the text for paragraph modes. You'll notice that the author uses statement/support, cause/effect, and definition/example frequently.

Rhetorical modes serve an essay's overall purpose; here, in an argument essay, the author chooses modes that help to clarify a thesis and support it logically, and illustrates it concretely.

Complete our marking of the text by underlining statements and supports in paragraphs one and two; numbering the chronological events in paragraph three; identifying the causes and effects in paragraph four; identifying the terms defined in paragraph four; identifying cause and effect again in paragraphs six and seven; underlining statement and support in paragraph eight.

The Athenian democracy is often held up for admiration and even adulation* in the Western world. Athens did institute the first democracy, but it contained what to modern eyes are two glaring flaws: slavery and female oppression. We point these flaws out not to condemn or minimize the achievements of Athenian society, but to illustrate the dangers of assuming that a theory of democracy precludes* inequities in practice. The ancient world did not share the modern view that "all men are created equal," a statement asserting belief in American democracy but whose wording conceivably excludes women from sharing in democratic rights.

extreme praise

prevents in advance

AMAURY DE RIENCOURT
"Women in Athens"

KEY CONCEPTS

A culture that practices **INFANTICIDE** controls its population by killing unwanted newborn infants at birth.

Freud theorized that humans, on both an individual level and a group level, may indulge in a **DEATH-WISH**, a desire for their own extinction.

● With the development of Greek culture came a steady regression* of woman's status; from Herodotus to Thucydides, she gradually faded into the home, and Plutarch takes pleasure in quoting Thucydides to the effect that "the name of a decent woman, like her person, should be shut up in the

loss

house." Greek literature was suddenly full of disparaging* remarks about woman and her innumerable faults — witness the writings of Hesiod, Lucian, Aristophanes, and Simonides of Amorgos. Her legal status deteriorated: inheritance through the mother disappeared; she could not make contracts or incur large debts or bring actions at law. Solon even went so far as to legislate that anything done under the influence of woman could not be legally binding. Furthermore, she did not even inherit her husband's property after his death. She retreated to a virtual purdah,* locked in her home and advised not to be seen near a window; she spent most of her life in the women's quarters and never appeared when male friends visited her husband.

discrediting

Hindu custom of keeping women in the house

Such downgrading at the height of Greek cultural achievements is striking, especially in Periclean Athens.* But Pericles himself approved; in his famous Funeral Speech, he summed up his views: "If I must also speak a word to those who are in widowhood on the powers and duties of women, I will cast all my advice in one brief sentence. Great will be your glory if you do not lower the nature which is within you — hers most of all whose praise or blame is least bruited* on the lips of men."

Golden Age of Athens

repeated

The strongly masculine character of Greek culture may in part account for this, but it is also weird reversal of the basic concepts of sexual creativity. In the old days men were suitably ignorant about their creative role in life. Athenian lore* claimed that before Cecrops, the legendary founder of Athens, "children did not know their own fathers." The discovery of their role as sexual inseminators gave them a new pride and stimulated the patriarchal revolution. Now the Greeks went a step further. They fancied that men alone were endowed with generative power, women being merely empty vessels or, at best, sort of incubators designed to carry their child and nurse it in life's early stages. Like the Persians' divine Ohrmazd, more than one Greek sighed and uttered the famous "If only we could have children without having recourse* to women!" This recurring theme of extreme misogynists* was echoed again, some two thousand years later, by Thomas Browne: "I could be content that we might procreate like trees, without conjunction, or that there were any way to perpetu-

folk tradition

assistance from women-haters

Statement & support

Statement & support and chronological

ate the World without this trivial and vulgar way of union."

Athenian women were hardly educated, in accord with Euripides' view that women were harmed by an overly developed intellect. In the sixth century B.C., women still contributed somewhat to Greek literature; by the fifth century B.C., they were culturally barren. Having turned their respectable women into bores, men then searched elsewhere for entertainment and inspiration — in the extraordinary development of homosexuality and in the company of the only free women in Athens, the hetairai,* the "companions," the most accomplished courtesans* of the times. Demosthenes summed up the Athenian view of woman's uses in the following statement: "We have courtesans for the sake of pleasure, concubines* for the daily health of our bodies, and wives to bear us lawful offspring and be the faithful guardians of our homes."

Cause & effect [handwritten margin note]

highly cultured females
"high-class" prostitutes kept by nobles

unmarried in-house female companions

The only attractive — and therefore influential — women were the hetairai, women of some social standing, endowed with a veneer* of culture, and capable of witty and learned conversation. They were denied civil rights but were entitled to the protection of their special goddess, Aphrodite Pandemos. Many of them left some mark on Greek history and literature — Aspasia, one of the precursors,* who seduced Pericles and opened a school of rhetoric and philosophy; the famous Clepsydra, who timed her lovers' visits with an hourglass; Thargelia, the great spy for the account of the Persians; Danae, who influenced Epicurus in his philosophic views; Archeanassa and Theoris, who amused respectively Plato and Sophocles; and countless others. Some whose plastic* beauty was breathtaking inspired artists and served as models — Phryne, who appeared stark naked at the Eleusinian festival and posed for Praxiteles' "Aphrodite"; and also Lais of Corinth, one of the great beauties of all time, whose eccentric adventures stunned her contemporaries. In fact, nothing symbolizes more aptly the Greek view of the female sex's social role and value as Praxiteles' two antipodal* statutes, "The Weeping Wife" and "The Laughing Hetairai."

Definition [handwritten margin note]

superficial appearance

those who come before

well-formed

directly opposing

Greek men held a contemptuous view of the opposite sex; even the best-endowed hetairai had a difficult time competing with their clients' male lovers. Even in Sparta, where women enjoyed more prestige and influence than in the rest of Greece, Alcman could pay no greater compliment to his women companions than to call them his "female boy-friends!" The poet-politician Critias stated that girls were charming only to the extent that they were slightly boyish — and vice versa. Homosexuality was both a cause and consequence of this steady downgrading of the female of the species; and rave against it as they might, the hetairai proved unable to curb it. At any rate, the Greek example makes it plain that the prevalence of male homosexuality in any given society is tightly linked with increasing misogyny and the social repression of woman; a kind of horror feminae* pervades the social atmosphere, springing from the fact that the typical feminine attributes — maternal procreativity and sexual-libidinal* endowments — are no longer appreciated. Havelock Ellis quite rightly pointed out the close connection between **infanticide** (birth control) and homosexuality, a connection that is stamped by an incipient* **death-wish** on the part of any society where they prevail. When the point is reached that woman is rejected, even as a sex object, this society is, psychologically, committing suicide — as the Greek example made plain a few generations after Pericles.

fear of woman

pertaining to pleasure

just starting

If we dig further, it becomes clear that one main reason for this degradation of the female sex is that, whereas we put the emphasis of love on its object and think of it in terms of the worthiness of the object, the ancient Greeks put it on the urge itself, honoring the feeling even if it happened to focus on an unworthy recipient. This made it easier for the Greeks to restrict their eroticism* largely to homosexual relations. Its prevalence was such that it became part of public education in Sparta and Crete; it became the essential element in Greek military formations where pairs of lovers and male beloved ones formed the basic tactical unit, fighting side by side — the Sacred Band at Thebes, presumed to be the finest fighting force in the Hellenic world, was made up entirely of homosexuals.

sexual feeling

Most Greeks had only pity for those few men who could fall in love with women with the same passion as with members of their own sex. Even the famous

[margin annotations: Cause & effect / Cause & effect / Statement & support]

Platonic love is, in fact, sublimated love of an exclusively homosexual nature. In the Symposium, Pausanias states:

> There are two goddesses of love, and therefore, also two forms of Eros. The Eros of the earthly Aphrodite is earthly, universal, common and casual. And everything common worships her. Both sexes, man and woman, had part in the creation and birth of the earthly Aphrodite. The higher love comes from the heavenly Aphrodite and she is the creation of man. Therefore all youths and men who are seized with this love strive after their own sex, full of longing for the manly; they love the stronger nature and the higher mind.

Such an outlook was devastating to feminine status, dignity, and influence.

The following essay has a strong thesis backed up by detailed historical evidence; its paragraphs, therefore, are mainly statement and support, or narrative, the retelling of events. Read the essay and paraphrase the author's thesis.

Robespierre's bloody career illustrates how one can be devoted to a seemingly admirable ideal while debasing its very premises. As a leader of the French Revolution, Robespierre ostensibly* fought for "liberty, fraternity, and   supposedly *equality" (the Revolution's motto). But he used tactics of oppression, violence, and terror. His "Reign of Terror," which may seem like a deviation from revolutionary ideals, finds parallels in the bloodletting of the Russian Revolution, the purges of China's Cultural Revolution, Idi Amin's rule in the newly independent Uganda, and other collisions of political ideals and atrocities.*

ALBERT PARRY
"Robespierre's Bloody Virtue"

KEY CONCEPTS
The next-to-last reading in this chapter explains the theory of **TERRORISM**; see page 374.

TYRANNICAL laws are those that oppress a people and are imposed without their consent.

As a negative term, **SOPHIST** means one who uses empty rhetoric and false reasoning.

The opening article in this chapter defines **INALIENABLE RIGHTS**; see page 305.

DISCIPLES OF ROUSSEAU are believers in the natural goodness, or

INBORN SINLESSNESS, of man. Rousseau was an eighteenth-century French writer and philosopher; his *Social Contract* treats the theory of representative democracy.

One common meaning of the word **IDEALIST** is someone who is unrealistically optimistic. The term is loosely related here to the philosophical notion of idealism; see Chapter 1, page 33.

What is happening now is related to what has happened in the past. And because **terrorism** so threatens our lives today, it is important for us to know its history and tradition.

Historically, terrorism's main stages have taken place in Western Europe and Russia; then, North America, and latterly, Asia and Latin America, followed by Africa.

First, this was the phenomenon chosen by Karl Marx, Friedrich Engels, and Vladimir Lenin as the subject of their intense study and the foremost model for their own preachments and activities. Since, overwhelmingly, Marx, Engels, and Lenin are the prime sources of inspiration for modern terrorists throughout the world, it is through them that these terrorists owe their beginnings to Maximilien Robespierre and his Reign of Terror.

Second, this Great Terror of 1793–94 was the first in history to attempt the elevation of primitive passion into a high-flown political philosophy, and to create an organization that tried to systematize murder and other lawlessness into a set of rules.

Of course, political slayers had, for thousands of years, tried to manipulate people through violence and fear. But Robespierre's reign was the first terror organized nationwide by revolutionaries actually seizing power and becoming a punitive* government proclaiming murder as the law of the land. The very terms "terror," "terrorism," and "terrorists," used in their modern sense in so many languages, have come to us mainly from Robespierre's Reign of Terror — one more confirmation that today's exercises of terror trace their lineage* to Robespierre. [*punishing*] [*ancestry*]

The French Revolution came with its guillotine* — history's first campaign of political terror to be legislated by a people's duly elected representatives into a state-authorized system. And so, though terror had been used by individuals and groups before Robespierre's rule, his Reign of Terror systematized violence, hallowed* it by the state's prestige, and created an intense fear in a way and on a scale heretofore unknown, a way that gave rise to the concept of modern terrorism. [*a device used for beheading*] [*made holy*]

As for the theory of terror, it was Danton who, among the first, formulated its purpose: terror was a most desirable, most urgent weapon to defend the young Republic against its foes, both foreign and domestic. To an extent he was echoed by Lazare Carnot, the revolutionist who had been trained as a military engineer, and who from 1792 on was to go into

SOURCE: *Terrorism: From Robespierre to Arafat* by Albert Parry. Copyright © 1976 by Vanguard Press. Reprinted by permission of the publisher.

history as the organizer of the new revolutionary armies of France and the architect of her eventual military victories over the Austrians and other foreign enemies. Carnot proclaimed that the Great Terror was the explanation of these triumphs. In truth, however, the principal successes of the French armies came before, not during, the Terror's sharpest crests. The Great Terror did not inspirit* the citizen-soldiers; it frightened not the invaders, but the French themselves.

give courage to

Danton, in his speech at the chaotic session of the Convention of August 12, 1793, urged, as one of the measures of stepping up the Terror, the arrest — as hostages — of all "suspects" in Paris and the provinces. In the Convention's session of September 5 commemorating the first anniversary of the Massacres, it was decided to expand the Revolutionary Tribunal and to form a special army of 6,000 infantrymen and 1,200 cannoneers to carry terror throughout the nation.

In addition, Danton proposed revolutionizing all worthy men, particularly in Paris, by providing every worker with a rifle. Revolutionaries everywhere were to have arbitrary* power to detain, judge, and execute any and all "suspects."

according to individual judgment

Bertrand Barere, an ardent Jacobin,* summarized: "Let us make terror the order of the day!" Terror was not to be an exception to the new life — it was to be its ambiance* and prime rule. People would have to accept it for their own welfare. Another Jacobin summarized: "Since neither our virtue nor our moderation nor our philosophic ideas have been of use to us, let us be brigands* for the good of the people." This was the phraseology* that would live for generations, and with such pithy* excuses generations of men would be made to suffer and die. Those excuses would reappear in the slogans of Lenin and Trotsky, of Hitler and Mussolini, of Mao Tse-tung and Ho Chi Minh, of Castro and Guevara, of DeFreeze and Arafat.

radical revolutionary

surrounding atmosphere

bandits
slogan / clear and direct

Thus, in France in 1793–94, terror was justified not alone as a means of the survival of the French people threatened by its enemies, but also as a path to the people's welfare and virtue. In November 1793, Jean Nicolas Billaud-Varenne, the secretary of the Jacobin club, elucidated the principles of a complete revolutionary centralization of state power to be based on the smiting* ax, so that the French government could be "purified" instead of remaining "a volcano of villainy." On December 4 these postulates were formally incorporated into a law of terror.

striking

Finally and authoritatively, Robespierre himself invoked the good of the people as the paramount reason for terror. In his speech of December 25, 1793, on "the Principles of the Revolutionary Government," the advocate from Arras intoned that the theory of this government was as new as the very revolution that gave it birth — it could be found in no books but only in the life and strife of that specific era. Robespierre explained the difference between two regimes as he saw them — the revolutionary and the constitutional. The former regime had as its task the creation of a republic; the latter, the safeguard of that republic. Robespierre viewed the world of politics quite narrowly: to him there were only two positive kinds of governments. He elucidated these two regimes: A revolution meant war by the legions of freedom against their adversaries. A constitution came after the triumph of the revolution — it was the regime of a victorious and peaceful freedom. This specific time in France was one of war. Therefore the nation's revolutionary government must defend good citizens with all possible force, implacably* dealing out death to the enemies of the people.

mercilessly

These concepts were enough, Robespierre declaimed, to make clear the origin and nature of revolutionary laws. But the opponents of these concepts and these laws, the captious* persons who called these laws **tyrannical**, were either stupid individuals or vice-ridden **sophists**. Robespierre asked: "If the revolutionary government must be more energetic in its actions and freer in its steps, does this mean that it is less just and less lawful?" He answered, "No! For it bases itself on the holiest of all laws — the good of the people; and on the most **inalienable of all rights** — necessity."

always finding petty faults

This argument served as an all-important part of almost every public statement by Robespierre, always ending in his call to improve yet further the work of the Revolutionary Tribunal and to bring to the guillotine blade yet another rollcall of persons, yet more categories of men and women.

Through all this, Robespierre claimed to be the truest of all the **disciples of Rousseau**. He reminded his listeners that Rousseau had described man as good by nature but corrupted by civilization. This idea was twisted by Robespierre into his burning conviction that man could be saved from himself, from his meanness and criminality, by the guillotine. Robespierre would help man get rid of the evil not recognized by man himself; he would restore man's pristine purity by the death penalty. By executing them en masse,* this provincial lawyer would be doing his victims the valiant favor of restoring virtue to them and to society. Their execution would be less of a punishment, more of a gift — the gift of the original, **inborn sinlessness** returned to them as their heads rolled off the bloody block. This Republic of Virtue via Blood, ushered in by Robespierre, would surely be blessed by the Supreme Being, by Robespierre's own version of the Supreme Being, the new revolutionary deity whose worship Robespierre decreed as a new state religion, in whose honor he arranged his peculiar pageants of worship.

together; in great numbers

Because of this singular fanaticism, he has been called by some a mistaken **idealist**. In sober reality he was mistaken, but he was not an idealist. To apply this noun to him is an insult to idealism. Robespierre was a sick, demented man who caused wholesale deaths while emitting high-sounding but vapid phrases. His was not an ideology; it was a phraseology.

And yet, at first, many Frenchmen and Frenchwomen took his oratory for an ideology as well as for a viable revolutionary religion. Many willingly, even enthusiastically, followed him. As an illness often overcomes an individual by degrees, so the Grand Terror, charged up and maintained by this extraordinary zealot,* grew in phases so insidious* that even de-

fanatic / treacherous

cent persons sometimes failed to notice they were being drawn in as his followers; too late did these followers realize that soon they were to join his victims on the tragic scaffold.* Their hysterical applause for the tyrant was replaced by sheer fright when, alas, nothing was left for them to do but mount the steps and submit to the blade.

platform for executing
people

First tried out in 1792, the guillotine was to gain worldwide fame as the most chilling memory of the French Revolution. For generations to come it would be a dreaded symbol. But in our own 1970s a weird North American counterculture entertainer, Vincent Damon Furnier, better known as "Alice Cooper," drew a mindless laugh out of his audiences by including a guillotine in his stage show: he would stick his repugnantly untidy head into Dr. Guillotin's machine, the stage crew substituting a fake head before the blade would fall. Thus old terror thrilled the mob of our violence-filled times. Fun, not fright, was the new response.

The following essay is an argument, and its paragraphs consist of statement and support in each case. We've underlined each statement. Examine and evaluate the support offered for each, marking any logical fallacy or false analogy. Your reading strategy should draw on your skill in recognizing bias and assumption, introduced in Chapter 2, page 94.

The Ku Klux Klan (KKK) was originally formed as a protective order to prevent Northern carpetbaggers* from exploiting the post-Civil War Southerners. Although it had benevolent intentions at its start, the KKK soon became synonymous with racism and segregation. Its members perpetrated violent acts on blacks, Jews, and other minorities. The white sheet and burning cross symbolize their policies of white supremacy through terrorist tactics. Again, as with Robespierre, a terrible irony appears in the clash of the group's asserted goal — defense of American democracy — with their actual beliefs and tactics that subvert the democratic system. The following essay, written by a KKK member, uses the language of justice and patriotism to disguise its radical WASP (White Anglo Saxon Protestant) bias.

travelling merchants

HIRAM WESLEY EVANS
"The Klan's Fight for Americanism"

KEY CONCEPTS

IMPERIALISM is defined in a later essay in this chapter; see page 364.

AUTOCRACY means absolute rule by a single person without the people's necessary consent.

In an **ARISTOCRACY**, the nobility, or titled class, holds political, economic, and social power.

SOURCE: "The Klan's Fight for Americanism" by Hiram Wesley Evans. Copyright © 1926 by The North American Review. Reprinted with permission of the University of Northern Iowa.

● First in the Klansman's mind is patriotism — America for Americans. He believes religiously that a betrayal of Americanism or the American race is treason to the most sacred of trusts, a trust from his fathers and a trust from God. He believes, too, that Americanism can only be achieved if the pioneer stock* is kept pure. There is more than race pride in this. Mongrelization* has been proven bad. It is only between closely related stocks of the same race that interbreeding has improved men; the kind of interbreeding that went on in the early days of America between English, Dutch, German, Huguenot, Irish and Scotch.

    Racial integrity* is a very definite thing to the Klansman. It means even more than good citizenship, for a man may be in all ways a good citizen and yet a poor American, unless he has racial understanding of Americanism, and instinctive loyalty to it. It is in no way a reflection on any man to say that he is un-American; it is merely a statement that he is not one of us. It is often not even wise to try to make an American of the best of aliens. What he is may be spoiled without his becoming American. The races and stocks of men are as distinct as breeds of animals, and every boy knows that if one tries to train a bulldog to herd sheep, he has in the end neither a good bulldog nor a good collie.

    Americanism, to the Klansman, is a thing of the spirit, a purpose and a point of view, that can only come through instinctive racial understanding. It has, to be sure, certain defined principles, but he does not believe that many aliens understand those principles, even when they use our words in talking about them. Democracy is one, fairdealing, impartial justice, equal opportunity, religious liberty, independence, self-reliance, courage, endurance, acceptance of individual responsibility as well as individual rewards for effort, willingness to sacrifice for the good of his family, his nation and his race before anything else but God, dependence on enlightened conscience for guidance, the right to unhampered* development — these are fundamental. But within the bounds they fix there must be the utmost freedom, tolerance, liberalism. In short, the Klansman believes in the greatest possible diversity and individualism within the limits of the American spirit. But he believes also that few aliens can understand that spirit, that fewer try to, and that there must be resistance, intolerance even, toward anything that threatens it, or the fundamental national unity based upon it.

    The second word in the Klansman's trilogy is "white." The white race must be supreme, not only in America but in the world. This is equally undebatable, except on the ground that the races might live together, each with full regard for the rights and interests of others, and that those rights and interests would never conflict. Such an idea, of course, is absurd; the colored races today, such as Japan, are clamoring not for equality but for their supremacy. The whole history of the world, on its broader lines, has been one of race conflicts, wars, subjugation or extinction. This is not pretty, and certainly disagrees with the maudlin* theories of cosmopolitanism,* but it is truth. The world has been so made that each race must fight for its life, must conquer, accept slavery or die. The Klansman believes

Margin glosses:

ancestry, lineage

mixture of races

wholeness

without interference

sentimental

representative of all the world

that the whites will not become slaves, and he does not intend to die before his time.

Moreover, the future of progress and civilization depends on the continued supremacy of the white race. The forward movement of the world for centuries has come entirely from it. Other races each had its chance and either failed or stuck fast, while white civilization shows no sign of having reached its limit. Until the whites falter, or some colored civilization has a miracle of awakening, there is not a single colored stock that can claim even equality with the white, much less supremacy.

The third of the Klan principles is that Protestantism must be supreme; that Rome shall not rule America. The Klansman believes this not merely because he is a Protestant, nor even because the Colonies that are now our nation were settled for the purpose of wresting* America from the control of Rome and establishing a land of free conscience. He believes it also because Protestantism is an essential part of Americanism; without it America could never have been created and without it she cannot go forward. Roman rule would kill it.

taking away

Protestantism contains more than religion. It is the expression in religion of the same spirit of independence, self-reliance and freedom which are the highest achievements of the Nordic* race. It sprang into being automatically at the time of the great "upsurgence" of strength in the Nordic peoples that opened the spurt of civilization in the fifteenth century. It has been a distinctly Nordic religion, and it has been through this religion that the Nordics have found strength to take leadership of all whites and the supremacy of the earth. Its destruction is the deepest purpose of all other peoples, as that would mean the end of Nordic rule.

Northern European Caucasian

It is the only religion that permits the unhampered individual development and the unhampered conscience and action which were necessary in the settling of America. Our pioneers were all Protestants, except for an occasional Irishman — Protestants by nature if not by religion — for though French and Spanish dared and explored and showed great heroism, they made little of the land their own. America was Protestant from birth.

She must remain Protestant, if the Nordic stock is to finish its destiny. We of the old stock Americans could not work — and the work is mostly ours to do, if the record of the past proves anything — if we became priestridden, if we had to submit our consciences and limit our activities and suppress our thoughts at the command of any man, much less of a man sitting upon Seven Hills* thousands of miles away. This we will not permit. Rome shall not rule us. Protestantism must be supreme.

the Seven Hills of Rome (the Pope)

Let it be clear what is meant by "supremacy." It is nothing more than power of control, under just laws. It is not **imperialism**, far less is it **autocracy** or even **aristocracy** of a race or stock of men. What it does mean is that we insist on our inherited right to insure our own safety, individually and as a race, to secure the future of our children, to maintain and develop our racial heritage in our own, white, Protestant, American way, without

interference. . . . We are accused of injecting old prejudices, hatred, race
and religion into politics, of creating an un-American class division, of
trying to profit by race and religious enmities,* of violating the principle   hostility
of equality, and of ruining the Democratic party.

Most of these charges are not worth answering. So long as politicians
cater to alien racial and religious groups, it is the merest self-defense to
have also a Protestant and an American "vote" and to make it respected.
The hatred and prejudice are, as has been evident to every candid person,
displayed by our enemies and not by us. As to the charge that the Klan
brought race and religion into politics, that simply is not true. That was
done by the very people who are now accusing us, because we are cutting
into the profits they had been making in politics out of their races and their
religions. Race and religion have for years been used by the aliens as
political platforms. The Klan is in no way responsible for this condition.
We merely recognized it when others dared not, and we fight it in the
open. Our belief is that any man who runs for office or asks political favors,
or advocates policies or carries on any other political activity, either as a
member of any racial or religious group, or in the interests of or under
orders from such a group or of any non-American interest whatever,
should be opposed for that very reason. The Klan's ambition is to get race
and religion out of politics, and that cannot be done so long as there is any
profit in exploiting them. It therefore fights every attempt to use them.

One of the Klan's chief interests is in education. We believe that it is
the duty of government to insure to every child opportunity to develop
its natural abilities to their utmost. We wish to go to the very limit in the
improvement of the public schools; so far that there will be no excuse
except snobbery for the private schools.

Further, the Klan wishes to restore the Bible to the school, not only
because it is part of the world's great heritage in literature and philosophy
and has profoundly influenced all white civilization, but because it is the
basis on which all Christian religions are built, and to which they must look
for their authority. . . . Jews or Catholics are lavish with their caustic*   sarcastic, biting
criticism of anything American. Nothing is immune; our great men, our
historic struggles and sacrifices, our customs and personal traits, our "Puri-
tan consciences" — all have been scarified* without mercy . . . we of the   inflicted with small cuts
Klan admit that we are intolerant and narrow in a certain sense. . . . We
are intolerant of everything that strikes at the foundations of our race, our
country or our freedom of worship. We are narrowly opposed to the use
of anything alien — race, loyalty to any foreign power or to any religion
whatever — as a means to win political power. We are prejudiced against
any attempt to use the privileges and opportunities which aliens hold only
through our generosity as levers to force us to change our civilization, to
wrest from us control of our own country, to exploit us for the benefit of
any foreign power — religious or secular — and especially to use America
as a tool of for the advantage of any side in the hatreds and quarrels of the
Old World. This is our intolerance; based on the sound instincts which

have saved us many times from the follies of the intellectuals. We admit it. More and worse, we are proud of it.

. . . The Negro, the Klan considers a special duty and problem of the white American. He is among us through no wish of his; <u>we owe it to him and to ourselves to give him full protection and opportunity</u>. But his limitations are evident; we will not permit him to gain sufficient power to control our civilization. Neither will we delude him with promises of social equality which we know can never be realized. The Klan looks forward to the day when the Negro problem will have been solved on some much saner basis than miscegenation,* and when every State will enforce laws making any sex relations between a white and a colored person a crime.

<u>For the alien in general we have sympathy, opportunity, justice,</u> but no permanent welcome unless he becomes truly American. It is our duty to see that he has every chance for this, and we shall be glad to accept him if he does. We hold no rancor* against him; his race, instincts, training, mentality and whole outlook of life are usually widely different from ours. We cannot blame him if he adheres to them and attempts to convert us to them, even by force. But we must see that he can never succeed.

The Jew is a more complex problem. His abilities are great; he contributes much to any country where he lives. This is particularly true of the Western Jew, those of the stocks we have known so long. Their separation from us is more religious than racial. When freed from persecution these Jews have shown a tendency to disintegrate and amalgamate.* We may hope that shortly, in the free atmosphere of America, Jews of this class will cease to be a problem. Quite different are the Eastern Jews of recent immigration, the Jews known as the Askhenasim. It is interesting to note that anthropologists now tell us that these are not true Jews, but only Judaized Mongols — Chazars. These, unlike the true Hebrew, show a divergence from the American type so great that there seems little hope of their assimilation.*

<u>The most menacing and most difficult problem facing America today is this of the permanently unassimilable alien.</u> The only solution so far offered is that of Dr. Eliot, president emeritus of Harvard. After admitting that the melting pot has failed — thus supporting the primary position of the Klan! — he adds that there is no hope of creating here a single, homogeneous* race-stock of the kind necessary for national unity. He then suggests that instead, there shall be a congeries* of diverse peoples, living together in sweet harmony, and all working for the good of all and of the nation! This solution is on a par with the optimism which foisted the melting pot on us. Diverse races never have lived together in such harmony; race antipathies* are too deep and strong. If such a state were possible, the nation would be too disunited for the progress. One race always ruled, one always must, and there will be struggle and reprisals* till the mastery is established — and bitterness afterwards. And, speaking for us Americans, we have come to realize that if all this could possibly be done, still within a few years we should be supplanted* by the "mere force

mixing of races

hatred

join into a whole

absorption into the dominant culture

of the same composition group

dislikes

revenge

removed and replaced

of breeding" of the low standard peoples. We intend to see that the American stock remains supreme.

What is Malcolm X's purpose (the thesis) in making this speech? What is the rhetorical mode? Read for a sense of how purpose and organization are logically connected.

_____

Malcolm X was a militant black nationalist during the early 1960s, the era of the civil rights movement. Malcolm's father was murdered by the Ku Klux Klan in Michigan when Malcolm was a child. At the height of his influence as a black leader, Malcolm was himself murdered by followers of his former associate, the black Muslim leader, Elijah Muhammad. Unlike Martin Luther King, Jr., who advocated nonviolent protest, Malcolm X preached militant, that is, radical black activism, as reflected in the rhetoric of the speech below. His formulation of "the ballot or the bullet" shows the ultimatum with which Malcolm X challenged the democratic system.

MALCOLM X
"The Ballot or the Bullet"

● The question tonight, as I understand it, is "The Negro Revolt, and Where Do We Go From Here?" or "What Next?" In my little humble way of understanding it, it points toward either the ballot or the bullet.

Before we try and explain what is meant by the ballot or the bullet, I would like to clarify something concerning myself. I'm still a Muslim, my religion is still Islam. That's my personal belief. Just as Adam Clayton Powell is a Christian minister who heads the Abyssinian Baptist Church in New York, but at the same time takes part in the political struggles to try and bring about rights to the black people in this country; and Dr. Martin Luther King is a Christian minister down in Atlanta, Georgia, who heads another organization fighting for the civil rights of black people in this country; and Rev. Galamison, I guess you've heard of him, is another Christian minister in New York who has been deeply involved in the school boycotts to eliminate segregated education; well, I myself am a minister, not a Christian minister, but a Muslim minister; and I believe in action on all fronts by whatever means necessary.

Although I'm still a Muslim, I'm not here tonight to discuss my religion. I'm not here to try and change your religion. I'm not here to argue or discuss anything that we differ about, because it's time for us to submerge our differences and realize that it is best for us to first see that we have the same problem, a common problem — a problem that will make you catch hell whether you're a Baptist, or a Methodist, or a Muslim, or a

SOURCE: From *Malcolm X Speaks: Selected Speeches and Statements,* Merit Publishers, 1965.

nationalist. Whether you're educated or illiterate, whether you live on the boulevard or in the alley, you're going to catch hell just like I am. We're all in the same boat and we all are going to catch the same hell from the same man. He just happens to be a white man. All of us have suffered here, in this country, political oppression at the hands of the white man, economic exploitation at the hands of the white man, and social degradation at the hands of the white man.

Now in speaking like this, it doesn't mean that we're anti-white, but it does mean we're anti-exploitation, we're anti-degradation, we're anti-oppression. And if the white man doesn't want us to be anti-him, let him stop oppressing and exploiting and degrading us. Whether we are Christians or Muslims or nationalists or agnostics* or atheists, we must first learn to forget our differences. If we have differences, let us differ in the closet; when we come out in front, let us not have anything to argue about until we get finished arguing with the man. If the late President Kennedy could get together with Khrushchev and exchange some wheat, we certainly have more in common with each other than Kennedy and Khrushchev had with each other.

religious doubters

If we don't do something real soon, I think you'll have to agree that we're going to be forced either to use the ballot or the bullet. It's one or the other in 1964. It isn't that time is running out — time has run out! 1964 threatens to be the most explosive year America has ever witnessed. The most explosive year. Why? It's also a political year. It's the year when all of the white politicians will be back in the so-called Negro community jiving* you and me for some votes. The year when all of the white political crooks will be right back in your and my community with their false promises, building up our hopes for a letdown, with their trickery and their treachery, with their false promises which they don't intend to keep. As they nourish these dissatisfactions, it can only lead to one thing, an explosion; and now we have the type of black man on the scene in America today — I'm sorry, Brother Lomax — who just doesn't intend to turn the other cheek any longer.

deceiving, talking nonsense

Don't let anybody tell you anything about the odds are against you. If they draft you, they send you to Korea and make you face 800 million Chinese. If you can be brave over there, you can be brave right here. These odds aren't as great as those odds. And if you fight here, you will at least know what you're fighting for.

I'm not a politician, not even a student of politics; in fact, I'm not a student of much of anything. I'm not a Democrat, I'm not a Republican, and I don't even consider myself an American. If you and I were Americans, there'd be no problem. Those Hunkies* that just got off the boat, they're already Americans; Polacks* are already Americans; the Italian refugees are already Americans. Everything that came out of Europe, every blue-eyed thing, is already an American. And as long as you and I have been over here, we aren't Americans yet.

derogatory term for Hungarians
derogatory term for Polish people

Well, I am one who doesn't believe in deluding myself. I'm not going to sit at your table and watch you eat, with nothing on my plate, and call

myself a diner. Sitting at the table doesn't make you a diner, unless you
eat some of what's on that plate. Being here in America doesn't make you
an American. Being born here in America doesn't make you an American.
Why, if birth made you American, you wouldn't need any legislation, you
wouldn't need any amendments to the Constitution, you wouldn't be
faced with civil-rights filibustering* in Washington, D.C., right now. They   blocking legislation by
don't have to pass civil-rights legislation to make a Polack an American.   making a very long speech

No, I'm not an American. I'm one of the 22 million black people who
are the victims of Americanism. One of the 22 million black people who
are the victims of democracy, nothing but disguised hypocrisy. So, I'm not
standing here speaking to you as an American, or a patriot, or a flag-
saluter, or a flag-waver — no, not I. I'm speaking as a victim of this American system. And I see America through the eyes of the victim. I don't see
any American dream; I see an American nightmare.

So it's time in 1964 to wake up. And when you see them coming up with
that kind of conspiracy, let them know your eyes are open. And let them
know you got something else that's wide open too. It's got to be the ballot
or the bullet. The ballot or the bullet. If you're afraid to use an expression
like that, you should get on out of the country, you should get back in the
cotton patch, you should get back in the alley. They get all the Negro vote,
and after they get it, the Negro gets nothing in return. All they did when
they got to Washington was give a few big Negroes big jobs. Those big
Negroes didn't need big jobs, they already had jobs. That's camouflage,
that's trickery, that's treachery, window-dressing. I'm not trying to knock
out the Democrats for the Republicans, we'll get to them in a minute. But
it is true — you put the Democrats first and the Democrats put you last.

I say again, I'm not anti-Democrat, I'm not anti-Republican, I'm not
anti-anything. I'm just questioning their sincerity, and some of the strategy
that they've been using on our people by promising them promises that
they don't intend to keep. When you keep the Democrats in power, you're
keeping the Dixiecrats* in power. I doubt that my good Brother Lomax   white Southern Democrats
will deny that. A vote for a Democrat is a vote for a Dixiecrat. That's why,
in 1964, it's time now for you and me to become more politically mature
and realize what the ballot is for; what we're supposed to get when we cast
a ballot; and that if we don't cast a ballot, it's going to end up in a situation
where we're going to have to cast a bullet. It's either a ballot or a bullet.

Malcolm X had a strong and direct thesis in his speech; James Farmer also
has a strong thesis, but it is implied. What is the rhetorical mode of the piece,
and how does it reflect Farmer's purpose?

---

*James Farmer was another civil rights activist in the 1960s who went on
to become the national leader of CORE (the Congress of Racial Equality). This
group, along with Martin Luther King's Southern Christian Leadership Confer-*

ence, the NAACP, and the Student Non-violent Coordinating Committee, led the nonviolent struggle for equality. This passage illustrates how blacks suffered under segregation and in many cases were denied even the right to vote. The civil rights workers used boycotts, sit-ins, and protest marches in their fight for justice. Farmer recounts one instance of the often violent treatment which civil rights workers faced.

JAMES FARMER
"A Night of Terror in Plaquemine, Louisiana, 1963"

● I went down to Plaquemine toward the end of August 1963 on the first day of what I innocently assumed would be a routine three-day trip. We staged a protest march into town after my speech. When the march was over, all the leaders, myself included, were arrested and taken off to jail in nearby Donaldsonville (which hospitably offered us its facilities in lieu*   in place of of the already overcrowded Plaquemine jail).

We stayed in jail for a week and a half. When we came out, the spirit of militancy was spreading in Plaquemine, and two days later a group of young people organized another demonstration, protesting segregation in public places as well as exclusion from the city. This time, however, the marchers did not even get into town. The chief of police stopped them halfway, arrested the leaders, and held the rest of the marchers where they were until state troopers arrived. The troopers came on horseback, riding like cowboys, and they charged into the crowd of boys and girls as if they were rounding up a herd of stampeding cattle. They were armed with billy clubs and cattle prods, which they used mercilessly. Many of the youngsters who fell under the blows were trampled by the horses. (The children of Selma, whose suffering at the hands of police appalled the nation two years later, were but a part of a spiritual community of brave Southern youngsters like these who for years have been deprived of national attention by inadequate press coverage.)

This gratuitous* savagery inflicted upon their children immediately   unnecessary aroused the adults to a pitch of militancy much more intense than anything the organizational effort had been able to achieve. The ministers, who had previously hung back, united for the first time. (Only one minister, the Rev. Jetson Davis, had been active in the movement. It was his Plymouth Rock Baptist Church to which the injured boys and girls had fled for comfort and medical assistance.) Apathy or fear or whatever had caused their reluctance dissolved in outrage. The next morning, Sunday, every minister in the Negro quarter preached a sermon extolling freedom and condemning police brutality. After church, according to agreement, they led their congregations to Reverend Davis' church and organized a massive march in protest against the rout of the previous day. As the time

SOURCE: From *Freedom — When?* by James Farmer. Copyright © 1965 by the Congress of Racial Equality, Inc. Reprinted by permission of Random House.

approached for the march to begin, some of the ministers began to waver. One of them hesitated on his way to the front of the line. "Where's my wife?" he said, looking around fearfully. "I don't see my wife. I think I'd better just go on home." His wife was standing right behind him. "Man," she said, "if you don't get up there in the front of that line, you ain't got no wife."

He marched, all right, but his presence could not alter the course of events. This time when the troopers intercepted the marchers there was nothing impromptu* about the confrontation. They did not even come on horseback; they came in patrol cars and the horses arrived in vans. The troopers mounted their horses and assembled their weapons as if the crowd of unarmed men and women before them were an opposing army; they charged into the mass as they had done the day before, flailing with billy clubs and stabbing with cattle prods. "Get up, nigger!" one would shout, poking a man with an electric prod and beating him to the ground with a club. "Run, nigger, run!"

unplanned, spontaneous

I was waiting at the Plymouth Rock Church. I watched the Negroes come running back, those who could run, bleeding, hysterical, faint, some of the stronger ones carrying the injured. The nurse started to bandage the wounds and the rest of us began to sing "We Shall Overcome," but the troopers rode roaring through the streets right up to the door of the church. The Freedom Rock Church, we call it now. They dismounted and broke into the church, yelling and hurling tear gas bombs in front of them — bomb after bomb, poisoning the air. The gas masks protecting the troopers' faces transformed them into monsters as they stood and watched our people growing more and more frantic, screaming with pain and teror, trampling on one another in their frenzied efforts to escape through the back door to the parsonage* behind the church. When the people had finally escaped, the troopers set about destroying the empty church. They knocked out the windows, overturned the benches, laid waste everything they could reach, and flooded the gutted building with high-pressure hoses until Bibles and hymnals floated in the aisles.

minister's house

Then they attacked the parsonage to which we had fled. They sent tear gas bombs smashing through the windows, until all the windows were shattered and almost everyone inside was blinded and choking. The screaming was unbearable, I caught sight of Ronnie Moore administering mouth-to-mouth resuscitation to a young woman. People writhed on the floor, seeking oxygen. A few managed to push through the rear door into the parsonage yard, but the troopers, anticipating them, had ridden around to the back with more bombs to force them in again. And then bombs thrown into the parsonage forced them back out into the yard. All these men and women, who just that morning had resolutely banded together to reach out for freedom and dignity, were reduced now to running from torment, helpless victims of a bitter game.

We tried to telephone for help, but the operators were not putting through any outgoing calls from the Negro section. Within the community, though, there was telephone service, and several calls got through to us at the parsonage. What had appeared to be random and mindless brutality proved to have had a mad purpose after all. It was a manhunt. Troopers were in the streets, kicking open doors, searching every house in the Negro community, overturning chairs and tables, looking under beds and in closets, yelling, "Come on out, Farmer, we know you're in there. Come on out, Farmer! We're going to get you." We could hear the screaming in the streets as the troopers on horseback resumed their sport with the cattle prods and billy clubs: "Get up, nigger! Run, nigger, run!" Holding their victims down with the cattle prod, they were saying, "We'll let you up nigger, if you tell us where Farmer is." Two of our girls, hiding beneath the church, overheard one trooper saying to another, "When we catch that goddam nigger Farmer, we're gonna kill him."

Spiver Gordon, CORE field secretary in Plaquemine, who, people say, looks like me, told me later that he wandered out of the church into the street at this time. Sighting him, state troopers ran up shouting, "Here he is boys. We got Farmer. We got their m — — — f — — — Jesus." A trooper beckoned to a crowd of hoodlums who were watching nearby, many holding chains, ropes, clubs. "What post we gonna hang him from?" said one. After Spiver convinced them he wasn't me, he took a good lacing*   beating for looking like me. An officer said, "He ain't Farmer. You've beat him enough. Put him in the car and arrest him."

There seemed no prospect of aid from any quarter.* We were all   side or person suffering intensely from the tear gas, and the troopers kept us running with the bombs. In desperation I sent two people creeping through the grass from the parsonage to a funeral hall half a block away to ask for refuge.* The owners of the hall agreed to shelter us (although I doubt that   shelter they knew what they were taking on). So we crawled on our bellies through the grass, in twos, threes, fours, making use of guerrilla* tactics   irregular, behind the lines that some remembered from the war but none of us had ever learned as   soldier a technique of non-violent demonstration, until we reached our new sanctuary.* Night had fallen by the time all three hundred of us were safely   shelter inside, jammed together like straws in a broom into two rooms and a hallway. The sound of screaming still echoed in the streets as the troopers beat down another Negro ("Run, nigger, run!") or invaded another house. The telephones were still useless.

Very shortly the troopers figured out where we were. One of them — a huge, raging, red-faced man — kicked open the back door of the funeral home and screamed, "Come on out, Farmer. We know you're in there. We're gonna get you." I was in the front room. I could look down the hallway, over all the heads, right into his face: it was flushed and dripping with sweat; his hair hung over his eyes, his mouth was twisted. Another trooper burst through the door to stand beside him. "Farmer! Come out!"

I had to give myself up. I felt like a modern Oedipus who, unaware, brought down a plague upon the city. In this hall, their lives endangered by my presence, were three hundred people, many of whom had never even seen me before that day. I began to make my way into the hall, thinking that I would ask to see the warrant for my arrest and demand to know the charges against me. But before I could take three steps the men around me grabbed me silently and pulled me back into the front room, whispering fiercely, "We're not going to let you go out there tonight. That's a lynch mob. You go out there tonight, you won't be alive tomorrow morning."

The trooper, meanwhile, had discovered a large Negro in the back room. He shouted triumphantly: "Here he is, we got that nigger Farmer! Come on in, boys. We got him here."

"I'm not Farmer," the man said. A third trooper came in.

"That ain't Farmer," he said. "I know that nigger." They went through his identification papers. He wasn't Farmer.

Suddenly, to everyone's astonishment, a woman pushed her way through the crowd to the back room and confronted the troopers. It was the owner of the funeral home, a "Nervous Nellie," as they say, who had previously held herself apart from the movement. I can never know — she herself probably does not know — what inner revolution or what mysterious force generated in that crowded room plucked her from her caul* of fear and thrust her forth to assert with such a dramatic and improbable gesture her new birth of freedom. A funeral hall is as good a place as any for a person to come to life, I suppose, and her action sparked a sympathetic impulse in everyone who watched as she planted herself in front of the first trooper and shook a finger in his face: "Do you have a search warrant to come into my place of business?"

    insulating membrane

The trooper stared down at her, confounded, and backed away. "No," he said.

"You're not coming into my place of business without a search warrant. I'm a taxpayer and a law-abiding citizen. I have a wake going on here."

"This ain't no wake," the trooper said, looking around at the throng* of angry, frightened people crushed together before him. "These people ain't at no wake."

    crowd

"Well, you're not coming into my place of business without a search warrant." The accusing finger pushed him back to the door, where he muttered for a moment to his men outside, then turned and yelled, "All right. We got all the tear gas and all the guns. You ain't got nothin'. We'll give you just five minutes to get Farmer out here. Just five minutes, that's all." He slammed the door.

The door clanged in my ears like the door of a cell in death row. "I'll go out and face them," I said, but once again I was restrained. They would stick by me, these strangers insisted, even if they all had to die, but they would not let me out to be lynched. Someone standing near me pulled out a gun. "Mr. Farmer," he said, "if a trooper comes through that door, he'll be dead."

"If a trooper comes through that door, he may be dead," I conceded. "But what about the trooper behind him and all the ones behind that one?

You'll only provoke them into shooting and we won't have a chance." Very reluctantly he allowed me to take the gun from him. It is hard for people to practice non-violence when they are looking death in the face.

———————

While most Blacks recognized the oppressive conditions of pre-civil rights America, the "women's liberation" movement, both at its start and to this day, has found unity among women a difficult goal to achieve. The feminist movement itself consists of several factions, such as radical feminism or social-ist feminism, some of whose ideology conflicts with that of other groups despite their similar political dissatisfactions. Feminism remains a potent politi-cal force in contemporary society, but the feminist struggle transcends politics: religion, medicine, psychology, education, business, law, all have had to re-spond to feminist issues.

MARLENE DIXON
"Why Women's Liberation"

KEY CONCEPTS

Domestic **TYRANNY**, like political tyranny, means oppressive rule by one person, in this case the male head of the household.

SOCIAL DARWINISM is construed here as racial discrimination; see Chapter 3, pages 185–188.

● The 1960s has been a decade of liberation; women have been swept up by that ferment* along with blacks, Latins, American Indians and poor whites — the whole soft underbelly of this society. As each oppressed group in turn discovered the nature of its oppression in American society, so women have discovered that they too thirst for free and fully human lives. The result has been the growth of a new women's movement, whose base encompasses poor black and white women on relief, working women exploited in the labor force, middle class women incarcerated* in the split level dream house, college girls awakening to the fact that sexiness is not the crowning achievement in life, and movement women who have dis-covered that in a freedom movement they themselves are not free. In less than four years women have created a variety of organizations, from the nationally-based middle class National Organization of Women (NOW) to local radical and radical feminist groups in every major city in North America. The movement includes caucuses* within nearly every New Left group and within most professional associations in the social sciences. Ranging in politics from reform to revolution, it has produced critiques of almost every segment of American society and constructed an ideology that rejects every hallowed cultural assumption about the nature and role of women.

agitation

imprisoned

special interest groups

SOURCE: Marlene Dixon, "Why Women's Liberation" in *Ramparts* Magazine 8:57–63, De-cember 1969.

The three major groups which make up the new women's movement — working women, middle class married women and students — bring very different kinds of interests and objectives to women's liberation. Each group represents an independent aspect of the total institutionalized oppression of women. Their differences are those of emphasis and immediate interest rather than of fundamental goals. All women suffer from economic exploitation, from psychological deprivation, and from exploitive sexuality. Within women's liberation there is a growing understanding that the common oppression of women provides the basis for uniting across class and race lines to form a powerful and radical movement.

Clearly, for the liberation of women to become a reality it is necessary to destroy the ideology of male supremacy which asserts the biological and social inferiority of women in order to justify massive institutionalized oppression. Yet we all know that many women are as loud in their disavowal* of this oppression as are the men who chant the litany* of "a woman's place is in the home and behind her man." In fact, women are as trapped in their false consciousness as were the mass of blacks 20 years ago, and for much the same reason.

denial / chanted prayer

As blacks were defined and limited socially by their color, so women are defined and limited by their sex. While blacks, it was argued, were preordained* by god or nature, or both, to be hewers* of wood and drawers of water, so women are destined to bear and rear children, and to sustain their husbands with obedience and compassion. The Sky-God tramples through the heavens and the Earth/Mother-Goddess is always flat on her back with legs spread, putting out for one and all.

decided beforehand / cutters

Indeed, the phenomenon of male chauvinism can only be understood when it is perceived as a form of racism, based on stereotypes drawn from a deep belief in the biological inferiority of women. The so-called "black analogy" is no analogy at all; it is the same social process that is at work, a process which both justifies and helps perpetuate the exploitation of one group of human beings by another.

The very stereotypes that express the society's belief in the biological inferiority of women recall the images used to justify the oppression of blacks. The nature of women, like that of slaves, is depicted as dependent, incapable of reasoned thought, childlike in its simplicity and warmth, martyred in the role of mother, and mystical in the role of sexual partner. In its benevolent form, the inferior position of women results in paternalism;* in its malevolent form, a domestic **tyranny** which can be unbelievably brutal.

condescending rule by a father-figure

It has taken over 50 years to discredit the scientific and social "proof" which once gave legitimacy to the myths of black racial inferiority. Today most people can see that the theory of the genetic inferiority of blacks is absurd. Yet few are shocked by the fact that scientists are still busy "proving" the biological inferiority of women.

In recent years, in which blacks have led the struggle for liberation, the emphasis on racism has focused only upon racism against blacks. The fact that "racism" has been practiced against many groups other than blacks has been pushed into the background. Indeed, a less forceful but more accurate term for the phenomenon would be **social Darwinism**. It was the opinion of the social Darwinists that in the natural course of things the "fit" succeed (i.e., oppress) and the "unfit" (i.e. the biologically inferior) sink to the bottom. According to this view, the very fact of a group's oppression proves its inferiority and the inevitable correctness of its low position. In this way each successive immigrant group coming to America was decked out in the garments of "racial" or biological inferiority until the group was sufficiently assimilated, whereupon Anglo-Saxon venom would turn on a new group filling up the space at the bottom. Now two groups remain, neither of which has been assimilated according to the classic American pattern: the "visibles" — blacks and women. It is equally true for both: "it won't wear off."

For those who believe in the "rights of mankind," the "dignity of man," consider that to make a woman a person, a human being in her own right, you would have to change her sex: imagine Stokely Carmichael* "Prone and silent"; imagine Mark Rudd* as a Laugh-In-girl; picture Rennie Davis* as Miss America. Such contradictions as these show how pervasive and deep-rooted is the cultural contempt for women, how difficult it is to imagine a woman as a serious human being, or conversely, how empty and degrading is the image of woman that floods the culture.

radical black activist
left wing student activist

Countless studies have shown that black acceptance of white stereotypes leads to mutilated identity, to alienation, to rage and self-hatred. Human beings cannot bear in their own hearts the contradictions of those who hold them in contempt. The ideology of male supremacy and its effect upon women merits as serious study as has been given to the effects of prejudice upon Jews, blacks, and immigrant groups.

It is customary to shame those who would draw the parallel between women and blacks by a great show of concern and chest beating over the suffering of black people. Yet this response itself reveals a refined combination of white middle class guilt and male chauvinism, for it overlooks several essential facts. For example, the most oppressed group within the feminine population is made up of black women, many of whom take a dim view of the black male intellectual's adoption of white male attitudes of sexual superiority (an irony too cruel to require comment). Neither are those who make this pious objection to the racial parallel addressing themselves very adequately to the millions of white working class women living at the poverty level, who are not likely to be moved by this middle class guilt-ridden one-upmanship while having to deal with the boss, the factory, or the welfare worker day after day. They are already dangerously resentful of the gains made by blacks, and much of their "racist backlash*" stems from the fact that they have been forgotten in the push for social change. Emphasis on the real mechanisms of oppression — on the commonality of the process — is essential lest groups such as these, which would work in alliance, become divided against one another.

strong reaction

White middle class males already struggling with the acknowledgement of their own racism do not relish* an added burden of recognition:

enjoy

that to white guilt must soon be added "male." It is therefore understand-able that they should refuse to see the harshness of the lives of most women — to honestly face the facts of massive institutionalized discrimi-nation against women. Witness the performance to date: "Take her down off the platform and give her a good f — ck," "Petty Bourgeois Revisionist Running Dogs," or in the classic words of a Berkeley male "leader," "Let them eat c — k."

Among whites, women remain the most oppressed — and the most unorganized — group. Although they constitute a potential mass base for the radical movement, in terms of movement priorities they are ignored; indeed they might as well be invisible. Far from being an accident, this omission is a direct outgrowth of the solid male supremist beliefs of white radical and left-liberal men. Even now, faced with both fact and agitation, leftist men find the idea of placing any serious priority upon women so outrageous, such a degrading notion, that they respond with a virulence*   hatred far out of proportion to the modest requests of movement women. This only shows that women must stop wasting their time worrying about the chauvinism of men in the movement and focus instead on their real prior-ity: organizing women.

SECTION READING QUESTIONS

The following pairs of questions all require you to relate Hook's definition of democracy to a textual issue and then to a hypothetical practical problem.

[1] How is the exclusion of women from the Athenian democratic process inconsistent with Hook's definition of democracy? How did those in power insure the exclusion of women?

[2] Is there a contradiction in defending democracy and being a misogynist*   hater of women at the same time?

[3] Hook paraphrases Plato and Santayana on democracy's relationship to tyranny and terror (pages 308–309, paragraph 17). Robespierre also discusses the link in paragraphs 12 and 13, pages 318–319, but explains it differently. Clarify the difference: which one professes to be defending democracy?

[4] Robespierre includes "necessity" among the inalienable rights protected by democracy. Can democracy function practically if a government accepts that the ends justify the means?

[5] On how many levels does Klan philosophy conflict with the theory of democracy as Hook defines it?

[6] Can a democratic society insist on assimilation (adopting the majority's language and culture) as a prerequisite to full participation in the democracy?

[7] What does Malcolm X mean by saying blacks face a choice between "the ballot and the bullet?"

[8] What would Hook see as the theoretical problem involved in a minority member using violence — "the bullet" — as a means of gaining equal rights in a democracy?

[9] In practice, minorities have often had to struggle for equal rights in theoretically democratic systems. What are the human costs of such a struggle as illustrated in James Farmer's narrative?

[10] Does democracy allow for civil disobedience, and why might it be necessary in a professedly democratic society?

[11] How does the historical oppression of blacks contradict the theoretical necessity of "freely given consent" in a truly democratic system? Consider blacks' and women's historical participation in the democratic process.

[12] What parallels does Dixon draw between the oppression of blacks and that of women?

[13] How does Social Darwinism provide a rationale for male chauvinism?

SECTION ESSAY ASSIGNMENTS

[1] Analyze and discuss the practical shortcomings that democratic systems have experienced from ancient Athens to contemporary America, drawing on the first seven readings in this chapter.

[2] Compare and contrast the oppression faced by blacks in the nineteenth and twentieth centuries with women's conditions in ancient Athens and present-day America.

[3] Democracy supposedly guarantees free speech and full representation. When an individual is deprived of those rights, is he or she justified in resorting to civil disobedience, ranging from nonviolent protest to terrorism, as a means of fighting oppression and gaining equal rights and full participation? Refer to Robespierre, Malcolm X, and James Farmer especially to support your views.

Monarchy and Excess

Survey the following article, which is an extended definition of monarchy. Your reading strategy should allow you to paraphrase and summarize the definition.

WILLIAM EDENSTEIN
"Monarchy"

KEY CONCEPTS

DESPOTISM, **TYRANNY**, and **AUTOCRACY** have all been defined in earlier readings; see pages 305 and 320.

IMPERIAL EXPANSION, like colonial expansion (page 363), involves a stronger nation taking power over a weaker one, exploiting it economically.

For a definition of **ARISTOCRACY**, see page 320.

The **BOURGEOISIE**, a Marxist term, is the middle class, or those above the working class.

● Monarchy is a form of government in which one person is the sovereign.* supreme ruler The word derives from the Greek "monarchia," the rule of one. The Greeks, however, distinguished the legitimate one-man government of monarchy from the illegitimate one-man dictatorship or **despotism** or **tyranny**. In the latter system the ruler rules in his own interest rather than in that of the governed. In a monarchy in its pure (and original) form, the ruler combined in his person the supreme authority and power in legislation as well as in administration and adjudication.* In later stages of evolu- judicial rule tion, the monarch frequently still retained his position as the supreme law-giver, but handed over the judicial and administrative functions to specialized agencies, generally subordinate to him. Above all, the monarch was originally, and long remained, the commander in chief of his nation's armed forces.

In early history, as among primitive peoples today, the monarchical form of government was virtually the only one known and practiced. Generally, monarchy was hereditary. In Asia and Africa monarchy persisted in its **autocratic** form until, beginning in the 17th century, **imperial expansion** by European states (England, France, Holland) put an end to native monarchical autocracies. Native monarchies were often retained, however, as instruments of control over conquered populations. Where such European imperial influence has been only short-lived — as in Saudi Arabia — the despotic or autocratic form of monarchy has survived.

In antiquity

The Greeks discarded the monarchical system of government beginning in the 7th century B.C., although Sparta persisted in monarchical rule of an elective type. Monarchy did not fit the individualistic, rational, inquiring mentality of the Greeks, who may be said to have invented repub-

SOURCE: "Monarchy" by William Edenstein from *The Encyclopedia Americana* by Grolier Inc. Copyright © 1984. Reprinted by permission of the publisher.

lican self-government in the Western World. Moreover, their main enemy in the 5th century B.C. was Persia, an empire under an absolute monarchy. Monarchy thus became in ancient Greece the symbol of external and internal servitude. Even after Philip and Alexander the Great had forced the Greek city-states into the Macedonian monarchy and empire, the institutions of self-government in the city-states were preserved by their Macedonian overlords.

The Jews opposed monarchy from very early times. According to the teachings of Judaism, God was sovereign, and no man could demand complete allegiance from his subjects. The Romans had their great period during their republican system of government. The establishment of monarchy in Rome coincided with the expansion of Rome from a relatively small city-state to a world empire. Although the Roman monarchy of the imperial type helped unite the empire, it symbolized the early decay of those civic qualities in Rome that were the foundations of its greatness.

In the middle ages

After the destruction of the Western Roman Empire in 476 A.D., monarchy continued in the Eastern Roman Empire centered in Constantinople. In the West, two types of monarchy gradually emerged. First, the bishop of Rome progressively established himself as the ruler of all Christendom, and he claimed monarchical prerogatives over all Christians in matters temporal as well as spiritual. Meanwhile, the German rulers sought to restore the Roman imperial monarchy under German leadership, claiming universal political allegiance throughout the Christian world. This Holy Roman Empire of the Teutonic* Nations was inaugurated* with the coronation of Charlemagne in 800 by the pope in Rome. Legally, it lasted until 1806, when Napoleon I destroyed it, but it had exercised little influence during the last few centuries of its existence.

Northern European, particularly German / formally begun

In the renaissance and modern times

The monarchy more than any other institution was instrumental in forging the modern nation-state. In general, the main force to be overcome was the **aristocracy**, which opposed increased royal power. But the new middle class, or **"bourgeoisie,"** which supplied much of the administrative personnel of the new nation-states, was willing to allow the monarch strong central authority so long as he could maintain law and order, efficient communications, a stable currency, and protection against internal and external enemies.

England, in the 17th century, was the first modern country to abandon the concept of the absolute monarchical authority. The Civil War culminated in the execution of King Charles I in 1649, the establishment of a republic under Oliver Cromwell, and the ascendancy* of the middle classes. The monarchy was restored in 1660, but the revolution of 1688 finally established the principle that political authority resides in Parlia-

rising power

ment. A century later, the French followed the English example and established a republic based on "liberty, equality, and fraternity." During the 19th century, monarchy was restored in France for short periods, but the concept of absolute monarchy deriving its authority from divine grace was dead.

Where liberalism was weak, the monarchical form of government lasted until World War I. In Russia the monarchy was destroyed in 1917, and the emperors of Germany and Austria abdicated in 1918. Today, monarchy exists in Western nations where it has allied itself with democracy and liberalism, as in Britain, Belgium, the Netherlands, Denmark, Norway, and Sweden. In liberal societies the monarchy served as a symbol of national unity and continuity.

QUESTIONS FOR DISCUSSION AND WRITING

[1] Summarize the definition of "monarchy."

[2] How can monarchy be interpreted as a "symbol of servitude?" Do you see any parallel in *Oedipus Rex?*

[3] Describe the various degrees of monarchical rule, from a figurehead monarch to one of absolute power.

Read Suetonius' narrative for its implied thesis on the decadent and cruel excesses that can corrupt an absolute monarch.

———————

In the first century B.C., *the Roman republic, a representative form of government, came to an end. Julius Caesar led Rome on its way to empire. He was succeeded by a series of Caesars: Augustus, Tiberius, Gaius, Claudius, and Nero, among others. The Roman empire stretched from England and Spain to Jerusalem and parts of Africa. The Roman conquerors offered* Pax Romana, *support and protection against aggression to those nations who accepted Roman rule. But this peace was hard to maintain, both abroad and at home, and the Roman emperors often succumbed to the temptation which absolute power placed before them. Rome fell in 476* A.D.

SUETONIUS
"Gaius (Caligula)"

● So much for the Emperor; the rest of this history must deal with the Monster.

SOURCE: *The Twelve Caesars,* trans. by Robert Graves. Copyright © 1957 by Robert Graves. Reprinted by permission of Robert Graves and Penguin Books Ltd.

He adopted a variety of titles: such as "Pious," "Son of the Camp," "Father of the Army," "Best and Greatest of Caesars." But when once, at the dinner table, some foreign kings who had come to pay homage were arguing which of them was the most nobly descended, Gaius interrupted their discussion by declaiming Homer's line:

Nay, let there be one master, and one king!

And he nearly assumed a royal diadem* then and there, turning the semblance of a principate* into an autocracy. However, after his courtiers reminded him that he already outranked any prince or king, he insisted on being treated as a god — sending for the most revered or artistically famous statues of the Greek deities (including that of Jupiter at Olympia), and having their heads replaced by his own.

> crown
>
> territory ruled by a prince

Next, Gaius extended the Palace as far as the Forum; converted the shrine of Castor and Pollux into its vestibule;* and would often stand beside these Divine Brethren to be worshipped by all visitants, some of whom addressed him as "Jupiter Latiaris." He established a shrine to himself as God, with priests, the costliest possible victims, and a life-sized golden image, which was dressed every day in clothes identical with those that he happened to be wearing. All the richest citizens tried to gain priesthoods here, either by influence or bribery. Flamingoes, peacocks, black grouse, guinea-hens, and pheasants were offered as sacrifices, each on a particular day of the month. When the moon shone full and bright he always invited the Moon-goddess to sexual intercourse in his bed; and during the day would indulge in whispered conversations with Capitoline Jupiter (a statue), pressing his ear to the god's mouth, and sometimes raising his voice in anger. Once he was overheard threatening the god: "If you do not raise me up to Heaven I will cast you down to Hell." Finally he announced that Jupiter had persuaded him to share his home; and therefore connected the Palace with the Capitol by throwing a bridge across the Temple of the God Augustus; after which he began building a new house inside the precincts of the Capitol itself, in order to live even nearer.

> entrance hall

Because of Agrippa's humble origin Gaius loathed being described as his grandson, and would fly into a rage if anyone mentioned him, in speech or song, as an ancestor of the Caesars. He nursed a fantasy that his mother had been born of an incestuous union between Augustus and his daughter Julia; and not content with thus discrediting Augustus' name, cancelled the annual commemorations of Agrippa's victories at Actium and off Sicily, declaring that they had proved the disastrous ruin of the Roman people. He called his great-grandmother Livia a "Ulysses in petticoats," and in a letter to the Senate dared describe her as of low birth — "her maternal grandfather Aufidius Lurco having been a mere local senator at Fundi" — although the public records showed Lurco to have held high office at Rome. When his grandmother Antonia asked him to grant her a private audience he insisted on taking Macro, the Guards Commander, as his escort. Unkind treatment of this sort hurried her to the grave though, according to some, he accelerated the process with poison and, when she died, showed so little respect that he sat in his dining-room and watched the funeral pyre burn. One day he sent a colonel to kill young Tiberius Gemellus without warning, on the pretext that Tiberius had insulted him by taking an antidote against poison — his breath smelled of it. Then he forced his father-in-law, Marcus Silanus, to cut his own throat with a razor, the charge being that he had not followed the imperial ship when it put to sea in a storm, but had stayed on shore to seize power at Rome if anything happened to himself. The truth was that Silanus, a notoriously bad sailor, could not face the voyage; and Tiberius's breath smelled of medicine taken for a persistent cough which was getting worse. Gaius preserved his uncle Claudius merely as a butt for practical jokes.

Nor was he any more respectful or considerate in his dealings with the Senate, but made some of the highest officials run for miles beside his chariot, dressed in their togas; or wait in short linen tunics at the head or foot of his dining couch. Often he would send for men whom he had secretly killed, as though they were still alive, and remark off-handedly a few days later that they must have committed suicide. When two Consuls forgot to announce his birthday, he dismissed them and left the country for three days without officers of state. One of his quaestors* was charged   public officials
with conspiracy; Gaius had his clothes stripped off and spread on the ground, to give the soldiers who flogged him a firmer foothold.

He behaved just as arrogantly and violently towards the other orders of society. A crowd bursting into the Circus about midnight to secure free seats angered him so much that he had them driven away with clubs; more than a score of knights, as many married women, and numerous others were crushed to death in the ensuing panic. Gaius liked to stir up trouble in the Theatre by scattering gift vouchers before the seats were occupied, thus tempting commoners to invade the rows reserved for knights. During gladiatorial shows* he would have the canopies* removed at the hottest   public fights between men
time of the day and forbid anyone to leave; or take away the usual equip-   and animals / roof-like
ment, and pit feeble old fighters against decrepit wild animals; or stage   covering
comic duels between respectable householders who happened to be physically disabled in some way or other. More than once he closed down the granaries and let the people go hungry.

Gaius made parents attend their sons' executions, and when one father excused himself on the ground of ill-health, provided a litter for him. Having invited another father to dinner just after the son's execution, he overflowed with good-fellowship in an attempt to make him laugh and joke. He watched the manager of his gladiatorial and wild-beast shows being flogged with chains for several days running, and had him killed only when the smell of suppurating* brains became insupportable.* A writer   giving off pus / unbearable
of Atellan farces was burned alive in the amphitheatre, because of a line

which had an amusing double-entendre.* One knight, on the point of being thrown to the wild beasts, shouted that he was innocent; Gaius brought him back, removed his tongue, and then ordered the sentence to be carried out.

double-meaning statement

Gaius' savage crimes were made worse by his brutal language. He claimed that no personal trait made him feel prouder than his "inflexibility" — by which he must have meant "brazen impudence." As though mere deafness to his grandmother Antonia's good advice were not enough, he told her: 'Bear in mind that I can treat anyone exactly as I please!' Suspecting that young Tiberius Gemellus had taken drugs as prophylactics* to the poison he intended to administer, he scoffed: "Can there really be an antidote against Caesar?" And, on banishing his sisters, he remarked: "I have swords as well as islands." One ex-praetor, taking a cure at Anticyra, made frequent requests for an extension of his sickleave; Gaius had him put to death, suggesting that if hellebore* had been of so little benefit over so long a period, he must need to be bled. When signing the execution list he used to say: "I am clearing my accounts." And one day, after sentencing a number of Gauls and Greeks to die in the same batch, he boasted of having "subdued Gallo-Graecia."

things that prevent or protect against

medicinal plant

The method of execution he preferred was to inflict numerous small wounds; and his familiar order: "Make him feel that he is dying!" soon became proverbial. Once, when the wrong man had been killed, owing to a confusion of names, he announced that the victim had equally deserved death; and often quoted Accius' line:

Let them hate me, so long as they fear me.

READING SKILL: *Using Logical Connectors to Improve Comprehension*

Writers use logical connectors in paragraphs or between paragraphs to show a logical relationship between two or more sentences. Perhaps you have learned about connectors in your writing classes. They are also important in lecture notetaking and, for our purposes here, in reading comprehension.

Connectors serve the following purposes:

1. Addition: used to signal addition, similarity, introduction, exemplification, and emphasis.

   EXAMPLES: moreover, also, furthermore, specifically, namely, similarly, equally, actually, indeed, above all

2. Contrast and contradiction: used to signal conflict, contrast, concession, dismissal, or displacement.

   EXAMPLES: but, however, on the other hand, in contrast, although, in spite of, nonetheless

3. Causal: used to signal cause/reason, effect/result, purpose, and condition.

   EXAMPLES: since, due to the fact that, therefore, thus, if, provided that, if so, in that case, as a result

4. Sequential: used to signal numerical order, beginning, continuation, conclusion, digression, resumption, and summation.

   EXAMPLES: first, initially, to start with, subsequently, at last, to conclude, by the way, in conclusion, to sum up

How can using logical connectors improve reading comprehension? If you pay attention to logical connectors while reading, they will signal how the author is arranging the information for you; they will help you to perceive the organizational patterns of paragraphs or portions of paragraphs, and as we mentioned before, they will aid you in understanding and remembering information. Identifying connectors can sometimes help you "unlock" difficult-to-understand sentences by showing you the logical relationship of ideas within the sentence. For example, a long complicated sentence like "Machiavelli was an Italian Renaissance writer who, in spite of his notoriety for the amoral system outlined in *The Prince,* represents the Renaissance spirit of achievement in all forms of art as well as practical accomplishment in the social graces" can be made more comprehendible by breaking it into one statement of contradiction and one of addition: "<u>In spite of</u> his notoriety, Machiavelli was artistically <u>as well as</u> socially accomplished."

Identifying connectors can also help you isolate the topic sentence of a paragraph, for instance, by signalling supporting details. If you are reading a paragraph containing connectors such as "first," "second," and "finally," it is very probable that a topic sentence precedes or, more infrequently, directly follows such a "shopping list" of examples. Being aware of connectors can also help lead you to the author's purpose or intention. "In conclusion" will signal the author's intention to sum up and conclude his or her position or a part of his or her argument. A connector of contrast or contradiction, such as "however" or "but," can warn you to be prepared for information even more important than what was just stated. Connectors of addition, such as "in addition" or "moreover," prepare you for additional information or some kind of repetition or restatement, something very common in writing. Cause and effect connectors, like "therefore" or "due to the fact that," will show you that something is the cause of an effect or action.

We've marked the first four paragraphs of the following reading passage for logical connectors. We also explain the function of those we've marked in the first paragraph at that paragraph's end. Read our explanation and then try explaining the function of the connectors in the other paragraphs we've marked. Then go on and mark the connectors in the rest of the essay, noting the function they serve within the text. Once you have identified the logical connectors and their function within a sentence or paragraph, you should have a sense of the paragraph's purpose.

One warning: we don't mean to imply that every time you read you should circle all the connectors. Instead, we want you to become aware of them when you read and perhaps focus on them when you are having difficulty with a particular text.

Machiavelli's The Prince *has enjoyed renown* and infamy* both, depend-*   fame / evil reputation
ing on its audience. The author offered his work to the leaders of Renaissance
states as a kind of guidebook to power through manipulation, deception, and
force. The term "Machiavellian" has come to mean a cunning, devious ap-
proach or attitude. Like the contemporary Castiglione's courtier, the ideal of
grace, the Prince embodies the ideal of power. The prince depicted here
became a model of pragmatic* and ruthless leadership. Some twentieth-   practical
century leaders who displayed a Machiavellian edge were Stalin, Hitler, and
Mussolini.

MACHIAVELLI
FROM *The Prince*

● Every prince should prefer to be considered merciful rather than cruel, yet (1) he should be careful not to mismanage this clemency* of his. People   mercy
thought Cesare Borgia* was cruel, but (2) that cruelty of his reorganized   Italian Cardinal, political
the Romagna,* united it, and established it in peace and loyalty. Anyone   and military leader / Italian
who views the matter realistically will see that this prince was much more   lands
merciful than the people of Florence, who, to avoid the reputation of
cruelty, allowed Pistoia to be destroyed. Thus (3), no prince should mind
being called cruel for what he does to keep his subjects united and loyal;
he may make examples of a very few, but (4) he will be more merciful in
reality than those who, in their tenderheartedness, allow disorders to
occur, with their attendant* murders and lootings. Such turbulence brings   accompanying
harm to an entire community, while (5) the executions ordered by a prince
affect only one individual at a time. A new prince, above all others, cannot
possibly avoid a name for cruelty, since (6) new states are always in danger.
And (7) Virgil, speaking through the mouth of Dido, says:

> My cruel fate and doubts attending an unsettled state force me to guard
> my coast from foreign foes.

[(1) "Yet" functions to signal that the author will contradict what he has just
said. Here Machiavelli says a prince should appear merciful and then he contra-
dicts that absolute statement and warns against being overly merciful.

(2) "But," a connector of contrast, subordinates or makes less important the

SOURCE: Reprinted from *The Prince* by Niccolò Machiavelli. A Norton Critical Edition.
Translated and edited by Robert M. Adams. By permission of W. W. Norton & Company,
Inc. Copyright © 1977 by W. W. Norton & Company, Inc.

fact that Cesare Borgia was thought cruel and emphasizes that his cruelty served an important political purpose.

(3) "Thus," a connector showing result, signals that Machiavelli will derive a logical result from his preceding examples: a prince shouldn't mind being called cruel when his goal is maintaining unity and loyalty. Borgia was called cruel but he gained his end; the people of Florence, wanting to avoid a reputation for cruelty, lost a city.

(4) "But," here a connector of contradiction, subordinates the idea that a prince may seem cruel in his methods to the idea that overall it is more important to achieve the end of maintaining order.

(5) "While" is a connector of contrast. Machiavelli says general turbulence harms everyone; an execution, in contrast, hurts only the person involved.
If you can't get the sense of what the connector does, try substituting a synonym. In this case, "however" or "on the other hand" may help clarify how "while" is being used.

(6) "Since," a cause and effect connector that, like "because," always names a cause, here sets up the logic that because a new state is always in danger, a new prince cannot avoid having a reputation for cruelty.

(7) "And" shows emphasis or addition. Machiavelli here adds another piece of evidence to support his main point.]

Yet a prince should be slow to believe rumors and to commit himself to action on the basis of them. He should not be afraid of his own thoughts; he ought to proceed cautiously, moderating his conduct with prudence* and humanity, allowing neither overconfidence to make him careless, nor overtimidity to make him intolerable.

careful judgment

Here the question arises: is it better to be loved than feared, or vice versa? I don't doubt that every prince would like to be both; but since it is hard to accommodate these qualities, if you have to make a choice, to be feared is much safer than to be loved. For it is a good general rule about men, that they are ungrateful, fickle,* liars, and deceivers, fearful of danger and greedy for gain. While you serve their welfare, they are all yours, offering their blood, their belongings, their lives, and their children's lives, as we noted above — so long as the danger is remote. But when the danger is close at hand, they turn against you. Then, any prince who has relied on their words and has made no other preparations will come to grief; because friendships that are bought at a price, and not with greatness and nobility of soul, may be paid for but they are not acquired, and they cannot be used in time of need. People are less concerned with offending a man who makes himself loved than one who makes himself feared: the reason is that love is a link of obligation which men, because they are rotten, will break any time they think doing so serves their advantage; but fear involves dread of punishment, from which they can never escape.

unstable, undecided

Still, a prince should make himself feared in such a way that, even if he gets no love, he gets no hate either; because it is perfectly possible to be feared and not hated, and this will be the result if only the prince will keep his hands off the property of his subjects or citizens, and off their women. When he does have to shed blood, he should be sure to have a strong justification and manifest cause; but above all, he should not confiscate people's property, because men are quicker to forget the death of a father than the loss of a patrimony. Besides, pretexts* for confiscation are always plentiful; it never fails that a prince who starts living by plunder can find reasons to rob someone else. Excuses for proceeding against someone's life are much rarer and more quickly exhausted.

false reasons

Returning to the question of being feared or loved, I conclude that since men love at their own inclination but can be made to fear at the inclination of the prince, a shrewd prince will lay his foundations on what is under his own control, not on what is controlled by others. He should simply take pains not to be hated, as I said.

The way princes should keep their word

How praiseworthy it is for a prince to keep his word and live with integrity rather than by craftiness, everyone understands; yet we see from recent experience that those princes have accomplished most who paid little heed to keeping their promises, but who knew how craftily to manipulate the minds of men. In the end, they won out over those who tried to act honestly.

You should consider then, that there are two ways of fighting, one with laws and the other with force. The first is properly a human method, the second belongs to beasts. But as the first method does not always suffice, you sometimes have to turn to the second. Thus a prince must know how to make good use of both the beast and the man.

Thus a prudent prince cannot and should not keep his word when to do so would go against his interest, or when the reasons that made him pledge it no longer apply. Doubtless if all men were good, this rule would be bad; but since they are a sad lot, and keep no faith with you, you in your turn are under no obligation to keep it with them.

Besides, a prince will never lack for legitimate excuses to explain away his breaches* of faith. Modern history will furnish innumerable examples of this behavior, showing how many treaties and promises have been made null and void by the faithlessness of princes, and how the man succeeded best who knew best how to play the fox. But it is a necessary part of this nature that you must conceal it carefully; you must be a great liar and hypocrite. Men are so simple of mind, and so much dominated by their immediate needs, that a deceitful man will always find plenty who are ready to be deceived.

failures

In actual fact, a prince may not have all the admirable qualities we listed, but it is very necessary that he should seem to have them. Indeed, I will venture to say that when you have them and exercise them all the time, they are harmful to you; when you just seem to have them, they are useful. It is good to appear merciful, truthful, humane, sincere, and religious; it is good to be so in reality. But you must keep your mind so disposed that, in case of need, you can turn to the exact contrary. This has to be understood: a prince, and especially a new prince, cannot possibly exercise all those virtues for which men are called "good." To preserve the state, he often has to do things against his word, against charity, against humanity, against religion. Thus he has to have a mind ready to shift as the winds of fortune and the varying circumstances of life may dictate. And as I said above, he should not depart from the good if he can hold to it, but he should be ready to enter on evil if he has to.

Hence a prince should take great care never to drop a word that does not seem imbued with the five good qualities noted above; to anyone who sees or hears him, he should appear all compassion, all honor, all humanity, all integrity, all religion. Nothing is more necessary than to seem to have this last virtue. Men in general judge more by the sense of sight than by the sense of touch, because everyone can see but only a few can test by feeling. Everyone sees what you seem to be, few know what you really are; and those few do not dare take a stand against the general opinion, supported by the majesty of the government. In the actions of all men, and especially of princes who are not subject to a court of appeal, we must always look to the end. Let a prince, therefore, win victories and uphold his state; his methods will always be considered worthy, and everyone will praise them, because the masses are always impressed by the superficial appearance of things, and by the outcome of an enterprise. And the world consists of nothing but the masses; the few have no influence when the many feel secure. A certain prince of our own time, whom it's just as well not to name, preaches nothing but peace and mutual trust, yet he is the determined enemy of both; and if on several different occasions he had observed either, he would have lost both his reputation and his throne.

As you read the next article, circle the logical connectors. Note how the author uses them for a particular logical or rhetorical purpose.

The European monarchs of the seventeenth century took over the power which the medieval church had once exercised. Grandeur and elegance characterized their rule, which Versailles, the elaborate palace/city of Louis XIV, the Sun King, most vividly depicts. Monarchs like Louis, Henry VIII, Elizabeth I, and Phillip II were more like the Roman emperors than the monarchs of today, who are mainly figurehead rulers.

W. H. LEWIS
"The Court"

KEY CONCEPTS

The statement, **L'ÉTAT, C'EST MOI**, or in English, "I am the state," means that the king is the living symbol of the nation, identical to it and therefore all-powerful.

STOIC ENDURANCE refers to the Stoic philosophical belief that one should avoid extremes and accept events as they happen without judging them immediately as good or evil.

● If Versailles was not all France, it was at least the place to which all French eyes were turned, the concretion* in stone and marble of the apocryphal dictum **l'état c'est moi**, a theory of life made visible. Regularity, dignity, magnificence, a bleak and comfortless splendor brooded* throughout the huge chateau* and the well-disciplined gardens, whose cost remains unknown to this day; for even Louis XIV blenched* at the figures, and burnt Mansart's accounts.

physical existence

hung over
castle or estate
flinched

We must not, however, reproach Versailles with its lack of comfort, for the idea of making it comfortable never entered the head of either builder or owner. By Louis and his contemporaries comfort was held in contempt, as an aspiration unworthy of a gentleman; the mark of the man of quality, as the King once said, is indifference to heat, cold, hunger and thirst. And if in the interior of the palace there was little indifference shown to hunger and thirst, there was at any rate ample opportunity for a **stoic endurance** of other discomforts. When the royal architect pointed out to his master that if certain chimneys were not raised, the fires would smoke, Louis replied that it was a matter of indifference to him whether they smoked or not, so long as the chimneys were not visible from the gardens. Madame de Maintenon complains bitterly of the discomfort of her room at Fontainebleau where there is a window the size of an arcade,* to which she is not allowed to fit a shutter because it would mar the external symmetry of the facade: with the result that the room was freezing in winter, and baking hot in summer. Magnificence was what was aimed at in a seventeenth-century house, not comfort.

covered passageway

The enormous chateau of Versailles, with its ten thousand inhabitants, in which was spent twelve out of every twenty shillings collected in taxes, was something more than a mere seat of government. To the man or woman of ambition it was a lottery in which the prizes were dazzling, and in which few could resist the temptation to take a ticket. So yet another squire would mortgage his estate, mount his horse, and set off on the road to Versailles, confident in his ability to make his way under the eye of the King and with the assistance of his patron. For the great man of his province was almost certain to be his distant relative, and the grand seigneur* would reluctantly admit his country cousin's claim to his assistance: probably not in cash, of which the great man himself would be uncommonly short, but he would feed him, perhaps find him a free garret* to sleep in, and would have no objection to the newcomer using his name to obtain credit with the Court tradespeople.

gentleman

attic

And so a new courtier has arrived at Versailles. Not of course to live in the chateau, for many weary years will have to pass before he is even considered for a vacant attic; unless some lucky accident befall him such as happened to the Marquis de Dangeau when impromptu* verse making was in fashion. The King one day jokingly offered him a room if he could

spontaneous

fill in a set of verses on the spot; Dangeau did so, and Louis, who never broke a promise, gave him the coveted* room. But this sort of thing came to few, and our new courtier could resign himself to an expensive lodging in the town, which he would never see by daylight in the winter months; to a life of rising in the shivering night to hurry to his patron's side and to follow him to the King's, of standing all day in the ante-rooms,* and of returning with aching feet to his bed in the small hours of the next morning.

desired

rooms leading into another larger room

But greater than his material sufferings would be those of a kind with which most of us are familiar, the embarrassments and agonies of a new boy at school; for there is a remarkable resemblance between the life of old Versailles and that of a public school.* At Versailles was the same complex unwritten law, the same struggle for trivial distinctions, an intricate and illogical code of privilege, with public shame and biting rebuke for the man who transgressed against its provisions. Even the most unpleasing of public school vices, though abhorred* by the King, flourished in that section of the Court which was under the influence of his depraved* brother, Monsieur, the Duc d'Orleans.

British: private educational institution

detested

perverted

Court etiquette was a life study. Who for instance could guess that at Versailles it was the height of bad manners to knock at a door? You must scratch it with the little finger of the left hand, growing the finger nail long for that purpose. Or could know that you must not tutoyer* an intimate friend in any place where the King was present? That if the lackey* of a social superior brought you a message, you had to receive him standing, and bare-headed? You have mastered the fact that you must not knock on a door, so when you go to make your first round of calls in the great houses in the town, you scratch: wrong again, you should have knocked. Next time you rattle the knocker, and a passing exquisite* asks you contemptuously if you are so ignorant as not to know that you give one blow of the knocker on the door of a lady of quality? Who could guess that if you encounter the royal dinner on its way from the kitchens to the table, you must bow as to the King himself, sweep the ground with the plume of your hat, and say in a low, reverent, but distinct voice, La viande du Roi*? Many times must the apprentice courtier have echoed the psalmist's* lament, "Who can tell how oft he offendeth?" And it behoved* you not to offend, for the King had an eye like a hawk, or shall we say, like a school prefect,* for any breach of etiquette, and not even the most exalted were safe from his reproof.* One night at supper his chatterbox of a brother put his hand in a dish before Louis had helped himself: "I perceive," said the King icily, "that you are no better able to control your hands than your tongue." In 1707 at Marly, Mme de Torcy, wife of a minister, took a seat above a duchess at supper. Louis, to her extreme discomfort, regarded her steadfastly throughout the meal, and when he reached Madame de Maintenon's room, the storm broke; he had, he said, witnessed a piece of insolence so intolerable that the sight of it had prevented him from eating: a piece of presumption which would have been unendurable in a woman of quality.

use familiar speech

low-ranking male servant

dandy

the king's dinner

writer of Biblical psalms

was necessary for

administrator

criticism

It took the combined efforts of Madame de Maintenon and the Duchess of Burgundy the rest of the evening to pacify him. Decidedly not a king with whom to take liberties, or even make mistakes. This is Louis, or one side of Louis, at the height of his arrogance and prosperity: the Grand Monarque of the middle 'eighties, now forty-five or so, and in reluctant transition from Prince Charming to the impenetrably dignified king. Louis and Louis' Court had both been very different twenty years earlier, when the King's ambition had been to be the smartest of the smart set, homme à bonnes fortunes in his own right, owing his successes not to his crown but to his own graces. The king who climbed about the roofs of the Louvre at night to find an unbarred window in the quarters of the Maids-of-Honour was a very different man from the King who married Madame de Maintenon; and for old courtiers it must have been difficult to realize that the new Louis was the same man who, when pinched a tergo* by a *from behind* pretty girl in full Court, sprang upwards with a shout of "Damn the bitch!" In this new court, a freezing but superficial decorum and a rigid etiquette had become the rule.

SECTION READING QUESTIONS

[1] Did the fact that Caligula was an absolute monarch who inherited his power promote the decadence that we see in his personal and public life? Consider his relationship with his family, the senate, the Roman populace, and the Roman gods.

[2] Must all monarchs be despots?

[3] Explain Machiavelli's justification for the Prince's use of fear and cruelty.

[4] Historically, many monarchs have been cruel and oppressive. Why might a populace tolerate such treatment from their monarch? Refer especially to paragraph six in Edenstein's essay.

[5] Louis XIV built Versailles as a symbol of his royal splendor and greatness. How can you interpret Versailles as both a positive and negative symbol for the people under Louis' rule?

[6] How did the stylistic excesses of court life serve to maintain the monarch's power? Think of the lavish court architecture seen in Versailles and Buckingham Palace. Consider the court dress, the King's robes and crown, the elaborate court etiquette, the busy cultural scene. How might the King's subjects, many of them peasants, view their monarch?

SECTION ESSAY ASSIGNMENTS

[1] How do Machiavelli's *The Prince* and Louis' court at Versailles reflect Castiglione's aesthetics of *sprezzatura* and the ideal courtier?

[2] Both Robespierre and Caligula shared certain political tactics, despite the fact that they defended different political systems. Compare and contrast their tactics, goals, and personal behavior.

[3] Despite Caligula's perversions, the Prince's deceptions, and Louis XIV's excesses, monarchy as a political system has thrived throughout history. Develop an argument defending monarchy as a viable form of government.

Costs of Communism

LEWIS L. LORWIN
"Communism"

KEY CONCEPTS

CAPITALISM is an economic system characterized by private industry instead of state-controlled production.

The Marxist theory of **MATERIALISM** states that all social and political institutions have an economic basis.

A **DIALECTICAL PROCESS** involves a thesis and antithesis evolving into a synthesis: one thing clashes with its opposite and some new thing derives from the clash.

For a definition of **IMPERIALISM** and **COLONIALISM**, see page 364.

In a **PROLETARIAN DICTATORSHIP** the working class holds political control.

COLLECTIVE WAYS OF LIVING are cooperative efforts for the common good, or people working on a communal level, sharing both the work and the profits.

● Communism is the term used broadly to designate a theory or system of social organization used on the holding of all property in common. Specifically and currently, it refers to the doctrines underlying the revolutionary movement that aims to abolish **capitalism** and ultimately to establish a society in which all goods will be socially planned and controlled, and in which distribution will be in accordance with the maxim "from each according to his capacity, to each according to his needs." It is to be distinguished from socialism, which means, by constitutional and democratic methods, to nationalize gradually only the essential means of production and to organize distribution on the basis of a just reward to each person for the amount and quality of his or her work.

Marx and Engels

The theoretical foundations of modern communism were laid by the Germans Karl Marx and Friedrich Engels in *The Communist Manifesto* (1848). Marx and Engels took over and modified the then current concepts of **materialism**, the Hegelian view of historic evolution as a **dialectical process** moving from thesis through antithesis to synthesis, the labor theory of value of David Ricardo, the critique of capitalism of the "utopian" French socialists, and the tactics of Blanqui. The synthesis of Marx and Engels consisted in formulating these and the dynamics of "world revolution." After Lenin's death, Joseph Stalin added to Communist doctrine his special ideas that socialism could be built in one country, particularly Russia, and that the Soviet Union was the base of the "world revolution."

According to these Communist elaborations, the present stage of world history is that of "finance capitalism" or **"imperialism,"** marked by the growth of monopoly and the control of industry by finance. It is the epoch* of the decay or "general crisis" of capitalism on the one hand, and of the "world revolution" on the other. The "general crisis" of capitalism, say the Communists, began with World War I. It is to be a prolonged process, during which there may be brief periods of world economic stabilization and development, but every such period will be followed by a new crisis and decline, bringing the final collapse of capitalism nearer. The "general crisis" of capitalism cannot be overcome, argue the Communists, because "finance capitalism" aggravates the disparity between the growing productive forces of society and the restrictive methods of distribution, between the capacity to produce and the ability of the people to purchase the products of industry. The Communists view these disparities as the cause of industrial and social conflicts within each country, and as the cause of increasing struggles between nations for the control of raw materials and markets. International animosities are further accentuated, they maintain, by political antagonisms between the great powers and the **colonial** and underdeveloped countries.

World War II, according to their theory, sharpened these antagonisms in such a way as to divide the world into two opposing camps — the "capitalist-imperialist" states led by the United States on one side, and the "socialist" countries led by the USSR on the other side. Between these two camps struggle is inevitable, though for temporary periods the peaceful coexistence of the two systems and an easing of international tensions are possible.

As a result of the "general crisis" of capitalism, the "world revolution," which, the Communists maintain, began with the Russian Revolution of 1917, is "maturing." This "world revolution" is conceived by the Communists as a whole epoch of class struggles, national wars, revolutions, and **proletarian dictatorships** in different countries, some of which may fail temporarily while others are successful. For an indefinite period, there-

*period of time

fore, the Communists expect the world to present a spectacle of conflicting socioeconomic systems existing side by side.

Though their ultimate aim in each country is the establishment of a Communist society, the achievement of this aim, according to their theory, must be preceded by a transition period, during which industry will be nationalized, a planned economy organized, and the people accustomed to **collective ways of living**. The Communists call this period the "building of socialism" as the "first phase of communism." During the transition period the government will be organized as a "proletarian dictatorship," that is, as the class rule of the workers under the control of the Communist party which claims to be the "vanguard of the proletariat." Such a government will use all the powers of the state to crush resistance to its program. Thus, though the Communists claim that in some countries the revolution may initially be carried through by peaceful means, the fulfillment of the program involves the employment of violent and dictatorial methods.

Communism versus Socialism

Though both derive from Marx, socialism and communism parted ways in 1917–1919 and are now farther apart than ever. To the extent that they still hold to Marxian ideas, the democratic socialists have revised them to fit modern conditions of democratic freedom and social progress. The democratic socialists consider Leninism a Russian distortion of Marx and denounce Communist methods as antidemocratic and immoral. Nor do they regard the Soviet Union as a socialist country simply because it has nationalized its industries and introduced economic planning.

QUESTIONS FOR DISCUSSION AND WRITING

[1] According to Marx and Engels, how will communism come to replace the present political system?

[2] Describe the "general crisis" of capitalism according to Marxist theory.

[3] What is the dictatorship of the proletariat? Why do Marxists view it as a necessary stage?

Communism is an ideal of communal or popular rule. Stalin's leadership illustrates how, despite this ideal, power can corrupt. As a communist leader, he instituted a reign of terror far surpassing Robespierre's. Under his rule, Russia came to epitomize the modern totalitarian state.

ALEXANDER WEISSBERG
FROM *The Accused*

KEY CONCEPTS

For definitions of **TOTALITARIANISM, DICTATORSHIP**, and **TYRANNY**, see page 305.

In a **SOCIALIST REVOLUTION**, the people seize power from a centralized government and replace it with communal rule.

● From the middle of 1936 to the end of 1938 the **totalitarian** state took on its final form in the Soviet Union. In this period approximately eight million people were arrested in town and country by the secret police, the G.P.U. The arrested men were charged with high treason, espionage, sabotage, preparation for armed insurrection* and the planning of at- | rebellion, uprising
tempts on the lives of Soviet leaders. After periods of examination which rarely exceeded three months, all these men, with very few exceptions, pleaded guilty, and where they were actually brought before the courts they confirmed their confessions in public. They were all sentenced to long terms of forced labor in the concentration camps of the Far North or of the Central Asiatic desert districts.

They were all innocent.

The victims were accidental. In those days the G.P.U. operated in such a fashion that there was no probability that the arrested would really be enemies of the Soviet power rather than harmless citizens. But still further, the general atmosphere of fear created by Stalin's slogan "Vigilance!," the spy scare and the encouragement of denunciation crippled the activity of those whose official task it was to track down the real enemies of the state.

They were doubly innocent. Not one of them was guilty of spying; not one of them had betrayed his country to the Germans or to the Japanese; not one of them had planned or carried out any act of sabotage.

But perhaps they were guilty in the sense of Soviet public policy at the time while not being actually guilty of the crimes with which they were charged? Perhaps they really were conspirators, not against the Soviet power as such, but against the Party leaders and the Party regime? Perhaps they had attempted by underground methods to overthrow Stalin's **dictatorship** in the Party? Perhaps the dictator's secret police had nipped their conspiracy in the bud and then denounced them as counterrevolu-
tionaries* and agents of a foreign power in order to deprive them of that | people opposed to a revolution
general sympathy on which the enemies of **tyranny** can reckon at all times and in all countries?

SOURCE: *The Accused,* Chapter 1, by Alexander Weissberg, trans. by Edward Fitzgerald. Copyright © 1951 by Alexander Weissberg. Reprinted by permission of Simon & Schuster, Inc.

Nothing of the sort. The arrested men were not enemies of the **socialist revolution** but its most ardent* supporters. And the overwhelming major-   enthusiastic
ity of them were not even opponents of the dictator. Very few of them had
actually been in opposition, and even these had long since capitulated*   given up
and abandoned all illegal activity. The overwhelming majority had neither
belonged to the opposition nor sympathized with it. Many of them were
actually enthusiastic Stalinists who had vigorously opposed the opposition.
In short, the general political attitude of the arrested men was not one
whit* different from that of the millions who had been lucky enough to   little bit
escape.

The arrests were made indiscriminately. In the depths of their hearts
the victims certainly opposed the dictator, but even this carefully repressed feeling was shared with the great majority of the population, and
they never allowed it expression because they knew what an ill-considered
word could mean to them and their families. If this carefully repressed
feeling was the criterion for the arrests, then the G.P.U. arrested not eight
million too many, but 152 million too few. After the happenings of 1932
and 1933 the feelings of the people certainly turned against the dictator.
The peasants had not forgiven him the hunger years and the death by
starvation of millions of their fellows. The workers and intellectuals in the
towns had not forgiven him for stifling all liberty. But all these feelings
were repressed. The hunger years came to an end. The economic system
gradually recovered. And the Russian people began to hope that they
would regain their lost freedom. Men began to forget the bitter years and
to take pleasure in the progress of their country. This process of emotional
recuperation was interrupted in August, 1936. A new era opened up in the
development of the Soviet Union, the era of the Great Purge.

But liquidation of the politically conscious sections of Soviet society was
only the preliminary to happenings which were so fantastically senseless
that it is difficult to describe them — and still more difficult to persuade
Western minds to believe them. Hundreds of thousands of old revolutionaries and old members of the Bolshevik* Party had been arrested. The   communist
very foundations of Soviet life had been shaken. But ordinary people still
believed it was exclusively a conflict within the ranks of the ruling party.
Then in the second half of 1937 the character of the action changed. The
scale of the arrests increased enormously and extended to those who had
never been members of any political party. Day and night G.P.U. vans
raced through the streets of town and village, taking their victims from
their homes, factories, universities, laboratories, workshops, barracks and
Government offices. All walks of life were involved, and workmen, peasants, officials and professional men, artists and officers found themselves
together in the cells. All branches of the economic system were affected.
Officials of heavy industry, agriculture, education and the armed forces
were among the arrested. There were fifty republics and autonomous
districts in the Soviet Union with their separate governments, and about
five hundred People's Commissars. Very few of these Commissars* sur-   administrators

vived the storm. Not a single one of all the big Soviet undertakings retained its director or its leading engineers. New men took their places, but within a few weeks they too were arrested.

The arrest of Marshal Tukhachevsky and eight leading generals opened the prison gates to the officers corps. The commanders of all Russian military districts, the strategic units of the whole system, changed their commands for prison cells. Their successors joined them a few weeks later before they had even had time to settle down in their new commands. Within the space of a few months some military districts changed their commanders half a dozen times, until before long there were not enough generals left and colonels took over, only to be relieved in their turn by majors. In the end many regiments were commanded by lieutenants.

The purge in the higher reaches of the Party and the labor unions was complete. At the head of the Communist Party is its Central Committee, which then consisted of seventy-one members and sixty-one deputies. These men had proved their revolutionary loyalty on a score of occasions. They had been picked out of hundreds of thousands of their fellow Party members. Every day of their lives had been carefully examined by the control organs of the Party and by the G.P.U. And yet more than three-quarters of them were arrested as spies. The Politburo* of the Party, which consisted of ten members and five deputies, is an even narrower elite. It is the personal staff of the dictator, the actual government of the country. And yet at least five of these men fell victim to the G.P.U.

executive committee of the Communist party

Soviet cultural life was temporarily paralyzed and it never fully recovered. The control organs of the Party closely examined every new literary and scientific publication for "Trotskyist* contraband." An unhappy formulation was enough to seal the fate of its author. Many leading Soviet writers joined the masses in the concentration camps. Many of those who were spared stopped writing altogether for fear of suffering the same fate. Still others sought safety in writing only of the past and avoiding even the slightest reference to current affairs. Those who were totally unprincipled "fulfilled their social task," i.e., they wrote whatever the ruling group required of them. They turned their coats again and again, condemned today what they had held sacred yesterday, only to damn tomorrow what they praised today. The result was a deplorable decline in literary standards, and such books as were published were no longer products of imagination and talent but belletristic* comments on the decisions of the latest Party Congress. Ordinary people stopped reading them.

followers of Trotsky, who opposed Stalin

artistic but lacking informative content

Scientific work suffered greatly from the G.P.U. excesses. The Terror paralyzed every creative endeavor. During the construction period the Soviet Government had spared neither money nor energy to build up a great network of scientific institutions. The scientist was the favored child of Soviet society. But when the Great Purge came he was not exempt. Many leading scientists were arrested and their colleagues were so intimidated that they stopped their work on the urgent problems of the day and turned to mere routine work in which they could not go wrong.

The victims of the purge came from all the peoples of the Union, but the national minorities were singled out for special attention. In all big towns there were small minorities whose main stock lived elsewhere, perhaps even outside the frontiers. The Germans had their independent republic on the Volga, the Armenians theirs in Southern Caucasia, the Uzbeks theirs in Central Asia. The origins of the groups of Letts, Lithuanians, Finns, Greeks, Bulgarians, Poles, Persians, and Chinese lay outside the Soviet Union. Groups of these peoples had lived for hundreds of years scattered over Russian territory without ever becoming fully assimilated. When they lived together in agricultural colonies, like the Germans in the Southern Ukraine, they obstinately retained their old national customs and their way of life. Lenin's nationality policy not only gave the oppressed nationalities political independence in their homogeneous colonies, but it also gave cultural autonomy to the smaller groups scattered over the territory of the bigger nationalities. It gave them their own schools, their own clubs and their own national theatres in which they could hear pieces performed in their own tongue, and it ensured them equality before the law. In the first years of the revolution none other than Stalin was People's Commissar for Nationalities, and under Lenin's guidance he implemented this just and far-sighted policy which ended the everlasting nationality squabbles in Russia and won the oppressed peoples for the revolution. And now all these minorities were liquidated by Stalin's own order. The men were all arrested, the women were banished from European Russia to Asiatic Russia and the children were often carried off to be brought up as Russian orphans in the children's homes of the G.P.U.

A small colony of about six hundred Armenians lived in Kharkov. One day in the autumn of 1937 over three hundred of them were arrested. Within six weeks the rest followed. Most of them were illiterate or semiliterate shoeshine boys, cobblers* or petty blackmarketeers. For a long time they were unable to understand what had brought them into prison. The Letts and the Germans had preceded them, and the Greeks and Bulgarians (who were among the most skillful gardeners in the country) followed them. After that came Poles and Lithuanians, Finns and Estonians, Assyrians and Persians, Uzbeks and Chinese, and many other ethnic groups Europe has never heard of. It almost seemed as though the G.P.U. were determined to ensure the racial purity of Russia's towns by administrative action. All these people had to be spies, the G.P.U. insisted. Germans, Poles and Letts had to have spied for Hitler; Chinese, Koreans and Mongolians for Japan; while Armenians, Assyrians and Persians had to have spied for the British Intelligence Service. The G.P.U. was a stickler* for order. The fact that the G.P.U. insisted that the Chinese should have spied for Japan, the archenemy of their own country, was a national injustice about which my Chinese cellmates — they were poor laundrymen — complained bitterly. On the other hand, in the examiner's office the Armenians entered the service of the British without much protest.

The final organization to go through the mincing machine* was the

shoemakers

stubbornly insistent

chopping machine

G.P.U. itself. The examiners came into their own cells to keep their former victims company. Prisoners would often find themselves in the same cell with the examiner who had been in charge of their cases. And then all the old questions would be asked again. But the G.P.U. men had no idea what they had done or why they had done it. They had no more idea of the significance of the happenings than their victims. It was only years later, when the whole thing was over, that the more intelligent prisoners gradually pieced together a general picture of the happenings and sought by analyzing innumerable incidents, which taken on their own seemed insignificant, to discover the motives of the dictator in launching the Great Purge.

I was the companion of these people for three years in the prisons of the G.P.U. in Kharkov, Kiev and Moscow. During that time I was held in a dozen different cells, and innumerable batches of prisoners came and went before my eyes. I remained. I was a careful observer of the unique process going on around me and I made a note of the facts with the intention of one day giving them to the outside world. I talked to hundreds of prisoners, classified them in the general framework of the events and sought an explanation. At no time did I ever lose hope that one day I should be free again. With calm certainty I waited for the change which I knew must come.

We all waited for that change. We all knew that things could not go on in the same way much longer. At some time or other the disastrous process would have to be curbed unless the country was to go down to ruin. Someone would have to put a stop to the G.P.U. madness. At some time or other the dictator would have to recognize the full extent of the damage which was being done by the purge he had ordered. For two terrible years we waited, and the whole country waited with us. Then the change came.

On December 8, 1938, the organizer of Stalin's Great Purge, Nikolai Ivanovitch Yezhov, People's Commissar for Home Affairs and head of the G.P.U., was removed from his post. A few months later he disappeared from the Central Committee and then he was arrested. We were never able to discover whether he was shot or not. At the same time a unique trial took place in the Moldavian Republic, in the southwest corner of the vast Soviet Union. The leader of the local G.P.U. and four of his examiners were charged before a military court with having arrested innocent people and forced them to make false confessions under torture. The accused pleaded guilty. But they did not defend themselves by saying that they had only carried out orders; instead, they confessed that they had acted under the instructions of a counterrevolutionary organization. They were found guilty, sentenced to death and shot. These men had done no more than every G.P.U. man had been doing with impunity* for two years from   without punishment
Arkhangelsk to Odessa and from Vladivostok to the Polish frontier. The indictment and execution of these minor G.P.U. officials was Stalin's signal for change. The Great Purge was over.

M. Feeley's essay, an argument, makes a strong statement about the future of the family, according to Marxist ideology. Read the essay to identify her thesis and the abstract logical support she offers for it.

———————

Although both Marxism and democracy profess a belief in equality, women under both systems suffer oppression. The author of the following article takes a radical position and criticizes the American Communist party for its acceptance of the family as the basic social unit, a revisionist* Marxist doctrine. To attain the first step toward a pure socialist state, Feeley supports the abolition of the family unit.

compromising or modifying revolutionary theory

DIANNE FEELEY
"The Family"

KEY CONCEPTS

The term **CLASS SOCIETY** refers to any nonsocialist society in which economic distinctions between groups exist, such as middle class versus working class.

For a definition of **CAPITALISM**, see page 351.

For a definition of **SIBLING RIVALRY**, see Chapter 2, page 107.

In a **PATRIARCHAL FAMILY SYSTEM** power is held by the father or eldest male relative.

● Marxists maintain that the family is basically characterized by its function as an economic institution. As an economic unit, each individual family is responsible for providing for its own members — from the care of the young to the welfare of the old. This is a tremendous economic responsibility; for example, to raise a child adequately from infancy through college in the United States requires anywhere from $75,000 to $150,000 according to current estimates. Add in the hours of unpaid labor that parents, usually women, perform in the home for tasks that could better be performed socially — such as laundering clothes — and one can begin to understand the financial commitment exacted from each family.

In vetoing a national child-care bill, Nixon was quoted by the December 10, 1971 *New York Times* as expressing distaste for the "family weakening implications of the system it envisions. . . ." Of course, as society provides more of its resources outside the structure of the family, the family as an economic unit will weaken. But although this course would be beneficial to society, it runs counter to the ideas of **class society** and its cornerstone, private property. And that is why those who rule this country

SOURCE: Excerpts from "The Family" by Dianne Feeley, pp. 73–86, selected from *Feminism and Socialism*, edited by Linda Jenness. Copyright © 1972 by Pathfinder Press Inc. Reprinted by permission of Pathfinder Press.

have fought so hard against such steps as free education, social security, comprehensive medical care, welfare benefits, and now, against child-care centers. In fact, the ruling class tries to take back wherever possible the few concessions already won from it.

Capitalism rules through its various institutions, which mirror and reinforce the values of the dominant class. Such institutions — whether the various agencies of the state, the church, or the family — function to repress the individual, to tell people that they must accept their lot in life, to spread the myth that things can't be changed. The family's reactionary ideological function complements its economic one. Nixon recognized this when in his speech vetoing child-care centers he announced:

> . . . good public policy requires that we enhance rather than diminish both parental authority and parental involvement with children — particularly in those decisive early years when social attitudes and a conscience are formed and religious and moral principles are first inculcated.

The family transmits a reactionary ideology through its hierarchical structure, training individuals to be submissive to "authority." Despite the window dressing about the "partnership of marriage," the man is the "head of the house," while the woman and children are economic dependents. The man's economic role gives him a position of authority within the household while the role of the woman turns her into a domestic slave. Although fully 43 percent of all married women are also wage earners, their jobs are considered supplementary to what is considered their primary responsibilities, the maintenance of the household and the care of the children. Since the family is only able to carry out its socially assigned responsibilities by using the woman's unpaid labor in the home, her servitude is justified by cultural assumptions about a woman's "nature."

The family structure itself does not produce revolutionary fighters. Its authoritarian ideology is designed to teach passivity, not rebellion. Given the economic and political function of the family, one must conclude that the revolutionaries' first steps toward rebellion are most often taken against strong opposition of their families. Wilhelm Reich, author of *The Sexual Revolution* and *The Mass Psychology of Fascism,* noted:

> It is not by accident that the attitude of adolescents toward the existing social order, pro or contra, corresponds to their attitude, pro or contra, toward the family. Similarly, it is not by accident that conservative and reactionary youths, as a rule, are strongly attached to their families, while revolutionary youths have a negative attitude toward the family and detach themselves from it.

Youth, after all, are under the control of their parents, without the protection of citizenship. Currently, an estimated half-million teenagers run away from home every year in rebellion against the oppressive and authoritarian atmosphere. Youth detention centers are filled with teen-agers whose only "crime" has been their "unruliness" or their attempt to leave home. The despair, alienation, and resentment that young people feel is a logical reaction to the pressures of operating within a social unit whose binding tie is economic. The competition, **sibling rivalry**, and smoldering resentment within the family are at least as frequent as the appearance of love and harmony.

Parents are also the victims of the family system. They — and especially the mother — must take full responsibility for their children, with little free time of their own. They suffer psychologically when they are not able to fully provide for the needs of their children.

As a result of these economic and psychological pressures, people are forced to take out their frustrations on those who live closest to them, their family. Each year statistics reveal several hundred thousand cases of battered children. In reporting on the first two months of 1971, the New York Medical Examiner noted that the largest number of victims in the city's murders were wives killed by husbands. Next came husbands killed by wives. These two groups were followed by parents, children, aunts, uncles, cousins, and in-laws killing each other. Such information tends to confirm the contention that the **patriarchal family system** serves to alienate family members from each other, rather than to promote concern for each other. Many feminists have concluded that the oppression women suffer through the institution of the family is not simply a wart on the nose of an otherwise healthy organism. This oppression is the very essence of the family institution. As they examine their own childhoods, they can see how the young girl is programmed to accept her role within the family. From the time she is wrapped in a pink blanket and given a name that defines her sex, she is reared differently from young boys.

The culture chooses to regard boys and girls as two separate species, and the family is given the primary responsibility for beginning the tracking system. Studies by Robert J. Stoller, Jerome Kagan and John Money indicate that by the time the child is eighteen months old, the family has successfully taught gender identification.* The family sends out gender based signals in the way it handles the child, or in the kind of language that it uses. As the child grows older, the masculine-feminine models within the home, in books, and on TV, are so easily absorbed that one need only look at the typical five-year-old at play in the doll corner for proof that the basic role differentiation has been learned.

knowing what male or female behavior society expects

The family, as the primary unit of society, has constricted the young girl's mind and emotions as effectively as the pre-revolutionary Chinese family bound the feet of its infant girls. Why, one must ask, have so many women submitted to this grotesque distortion of themselves? Precisely because woman's role has been limited to that of wife and mother. One can't escape what is one's destiny. But further, the very oppression of women has been glamorized. From childhood, girls are fed fairy tales and cinderella myths. It can happen to you, too, these stories proclaim. For those who see the reality a little more clearly, the woman is presented as selfless and all-giving.

How many individual women can dare to refuse what society tells them

it is their nature to be? Only with the development of the women's liberation movement have women come to see that the frustration they feel is
shared by others as well.

Unequal pay for women, the lack of child-care centers, the burden of
housework, and male supremacy — all derive from the family system as
an institution of class society. The only way to lay the basis for the disappearance of the family as an economic institution is by eliminating these
conditions — through allowing women to be fully integrated into social
production, abolishing unequal pay, establishing free, twenty-four-hour
child-care centers for all, setting up low-cost, high quality laundry services,
take-out food services and dining facilities, and creating a mechanized
public housecleaning service. These facilities are the socialist alternative
to the family system.

Capitalist society has made tremendous technological advances. For
the first time, society has developed the forces necessary to produce the
food, clothing, housing, and care people need. Why should these be the
responsibility of the biological parents, and most particularly, the woman?
The backward, insular* home is not able to provide the varied resources   isolated
of the total society. Today the family unit is more and more at odds with
the patterns of social interaction at work and at school. Narrow family
loyalty, like loyalty to one's country, is constricting. An anachronism* that   something outdated;
forces its members to limp along as best they can, the family unit con-   throwback to another time
demns women to the most isolated world of household slavery.

But in a technologically advanced society, the possibilities for good
medical care, a decent and stimulating environment, a broad education,
and the chance to be more than a workhorse are within reach. As a
consequence, socialists call for taking over the burdens that have been
traditionally "women's work" by socializing them. High quality child-care
centers, staffed by people who enjoy being with children, would be a
welcome replacement for the haphazard and almost non-existent care of
today. Free communal dining areas serving attractive, nutritious food or
prepared take-home meals would insure a better standard of health, and
a well-paid housekeeping service, utilizing scientific equipment, will help
end the servitude of women. All of these services, controlled by those who
use them, will free women from economic dependency on men and free
children from their oppressed status within the home.

While the Communist Party in the United States justifies and glorifies
the oppressive institution of the family, the rise of the women's liberation
movement has begun a critical examination of one of society's most sacred
institutions. Women will learn the truth about the Russian Revolution —
in its initial gains, in its setbacks, and in the bureaucracy's betrayal of the
revolution. More and more women are discovering the scathing Marxist
critique of the family. They see the shallowness, selfishness, and authoritarian attitudes that the family system imposes on its members. Women
are beginning to rebel against their oppressive roles. Women, including
women in the USSR, can see that there are alternatives to the savagery

of the individual household. There is a massive, and international feminist movement on the rise, demanding control by women over their lives.

It is absurd to speak of "magically" abolishing the family. The family institution must be replaced by something better. It can disappear only when society as a whole takes over the functions of the family in providing for people's needs.

SECTION READING QUESTIONS

[1] The Reign of Terror and Stalin's "Great Purge" resulted from different political ideologies. In addition to the bloodletting, they share many characteristics. Detail these similarities.

[2] How do communist theorists justify repressive political measures? Refer to Lorwin, paragraph six.

[3] As Feeley argues the point, why is the family system a contradiction to classic Marxist theory? How does capitalism perpetuate the family system, and how does the family system support the capitalist system?

SECTION ESSAY ASSIGNMENTS

[1] Lorwin's essay details the Marxist critique of capitalism and the defense of communism. Using his positive statements and negative criticisms, explain the probable Marxist reaction to monarchy as a political system.

[2] Compare the ideals and practical shortcomings of both communism and democracy. Do their proposed solution to social problems compare or contrast?

[3] Pure Marxist theory advocates abolishing the family unit. Argue the benefits or drawbacks of this position.

The Imperialist Heritage

Read the following passage for a definition of "imperialism," marking the text for the essential points.

ROBIN W. WINKS
"Imperialism"

KEY CONCEPT

EXPANSIONISM is a political and economic policy of one nation's increasing control over another through a growing physical domination.

● Imperialism is difficult to define or explain. This is so because, like the terms "republican" and "conservative," the word may be used in both praise and denunciation of the practice or policy for which it is the merest shorthand label. Further, "imperialism" often is taken as a synonym for "colonialism," with which it has a close relationship but from which it nonetheless should be distinguished.

Imperialism often is applied to the outward thrust of European society — the carrying of political, economic, and moral practices into non-European areas — which began in the 15th century. Most commonly, it refers to European **expansionism** in the period following the American Revolution, when Britain and France, in particular, shifted their interest from the New World and from colonies of white settlement to Asia and, later, to Africa, to colonies already populated by yellow, brown, or black men. Less often, imperialism is applied to ancient and medieval empires — to the growth of Rome, of China, of Islam, of the Mongols, or of the Incas. Preferably, the term should be used to describe the expansion of all technologically advanced peoples at the expense of the technologically backward, so that it embraces, for example, modern Japanese or even Indonesian expansion.

However applied, imperialism must involve at least three factors: the expansion of an advanced society at the expense of a society thought to be backward; the development of economic and political expertise in an area with an indigenous* population, without the intent of substantial colonial settlement; and the application of the imperial nation's force to areas well removed geographically from its base — with all the inherent problems of strategy and international diplomacy.

native

It is undeniable that all forms of imperialism, while often bringing stability, sanitation, education, and improved communications to an area, have also forced one people to advance at a pace set by another people. All imperialism, therefore, including that pointing toward the ultimate independence of the colony, implied that only the superior power could name the stages through which the inferior had to pass and would judge the degree and speed of that passing. As Kenya's one-time economics minister Tom Mboya remarked, "Efficiency is the last refuge of the imperialist." One might always find a test that another might not pass.

The most pervasive legacy* of imperialism was the assumption that someone else had, by nature, the right to judge the progress of another people. For this reason, while many scholars might well judge the physical benefits of imperialism to have been high for both power and colony alike, many also would judge the psychological effects to have been harmful to both. Anti-imperialism usually turns on this point. Although the age of "imperialism" has passed, the word imperialism remains a battle cry because its effects have yet to be measured fully.

something inherited from an ancestor

SOURCE: "Imperialism" by Robin W. Winks from *The Encyclopedia Americana*. Published by Grolier Inc. Copyright © 1984. Reprinted by permission of the publisher.

READING QUESTIONS

[1] Summarize the definition of "imperialism."

[2] Explain Tom Mboya's remark that "efficiency is the last refuge of the imperialist." Is he endorsing or criticizing imperialism?

[3] In paragraph three, Winks points out that imperialism involves three factors. Using those criteria, decide whether the founding of America is an instance of imperialism, given the presence of the American Indians.

W.E.B. Dubois (1868–1963) was a famous Black writer and educator. He was an eloquent critic of colonialism and an articulate social critic.

W.E.B. DUBOIS
"The White Masters of the World"

KEY CONCEPTS

The **SCIENCE OF DARWIN** refers to his theory of evolution and the doctrine of Social Darwinism; see Chapter 3, pages 186–187.

REALISTIC literature depicts common people in daily situations, using great detail to make scenes seem true to life.

● What are the real causes back of the collapse of Europe in the twentieth century?

One of the chief causes which thus distorted the development of Europe was the African slave trade, and we have tried to rewrite its history and meaning and to make it occupy a much less important place in the world's history than it deserves.

The result of the African slave trade and slavery on the European mind and culture was to degrade the position of labor and the respect for humanity as such. Not, God knows, that the ancient world honored labor. With exceptions here and there, it despised, enslaved, and crucified human toil. But there were counter currents, and with the Renaissance in Europe — that new light with which Asia and Africa illuminated the Dark Ages of Europe — came new hope for mankind. A new religion of personal sacrifice had been building on five hundred years of the self-efface-ment* of Buddha before the birth of Christ, and the equalitarianism of Mohammed which followed six hundred years after Christ's birth. A new world, seeking birth in Europe, was also being discovered beyond the sunset.

With this new world came fatally the African slave trade and Negro slavery in the Americas. There were new cruelties, new hatreds of human

*being withdrawn or self-denying

SOURCE: "The White Masters of the World," in *The World and Africa* by W.E.B. Dubois. Copyright © 1965 by International Publishers, Inc. Reprinted by permission of International Publishers.

beings, and new degradations of human labor. The temptation to degrade human labor was made vaster and deeper by the incredible accumulation of wealth based on slave labor, by the boundless growth of greed, and by world-wide organization for new agricultural crops, new techniques in industry and world-wide trade.

Just as Europe lurched forward to a new realization of beauty, a new freedom of thought and religious belief, a new demand by laborers to choose their work and enjoy its fruit, uncurbed greed rose to seize and monopolize the uncounted treasure of the fruits of labor. Labor was degraded, humanity was despised, the theory of "race" arose. There came a new doctrine of universal labor: mankind were of two sorts — the superior and the inferior; the inferior toiled for the superior; and the superior were the real men, the inferior half men or less. Among the white lords of creation there were "lower classes" resembling the inferior darker folk. Where possible they were to be raised to equality with the master class. But no equality was possible or desirable for "darkies." In line with this conviction, the Christian Church, Catholic and Protestant, at first damned the heathen blacks with the "curse of Canaan,*" then held out hope of freedom through "conversion," and finally acquiesced* in a permanent status of human slavery.

Despite the fact that the nineteenth century saw an upsurge in the power of the laboring classes and a fight toward economic equality and political democracy, this movement and battle was made fiercer and less successful and lagged far behind the accumulation of wealth, because in popular opinion labor was fundamentally degrading and the just burden of inferior peoples. Luxury and plenty for the few and poverty for the many was looked upon as inevitable in the course of nature. In addition to this, it went without saying that the white people of Europe had a right to live upon the labor and property of the colored peoples of the world.

In order to establish the righteousness of this point of view, science and religion, government and industry, were wheeled into line. The word "Negro" was used for the first time in the world's history to tie color to race and blackness to slavery and degradation. The white race was pictured as "pure" and superior; the black race as dirty, stupid, and inevitably inferior; the yellow race as sharing, in deception and cowardice, much of this color inferiority; while mixture of races was considered the prime cause of degradation and failure in civilization. Everything great, everything fine, everything really successful in human culture, was white.

In order to prove this, even black people in India and Africa were labeled as "white" if they showed any trace of progress; and, on the other hand, any progress by colored people was attributed to some intermixture, ancient or modern, of white blood or some influence of white civilization.

This logical contradiction influenced and misled science. The same person declared the mulattoes* were inferior and warned against miscegenation,* and yet attributed the pre-eminence of a Dumas, a Frederick Douglass, a Booker Washington, to their white blood.

suffering racial bias

quietly accepted or went along with

persons of Caucasian and black ancestry / mixing of races

A system at first conscious and then unconscious of lying about history and distorting it to the disadvantage of the Negroids became so widespread that the history of Africa ceased to be taught, the color of Memnon* was forgotten, and every effort was made in archeology, history, and biography, in biology, psychology, and sociology, to prove the all but universal assumption that the color line had a scientific basis.

famous Ethiopian king in Greek mythology

Without the winking of an eye, printing, gunpowder, the smelting* of iron, the beginnings of social organization, not to mention political life and democracy, were attributed exclusively to the white race and to Nordic Europe. Religion sighed with relief when it could base its denial of the ethics of Christ and the brotherhood of men upon the **science of Darwin**, Gobineau, and Reisner.

melting and combining

Together with the idea of a Superior Race there grew up in Europe and America an astonishing ideal of wealth and luxury: the man of "independent" income who did not have to "work for a living," who could indulge his whims and fantasies, who was free from all compulsion of either ethics or hunger, became the hero of novels, of drama and of fairy tale. This wealth was built, in Africa especially, upon diamonds and gold, copper and tin, ivory and mahogany, palm oil and cocoa, seeds extracted and grown, beaten out of the blood-stained bodies of the natives, transported to Europe, processed by wage slaves who were not receiving, and as Ricardo assured them they could never receive, enough to become educated and healthy human beings, and then distributed among prostitutes and gamblers as well as among well-bred followers of art, literature, and drama.

Cities were built, ugly and horrible, with regions for the culture of crime, disease, and suffering, but characterized in popular myth and blindness by wide and beautiful avenues where the rich and fortunate lived, laughed, and drank tea. National heroes were created by lopping off* their sins and canonizing* their virtues, so that Gladstone had no connection with slavery, Chinese Gordon did not get drunk, William Pitt was a great patriot and not an international thief. Education was so arranged that the young learned not necessarily the truth, but that aspect and interpretation of the truth which the rulers of the world wished then to know and follow.

cutting off
making saintly

In other words, we had progress by poverty in the face of accumulating wealth, and that poverty was not simply the poverty of the slaves of Africa and the peons of Asia, but the poverty of the mass of workers in England, France, Germany and the United States. Art, in building, painting, and literature, became cynical and decadent. Literature became **realistic** and therefore pessimistic. Religion became organized in social clubs where well-bred people met in luxurious churches and gave alms to the poor. On Sunday they listened to sermons — "Blessed are the meek"; "Do unto others even as you would that others do unto you"; "If thine enemy smite* thee, turn the other cheek"; "It is more blessed to give than to receive" — listened and acted as though they had read, as in very truth they ought to have read — "Might is right"; "Do others before they do you"; "Kill your enemies or be killed"; "Make profits by any methods and at any cost

strike, hit

so long as you can escape the lenient law." This is a fair picture of the decadence of that Europe which led human civilization during the nineteenth century and looked unmoved on the writhing* of Asia and of Africa.

contorting in pain

It would be unfair to paint the total modern picture of Europe as decadent. There have been souls that revolted and voices that cried aloud. Men arraigned* poverty, ignorance, and disease as unnecessary. The public school and the ballot fought for uplift and freedom. Suffrage* for women and laborers and freedom for the Negro were extended. But this forward-looking vision had but partial and limited success. Race tyranny, aristocratic pretense, monopolized wealth, still continued to prevail and triumphed widely. The Church fled uptown to escape the poor and black. Jesus laughed — and wept.

accused
right to vote

The dawn of the twentieth century found white Europe master of the world and the white peoples almost universally recognized as the rulers for whose benefit the rest of the world existed. Never before in the history of civilization had self-worship of a people's accomplishment attained the heights that the worship of white Europe by Europeans reached.

Orwell's essay is a narrative and therefore has an implied thesis. Read the essay and clarify Orwell's position on life under colonial rule. Like Dubois' essay, Orwell's essay treats the effects of imperialism, this time from the oppressed people's point of view. Beginning with imperialism as the cause, use a graphic organizer to show imperialism's effect on a colonized people. Remember that in a narrative you may not find abstract categories but rather concrete examples that you will have to name yourself. You may find some of Dubois' terms helpful.

GEORGE ORWELL
"Marrakech"

● As the corpse went past the flies left the restaurant table in a cloud and rushed after it, but they came back a few minutes later.

The little crowd of mourners — all men and boys, no women — threaded their way across the market-place between the piles of pomegranates* and the taxis and the camels, wailing a short chant over and over again. What really appeals to the flies is that the corpses here are never put into coffins, they are merely wrapped in a piece of rag and carried on a rough wooden bier* on the shoulders of four friends. When the friends get to the burying-ground they hack an oblong hole a foot or two deep, dump the body in it and fling over it a little of the dried-up, lumpy earth, which is like broken brick. No gravestone, no name, no identifying mark of any kind. The burying-ground is merely a huge waste of hummocky*

tropical fruit

portable frame for carrying a coffin

like a low rounded hill

earth, like a derelict* building-lot. After a month or two no one can even   abandoned
be certain where his own relatives are buried.

When you walk through a town like this — two hundred thousand
inhabitants, of whom at least twenty thousand own literally nothing except the rags they stand up in — when you see how people live, and still
more how easily they die, it is always difficult to believe that you are
walking among human beings. All colonial empires are in reality founded
upon that fact. The people have brown faces — besides, there are so many
of them! Are they really the same flesh as yourself? Do they even have
names? Or are they merely a kind of undifferentiated brown stuff, about
as individual as bees or coral insects? They rise out of the earth, they sweat
and starve for a few years, and then they sink back into the nameless
mounds of the graveyard and nobody notices that they are gone. And even
the graves themselves soon fade back into the soil. Sometimes, out for a
walk, as you break your way through the prickly pear, you notice that it
is rather bumpy underfoot, and only a certain regularity in the bumps tells
you that you are walking over skeletons.

I was feeding one of the gazelles* in the public gardens.   deer-like animals

Gazelles are almost the only animals that look good to eat when they
are still alive, in fact, one can hardly look at their hindquarters without
thinking of mint sauce. The gazelle I was feeding seemed to know that this
thought was in my mind, for though it took the piece of bread I was
holding out it obviously did not like me. It nibbled rapidly at the bread,
then lowered its head and tried to butt me, then took another nibble and
then butted again. Probably its idea was that if it could drive me away the
bread would somehow remain hanging in mid-air.

An Arab navvy* working on the path nearby lowered his heavy hoe and   laborer
sidled towards us. He looked from the gazelle to the bread and from the
bread to the gazelle, with a sort of quiet amazement, as though he had
never seen anything quite like this before. Finally, he said shyly in French:

"I could eat some of that bread."

I tore off a piece and he stowed it gratefully in some secret place under
his rags. This man is an employee of the Municipality.

When you go through the Jewish quarters you gather some idea of what
the medieval ghettoes were probably like. Under their Moorish rulers the
Jews were only allowed to own land in certain restricted areas, and after
centuries of this kind of treatment they have ceased to bother about
overcrowding. Many of the streets are a good deal less than six feet wide,
the houses are completely windowless, and sore-eyed children cluster
everywhere in unbelievable numbers, like clouds of flies. Down the centre
of the street there is generally running a little river of urine.

In the bazaar huge families of Jews, all dressed in the long black robe
and little black skull-cap, are working in fly-infested booths that look like
caves. A carpenter sits cross-legged at a prehistoric lathe, turning chair-
legs at lightning speed. He works the lathe with a bow in his right hand
and guides the chisel with his left foot, and thanks to a lifetime of sitting

in this position, his left leg is warped out of shape. At his side his grandson, age six, is already starting simpler parts of the job.

I was just passing the coppersmiths' booths when somebody noticed that I was lighting a cigarette. Instantly, from the dark holes all round, there was a frenzied rush of Jews, many of them old grandfathers with flowing grey beards, all clamouring for a cigarette. Even a blind man somewhere at the back of one of the booths heard a rumour of cigarettes and came crawling out, groping in the air with his hand. In about a minute I had used up the whole packet. None of these people, I suppose, works less than twelve hours a day, and every one of them looks on a cigarette as more or less an impossible luxury.

As the Jews live in self-contained communities they follow the same trades as the Arabs, except for agriculture. Fruit-sellers, potters, silversmiths, blacksmiths, butchers, leather-workers, tailors, water-carriers, beggars, porters — whichever way you look you see nothing but Jews. As a matter of fact there are thirteen thousand of them, all living in the space of a few acres. A good job Hitler isn't here. Perhaps he is on his way, however. You hear the usual dark rumours about the Jews, not only from the Arabs but from the poorer Europeans.

"Yes, mon vieux,* they took my job away from me and gave it to a Jew.   old fellow
The Jews! They're the real rulers of this country, you know. They've got all the money. They control the banks, finance — everything."

"But," I said, "isn't it a fact that the average Jew is a labourer working for about a penny an hour?"

"Ah, that's only for show! They're all moneylenders really. They're cunning, the Jews."

In just the same way, a couple of hundred years ago, poor old women used to be burned for witchcraft when they could not even work enough magic to get themselves a square meal.

All people who work with their hands are partly invisible, and the more important the work they do, the less visible they are. Still, a white skin is always fairly conspicuous. In northern Europe, when you see a labourer ploughing a field, you probably give him a second glance. In a hot country, anywhere south of Gibraltar or east of Suez, the chances are that you don't even see him. I have noticed this again and again. In a tropical landscape one's eye takes in everything except the human beings. It takes in the dried-up soil, the prickly pear, the palm-tree and the distant mountain, but it always misses the peasant hoeing at his patch. He is the same colour as the earth, and a great deal less interesting to look at.

It is only because of this that the starved countries of Asia and Africa are accepted as tourist resorts. No one would think of running cheap trips to the Distressed areas. But where the human beings have brown skins their poverty is simply not noticed. What does Morocco mean to a Frenchman? An orange-grove or a job in government service. Or to an Englishman? Camels, castles, palm-trees, Foreign Legionnaires, brass trays and bandits. One could probably live here for years without noticing that for nine-tenths of the people the reality of life is an endless, back-breaking struggle to wring a little food out of an eroded soil.

Most of Morocco is so desolate that no wild animal bigger than a hare can live on it. Huge areas which were once covered with forest have turned into treeless waste where the soil is exactly like broken-up brick. Nevertheless a good deal of it is cultivated, with frightful labour. Everything is done by hand. Long lines of women, bent double like inverted capital Ls, work their way slowly across the fields, tearing up the prickly weeds with their hands, and the peasant gathering lucerne for fodder pulls it up stalk by stalk instead of reaping it, thus saving an inch or two on each stalk. The plough is a wretched wooden thing, so frail that one can easily carry it on one's shoulder, and fitted underneath with a rough iron spike which stirs the soil to a depth of about four inches. This is as much as the strength of the animals is equal to. It is usual to plow with a cow and a donkey yoked together. Two donkeys would not be quite strong enough, but on the other hand two cows would cost a little more to feed. The peasants possess no harrows,* they merely plough the soil several times over in different directions, finally leaving it in rough furrows, after which the whole field has to be shaped with hoes into small oblong patches, to conserve water. Along the edges of the fields channels are hacked out to a depth of thirty or forty feet to get at the tiny trickles which run through the subsoil.

large frame with discs used for plowing

Every afternoon a file of very old women passes down the road outside my house, each carrying a load of firewood. All of them are mummified with age and the sun, and all of them are tiny. It seems to be generally the case in primitive communities that the women, when they get beyond a certain age, shrink to the size of children. One day a poor old creature who could not have been more than four feet tall crept past me under a vast load of wood. I stopped her and put a five-sou piece (a little more than a farthing*) into her hand. She answered with a shrill wail, almost a scream, which was partly gratitude but mainly surprise. I suppose that from her point of view, by taking any notice of her, I seemed almost to be violating a law of nature. She accepted her status as an old woman, that is to say as a beast of burden. When a family is travelling it is quite usual to see a father and a grown-up son riding ahead on donkeys and an old woman following on foot, carrying the baggage.

British coin worth half a cent

But what is strange about these people is their invisibility. For several weeks, always at about the same time of day, the file of old women had hobbled past the house with their firewood, and though they had registered themselves on my eyeballs I cannot truly say that I had seen them. Firewood was passing — that was how I saw it. It was only that one day I happened to be walking behind them, and the curious up-and-down motion of a load of wood drew my attention to the human being underneath it. Then for the first time I noticed the poor old earth-coloured bodies, bodies reduced to bones and leathery skin, bent double under the crushing weight. Yet I suppose I had not been five minutes on Moroccan soil before I noticed the overloading of the donkeys and was infuriated by it. There is no question that the donkeys are damnably treated. The Moroccan donkey is hardly bigger than a St. Bernard dog, it carries a load which in the British army would be considered too much for a fifteen-hands* mule, and very often its pack-saddle is not taken off its back for weeks together. But what is peculiarly pitiful is that it is the most willing creature on earth, it follows its master like a dog and does not need either bridle or halter. After a dozen years of devoted work it suddenly drops dead, whereupon its master tips it into the ditch and the village dogs have torn its guts out before it is cold.

way of measuring a horse

This kind of thing makes one's blood boil, whereas — on the whole — the plight of the human beings does not. I am not commenting, merely pointing to a fact. People with brown skins are next door to invisible. Anyone can be sorry for the donkey with its galled* back, but it is generally owing to some kind of accident if one even notices the old woman under her load of sticks.

rubbed raw

As the storks flew northward the Negroes were marching southward — a long, dusty column, infantry, screw-gun batteries and then more infantry, four or five thousand men in all, winding up the road with a clumping of boots and a clatter of iron wheels.

They were Senegalese, the blackest Negroes in Africa, so black that sometimes it is difficult to see whereabouts on their necks the hair begins. Their splendid bodies were hidden in reach-me-down* khaki uniforms, their feet squashed into boots that looked like blocks of wood, and every tin hat seemed to be a couple of sizes too small. It was very hot and the men had marched a long way. They slumped under the weight of their packs and the curiously sensitive black faces were glistening with sweat.

hand-me-down

As they went past a tall, very young Negro turned and caught my eye. But the look he gave me was not in the least the kind of look you might expect. Not hostile, not contemptuous, not sullen, not even inquisitive. It was the shy, wide-eyed Negro look, which actually is a look of profound respect. I saw how it was. This wretched boy, who is a French citizen and has therefore been dragged from the forest to scrub floors and catch syphilis in garrison towns, actually has feelings of reverence before a white skin. He has been taught that the white race are his masters, and he still believes it.

But there is one thought which every white man (and in this connection it doesn't matter twopence if he calls himself a Socialist) thinks when he sees a black army marching past. "How much longer can we go on kidding these people? How long before they turn their guns in the other direction?"

It was curious, really. Every white man there has this thought stowed somewhere or other in his mind. I had it, so had the other onlookers, so had the officers on their sweating chargers and the white NCOs* marching in the ranks. It was a kind of secret which we all knew and were too clever to tell; only the Negroes didn't know it. And really it was almost

officers

like watching a flock of cattle to see the long column, a mile or two miles of armed men, flowing peacefully up the road, while the great white birds drifted over them in the opposite direction, glittering like scraps of paper.

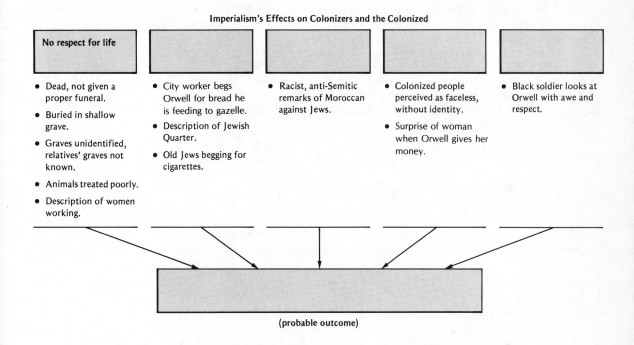

Imperialism's Effects on Colonizers and the Colonized

No respect for life			
• Dead, not given a proper funeral. • Buried in shallow grave. • Graves unidentified, relatives' graves not known. • Animals treated poorly. • Description of women working.	• City worker begs Orwell for bread he is feeding to gazelle. • Description of Jewish Quarter. • Old Jews begging for cigarettes.	• Racist, anti-Semitic remarks of Moroccan against Jews.	• Colonized people perceived as faceless, without identity. • Surprise of woman when Orwell gives her money.	• Black soldier looks at Orwell with awe and respect.

(probable outcome)

We've set up one possible graphic organizer for this piece. We've named some of the abstract headings for you, and we've listed some of the story's concrete examples. Complete the organizer, filling in the rest of the category headings.

SECTION READING QUESTIONS

[1] Explain how the slave trade has led to the moral collapse of Europe, according to Dubois.

[2] List the probable motives leading to a nation's imperialism.

[3] What are the daily personal effects of colonialism as Orwell describes them?

[4] Winks says that imperialism always involves "the expansion of an advanced society at the expense of a society thought to be backward." Explain the reasons for the colonizers' assumption that the colonizing are superior and the colonized are inferior.

SECTION ESSAY ASSIGNMENTS

[1] In paragraph three of Winks' essay, Winks lists three factors that define imperialism. Analyze the imperialistic nature of the European presence in Africa described in Dubois' essay.

[2] Both democracies and communist states have adopted imperialist policies. Develop a defense of/a rationale for imperialism from a democratic or communist point of view.

[3] You have studied several kinds of political oppression, sexism and racism being two major forms. Compare and contrast the attitude of the imperialistic oppressor to that of the sexist or racist. Consider also the effects of oppression in each case and the means available to the oppressed for fighting back.

Contemporary Terror

The author of the following essay analyzes the purposes, tactics, and effects of terrorism. Mark the text for these analytical passages.

BALJIT SINGH
"An Overview of Terrorism"

● Sigmund Freud has argued that civilization, with its institutional restraints and the repression of human nature, guarantees discontent. His vision of the human condition suggests that society must be continually prepared to accept change and expand human freedoms or must face many forms of resistance as an unavoidable reaction for its intransigence.*

refusal to compromise

The agents of change, however, are often victimized by society which tends to label them as traitors and treats their ideas and actions as dangerous threats to civilization itself. The most dangerous element in a situation of change is not that a resister is victimized or killed for his ideas or acts but that it is often done without recognizing it or saying so and is hidden behind the mask of a "penal code." Resistance and violence, therefore, may well have begun with Creation and may not end even on judgement day.

There is almost an infinite variety of violence of anti-social nature — homicide, acts of vandalism, arson, destructive rage, or other expressions of an essentially irrational urge to strike at someone or something. Political violence, on the other hand, occurs in acts designed to bring about social and political change both among and within nations.

Political violence may be grouped into two types: 1. conventional wars
and intervention, that is, those actions that are related to achieving national objectives and that essentially fall within the Napoleonic mode, and
2. unconventional, an unimaginative category that encompasses all varie-
ties of political warfare from subversion* to guerrilla warfare.

Political terrorism comprises only one type of violence activity sub-
sumed* under the general heading of unconventional warfare. Furthermore, the scope of political terrorism has expanded radically through
history. Perhaps the best known terrorists of yesteryear belonged to the
Arab world's "Society of the Assassins." The Assassins were founded some
900 years ago by the religious teacher Hassan Ibn Sabah. Their Arabic
name, Hashshasin, sprang from the terrorists' addiction to hashish. Because of their activities as killers, the word, assassination, came to mean
political murder. The Assassins were a religious-political group whose
power rested on the membership of fedawi (devoted ones) who killed at
the command of their religious leader, believing that killing the unright-
eous guaranteed their own salvation and assisted in overthrowing a corrupt order.

The Assassins remained a powerful force in the Arab world for 200
years and pitted their new weapon against their religious and political
opponents, the Turkish military forces and Sunni Islam. Ultimately, they
were destroyed by Mongol invaders, but two of their organizational practices — 1. popular agitation or their attempts to spread their beliefs among
the populace and 2. a strict code of secrecy among all members of the
organization — have an exceptionally modern ring.

Political terrorism as an instrument of power came of age during the
French Revolution of 1793–1794. Despite some indiscriminate killings
during the early phases of the Revolution, a policy of revolutionary terror
evolved clearly with the Jacobins. Robespierre, Saint-Just, and the Committee of Public Safety played a vital role in the organization and direction
of what came to be known as the Reign of Terror. As Fromkin has remarked:

> Robespierre had coerced a nation of 27 million people into accepting
> his dictatorship. His followers sent many thousands either to jail or to
> their deaths; one scholar's estimate is 40,000 deaths and 3,000,000
> arrests. Yet when retribution came and Robespierre and his group of
> supporters were executed, it turned out that in all there were only 22 of
> them.

By no means is this the entire story of political terror during the French
Revolution. The important point, however, is that a political group which
should have been weak when judged objectively could wield such dispro-
portionate amount of power. What made such a development possible can
be explained only by analyzing the phenomena of terror.

Terror incorporates two facets: 1. a state of fear or anxiety within an
individual or a group and 2. the tool that induces the state of fear. Thus,
terror entails that threat or use of symbolic violent acts aimed at influenc-

(margin notes)

undermining of a
government

included

ing political behavior. Despite its long history of use in many countries, political terror failed to score any significant successes after the French Revolution until 1921 when the British were forced to bow to the terrorist campaign in Ireland and granted that country independence under the terms of the Irish Treaty. The period between the Irish Treaty and the end of World War II saw little political terrorism, except as an adjunct* to   addition conventional warfare. The Germans, Russians, Yugoslavs, Japanese, French, British, and even Americans all engaged in some type of terrorist activity. The scope of it, however, was rather limited, and the objectives were well-defined.

Following World War II, political terrorism reemerged on the international scene. With notable exceptions in Cyprus and Algeria, it became one of the many tools used within the larger arena of nationalist movements for independence. From its minimal application in India to a substantial reliance upon it in Algeria, Cyprus, and Kenya, political terrorism encompassed a wide range of activities, including intimidation, abduction, sabotage, selective assassination, and indiscriminate killing.

During the 1960s, political terrorism appears to have entered into another phase. Perhaps the two most significant qualitative changes were: 1. its trans-national character and 2. its emergence as a self-sufficient strategy — that is, terrorists attempted to operate independently of the larger political arena. Several developments help explain this new direction.

The growth of political terrorism into a trans-national phenomena has been greatly facilitated through a revolution in communication — radio, satellite television, air travel, and tourism. Terrorist acts committed in the remotest parts of the world now receive instant coverage and their "propaganda by deed" is exploited to full advantage. The growth in international tourism has radically changed the composition of passengers aboard international airlines. Consequently, skyjackings emerged as tempting activities for contemporary political terrorists.

Terrorism's emergence as a self-sufficient tool to achieve political objectives is largely due to the vulnerability of our modern urban civilization. While Mao Tse Tung emphasized rural, peasant-based guerrilla warfare and thought in terms of an ultimate, armed, and open revolutionary conflict to attain victory, today's urban guerrillas view the modern city as the new battleground. Carlos Marighella in his Minimanual of the Urban Guerrilla exhibits considerable insight into the delicate nature and the interrelationship of vital services in our modern cities. He also provides a detailed list of terror tactics and their most efficient usage, including political kidnapping, selective assassination, bombing, hijackings, and bank robbery.

The strategies and tactics employed by political terrorists are generally directed at three groups: the populace, the regime* in power, and the   ruling system terrorist organization itself. The overall objectives of these strategies and tactics are to: 1. gain popular support, 2. disrupt and destroy the military and psychological strength of the regime, and 3. achieve internal stability and growth.

If we accept the premise that political terror is primarily aimed at the psyche* rather than at "military hardware" per se,* a carefully selected assassination of an "important but unpopular" public official may boost terrorists' morale, create sympathy among the populace, and provoke the regime to adopt repressive measures that further alienate the populace.

mind / by itself

These objectives are closely interrelated and are mutually reinforcing. Nascent* terrorist groups often attempt to accomplish multiple objectives through a single act. George Habash of the Popular Front for the Liberation of Palestine (P.F.L.P.) once remarked that "The main point is to select targets where success is 100% assured. . . . You should see how my people react to a successful operation! Spirits shoot sky-high." A successful operation therefore may also help achieve the long-term objective of gaining popular support.

just developing

Political terrorism essentially is propaganda by deed. Consequently, advertising the movement becomes an integral part of its tactics. The weak, who generally resort to terrorism as a weapon, have a great need for their cause to be widely noticed. Ramdane Abbane of the Algerian F.L.N. succinctly* summarized this tactic when he said:

concisely

> Is it better for our cause to kill ten of our enemies in a remote village where this will not cause comment, or to kill only one man in Algiers where the American press will get hold of the story the next day? . . . We must ensure that people learn about our struggle.

During the past few years the communication media has reported a wide variety of politically motivated terrorist acts designed both to gain publicity and to build organizational morale. The P.F.L.P.'s simultaneous skyjacking and subsequent destruction of four international airliners in September 1970, the Palestine Liberation Organization (P.L.O.) Commando's seizure of a Jewish high school at Maalot in May 1974 resulting in the death of two dozen children, and the death of some twenty innocent pedestrians in May 1974 when stolen cars packed with time bombs exploded in downtown Dublin, are but a few grim reminders of this tactic. However, to create a favorable image, such acts must be carefully targeted and efficiently executed; otherwise they may create an unfortunate first impression of the group and antagonize the populace. The so-called Symbionese Liberation Army's mindless abduction of Patricia Hearst followed by confused political rhetoric and material demands exemplifies the latter result.

Another important objective of political terrorism is the disorientation and psychological isolation of the individuals in the populace. The tactic of inducing* an atmosphere of fear and general nervousness is designed to detach the individual from his social context "whereby he has only himself upon whom to rely and cannot draw strength from his customary social supports." To create a disrupted psychological behavior through

bringing on

inducing a state of fear and anxiety among the populace, terrorists engage in random, intense, and unpredictable violent acts. These tactics create an atmosphere of ever-present danger to the public's physical safety and tend to undermine its confidence in the ability of the regime to maintain stability and order. When a regime continually fails to maintain order, the populace is forced to accept whatever protection, cohesion, or guarantees may be extended by the terrorists. In their search for stability and safety, the populace submits to a new authority structure that can alleviate their anxieties, as they did in Algeria, Cuba, and Northern Ireland. In such a situation, however, the terrorists' authority to govern is highly tenuous, and they must continually engage in acts of terror to remain in control, thereby repeatedly testing their resourcefulness. Since excessive acts of physical violence to induce fear and psychological disorientation can be both costly and often are counterproductive, they generally occur with heavy doses of propaganda, the main purpose of which is to break the bonds that exist between the populace and the incumbent* regime. Fear,   *ones in power* anxiety, and psychological disorientation among the populace greatly contribute to undermining a regime's authority and its ability for effective control.

The individual political terrorist, on the other hand, articulates* himself   *expresses* through group participation. Group acts enhance his sense of political purpose and direction, his dignity and identity. Individual consciousness is welded into a group ideology that provides needed social and political supports.

Most political terrorists themselves lead a life of uncertainty and strain. Power struggles, factional fights, ideological debates, strategy disputes and discipline problems are common within these clandestine* organizations.   *secret* The need for obedience to commands and conformity in the organization often requires enforcement action, generally the actual physical liquidation of wavering members. The Irish Republican Army and Black September, for instance, have consistently eliminated dissident* members. A   *those who disagree* similar fate also awaits enemy agents, reformers, and collaborators. The objective of all these acts is to demonstrate, both within and outside the group, the determination and the uncompromising stance of the leadership. In Algeria "executions of the traitors" by the F.L.N. far exceeded the number of French killed during the period of conflict.

The dominant forms of political terrorism today are but a reflection of the politics of our time. As the national independence movements were the natural products of colonialism, the contemporary political terrorists symbolize, often mistakenly, resistance against discrimination, exclusion, suppression, and abusive power and privilege all too manifest in social, economic, ethnic, cultural, and political spheres of society.

QUESTIONS FOR DISCUSSION AND WRITING

[1] Why should a terrorist organization engage in random violence against innocent citizens, possibly alienating those sympathetic to their cause? Explain the rationale for violence against an innocent population.

[2] The author states that terrorism underwent a change during the 1960s. Explain terrorism's modern characteristics.

[3] At the essay's end the author describes the psychological profile of a terrorist. What beliefs must a person hold for him/her to become a terrorist?

You will apply Singh's theoretical analysis of terrorism to this newspaper account of the terrorist bombing in Dublin, which Singh refers to on page 377.

RICHARD EDER
"23 Killed in Dublin Blast"

● At least 23 people were killed and about 80 were critically injured at the height of Dublin's rush hour tonight by bombs planted in three automobiles.

Shortly afterward, five people were killed and and more than 20 injured in a bombing in Monaghan, a small town 80 miles to the north.

The bombs, carefully calculated to kill as many people as possible, according to Ireland's Communications Minister, Connor Cruse O'Brian, caused more casualties than any other attack since the fighting over Northern Ireland began five years ago.

For the people of the Irish Republic, almost untouched by the troubles, the scenes of death and mutilation among the rush hour crowds of this pleasant and peaceful city brought the conflict suddenly and violently close.

Tonight the Irish Prime Minister, Liam Cosgrave, looking grim but collected, went on television to tell his people: "This will help to bring home to us here in this part of our island what the people in Northern Ireland have been suffering for five long years. Today's evil deeds will only serve to strengthen the resolve of those north and south who have been working for peace."

Neither Mr. Cosgrave nor any other official has indicated which side is suspected of planting the bombs, but there is a widespread if unproven conviction in Dublin that it was the work of Protestant extremists. This was bolstered by reports that at least two of the cars used were stolen from Protestant areas of Belfast.

A spokesman for the militant Provisional Irish Republican Army said that his organization had had nothing to do with the bombings and denounced them as "vile."

The bombs in Dublin went off just before 5:30 P.M., when crowds coming out of work were thickest on the sidewalks. The explosions were timed so closely that most witnesses thought there had been only one.

One was on Parnell Street, not far from the statue to Charles Stewart Parnell, a 19th century Irish hero. The second was on Talbot Street, a few blocks away. The third was farther off, on South Leinster Street on Dublin's south side.

The blasts, from bombs estimated to contain 200 to 300 pounds of gelignite* each, hurled bodies through shop windows and left one man crouched on South Leinster Street in flames. Dozens of cars were smashed.

a plastic explosive

More than half an hour later, as the Irish police were broadcasting a warning that "all points of the country are at risk," a bomb went off in Monaghan, a town near the Ulster border that has been the scene of considerable across-the-border armed activity. The bomb exploded in front of a pub, killing five persons and injuring more than 20.

On Parnell Street, Patrick Duffy was drinking in the Welcome Inn when the bomb went off outside. "I saw a red flash," he said later. "I thought the place was coming in on me. The cash register was blown off the counter."

Dominick O'Shea, the manager recalled: "Just before the bomb went off I saw a lady with a pram going by the door. Afterward we found the child in the cellar of the bar. I don't know how it got there."

Because it was Friday afternoon, people were doing their weekend shopping and the crowds were thicker than usual on the sidewalks. There was a bus strike in Dublin, and many workers who normally would have been out of the area were walking along slowly looking for taxis or lifts.

Almost all the deaths took place among the street crowds. Those inside shops were relatively unharmed, though one young man, staggering in tears down Talbot Street, had been with his wife inside a shoe store. She disappeared in the explosion.

On the corner of Talbot and Gardinier Streets a newsstand was blown into the air. Bodies nearby lay covered with torn and drifting newspapers. Two girls, window shopping further down Talbot Street, were blown through a window and were found with their bodies fused together by the blast.

Fire engines and ambulances, operating according to a plan devised after bombings in Dublin in December, 1972, and January, 1973, had killed three persons, arrived quickly and shuttled the wounded to hospitals. Fifteen persons had been killed instantly and eight more died in hospitals or on the way. About 80 persons were seriously injured.

Policemen struggled to hold back survivors looking desperately for an injured friend or relative. One man on Parnell Street picked up a dead baby, examined it, put it down and went on searching.

At the Temple Street Children's Hospital more than a dozen children were being treated. A 12-year-old boy, hit by a paving stone, sat white-faced waiting for his family to come for him. Justin McHugh, his left hand bandaged and waiting for a cut to be stitched, sat wordlessly with his parents.

"We used to live in Belfast, in the Ardoyne," his mother said. "Our house was blown to bits." Justin has stammered ever since. "Now," his mother said, "you see he doesn't talk at all."

The Blood-Transfusion Service sent out immediate calls for donors. The response was so great that the appeal was called off and Leeson Street, in front of its headquarters, was clogged with donors' cars.

The Cabinet met this evening after the explosions. No announcement was made, and Mr. Cosgrave, when he went on television afterward, confined himself to a brief message. Either he or one of his ministers is expected to hold a news conference tomorrow, when some of the hard questions about the implications of the attacks will come out.

The bombings took place just as Protestant militants* in Northern Ire-   activists who use violence
land have embarked on what seems to be building up into a climactic struggle. They are aiming their action against the moderate Protestant-Catholic coalition government and against plans by London and Dublin to set up a Council of All Ireland that will provide some link between north and south.

The fact that the bombs went off just as this was happening fortifies the belief here that Protestant extremists were responsible. Some spokesmen for paramilitary groups in the north have denied responsibility. But one of them, Sammy Smyth, of the Ulster Defense Association, was quoted as saying he was "happy" about the explosion.

SECTION READING QUESTIONS

[1] According to Singh's definition, what makes the Dublin bombing a terrorist act?

[2] Is Eder's report designed to inflame public opinion against the terrorists? Cite examples from the text that might particularly enrage or upset the reader.

WRITING SKILL: *Writing with Logical Connectors*

Logical connectors are the logical glue of a paragraph and essay. Identifying them as you read helps your comprehension, and using them as you write makes your ideas hang together from sentence to sentence, paragraph to paragraph. Without logical connectors, sentences and paragraphs may seem to be simple listings of unclearly related bits of information. If you write "Terrorists manipulate the media. They want to influence public opinion," you've only implicitly connected the two thoughts, and you end up relying on the reader to figure out how one sentence logically connects to the other. If, on the other hand, you write, "Terrorists manipulate the media because they want to influence public opinion," the formerly unconnected statements form a logical unit, and you send your audience a complete and clear message.

The words and expressions detailed earlier in this chapter under the reading skill "Using Logical Connectors to Improve Comprehension" are some commonly used connectors, listed according to logical purpose. When you use comparison or contrast to develop an idea, for example, you should draw on the list geared to that rhetorical purpose — "however," "unlike," "in contrast" — to signal your intention to your reader. When you've analyzed and argued a point, draw on words that show logical conclusion: "thus," therefore," "as a result." Clarify for yourself what rhetorical mode you're using and then tell the reader by including appropriate logical connectors.

Look at the following paragraph written by one of our students. In its original form, it has good individual thoughts but lacks logical coherence. The student revised it mainly for logical connection between ideas and sentences. By revising for logical connection, he was able to identify for himself some sections of the paragraph that needed rethinking. We've marked the logical connectors he included in the revised version of the paragraph. (This paragraph comes from an essay that analyzed the shortcomings of democracy.)

Original version:

The ample amount of freedom a democracy offers may lead to an anarchic society. People within the society may have many different views. They have freedom of speech, too. They may not accept the majority view and may reject it. Everyone is an individual and a widely accepted view may not exist. We have a society with many individuals with different views. Without a widely accepted view, we can't have a specific leader or government. Many different individuals will want to establish their view as the dominant one. They will lead us into an anarchy.

Revised version:

Because a democracy guarantees freedom of information, thought, and expression, it can ultimately lead to an anarchic society. People in a democracy may hold conflicting political views. Since they all have the freedom to think individually, they may not only reject the majority view but also deprecate it.In fact, due to everyone's individuality, a widely accepted view may never even come to exist. The outcome of such a situation might be a society made up of opposing voices. And because they may never reach agreement, the people may be unable to appoint a set leader or government. As a result, many different individuals may try to establish their views. In the end, democracy may lead to anarchy.

Using logical connectors when you write helps both you, the writer, and your audience, the reader, to follow a paragraph or essay's ideas more easily. Revising for logical connection can help you improve the thought of a paragraph or essay, just as noting logical connectors as you read can improve your comprehension. When you revise your written work, check it for coherence between its ideas, and revise your sentences and paragraphs for logical connection.

CHAPTER 5 ESSAY ASSIGNMENTS

[1] Often a nation's political system shapes its religious and artistic practices. Think about why a particular government might want to control its

citizens' beliefs and practices, and how the government could impose and enforce its views. Refer specifically to monarchy and communism to demonstrate motives for and means of political repression in religion and art. Which religious beliefs and works of art might such political systems find especially dangerous? Which might they actually promote?

[2] Both religion and politics are often sensitive and highly emotional issues. Some people and groups hold strong beliefs in the two areas, in some cases so strongly that they're willing to fight and die or kill others to defend them. Compare political commitment and religious fervor: What do people get from each, what psychological and social needs do they both fill, what kind of devotion do they exact? Contrast the purposes and practical effects of each. Refer to essays in Chapters 1–4.

[3] Choose three representative figures from the spheres of religion, art, and politics. Argue a case for the most influential figure. The real issue here is which sphere of experience has the greatest historical influence.

CHAPTER *6*

Philosophical Attitudes

INTRODUCTION

Many students assume that philosophy mainly involves studying the meaning of life. To some extent, that's true: it does examine issues such as why we exist, how we ought to behave, and what the world is. But it is also an academic discipline, meaning that it, like science, follows some method, employs evidence and logic, and attempts to be objective. In this chapter, we'll look at philosophy in both its definitions, as a set of attitudes toward life and as systems of thought.

Of all the subject areas covered in this book, philosophy is the most abstract, diverse, and interrelated with other fields. Its abstract nature makes philosophy difficult to understand in some cases, and its interconnections with religion, science, art, politics, and even history may make it seem a vast field that can be difficult to clarify.

No single historical continuum of philosophy exists, but most philosophical schools derive from or use earlier philosophical theories. The first article in this chapter, D. P. Dirk, "An Overview of Western Philosophy," sketches a broad historical and thematic overview of Western philosophy. It offers a sense of the philosophical identity of each historical period, from antiquity to the twentieth century, although it touches on only the most prominent philosophical thinkers and schools of each period. The rest of the chapter readings, instead of giving historically representative philosophical doctrines, present some major philosophical attitudes deriving from various periods and theories. Note that this chapter follows a different pattern from that of the preceding ones. By this point, *you should have a good sense of the Western historical ages. As you read about each philosophical school covered in this chapter, try to fit it into its particular historical time period.*

Stoicism, Epicureanism, cynicism, and mysticism all began as philosophies in ancient times, but as attitudes they surface in the thought of some modern writers and thinkers. Nihilism, aestheticism, and existentialism are mainly the products of modern thought. We can see these attitudes as reactions to or reflections of the realities of life at a specific time in history, just as we can see art or religious movements as expressions of an age's beliefs about human life and purpose. Following the theoretical discussion of each philosophy, you'll find readings that you can analyze according to the attitude it expresses. By applying theory to specific situations, you can develop the skill of identifying abstract structures in varied human experiences. In other words, you can name the abstract categories that underlie concrete details, which is an important and often-used academic skill. The readings that follow each philosophical piece are not intended to represent a specific philosophical outlook, although you'll be asked to interpret their content from the philosophical point of view you've just studied.

For some of the pieces we've suggested specific reading techniques. On others you'll have to devise a strategy that best suits your reading purposes. The writing assignments require you to draw on all the skills you've practiced so far: summary, definition, analysis, comparison, contrast, and argumentation.

Many of the key concepts in the following article should be familiar to you now, and many new ones are defined by the author. The article is organized chronologically and thematically; its content is dense, so you need to clarify by categorizing. A graphic organizer can help you map the concepts and their historical period. You should include as part of the organizer a brief description of each doctrine/theme/period.

D. P. DIRK
An Overview of Western Philosophy

● The philosophical schools of ancient Greece never ceased to be a significant influence in Western thought and culture. Throughout the history of Western philosophy one frequently finds that the great thinkers placed themselves in the thought-world of ancient Greece, making alliances with some figure or school and opposing others. At the same time, the advent of new ideas provided continuously varying textures to the great philosophies, often moving them further away from their ancient Greek roots. There have been many such new ideas over the past two millennia,* yet three stand out as most significant — religion, humanism, and scientific naturalism. With the ancient Greek schools as a base and these three ideas as themes of change, it is possible to sketch the story of Western philosophy from the time of the ancient world's end.

a thousand years

Religion, in particular Christianity, was quite clearly the most important catalyst for change in philosophical thought during the decline of the Roman Empire and for quite a long time afterwards. During this period the ancient Greek figure who enjoyed greatest prominence was Plato. What has turned out to be an extremely influential revival of his philosophy which we call Neoplatonism began in the third century A.D. The most important figure in this movement was Plotinus, (c. 203–296) a native of Egypt who had moved to Rome. The Neoplatonists adopted Platonic ideas like the exaltation of the rational aspect of humans and the denigration* of sensation and desire, while they embellished the doctrine of the Forms and that of the Platonic theory of creation. These latter doctrines were given a new shape in the theory of emanation. According to Plotinus, everything has its ultimate origin in The One, or the First Principle, which is simple, without parts, and which performs no actions. Everything ultimately emanates as rays from the sun, from The One, but it does so in successive stages. What emanates directly from The One is Nous or Mind, which is identical to the Platonic Forms. Psyche or Soul emanates from Nous, and everything else gradually emanates from Psyche. As in Plato, the soul's highest office is to contemplate the Forms, so for Plotinus, the role of the soul is to contemplate Nous. But there is a higher purpose to the contemplation of Nous, or the Forms: mystical, ecstatic, communion with The One.

criticism

One of philosophy's most important features in these early times was

Christianity's adaptation and transformation of Neoplatonism. For early Christian Platonists like St. Augustine (354–430), a native of North Africa, The One is roughly identified with God the Father, Nous with God the Son Jesus Christ, and Psyche with the Holy Spirit. Because Christ is consequently identified with the Forms, Christ for Augustine becomes the proper object of contemplation, the Teacher who in turn allows one to achieve communion with God. Despite these changes, Christian Platonism retains many of the themes of the older Platonisms. Possibly the most significant theme that it retains is what might be called the unifying idea of Platonism: human beings are radically dependent on something that transcends us for the good in life. Plato held that goodness in human life is ultimately to be attained through controlling sensation and desire, and living the life of reason through intellectual contemplation of the Forms which transcend us, which are higher than us. The Forms should be authorities in our lives. Augustine believes the same, except that he thinks the transcendent authority on whom we are radically dependent is the trinity God of Christianity.

Christian Platonism was the dominant philosophy in the West until the thirteenth century. In the twelfth and thirteenth centuries, however, the renewed availability of Aristotle's works occasioned a profound change in Western thought. Aristotle's works had up to this time been studied especially by Islamic philosophers, but they had not, for the most part, been translated into Latin, the intellectual language of the West. Around the time that these works became available, the University of Paris developed into the most important center for theological and philosophical studies in Europe. The most famous thinker to work there was Thomas Aquinas (1225–1274), who remains the most important philosopher and theologian for the Roman Catholic faith.

The thinkers at Paris created a synthesis of Christianity, Aristotelianism, and the Augustinian/Neoplatonic tradition that had prevailed until then. Aristotelian thought encouraged humanistic change. Aristotle, and consequently his medieval followers, did not share Plato's idea of human radical dependence on the transcendent nor Plato's exaltation of the rational at the expense of the sensation and desires. As did Aristotle, Aquinas thought that we apprehend truth through our sensation and reason working together, that the apprehension of truth is not to be achieved just through the purely rational contemplation of transcendent Forms of God. Analogously, the nature of the good for humans is not to be found by means of rational contemplation alone, but through human desire modified by reason. Thus, in contrast with the various Platonisms, truth and the good are not to be acquired through denying part of human nature and focusing on the transcendent, but through the use of all of the human faculties — reason, desire, and sensation. It should be emphasized, however, that the thinking of Aquinas and of other medieval Aristotelians was to a significant extent still influenced by Neoplatonism. Possibly the most significant example is their retention of the idea of a mystical communion with God, in the beatific* vision, at the close of life's spiritual journey.

showing blessedness

From this time until the sixteenth century, the history of Western philosophy is mainly that of the development and entrenchment* of medieval Aristotelianism. There are exceptions, however. For instance, Neoplatonism was quite popular in early Renaissance Italy and was an important influence on the art of that time and place. During the Renaissance, in the fifteenth century, Platonic currents made more significant gains. Within the Catholic Church there was a revival of Augustinian thought; this was an important catalyst of the Protestant Reformation. Both the Lutheran and the Calvinist branches of the Reformation leaned heavily on Augustinian ideas, such as radical human dependence on God for truth, the goodness and the idea of God as a transcendent authority (although these movements are much more complex than this characterization may indicate). Possibly a sign of the Platonic tendencies of Calvinists and Lutherans is their shunning of "sensual" adornment in their churches, their elimination of stained glass windows, paintings, and images from places of worship. In the Catholic Church itself, splits between Platonic and Aristotelian groups occurred, possibly the most famous of which was the division between the Jesuits, a religious order greatly influenced by Aquinas, and the Augustinian Jansenists in France.

establishment

The seventeenth and eighteenth centuries were a period in which European philosophy flourished. This period is called the period of modern philosophy, probably because this is what the early nineteenth-century philosopher Hegel called it. The Frenchman Rene Descartes (1596–1650) is usually thought of as the founder of modern philosophy. Descartes' thought, though influenced by the Aristotelian tradition, is more heavily Platonic, especially in that it exalts reason and denigrates sensation as faculties in the quest for truth. It is partly for this reason that Descartes is called a rationalist. One aspect of Descartes' philosophy that makes it revolutionary is its emphasis on science. Descartes not only lived during the scientific revolution, but also was one of its most important catalysts. In contrast to the Platonists, what Descartes focuses on as apprehensible by reason are the properties of bodies that are clearly geometrically describable, such as extension, shape, size, duration, and motion. These are the properties that figure into a mechanistic account of the physical universe. Nongeometrical properties, such as color, taste, and smell, are not apprehensible by reason and thus, following the Platonic tradition, are not real. The image for the physical universe which Descartes helped to bring to dominance in the seventeenth century was that of a clock, a complex machine, all of whose parts interact mechanically.

But there is more than mechanistic matter in Descartes' universe. Descartes is dualistic; he divides the universe into two kinds of substances — material and mental. Human beings have both a mind, a mental part, and a body, a material part. Thus, in an account of the entire universe there must appear two kinds of explanation — a mechanistic explanation for the material part, and a mentalistic explanation (an explanation that employs notions such as ideas, sensations, desire, reasons, and choices) for the mental part. John Locke (1632–1704), an English philosopher, basically accepted this dualistic framework. He differs from Descartes in an important way, however, in that he is less rationalistic than Descartes. Locke believes, like the Aristotelians, that sensory ideas are those from which one must proceed to acquire knowledge. This theory about knowledge is called <u>empiricism</u> and is often opposed to a rationalist theory of knowledge according to which reason can apprehend truth directly without having to rely on sensory ideas. Both Descartes and Locke were forerunners of the eighteenth century period called the Enlightenment. The seventeenth century scientific revolution culminated in the successes of Isaac Newton, who became the greatest intellectual hero of the eighteenth century. The Enlightenment was an age celebrating scientific and eventually moral reason as well. Old authorities like religion were no longer considered necessary. Religion, if maintained at all, was reinterpreted so as not to include the idea of radical dependence on a transcendent God. Infinite scientific and moral progress was thought to be possible, through human reason alone, liberated from any external tutelage.*   guidance

Many regard the Enlightenment thinker Immanuel Kant (1724–1804) as the most influential philosopher of the modern era. Kant tried to orchestrate an agreement between the various philosophical theories; for instance, he incorporated elements of both empiricism and rationalism into his system. At the same time he attempted to make room for science on the one side and, on the other, religion and humanistic morality, which according to many were being threatened by the idea that natural science explains everything. He did this by arguing that the realm of scientific explanation is only the realm of appearance and that behind the appearances, there is a realm of things in themselves about which science has nothing to say. We can't have any experience of things in themselves, but we can, we even must, have beliefs about this realm. In particular, we can hold the humanistic belief that we in ourselves are free and that God, even though he is not an object in the realm of science, exists as a thing-in-itself.

Kant had a tremendous influence on the thought of the nineteenth and twentieth centuries. To the one side, those who were interested in maintaining the integrity of religion and morality in the face of science often sought a Kantian solution to their problem. Conversely, those who were interested in a theory of science and knowledge also frequently looked to Kant's theory for guidance. Although Kant was an Enlightenment figure, he helped usher in a new period, Romanticism. The most important philosopher of the Romantic period was G.W.F. Hegel. His Romantic emphases included the importance of feeling and desire in acquiring knowledge of truth and the good, the cultural and historical factors that contribute to human nature, and the importance of seeing the history of thought and the history of the world as a single big picture with unifying themes.

It is important to note that Hegel's thought does not represent a complete break with the Enlightenment. For instance, two Enlightenment ideas that are central to Hegelian philosophy are the belief that everything can be rationally explained and the notion that the human race will progress as far as possible through reason.

Karl Marx (1818–1883)) was a German Jewish philosopher who received his philosophical education when Hegelianism was dominant. His own thought is indebted to Hegel and yet is very different. Among the cultural and historical factors that mold human beings, Marx thinks the economic to be the most important. Marx believes that progress to a communist classless society, from his point of view a utopia, is inevitable. This progress will take place through internal conflicts and inconsistencies, in all of the economic systems that precede communism. Marx's thought remains influential in the world today, and a large scholarly community continues to interpret and reformulate his ideas.

It is often thought that existentialism had its origins in the nineteenth century, and the Danish philosopher, Soren Kierkegaard (1813–1855), is sometimes said to be the first existentialist philosopher. In his writings, two major existentialist themes can be found; an emphasis on the role of the individual in the determination of meaning in life, and an emphasis on free choice. Kierkegaard is unlike many twentieth-century existentialists in that he thinks that the best life to choose is a Christian life of commitment to God. The German philosopher Nietzsche (1844–1900) is also often considered to be a forerunner of existentialism. In contrast to Kierkegaard, he attacked the Christian religion and Christian religious morality, saying that they cultivated weak aspects of human character like humility, pity, and repression of desire. Christian morality is a slave morality, he said. What people should try to develop is a morality of the superman Ubermensch, emphasizing the strength and nobility of human character.

The twentieth century is a century of great philosophical and intellectual variation. There are many divisions and differences among schools and individual thinkers. Yet, one can identify powerful thematic currents, one of the most prominent being scientific naturalism, which states that everything there is can be explained by natural science, by physics in particular. The logical positivists of the Vienna Circle developed this idea in the first half of the century. According to them, all talk of the transcendent, for instance, all talk about religion, is meaningless; all meaningful language must be linked to sensory experience. Logical positivism lost much of its influence after the first half of the century, but in its place came possibly more rigorous scientific naturalisms. For the scientific naturalists, the most difficult aspect of the universe to accommodate is the mental. An early attempt to naturalize theory of mind was behaviorism; after that failed, the computer soon became the scientific naturalist's favorite model of the mind.

Existentialism and phenomenology represent an important humanist current of thought in the twentieth century. Martin Heidegger and Jean-

Paul Sartre are possibly the two most famous philosophers of this tradition. Sartre believes that life in itself is meaningless, that there is no God, no eternal moral order to give it meaning. Meaning in life is achieved through individual free choice, through the choice of a project. The existentialists typically do think, however, that there are restrictions on the type of project that can make one's life meaningful. For Sartre the choice of project must not be in bad faith: one cannot be self-deceptive in one's choice. This allows Sartre to rule out projects that we would generally think of as evil from the realm of those that can give meaning to life.

Sartrian existentialism, like scientific naturalism, rejects the transcendentalism of Platonism and religion. Possibly the most unique aspect of twentieth-century thought is the fairly widespread acceptance of the loss of God and the loss of intellectual and moral standards that hold for everyone at all times. To be sure, not everyone in the present-day philosophical community rejects the transcendent in this way; there are still many religious thinkers and others who argue for theories that include transcendent intellectual and moral standards. The present age in philosophy is pluralistic;* to say that there is a single identifiable direction to modern thought would be a mistake.

more than one

QUESTIONS FOR DISCUSSION AND WRITING

[1] Platonism posits the existence of ideal forms and states that man's goal should be the contemplation and understanding of them. How did the Neoplatonists add to Platonic theory? How did the early Christian philosophers adapt and transform Neoplatonism for their purposes?

[2] What are the characteristics of "modern philosophy"?

[3] What is twentieth-century philosophy's most radical departure from almost all preceding theories and beliefs?

Ancient Philosopical Attitudes and Contemporary Situations

Stoicism remains a very common attitude toward life, though today we take it to mean self-containment and forbearance, the calm acceptance of things that happen to us and around us. The original Stoic attitude emphasized the relativity of virtue and the use of reason, as the article below details. Classical Latin authors kept the Stoic philosophy alive, mainly in literary works; Seneca is the most well known of the Roman Stoics. His philosophy perhaps attempted to add balance to the cruelty and decadence of Caligula's Rome, and may have helped Seneca himself carry out his own execution at Caligula's demand. Stoicism as a systematic philosophy no longer exists, but traces of it mark Christian thought, and as an attitude it colors some modern philosophies.

FRANCIS HENRY SANDBACH
"Stoicism"

● Philosophy is the pursuit of the correct way of life, and the center of gravity of stoicism lies in ethics. To be virtuous is necessarily good, to be vicious is bad. Everything other than virtue or vice is neither good nor bad, for nothing else necessarily affects the moral nature of man for good or bad. The usual objects of desire, health, wealth, honors, a spouse, children, etc., are not necessary to a virtuous life and often in fact lead to vice. They are therefore morally indifferent. So far the stoics reproduce the attitude of the cynics, but they realized that to stop there would make of virtue and vice names without any positive meaning; virtue cannot merely be a refusal to consider anything good except virtue or bad except vice. Those things which are morally indifferent and cannot be called good or bad are for the most part not absolutely indifferent, but possess relative values; these values are not permanent, but some things, e.g. health or friends, usually have "worth" and are "preferred," while others, e.g. sickness or friendlessness, usually have "unworth" and are, to imitate the somewhat uncouth stoic terminology, "demoted." Exceptional circumstances may change the usual values: disease might be preferred to health if one might thereby escape conscription* to fight in an unjust war. Such things, in themselves morally indifferent, constitute the field of action in which virtue and vice can be displayed; virtue consists in making the right choices, in recognizing the true values and attempting to secure them.

the draft

Man shares with other animals impulses that cause him to choose among the morally indifferent things; these impulses are directed not, as the Epicureans maintained, towards pleasure but towards self-preservation and preservation of the species. But man differs from animals in that he is rational, and his reason should shape his impulses and his choices. This means not only that he can take a long-term view of his own interests and so on occasion reject what appears immediately advantageous, but also that, knowing himself to be but a part of the universe, he should realize that the apparent interests of the part must be subordinate to the interests of the whole. Zeno defined the end at which man should aim as "life in accordance with nature": by "nature" he meant not only man's instincts which lead him to choose "the primarily natural," i.e., life, health, etc., but also the whole nature of the universe, which is identical with God. Every event in the whole universe is necessary, providential and due to the divine will. Since man cannot wholly foresee the future, he is bound sometimes to choose what his own nature suggests but what fate will prevent his attaining. "So long as the future is uncertain," wrote Chrysip-

SOURCE: "Stoicism" by Francis Henry Sandbach from *Chamber's Encyclopedia* (1964 ed.).

pus, "I shall cleave* to those things that best promise to give me what is   stick, keep
in accordance with nature; God himself has made me a creature that
chooses so. But if I knew that it was fated for me to fall ill today, I should
have an impulse to fall ill."

Actions chosen by man's reason are called "appropriate" actions; they
are actions which, though not necessarily right, can be reasonably defended. Some actions, e.g., to be brave, are always appropriate; others,
e.g., to take care of one's health, are usually so; others, e.g., to give away
one's possessions, only exceptionally so. If a man were completely wise, his
choices would always be right and evinced* as such by the course of events.   demonstrated clearly
His actions therefore would be not only "appropriate" but "correct" too.
Externally they might not differ from the merely appropriate, but in
essence they would be distinct, as being the product of knowledge and not
of guesswork.

Wickedness is closely associated with the passions; these arise from
mistaken judgments by which we suppose that indifferent things are good
or bad; on these judgments follow unreasonable and uncontrolled movements of the soul. There are four cardinal passions: desire, pleasure, fear
and sorrow. Desire arises when an object of choice is thought to be intrinsically* good; the true stoic knows that he does right in usually choosing, for   by its real nature
example, the course of action that promises to secure him his health, but
his goodness does not depend on his actually being healthy; therefore he
is emotionally detached, he neither desires to be well nor fears sickness,
neither feels glad in health nor sorrows if he falls ill. The passions are
wrong from their inception* in the false judgement and must therefore   beginning
be, not moderated, but extirpated* along with the falsehood. The wise   destroyed
man is not, however, without emotions; his correct judgments (that virtue
and vice are good and bad) lead to moderate movements of his soul; he
feels joy in his own virtue, repugnance* for ill-doing and a wish to help   disgust
his fellow-men to be good.

QUESTIONS FOR DISCUSSION AND WRITING

[1] Summarize the major Stoic beliefs. How is Stoicism a fatalistic*   believing that Fate
doctrine?   predetermines life

[2] Stoic philosophy is often characterized as one of self-containment,
endurance, and avoidance of pleasure. How correct is this common
perception?

[3] How might a Stoic react in the following situations?
a. The loss of a family member or other loved one
b. Severe financial problems
c. A terrorist attack

[4] In Chapter 5, you read a passage from Suetonius' "Gaius (Caligula)."
Given the often horrifying conditions of life under the mad Emperor, how

might a Stoic attitude have helped someone to make sense of his or her experience?

[5] "Every event in the whole universe is necessary, providential and due to the divine will" (page 393). This classical Stoic belief surfaces in later Christian thought, though at some times it is rejected, at others accepted. Is it a characteristic belief of medieval Christianity? Think about the material you read in Chapter 2: Tertullian, Venerable Bede, Dante, and others.

We're probably all familiar with "street people," people who have no established home and who live mainly on our city streets. Sharon Curtin interviewed one such woman. As you read her account, consider both the person and the situation from a Stoic's point of view. Which of Letty's beliefs and actions suggest a Stoic attitude? How would a Stoic react to the social condition of "street people"?

SHARON CURTIN
"Letty the Bag Lady"

● Letty the Bag Lady lived in a "Single Room Occupancy" hotel approved by the New York City welfare department and occupied by old losers, junkies, cockroaches and rats. Whenever she left her room — a tiny cubicle with a cot, a chair, a seven-year-old calendar and a window so filthy it blended with the unspeakable walls — she would pack all her valuables in two large shopping bags and carry them with her. If she didn't, everything would disappear when she left the hotel. Her "things" were also a burden. Everything she managed to possess was portable and had multiple uses (a shawl is more versatile than a sweater, and hats are no good at all, although she used to have lots of nice hats, she told me). Or was something she had to have, like the oversized leatherette covered Bible occupying a full quarter of one bag, in five-color-illustrated glory.

Letty was pretty crazy and she knew it. I think she even liked being old and frightening. "Scare babies in the womb, I do, this face of mine never was pretty, and time pulls and tugs it in all different directions like an old sweater sagging; and people stop and stare at me in the street. Stupid bastards, I say, someday you'll be old and ugly and hungry. And I'll be among the heavenly hosts, laughing my fool head off — at all of you with your wrinkle cremes and diet soda and wigs and paint. Dead before you live, I say, all of you are dead before you live. Ugly as sin but leastways I had a real life!"

So Letty and I agreed that she was pretty crazy, and she thought I was insane. Should be locked up for morbid interests in old rotten bodies. Tested for queer ideas, and stopped from bothering people. She couldn't

SOURCE: "Letty the Bag Lady" in *Nobody Ever Died of Old Age* by Sharon Curtin. Copyright © 1972 by Sharon Curtin. Reprinted by permission of Little Brown & Co.

accept my simple-minded well-I-just-want-to-know explanation. And if I made things more complicated she'd shake her head and call me a mind-bending fool.

The first day I saw Letty I had left my apartment in search of a "bag lady." I had seen these women around the city frequently, had spoken to a few. (Including one episode early in my New York experience when I offered, Wyoming Girl Scout fashion, to carry an old woman's bags. Her response was direct, sudden, and a true learning experience. She whomped me with her umbrella.) Sitting around the parks — Tompkins Square, upper Broadway, Union Square — had taught me more about these city vagabonds. As a group, few were eligible for social security. They had always been flotsam and jetsam, floating from place to place and from job to job — waitress, short order cook, sales clerk, stock boy, maid, mechanic, porter — all those jobs held by faceless people. The "bag ladies" were a special breed. They looked and acted and dressed strangely in some of the most determinedly conformist areas of the city. They frequented Fourteenth Street downtown, and the fancy shopping districts uptown. They seemed to like crowds but remained alone. They held long conversations with themselves, with telephone poles, with unexpected cracks in the sidewalk. They hung around lunch counters and cafeterias, and could remain impervious to the rudeness of a determined waitress and sit for hours clutching a coffee cup full of cold memories.

Letty was my representative bag lady. I had picked her up on the corner of Fourteenth and Third Avenue. She had the most suspicious face I had encountered; her entire body, in fact, was pulled forward in one large question mark. She was carrying a double plain brown shopping bag and a larger white bag ordering you to vote for some obscure man for some obscure office and we began talking about whether or not she was an unpaid advertisement. This immediately caught her interest, because part of her code was that nobody could ever cheat her to take advantage of her. I asked her if she would have lunch with me, and let me treat, as a matter of fact. After some hesitation and a few sharp glances over the top of her glasses (this is at high noon in a big city. I don't know what she was afraid of; I guess I just looked weird to her), Letty the Bag Lady let me come into her life. We had lunch that day, the next, and later the next week.

Being a bag lady was a full-time job. Take the problem of the hotels. You can't stay too long in any one of those welfare hotels, Letty told me, because the junkies figure out your routine, and when you get your checks, and you'll be robbed, even killed. So you have to move a lot. And every time you move, you have to make three trips to the welfare office to get them to approve the new place, even if it's just another cockroach-filled, rat-infested hole in the wall. During the last five years, Letty tried to move every two or three months. "You can't ever fix a place up, you know, really clean it or put up curtains and maybe a picture or two because you can't stay, can't get attached. Seems to me I been moving in and out of the same hotel room for the last seven years. Shit-colored floors, shit-colored walls, and the john down the hall a mile, with no lock on the door. Never any time to just settle in, or make a friend. You can't trust anyone, they'll say they're your friend today and tomorrow be pounding you on the head and stealing your things. Like I didn't want to talk to you, you didn't look like a junkie or a pross, but I was afraid you thought I was some rich eccentric, I walk around in these rags because I want to, and the bags are full of money. I been mugged so many times by kids thinking I had money. I may be plenty eccentric, but I sure ain't rich. Maybe I could get a sign or a button like all the kids wear that says I am just as poor as I look, and I look this way because I'm poor. I used to love pretty clothes, I'd save all my money to buy a dress to wear just once. And now I'm lucky to have a change of clothes for the change in seasons."

Most of our conversations took place standing in line. New York State had just changed the regulations governing Medicaid cards and Letty had to get a new card. That took two hours in line, one hour sitting in a large dank-smelling room, and two minutes with a social worker who never once looked up. Another time, her case worker at the welfare office sent Letty to try and get food stamps, and after standing in line for three hours she found out she didn't qualify because she didn't have cooking facilities in her room. "This is my social life," she said. "I run around the city and stand in line. You stand in line to see one of them fancy movies with people making love right in front of everybody and calling it art; I stand in line for medicine, for food, for glasses, for the cards to get pills, for the pills; I stand in line to see people who never see who I am; at hotel, sometimes I even have to stand in line to go to the john. When I die there'll probably be a line to get through the gate, and when I get up to the front of the line, somebody will push it closed and say, "Sorry. Come back after lunch." These agencies, I figure they have to make it as hard for you to get help as they can, so only really strong people or really stubborn people like me can survive. All the rest die. Standing in line."

Letty would talk and talk; sometimes, she didn't seem to know I was even there. She never remembered my name, and would give a little start of surprise whenever I said hers, as if it had been a long time since anyone had said "Letty." I don't think she thought of herself as a person, anymore, I think she had accepted the view that she was a welfare case, a Medicaid card, a nuisance in the bus depot in the winter time, a victim to any petty criminal, existing on about the same level as cockroaches.

Over and over again, she would ask me why I bothered to talk to her, and when I said that I just wanted to get to know a "bag lady" she would laugh and say, "Yeah. A bag lady. To you I'm a bag lady."

Letty didn't show for our next meeting. I walked the streets, seeing hundreds of old ladies like her, but no Letty. I didn't know where she lived, didn't even know her last name. There was no way to find her; I couldn't go to the police or any agency. She may have died in one of those weekly fires New York has in old hotels; she may have become so freaky she was locked up in Bellevue. Her body could have been in any one of the alleys on the lower East Side, or she could be buried in Potter's Field.

QUESTIONS FOR DISCUSSION AND WRITING

[1] Define the term "bag lady," using Letty's situation for illustration, and analyze how her attitudes toward possessions, daily survival, and life in the "big city" can be considered Stoic.

[2] Analyze the parts of Letty's lifestyle that would be endorsed by a Stoic and contrast the parts and beliefs that would be counter to Stoic philosophical beliefs.

[3] Street people, people who are homeless, jobless, without social connection, are sometimes held up as examples of how our government fails to provide for the poor. Others view street people as lazy, irresponsible sponges on society. Pursue one of these arguments from a Stoic point of view, using Letty the bag lady as a representative street person.

Ambition by its very nature seems an un-Stoic pursuit, for ambitious people must believe that some absolute good worth striving for exists. Joseph Epstein, in the essay below, presents an ethical argument on the value of ambition. Some of his points border on Stoic attitudes. Read the essay to determine the extent to which Epstein's argument agrees with Stoicism, and identify the points that can't be reconciled with it.

JOSEPH EPSTEIN
"The Virtues of Ambition"

● Ambition is one of those Rorschach* words: define it and you instantly reveal a great deal about yourself. Even that most neutral of works, Webster's, in its Seventh New Collegiate Edition, gives itself away, defining ambition first and foremost as "an ardent desire for rank, fame, or power." Ardent immediately assumes a heat incommensurate* with good sense and stability, and rank, fame, and power have come under fairly heavy attack for at least a century. One can, after all, be ambitious for the public good, for the alleviation of suffering, for the enlightenment of mankind, though there are some who say that these are precisely the ambitious people most to be distrusted.

Surely ambition is behind dreams of glory, of wealth, of love, of distinction, of accomplishment, of pleasure, of goodness. What life does with our dreams and expectations cannot, of course, be predicted. Some dreams, begun in selflessness, end in rancor; other dreams, begun in selfishness, end in large-heartedness. The unpredictability of the outcome of dreams is no reason to cease dreaming.

psychological personality test

not equal

To be sure, ambition, the sheer thing unalloyed* by some larger pur-   pure; unmixed
pose than merely clambering up, is never a pretty prospect to ponder. As
drunks have done to alcohol, the single-minded have done to ambition —
given it a bad name. Like a taste for alcohol, too, ambition does not always
allow for easy satiation.* Some people cannot handle it; it has brought grief   fulfillment, satisfaction
to others, and not merely the ambitious alone. Still, none of this seems
sufficient cause for driving ambition under the counter.

What is the worst that can be said — that has been said — about ambition? Here is a (surely) partial list:

To begin with, it, ambition, is often antisocial, and indeed is now out-
moded, belonging to an age when individualism was more valued and
useful than it is today. The person strongly imbued* with ambition ignores   colored with
the collectivity; socially detached, he is on his own and out for his own.
Individuality and ambition are firmly linked. The ambitious individual, far
from identifying himself and his fortunes with the group, wishes to rise
above it. The ambitious man or woman sees the world as a battle; rivalrous-
ness is his or her principal emotion: the world has limited prizes to offer,
and he or she is determined to get his or hers. Ambition is, moreover,
jesuitical;* it can argue those possessed by it into believing that what they   imposing one's values
want for themselves is good for everyone — that the satisfaction of their
own desires is best for the commonweal.* The truly ambitious believe that   everyone's well-being
it is a dog-eat-dog world, and they are distinguished by wanting to be the
dogs that do the eating.

From here it is but a short hop to believe that those who have achieved
the common goals of ambition — money, fame, power — have achieved
them through corruption of a greater or lesser degree, mostly a greater.
Thus all politicians in high places, thought to be ambitious, are understood
to be, ipso facto,* without moral scruples. How could they have such   by the facts themselves
scruples — a weighty burden in a high climb — and still have risen as they
have?

If ambition is to be well regarded, the rewards of ambition — wealth,
distinction, control over one's destiny — must be deemed worthy of the
sacrifices made on ambition's behalf. If the tradition of ambition is to have
vitality, it must be widely shared; and it especially must be esteemed by
people who are themselves admired, the educated not least among them.
The educated not least because, nowadays more than ever before, it is
they who have usurped the platforms of public discussion and wield the
power of the spoken and written word in newspapers, in magazines, on
television. In an odd way, it is the educated who have claimed to have
given up on ambition as an ideal. What is odd is that they have perhaps
most benefited from ambition — if not always their own then that of their
parents and grandparents. There is a heavy note of hypocrisy in this; a case
of closing the barn door after the horses have escaped — with the educated themselves astride them.

Certainly people do not seem less interested in success and its accoutre-
ments* now than formerly. Summer homes, European travel, BMWs —   accompanying objects
the locations, place names and name brands may change, but such items

do not seem less in demand today than a decade or two years ago. What has happened is that people cannot own up to their dreams, as easily and openly as once they could, lest they be thought pushing, acquisitive, vulgar. Instead we are treated to fine pharisaical* spectacles, which now more than ever seem in ample supply: the revolutionary lawyer quartered in the $250,000 Manhattan condominium; the critic of American materialism with a Southampton summer home; the publisher of radical books who takes his meals in three-star restaurants; the journalist advocating participatory democracy in all phases of life, whose own children are enrolled in private schools. For such people and many more perhaps not so egregious,* the proper formulation is, "Succeed at all costs but refrain from appearing ambitious."   *hypocritically self-righteous*   *very bad*

The attacks on ambition are many and come from various angles; its public defenders are few and unimpressive, where they are not extremely unattractive. As a result, the support for ambition as a healthy impulse, a quality to be admired and inculcated in the young, is probably lower than it has ever been in the United States. This does not mean that ambition is at an end. That people no longer feel its stirrings and promptings, but only that, no longer openly honored, it is less often openly professed. Consequences follow from this, of course, some of which are that ambition is driven underground, or made sly, or perverse. It can also be forced into vulgarity, as witness the blatant pratings of its contemporary promoters. Such, then, is the way things stand: on the left angry critics, on the right obtuse supporters, and in the middle, as usual, the majority of earnest people trying to get on in life.

Many people are naturally distrustful of ambition, feeling that it represents something intractable* in human nature. Thus John Dean entitled his book about his involvement in the Watergate affair during the Nixon administration *Blind Ambition,* as if ambition were to blame for his ignoble actions, and not the constellation of qualities that make up his rather shabby character. Ambition, it must once be underscored, is morally a two-sided street. Place next to John Dean Andrew Carnegie, who, among other philanthropic acts, bought the library of Lord Acton, at a time when Acton was in financial distress, and assigned its custodianship to Acton, who never was told who his benefactor was. Need much more be said on the subject than that, important though ambition is, there are some things that one must not sacrifice to it?   *hard to control*

But going at things the other way, sacrificing ambition so as to guard against its potential excesses, is to go at things wrongly. To discourage ambition is to discourage dreams of grandeur and greatness. All men and women are born, live, suffer, and die; what distinguishes us one from another is our dreams, whether they be dreams about worldly or unworldly things, and what we do to make them come about.

It may seem an exaggeration to say that ambition is the linchpin* of society, holding many of its disparate* elements together, but it is not an exaggeration by much. Remove ambition and the essential elements of   *important central part*   *different* society seem to fly apart. Ambition, as opposed to mere fantisizing about desires, implies work and discipline to achieve goals, personal and social, of a kind society cannot survive without. Ambition is intimately connected with family, for men and women not only work partly for their families; husbands and wives are often ambitious for each other, but harbor some of their most ardent ambitions for their children. Yet to have a family nowadays — with birth control readily available, and inflation a good economic argument against having children — is merely an expression of ambition in itself. Finally, though ambition was once the domain chiefly of monarchs and aristocrats, it has, in more recent times, increasingly become the domain of the middle classes. Ambition and futurity — a sense of building for tomorrow — are inextricable. Working, saving, planning — these, the daily aspects of ambition — have always been the distinguishing marks of a rising middle class. The attack against ambition is not incidentally an attack on the middle class and what it stands for. Like it or not, the middle class has done much of society's work in America; and it, the middle class, has from the beginning run on ambition.

It is not difficult to imagine a world shorn of ambition. It would probably be a kinder world: without demands, without abrasions, without disappointments. People would have time for reflection. Such work as they did would not be for themselves but for the collectivity. Competition would never enter in. Conflict would be eliminated, tension become a thing of the past. The stress of creation would be at an end. Art would no longer be troubling, but purely celebratory in its functions. The family would become superfluous as a social unit, with all its former power for bringing about neurosis drained away. Longevity would be increased, for fewer people would die of heart attack or stroke caused by tumultuous endeavor. Anxiety would be extinct. Time would stretch on and on, with ambition long departed from the human heart.

Oh, how unrelievedly boring life would be!

There is a strong view that holds that success is a myth, and ambition therefore a sham. Does this mean that success does not really exist? That achievement is at bottom empty? That the efforts of men and women are of no significance alongside the force of movements and events? Now not all success, obviously, is worth esteeming, or all ambition worth cultivating. Which are and which are not is something one soon enough learns on one's own. But even the most cynical secretly admit that success exists; that achievement counts for a great deal; and that the true myth is that the actions of men and women are useless. To believe otherwise is to take on a point of view that is likely to be deranging. It is, in its implications, to remove all motive for competence, interest in attainment, and regard for posterity.

We do not choose to be born. We do not choose our parents. We do not choose our historical epoch, the country of our birth or the immediate circumstances of our upbringing. We do not, most of us, choose to die; nor do we choose the time or conditions of our death. But within all this realm of choicelessness, we do choose how we shall live: courageously or in cowardice, honorably or dishonorably, with purpose or in drift. We decide what is important and what is trivial in life. We decide that what makes us significant is either what we do or what we refuse to do. But no matter how indifferent the universe may be to our choices and decisions, these choices and decisions are ours to make. We decide. We choose. And as we decide and choose, so are our lives formed. In the end, forming our own destiny is what ambition is about.

QUESTIONS FOR DISCUSSION AND WRITING

[1] Epstein analyzes the "virtues" of ambition. Analyze ambition's dangers or evils from a Stoic's perspective.

[2] To what extent would a Stoic endorse Epstein's defense of ambition? Is ambition ultimately compatible with Stoicism?

[3] Draw on Epstein's views and the arguments of Social Darwinism to develop a case against Stoicism as a philosophy of life.

_____

Like Stoicism, Epicureanism has also become obsolete as an actual philosophical school, but as an attitude it too has influenced post-classical philosophical thought. In common use, the term "Epicureanism" suggests an attitude of abandon and pleasure-seeking, and an "Epicurean" sometimes means a person of sophistication, sensuality, and refined taste. These modern connotations have very little to do with the ancient philosophy, which emphasized avoidance of pain, not indulgence in pleasure; balance, not excess. In the following passage, the author clarifies the original doctrine and distinguishes it from hedonism, the more accurate term for "pleasure-seeking."

GEORGE K. STRODACH
FROM *The Philosophy of Epicurus*

● The Epicurean theory of the good life — that is, the life that is simultaneously satisfying and moral — had two aspects, one negative and the other positive. Before one can enjoy the fruits of living, one must free oneself of certain crippling liabilities. These liabilities, specifically, are the fear of gods, the fear of death, and the fear of the torments of hell. Both Epicurus and Lucretius took great pains to neutralize these fears and to show that they were utterly groundless.

The positive aspect of Epicurus' ethical teaching is known as hedonism, from the Greek noun for "pleasure." His hedonism has two basic assumptions, both materialistic in character: (a) that moral good is the same as

SOURCE: From *The Philosophy of Epicurus* by George K. Strodach. Copyright © 1963 by Northwestern University Press. Reprinted by permission of Northwestern University Press.

pleasure, either physical or mental, since the experienceable range of pleasure is very wide and extends to more than one level; and (b) that moral evil is the same as pain, whether physical or mental.

Moral acts involve deliberate "choices" of possible concrete pleasures and "aversions," i.e., the deliberate avoidance of prospective pain. An act is moral if in the long run, all things considered, it produces in the agent a surplus of pleasure over pain; otherwise it is immoral. This working principle is applicable in literally thousands of cases of individual "choice and aversion" and can readily be illustrated by examples from our life today:

1. A student decides to cheat in a college exam in order to pull up his grade. Is this act moral by Epicurus' standards? (We will forget, for the time being, all other possible standards.) Suppose the student "gets away with it" this time. His "pleasure" is increased, but at the same time he is a little worried that he may have aroused the instructor's suspicions. Pleasure and pain are more or less evenly balanced, and it is impossible to tell in this instance whether the act is moral or immoral. Encouraged by his previous success, the same student decides to make a habit of cheating. Several alternatives are now possible: (a) The student may finally be detected and thrown out of college, in which case pain outweighs pleasure and the act is immoral. (b) The student may be clever and consistently avoid detection but at the same time experience a nagging anxiety, in which case pain probably is greater than pleasure and the act immoral. Or (c) he may consistently avoid detection and feel no qualms or anxiety whatever (and there seems to be plenty of this kind of student in the colleges today). In this case Epicurus would be forced to admit that the act is completely moral, since only pleasure is produced by it! However, the habit of successful cheating in college may well be carried over later into cheating in marriage and dishonesty in business, where the consequences may turn out to be more painful than pleasurable. The long-term effects of our habits are always pertinent judgments of moral and immoral.

2. A convivial* drinker who loves martinis may consume ten or more at a party and stay on his feet. Is this act moral by Epicurus' standards? We have to take into account not only the short-term effects (our friend enjoys himself hugely for two hours) but all the consequences. If he suffers no ill effects during the night or the next morning, the act is wholly pleasurable and therefore wholly moral; otherwise it is probably immoral, depending on the intensity of his hangover. (It was this sort of example that gave Epicureanism a "black eye." Epicurus himself would have frowned on it, since he disapproved, on principle, of sensuality, raw pleasure, and overindulgence. Nevertheless it is characteristic of "epicures" in every age and is certainly pertinent to modern living.)

liking food, drink, and good company

This basic description of hedonism still needs certain important qualifications in order to fit Epicurus' own meaning of the term, but for the time being it is obvious that: (1) The pleasure-pain principle is extremely flexible and can be used to uphold both conventional and unconventional moral values. (2) Hedonism proceeds to judge an act as moral or immoral not by the act itself, nor by any hard and fast rules of behavior, nor by the dictates* of reason, but by the experience it produces, specifically the feelings of pleasure and pain resulting from the act. For Epicurus believed that these feelings were the only true and natural foundation for an empirical ethics. "Every pleasure is a good by reason of its having a nature akin to our own, but not every pleasure is desirable. In like manner every state of pain is an evil, but not all pains are uniformly to be rejected. (3) The ethics of hedonism is relative and not absolute, and the morality of many acts is ambiguous, since the value of a given act does not depend on the a priori* character of the act itself but on its psychological consequences, which of course differ from person to person and from time to time.

orders or commands

theoretical

a. Pleasure is neutral or negative in meaning. The doctrine that pleasure is the highest ethical good lends itself immediately to serious misunderstanding because of the unfortunate ambiguity of the key term "pleasure." The Epicureans have been purposely misrepresented as sensualists and "high livers" by their rivals and detractors, both ancient and modern; for "pleasure" has been a "dirty word" in the eyes of many moralists and laymen in all periods of history. Actually the strict Epicurean sectarian* was rather ascetic* and even puritanical, both in teaching and in practice, and this fact is borne in on anyone who reads the surviving texts sympathetically. Epicurus regarded "pleasure" as the logical opposite of "pain"; in other words, for him pleasure meant nonpain, or the relative absence of pain in mind and body, i.e., both physical comfort or well-being and peace of mind. The good life, then, is quite simply one that daily and yearly conduces* to these ends. It is emphatically not a life of sensual enjoyments, excitement, competition, social prestige, and monetary success — all of which we in this country tend to believe constitute the good life, or what we call the "American way of life."

member of a group
strictly disciplined

leads

The good life for the Epicurean involved disciplining of the appetites, curtailment of desires and needs to the absolute minimum necessary for healthy living, detachment from most of the goals and values that are most highly regarded, and withdrawal from active participation in the life of the community, in the company of a few select friends — in a word, plain living and high thinking.

It will be seen from this that the Epicurean ideal is hardly what we mean by a life of pleasure or even a pleasant life. The conception of pleasure is wholly negative — the minimizing of all the pains of living, great and small, and of the three besetting fears, and the maximizing of inner peace, serenity, and well-being. The ideal, then, in its strict interpretation is practically Oriental — the achieving of a Buddha-like tranquillity — with the difference, of course, that the Epicurean asserted the full reality of the physical world and did not seek to be absorbed into a mystical nirvana.*

union with God

b. Hedonism emphasizes rational selection of pleasures and pains. Al-

though every pleasure is a natural good in itself and every pain a natural evil, not every pleasure is desirable, nor is every pain to be avoided. At this point a kind of prudential* process of calculation enters in, to pre-   careful
scribe the necessary conditions for a mature hedonism. Reasoning over-
lays the naivete* of nature with wisdom and tries to guide it aright. Thus   simplicity, unsophistication
if one knows beforehand that ten martinis will result in a hangover, it is the part of wisdom to take only five. By the same token if surgery is indicated, it should be undergone for the sake of future comfort and safety. And if the typical American wants to "succeed" today, he must be sensible and undergo the pains of four years of a college education. His present discomforts will pay handsome dividends in the future.

For example, if confronted with a choice between a simple and a luxurious diet, between obscurity and fame, between a life of contemplation and a life in politics, the strict Epicurean would always choose the less obvious value — simple diet, obscurity, and contemplation. He would much prefer to be a Thoreau or a Frost than board chairman of U.S. Steel or President of the United States. And indeed to choose the simple life has a certain wisdom, though from the American point of view it looks like sheer inertia, defeatism, or stupidity. It means choosing the way that very probably presents the fewest pains and disappointments rather than the way that seems to promise the largest number of positive satisfactions but contains many hidden frustrations, not to mention ulcers. The defensive and negative attitude to life was wisdom distilled from an age of troubles, when it did not pay to be either optimistic or enterprising.

c. Hedonism is deficient as a social ethic. The self-protective and individualistic attitude of Epicurus' hedonism prevented it from turning outward toward society at large and developing into a mature social ethic. True, it did emphasize friendship and the practice of gentleness and loving kindness among its members, and in fact actual religious fervor, in spreading the gospel of atomism* as a counterirritant to the phobias gen-   individualism
erated by popular religion. But these are not the same as a comprehensive theory for the welfare of society as a whole, such as John Stuart Mill developed in Victorian England from a hedonistic base. The altruistic*   selfless concern for others
spirit of Mill's "greatest good for the greatest number" (which, incidentally, included the British working classes) was far different from Epicurus' introverted escapism: "Withdraw from the world; avoid the pains and dangers of involvement; seek your own security and serenity."

From the egocentric question, What acts are likely to bring me pain or pleasure? it seems not too huge a step to the altruistic questions, What acts of mine are likely to bring pain or pleasure to others? Do I have a duty to increase the happiness of others as well as my own happiness? Can I be happy myself if I ignore the unhappiness of others around me? Am I ever to suppress and sacrifice my own pleasure for the good of others, including at times the community? A modern hedonist, with his social conscience enlarged by the impact of Mill and others, would be bound to seek answers to these questions and then go on to apply a new version of the pleasure-pain principle to pressing current problems such as anti-Semitism, racial discrimination, world overpopulations, thermonuclear war, the growth of Communism, and others. The student should let his mind play over the whole range of these social and political problems, consider their vast implications for human happiness and unhappiness, and then finally ask himself whether Epicurus' advice — "Seek your own security and peace of mind" — is adequate for our own age of troubles.

QUESTIONS FOR DISCUSSION AND WRITING

[1] Summarize the major Epicurean beliefs. Does the author finally approve or disapprove of Epicureanism as a moral philosophy?

[2] Define "hedonism" and explain how it is not an accurate reflection of Epicurean philosophy.

[3] Both Stoics and Epicureans seek balance in life and avoid extremes as a way of creating happiness. What beliefs show the differences in the two philosophies?

[4] Look at Strodach's short summary of Epicureanism in paragraph eight, page 404. Apply this definition to the beliefs of the following writers to determine to what extent Epicureanism can be found in their thought:

  a. Socrates, as Plato depicts him   g. Castiglione (Chapter 4)
     (see Chapter 1)   h. Montaigne (Chapter 4)
  b. Tertullian (Chapter 2)   i. Jackson Pollock (Chapter 4)
  c. Martin Luther (Chapter 2)   j. Robespierre (Chapter 5)
  d. Puritans (Chapter 2)   k. Malcolm X (Chapter 5)
  e. Emerson (Chapter 2)   l. Caligula (Chapter 5)
  f. Freud (Chapter 3)   m. Machiavelli (Chapter 5)

The following essay appeared in Newsweek *in the section titled "My Turn." Margaret Halsey is a contemporary voice who challenges the self-indulgence and lack of discipline that she believes permeates our culture. Read her essay from the point of view of a classical Epicurean: does her argument agree with the ancient Epicurean attitude?*

MARGARET HALSEY
"What's Wrong with 'Me, Me, Me'?"

● Tom Wolfe has christened today's young adults the "me" generation, and the 1970's — obsessed with things like consciousness expansion and

SOURCE: "What's Wrong with 'Me, Me, Me'?" by Margaret Halsey. Copyright ⓒ 1978 by *Newsweek* Magazine April 17, 1978, (91) p 25 Reprinted by permission of *Newsweek*.

self-awareness — have been described as the decade of the new narcissism. The cult of "I," in fact, has taken hold with the strength and impetus of a new religion. But the joker in the pack is that it is all based on a false idea.

The false idea is that inside every human being, however unprepossessing, there is a glorious, talented and overwhelmingly attractive personality. This personality — so runs the erroneous belief — will be revealed in all its splendor if the individual just forgets about courtesy, cooperativeness and consideration for others and proceeds to do exactly what he or she feels like doing.

Nonsense.

Inside each of us is a mess of unruly primitive impulses, and these can sometimes, under the strenuous self-discipline and dedication of art, result in notable creativity. But there is no such thing as a pure, crystalline and well-organized "native" personality, though a host of trendy human-potential groups trade on the mistaken assumption that there is. And backing up the human-potential industry is the advertising profession, which also encourages the idea of an Inner Wonderfulness that will be unveiled to a suddenly respectful world upon the purchase of this or that commodity.

However, an individual does not exist in a vacuum. A human being is not an isolated, independent thing-in-itself, but inevitably reflects the existence of others. The young adults of the "me" generation would never have lived to grow up if a great many parents, doctors, nurses, farmers, factory workers, teachers, policemen, firemen and legions of others had not ignored their human potential and made themselves do jobs they did not perhaps feel like doing in order to support the health and growth of children.

And yet, despite the indulgence of uninhibited expression, the "self" in self-awareness seems to cause many new narcissists and members of the "me" generation a lot of trouble. This trouble emerges in talk about "identity." We hear about the search for identity and a kind of distress called an identity crisis.

"I don't know who I am." How many bartenders and psychiatrists have stifled yawns on hearing that popular threnody* for the thousandth time!   sad, grieving song

But this sentence has no meaning unless spoken by an amnesia victim, because many of the people who say they do not know who they are actually do know. What such people really mean is that they are not satisfied with who they are. They feel themselves to be timid and colorless or to be in some way or other fault-ridden, but they have soaked up enough advertising and enough catch-penny ideas of self-improvement to believe in universal Inner Wonderfulness. So they turn their backs on their honest knowledge of themselves — which with patience and courage could start them on the road to genuine development — and embark on a quest for a will-o'-the-wisp called "identity."

But a search for identity is predestined to fail. Identity is not found, the way Pharoah's daughter found Moses in the bulrushes. Identity is built. It is built every day and every minute throughout the day. The myriad*   many choices, small and large, that human beings make all the time determine identity. The fatal weakness of the currently fashionable approach to personality is that the "self" of the self-awareness addicts, the self of Inner Wonderfulness, is static. Being perfect, it does not need to change. But genuine identity changes as one matures. If it does not, if the 40-year-old has an identity that was set in concrete at the age of 18, he or she is in trouble.

The idea of a universal Inner Wonderfulness that will be apparent to all beholders after a six-week course in self-expression is fantasy.

But how did this fantasy gain wide popular acceptance as a realizable fact?

Every society tries to produce a prevalent psychological type that will best serve its ends, and that type is always prone to certain emotional malfunctions. In early capitalism, which was a producing society, the ideal type was acquisitive, fanatically devoted to hard work and fiercely repressive of sex. The emotional malfunctions to which this type was liable were hysteria and obsession. Later capitalism, today's capitalism, is a consuming society, and the psychological type it strives to create, in order to build up the largest possible markets, is shallow, easily swayed and characterized much more by self-infatuation than self-respect. The emotional malfunction of this type is narcissism.

It will be argued that the cult of "I" has done some individuals a lot of good. But at whose expense? What about the people to whom these "healthy" egoists are rude or even abusive? What about the people over whom they ride roughshod*? What about the people they manipulate and   roughly, without respect exploit? And — the most important question of all — how good a preparation for inevitable old age and death is a deliberately cultivated self-love? The psychologists say that the full-blown classic narcissists lose all dignity and go mad with fright as they approach their final dissolution. Ten or fifteen years from now — when the young adults of the "me" generation hit middle age — will be the time to ask whether "self-awareness" really does people any good.

A long time ago, in a book called *Civilization and Its Discontents,* Freud pointed out that there is an unresolvable conflict between the human being's selfish, primitive, infantile impulses and the restraint he or she must impose on those impulses if a stable society is to be maintained. The "self" is not a handsome god or goddess waiting coyly to be revealed. On the contrary, its complexity, confusion and mystery have proved so difficult that throughout the ages men and women have talked gratefully about losing themselves. They lose the self in contemplating a great work of art, or in nature, or in scientific research, or in writing poetry, or in fashioning things with their hands or in projects that will benefit others rather than themselves.

The current glorification of self-love will turn out in the end to be a no-win proposition, because in questions of personality or "identity," what counts is not who you are, but what you do. "By their fruits, ye shall know them." And by their fruits, they shall know themselves.

QUESTIONS FOR DISCUSSION AND WRITING

[1] One tenet of the 1970s "me generation" was, "If it feels good, do it." To what extent is the "me generation's" attitude an Epicurean one? Are any major differences apparent?

[2] One can argue that the "me generation" is a modern form of Epicureanism, though perhaps in a debased form. Using the theory of Epicureanism in Strodach's article and Halsey's essay, analyze the probable impact which Epicureanism would have on a country's political life. Decide whether that impact would be mostly beneficial or harmful.

Gwendolyn Brooks, a well-known black American poet, wrote the following poem in 1959. Part of the poem's power comes from the skilled use of diction and meter to underline the poem's content, or meaning. It reflects the attitudes, beliefs, and values of the seven young pool players.

GWENDOLYN BROOKS,
"The Pool Players"

Seven at the Golden Shovel

We real cool. We
Left school. We

Lurk late. We
Strike straight. We

Sing sin. We
Thin gin. We

Jazz June. We
Die soon.

QUESTIONS FOR DISCUSSION AND WRITING

[1] What is the philosophical attitude expressed by the young pool players?

[2] Explain the pool players' attitude toward death as it is suggested in the final line. Does the author share their view?

[3] Does their view suggest an Epicurean or a hedonistic attitude?

SOURCE: From The World of Gwendolyn Brooks *by Gwendolyn Brooks. Copyright © 1959 by Gwendolyn Brooks. By Permission of Harper & Row Publishers, Inc.*

Cynicism was not a systematic philosophy in the same way as Stoicism or Epicureanism. Because indifference and apathy characterize the Cynic's attitude, none of the classical Cynics chose to write down any formal theory. The modern connotations of the term "cynic" imply an attitude of distrust and pessimism.

FARRAND SAYRE
FROM *The Greek Cynics*

● The object of Cynicism was happiness.

The Cynics sought happiness through freedom.The Cynic conception of freedom included freedom from desires, from fear, anger, grief and other emotions, from religious or moral control, from the authority of the city or state or public officials, from regard for public opinion and freedom also from the care of property, from confinement of any locality and from the care and support of wives and children.

As a result of the quest for freedom the Cynics were extreme individualists. The quest was personal and the Cynic had no loyalty to family, state, or race. He did not discriminate against any race or nationality because he did not favor any. "We should not give thanks to our parents — either because we were born, since creatures are generated by nature — nor on account of what we are for this results from a combination of elements. And there should be no gratitude for what comes by choice and purpose." "Whoever trusts us will remain single, those who do not trust us will rear children. And if the race of men should cease to exist, there would be as much cause for regret as there would be if the flies and wasps should pass away."

The Cynic virtues were the qualities through which freedom was attained. The description of Cynicism as "the pursuit of virtue" mistakes the means for the end and is misleading. The most important of these virtues was callousness, insensibility or apathy; it was associated with indifference. Julian is inconsistent in saying; "Apathy they (Cynics) regard as the end and aim," for apathy was only a means to the end. The Cynics regarded peace of mind as happiness or an essential element of it.

An important Cynic virtue was hardihood, ruggedness or endurance. It may be regarded as the physical form of apathy. It was said to have been attained or promoted by hardening exercises but with the later Cynics it came to mean the ability to endure the hardships incident to the Cynic form of life. The opposite of this virtue was softness, effeminacy or foppery, the vice most frequently and most severely denounced by the Cynics. Diogenes was said to have rolled in his earthenware jar over hot sand, to have walked barefooted over snow and to have embraced a bronze statue in freezing weather.

The Cynic principle of apathy naturally led to idleness, for if a Cynic engaged in any form of work he would thereby show a lack of apathy; and work under the control of an employer was inconsistent with the Cynic conception of freedom. Diogenes was quoted as saying; "Instead of useless toils men should choose such as nature recommends, whereby they might have lived happily." Chrysippus was credited with expressing many Cynic ideas and the following seems to be one of them; "What reason is there that he (the wise man) should provide a living? For if it be to support life, life itself is after all a thing indifferent. If it be for pleasure, pleasure too is a thing indifferent. While it be for virtue, virtue in itself is sufficient to constitute happiness. The modes of getting a livelihood are also ludicrous."

Poverty was an important Cynic virtue; it freed the Cynic from the care of property, from worry over losses and from confinement to any locality. It left him free to wander from city to city, from state to state and from country to country. It also partially explains the Cynic idleness, for he did not have the ordinary incentive to labor.

The Cynics did not express any sympathy for the poor for, in their opinion, the poor possessed the conditions of happiness, freedom and virtue. Neither were they friends, advocates and defenders of the poor, as they have sometimes been said to be. The possession of property was an encumbrance and a disadvantage. The Cynic's repudiation of possessions led them to ignore the property rights of other men and explains their thievery. One of the best known traditions of the Cynics was the following, which was attributed to Diogenes: "All things belong to the gods; the gods are friends of the wise and friends share all property in common; therefore all things are the property of the wise." The Cynics interpreted this to mean that they were free to take anything they wanted and could lay their hands on.

The Cynics held that laws were made by men no wiser than themselves and that customs and conventionalities differed in different countries and consequently had no validity. Their quest of freedom led them to disregard both; it also led them to disregard public opinion, reputation, honor and dishonor.

Disregard of honor and reputation was developed into open defiance of public opinion by shamelessness. "It was his (Diogenes) habit to do everything in public, the works of Demeter* and of Aphrodite* alike ... Behaving indecently in public, he wished it were as easy to banish hunger by rubbing the belly." Epictetus says: "He ought not to wish to hide anything that he does, and if he does, he is gone, he has lost the character of a Cynic, of a man who lives under the open sky, of a free man." Julian said, "The cities of Greece were averse to the excessive plainness and simplicity of the Cynic freedom of manner." Lucian represents a Cynic as saying: "Away with modesty, good nature and forbearance.* Wipe the blush from your cheek forever ... Scruple not to perform

*relieving oneself / making love

*self-restraint

the deeds of darkness in broad daylight. Select your love adventures with a view to public entertainment." Dio Chrysostom described Diogenes as terminating a discourse by squatting down and evacuating his bowels in the presence of his hearers. Epictetus said: "The present Cynics are dogs that wait at tables and in no respect imitate the Cynics of old, except perchance in breaking wind but in nothing else." This seems to have been a Cynic characteristic. Julian describes Diogenes as striking a youth with his staff for breaking wind in public and thus infringing on a Cynic prerogative. The Cynic displayed his hardihood, his apathy, his courage and his freedom by affronting and shocking public opinion.

The Cynics scoffed at the customs and conventionalities of others, but were rigid in observance of their own. The Cynic would not appear anywhere without his wallet, staff and cloak, which must invariably be worn, dirty and ragged and worn so as to leave the right shoulder bare. He never wore shoes and his hair and beard were long and unkempt.

Although the Cynics repudiated learning, they claimed to possess wisdom; for, did they not know the road to happiness? "To the man who said to him (Diogenes), 'You don't know anything, although you are a philosopher,' he replied, 'Even if I am but a pretender to wisdom, that in itself is philosophy'." This seems to be an admission that the Cynic claim to possess wisdom was not based on learning. The Cynics asserted their superior wisdom by criticising and denouncing other men. Epictetus describes the ordinary conduct of a Cynic of his time as follows; "I will take a little bag and a staff and I will go about and begin to beg and to abuse those whom I meet; and if I see any man plucking their hair out of his body, I will rebuke him, or if he has dressed his hair or if he walks about in purple." "They (Cynics) are full of empty boasting and if one of them grows a long beard and elevates his eyebrows and throws his cloak over his shoulder, and goes barefooted, he claims straightway wisdom and courage and virtue, and gives himself great airs, though he may not know his letters, nor, as the saying goes, how to swim. They despise everyone, and call the man of good family effeminate, the low born poor spirited, the handsome man a debauchee,* the ugly person simple minded, the rich covetous and the poor greedy." Lucian wrote: "As soon as I came to Elis, in going up by way of the gymnasium, I overheard a Cynic bawling out the usual street corner invocation to Virtue in a loud harsh voice and abusing every one without exception."

someone perverted or morally corrupt

The Cynics claimed that, as wise men, they formed a class having special privileges; among these privileges was the right to collect contributions from every one, the right to be supported by the community and the right to express themselves fully to every one at all times. "Being asked what was the most beautiful thing in the world, he (Diogenes) replied, 'Freedom of speech'."

The Cynic claim to wisdom raised a question as to how they attained it. Dio Chrysostom says that the wise man is "noble by nature" and "does not have to learn." Julian said that Cynicism, being a natural philosophy, "demands no special study whatever." Plutarch says: "The wise man, in a moment of time, changes from the lowest possible depravity to an unsurpassable state of virtue. . . . The man who was the very worst in the morning becomes the very best at evening. . . . He who was a worthless dolt when he fell asleep awakes wise." Plutarch ascribes this theory to the Stoics and he is opposing it, but he must have been referring to Cynics, for the Stoics did not class any one as wise, except Socrates and Antisthenes. For the Stoics, the wise man was an ideal. Wisdom was a goal which they might seek but could not attain.

The Cynics showed their apathy also in their attitude toward death and suicide. "Diogenes somewhere says that there is only one way to freedom and that is to die content." It is only in death that a man can attain complete apathy. "Diogenes, being asked who were the noblest men, said, 'Those despising wealth, learning, pleasure and life; esteeming above them poverty, ignorance, hardship and death'." An empty, idle and aimless life leads to nothing but boredom and misery; the Cynics may have shown some acknowledgment of this in their mention of suicide as "The open door." Teles says; "A man can readily find release, for just as he leaves an assembly, so he can take his departure from life — as Bion says 'to go out-doors'. . . Just as I depart from a banquet, so I will depart from life . . . I am not overly fond of life and I do not desire to prolong it, but as I am unable to find happiness, I will depart." Athenaeus quoted Antisthenes as saying, "Deliver your selves from life." Some of the stories of the death of Diogenes represented him as committing suicide.

The Cynics, in seeking freedom, rejected marriage and the rearing of children, repudiated obligations to parents and the state and avoided friendships. Lucian represents a Cynic as saying: "With wife and children and country you will not concern yourself. . . . You will live alone in the midst of the city, holding communion with no one, admitting neither friend nor guest, for such would undermine your power." "They (Cynics) consider friends as insincere and faithless, consequently they trust no one." Tertullian represents a Cynic as saying: "I have withdrawn from the populace. My only business is with myself . . . None is born for another, being destined to die for himself."

The Cynics were not Socratics; their teaching was opposed to that of Socrates in almost every respect. The distinction between right and wrong did not enter into Cynicism. It was the problem of the Cynic to seek happiness and freedom and the avoidance of what was wrong would restrict his freedom. The Stoics claimed succession from Socrates but we have no evidence that the Cynics did so.

The Cynics had no canon or authoritative writing, such as the Epicureans had in the writings of Epicurus. They were illiterates and wrote nothing. Julian said: "If the Cynics had composed treatises with any serious purposes . . . it would have been proper for my opponent to be guided by them . . . but nothing of that sort exists." Our knowledge of them is derived from observers who were not Cynics; but these were not all antagonistic. The Stoics regarded their origin as connected with that of the Cynics and were inclined to take a favorable view of them.

The Cynic traditions were oral and consisted for the most part of stories of Diogenes, a semi-mythical character; since little was known about him, he was a convenient vehicle on which the Cynics could locate stories expressing their ideas.

The Cynics attacked and ridiculed religion, philosophy, science, art, literature, love, friendship, good manners, loyalty to parents and the state, and even athletics — everything which tended to embellish and enrich human life, to give it significance and make it worth living. The callous amoralism expressed by the word "cynicism" reflects the impression made by them upon their contemporaries.

The Cynics did much to prepare the way for Christianity by destroying respect for existing religions, by ignoring distinctions of race and nationality and by instituting an order of wandering preachers claiming exceptional freedom of speech. Tertullian says that early Christian preachers adopted the Cynic cloak, and Augustine mentioned the club or staff as the only distinctive feature of the Cynics. Julian mentioned the similarity of methods of the Cynics and the Christians in their public discourses and their collections of contributions. Lucian describes cooperation between Cynics and Christians (Peregrinus). The early Christians worked side by side with Cynics for three hundred years and were to some extent influenced by them. We do not know of any early Christian arts, music, literature or sciences. Early Christian orders of priesthood accepted celibacy and poverty as virtues. The Dominicans explained their designation by saying that they were "Domini canes" (dogs of the Lord).

QUESTIONS FOR DISCUSSION AND WRITING

[1] Define Cynicism.

[2] To which philosophy is Cynicism most closely related in terms of beliefs, Stoicism or Epicureanism?

[3] Given your knowledge of street people from Curtin's "Letty the Bag Lady," can you consider the lifestyle of such individuals a form of modern-day cynicism?

[4] In Chapter 1, Aesop relates a legendary incident in the life of Diogenes. Review the fable (see pages 69–70) and explain how it illustrates Diogenes' Cynical attitude.

[5] In the final paragraph, Sayre states that Cynicism "did much to prepare the way for Christianity." In your own words, explain how Cynicism laid a foundation for the emerging Christian religion.

Eric Hoffer was a longshoreman as well as an author. His essay mixes practical experience and historical learning. This piece on the value of shame might be taken as an argument against the classical Cynic attitude. Read it as a refutation of indifference and apathy.

ERIC HOFFER
"Long Live Shame!"

● The ancient Hebrews were alone in envisioning a troubled paradise. The Garden of Eden was not an abode of bliss but a place tense with suspicion and anxiety. For no sooner did God, in a moment of divine recklessness, create man in His own image than He was filled with misgivings. There was no telling what a creature thus made would do next. So God placed Adam and Eve in the Garden of Eden where he could watch them.

It is plain that Adam and Eve were ill at ease under constant observation, and in their isolation from other living things. They welcomed the snake's visit, confided in him, and listened to his advice. The expulsion from Eden was not the terrible fall it has been made out to be. It was actually a liberation from the stifling confines of a celestial zoo.

Now, what concerns me is the puzzling fact that when Adam and Eve followed the snake's advice, disobeyed God's commandment, and ate from "the tree of the knowledge of good and evil" they felt not guilty but ashamed — ashamed of their nakedness.

What connection could there be between the knowledge of good and evil and the impulse to cover the genitals with fig leaves?

It is conceivable that, to begin with, good and evil were not individual but social concepts. That was good which preserved the group, and evil that which threatened its survival. Now, there is one dangerous threat that no society can escape: namely, the recurrent threat of disruption by juveniles as a young generation passes from boyhood to manhood.

Since sexual drives are at the core of the destructive impulses characteristic of the juvenile phase, sex is seen as a threat, hence an evil. The primeval association of sex with shame is, like the taboos of incest and endogamy,* part of an apparatus devised to defend a society against rape by juveniles inside the tribe.

marriage within a social class or group

Through the millennia societies acted as if their safety depended upon the preservation of female chastity. Sex, of course, is not the sole threat to the group. Cowardice, weakness, bad manners are as dangerous, and they, too, are associated with shame.

Shame, far more than guilt, involves an awareness by the individual of being watched and judged by the group. It is to be expected, therefore, that the more compact the group, the more pronounced the sense of shame. The member of a compact group carries the group within him, and never feels alone.

Anthropologists distinguish between the "shame culture" of primitive groups and "guilt culture" of advanced societies. Actually, what comes here in question is not social primitiveness but social compactness.

It is true that the most perfect examples of social compactness are found in primitive societies. But a technically advanced country like Japan, in which the individual is totally integrated with the group, has as strong a sense of shame as any primitive tribe.

By the same token one should expect the sense of shame to be blurred where socialization of the young becomes ineffectual, and social cohesion is weakened.

In this country at present the inability of adults to socialize their young has made it possible for juveniles to follow their bents, act on their impulses, and materialize their fantasies.

The result has been a youth culture flauntingly shameless. You see well-fed good-looking youngsters, obviously the sons and daughters of well-to-do parents, beg in the streets, pet in public, line up for pornographic movies, and vie* with each other in taking advantage of every opening for skullduggery* offered by a social system based on trust.

compete
deceitful acts

The disconcerting thing is that loss of shame is not confined to juveniles. The adult majority is not ashamed of its cowardice, workers are not ashamed of negligence, manufacturers of marketing shoddy products, and the rich of dodging taxes. We have become a shameless society.

Our intellectual mentors strive to infect us with a sense of guilt — about Vietnam, the Negro, the poor, pollution — and frown on shame as reactionary and repressive. But whether or not a sense of guilt will make us a better people, the loss of shame threatens our survival as a civilized society. For most of the acts we are ashamed of are not punishable by law, and civilized living depends upon the observance of unenforceable rules.

One also has the feeling that shame is more uniquely human than guilt. There is more fear in guilt than in shame, and animals know fear. We blanch with guilt as we do with fear, but we blush with shame.

The fabulous Greeks made of shame a goddess — Aidos. She was the source of dignity, decency, and good manners. An offense committed against Aidos was avenged by the goddess Nemesis. Long live shame!

QUESTIONS FOR DISCUSSION AND WRITING

[1] Analyze the major social values promoted by Hoffer and show how they are incompatible with the Cynic view of society and individual behavior.

[2] Would the concept of shame be compatible with Epicurean philosophy? Focus on the Epicurean sense of community and relative good and evil.

Herman Hesse was a twentieth-century German writer. His work has found particular popularity among young people, perhaps because his stories, novels, and poems often deal with the search for personal identity and a sense of meaning, and often bring in mystical and Eastern thought. Siddhartha and Steppenwolf *are among his most well-known works. In the following excerpt from* Steppenwolf, *Harry Haller, a middle-aged man who has cut himself off*

from his family and society, describes the discontent and sense of purposeless-
ness he finds in modern life. He calls himself the "Steppenwolf," German for
"wolf of the steppes," a figure that suggests alienation, unease with society,
and loneliness.

HERMAN HESSE
FROM *Steppenwolf*

● There is much to be said for contentment and painlessness, for these
bearable and submissive days, on which neither pain nor pleasure cry out,
on which everything only whispers and tiptoes around. But the worst of
it is that it is just this contentment that I cannot endure. After a short time
it fills me with irrepressible loathing and nausea. Then, in desperation, I
have to escape into other regions, if possible on the road to pleasure, or,
if that cannot be, on the road to pain. When I have neither pleasure nor
pain and have been breathing for awhile the lukewarm insipid* air of   lifeless
these so-called good and tolerable days, I feel so bad in my childish soul
that I smash my rusty lyre* of thanksgiving in the face of the slumbering   small harp-like instrument
god of contentment and would rather feel the most devilish pain burn in
me than this warmth of a well-heated room. A wild longing for strong
emotions and sensations seethes in me, a rage against this toneless, flat,
normal and sterile life. I have a mad impulse to smash something, a ware-
house perhaps, or a cathedral, or myself, to commit outrages, to pull off
the wigs of a few revered idols, to provide a few rebellious schoolboys with
the longed-for ticket to Hamburg, to seduce a little girl, or to stand one
or two representatives of the established order on their heads. For what
I always hated and detested and cursed above all things was this contentment, this healthiness and comfort, this carefully preserved optimism of
the middle classes, this fat and prosperous brood* of mediocrity.   family group

It was in such a mood then that I finished this not intolerable and very
ordinary day as dusk set in. I did not end it in a manner becoming a rather
ailing man and go to bed tempted by a hot water bottle. Instead I put on
my shoes ill-humoredly, discontented and disgusted with the little work
I had done, and went out into the dark and foggy streets to drink what men
according to an old convention call "a glass of wine," at the sign of the
Steel Helmet.

Thus I went down the steep stairs from my attic among strangers, those
smug and well-brushed stairs of a three-story house, let* as three flats* to   rented / apartments
highly respectable families. I don't know how it comes about, but I, the
homeless Steppenwolf, the solitary, the hater of life's petty conventions,
always take up my quarters in just such houses as this. It is an old sentimental weakness of mine. I live neither in palatial houses nor in those of the

humble poor, but instead and deliberately in these respectable and weari-
some and spotless middle class homes, which smell of turpentine and soap
and where there is a panic if you bang the door or come in with dirty shoes.
The love of this atmosphere comes, no doubt, from the days of my childhood, and a secret yearning I have for something homelike drives me,
though with little hope, to follow the same old stupid road. Then again,
I like the contrast between my lonely, loveless, hunted, and thoroughly
disorderly existence and this middle-class family-life. I like to breathe in
on the stairs this odor of quiet and order, of cleanliness and respectable
domesticity.* There is something in it that touches me in spite of my   homekeeping
hatred for all it stands for. I like to step across the threshold of my room
and leave it suddenly behind; to see, instead, cigar-ash and wine-bottles
among the heaped-up books and nothing but disorder and neglect; and
where everything — books, manuscript, thoughts — is marked and satu-
rated with the plight of lonely men, with the problem of existence and
with the yearning after a new orientation for an age that has lost its
bearings.

Once, I had lost my reputation and livelihood. I had had to forfeit the
esteem of those who before had touched their caps to me. Next, my family
life fell in ruins over night, when my wife, whose mind was disordered,
drove me from house and home. Love and confidence had changed all of
a sudden to hate and deadly enmity and the neighbors saw me go with
pitying scorn. It was then that my solitude had its beginning. Years of
hardship and bitterness went by. I had built up the ideal of a new life,
inspired by the asceticism* of the intellect. I had attained a certain seren-   sensual denial
ity and elevation of life once more, submitting myself to the practice of
abstract thought and to a rule of austere meditation. But this mold, too,
was broken and lost at one blow all its exalted and noble intent. A whirl
of travel drove me fresh over the earth; fresh sufferings were heaped up,
and fresh guilt. And every occasion when a mask was torn off, an ideal
broken, was preceded by this hateful vacancy and stillness, this deathly
constriction and loneliness and unrelatedness, this waste and empty hell
of lovelessness and despair, such as I had now to pass through once more.

It is true that every time my face was shattered in this way I had in the
end gained something, it could not be denied, some liberty, spiritual
growth and depth, but with it went an increased loneliness, an increasing
chill of severance* and estrangement. Looked at with the bourgeois eye,   being cut off
my life had been a continuous descent from one shattering to the next that
left me more remote at every step from all that was normal, permissible
and healthful. The passing years had stripped me of my calling, my family,
my home. I stood outside all social circles, alone, beloved by none, mis-
trusted by many, in unceasing and bitter conflict with public opinion and
morality; and though I lived in a bourgeois setting, I was all the same an
utter stranger to this world in all I thought and felt. Religion, country,
family, state all lost their value and meant nothing to me any more. The

pomposity* of the sciences, societies, and arts disgusted me. My views and   snobbishness
tastes and all that I thought, once the shining adornments of a gifted and
sought-after person, had run to seed in neglect and were looked at
askance.* Granting that I had in the course of all my painful transmuta-   with disapproval
tions made some invisible and unaccountable gain, I had had to pay dearly
for it; and at every turn my life was harsher, more difficult, lonely and
perilous. In truth, I had little cause to wish to continue in that way which
led on into ever thinner air, like the smoke in Nietzsche's autumn song.

Oh, yes, I had experienced all these changes and transmutations that
fate reserves for her difficult children, her most sensitive children. I knew
them only too well. I knew them well as a zealous* but unsuccessful   fanatically enthusiastic
sportsman knows the stands at a shoot; as an old gambler on the Exchange
knows each stage of speculation, the scoop, the weakening market, the
break and bankruptcy. Was I really to live through all this again? All this
torture, all this pressing need, all these glimpses into the paltriness* and   insignificance
worthlessness of my own self, the frightful dread lest I succumb, and the
fear of death. Wasn't it better and simpler to prevent a repetition of so
many sufferings and to quit the stage? Certainly, it was simpler and better.
Whatever the truth of all that was said in the little book on the Steppenwolf about "suicides," no one could forbid me the satisfaction of invoking
the aid of a gas-stove or a razor or revolver, and so sparing myself this
repetition of a process whose bitter agony I had to drink often enough,
surely, and to the bitter end. No, in all conscience, there was no power in
the world that could prevail with me to go through the mortal terror of
another encounter with myself, to face another reorganization, a new
incarnation, when at the end of the road there was no peace or quiet —
but forever destroying the self in order to renew the self. Let suicide be
as stupid, cowardly, shabby as you please, call it an infamous and ignominious* escape; still, any escape, even the most ignominious, from this tread-   shameful
mill of suffering was the only thing to wish for. No stage was left for the
noble and heroic heart. Nothing was left but the simple choice between
a slight and swift pang and an unthinkable, a devouring and endless suffering. I had played Don Quixote often enough in my difficult, crazed life,
had put honor before comfort, and heroism before reason. There was an
end of it!

QUESTIONS FOR DISCUSSION AND WRITING

[1] Harry Haller laments the conditions of his life; a Cynic, however, might
say that Harry's experiences confirm Cynic perceptions and values. Analyze
those parts of Harry's life and feelings that a Cynic might endorse. Would
the Cynics ultimately claim him as one of their own?

[2] Contrast Harry Haller's view of social conventions with those expressed
by Eric Hoffer in "Long Live Shame!" Which Cynic precepts might support
Haller's view over Hoffer's?

Like some of the other philosophies discussed in this chapter, mysticism was never developed as systematic thought; in fact, "thought" may be alien to the mystical attitude or experience insofar as "thought" names an analytical process. One possible way to define mysticism is as an intuitive sense of truth or God, a sense of oneness with a higher being, and direct experience or knowledge of the divine world or life force. Mysticism can be found in all major religions, although the basic concept can't be tied to a particular set of beliefs, nor can mysticism as a whole be restricted to religious experience. In Star Wars, *Luke Skywalker learns to use "the force" through "mystical" discipline. Some of the incredible power demonstrated by martial arts masters has been attributed to a similar inner discipline and spiritual connection.*

MARGARET SMITH
"The Nature and Meaning of Mysticism"

● The word "Mysticism" itself comes down to us from the Greeks and is derived from a root meaning "to close." The mystic was one who had been initiated into the esoteric* knowledge of Divine things, and upon whom   secret
was laid the necessity of keeping silence concerning his sacred knowledge. The term "mystical," then, might be applied to any secret cult revealed only to the initiated. The philosophers took over the word from the priests and applied it to their own speculative doctrines and thence it passed over into the Christian Church, which held itself to be a body of initiates into a truth not possessed by mankind at large. The derivation of the word was later held to give it the meaning of closing the mind to the influence of all external things, so that it might be withdrawn into itself, and so be fitted to receive the Divine Illumination.

But the real meaning of the word, as we use it now, represents something much wider than its derivation. That for which it stands is a tendency not limited to the Greeks, either priests or philosophers, nor bounded by the far-reaching comprehensiveness of the Christian Church. It denotes something which is to be found, in a highly developed state, in the early religious doctrines of the East; in the Vedic* literature; in Bud-   ancient Hindu religious
dhism both in India and in China; in a form strangely attractive, consider-   writing
ing the apparently barren soil in which this flower has bloomed, in Sufism, the mysticism of Islam, which has spread itself and taken firm root in Persia, Turkey and India as well as in Arab lands; in Judaism, again an unpromising environment to all appearances; and finally, as we have seen, in Greece and in the West.

"There is hardly any soil, be it ever so barren, where Mysticism will not strike root; hardly any creed, however formal, round which it will not twine itself. It is, indeed, the eternal cry of the human soul for rest; the

SOURCE: "The Nature and Meaning of Mysticism," in *An Introduction to the History of Mysticism* by Margaret Smith. Copyright © 1977 by Society for Promoting Christian Knowledge. Reprinted by permission of Sheldon Press.

insatiable longing of a being wherein infinite ideals are fettered* and cramped by a miserable actuality; and so long as man is less than an angel and more than a beast, this cry will not for a moment fail to make itself heard. Wonderfully uniform, too, is its tenor: in all ages, in all countries, in all creeds, whether it come from the Brahmin* sage, the Persian poet, or the Christian quietist,* it is in essence an enunciation more or less clear, more or less eloquent, of the aspiration of the soul to cease altogether from self and to be at one with God."

Mysticism, therefore, is not to be regarded as a religion in itself, but rather as the most vital element in all true religions, rising up in revolt against cold formality and religious torpor.* Nor is it a philosophical system, though it has its own doctrine of the scheme of things. It is to be described rather as an attitude of mind; an innate tendency of the human soul, which seeks to transcend reason and to attain to a direct experience of God, and which believes that it is possible for the human soul to be united with Ultimate Reality, when "God ceases to be an object and becomes an experience." Mysticism has been defined as "the supernatural union of likeness, begotten of love, which is the union of the human will with the Divine. They seek to realize the unfelt natural presence of God in creation — by entering into a personal relationship with the concealed Presence which is the Source of being." While religion in general separates the Divine from the human, Mysticism, going beyond religion, aspires to intimate union with the Divine, to a penetration of the Divine within the soul and to a disappearance of the individuality, with all its modes of acting, thinking and feeling, in the Divine substance. The mystic seeks to pass out of all that is merely phenomenal, out of all lower forms of reality, to become Being itself.

Mysticism, then, is spiritual and transcendent in its aims, but it holds that the Object of its quest, the World-Soul, the Absolute, the One Reality, is also the Beloved, and as lovers the mystics seek for unions with the One. That union they believe can be attained only by passing through certain definite stages, which they call the treading of the Mystic Way, so that Mysticism is active and practical; it means discipline and rule of life, and much upward striving before the mystic can hope to attain the heights. Mysticism since it is permeated* through and through by the power of Love, can never be self-seeking, for the end can only be attained by self-stripping; moreover, what is given in full measure to the mystic must be shared with others. That flooding of the mystic's soul with the Divine Life must mean a fuller, richer life lived in contact with other human lives. "The perfect life," said Plato, "would be a life of perfect communion with other souls, as well as with the Soul which animates the universe." This mystic consciousness of the Presence of God is not given simply to delight in as the most exquisite of pleasures, but is to inspire the mystic to a finer service of humanity; the purest Mysticism is found where the mystic "throws himself into action and life as though it were forever, and does it simply, without attempts to be isolated with the Absolute out of Time." So the active life of service in the world has been found necessary to the

chained down

Hindu priest
one who passively accepts the world

dullness

soaked, filled

greatest of the mystics, who have felt themselves to be living in God, as
in some measure deified in all their being and so in all their acts to be only
instruments of God.

To sum up, then, in the words of a great modern teacher of Mysticism:
"To be a mystic is simply to participate here and now in real and eternal
life, in the fullest, deepest sense which is possible to man. It is to share as
a free and conscious agent in the joyous travail* of the universe, its mighty,   intense work
onward sweep through pain and glory to its home in God. The ordered
sequence of states, the organic development, whereby his consciousness
is detached from illusion and rises to the mystic freedom which conditions,
instead of being conditioned by, its normal world, is the way he must tread
in order to attain. Only by this deliberate fostering of his deeper self, this
transmutation of the elements of character, can he reach those levels of
consciousness upon which he hears and responds to the measure 'where
to the worlds keep time' on their great pilgrimage towards the Heart of
God. The mystic act of union, that joyous loss of the transfigured self in
God, which is the crown of man's conscious ascent towards the Absolute,
is the contribution of the individual to this, the destiny of the Cosmos."

QUESTIONS FOR DISCUSSION AND WRITING

[1] Define mysticism.

[2] What is the major difference between mysticism and any of the other
philosophical attitudes covered in this chapter?

[3] What is the role of discipline in the mystic's life? How is it a step
toward union with the Divine or Absolute?

[4] Romanticism and mysticism have much in common. Review the works
of Emerson (pages 131–133), Coleridge (pages 290–291), and Bowra (pages
292–294). What are Romanticism's mystical elements?

[5] How does "The Golden Calf" (see pages 88–89) reflect a view that
opposes mysticism? Review your notes on the Bible story's implied thesis.

---

*Chief Seattle, a nineteenth-century Native American, describes his reaction
to the decimation of the Indians by the white settlers' westward expansion. He
acknowledges the coming of a new historical age, but he teaches that in spirit
the Indians live on; he says, "There is not death, only a change of worlds." As
you read, identify the mystical elements of Chief Seattle's thought.*

CHIEF SEATTLE
"My People"

● Yonder sky that has wept tears of compassion upon my people for
centuries untold,* and which to us appears changeless and eternal, may   beyond description

change. Today is fair. Tomorrow may be overcast with clouds. My words are like the stars that never change. Whatever Seattle says the great chief at Washington can rely upon with as much certainty as he can upon the return of the sun or the seasons. The White Chief says that Big Chief* at Washington sends us greetings of friendship and goodwill. That is kind of him for we know he has little need of our friendship in return. His people are many. They are like the grass that covers vast prairies. My people are few. They resemble the scattering trees of a storm-swept plain. The great, and — I presume — good, White Chief sends us word that he wishes to buy our lands but is willing to allow us enough to live comfortably. This indeed appears just, even generous, for the Red Man no longer has rights that he need respect, and the offer may be wise also, as we are no longer in need of an extensive country. . . . I will not dwell on, nor mourn over, our untimely decay, nor reproach our paleface brothers with hastening it, as we too may have been somewhat to blame.

U.S. President

Youth is impulsive. When our young men grow angry at some real or imaginary wrong, and disfigure their faces with black paint, it denotes that their hearts are black, and then they are often cruel and relentless,* and our old men and old women are unable to restrain them. Thus it has ever been. Thus it was when the white men first began to push our forefathers further westward. But let us hope that the hostilities between us may never return. We would have everything to lose and nothing to gain. Revenge by young men is considered gain, even at the cost of their own lives, but old men who stay at home in times of war, and mothers who have sons to lose, know better.

unstoppable

Our good father at Washington — for I presume he is now our father as well as yours, since King George has moved his boundaries further north — our great good father, I say, sends us word that if we do as he desires he will protect us. His brave warriors will be to us a bristling wall of strength, and his wonderful ships of war will fill our harbors so that our ancient enemies far to the northward — the Hydas and Tsimpsians — will cease to frighten our women, children, and old men. Then in reality will he be our father and we his children. But can that ever be? Your God is not our God! Your God loves your people and hates mine. He folds his strong and protecting arms lovingly about the paleface and leads him by the hand as a father leads his infant son — but He has forsaken His red children — if they really are his. Our God, the Great Spirit, seems also to have forsaken us. Your God makes your people wax strong every day. Soon they will fill the land. Our people are ebbing away like a rapidly receding tide that will never return. The white man's God cannot love our people or He would protect them. They seem to be orphans who can look no-where for help. How then can we be brothers? How can your God become our God and renew our prosperity and awaken in us dreams of returning greatness? If we have a common heavenly father He must be partial — for He came to his paleface children. We never saw Him. He gave you laws but He had no word for His red children whose teeming multitudes once filled this vast continent as stars fill the firmament. No; we are two distinct races with separate origins and separate destinies. There is little in common between us.

To us the ashes of our ancestors are sacred and their resting place is hallowed ground. You wander far from the graves of your ancestors and seemingly without regret. Your religion was written upon tables of stone by the iron finger of your God so that you could not forget. The Red Man could never comprehend nor remember it. Our religion is the traditions of our ancestors — the dreams of our old men, given them in solemn hours of night by the Great Spirit; and the visions of our sachems;* and it is   chiefs
written in the hearts of our people.

Your dead cease to love you and the land of their nativity as soon as they pass the portals of the tomb and wander way beyond the stars. They are soon forgotten and never return. Our dead never forget the beautiful world that gave them being.

Day and night cannot dwell together. The Red man has ever fled the approach of the White Man, as the morning mist flees before the morning sun. However, your proposition seems fair and I think that my people will accept it and will retire to the reservation you offer them. Then we will dwell apart in peace, for the words of the Great White Chief seem to be the words of nature speaking to my people out of dense darkness.

It matters little where we pass the remnant of our days. They will not be many. A few more moons; a few more winters — and not one of the descendants of the mighty hosts that once moved over this broad land or lived in happy homes, protected by the Great Spirit, will remain to mourn over the graves of a people once more powerful and hopeful than yours. But why should I mourn at the untimely fate of my people? Tribe follows tribe, and nation follows nation, like the waves of the sea. It is the order of nature, and regret is useless. Your time of decay may be distant, but it will surely come, for even the White Man whose God walked and talked with him as friend with friend, cannot be exempt from the common destiny. We may be brothers after all. We will see.

We will ponder your proposition, and when we decide we will let you know. But should we accept it, I here and now make this condition that we will not be denied the privilege without molestation of visiting at any time the tombs of our ancestors, friends and children. Every part of this soil is sacred in the estimation of my people. Every hillside, every valley, every plain and grove, has been hallowed by some sad or happy event in days long vanished. . . . The very dust upon which you now stand responds more lovingly to their footsteps than to yours, because it is rich with the blood of our ancestors and our bare feet are conscious of the sympathetic touch. . . . Even the little children who lived here and rejoiced here for a brief season will love these somber solitudes and at eventide they greet shadowy returning spirits. And when the last Red Man shall have perished, and the memory of my tribe shall have become a myth among the White Men, these shores will swarm with the invisible dead of my tribe, and when your children's children think themselves alone in the field, the store, the shop, upon the highway, or in the silence of the pathless woods, they will not be alone. . . . At night when the streets of your cities and villages are silent and you think them deserted, they will throng with the returning hosts that once filled and still love this beautiful land. The White Man will never be alone.

Let him be just and deal kindly with my people, for the dead are not powerless. Dead, did I say? There is not death, only a change of worlds.

QUESTIONS FOR DISCUSSION AND WRITING

[1] Analyze Chief Seattle's view of his people's relationship to their ancestors as a mystical attitude.

[2] How would a Cynic's view of the Indian people's annihilation compare and contrast with the mystical interpretation?

During the 1960s, many Americans turned to Eastern religions and philosophies in an attempt to find a new (to them) way of dealing with the issues of personal meaning, values, and experience. The beatniks of the 1950s (Jack Kerouac, Allan Ginsburg, and Gregory Corso, among others) first looked to Zen as an alternative view to the Western rational tradition. Daisetz Suzuki is a famous professor of Eastern religion and philosophy, and Eugene Herrigel was a German living in Japan who studied Zen and archery with a Japanese Zen master over a period of ten years. In his introduction to Herrigel's book, Suzuki outlines the precepts of Zen.

DAISETZ T. SUZUKI
"Introduction to Eugene Herrigel's Zen*"*

● One of the most significant features we notice in the practice of archery, and in fact of all the arts as they are studied in Japan and probably also in other Far Eastern countries, is that they are not intended for utilitarian* purposes only or for purely aesthetic enjoyments, but are meant to train the mind; indeed, to bring it into contact with the ultimate reality. Archery is, therefore, not practiced solely for hitting the target; the swordsman does not wield the sword just for the sake of outdoing his opponent; the dancer does not dance just to perform certain rhythmical movements of the body. The mind has first to be attuned to the Unconscious.

functional

If one really wishes to be master of an art, technical knowledge of it is not enough. One has to transcend technique so that the art becomes an "artless art" growing out of the Unconscious.

SOURCE: "Introduction to Eugene Herrigel's *Zen*," by Daisetz T. Suzuki, in *Zen in the Art of Archery* by Eugen Herrigel. Copyright © 1953, by Pantheon Books, Inc., New York. Reprinted by permission of the publisher.

In the case of archery, the hitter and the hit are no longer two opposing objects, but are one reality. The archer ceases to be conscious of himself as the one who is engaged in hitting the bull's-eye which confronts him. This state of unconsciousness is realized only when, completely empty and rid of the self, he becomes one with the perfecting of his technical skill, though there is in it something of a quite different order which cannot be attained by any progressive study of the art.

What differentiates Zen most characteristically from all other teaching, religious, philosophical, or mystical, is that while it never goes out of our daily life, yet with all its practicalness and concreteness Zen has something in it which makes it stand aloof from the scene of worldly sordidness and restlessness.

Here we come to the connection between Zen and archery, and such other arts as swordsmanship, flower arrangement, the tea ceremony, dancing, and the fine arts.

Zen is the "everyday mind," as was proclaimed by Baso (Ma-tsu, died 788); this "everyday mind" is no more than "sleeping when tired, eating when hungry." As soon as we reflect, deliberate, and conceptualize, the original unconsciousness is lost and a thought interferes. We no longer eat while eating, we no longer sleep while sleeping. The arrow is off the string but does not fly straight to the target, nor does the target stand where it is. Calculation which is miscalculation sets in. The whole business of archery goes the wrong way. The archer's confused mind betrays itself in every direction and every field of activity.

Man is a thinking reed but his great works are done when he is not calculating and thinking. "Childlikeness" has to be restored with long years of training in the art of self-forgetfulness. When this is attained, man thinks yet he does not think. He thinks like the showers coming down from the sky; he thinks like the waves rolling on the ocean; he thinks like the stars illuminating the nightly heavens; he thinks like the green foliage shooting forth in the relaxing spring breeze. Indeed, he is the showers, the ocean, the stars, the foliage.

When a man reaches this stage of "spiritual" development, he is a Zen artist of life. He does not need, like the painter, a canvas, brushes, and paints; nor does he require, like the archer, the bow and arrow and target, and other paraphernalia. He has his limbs, body, head, and other parts. His Zen-life expresses itself by means of all these "tools" which are important to its manifestation. His hands and feet are the brushes and the whole universe is the canvas on which he depicts his life for seventy, eighty, or even ninety years. This picture is called "history."

Hoyen of Gosozen (died 1140) says: "Here is a man who, turning the emptiness of space into a sheet of paper, the waves of the ocean into an inkwell, and Mount Sumeru into a brush, writes these five characters: so-shi-sai-rai-i. To such, I spread my zagu (a Zen religious article) and make my profound bow."

One may well ask, "What does this fantastic pronouncement mean? Why is a person who can perform such a feat considered worthy of the utmost respect?" A Zen master would perhaps answer, "I eat when hungry, I sleep when tired." If he is nature-minded, he may say, "It was fine yesterday and today it is raining."

QUESTIONS FOR DISCUSSION AND WRITING

[1] Suzuki discusses the major difference between Zen and mysticism. Explain this difference but also show the similarities in the two practices.

[2] Compare the archer's Zen experience with the mystical vision of Chief Seattle.

Modern Attitudes Toward Modern Evils

Nihilism is antithetical* to mysticism, for it denies the existence of any absolute power, being, or value. As an attitude it has probably existed as long as religious belief has, for once the notion of faith exists, the notion of doubt inevitably arises. Nihilism extends doubt to its logical extreme: disbelief in any meaning or purpose in life. Certain aspects of the contemporary "punk" culture seem nihilistic: its disconnection with mainstream values, its quest for immediate gratification, violence, and valuing of shock for shock's sake. The gang members in Anthony Burgess' novel (and Stanley Kubrick's film) A Clockwork Orange are nihilistic; one can see the same nihilistic attitude expressed by the pool players in Gwendolyn Brooks' poem.

opposite

CHARLES L. GLICKSBERG
"Nihilism"

● What is generally meant by nihilism? Nihilism is difficult to define because it takes so many different forms, but it is a real enough experience. It is a spiritual crisis through which all thinking people pass at some time in their lives; and very few come through this ordeal unscathed.* There is the passive nihilism of the buddhist variety: life is an empty dream, action is futile, and striving for happiness, fulfillment, or perfection betrays the fact that one is still the slave of illusion. The second type, the nihilism of negativity, is derived from the special brand of nihilism that sprang up in Europe, especially in Russia, in the nineteenth century; it was a nihilism that, despite its professed rejection of all belief, rested its faith in the scientific method.

unharmed

Then there is a species of nihilism that is active, Dionysian:* Nietzsche speaks of ecstatic nihilism. Nietzsche's nihilism is metaphysical rather than ideological. His attitude toward science is therefore not worshipful; sci-

pleasure-seeking

SOURCE: "Nihilism," in *The Literature of Nihilism* by Charles L. Glicksberg. Copyright © 1975 by Associated Unn. Presses. Reprinted by permission of Associated University Presses.

ence is no more than a body of fictions, a set of conventions; it did not presuppose that it was based on truth. Nietzsche's nihilism was all-inclusive. He perceived no meaning in the world, no ultimate purpose, no sustaining principle of order. Man is saddled with the task of imposing order on a senseless universe. There is also the type of nihilism that is carried to the logical extreme of suicide. Finally, there is the nihilism that promotes and justifies an unconscionable* struggle for power. Life on earth is completely amoral in character; categorical imperatives* are human constructs; no law exists to prevent the rule of the strong — a doctrine that motivated the Nazi reign of terror.

inexcusable

necessary actions

Webster's New International Dictionary defines nihilism as "a viewpoint that all traditional values and beliefs are unfounded and that all existence is consequently senseless and useless: a denial of intrinsic meaning and value in life." Another definition that this dictionary gives is that nihilism is "a doctrine that denies or is taken as denying any objective or real ground of truth. In a more specific context this includes the philosophy of moral nihilism, which denies the objective ground of morality."

But if the truth that man pursues so eagerly is only a solipsist* illusion, then he finds himself trapped in a vicious circle of contradictions. Why speak? Why recommend one illusion as vastly superior to another? If truth is a myth, then all distinctions are abolished, and one might as well follow the erratic guidance of instinct and feeling instead of the promptings of reason.

egotistical

The cult of nihilism tends swiftly to grow into a cult of violence and terror on the political scene, "expressing a total contempt for life . . . In an active or latent state, nihilism is at work throughout our civilization." Important, however, as is the social and historical background, it does not appear that nihilism is the special creation of the twentieth century, this age of crisis and catastrophe. The historical crisis of our time colors and accentuates the dominant motif of doom that crops up, but the nihilist strain has made itself felt in other cultures during the past, though in a less virulent* manner. Before the advent of the horrors of the holocaust, there were poets, dramatists, and philosophers, who faced the nihilist dilemma. From Sophocles and Lucretius to Schopenhauer, Nietzsche, Dostoevski, Kierkegaard, and Tolstoy, there is scarcely an important creative figure who has not at some time been stricken with the fever of nihilism. It is always there to be faced — and overcome.

angry

I am assuming that the spiritual conflict that culminates in nihilism, far from being the mark of an unhinged mind or craven temperament or the characteristic but short-lived product of a time of trouble, is an archetypal* experience. The individual either passes through the dark night of the soul and beholds finally the glimmer of the light beyond, however ambiguously it shines forth, or he never emerges from the darkness that hems him in. Though the nihilist has presumably abandoned the quest for ultimate meaning, he never actually ceases to question or cry out or seek a solution to the mystery of being. The dialectic of nihilism is charged with unresolvable elements of complexity. It is not the formal expression of a philosophi-

original, basic

cal position nor is it a logically elaborated system of thought. If it embodies a world vision that is in the end forced to say No to life, it utters this categorical negation with different accents of conviction.

The rage of the nihilist against the ineradicable* absurdity of existence is an inverted expression of his love of life. Since his life goes on — he rejects, as does Camus, the expedient of suicide — he stops at some point in his career to ask himself: "How am I to live? What is to be done?"

It is apparent that the nihilist and the humanist share a common body of assumptions. Both believe that man is alone, both reject faith in the supernatural. But whereas the secular humanist then proceeds to declare that man is the measure, the sole source and touchstone of value, the nihilist repudiates all such man-made values as illusions, mere as-if fictions designed to hide from human eyes the emptiness and futility of existence. The nihilist will not conceal from himself the desolating "truth" of human dereliction. He will proclaim far and wide his discovery that the idea of progress, like the romantic faith in the perfectibility of man, is a spurious* myth. He harbors no revolutionary hopes; he does not look forward to the future for the redemption of mankind.

It is at this point of no return that the nihilist reverses his field, as it were, and takes up a position that, in defiance of the canons* of logic, brings him to a closer understanding of the intense spiritual battle the religious Existentialist must wage before he can affirm his faith in God. Faced with the ultimate issue of death — his death — as annihilation, the nihilist wants to know how best to live the time of his life. But what is "good," what is "best"? Intellectually he is convinced that he has purged his mind of all religious traces, though his longing for God, as was true in the case of Nietzsche, never leaves him. But longing that never goes beyond that stage is not the same thing as the actuality of faith. The nihilist distrusts the coinages of the mind, the stratagems* of the duplicitous* self, the abstractions that it creates and then hypostatizes* as sacred realities. He applies the same stringent skepticism to his own negative conclusions.

This encounter with nothingness forms the crux of nihilist literature, just as the experience of the dark night of the soul lies at the heart of Christian mysticism. Most people are sleepwalkers who take it for granted that life has a meaning beyond the mere living of it. It is this instinctive faith that the nihilist begins by questioning and then finally decides to reject. As soon as he does so, he finds himself trapped in a spiritual cul-de-sac. He is unable either to affirm or to deny. He can neither act nor refrain from acting. How shall he act on his negative beliefs?

This life-negating dementia* constitutes a theme that has been pondered by poets, philosophers, mystics, and saints for over two thousand years. It is the archetypal concern of the tragic vision, the central, though not sole, preoccupation of religion. When human consciousness first arose, man must have formulated the question of questions: Who am I in relation to the cosmos? What am I doing here on earth? What purpose am I supposed to serve?

Nietzsche announced that God was dead and wrestled with the prob-

---

unable to be destroyed

false

rules

tricks / deceptive
makes an idea into something concrete

mindlessness

lem of what was to take the place of God. He sought to grasp the truth bearing on the human condition, without regard for the harmful consequences it might have for mankind. The relentless search for the truth at all costs is sustained by a moral principle, but it led Nietzsche to the ultimate of disillusionment. If truth is a myth, then the pursuit of truth must cease, for it leads nowhere. Nothing is to be believed, not even the empirically warranted conclusions of science. The upshot in Nietzsche's case is a nihilism that cannot be borne because it cannot be lived. As Karl Jaspers points out: "Even if his thinking appears as a self-destructive process in which no truth can last, even if the end is always nothingness, Nietzsche's own will is diametrically opposed to this nihilism. In empty space he wants to grasp the positive." He endeavors to formulate a vital faith, a transcendent affirmation that can inspire human life to nobler effort. Hence he glorifies strength, the elan vital,* the will to power, the [life force] ideal of eternal recurrence. This is a far cry, however, from any religious gospel that the general run of mankind can embrace. But the passion of striving, the stubborn hankering after the ideal, is abundantly present in his work; he is not satisfied with the finite, the merely human; he must break out of the nihilistic impasse.

QUESTIONS FOR DISCUSSION AND WRITING

[1] Define nihilism.

[2] How is nihilism a particularly modern philosophical attitude? Refer to Dirk's article.

[3] To what extent is Cynicism a nihilistic doctrine? Which if any of its tenets make it nonnihilistic?

[4] Explain the nihilistic content of "The Pool Players" (page 409).

[5] Is atheism <u>necessarily</u> nihilistic? Refer to Madalyn Murray O'Hair's argument in Chapter 2.

Joan Didion is a prominent contemporary American writer. She's famous as a stylist, a writer whose lean style embodies her sense of the emptiness, alienation, and almost moral bleakness of modern-day life. Note the physical descriptions that she includes in her essay, and consider how they serve to reveal the feeling she associates with El Salvador's current state of political crisis.

JOAN DIDION
"Death in El Salvador"

● The three-year-old El Salvador International Airport is glassy and white and splendidly isolated, conceived during the waning of the Molina "National Transformation" as convenient less to the capital (San Salvador is forty miles away, until recently a drive of several hours) than to a central hallucination of the Molina and Romero regimes, the projected beach resorts, the Hyatt, the Pacific Paradise, tennis, golf, water-skiing, condos, Costa del Sol, the visionary intervention of a tourist industry in yet another republic where the leading natural cause of death is gastrointestinal infection. In the general absence of tourists these hotels have since been abandoned, ghost resorts on the empty Pacific beaches, and to land at this airport built to service them is to plunge directly into a state in which no ground is solid, no depth of field reliable, no perception so definite that it might not dissolve into its reverse.

The only logic is that of acquiescence.* Immigration is negotiated in a thicket of automatic weapons, but by whose authority the weapons are brandished* (Army or National Guard or National Police or Customs Police or Treasury Police or one of a continuing proliferation of other shadowy and overlapping forces) is a blurred point. Eye contact is avoided. Documents are scrutinized upside down. Once clear of the airport, on the new highway that slices through green hills rendered phosphorescent* by the cloud cover of the tropical rainy season, one sees mainly underfed cattle and mongrel dogs and armored vehicles, vans and trucks and Cherokee Chiefs fitted with reinforced steel and bulletproof Plexiglas an inch thick. Such vehicles are a fixed feature of local life, and are popularly associated with disappearance and death. There was the Cherokee Chief seen following the Dutch television crew killed in Chalatenango province in March of 1982. There was the red Toyota three-quarter-ton pickup sighted near the van driven by the four American Catholic workers on the night they were killed in 1980. There were, in the late spring and summer of 1982, the three Toyota panel trucks, one yellow, one blue, and one green, none bearing plates, reported present at each of the mass detentions (a "detention" is another fixed feature of local life, and often precedes a "disappearance") in the Amatepec district of San Salvador. These are the details — the models and colors of armored vehicles, the makes and calibers of weapons, the particular methods of dismemberment and decapitation used in particular instances — on which the visitor to Salvador learns immediately to concentrate, to the exclusion of past or future concerns, as in a prolonged amnesiac fugue.*

Terror is the given of the place. Black-and-white police cars cruise in pairs, each with the barrel of a rifle extruding from an open window. Roadblocks materialize at random, soldiers fanning out from trucks and taking positions, fingers always on triggers, safeties clicking on and off. Aim is taken as if to pass the time. Every morning El Diario de Hoy and La Prensa Grafica carry cautionary stories. "Una madre y sus dos hijos fueron asesinados con arma cortante (corvo) por ocho sujetos desconocidos el lunes en la noche": A mother and her two sons hacked to death in their beds by eight desconocidos, unknown men. The same morning's paper: the unidentified body of a young man, strangled, found on the shoulder of the road. Same morning, different story: the unidentified bodies of three

passive acceptance

carried threateningly

giving off light

musical work with a repeatedly developed theme

young men, found on another road, their faces partially destroyed by bayonets, one face carved to represent a cross.

It is largely from these reports in the newspapers that the United States embassy compiles its body counts, which are transmitted to Washington in a weekly dispatch referred to by embassy people as "the grimgram." These counts are presented in a kind of tortured code that fails to obscure what is taken for granted in El Salvador, that government forces do most of the killing. In a January 15, 1982 memo to Washington, for example, the embassy issued a "guarded" breakdown on its count of 6,909 "reported" political murders between September 16 1980 and September 15 1981. Of these 6,909, according to the memo, 922 were "believed committed by security forces," 952 "believed committed by leftist terrorists," 136 "believed committed by the rightist terrorists," and 4,889 "committed by unknown assailants," the famous desconocidos favored by those San Salvador newspapers still publishing. (The figures actually add up not to 6,909 but to 6,899, leaving ten in a kind of official limbo.) The memo continued:

> The uncertainty involved here can be seen in the fact that responsibility cannot be fixed in the majority of cases. We note, however, that it is generally believed in El Salvador that a large number of the unexplained killings are carried out by the security forces, officially or unofficially. The Embassy is aware of dramatic claims that have been made by one interest group or another in which the security forces figure as the primary agents of murder here. El Salvador's tangled web of attack and vengeance, traditional criminal violence and political mayhem make this an impossible charge to sustain. In saying this, however, we make no attempt to lighten the responsibility for the deaths of many hundreds, and perhaps thousands, which can be attributed to the security forces. . . .

The body count kept by what is generally referred to in San Salvador as "the Human Rights Commission" is higher than the embassy's, and documented periodically by a photographer who goes out looking for bodies. These bodies he photographs are often broken into unnatural positions, and the faces to which the bodies are attached (when they are attached) are equally unnatural, sometimes unrecognizable as human faces, obliterated by acid or beaten to a mash of misplaced ears and teeth or slashed ear to ear and invaded by insects. "Encontrado en Antiguo Cuscatlan el dia 25 de Marzo 1982: camison de dormir celeste," the typed caption reads on one photograph: found in Antiguo Cuscatlan March 25 1982 wearing a sky-blue nightshirt. The captions are laconic.* Found in   using few words
Soyapango May 21 1982. Found in Meficanos June 11 1982. Found at El Playon May 30 1982, white shirt, purple pants, black shoes. . . .

All forensic* photographs induce in the viewer a certain protective   used for legal proceedings
numbness, but dissociation is more difficult here. In the first place these are not, technically, "forensic" photographs, since the evidence they document will never be presented in a court of law. In the second place the

disfigurement is too routine. The locations are too near, the dates too recent. There is the presence of the relatives of the disappeared: the women who sit every day in this cramped office on the grounds of the archdiocese, waiting to look at the spiral-bound photo albums in which the photographs are kept. These albums have plastic covers bearing softfocus color photographs of young Americans in dating situations (strolling through autumn foliage on one album, recumbent in a field of daisies on another), and the women, looking for the bodies of their husbands and brothers and sisters and children, pass them from hand to hand without comment or expression.

QUESTIONS FOR DISCUSSION AND WRITING

[1] Given historical events like the Holocaust, Stalin's purges, the Reign of Terror, the Hiroshima atomic attack, and the El Salvador murders, develop an argument supporting or rejecting the nihilist attitude. If you choose to argue against nihilism, you may draw on material in Chapter 2 or Pope's *Essay on Man* in Chapter 4.

[2] You've read several articles that deal with political revolutionaries — terrorists, Robespierre, Marxists/communists, Malcolm X. Define the term "revolutionary" and argue whether a revolutionary can subscribe to nihilism.

During World War II, the German Nazis systematically exterminated people whom they believed to be racially or socially inferior. Auschwitz was one of many death-camps where prisoners were kept, often as slave-labor, until they were executed. The modern world had never witnessed such wide-scale, organized genocide. As the horrible evidence of the Nazi crimes continues even today to be documented, it reinforces the perception of the atrocity as one of the most evil acts ever committed by human beings. As you read the essay, note how it might support a nihilistic view of modern life.

VIKTOR E. FRANKL
"Arrival at Auschwitz"

● Fifteen hundred persons had been traveling by train for several days and nights: there were eighty people in each coach. All had to lie on top of their luggage, the few remnants of their personal possessions. The carriages were so full that only the top parts of the windows were free to let in the gray of dawn. Everyone expected the train to head for some munitions factory, in which we would be employed as forced labor. We did not know whether we were still in Silesia or already in Poland. The engine's whistle had an uncanny sound, like a cry for help sent out in

SOURCE: "Arrival at Aushwitz" in *Man's Search for Meaning*. Copyright © 1962 by Viktor Frankl. Reprinted by permission of Beacon Press.

commiseration for the unhappy load which it was destined to lead into
perdition.* Then the train shunted, obviously nearing a main station.   hell
Suddenly a cry broke from the ranks of the anxious passengers, "There is
a sign, Auschwitz!" Everyone's heart missed a beat at that moment. Auschwitz — the very name stood for all that was horrible: gas chambers,
crematoriums, massacres. Slowly, almost hesitatingly, the train moved on
as if it wanted to spare its passengers the dreadful realization as long as
possible: Auschwitz!

With the progressive dawn, the outlines of an immense camp became
visible: long stretches of several rows of barbed wire fences; watch towers;
search lights; and long columns of ragged human figures, gray in the
grayness of dawn, trekking along the straight desolate roads, to what
destination we did not know. There were isolated shouts and whistles of
command. We did not know their meaning. My imagination led me to see
gallows with people dangling on them. I was horrified, but this was just as
well, because step by step we had to become accustomed to a terrible and
immense horror.

Eventually we moved into the station. The initial silence was interrupted by shouted commands. We were to hear those rough, shrill tones
from then on, over and over again in all the camps. Their sound was almost
like the last cry of a victim, and yet there was a difference. It had a rasping
hoarseness, as if it came from the throat of a man who had to keep shouting
like that, a man who was being murdered again and again. The carriage
doors were flung open and a small detachment of prisoners stormed inside. They wore striped uniforms, their heads were shaved, but they
looked well fed. They spoke in every possible European tongue, and all
with a certain amount of humor, which sounded grotesque under the
circumstances. Like a drowning man clutching a straw, my inborn optimism (which has often controlled my feelings even in the most desperate
situations) clung to this thought: These prisoners look quite well, they
seem to be in good spirits and even laugh. Who knows? I might manage
to share their favorable position.

In psychiatry there is a certain condition known as "delusion of re-
prieve.*" The condemned man, immediately before his execution, gets   postponement of execution
the illusion that he might be reprieved at the very last moment. We, too,
clung to shreds of hope and believed to the last moment that it would not
be so bad. Just the sight of the red cheeks and round faces of those prisoners was a great encouragement. Little did we know then that they formed
a specially chosen elite, who for years had been the receiving squad for
new transports as they rolled into the station day after day. They took
charge of the new arrivals and their luggage, including scarce items and
smuggled jewelry. Auschwitz must have been a strange spot in this
Europe of the last years of the war. There must have been unique treasures of gold and silver, platinum and diamonds, not only in the huge
storehouses but also in the hands of the SS.

Fifteen hundred captives were cooped up in a shed built to accommodate probably two hundred at the most. We were cold and hungry and there was not enough room for everyone to squat on the bare ground, let alone to lie down. One five-ounce piece of bread was our only food in four days. Yet I heard the senior prisoners in charge of the shed bargain with one member of the receiving party about a tie-pin made of platinum and diamonds. Most of the profits would eventually be traded for liquor — schnapps. I do not remember any more just how many thousands of marks were needed to purchase the quantity of schnapps required for a "gay evening," but I do know that those long-term prisoners needed schnapps. Under such conditions, who could blame them for trying to dope themselves? There was another group of prisoners who got liquor supplied in almost unlimited quantities by the SS: these were the men who were employed in the gas chambers and crematoriums, and who knew very well that one day they would be relieved by a new shift of men, and that they would have to leave their enforced role of executioner and become victims themselves.

Nearly everyone in our transport lived under the illusion that he would be reprieved, that everything would yet be well. We did not realize the meaning behind the scene that was to follow presently. We were told to leave our luggage in the train and to fall into two lines — women on one side, men on the other — in order to file past a senior SS officer. Surprisingly enough, I had the courage to hide my haversack* under my coat. My line filed past the officer, man by man. I realized that it would be dangerous if the officer spotted my bag. He would at least knock me down; I knew that from previous experience. Instinctively, I straightened on approaching the officer, so that he would not notice my heavy load. Then I was face to face with him. He was a tall man who looked slim and fit in his spotless uniform. What a contrast to us, who were untidy and grimy after our long journey! He had assumed an attitude of careless ease, supporting his right elbow with his left hand. His right hand was lifted, and with the forefinger of that hand he pointed very leisurely to the right or to the left. None of us had the slightest idea of the sinister meaning behind that little movement of a man's finger, pointing now to the right and now to the left, but far more frequently to the left.

It was my turn. Somebody whispered to me that to be sent to the right side would mean work, the way to the left being for the sick and those incapable of work, who would be sent to a special camp. I just waited for things to take their course, the first of many such times to come. My haversack weighed me down a bit to the left, but I made an effort to walk upright. The SS man looked me over, appeared to hesitate, then put both his hands on my shoulders. I tried very hard to look smart, and he turned my shoulders very slowly until I faced right, and I moved over to that side.

The significance of the finger game was explained to us in the evening. It was the first selection, the first verdict made on our existence or non-existence. For the great majority of our transport, about 90 per cent, it meant death. Their sentence was carried out within the next few hours.

*pack

Those who were sent to the left were marched from the station straight to the crematorium. This building, as I was told by someone who worked there, had the word "bath" written over its doors in several European languages. On entering, each prisoner was handed a piece of soap, and then — but mercifully I do not need to describe the events which followed. Many accounts have been written about this horror.

We who were saved, the minority of our transport, found out the truth in the evening. I inquired from prisoners who had been there for some time where my colleague and friend P — — — had been sent.

"Was he sent to the left side?"

"Yes," I replied.

"Then you can see him there," I was told.

"Where?" A hand pointed to the chimney a few hundred yards off, which was sending a column of flame up into the gray sky of Poland. It dissolved into a sinister cloud of smoke.

"That's where your friend is, floating up to Heaven," was the answer. But I still did not understand until the truth was explained to me in plain words.

But I am telling things out of their turn. From a psychological point of view, we had a long, long way in front of us from the break of that dawn at the station until our first night's rest at the camp.

Escorted by SS guards with loaded guns, we were made to run from the station, past electrically charged barbed wire, through the camp, to the cleansing station; for those of us who had passed the first selection, this was a real bath. Again our illusion of reprieve found confirmation. The SS men seemed almost charming. Soon we found out their reason. They were nice to us as long as they saw watches on our wrists and could persuade us in well-meaning tones to hand them over. Would we not have handed over all our possessions anyway, and why should not that relatively nice person have the watch? Maybe one day he would do one a good turn.

We waited in a shed which seemed to be the anteroom to the disinfecting chamber. SS men appeared and spread out blankets into which we had to throw all our possessions, all our watches and jewelry. There were still naive prisoners among us who asked, to the amusement of the more seasoned ones who were there as helpers, if they could not keep a wedding ring, a medal or a good-luck piece. No one could yet grasp the fact that everything would be taken away.

I tried to take one of the old prisoners into my confidence. Approaching him furtively,* I pointed to the roll of paper in the inner pocket of my coat and said, "Look, this is the manuscript of a scientific book. I know what you will say; that I should be grateful to escape with my life, that that should be all I can expect of fate. But I cannot help myself. I must keep this manuscript at all costs; it contains my life's work. Do you understand that?"   sneakily

Yes, he was beginning to understand. A grin spread slowly over his face, first piteous,* then more amused, mocking, insulting, until he bellowed   full of pity one word at me in answer to my question, a word that was ever present in the vocabulary of the camp inmates: "Shit!" At that moment I saw the plain truth and did what marked the culminating point of the first phase of my psychological reaction: I struck out my whole former life.

Suddenly there was a stir among my fellow travelers, who had been standing about with pale, frightened faces, helplessly debating. Again we heard the hoarsely shouted commands. We were driven with blows into the immediate anteroom of the bath. There we assembled around an SS man who waited until we had all arrived. Then he said, "I will give you two minutes, and I shall time you by my watch. In these two minutes you will get fully undressed and drop everything on the floor where you are standing. You will take nothing with you except your shoes, your belt or suspenders, and possibly a truss.* I am starting to count — now!"

supporter worn for a hernia

With unthinkable haste, people tore off their clothes. As the time grew shorter, they became increasingly nervous and pulled clumsily at their underwear, belts and shoelaces. Then we heard the first sounds of whipping; leather straps beating down on naked bodies.

Next we were herded into another room to be shaved: not only our heads were shorn, but not a hair was left on our entire bodies. Then on to the showers, where we lined up again. We hardly recognized each other; but with great relief some people noted that real water dripped from the sprays.

While we were waiting for the shower, our nakedness was brought home to us: we really had nothing now except our bare bodies — even minus hair; all we possessed, literally, was our naked existence. What else remained for us as a material link with our former lives? For me there were my glasses and my belt; the latter I had to exchange later on for a piece of bread. There was an extra bit of excitement in store for the owners of trusses. In the evening the senior prisoner in charge of our hut welcomed us with a speech in which he gave us his word of honor that he would hang, personally, "from that beam" — he pointed to it — any person who had sewn money or precious stones into his truss. Proudly he explained that as a senior inhabitant the camp laws entitled him to do so.

Where our shoes were concerned, matters were not so simple. Although we were supposed to keep them, those who had fairly decent pairs had to give them up after all and were given in exchange shoes that did not fit. In for real trouble were those prisoners who had followed the apparently well-meant advice (given in the anteroom) of the senior prisoners and had shortened their jackboots by cutting the tops off, then smearing soap on the cut edges to hide the sabotage. The SS men seemed to have waited for just that. All suspected of this crime had to go into a small adjoining room. After a time we again heard the lashings of the strap, and the screams of tortured men. This time it lasted for quite a while.

Thus the illusions some of us still held were destroyed one by one, and then, quite unexpectedly, most of us were overcome by a grim sense of humor. We knew that we had nothing to lose except our so ridiculously naked lives. When the showers started to run, we all tried very hard to make fun, both about ourselves and about each other. After all, real water did flow from the sprays!

Apart from that strange kind of humor, another sensation seized us: curiosity. I have experienced this kind of curiosity before, as a fundamental reaction toward certain strange circumstances. When my life was once endangered by a climbing accident, I felt only one sensation at the critical moment: curiosity, curiosity as to whether I should come out of it alive or with a fractured skull or some other injuries.

Cold curiosity predominated even in Auschwitz, somehow detaching the mind from its surroundings, which came to be regarded with a kind of objectivity. At that time one cultivated this state of mind as a means of protection. We were anxious to know what would happen next; and what would be the consequence, for example, of our standing in the open air, in the chill of late autumn, stark naked, and still wet from the showers. In the next few days our curiosity evolved into surprise; surprise that we did not catch cold.

There were many similar surprises in store for new arrivals. The medical men among us learned first of all: "Textbooks tell lies!" Somewhere it is said that man cannot exist without sleep for more than a stated number of hours. Quite wrong! I had been convinced that there were certain things I just could not do: I could not sleep without this or I could not live with that or the other. The first night in Auschwitz we slept in beds which were constructed in tiers. On each tier (measuring about six-and-a-half to eight feet) slept nine men, directly on the boards. Two blankets were shared by each nine men. We could, of course, lie only on our sides, crowded and huddled against each other, which had some advantages because of the bitter cold. Though it was forbidden to take shoes up to the bunks, some people did use them secretly as pillows in spite of the fact that they were caked with mud. Otherwise one's head had to rest on the crook of an almost dislocated arm. And yet sleep came and brought oblivion and relief from pain for a few hours.

I would like to mention a few similar surprises on how much we could endure: we were unable to clean our teeth, and yet, in spite of that and a severe vitamin deficiency, we had healthier gums than ever before. We had to wear the same shirts for half a year, until they had lost all appearance of being shirts. For days we were unable to wash, even partially, because of frozen water pipes, and yet the sores and abrasions on hands which were dirty from work in the soil did not suppurate* (that is, unless — give off pus — there was frostbite). Or for instance, a light sleeper, who used to be disturbed by the slightest noise in the next room, now found himself lying pressed against a comrade who snored loudly a few inches from his ear and yet slept quite soundly through the noise.

If someone now asked of us the truth of Dostoevski's statement that flatly defines man as a being who can get used to anything, we would reply, "Yes, a man can get used to anything, but do not ask us how." But our psychological investigations have not taken us that far yet; neither had we prisoners reached that point. We were still in the first phase of our psychological reactions.

QUESTIONS FOR DISCUSSION AND WRITING

[1] Summarize the prisoners' prevailing mental state at the start of their internment, and analyze their increasingly nihilistic frame of mind as they adapt to their new circumstances.

[2] Compare the situation faced by Chief Seattle and his people with that of the Jews in Auschwitz. What aspects of each experience would confirm the nihilist world view?

"Aestheticism" as a personal philosophy emerged in the late nineteenth century, but in its upper-class exclusivity and emphasis on style, it has forerunners in hedonistic and elitist thought over the centuries. The term can simply mean "love of beauty and the arts," but its modern connotations usually suggest a superior, perhaps pretentious, perhaps self-indulgent attitude. In contemporary pop culture, aestheticism underlies some rock groups' extravagant, often shocking stage appearance (Prince, Kiss, and Boy George are notable). The author of the following essay explains aestheticism's excesses but also clarifies its importance as a force liberating the individual from overly restrictive social codes.

R. V. JOHNSON
"Aspects of Aestheticism"

● An aesthete is often defined as somebody who appreciates beauty; but aesthetes, in this broad sense, have obviously existed before and since the nineteenth century. What was so special about "the Aesthetes"? As for the word, "aestheticism": this is used to denote different features of nineteenth-century culture. How do these different features relate to each other?

Aestheticism was not one simple phenomenon, but a group of related phenomena, all reflecting a conviction that the enjoyment of beauty can by itself give value and meaning to life.

Aestheticism as a view of life implies taking life "in the spirit of art," as something to be appreciated for its beauty, its variety, its dramatic spectacle. The classic statement of this view in English is the concluding essay in Walter Pater's *The Renaissance*, a collection of essays on art and literature first published in one volume in 1873. To pursue the aesthetic life, as Pater describes it, we must cultivate our whole area of awareness,

SOURCE: "Aspects of Aestheticism," in *Aestheticism* by R. V. Johnson. Copyright © 1969 by R.V. Johnson. Reprinted by permission of Methuen & Co., Ltd.

sharpening intelligence, sense-perception and powers of introspection. Pater was accused of advocating selfishness and sensuality. The first charge had some truth in it, the second was less just. He advocated the cultivation of a varied sensibility, not unreflecting self-abandonment or the unbalanced concentration on one area of experience only. However, Pater's aestheticism could easily fall foul of any rigid moral prohibitions; and it was genuinely opposed to the spirit of puritan morality. Hostile critics of *The Renaissance* were right to recognize something subversive* of commonly received standards.

overthrowing something
established

I take the "puritan morality" mentioned above (or what is sometimes nowadays called "the protestant ethic") to be a code of behavior, deriving from the Puritanism of the sixteenth and seventeenth centuries, and stressing industry, temperance,* useful activity. The good life, in this view, is essentially active; life is a moral struggle, represented metaphorically as a pilgrimage or a battle. This puritan ethic was generally accepted in the largely Nonconformist middle class that was increasingly setting the public tone of Victorian society. By contrast, the aesthetic viewpoint involved detachment, an avoidance of wholehearted involvement in practical affairs. The aesthete aspires to treat life, not as a battle but as a spectacle. As so often, it is a French writer, here Villiers de l'Isle-Adam, who, through the hero of *Axel* (1890), expresses the viewpoint with the most resounding effect: "Live? Our servants will do that for us." Only by detachment can the aesthete "appreciate" life as a spectator; he is the spectator even of his own emotions. (This, presumably, involved the difficulty of being simultaneously inside and outside his own skin.) The aesthetic approach to life is thus contemplative, not active. I shall use the term "contemplative aestheticism" both to stress this point, and to distinguish aestheticism as a view of life from art for art's sake, which is largely a statement of policy to be followed by active practitioners of art.

moderation

In the conclusion of *The Renaissance* Pater conveys a world-weary skepticism. We seek reality and find, in the world about us, only change, a constant succession of phenomena. Turning inwards, we find that our own consciousness is equally fugitive, a drift of momentary sensations and thoughts. We cannot be sure of any enduring reality behind the flow of phenomena; we cannot be sure that we ourselves have any stable identity. The world is constantly slipping away, and we with it. What, then, can we do but make the most of experience as it passes?

We are certain of one thing only: death. "We are all under the sentence of death but with a sort of indefinite reprieve." Let us, then, make the most of life while we have it.

Practically, much depends on what we think is the best way of making the most of life. For Pater, all depends on "a quickened, multiplied consciousness," an experience that is at once intense and varied. Anything in the nature of repetition — including, one would think, the compulsive behavior of the vulgar sensualist — is to be minimized. "In a sense it might even be said that our failure is to form habits; for, after all, habit is relative to a stereotyped world, and meantimes it is only the roughness of the eye that makes any two persons, things, situations seem alike." How, then, are we to maintain such alert sensitivity? Pater does not positively prescribe any single way; and his interests were wider than his reputation as the high priest of English aestheticism might suggest. Thus he commends the study of philosophy; but, significantly, he does not commend it as a means of arriving at truth — "truth" is unattainable — but because it highlights features of experience. (Thus a study of the problem of free-will and determinism may not yield an answer; but it will heighten our awareness of the human condition, of which "freedom" and "determinism" represent different aspects.) "Philosophical theories or ideas, as points of view, instruments of criticism, may help us to gather up what might otherwise pass unregarded by us." This, however, is a rather limited endorsement of philosophy. And it is art that, for Pater, adds most to our experience:

> Of such wisdom, the poetic passion, the desire of beauty, the love of art for its own sake, has most. For art comes to you, proposing frankly to give nothing but the highest quality to your moments as they pass, and simply for those moments' sake.

Here the reference to "the love of art for its own sake" has fairly clear implications: art is to be valued for the immediate impression it affords, for something received at the moment of appreciation, not for any purely hypothetical after-effects. This is in keeping with his earlier remark: "not the fruit of experience but experience itself is the end."

While contemplative aestheticism may commend a rich and varied experience, it may also prompt a retreat from life — from what most people, pressed by circumstances, involved in personal relationships and engaged in definite occupations, would regard as life. It obviously presupposes leisure and a freedom from humdrum pressures. The supreme exemplar* of the aesthetic retreat from ordinary life is, perhaps, Des Esseintes, the hero of the French novel by J. K. Huysmans, *A Rebours* (*In Reverse*, 1884). Des Esseintes shuts himself in his room, and, with the aid of various stimuli, including medieval ecclesiastical objects and the novels of Dickens, seeks to objectify the private world of his imagination. Once, he is sufficiently stirred by his enthusiasm for Dickens to start on a journey to London; however, he sees so much of English tourists and their habits in Paris that he decides he has seen enough of England to enhance his appreciation of Dickens, and returns home.

Contemplative aestheticism can, however, assume more positive moral implications than it does in the conclusion of *The Renaissance.* The appreciation of life involves the appreciation of people and, if this is more than superficial, an enhanced understanding of them. Thus Pater pleads elsewhere for a morality of sympathy, one that dissolves hard and inflexible moral rules and estimates people with due regard to circumstances and individual temperament. Here again aestheticism diverges from a puritan ethic of rigid "thou shalt nots."

model

Contemplative aestheticism reflects a common Victorian aspiration after personal culture — "self-culture" as it was sometimes called. In the conclusion of *The Renaissance,* the ideal of self-culture receives an extreme statement. For Pater, the cultivation of sensibility is not merely a desirable thing; it is the only thing that can make sense of life, and, ideally, embraces the whole of it.

> To burn always with this hard, gemlike flame, to maintain this ecstasy, is success in life.

This is hardly a conventional concept of success. Like Matthew Arnold, in *Culture and Anarchy* (1869) and elsewhere, Pater deplores the preoccupation with what Arnold called "machinery," the attitude which envisages life in terms of means and ends; so that in practice, everything tends to become only a means to something else; personal fulfilment is put off till tomorrow, which never comes. People, as Pater remarks in an essay on Wordsworth, become "like thorns in their anxiety to bear grapes." In his attack on such short-sighted "practicality," Pater is with Arnold, though without Arnold's social awareness: he writes for a few kindred spirits. None the less, we can recognize the point of his challenging maxim: "not the fruit of experience but experience itself is the end" — that it is possible to become pre-occupied with the means of living, to the neglect of living itself.

QUESTIONS FOR DISCUSSION AND WRITING

[1] Define an "aesthete."

[2] Compare and contrast the main points of nihilism and aestheticism.

[3] Is the ancient Greek doctrine of "the useful and beautiful" completely antithetical to aestheticism?

[4] In what ways is Castiglione's ideal courtier (see page 273) similar to the modern aesthete?

[5] Discuss how Louis XIV's court (page 347) exemplifies institutionalized aestheticism.

During the nineteenth century in France, a group of young men styled themselves "dandies." These dandies were flamboyant in dress and manner. They were similar in a sense to Castiglione's courtier in that they purposely cultivated a false front, asserting that surface was more important than substance — one's "look" mattered more than one's real self. Partly they were rebelling against bourgeois (middle-class) society. One young dandy supposedly liked to shock polite Parisian society by taking a lobster for a walk through the park. Writers of this generation began the Symbolist movement

*in literature. Charles Baudelaire is the most famous forerunner of Symbolism;
Arthur Rimbaud, another French writer, is among its greatest poets. Rimbaud's
poetry is made up of visions and sounds that evoke a private world of experience. He wrote, " 'I' is another," which is one way of expressing the difference
between a person's real self and his or her outward image. The following
passage comes from a Symbolist novel by J. K. Huysmans, a French writer of
the late nineteenth century. The title of his book suggests the main character's
attitude and manner toward established society, an attitude of nonconformity
and individuality.*

J. K. HUYSMANS
FROM *Against the Grain*

● More than two months slipped by before the time came when Des
Esseintes found it feasible to immerse himself definitely in the peace and
silence of his house at Fontenay; purchases of all kinds still kept him
perambulating* the Paris streets, tramping the town from end to end.   walking

He had long been an expert in the right and wrong combinations and
contrasts of tints. In other days, when he was still in the habit of inviting
women to his house, he had fitted up a boudoir* where, amid dainty   bedroom
carved furniture of the light yellow camphor-wood of Japan, under a sort
of tent of pink Indian satin, the flesh tints borrowed a soft, warm glow from
the artfully disposed lights sifting down through the rich material.

This room, where mirrors hung on every wall, reflecting backwards and
forwards from one to another an infinite succession of pink boudoirs, had
enjoyed a great renown among his various mistresses, who loved to bathe
their nakedness in this flood of warm crimson amid the aromatic odors
given off by the Oriental wood of the furniture.

Then, in the days when Des Esseintes still deemed it incumbent* on   necessary
him to play the eccentric, he had also installed strange and elaborate
dispositions* of furniture and fittings, partitioning off his salon* into a   arrangements / parlor
series of niches,* each differently hung and carpeted, and each harmoniz-   recesses in a wall
ing in a subtle likeness by a more or less vague similarity of tints, gay or
sombre, refined or barbaric, with the special character of the Latin and
French books he loved. He would then settle himself down to read in
whichever of these recesses displayed in its scheme of decoration the
closest correspondence with the intimate essence of the particular book
his caprice* of the moment led him to peruse.*   impulse / read

Last fancy of all, he had prepared a lofty hall in which to receive his
tradesmen. These would march in, take seats side by side in a row of
church stalls; then he would mount an imposing pulpit and preach them
a sermon on dandyism,* adjuring* his bookmakers and tailors to conform   extreme concern with
with the most scrupulous fidelity to his commandments in the matter of   one's clothes and
                                                                            appearance / making
                                                                            someone swear under oath

SOURCE: Huysmans, J.K. *Against the Grain*, New York: 3 Sirens Press. Originally published
in 1884.

cut and fashion, threatening them with the penalty of pecuniary* excom-   financial
munication if they failed to follow out to the letter the instructions embodied in his monitories* and bulls.*   letters of warning / official
                                          documents from the Pope

He won a great reputation as an eccentric, — a reputation he crowned
by adopting a costume of black velvet worn with a gold-fringed waistcoat
and sticking by way of cravat* a bunch of Parma violets in the opening of   neck tie
a very low-necked shirt. Then he would invite parties of literary friends
to dinners that set all the world talking. In one instance in particular,
modelling the entertainment on a banquet of the eighteenth century, he
had organized a funeral feast in celebration of the most unmentionable of
minor personal calamities. The dining-room was hung with black and
looked out on a strangely metamorphosed* garden, the walks being   changed
strewn with charcoal, the little basin in the middle of the lawn bordered
with a rim of black basalt* and filled with ink; and the ordinary shrubs   volcanic rock
superseded* by cypresses and pines. The dinner itself was served on a   made less significant
black cloth, decorated with baskets of violets and scabiosa* and il-   kind of plant
luminated by candelabra in which tall tapers* flared.   candles

While a concealed orchestra played funeral marches, the guests were
waited on by naked negresses wearing shoes and stockings of cloth of silver
besprinkled with tears.

The viands* were served on black-bordered plates, — turtle soup, Rus-   food
sian black bread, ripe olives from Turkey, caviar, mule steaks, Frankfurt
smoked sausages, game dished up in sauces coloured to resemble liquorice
water and boot-blacking, truffles in jelly, chocolate-tinted creams, pud-
dings, nectarines, fruit preserves, mulberries and cherries. The wines
were drunk from dark-tinted glasses. After the coffee and walnuts came
other unusual beverages, kwas, porter and stout.

The invitations, which purported to be for a dinner in pious memory
of the host's (temporarily) lost virility, were couched* in the regulation   worded
phraseology of letters summoning relatives to attend the obsequies* of a   funeral services
defunct* kinsman.   dead

He had had the boudoir hung with tapestry of a vivid red, and on each
of the four walls were displayed in ebony frames prints by Jan Luyken, an
old Dutch engraver, almost unknown in France.

The works he possessed of this artist, at once fantastic and depressing,
vigorous and brutal, included the series of his "Religious Persecutions," a
collection of appalling plates representing all the tortures which the savagery of religious intolerance has invented, plates exhibiting all the horrors of human agony, — men roasted over braziers,* skulls laid open by   coal grills
sword cuts, pierced with nails, riven asunder* with saws, bowels drawn out   torn apart
of the belly, and twisted round rollers, finger-nails torn out one by one
with pincers, eyes put out, eyelids turned back and transfixed with pins,
limbs dislocated or carefully broken bones laid bare and scraped for hours
with knives.

These productions, replete* with abominable imaginations, stinking of   filled
the stake, reeking with blood, echoing with curses and screams of agony,
made Des Esseintes' flesh creep as he stood stifled with horror in the red
boudoir.

These prints were mines of curious information; a man could look at
them for hours and never weary; profoundly suggestive of ideas, they
often helped Des Esseintes to kill the time on days when books refused
to interest him.

He must contrive a bed-chamber to resemble a monk's cell in a Religious House; but here came difficulty upon difficulty, for he refused absolutely to endure for his personal occupation the austere ugliness that
marks such refuges for penitence and prayer.

By dint* of turning the question over this way and that and looking at   through the effort
it from every side, he arrived at the conclusion that the result to be aimed
at amounted to this — to arrange by means of objects cheerful in themselves a melancholy whole, or rather, while preserving its character of
plain ugliness, to impress on the general effect of the room thus treated
a kind of elegance and distinction; to reverse, in fact, the optical delusion
of the stage, where cheap tinsel plays the part of expensive and sumptuous*   rich
robes, to gain indeed precisely the opposite effect, using costly and magnificent materials so as to give the impression of common rags; in a word,
to fit up a Trappist's cell that should have the look of the genuine article,
and yet of course be nothing of the sort.

He set about the task as follows: to imitate the ochre wash* that is the   color
invariable mark of administrative and clerical direction, he had the walls
hung with saffron silk; to represent the chocolate brown of the wainscot,*   wood paneling
the regulation colour for such like places, he panelled the lower part of
these same walls with wood painted a rich, deep purple. The effect was
charming, recalling — though how different really! — the bald stiffness of
the pattern he was copying, — with modifications. The ceiling, in the same
way, was covered with unbleached white cloth, giving the appearance of
plaster, but without its crude shiny look; then for the cold tiles of the floor,
he mimicked these very successfully, thanks to a carpet with a pattern of
red squares, interspersed with spots of a whitish hue* where the occu-   color
pants' sandals might have been supposed to leave their mark.

This room he furnished with a little iron bedstead, a sham* hermit's   phony
couch, constructed out of old pieces of wrought and polished iron, its
plainness relieved at head and foot by a leaf and flower ornamentation,
— tulips and vine-tendrils intertwined, once part of the balustrade* of the   railing
great staircase of an old chateau.

By way of night-table, he installed an antique prie-Dieu, the inside of
which would hold a utensil, while the top supported a book of offices of
the Church; he erected against the opposite wall a state pew, surmounted
by an open-work canopy decorated with ornaments carved in the solid
wood; he used candelabra that had come from a desecrated* church, in   vandalized

which he burned real wax tapers purchased at a special house patronized by the clergy, for he felt a genuine repugnance for all the modern methods of illumination, whether petroleum, rock-oil, gas or composite candles, all alike in their crude, dazzling effects.

In bed in the morning, as he lay with his head on the pillow before falling asleep, he would gaze at his Theocopuli, the painful colouring of which modified to some degree the soft cheerfulness of the yellow silk on the walls and gave it a graver tone; at these times, he could easily picture himself living a hundred leagues from Paris, far from the world of men, in the depths of a Monastery.

And, after all, the illusion was not difficult to sustain for truly he was living a life largely analogous to that of a Monk. In this way, he enjoyed the advantages of confinement in a cloister, while he escaped its inconveniences, — the quasi-military discipline, the lack of comfort, the dirt and herding together and the monotonous idleness. Just as he had made his cell into a warm, luxurious bedchamber, so he had procured himself an existence carried on under normal conditions, without hardship or incommodity, sufficiently occupied, yet free from irksome restraints.

Like an eremite,* he was ripe for solitude, harassed by life's stress,   hermit
expecting nothing more of existence; like a monk again, he was overwhelmed with an immense fatigue, a craving for peace and quiet, a longing to have nothing more to do henceforth with the vulgar, who were in his eyes all utilitarians and fools.

In short, though he was conscious of no vocation for the state of grace, he felt in himself a genuine sympathy for the folks shut up in Monasteries, persecuted by a society that hates them and can never forgive the well-grounded contempt they entertain for it nor the wish they manifest to redeem, to expiate* by long years of silence the ever-increasing licentious-   make amends for
ness* of its grotesque or silly conversations.   lustfulness

QUESTIONS FOR DISCUSSION AND WRITING

[1] Des Esseintes represents a decadent aesthete, one who deviates from the original doctrine of aestheticism. Inferring from Des Esseintes' lifestyle and sensibility,* define "decadent aestheticism" and analyze the beliefs or   aesthetic responses
practices it has in common with the doctrine as Johnson describes it.

[2] Both Des Esseintes and Castiglione's ideal courtier cultivate a sense of style. The courtier is supposed to practice *sprezzatura;* Des Esseintes practices excess. Examine the relationship between the two styles. In what ways does Des Esseintes display "nonchalance"?

Benvenuto Cellini, a Renaissance Italian artist, is as well known for his Autobiography *(pub. 1734) as he is for his sculpture and metalwork. His book reflects a combination of the realities of life in sixteenth-century Italy and the Renaissance sense of personal style. As you read the following selection, note Cellini's sense of himself as an artist and a man of honor. Read also for the state view of the artist, represented by the powerful Italian cardinals and the Pope himself.*

BENVENUTO CELLINI
FROM *The Autobiography of Benvenuto Cellini*

● While I was sitting with several of my friends, Pompeo, my enemy, passed by, in the midst of ten heavily armed men. When he was just opposite me he stopped, looking like he was going to pick a fight with me. My friends, who were all strong and brave men, signaled me to arm myself, but it suddenly occurred to me that if I took out my sword, something terrible might happen to them, even though they had done nothing. I therefore decided that it would be better for me to risk my life alone.

Pompeo stood there hardly long enough to say two Hail Mary's;* then he turned toward me and laughed sneeringly. And as he moved on, the men with him also began to laugh, waving their hats in the air, and making other insulting gestures. My friends would have started a fight right then, but I angrily told them that I could take care of myself and had no need of anyone else's help, and that they should mind their own business. They got angry and went off, grumbling to themselves.

Catholic prayers

Among them was my dearest friend, Albertaccio del Bene, whose brothers were Alessandro and Albizo (today a very rich man in Lyons). Albertaccio was the most remarkable young man I ever knew, and the most courageous, and he thought as much of me as he did of himself. Because he was well aware that what I had done came not from lack of courage but from the greatest bravery, knowing me as he did, he responded by asking me to consider him part of whatever I chose to do. I said to him, "Albertaccio, my dearest friend, a time may come when I need to ask for your help, but in this case, if you care for me, let me take care of my business, and you take care of yours. Go along with the others — there's no time to lose." I spoke these words in a great hurry.

Meanwhile, my enemies had moved slowly toward a place called the Chiavaca and stopped in an intersection from which several roads led off in different directions. But the one on which stood the house of my enemy Pompeo led directly to the Campo di Fiore. For some reason Pompeo had gone into a shop on the corner of the Chiavaca. He stayed in there a while, taking care of some business. While people said he had been boasting about the "great insult" he believed he had given me, in reality it was his own bad luck that he ended up causing, because I reached the corner just as he came out of the shop.

His friends made room for him in their midst. I took out a sharp little dagger and, breaking through the line of his henchmen, stabbed him with such speed and force that no one was able to stop me. I had aimed to strike him in the face, but in his fright he turned, and I stabbed him just below

Translated by Jeanne Gunner.

the ear. I stabbed him there two times only, for the second time he died on the spot, which had never been my intention. But as they say, sometimes you don't know your own strength.

I pulled back the dagger with my left hand and drew my sword with the right, in order to defend myself. However, his gang had run up to the dead body and not one made a move against me. So I walked back up the street alone, thinking about where I could hide. When I had gone a few hundred feet, I was joined by my very good friend Piloto, a goldsmith,* who said to me, "My brother, now that the damage is done, let's see what we can do about saving you." I said to him, "Let's go to Albertaccio del Bene's house. I told him just a short while ago that the time would come when I needed him."

gold worker

We arrived at Albertaccio's house, and I embraced him with great affection. Soon the best young men of all the Italian states except Milan appeared. Each offered to give his life in order to save mine. Even Luigi Rucellai sent a wonderful offer of his services, as did many others of his station, because they all condoned my action, holding that Pompeo had insulted me deeply, and marvelling that I had put up with it so long.

Cardinal Cornaro, when he learned of the incident, sent thirty soldiers loaded with weapons to bring me to his quarters, with all due respect. I accepted his offer and went with the soldiers, and the same number of my young friends kept me company. In the meantime, Traiono, Pompeo's relative and first chamberlain* to the pope, sent a Milanese gentleman of high rank to Cardinal de' Medici, who told the Cardinal about the grave crime I had committed. He insisted that the Cardinal punish me.

officer in charge of a lord's home

The Cardinal answered quickly, saying, "He would indeed have committed a great crime had he not committed this minor one; thank Mr. Traiano for me for having told me what I did not know." Then, in front of this gentleman, he turned to the bishop of Frulli, his assistant and good friend, and said, "Look everywhere for my dear Benvenuto, and bring him to me; I want to help him and defend him. Whoever is against him, is also against me." Flushing with anger, the Milanese gentleman departed.

The bishop of Frulli found me in the house of Cardinal Cornaro and, finding the Cardinal as well, told him how the Cardinal de' Medici had sent for Benvenuto, and that he wanted to be of help to him. This Cardinal Cornaro was as touchy as a bear. He answered the bishop very angrily, saying that he was as able to help me as was Cardinal de' Medici. To this the bishop replied that he hoped he would be able to speak a few words to me about some unrelated business of the Cardinal's. Cornaro told him that he had already spoken to me as much as he was going to that day.

The Cardinal de' Medici was outraged. But the next evening, without Cornaro's knowledge and under heavy guard, I went to visit him. I begged him to do me the favor of letting me stay in Cornaro's house, and I told him of the great courtesy Cornaro had shown me; I said that if his most holy lordship would let me remain with Cornaro, I would have one more friend in my time of need; in all other things his lordship might do with me what he pleased. To this he answered that I should do whatever I judged best.

I returned to Cornaro's house. There, a few days later, Cardinal Farnese was made pope. As soon as he had taken care of some more important matters, the pope sent for me, saying that he wanted no one but me to coin his money. To these words of his holiness a certain gentleman, one of the pope's closest associates, a man named Latino Juvinale, said that I was in hiding, having murdered a Milanese, Pompeo by name, and he added all the details of the case that were favorable to me.

To these words the pope replied: "I know nothing about the death of Pompeo, but I do know the justifications of Benvenuto very well. Give him a safe-conduct* at once, so that he will be secure from all harm." pass

In attendance there was a great friend of Pompeo, called Mr. Ambrogio, who was also an intimate of the pope and a Milanese. He said to the pope: "In the first days of your papacy it would not be wise to grant favors of this sort." The pope turned to him and said: "You don't understand this business as well as I do. Know that men like Benvenuto, unique in their profession, are not subject to the law. And even more so in the case of one who has been so provoked." He gave me the safe-conduct, and I entered his service at once, enjoying the highest favor.

QUESTIONS FOR DISCUSSION AND WRITING

[1] Cellini commits a murder; the Pope, the embodiment of Christian morality, absolves him of any crime, spiritual or legal. Examine the Pope's justification of his pardon as a possible outgrowth of aestheticism. How does his judgment illustrate the aestheticist belief that beauty and art are the highest good?

[2] Johnson cites one form of aestheticism as "aspiration after personal culture." Define the personal aesthetic of Cellini, Des Esseintes, and Castiglione's courtier. How does each cultivate personality or style as an aesthetic ideal? Compare the three aesthetics and decide which of the three is the most extreme.

Jean Paul Sartre's reputation is fixed as one of the twentieth century's most influential philosophers. His existential theories had their greatest popularity in post-World War II Europe, especially in Sartre's native France. Often, new philosophies come into being during times of political turmoil, uncertainty, and change, when wars or other catastrophic events challenge the old order. Postwar Europe had suffered through two global conflicts, the coming of the atomic age, the partition of Germany and Eastern Europe, and the failure of many economies and governments. Existentialism teaches that such a disordered reality reflects life's universal absurdity, and places all responsibility for value and meaning on the individual, who must act in order to define his or her image of humanity.

JEAN PAUL SARTRE
"Existentialism"

● Man is nothing else but what he makes of himself. Such is the first
principle of existentialism. It is also what is called subjectivity. But what
do we mean by this, if not that man has a greater dignity than a stone or
table? For we mean that man first exists, that is, that man first of all is the
being who hurls himself toward a future and who is conscious of imagining
himself as being in the future. Man is at the start a plan which is aware
of itself, rather than a patch of moss, a piece of garbage, or a cauliflower;
nothing exists prior to this plan; there is nothing in heaven; man will be
what he will have planned to be. Not what he will want to be. Because by
the word "will" we generally mean a conscious decision, which is subsequent to what we have already made of ourselves. I may want to belong
to a political party, write a book, get married; but all that is only a manifestation of an earlier, more spontaneous choice that is called "will." But if
existence really does precede essence, man is responsible for what he is.
Thus, existentialism's first move is to make every man aware of what he
is and to make the full responsibility of his existence rest on him. And
when we say that a man is responsible for himself, we do not only mean
that he is responsible for his own individuality, but that he is responsible
for all men.

The word "subjectivism" has two meanings. Subjectivism means, on
the one hand, that an individual chooses and makes himself; and, on the
other, that it is impossible for man to transcend human subjectivity. The
second of these is the essential meaning of existentialism. When we say
that man chooses his own self, we mean that every one of us does likewise;
but we also mean by that that in making this choice he also chooses all
men. In fact, in creating the man that we want to be, there is not a single
one of our acts which does not at the same time create an image of man
as we think he ought to be. To choose to be this or that is to affirm at the
same time the value of what we choose, because we can never choose evil.
We always choose the good, and nothing can be good for us without being
good for all.

If, on the other hand, existence precedes essence, and if we grant that
we exist and fashion our image at one and the same time, the image is valid
for everybody and for our whole age. Thus, our responsibility is much
greater than we might have supposed, because it involves all mankind. If
I am a workingman and choose to join a Christian trade union rather than
be a Communist, and if by being a member, I want to show that the best
thing for a man is resignation, that the kingdom of man is not of this world,
I am not only involving my own case — I want to be resigned for everyone.
As a result, my action has involved all humanity. To take a more individual

matter, if I want to marry, to have children, even if this marriage depends solely on my own circumstances or passion or wish, I am involving all humanity in monogamy and not merely myself. Therefore, I am responsible for myself and for everyone else. I am creating a certain image of man of my own choosing. In choosing myself, I choose man.

The existentialist thinks it very distressing that God does not exist, because all possibility of finding values in a heaven of ideas disappears along with Him; there can no longer be an a priori Good, since there is no infinite and perfect consciousness to think it. Nowhere is it written that the good exists, that we must be honest, that we must not lie; because the fact is we are on a plane where there are only men. Dostoievsky said, "If God didn't exist, everything would be possible." That is the very starting point of existentialism. Indeed, everything is permissible if God does not exist, and as a result man is forlorn,* because neither within him nor without does he find anything to cling to. He can't start making excuses for himself.

hopeless; alone

If existence really does precede essence, there is no explaining things away by reference to a fixed and given human nature. In other words, there is no determinism, man is free, man is freedom. On the other hand, if God does not exist, we find no values or commands to turn to which legitimize our conduct. So, in the bright realm of values, we have no excuse behind us, nor justification before us. We are alone, with no excuses.

That is the idea I shall try to convey when I say that man is condemned to be free. Condemned, because he did not create himself, yet, in other respects is free; because, once thrown into the world, he is responsible for everything he does.

To give you an example which will enable you to understand forlornness better, I shall cite the case of one of my students who came to see me under the following circumstances: his father was on bad terms with his mother, and, moreover, was inclined to be a collaborationist;* his older brother had been killed in the German offensive of 1940, and the young man, with somewhat immature but generous feelings, wanted to avenge him. His mother lived alone with him, very much upset by the half-treason of her husband and the death of her older son; the boy was her only consolation.

person who works with enemy invaders

The boy was faced with the choice of leaving for England joining the Free French forces — that is, leaving his mother behind — or remaining with his mother and helping her to carry on. He was fully aware that the woman lived only for him and that his going off — and perhaps his death — would plunge her into despair. He was also aware that every act that he did for his mother's sake was a sure thing, in the sense that it was helping her to carry on, whereas every effort he made toward going off and fighting was an uncertain move which might run aground and prove completely useless; for example, on his way to England he might, while passing through Spain, be detained indefinitely in a Spanish camp; he might reach England or Algiers and be stuck in an office at a desk job. As a result, he was faced with two very different kinds of action: one, concrete, immediate, but concerning only one individual; the other concerned an incomparably vaster group, a national collectivity, but for that very reason was dubious, and might be interrupted en route. And, at the same time, he was wavering between two kinds of ethics. On the one hand, an ethics of sympathy, of personal devotion; on the other, a broader ethics, but one whose efficacy* was more dubious. He had to choose between the two.

effectiveness

Who could help him choose? Christian doctrine? No. Christian doctrine says, "Be charitable, love your neighbor, take the more rugged path, etc., etc." But which is the more rugged path? Whom should he love as a brother? The fighting man or his mother? Which does the greater good, the vague act of fighting in a group, or the concrete one of helping a particular human being to go on living? Who can decide a priori? Nobody. No book of ethics can tell him. The Kantian ethics says, "Never treat any person as a means, but as an end." Very well, if I stay with my mother, I'll treat her as an end and not as a means; but by virtue of this very fact, I'm running the risk of treating the people around me who are fighting, as means; and conversely, if I go to join those who are fighting, I'll be treating them as an end, and, by doing that, I run the risk of treating my mother as a means.

If values are vague, and if they are always too broad for the concrete and specific case that we are considering, the only thing left for us is to trust our instincts. That's what this young man tried to do; and when I saw him, he said, "In the end, feeling is what counts. I ought to choose whichever pushes me in one direction. If I feel that I love my mother enough to sacrifice everything else for her — my desire for vengeance, for action, for adventure — then I'll stay with her. If, on the contrary, I feel that my love for my mother isn't enough, I'll leave."

But how is the value of a feeling determined? What gives his feeling for his mother value? Precisely the fact that he remained with her. I may say that I like so-and-so well enough to sacrifice a certain amount of money for him, but I may say so only if I've done it. I may say "I love my mother well enough to remain with her" if I have remained with her. The only way to determine the value of this affection is, precisely, to perform an act which confirms and defines it. But, since I require this affection to justify my act, I find myself caught in a vicious circle.

Given that men are free and that tomorrow they will freely decide what man will be, I cannot be sure that, after my death, fellow-fighters will carry on my work to bring it to its maximum perfection. Tomorrow, after my death, some men may decide to set up Fascism,* and the others may be cowardly and muddled enough to let them do it. Fascism will then be the human reality, so much the worse for us.

a form of totalitarianism

Actually, things will be as man will have decided they are to be. Does that mean that I should abandon myself to quietism? No. First, I should involve myself; then, act on the old saw, "Nothing ventured, nothing gained." Nor does it mean that I shouldn't belong to a party, but rather that I shall have no illusions and shall do what I can. For example, suppose I ask myself, "Will socialization, as such, ever come about?" I know nothing about it. All I know is that I'm going to do everything in my power to bring it about. Beyond that, I can't count on anything. Quietism is the attitude of people who say, "Let others do what I can't do." The doctrine I am presenting is the very opposite of quietism, since it declares, "There is no reality except in action." Moreover, it goes further, since it adds, "Man is nothing else than his plan; he exists only to the extent that he fulfills himself; he is therefore nothing else than the ensemble of his acts, nothing else than his life."

Now, for the existentialist there is really no love other than one which manifests itself in a person's being in love. There is no genius other than one which is expressed in works of art; the genius of Proust is the sum of Proust's works; the genius of Racine is his series of tragedies. Outside of that, there is nothing. Why say that Racine could have written another tragedy, when he didn't write it? A man is involved in life, leaves his impress on it, and outside of that there is nothing. To be sure, this may seem a harsh thought to someone whose life hasn't been a success. But, on the other hand, it prompts people to understand that reality alone is what counts, that dreams, expectations, and hopes warrant no more than to define a man as a disappointed dream, as miscarried hopes, as vain expectations. In other words, to define him negatively and not positively. However, when we say, "You are nothing else than your life," that does not imply that the artist will be judged solely on the basis of his works of art; a thousand other things will contribute toward summing him up. What we mean is that a man is nothing else than a series of undertakings, that he is the sum, the organization, the ensemble of the relationships which make up these undertakings.

When all is said and done, what we are accused of, at bottom, is not our pessimism, but an optimistic toughness. If people throw up to us our works of fiction in which we write about people who are soft, weak, cowardly, and sometimes even downright bad, it's not because these people are soft, weak, cowardly, or bad; because if we were to say, as Zola did, that they are that way because of heredity, the workings of environment, society, because of biological or psychological determinism, people would be reassured. They would say, "Well, that's what we're like, no one can do anything about it." But when the existentialist writes about a coward, he says that this coward is responsible for his cowardice. He's not like that because he has a cowardly heart or lung or brain; he's not like that on account of his physiological make-up; but he's like that because he has made himself a coward by his acts. There's no such thing as a cowardly constitution; there are nervous constitutions; there is poor blood, as the common people say, or strong constitutions. But the man whose blood is poor is not a coward on that account, for what makes cowardice is the act of renouncing or yielding. A constitution is not an act; the coward is defined on the basis of the acts he performs. People feel, in a vague sort of way, that this coward we're talking about is guilty of being a coward, and the thought frightens them. What people would like is that a coward or a hero be born that way.

Existentialism is nothing else than an attempt to draw all the consequences of a coherent atheistic position. It isn't trying to plunge man into despair at all. But if one calls every attitude of unbelief despair, like the Christians, then the word is not being used in its original sense. Existentialism isn't so atheistic that it wears itself out showing that God doesn't exist. Rather, it declares that even if God did exist, that would change nothing. There you've got our point of view. Not that we believe that God exists, but we think that the problem of His existence is not the issue. In this sense existentialism is optimistic, a doctrine of action, and it is plain dishonesty for Christians to make no distinction between their own despair and ours and then to call us despairing.

QUESTIONS FOR DISCUSSION AND WRITING

[1] Summarize the main points of Sartre's essay to arrive at a definition of existentialism.

[2] Explain why the existence or nonexistence of God is not an issue for the existentialist.

[3] Why is existentialism often called a pessimistic doctrine? How does the existentialist counter that charge?

[4] Which other philosophical attitudes are most unlike existentialism? Explain your interpretation.

[5] Sartre refers to the Resistance fighters, a group of people during World War II who fought against the Germans to free occupied France. He used an existential argument to justify their activities. Could an existential argument also be used to justify terrorism as it is practiced today? Refer to Singh's essay in Chapter 5.

Jack Henry Abbott wrote In the Belly of the Beast, *a collection of essays, while he was in jail (where he remains today). He is known not only for this book but also for his friendship with Norman Mailer, a famous American writer. Mailer began corresponding with Abbott and encouraged him to continue writing. Later he assisted in gaining Abbott's release on parole. Within six weeks, Abbott murdered a young waiter in New York City in a dispute over the use of a restroom. Abbott questions whether he can ever survive outside of prison society, and he poses the issue of responsibility: society, he says, created him, and thus he reflects society's problems and corruption. The title of his book symbolizes his position in society as well as his view of it. In the selection below, Abbott explores the issue of how one remains — or can even become — human in an inhuman environment.*

JACK HENRY ABBOTT
"Gods and Drugs"

● Yogis starve their needs to death. I feed mine dreams. I put them asleep, but they always awaken again and try to move me about like a puppet on their strings. I am a white man, a civilized man, like you and all white men. The need to live close to God, the necessity, in other words, that breeds the certainty in our breasts that God exists, has been washed from our genes through history. Unlike you and most white men, my despair of God drives me from even the ritual conventions of religion, because, unlike others, I do not feel the necessity within me of social conventions that respect the dead. Unlike modern white men, philosophers, who despair of God, my despair does not drive me to the existential act of belief.

I do not believe in God, not because I do not want to but because I cannot. I do not believe in religious ethics because I cannot, and the same goes for all of my "beliefs." And for my "feelings," I cannot choose what I envy, hate, love or desire. If I believed the death penalty to be absolutely "immoral," I would not hesitate to save anyone from execution. Otherwise, my conscience would haunt me. Is all this a psychological aberration? Is it "idealism?" I do not think so. But I think all modern existentialist philosophy unconsciously aims at finding a way for a man to live with a guilty conscience, a conscience that haunts him. Man is a coward, plain and simple. He loves life too much. He fears others too much. And I would too, if I could, but I cannot live with a lie. But I have seen men who are such facile* liars they can stick to their story for decades.   easy, casual

. . . It just occurred to me that any brand of theism must be rooted in some parallel brand of "faith." Displaced faith in society (mankind) and in personal beings always results in faith in some metaphysical world. Faith is a hell of a concept, a hell of a phenomenon. Existential faith for Sartre meant faith only in the distinction between one's ass and a hole in the ground (rather literally). For strange reasons too trite to go into here, he actually said that loss of faith (i.e., fear; phobia) in a hole (I mean that also literally) results (by displacement) in the phenomenon known as homosexuality. He really said that toward the last two hundred pages of *Being and Nothingness.* I read that thirteen years ago and still I have trouble believing anyone (even he) could be so crass, so stupid, as to say such a thing — even if it were, in a way, true. Idealists are so naive when they talk about material reality.

. . . I find the human element in all religions very beautiful and touching. Religious ideas move me very much, almost as much as the people who hold those beliefs. I am moved by the knowledge that you find consolation in religious existentialism. I wish I could. You are a very lucky man. My readings of Kierkegaard, Buber and Jasper — to name three — left me inspired and changed me. What little emotional maturity I have I feel I owe to Soren Kierkegaard's works (after Nietzsche's childish ravings).

I want consolation more than anything in this world. I cannot help it if I have not been consoled by God, by a vision of the true Glory of God. I mean this with all my heart. Science is not consolation to me, any more than any abstract knowledge of the world can be a consolation.

The truth of religious existentialism is of a different nature than the truth of science. My problem is to live with both, because for some perverse reason, my life has been such that I cannot be happy, cannot be consoled, with just one of those. The two must be reconciled, and that is what Marxism has all the indication of possibly doing.

. . . God, I need a fix now. It is the only respite possible after so many years. Next month I begin working on my seventeenth year behind bars.

To feel the glow that begins like a fire in my belly and rises up through my nerves and organs, up to my temples, is something nothing else can give me. It gives me what I need to live with all this.

The other gods are nothing compared to this. You do not have to believe in anything. When it becomes necessary out of despair to believe in God, you have cheated oppression when you can live beside the beast without twisting your mind into believing it is God.

Someone said that if there was no God, men would invent one. The man who invented opium must have been the most rebellious. I believe the word, in this religious context, is damned.

Have you noticed how, in this hemisphere, drugs are tied into revolutionary matters somehow? This is true clear to the tip of South America.

I sometimes think it is our antidote to the devil. The "atmosphere" is so stifling in this the most powerful monolithic capitalist empire in the entire world. I do not "need" what the devil alone can give me if I have a few drugs (a little marijuana, mushroom, hash).

I wish revolution in this country were as simple as that in industrially underdeveloped countries. I would otherwise end my life in the act of murdering a pig in the prison corridor. Especially nowadays, when prisons are so much "easier" (i.e., psychologically an inferno for an American communist). I would not last long without respites once in a while. These respites are only available through drugs.

Ole!

What if I am only justifying myself unconsciously with these words and they are silly excuses to be an asshole?

I realize, but not as fully as I should, that all these doubts about myself are only expressions of my isolation. Given the material freedom to act, to organize and develop situations and ties, no such self-doubt would enter my mind. I would laugh to remember these (present) days of my "reflections on my reflections"!

A comrade arrived here the other day from another prison. He thinks of discipline in terms of physical health (no smoking, no drugs, no punks,* etc.). In terms of calisthenics almost. This attitude expresses an ultra-leftist tendency which has come 180 degrees; so far to the left, it is identical to the right.

submissive homosexual lovers

He came to prison with a natural life sentence. This is his first time in prison. Although he has been in prison five or six years now, a lot of circumstances have, it seems, conspired to protect him from many of the realities of prison: other prisoners — and, therefore, himself.

He does not understand vice. He had the conscience of a bourgeois, i.e., he has an obviously bad conscience, which means guilty feelings.

He wants to stand aloof from the predicament of prisoners and yet he is one of them. Naturally, he has felt a few of their most pressing needs (to him very humiliating, shameful, disgraceful needs). He denies to himself he feels them and seems to enjoy denouncing anyone who does not deny such needs in himself.

He does not understand that men who are deprived of the most basic forms of happiness will always find that happiness in other forms. Happiness is a serious need: a need as final, as inevitable, to the support of human life as sleep.

As long as he is a part of a people who can only find happiness in what people in other parts of the world call vices, he must feel the need for indulgence in those vices.

There are several escape routes out of it. There is insanity (I mean lumbering, slobbering insanity). There is suicide. There is co-existence, and by this I mean becoming a tool of those who govern us in prison.

None of these routes can get you away in one piece. All of them stem from fear of yourself, uncertainty about yourself.

I told him once: "You cannot as a communist revolutionary bring your spick-and-span ass into a Peruvian bohio and denounce the peasant-serfs for chewing the cocoa leaves for the cocaine and order them to first stop eating cocaine and wasting their bodies before they can organize for revolution."

It is one of the only forms of happiness possible for them. To demand such a thing is to demand they join forces with their oppressors, their patrons — who make the same demands.

. . . I started taking heroin a long time ago in prison. I had just knocked back three years in the hole, solitary confinement. I came out skin and bones, a nervous wreck (as usually occurs). My friends sent a kid to my cell for a present. He was excited about me and eager. I broke up the whole thing and sent him away and cooked up a fix. I used for emotional reasons, I guess. We all need emotional security. It's the only way I can get it, so I do it. It's practical and most convicts serving long sentences use heroin for that purpose. It is therapeutic.

. . . There is a kind of marijuana that is very good, very potent and expensive. It is the leaves of a sex-starved cannabis plant. A female cannabis plant is placed to grow among male plants, surrounded by male plants. Pins are inserted at various points of its stems to prevent the seeds from passing along the stalks to be fertilized by the males. She begins to quiver and suffer.

They say this plant, after several weeks, contorts in pain. They say at night, when the sun goes down, you can see it actually move. It pulls its leaves into itself as though wrapping its arms about its body for warmth. The idea of tragedy in plant life is created by man.

Everywhere I see suffering, I see someone who derives pleasure from the fruits of suffering.

It is as though I were weathering everything in this world. Everything. Even my pleasures. Even when I am so happy I wish the moment could last forever, still I have an appetite to see it pass away. I weather even my greatest happiness.

QUESTIONS FOR DISCUSSION AND WRITING

[1] Abbott is currently a prisoner in a federal penitentiary where, in addition to writing, he's been involved with the "hard" side of prison life: violence, drugs, homosexuality. In what ways can he maintain an existential philosophy, given the environment he inhabits? What values does he assert through his behavior?

[2] How might Abbott view his situation if he were a nihilist? Which doctrine, nihilism or existentialism, would be most useful to him in confronting his life and making sense of it?

Dick Gregory has been making headlines for three decades. Most recently, he's been in the news as a political activist protesting apartheid and as a nutritionist advocating a vegetarian diet. Gregory has survived several hunger strikes which he undertook as a means of drawing attention to racism in this country and abroad. He started out his public career as a stand-up comedian, and even then race relations was a major theme in his work. The passage reprinted below comes from his autobiography; it details the poverty of his early years.

DICK GREGORY
"Not Poor, Just Broke"

● I got picked on a lot around the neighborhood; skinniest kid on the block, the poorest, the one without a Daddy. I guess that's when I first began to learn about humor, the power of a joke.

"Hey, Gregory."

"Yeah."

"Get your ass over here, I want to look at that shirt you're wearing."

"Well, uh, Herman, I got to . . ."

"What you think of that shirt he's wearin', York?"

"That's no shirt, Herman, that's a tent for a picnic."

"That your Daddy's shirt, Gregory?"

"Well, uh . . ."

"He ain't got no Daddy, Herman, that's a three-man shirt."

"Three-man shirt?"

"Him 'n' Garland 'n' Presley supposed to wear that shirt together."

At first, if Boo wasn't around to help me, I'd just get mad and run home and cry when the kids started. And then, I don't know just when, I started to figure it out. They were going to laugh anyway, but if I made the jokes they'd laugh with me instead of at me. I'd get the kids off my back, on my side. So I'd come off that porch talking about myself.

"Hey, Gregory, get your ass over here. Want you to tell me and Herman how many kids sleep in your bed."

"Googobs of kids in my bed, man, when I get up to pee in the middle of the night gotta leave a bookmark so I don't lose my place."

Before they could get going, I'd knock it out first, fast, knock out those jokes so they wouldn't have time to set and climb all over me.

"Other night I crawled through one of them rat holes in the kitchen, would you believe it them rats were sleeping six to a bed just like us."

And they started to come over and listen to me, they'd see me coming and crowd around me on the corner.

"We don't worry about knocking the snow off our shoes before we go into my house. So cold in there, no snow's going to melt on the floor anyway."

Everything began to change then. Once you get a man to laugh with you, it's hard for him to laugh at you. The kids began to expect to hear funny things from me, and after a while I could say anything I wanted. I got a reputation as a funny man. And then I started to turn the jokes on them.

"Hey, Gregory, where's your Daddy these days?"

"Sure glad that mother-fucker's out the house, got a little peace and quiet. Not like your house, York."

"What you say?"

"Yeah, man, what a free show I had last night, better than the Muni, laying in bed with the window open, listening to your Daddy whop with your Mommy. That was your Daddy, York, wasn't it?"

And then I'd turn, real quick, to another kid.

"Hey, Herman, did the police wagon ever get by your house last night? They stopped by my house and asked where you lived. . . ."

I got to be good, the champ of the block, the champ of the neighborhood as I got older. I'd stand on the corner, hands in my pockets, feet on the sewer lid, back to the street, Boo right next to me. After a while, they'd come from all around to try to score on the champ.

"You Richard Gregory?"

"Yeah."

"I'm George. . . ."

"You're midnight, blackest cat I ever saw, bet your Mammy fed you buttermilk just so you wouldn't pee ink."

Sometimes I could even use the humor on myself. Like when I was delivering papers and I broke my arm and I couldn't cry from laughing over the run-down heels on my shoes that made me slip when I turned the corner. A worn heel could break an arm, but I never heard of an arm could break a heel.

But mostly I'd use family jokes, about how my mother was such a bad cook, maybe the worst cook in the whole world. "Who ever heard of burning Kool-Aid?"

QUESTIONS FOR DISCUSSION AND WRITING

[1] Gregory was looked down on in his social group as "the poorest, the one without a Daddy," which meant he was a member of the underclass, powerless and without value. But he used humor to change his own and others' perception of him, to add value and meaning to his life. What makes his action existential, and would an existentialist condone his use of humor?

[2] Gregory and Abbott both suffer in extreme situations where human decency and a sense of meaning seem nearly impossible. Does existentialism offer any special comfort to people in extreme situations such as these? Why might a person in such a situation choose existential philosophy over faith in God?

CHAPTER 6 ESSAY ASSIGNMENTS

[1] After reviewing the last six chapter readings, select a religious belief, aesthetic theory, political doctrine, or philosophical attitude that you think offers a particularly beneficial approach to the daily pressures and problems of life. First sum up the particular approach and then analyze its positive influence and practical helpfulness.

[2] Compare and contrast the concerns, degree of involvement in world affairs, and other attitudes and actions of a person committed to a political approach to life versus one who proceeds philosophically. You can tie this discussion to any specific political ideology or philosophical attitude; its focus should be on analyzing the elements of political and philosophical commitment and then on comparing and contrasting them.

[3] Set up an opposition of two philosophical attitudes covered in this chapter. Develop an argument against one and for the other.